CW00595151

The Investigation of Crime: A G

The Investigation of Crime: A Guide to Police Powers

Vaughan Bevan
MA, LLB, Barrister
Senior Lecturer in Law
at the University of Sheffield

Ken Lidstone
LLB, Inspector South Wales Constabulary 1961–1971
Senior Lecturer in Law
at the University of Sheffield

Butterworths
London, Dublin, Edinburgh
1991

United Kindgom	Butterworth & Co (Publishers) Ltd, 88 Kingsway, London WC2B 6AB and 4 Hill Street, Edinburgh EH2 3JZ
Australia	Butterworths Pty Ltd, Sydney, Melbourne, Brisbane, Adelaide, Perth, Canberra and Hobart
Canada	Butterworths Canada Ltd, Toronto and Vancouver
Ireland	Butterworth (Ireland) Ltd, Dublin
Malaysia	Malayan Law Journal Sdn Bhd, Kuala Lumpur
New Zealand	Butterworths of New Zealand Ltd, Wellington and Auckland
Puerto Rico	Equity de Puerto Rico, Inc, Hato Rey
Singapore	Malayan Law Journal Pte Ltd, Singapore
USA	Butterworth Legal Publishers, Austin, Texas; Boston, Massachusetts; Clearwater, Florida (D & S Publishers); Orford, New Hampshire (Equity Publishing); St Paul, Minnesota; and Seattle, Washington

A CIP Catalogue record for this book is available from the British Library.

ISBN 0 406 10401 8

Printed and bound in Great Britain by
Mackays of Chatham PLC, Chatham, Kent

Dedication

In memory of Jean

Preface

The Police and Criminal Evidence Act 1984 came into force in January 1986. It was revolutionary in that it was the first legislative attempt to define comprehensively the investigative powers of the police, more so because it was accompanied by Codes of Practice which were intended to 'provide clear and workable guidelines for the police as well as strong safeguards for the individual'. The passage of the legislation attracted considerable controversy. Its implementation has been equally controversial, the Act being blamed by some police officers for the loss of efficiency as evidenced by a drop in detection rates. The main provisions of the 1984 Act have now been applied to Northern Ireland by the Police and Criminal Evidence (Northern Ireland) Order 1989 and the original Codes of Practice have been revised after much consultation and in the light of four years' experience of the Act and Codes in operation. These Codes are Crown Copyright and are reproduced with the kind permission of the Controller of Her Majesty's Stationery Office. Despite the setting up in 1991 of another Royal Commission to examine the criminal process in England and Wales following the acquittal of the Birmingham Six and other concerns, the PACE Act and Order are unlikely to be changed substantially and will continue to have far-reaching consequences for the investigation of crime and for the style of policing well into the next century.

This book, which now includes investigative powers contained in Acts passed since 1984, is intended as a practical guide for those involved in the investigation of crime or affected by, or interested in, the exercise of police powers.

We owe a debt of gratitude to the secretarial staff in the Department of Law, in particular Mrs Jean Hopewell and Mrs Shirley Peacock, whose considerable typing feats turned our illegible scribble into legible typescript. We would also like to thank the many police officers who rang or wrote to us with problems and queries and in particular Sergeant Gordon Bibby of the Merseyside Police and Detective Chief Inspector Jack Wadd of the Metropolitan Police whose wide-ranging knowledge of and insight into the practicalities of policing were shared unstintingly. We

vii

would encourage police officers and members of the legal profession to contact us with any problem or query at the address below. Finally we must thank our publishers for their encouragement and patience.

The law is stated as at 31 July 1991.

Vaughan Bevan
Ken Lidstone
Faculty of Law
University of Sheffield

August 1991

Contents

Table of Statutes

References to *Statutes* are to Halsbury's Statutes of England (Fourth Edition) showing the volume and page at which the annotated text of the Act may be found.

Table of Cases

1 Introduction

1.01 Before January 1st 1986, when the Police and Criminal Evidence Act 1984 came into effect, the law governing police powers for the investigation of crime was unclear and antiquated. It had developed piecemeal since the establishment of professional police forces in the nineteenth century. Parliament had added fitfully to the few common law principles but there was no clear statement of police powers. This varied and scant law was supplemented by (a) rules of guidance as to the admissibility of confessions provided by the Lord Chief Justice (the Judges' Rules); (b) national administrative guidance in the form of Home Office Circulars (notably that attached to the Judges' Rules); and (c) local administrative guidance in the shape of standing orders issued within each police force. The result was patchy legal obligations and powers for the police and local variations in powers (eg some police forces had wide stop and search powers whereas others were tied to a few narrow national powers). A wide ranging overhaul of the system had been due for many years. New and heavier pressures on the police and a more critical public opinion demanded that the powers of the police be placed on a modern statutory footing. Eventually, in 1978, a Royal Commission on Criminal Procedure was appointed to consider, inter alia, 'the powers and duties of the police in respect of the investigation of criminal offences and the rights and duties of suspects and accused persons, including the means by which they are secured'. With commendable speed the Commission reported within 3 years, having commissioned and received 12 Research Studies, which did much to increase public awareness of police powers and procedures.

1.02 The Royal Commission's recommendations formed the basis of the Police and Criminal Evidence Act 1984 but the Government chose not to implement the Commission's proposals in their entirety, preferring its own package of measures; similarly with the Royal Commission's proposals for an independent prosecutions system, which was enacted by the Prosecution of Offences Act 1985. Both Acts took effect from 1986, a year which will go down in police history. The years since then will also go down in police history, but for different reasons. The acquittal of the Birmingham Six, the Guildford Four and the Maguire Seven reflected

1

badly on the much vaunted fairness of the criminal justice system. The inquiry into the West Midland Serious Crime Squad leading to the over-turning of convictions based on false confessions, together with those acquittals, has cast doubt on the integrity not only of the police, but of the entire criminal justice system. Following the acquittal of the Birmingham Six, the Home Secretary announced the setting up of another Royal Commission. This Commission, under the chairmanship of Lord Runciman, began sitting in June 1991. Its principal aim appears to be to minimise, as far as is possible, the likelihood of such events happening again. The Commission will examine the pre-trial stage, the role of the police and prosecutors, and the possible use of investigative magistrates similar to those in other jurisdictions such as France. Its terms of reference also include looking at expert and scientific evidence and the conduct of trials and appeals. Following so closely upon the 1981 Royal Commission, the 1991 Royal Commission is unlikely to recommend radical changes in the investigative powers of the police with which this book is concerned.

1.03 Of more immediate concern are events in England and Wales, Northern Ireland and abroad which affect police powers. The old adage 'crime does not pay' was seldom true for major criminals. This has been recognised and the emphasis is now on the confiscation of the proceeds of crime, particularly drug related crime. Such crimes are international and the onset of a single European market in 1992 has added impetus to the growth of international cooperation. The Drug Trafficking Act 1986, the Criminal Justice Act 1988 and the Criminal Justice (International Co-operation) Act 1990 provide powers which enable the police to trace the proceeds of crime both here and abroad and to assist foreign governments in tracing such proceeds. The Prevention of Terrorism (Temporary Provisions) Act 1989 provides similar powers to trace and confiscate monies used to fund terrorism. Nearer home the Police and Criminal Evidence (Northern Ireland) Order 1989 applied most of the PACE Act 1984 powers and duties to Northern Ireland. New Codes of Practice took effect in 1991 and tape-recording of interviews has been introduced with the prospect of video-recording in the future. Parliament has also been active on a more mundane level with the creation of new offences and the addition or extension of powers to deal with these offences.

1.04 It is no longer sufficient to offer a guide to the PACE Act. Instead we offer a guide to the investigative powers of the police. Though the bulk of such powers are contained in PACE, as para 1.03 indicates there are many such powers outside that Act. We have, of course, taken account of the numerous judicial decisions on the PACE Act and the large body of research which has been conducted since 1986, including our own study of the use of powers of search and seizure. In order to accommodate this new material we have decided to drop consideration of complaints and discipline which formed Part IX of PACE, and the general matters which made up Part X. Evidential matters dealt with by Part VII and VIII of PACE, with the exception of confessions and the exclusion of evidence, are similarly dropped on the basis that such matters are better dealt with in a textbook on the law of evidence. Confessions and the exclusion of evidence are dealt with in Chapter 8 together with the Codes governing interviewing and tape-recording of interviews.

1.05   The investigative powers dealt with are those directed toward the investigation of crime in general but excluding road traffic offences. For a consideration of these powers, together with an examination of the offences in respect of which many of the powers discussed will be used, see English and Card, *Butterworths Police Law*, 3rd Edition, 1991. The format of this book follows the order of the PACE Act and Order with additional powers considered in the appropriate chapter, see for example, Chapter 4, Part C which incorporates search and seizure powers contained in other statutes. As with the first edition, for ease of use footnotes have been avoided and cases have only been given their date in the text. A complete list of cases and their citations is found in the Table of Cases. The text of the PACE Act 1984 and the relevant parts of the other statutes referred to, are to be found in the Appendices together with the Codes of Practice. The Northern Ireland Order is not included, the text being almost identical with the PACE Act 1984. The Northern Ireland Codes of Practice, issued in 1989, differ in some respects from the revised Codes for England and Wales issued in 1991. Since the Northern Ireland Office intends to adopt the 1991 Codes, including the Code on Tape-recording, as soon as convenient, only the 1991 Codes are included. References to Codes of Practice will therefore be to the 1991 revised Codes. References to the Articles of the Northern Ireland Order follow references to the PACE Act, eg (s 1, Art 3).

2 Themes and definitions

2.01 There are some concepts and definitions which appear throughout the study of police powers. To avoid unnecessary repetition and to highlight their importance, they are dealt with separately in this chapter.

Reasonable suspicion

2.02 'There must be safeguards to protect members of the public from random, arbitrary and discriminatory searches. Clarification of powers will help but the principal safeguard must be found in the requirement for and stricter application of the criterion of reasonable suspicion.' (Royal Commission 1981, para 324–25)

The criterion of reasonable suspicion, or more properly, of reasonable grounds to believe or suspect, is the legal threshold for the exercise of almost all the coercive powers available under the PACE Act and other relevant legislation and for the non-coercive powers such as delaying the detained person's right to consult with a solicitor. Magistrates and senior police officers who may authorise the exercise of certain powers must also be satisfied that there are reasonable grounds to believe that the exercise of those powers is justified. In the absence of reasonable grounds to believe or suspect, the exercise of those powers is not permitted and any consequential interference with the liberty of the individual is unlawful. The importance of the criterion can not therefore be overstated.

'Believe' or 'suspect'

2.03 Two formulations of 'reasonable grounds' are used in the PACE Act and N.I. Order. 'Reasonable grounds to believe' is used, for example, in respect of:

(a) the issuance of warrants to search premises (s 8, Art 10);
(b) the issuance of orders or warrants to produce or search for evidence held in confidence (Sch 1);

4

(c) the issuance of orders or warrants to detain a person without charge (ss 42, 43 and 44, Arts 43, 44 and 45);

(d) entry to premises without a warrant to arrest persons or recapture them (s 17, Art 19);

(e) the search of persons or premises following an arrest (s 32, Art 34);

(f) the seizure of evidence found in consequence of a search of premises (s 19, Art 21), or persons (s 32, Art 34);

(g) authorising detention in police custody (s 37(3), Art 38(3));

(h) the intimate search of persons in police detention (s 55, Art 56);

(i) the power to delay informing someone of the fact of arrest (s 56, Art 57);

(j) the power to delay access to a solicitor (s 58, Art 59).

In addition, whenever a power is conditional upon the offence being a serious arrestable offence (as defined by s 116 and Sch 5, Art 87 and Sch 5, see para 2.24, post), the person who is to exercise the power must have reasonable grounds to believe that the offence is a serious arrestable offence. 'Reasonable grounds to suspect', on the other hand, is used, for example, in respect of:

(a) the power to stop and search a person or vehicle (s 1(3), Art 3(3));

(b) powers of arrest under ss 24 and 25 (Arts 26 and 27) and in respect of the powers of arrest preserved by Sch 2;

(c) search of premises following an arrest for an arrestable offence (s 18, Art 20) (cf s 32, where a search of premises following an arrest for any offence requires reasonable grounds to believe).

Occasionally there is a dual formulation; for example, in s 4 (Art 6) (the setting up of road blocks) there must be reasonable grounds for believing that the offence is a serious arrestable offence; and for suspecting that the person sought is, or is about to be, in the area in which the vehicle is to be stopped.

2.04 The different formulations seek to impose a higher threshold for those powers which require the existence of reasonable grounds to believe and it is no coincidence that those powers involve the invasion of a person's privacy, his continued detention or delay in the exercise of one of his rights. In contrast, those powers which are exercised most frequently, for example, stop and search and arrest powers, are conditional upon the existence of reasonable grounds to *suspect*. This is a much lower standard than reasonable grounds to believe. In legal theory the latter standard requires something close to certainty. In *Johnson v Whitehouse* (1984), Nolan J, speaking of the requirement of a reasonable belief as the threshold to the requirement of a breath test under the Road Traffic legislation, said:

> 'The greater force of the word "believe" is an essential part of the law and

the request for a breath test . . . can only be justified if there are reasonable grounds for believing — *in the full sense of the word* — that the person was the driver of the vehicle.' (Emphasis supplied)

In *Baker v Oxford* (1980) the Divisional Court also accepted that there was a distinction between 'believe' and 'suspect' but did not indicate what it was. However, in argument it had been suggested that 'suspect' implied an imagination that something exists without proof, whereas 'believe' implied an acceptance of what was true. As Lord Devlin put it in *Hussien v Chong Fook Kam* (1970), 'suspicion in its ordinary meaning is a state of conjecture or surmise where proof is lacking: I suspect but I cannot prove'. It is not necessary to have substantial proof before one can be said to 'believe', but the existence of a belief implies that there is more information available which turns conjecture or surmise into an acceptance that something is true. If, therefore, there are ten steps from mere suspicion to a state of certainty, or an acceptance that something is true, then reasonable suspicion may be as low as step 2 or 3, whilst reasonable belief may be as high as step 9 or 10. In the main, those powers in the PACE Act for which the threshold requirement is a reasonable belief, can be exercised in the comparative calm of the courtroom or police station and this justifies the use of the higher standard. Those powers for which reasonable suspicion is required are, in the main, exercisable in the street in circumstances which may not permit of mature reflection. The exercise of those powers is nonetheless a serious infringement of the liberty of the citizen and affects the greatest number of people. It is therefore imperative that the criterion be strictly applied if it is to be a safeguard against the arbitrary exercise of police powers. The different categories of powers will now be considered.

Arrest powers

2.05 The threshold requirement for a valid arrest at common law was 'reasonable cause to suspect that the person was guilty of a felony'. The use of the phrase 'was guilty' is unfortunate since it contradicts the presumption of innocence. However, it probably reflects the reality of the exercise of arrest powers, which is that a police officer arrests a presumptively guilty person. Be that as it may, this test was given statutory force by s 2(4) of the Criminal Law Act 1967 which abolished felonies and created the concept of an 'arrestable offence'. This concept was perpetuated by s 24 of the PACE Act (Art 26 of the N.I. Order) and the threshold requirement of a valid arrest under the PACE Act and Order is reasonable cause to suspect that a person is committing, or has committed, an offence. Recent cases suggest a lowering of the threshold.

2.06   In *Castorina v Chief Constable of Surrey* (1988), a civil action for false arrest and imprisonment, Woolf LJ suggested that, when it is alleged that an arrest was unlawful, three questions must be asked:

1)   Did the arresting officer suspect that the person arrested was guilty of the offence? The answer to this question depends on the findings of fact as to the officer's state of mind and is in that sense subjective.

2)   Assuming that the officer had the necessary suspicion, was there reasonable cause for that suspicion? This is an objective requirement to be determined by the trial judge (therefore a matter of law) though it may fall to be determined on the basis of facts found by the jury.

3)   If the answer to these questions is in the affirmative, then the officer has a discretion to arrest (ss 24 and 25, Arts 26 and 27, use the words 'may arrest' not 'must') and discretion must be exercised in accordance with the principles set down in *Associated Provincial Picture Houses Ltd v Wednesbury Corporation* (1948) (the Wednesbury principles). This 'three questions approach' can be applied to the exercise of all powers conditional on the requirement of reasonable cause to believe by replacing the word 'suspect' or 'suspicion' with 'believe' or 'belief'.

2.07   Suspicion — In *Siddiqui v Swain* (1979) the Division Court said '. . . the words "has reasonable cause to suspect" [or believe] import the requirement that the constable in fact suspects [or believes] . . .' That suspicion in the context of arrest may arise from his own observation or from information supplied to him from other sources. However, though this is a subjective requirement, the question is not answered by the constable's assertion that he in fact suspected. There must be objectively verifiable facts which led him to suspect that the person had committed the offence in question. It may be that his conclusions from those facts are not reasonable, there is then suspicion but not reasonable suspicion. Questions 1 and 2 are therefore not entirely separate. The judge or jury may determine that the absence of any reasonable grounds for the suspicion means that the constable did not in fact suspect. This is similar to the defence of mistaken belief in the general criminal law. If a defendant says that he was labouring under a mistake of fact and therefore held a particular belief, he must be judged on the facts as he believed them to be (the subjective approach). However, if there are no reasonable grounds for such a belief, the jury may well conclude that the defendant did not in fact hold that belief (*DPP v Morgan* (1976); *R v Williams (Gladstone)* (1984)). The question whether a constable actually suspected is therefore not answered by his assertion that he did. If there is no reasonable basis upon which he could have suspected, the judge or jury may conclude that he did not in fact suspect.

'Reasonable'

2.08   The adjective 'reasonable' imports an objective standard and requires facts and circumstances which would lead an impartial third party to form the belief or suspicion in question. In a civil action arising out of the exercise of a power which requires a reasonable belief or suspicion, the question whether there were reasonable grounds will be decided by the judge, as it will in the rare criminal cases in which the question arises (cf *Herniman v Smith* (1938)). In forming that belief or suspicion the person is not constrained, as is a court, by rules of evidence. Consequently inadmissible evidence may be taken into account; for example, hearsay, the previous character of the accused, including any previous conviction, or information from an informant. The hearsay or information must itself be reasonable and the constable must be satisfied that it is true, or possibly true, depending on whether the standard is 'believe' or 'suspect'. An anonymous telephone call would satisfy neither standard and reasonable steps must be taken to verify that information. How far the person should go in seeking verification also depends upon whether the standard is reasonable grounds to believe or to suspect. Clearly the latter standard will be satisfied by taking fewer steps than will the former. Informants are a regular source of information giving rise to a reasonable belief or suspicion. How much verification is necessary will depend in part upon the type of information, and in part upon the credibility of the informer. The more often the informant gives credible information the greater his credibility and the fewer steps which need to be taken to verify it, though much will depend on the nature of the information and of the informant. It has been suggested that information from a principal or accomplice in the crime cannot be the basis of reasonable cause to believe or suspect (*Isaacs v Brand* (1817)). If this was the ratio of that case, which is doubtful, it cannot in modern times be good law. As with the case of one party to a crime giving evidence against another party, one must be aware that the person has, or may have, a purpose of his own to serve and take appropriate steps to verify the information. However, the supplier of drugs or seller of stolen goods can often provide more reliable information than those who are not involved and who have a better reputation. Where the information comes from fellow police officers, a constable may be justified in acting on it without any verification. For example, constable A hears a crash of glass at 2 a.m. He turns a corner to see a shop window broken and a youth running away. He communicates this information, together with a description of the youth, to his radio operator who in turn passes it to all constables in the area. At 2.05 a.m. constable B sees D, who answers the description, running from the direction of the incident. Constable B has reasonable grounds to suspect, (a) that an arrestable offence (criminal damage and/or theft) has been committed, and (b) that D has committed it.

He may then arrest D under s 24(6) of the 1984 Act (Art 26(6) of the 1989 Order) (see para 5.15, post). Note that the constable is under a duty to tell D why he is being arrested, in effect to state the reasonable grounds justifying the arrest. If D is able to satisfy the constable that those grounds are not in fact reasonable, there is a duty to release D if he has not yet reached a police station (see s 30(7), Art 32(10) discussed in para 5.53, post; and see *King v Gardner* (1979), considered in para 2.16, post, which suggests that the original observer (constable A above) should give evidence of what he saw if reasonable suspicion is in issue).

2.09   The need to make further inquiries — In *Castorina v Chief Constable of Surrey* (1988) Purchas LJ said:

'There is ample authority for the proposition that courses of inquiry which may or may not be taken by the investigating officer before arrest are not relevant to the consideration whether on the information available to him at the time of arrest he had reasonable cause for suspicion. Of course, failure to follow an obvious course in exceptional circumstances may well be grounds for attacking the executive exercise of that power under the *Wednesbury* principle.'

This approach was supported by Woolf LJ and Sir Frederick Lawton. However, despite the judicial unanimity, this cannot be accepted as a correct statement of the law. The authorities cited in support (*Mohammed-Holgate v Duke* (1984) and *Ward v Chief Constable of Avon and Somerset Constabulary* (1986)) do not in fact support the proposition that further inquiries are not relevant to the issue of whether there was reasonable cause for suspicion. In both these cases it was held that, once the arresting officer has reasonable suspicion, there is no legal requirement to make further inquiries before exercising the power to arrest. That is a far cry from saying that there is no legal requirement to make further inquiries in order to establish reasonable suspicion. In *Castorina*, there had been a burglary at C's former workplace which was considered to be an 'inside job'. The managing director, when asked whether there was anyone with a grudge, stated that C had recently been dismissed but he did not think she was responsible. Having established that C was of good character and without further inquiry, the police went to C's home and arrested her. Her subsequent action for false imprisonment succeeded at first instance but was overturned on appeal, the Court of Appeal ruling that the trial judge had applied the wrong definition of false imprisonment and reasonable cause to suspect. Having made the above statement on further inquiries, Purchas LJ went on to determine that:

'In the circumstances of this case, and I emphasise that every case has to be determined upon its particular facts, I am satisfied that the arresting officers had reasonable cause to suspect that the plaintiff was guilty of this unusual burglary.'

It is, with respect, difficult to see how the officers could have actually suspected that C had committed the burglary, still less that a reasonable man, in the position of the constables at the time of the arrest, would have thought so. If the fact that a middle-aged woman of good character had been dismissed from the firm recently was sufficient grounds for reasonable suspicion, that test ceases to be a proper safeguard against the exercise of police powers. A judge must be satisfied that the officer actually held the requisite suspicion. That can only be determined of course by reference to the facts of a particular case, but there must be some facts which lead to that suspicion. A constable may in fact suspect but, unless there are reasonable grounds upon which that suspicion can be founded, there is no reasonable cause for suspicion. Consequently a police officer who has a suspicion which is not based on reasonable grounds must make further inquiries in order to provide that basis.

Suspicion based on unrelated matters

2.10   In *Monaghan v Corbett* (1983) a constable spoke to D, whose car was parked outside his house. The constable smelt alcohol in D's breath. Next day, a Sunday, he was informed by a neighbour that D habitually drove to a public house at Sunday lunchtime and that D had just done so. The constable awaited D's return and asked him for a breath test. His reasonable suspicion (that D was driving with excess alcohol in the blood) was founded on the smell of alcohol on D's breath the previous day, together with his alleged habitual visits to the public house. The court accepted that information grounding reasonable suspicion could come from sources other than the constable's own observation, for example, from members of the public or fellow police officers. However, it held that it would be a very dangerous extension of the law to permit reasonable suspicion to be founded on facts wholly unconnected with the driving of a motor vehicle at the time to which the suspicion relates. It followed that there were no reasonable grounds to suspect that D was driving with excess alcohol in the blood and a breath test had not been lawfully required (cf. *DPP v Wilson* (1991)). In other contexts, the principle would exclude reasonable suspicion being based solely on the fact that D has previous convictions. One cannot, for example, reasonably suspect that D, who has previous convictions for theft, is guilty because he habitually visits a local store. There must be some conduct relating to a particular visit, which may be added to the fact of previous convictions, and together they may found reasonable cause to believe or suspect. Similarly the fact that an area is a high crime area is insufficient. A person passing through an area in which a number of burglaries have been committed cannot, without more, be suspected of burglary. If the person is a known burglar, there is suspicion, but other conduct (or information) is required before it can be said that such suspicion is reasonable.

Reasonable suspicion — stop and search

2.11   The power to stop and search persons or vehicles under s 1(1) of the PACE Act 1984 (Art 3(3) of the N.I. Order), and the powers to stop and search under other statutes (see Ch 3, post) are only exercisable if the constable has reasonable grounds for suspecting that he will find articles to which the power relates. It is in this area that the requirement of reasonable suspicion has caused most difficulty. A definition has proved elusive. The Committee on Drug Dependency (1970), considering the stop and search power under the misuse of drugs legislation, concluded that reasonable suspicion could not be positively defined. They were urged to define it negatively, that is, to state what was not reasonable suspicion. They could, however, only agree that dress and hair style should be excluded as sole grounds for suspicion. The Royal Commission on Criminal Procedure (1981) also concluded that the criterion of reasonable suspicion could not be defined and recommended instead, in relation to stop and search powers, the giving of reasons, the recording of those reasons and supervision of junior officers in order to ensure that the criterion was not devalued by the lack of definition (para 3.25). The implementation of that recommendation by ss 2 and 3 of the Act may be seen as accepting that the criterion is not an effective safeguard. On the other hand, by giving guidance as to what was, or was not, reasonable suspicion in relation to the stop and search powers in the first edition of the Code of Practice, the government sought to make it effective. Even that limited guidance was seen by the police as too restrictive. The second edition (1991) gives less guidance and, crucially, does not repeat the statement, that the degree or level of suspicion required to establish reasonable grounds for a stop and search is no less than that required to justify an arrest. This may be seen as an indication that the threshold requirement for a stop and search is lower than that for an arrest. However, this is not so. Reasonable cause for suspicion is a legal concept and as such it is for the courts, rather than administrators, to determine what it is in a particular case. There can be no justification for a different interpretation of an identical criterion according to the power to be exercised.

2.12   That said, the Code of Practice seeks to prevent stop and search powers being exercised against people of a particular racial or ethnic origin or whose mode of dress sets them apart. Code A, para 1.7 states:

> 'Reasonable suspicion can never be supported on the basis of personal factors alone. For example, a person's colour, age, hairstyle or manner of dress, or the fact that he is known to have a previous conviction for possession of an unlawful article, cannot be used alone or in combination with each other as the sole basis on which to search that person. Nor may it be founded on the basis

of stereotyped images of certain persons or groups as more likely to be committing offences.'

It should be noted that the exercise of arrest or stop and search powers in a racially discriminatory manner is a disciplinary offence. The guidance needs to be read carefully. None of the above factors can be used *alone or in combination with each other as the sole basis* for searching a person. Some of them can be used in combination with other factors. For example, if information is received that a youth of a particular colour, age and dress was seen waving a machete and a person of that description is seen in the vicinity, there are reasonable grounds justifying a search. Similarly if a description is given of a person seen carrying a knife and a person of a similar description is known to have a propensity to carry knives, having been stopped and searched before, there are reasonable grounds justifying a search. Code A, para 1.6 is a significant relaxation of earlier guidance. It states:

> 'Whether reasonable grounds for suspicion exist will depend on the circumstances in each case, but there must be some objective basis for it. An officer will need to consider the nature of the article suspected of being carried in the context of the factors such as the time and the place, and the behaviour of the person concerned or those with him. Reasonable suspicion may exist, for example, where information has been received such as a description of an article being carried or of a suspected offender; a person is seen acting covertly or warily or attempting to hide something; or a person is carrying a certain type of article at an unusual time or in a place where a number of burglaries or thefts are known to have taken place recently. But the decision to stop and search must be based on all the facts which bear on the likelihood that an article of a certain kind will be found.'

The final sentence is the most significant. There must be objectively verifiable facts which point to the likelihood that an article will be found. The reality is that there seldom will be such facts. Knives and similar offensive or potentially offensive weapons can be carried on the person with no outward sign. (Similarly articles intended for use in theft.) In some cases there will be no reasonable grounds justifying a search until an offence is committed. For example, a youth with previous convictions for theft from cars has a screwdriver, which he intends using to break into cars, hidden in his bomber jacket. He is seen by a constable, who knows of the convictions, standing near a line of parked cars in mid-afternoon. He does nothing untoward while under observation. At this point there is strong suspicion that he has an article for use in theft on his person but no reasonable suspicion justifying a search. If he starts trying the doors of cars there is now reasonable suspicion but he may then be arrested for interfering with motor vehicles (s 9, Criminal Attempts Act 1981). Similarly a person with previous convictions for causing harm using knives only raises a suspicion that he may have a knife with him. In the absence of information that he is actually carrying one, a constable must wait until some overt use is made of it, by which time he has a power of arrest under the Prevention of Crime Act 1953. This requirement of reasonable suspicion may then be seen by the police as an unwarranted constraint on policing and in practice reliance may be placed on 'consent' or that old stalwart 'the Ways and Means Act'.

2.13 The above discussion applies to the other requirements of reasonable grounds to suspect or believe whether contained in the PACE Act or Order or other statutes. For example, an application for a search warrant under s 23(3) of the Misuse of Drugs Act 1971, requires 'reasonable ground for suspecting that any controlled drugs are unlawfully in the possession of a person on any premises . . .'. In such a case the applicant must have a reasonable ground for the suspicion and the magistrate must be satisfied that there is such a ground.

2.14 Reasonableness in the exercise of the discretion to exercise a power — As indicated above (para 2.05), if there is a reasonable cause to suspect which then justifies the exercise of a power, the constable generally has a discretion (an executive discretion as opposed to judicial discretion) as to whether to exercise it. This is imported by the word 'may'; for example, 'may arrest'; 'may stop and search'. Where there is reasonable cause to suspect that stolen or prohibited articles will be found on a person or vehicle, in practice the choice is between obtaining the person's consent or exercising the power. Where there is reasonable cause to suspect an offence and an offender, again the choice will be between obtaining the person's consent to accompany the constable to a police station, proceeding by summons or arresting (as to whether consent should be sought, see para 2.21). In all cases in which a constable exercises his discretion, it must be exercised reasonably in accordance with the principles laid down in *Associated Provincial Picture Houses Ltd v Wednesbury Corporation* (1948). Put simply, 'unreasonableness' in the Wednesbury context means acting in a way in which no reasonable person would act, or in this context, the way in which no reasonable policeman would act. The courts have been slow to find that the police have contravened this principle. In *Mohammed-Holgate v Duke* (1984) the House of Lords held that a constable had not acted unreasonably (and therefore unlawfully) by arresting a person, in respect of whom there was reasonable suspicion, simply because he believed that he would be more likely to confess and tell the truth while in custody. Similarly in *Ward v Chief Constable of Avon and Somerset Constabulary* (1986) (see below para 2.16(i)).

Statutory protection for a lawful constable

2.15 Section 38 of the Offences against the Person Act 1861 makes it an offence to assault any person with intent to resist a *lawful* arrest. Section 51 of the Police Act 1964 makes it an offence to assault, resist or wilfully obstruct a constable *in the execution of this duty*. The respective requirements that the arrest be lawful and the constable be in the execution of his duty are essential. It is not an offence under these sections to assault, resist or wilfully obstruct a constable who is acting unlawfully. One is entitled to resist an unlawful arrest and a constable acting unlawfully cannot be in the execution of his duty. The importance of these offences lies not only in the protection given to constables acting lawfully, but also in that they give the criminal courts the opportunity to examine the conduct of a constable and to give guidance on the meaning of 'reasonable grounds to believe or suspect' in the context of arrest powers, powers to enter premises to effect an arrest, and powers to stop and search. Some of the decisions are set out below. The unlawful actions of a constable may also result in a civil action, in the context of arrest, for wrongful arrest and false imprisonment. The question whether or not there was reasonable cause to suspect so as to justify the arrest is often the issue in such cases and so these cases also offer guidance on the meaning of the criterion.

Reasonable suspicion — some pre- and post-PACE Act decisions

2.16   The criterion of reasonable suspicion was, as indicated in para 2.05, ante, adopted from the common law and given statutory form in relation to arrest, by the Criminal Law Act 1967 and now the PACE Act and Order, and is similarly used in numerous statutory powers. The following decisions give an indication of how it is interpreted in practice.

(a)   *King v Gardner* (1979) — Police officers received a radio message that suspects had been seen loitering. They were described as two males and one female, one with a dog. One male was described as wearing blue jeans and as having long hair. The police officers saw D who was walking with a woman and a dog. D refused to show them what he had in a large canvas bag and was prosecuted for assaulting a policeman in the scuffle which followed. No evidence was called other than the policeman's bare assertion that D fitted the description. The stipendiary magistrate's decision that there was no evidence of reasonable suspicion justifying the stop was upheld by the Divisional Court. The constable was not therefore acting in the execution of his duty and D was acquitted. Note that the case turned on the absence of any evidence of reasonable grounds to suspect that D was carrying stolen goods in his bag. Even if he did fit the description of a man seen loitering that, in itself, was not reasonable grounds to suspect that D was carrying stolen goods. There would have to be some evidence to suggest that some goods may have been stolen. For example, signs of forced entry to a house where they were seen loitering or some other conduct which provides a reasonable basis for the suspicion that the loiterers were involved in some criminal activity.

(b) *R v Prince* (1981) — P and another youth were being followed by two police officers suspicious of them. P was seen to go into two post offices in succession. Whilst inside, he spoke to the cashier concerning a document in his possession. In the second post office he was challenged by a police officer who had seen that the document was a giro cheque. Both officers demanded to see the giro cheque. P refused to part with it and made to leave the post office. The prosecution alleged that P was being detained under s 66 of the Metropolitan Police Act 1839, which provided a power similar to that contained in s 1 of the PACE Act. The officers were blocking P's way out so he assaulted them. He was charged with assault occasioning actual bodily harm. It was held that there was no case to answer. There were, in the circumstances, no reasonable grounds for suspecting that P was in possession of the giro cheque unlawfully. P's behaviour, coupled with the officer's hunch, was no basis for detention. A person is entitled to use reasonable force to resist unlawful detention but, while there was some evidence of the use of unreasonable force, it was unsafe to leave it to the jury.

(c) *Daniel v Morrison* (1979) — A police constable stopped a car in the exercise of his power under the Road Traffic Act. The car was not displaying a vehicle excise licence (it had fallen off inside the vehicle). D refused to answer questions and tried to walk away saying, as he did so, that the car was stolen. The constable then detained D under s 66 of the Metropolitan Police Act 1839. D punched the constable and was charged with assaulting him in the execution of his duty. He was convicted. His conduct, and perhaps most importantly, his remarks, gave the constable reasonable grounds to suspect that D was in possession of a stolen car. He was then entitled to detain him while further questioning or inquiries took place.

(d) *Pedro v Diss* (1981) — Police officers in a police car observed three youths 'loitering' near the doorway of a private house. As the police car approached, the youths moved off. D refused to answer any questions and was abusive. He was searched and two yale keys were found. He made to walk off but was restrained after a struggle. It was subsequently discovered that D's brother lived at the address where D was first seen. His conviction for assaulting the constable was quashed on appeal. The court held that there was a duty to inform D of the reasons for his detention under s 66 of the Metropolitan Police Act 1839 and the failure to carry out this duty rendered the detention unlawful. Therefore the police were not acting in the execution of their duty in detaining D. The Divisional Court did not consider whether there had been reasonable grounds to suspect that D was in possession of housebreaking implements, but the magistrates clearly thought there were. However, it appears to be more a case of suspicion based on D's hostility and abusiveness, rather than reasonable suspicion. Note that while the finding of the keys may turn suspicion into 'reasonable' suspicion in order to justify a search, an officer must have reasonable grounds to suspect *before* the search takes place (see the discussion in para 3.17, post).

(e) *McBean v Parker* (1984) — Two police officers on duty in the early hours of the morning stopped to speak to a group of youths. They approached D and asked for his name and address which he refused to give. He also refused to empty his pockets when asked to. One officer then tried to search D without giving any reason for the search. D resisted. The second officer joined in and D butted him with his head. D was then arrested and charged (a) with damaging the first officer's jacket, and (b) assaulting the second officer in the execution of his duty. D was convicted on both charges but the Divisional Court allowed an appeal against conviction on the ground that the constable had not stated the reason for the search which was therefore unlawful (see *Pedro v Diss* (1981), ante). D was then entitled to resist. The first officer's jacket was torn while D used reasonable force to resist the unlawful search. Headbutting the second officer was probably not reasonable force, and had D been charged with common assault the court would have found it difficult to justify. However, the charge was assaulting the officer in the execution of his duty and he clearly was not so acting. An alternative ground for allowing the appeal would have been the total absence of reasonable grounds to suspect D. Under s 1 of the 1984 Act there must be reasonable grounds to suspect D has stolen goods or prohibited articles on him and the constable must under s 2 give D the reasons for the search. If the facts of this case were to be repeated under the Act, one would expect the same result, though it is to be hoped that there would be an acquittal at first instance.

(f) *Holtham v Commissioner of Police of the Metropolis* (1987) — The police were investigating a murder. The plaintiffs were the parents of the suspect and the police came to search their house for goods stolen from the victim. The parents were extremely co-operative. The loft was surprisingly clean, leading the police to suspect that they were expected, hence the search proved negative. It became apparent that the parents were aware of their son's arrest. They told the police that he had not visited them in July or August, contradicting a statement from a neighbour. This was taken as confirming the suspicion that the parents, being aware of the son's arrest, had removed the evidence and they were arrested for doing acts intended to impede the son's prosecution, contrary to s 4(1) of the Criminal Law Act 1967. In an action for false imprisonment, Peter Pain J held that the police did not have reasonable grounds to suspect and the arrest was, therefore, unlawful. Reasonable grounds for suspicion are, he said, 'something a good deal more than suspicion'. He concluded that 'further inquiry should have been made following the negative search'. The Court of Appeal rejected this conclusion holding that there was reasonable suspicion. Sir John Donaldson MR thought the trial judge was in error because:

'Suspicion may or may not be based upon reasonable grounds but it still remains suspicion and nothing more.'

He went on to hold that the police had good cause to suspect that the plaintiffs were lying and that the likeliest explanation for their lying was that they were doing so with intent to impede their son's prosecution.

(g) *Kynaston v DPP* (1987) — Police officers entered premises in the exercise of their power under s 17(1)(b) of PACE to arrest D for armed robbery (an arrestable offence). The occupants resisted the entry and were charged with and convicted of obstructing and assaulting the police in the execution of their duty (s 51(3) Police Act 1964). At the trial the defence submitted that there was no case to answer because a constable entering premises under s 17(1)(b) and (2)(a) was required to have not only reasonable grounds for believing that the person was on the premises (s 17(2)(a)) but also reasonable grounds for suspecting that the person sought had committed the arrestable offence. The magistrates rejected this submission. One defendant then pleaded guilty, the others were convicted. On appeal by way of case stated the Divisional Court held that, whilst a constable must have reasonable suspicion justifying the arrest, it was not necessary that it be proved by positive evidence, it can be inferred. The court further found that there were reasonable grounds to believe that the person sought was in the premises entered, as required by s 17(2)(a). He had been chased by an off-duty police officer who lost him in the area, and information was then received that he had entered the house occupied by one of the defendants. It was further held that the facts found by the justices were more than ample to justify the inference that the police had reasonable grounds for suspecting that D had committed the offence of robbery. However, no facts were cited by the justices which could support this inference. So the Divisional Court relied on the evidential presumption that, unless the contrary is proved, a man acting in a public capacity or situation, was duly appointed and has properly discharged his official duties (*praesumuntur rite esse acta*). This, it is submitted, is an improper application of the principle. It cannot be presumed that a police officer has lawfully arrested a person simply because he is acting in his public capacity as a police officer. There must be some facts before the court justifying such an inference (see *Chapman v DPP* below).

(h) *Chapman v DPP* (1988) — While on duty plain-clothed police officers received a radio message from a colleague that he had been assaulted by youths who had run away. They went to the scene and learned that one of the youths had entered a nearby flat. Two police officers went to the flat, explained to the occupier that one of their number had been assaulted by six youths, one of whom had run into the flat, and requested entry. The occupier refused and resisted the entry by the police officers. He was subsequently arrested for assaulting and obstructing the police in the execution of their duty (s 51 Police Act 1964). The magistrates accepted that the only legal basis for entry was that under s 17 of the PACE Act 1984 to arrest a person for an arrestable offence. The magistrates were referred to the offence under s 2 of the Public Order Act 1986 and held that the words used by the constable to the occupier ('one of my officers has been assaulted by six youths, one of whom ran into this flat') reasonably disclosed an arrestable offence of violent disorder, and convicted the defendant. The Divisional Court quashed the conviction. There was no reason to doubt that the constable believed his colleague had been assaulted, but common assault was not an arrestable offence and there was no finding of fact as to any injuries sustained by the constable, nor were any mentioned to the defendant. It was not therefore open to the court to infer that an assault of arrestable seriousness had occurred. Nor in the absence of the necessary evidence were the justices entitled to conclude that the constable reasonably suspected violent disorder or any other arrestable offence had been committed. In the absence of the necessary evidence, the court could not conclude that the constable had been acting in the execution of his duty when assaulted by the defendant.

(i) *Ward v Chief Constable of Avon and Somerset Constabulary* (1986) — An action for wrongful arrest and false imprisonment followed the arrest of W for theft. Riots took place in April 1980. Shops were looted. Confectionery, including Easter eggs, valued at £10,000, was among the articles stolen. A detective sergeant received information from a reliable source that a television set had been carried into premises occupied by the person with whom W cohabited. He went to the premises and was admitted voluntarily. He searched the house and found 13 Easter eggs. W claimed that she bought them from a supermarket for 37p each. The detective sergeant was suspicious, the price was too low and there were no price labels on the eggs nor any sign that labels had been on them. He then arrested her on suspicion of theft. The trial judge found against W and the Court of Appeal dismissed her appeal. It had been argued on her behalf that the detective sergeant should have made further inquiries and in the absence of such inquiries there was no reasonable cause to suspect theft. The Court of Appeal held that there was reasonable cause, it was thin but the question was, was it sufficient. Holding that it was the Court said:

> 'Looking objectively, as one should, D.S. Edwards did have reasonable cause for making the arrest. He had found the eggs in circumstances which aroused his suspicion and called for an explanation. He was given an explanation which was apparently untrue. He disbelieved it, and on good grounds. It could not be said that no reasonable constable should not have exercised his discretion so as to make the arrest. He might have decided not to arrest, but he was entitled to do what he did.'

2.17 Despite the fact that the courts are often not setting an exacting standard, the requirement of reasonable suspicion will not permit the exercise of certain powers (particularly the power of stop and search) in circumstances in which the police wish to exercise them. However, the operational need for the exercise of such a power remains, thus creating pressure to exercise them despite that requirement, or to seek to avoid the requirement altogether by purporting to act with the consent of the person involved. Either course leads to illegality if, as must often be the case, the person is not 'consenting' but submitting to authority. A strict interpretation of the criterion of reasonable suspicion must result in considerably fewer stops and searches than the police would wish to do. This results in fewer arrests and a drop in detection rates. This may be unpalatable but must not be seen as a sign of police inefficiency, indeed the Audit Commission (1990) has concluded that as an indicator of efficiency, 'The simple measure of the clear up rate of recorded crime is of limited use'. Senior officers have long been aware of this yet pressure continues to be put upon junior officers to exercise their powers on the basis of mere suspicion or to circumvent the requirement by the pretence of consent (see below).

Consent and powers

2.18 Consent is one of the most important and effective 'powers' in the armoury of the police. That which can only be done within limits laid down by statute and code of practice, and that which statute prohibits expressly or impliedly, may be done free of such constraints with the consent of the individual or body concerned. For example, persons in a public or private place may be searched for stolen or prohibited articles (or anything else) if that person consents. Searches of premises may take place with the consent of the occupier or other person entitled to give consent. As indicated in Ch 4, research suggests that almost a third of searches carried out without a search warrant were recorded as being undertaken with consent. Material which under Part II of the PACE Act 1984 (Part III of the PACE (N.I.) Order 1989) is excluded from police access, can be obtained with the consent of the person in possession. The PACE Act and Order provide for the voluntary attendance of persons at a police station 'to assist police with their inquiries'. This gives the police a period of 'detention' which is in most respects the same as that following arrest but without the time limits imposed by the Act and Order. Some of the protections for the arrested person in a police station are only available on request, for example, the right of access to a solicitor. The person in custody may by signature on the custody record indicate that he does not want such protection, and if he does, he is clearly in a more vulnerable position. The incentive to seek consent or voluntary attendance is clear. The constable is able to act in circumstances in which a statutory power could not be exercised or, if such a power could have been exercised, the limitations imposed no longer exist and the paperwork which accompanies such exercise is reduced or eliminated.

2.19   There is a body of evidence that the concepts of consent and voluntariness are being used with increasing frequency, and in many cases being abused because the person is not freely consenting or volunteering but is in truth submitting to authority. The reliance on consent and voluntary cooperation has been justified as being consistent with the aims of the PACE Act and with the concept of policing by consent (see para 4.27, post). It is, however, consistent with neither. The PACE Act attempts to achieve a balance between police powers and individual liberty. It contains effective controls to limit the circumstances in which a police power may be exercised and the manner in, and the extent to, which it is exercised. Consent avoids such limitations. Two particular issues are raised: first, the true meaning of consent, and second whether consent is being improperly used as an alternative to the exercise of a power.

2.20   What is 'real consent'? In *Chatterton v Gerson* (1980), Bristow J said:

'It is clear law that in any context in which consent of an injured party is a defence to what would otherwise be a crime or civil wrong the consent must be real.' (at p 1012)

'A man cannot be said to be truly willing unless he is in a position to choose freely, and freedom of choice predicates, not only full knowledge of the circumstances on which the exercise of choice is conditional, so that he may be able to choose wisely, but the absence of any feeling of constraint so that nothing shall interfere with the freedom of his will.' *Bowater v Rowley Regis Corp* (1944) cited with approval by Lord Hodson in *ICI v Shatwell* (1965)

Freedom of choice is at the heart of real consent. It would follow that the person who responds to the statement 'I must ask you to accompany me to a police station', without more, is not really consenting but submitting to authority in ignorance of the fact that he has a choice; that he can say no. On the other hand, a person who is made fully aware that he is under investigation, who is aware of the crime under investigation, who knows that he is not being arrested, and who agrees to attend at a police station, is a true volunteer (Reiner et al (1990) Crim.L.R. 22 at p 28 argue that the true distinction is between suspects and witnesses, the suspect never being a true volunteer. This ignores the fact that many knowledgeable suspects, solicitors for example, have submitted to questioning at a police station without being arrested. The true volunteer is in the minority but, it is submitted, he does exist). Code of Practice B seeks to ensure that consent to a search of premises is real by requiring that the officer 'state the purpose of the search and inform the person concerned'. Code B 4.3 makes it clear that consent obtained by duress is of no effect. Research carried out by the authors showed that in a majority of searches of premises carried out with consent, the 'consent' was obtained from a person in police detention having been arrested for an offence, by obtaining a signature on a form of consent. The fact of arrest and detention may well be sufficient duress to negative such 'consent', but in addition it may be doubted whether a standard form is a sufficient compliance with the Code B which requires (para 4.2) that the officer in charge of the search 'shall state' the purpose of the search and that D need not consent to it. In *A-G of Trinidad and Tobago v Whiteman* (1991) the Privy Council, referring to the right to communicate with a legal adviser, held that it is incumbent upon a police officer to see that the arrested person was informed of his right in a way in which he understood it. The mere exhibition of notices in the police station is not enough. It is submitted that simply obtaining a signature without an oral statement of the person's rights is not enough. The use of ploys to ensure that the form is not read and its contents assimilated merely adds emphasis to the lack of real consent in such a process (see *Sanders* (1989) where more than 20 such ploys were apparently used to prevent a suspect from taking in the statement of his right of access to legal advice). Home Office statistics show that 256,900 searches of persons or vehicles under s 1 of the PACE Act 1984 were carried out in 1990. These are only searches carried out in the exercise of the s 1 power and do not include those carried out 'with consent'. It is impossible to state how many of the latter took place but the limitation imposed by the requirement of reasonable suspicion, the administrative burden that records be kept when the power is exercised, and the general ethos which sees consent as more in keeping with modern policing, suggest that almost as many are searched with 'consent' as under the s 1 power. However, all too often the 'request' for consent takes the form of an offer which cannot be refused. A search will take place with or without consent and a refusal merely serves to increase the suspicion (though it cannot alone amount to reasonable suspicion). The reality often is that the person whose premises are being searched, or who accompanies a constable to a police station, believes that a power is being exercised, perhaps more politely than he had expected but no less an exercise of power for that.

Consent v power

2.21   The Royal Commission on Criminal Procedure 1981 anticipated the continued use of consent but not as an alternative to available powers and certainly not as a means of evading the constraints on such powers and the safeguards against their abuse. In relation to the search of premises, it said:

> '. . . there will no doubt continue to be circumstances when premises are searched with the occupier's consent, where, for example, no arrest has been made and in the course of general police inquiries.' (para 3.50)

Consent should not be seen as an alternative to an available power. It should be sought only when no power is available and the action which the police wish to take is necessary for the prevention or detection of crime — necessary, not because there is pressure to achieve specific results which cannot be achieved within the available powers, but because it is in the public interest that the contemplated action be taken. If such necessity exists and no power is available the person whose consent is sought should be told what action the police wish to take, why it is thought necessary to take that action, that he is not obliged to permit that action to be taken and the consequences of the action as they affect him (see, for example, Code B, 4.2 which requires that the person be told that anything seized may be produced in evidence). Consent obtained following the giving of such information is likely to be seen as real (or informed) consent.

2.22   It must be accepted that the person will sometimes refuse consent. There will then be a temptation, often severe, to stretch, bend or break the law in order to achieve the objective. Such temptation must be resisted. Policing within the law means that actions which the police wish to take cannot always be taken within the law. To ignore this and to abuse the concept of consent or voluntariness is counter-productive and ultimately as damaging to the police as to the public. The public is harmed because the carefully judged balance between the public interest in the effective investigation of crime and the public interest in protecting the rights of the individual is destroyed. The police, under understandable pressure to obtain results, are also harmed by the exposure to civil, criminal and/or disciplinary action and by acquittals if the court excludes evidence obtained by their improper conduct. The pressure to obtain results explains, but never justifies, much police misconduct. The statutory rules and codes of practice with which this book is concerned go a long way toward achieving the balance between the twin public interests mentioned above. Almost all legitimate policing objectives relating to the investigation of crime can be achieved within this framework. If there are objectives which cannot be, then the police must argue for a change in the law.

2.23   The foregoing does not mean that police powers have to be used officiously and coercively. On the contrary, good policing requires that the cooperation of the citizen in the exercise of the power be sought before coercive measures are taken. Only when cooperation is not forthcoming, or is not likely to be forthcoming, can reasonable force be used. In this way the slogan 'policing with consent' becomes policing with cooperation. In other words the public cooperate with the exercise of police powers.

Serious arrestable offence (s 116 and Sch 5, Art 87)

2.24   '. . . circumstances may arise requiring the application of a power which of its nature would be unacceptable in the normal run of cases: intimate personal searches, the taking of certain body samples, prolonged detention or detention without allowing access to legal advice. In assessing whether such powers should be available and the special safeguards to be applied to them if they are, we concluded that account must be taken of the effectiveness of the power in investigating the offence concerned and of the importance that society places upon bringing those suspected of it to trial. The seriousness of the offence is, accordingly, a critical consideration.' (Royal Commission on Criminal Procedure, para 3.5)

Consequently Parliament, in the PACE Act 1984, decreed that the police can only exercise the following powers if there are reasonable grounds to believe that the offence for which the person is arrested and detained, or in respect of which the power is to be exercised, is a 'serious arrestable offence':

> s 4, (Art 6) Road checks
> s 8, (Art 10) The issue of search warrants by magistrates
> s 9, (Art 11) and Sch 1 The issue of an order for production of, or warrant to search for, special procedure material

s 42, (Art 43) Authorisation by a superintendent or above of the continued detention of a person

s 43, (Art 44) The issue by a magistrates' court of a warrant of further detention

s 44, (Art 45) The extension by a magistrates' court of a warrant of further detention

s 56, (Art 57) Delay in notifying someone of the person's arrest

s 58, (Art 59) Delay in permitting access to legal advice

s 62, (Art 62) Taking an intimate sample from a person with his consent

s 63, (Art 63) Taking a non-intimate sample from a person without his consent

The limitation on the exercise of these powers followed the recommendation of the Royal Commission. It concluded that the exercise of the powers must be warranted by the specific circumstances of a particular case and must be capable of immediate challenge and subsequent review. 'Only thus can adequate safeguards be provided against the arbitrary and indiscriminate use of such powers' (Royal Commission, para 3.10). The reasonable belief that an offence is a serious arrestable offence is an *essential precondition* to the exercise of the above powers. It follows that the exercise of these powers in respect of an offence, which is *not* reasonably believed to be a serious arrestable offence, *is unlawful*. Consequently, the interference with the liberty of the citizen will be a tort, and/ or a defence to a criminal charge arising out of a failure to comply with a constable's instructions or to a charge of assaulting or obstructing a constable in the execution of his duty. For example, if a serious arrestable offence is not involved, the taking of non-intimate samples will be an assault upon the individual, and, correspondingly, the use of reasonable force by the citizen to resist the taking will not be an assault on the constable in the execution of his duty. In contrast, if a serious arrestable offence is not involved, then delay in notifying someone of the arrest or in permitting access to a solicitor is not tortious, but it can be taken into account in considering the admissibility of any confession (see ss 76 and 78 (Arts 74 and 76), discussed in para 8.41, post).

Meaning of serious arrestable offence

2.25   The Royal Commission recommended that the exercise of the above powers be limited to 'grave offences' but could only produce a very imprecise definition of what that meant. The Government preferred the term 'serious arrestable offence'. This is based upon the concept of 'arrestable offence' defined in s 24 (Art 26, discussed in para 5.09–13, post). That definition incorporates all the most serious offences and a number of offences which can be serious because of their circumstances and their consequences. The definition of a 'serious arrestable offence' follows a similar pattern and is based on a proposal made by the Law Society that certain arrestable offences should always be regarded as serious, whilst others should be serious only if they satisfy one or more criteria. Statutes passed since 1986 have added to or amended the original definition. These changes are taken account of in the following discussion.

2.26   Serious arrestable offences fall into four categories:

(A)   Offences which are always serious arrestable offences.
1) Treason
2) Murder
3) Manslaughter
4) Rape
5) Kidnapping
6) Incest with a girl under the age of 13 (under 14 in N.I.)
7) Buggery with -
    (a)   a boy under the age of 16; or
    (b)   a person who has not consented
8) Indecent assault which constitutes an act of gross indecency
9) Any of the offences mentioned in paragraphs (a) to (d) of the definition of 'drug trafficking offence' in s 38(1) of the Drug Trafficking Act 1986
    (s 116(2)(a), (aa), (Art 87))

1) Explosive Substances Act 1883, s 2 (causing an explosion likely to endanger life or property)
2) Sexual Offences Act 1956, s 5 (intercourse with a girl under the age of 13) (NI Criminal Law Amendment Act 1885, s 4 (intercourse with girl under 14))
3) Firearms Act 1968, s 16 (possession of firearms with intent to injure) (Firearms (NI) Order 1981, Art 17)
4) Firearms Act 1968, s 17(1) (use of firearms or imitation firearms to resist arrest) (Firearms (NI) Order 1981, Art 18(1))
5) Firearms Act 1968, s 18 (carrying firearms with criminal intent) (Firearms (NI) Order 1981, Art 19)
6) Road Traffic Act 1988, s 1 (causing death by reckless driving) (Road Traffic (NI) Order 1981, Art 139(1))
7) Taking of Hostages Act 1982, s 1
8) Aviation Security Act 1982, s 1 (hi-jacking of aircraft)
9) Criminal Justice Act 1988, s 134 (Torture) (added by s 170, Sch 15 of the Criminal Justice Act 1988)
    (s 116(2)(b) (Art 87 (2)(b)); Sch 5, Part II)

(B)   Offences which are serious arrestable offences in respect of the

powers to delay notification of arrest (s 56 (Art 57)) and access to a
solicitor (s 58 (Art 59)).
(1) Prevention of Terrorism (Temporary Provisions) Act 1989, ss 2,
   8, 9, 10 or 11
(2) Attempting or conspiring to commit any of the above offences
   (s 116(5) (Art 87(5))

(C) *All other arrestable offences* are serious arrestable offences *only* if
their commission leads to, or is intended to lead to, or is likely to lead
to, any of the following consequences:
(a) Serious harm to the security of the State or public order
(b) Serious interference with the administration of justice or with
   the investigation of offences or of a particular offence
(c) The death of any person
(d) Serious injury to any person
(e) Substantial financial gain to any person; and
(f) Serious financial loss to any person
   (s 116(3)(a) and (b), and (6) (Art 87(3)(a) and (b))

(D) An arrestable offence which consists of making a threat is serious if
carrying out the threat would be likely to lead to any of the consequences mentioned in (C) above. For example, threatening to kill,
contrary to s 16 of the Offences Against the Person Act 1861, or
blackmail contrary to s 21 of the Theft Act 1968, if the demand is
likely to lead to substantial gain and serious financial loss
(s 116(4) (Art 87(4)).

2.27 There was little disagreement during Parliamentary debates on
the seriousness of offences falling into category (A). However, some
concern was expressed during the third reading of the Bill in the House of
Lords over the offence of indecent assault which constitutes an act of
gross indecency. It was feared that this would be used by the police in
order to harass homosexuals. However, the Government minister made it
clear that this was not the intention. The offence of committing an act of
gross indecency under s 13 of the Sexual Offences Act 1956 is not an
arrestable offence unless one man is over 21 and the other is not. Homosexual conduct between persons over 21 is not therefore an arrestable, let
alone serious arrestable, offence.

'The terms "assault" and "gross" in relation to the indecent act which it
involves, taken together pick out the range of activity in relation to the sexual
abuse of young people which brings these offences into the category which
justifies the use of reserved power.' (House of Lords Debates, 19 October 1984,
col 1236)

Category (C) offences are likely to prove the most difficult to identify.
Terms such as 'serious harm', 'serious interference', 'serious injury',

'serious financial loss' and 'substantial gain' do not lend themselves to precise definition. Some assistance is provided by s 116(8) (Art 87(8)) which states that injury includes 'any disease and any impairment of a person's physical or mental condition' (see *R v Miller* (1954) where 'bodily harm' was held to include the inducement of a hysterical or nervous condition). Rape is a serious arrestable offence under s 116(2)(a) (Art 87(2)(a)) and Sch 5, Part I, but lesser assaults which affect the victim's mental condition can be a serious arrestable offence. Determining whether a financial loss is a serious loss requires consideration of the circumstances of the particular loser. S 116(7) (Art 87(7)) makes this clear by stating that 'Loss is serious . . . if, having regard to all the circumstances, it is serious for the person who suffers it.' There is no similar provision in respect of financial gain which suggests that an objective test applies. Thus, theft of £1,000 from a bank with assets of £millions will not be a serious financial loss to the bank, whereas theft of the same amount from an impoverished widow clearly would be. Whether the theft from the bank is a serious arrestable offence will therefore depend on whether £1,000 is a substantial financial gain to the thief. This is to be judged by the standards of ordinary reasonable people. In *R v McIvor* (1987), the theft of 28 dogs, owned collectively by a hunt and worth in total £800, was not a serious arrestable offence, the loss not being serious to the collective owners. In *R v Smith (Eric)* (1987), the Walsall branch of a nationwide chain of stores selling electrical equipment was robbed of two video recorders, worth £400 each, and £116 in cash. The learned Recorder doubted whether the loss of goods and cash totalling £916 was a serious loss to such a large company and thought the gain to the two robbers involved was not necessarily substantial. *Quaere*, in determining whether the gain to the person is substantial, the fact that the proceeds were shared between the participants is to be taken into account; eg in *Smith* (above) the two robbers would have each received property and cash valued at £458. If four men steal £4,000 from a branch of a nationwide chain of bookmakers, the loss to the bookmakers will not be serious and the gain to the individual thief may not be substantial if the proceeds are shared equally. Though s 116(6)(e) (Art 87(6)(e)) uses the singular 'any person', in this context the singular includes the plural (Interpretation Act 1978 s 6(c)) suggesting that the total proceeds is the determinant. Additionally, the police must often decide whether the offence is a serious arrestable offence in ignorance of these facts. It is therefore submitted that the fact that the proceeds have been, or may be, shared among the participants in the crime is to be ignored.

2.28 *Multiple offences* — In determining whether the financial loss is serious or the gain substantial, offences must be considered individually. Thus D may have committed a series of burglaries and stolen property worth £50,000 in total. That in itself does not make the burglaries serious arrestable offences. The loss or gain in respect of each burglary must be considered in isolation and, while some will be serious arrestable offences, others may not. For example, burglary 1 of a house in the stockbroker belt in which property valued at £3,000 was stolen, may not be a serious loss to the occupier. Burglary 2 of a modest cottage, owned by a retired couple and in which half that amount was stolen, probably will be a serious loss to them. £3,000 will probably be seen as a substantial gain to the burglar so that both burglaries will be serious arrestable offences. On the other hand, if only £1,000 is stolen from a rich stockbroker it will probably not be a serious loss to him, nor a substantial gain to the thief.

2.29 The following examples indicate the application of the category (C) criterion, bearing in mind that the offence must *first* be an arrestable offence:

(a) D, a civil servant, takes a copy of a document marked 'secret' which he believes discloses malpractice by a Government minister. He passes it to a newspaper. It may be an offence under the Official Secrets Act 1989. These are arrestable offences, even though punishable by only 2 years imprisonment (s 24(2)(bb) (Art 26(2)(c)) discussed in para 5.09, post). The Government, who are 'the sole judges of what the national security requires' (*The Zamora* (1916)), describe the disclosure as 'causing serious harm to national security'. The offence may then be a serious arrestable offence (s 116(6)(a) Art 87(6)(a)).

(b) D approaches jurors and offers them money to bring in a not guilty verdict. This is an offence at common law of attempting to pervert the course of justice and an arrestable offence under s 24(1)(b), (Art 26(1)(b)). Such conduct is always a serious interference with the course of justice and will therefore be a serious arrestable offence (s 116(6)(b) Art 87(6)(b)).

(c) D is driving his motor car at a normal speed through a town centre. He is momentarily distracted by a shop window display and fails to see a pedestrian crossing the road. The pedestrian dies from injuries inflicted when the car struck him. D is guilty of, at most, driving without due care and attention contrary to s 3 of the Road Traffic Act 1988. Although the offence has led to the death of a person, it is not an arrestable offence and cannot therefore be a serious arrestable offence (s 116(6)(c) Art 87(6)(c)).

(d) D sets fire to his factory intending to claim on his insurance. He does not warn the night watchman, his intention being that the watchman should discover the fire and raise the alarm. The watchman is asleep and is severely burnt. D has committed arson contrary to s 1(2) of the Criminal Damage Act 1971. It is a serious arrestable offence in view of the consequences (s 116(6)(d) Art 87(6)(d)).

(e) D and others hijack a bullion van and steal gold bullion worth £1 million. It is robbery (s 8 of the Theft Act 1968), involves a substantial financial gain to D and the others, and is a serious financial loss to the owners of the bullion (s 116(6)(e) and (f) Art 87(6)(e) and (f)).

(f)   D steals £1,000 from a bank with assets of £12 million. This is a serious arrestable offence only if it is a substantial gain to D, because the loss of £1,000 can hardly be described as a serious loss to the bank. On the other hand, if force or threat of force is used, it *will* be a serious arrestable offence, regardless of the amount stolen, if serious injury is caused or is the intended or likely result (see s 116(6)(d) Art 87(6)(d) and para 2.30 below).

'Is intended or is likely to lead' to any of those consequences

2.30   This phrase would bring within the ambit of 'serious arrestable offence' attempts, conspiracies and other inchoate offences which involve arrestable offences and which are intended, or are likely, to produce any of the consequences listed in s 116(6) (Art 87(6)). For example, murder is always a serious arrestable offence under category (A) and attempted murder is also always such an offence under category (C). Conspiracy to commit treason will similarly always be a serious arrestable offence under category (C) because it is always intended, or is likely, to result in serious harm to the security of the State. Armed robbery, attempted armed robbery or a conspiracy to rob in which violence or firearms are to be used, will be serious arrestable offences because these offences either result in serious injury to persons, or are intended or likely to do so, or will result, or are intended, or likely to, result in substantial financial gain and serious financial loss. 'Likely' suggests a balance of probabilities, more than a 50–50 chance, and whenever firearms are carried or violence is contemplated, there is a 'likelihood' that serious injury or death will be a consequence. Thus, almost every offence which the police, or the general public, would describe as serious, will be a serious arrestable offence under this definition. (NB Possession of firearms with intent to injure, to resist arrest, or with criminal intent, are arrestable offences under s 116(2)(b) (Art 87(2)(b)) and Sch 5.

2.31   It should be noted that the fact that the offence is defined as a serious arrestable offence does not mean that the powers available will be exercised. In some cases the reasonable belief that the offence is a serious arrestable offence is one of a number of requirements. Even if the theft of £50 from an old age pensioner is a serious arrestable offence, the police are unlikely to invoke the extended powers of detention or to delay access to a solicitor. It is even less likely that magistrates could be persuaded to issue a warrant of further detention. However, if there are reasonable grounds to suspect that the offender in such a case is, or is about to be in an area, a road check under s 4 (Art 6) may be authorised. This may not be what the Royal Commission or the Government intended, but it is a consequence of the definition of serious arrestable offence together with the minimal requirements for the setting up of road checks.

Reasonable force (s 117) (Art 88)

2.32   Section 3 of the Criminal Law Act 1967 (s 3, Criminal Law Act (N.I.) 1967) provides that anyone may use such force as is reasonable in the circumstances to prevent crime, or its effect or assist in the lawful arrest of offenders, suspected offenders, or persons unlawfully at large (the use of force in order to effect an arrest is discussed in para 5.64, post). However, the 1984 Act (1989 Order) gives constables a number of powers which do not fall within s 3 of the 1967 Acts in that they are not used in the prevention of crime or in effecting an arrest; for example, the power to search a person, or to take his fingerprints. These powers would be useless against the obdurate or hostile person who refuses to cooperate. They must therefore be backed by the application of force and s 117 (Art 88) bestows a general power to use 'reasonable force, if necessary' in relation to any coercive power under the Act (Order). The word 'reasonable' limits the amount of force by requiring objective facts which in turn justify the application of the degree of force. 'Necessary' imports a similar limitation but also means that other non-coercive means have been used in an attempt to exercise the power or that these other means are likely to fail. This suggests that a reasonable explanation should be given, if practicable, to the person against whom the power is to be exercised. Thus, in *Brazil v Chief Constable of Surrey* (1983), it was held that, where a person is to be searched at a police station following an arrest, there is a duty to state the reasons for that search. Section 54(5) (Art 55(5)) gives effect to that decision (see para 7.18, post), but it is submitted that the principle underlying it, that no coercive power should be exercised without, where practicable, giving reasons, is of general application. If such reasons are not given, then the exercise of the power is unlawful and, it is submitted, the use of force is not 'necessary'.

2.33   Three factors flowing from the use of the words 'reasonable' and 'necessary' deserve special emphasis. First, the amount of force used must be related to the purpose for which the power is to be exercised. Whilst in the context of arrest or the prevention of crime lethal force may be used to prevent a serious crime or the escape of a dangerous offender, many of the powers to which s 117 (Art 88) relates can never justify the use of such a degree of force. For example, the taking of a person's fingerprints would not justify the use of a degree of force sufficient to break that person's fingers. Second, the context in which many of the powers will be exercised (at the police station) suggest that there will usually be sufficient constables at hand to subdue a person effectively without the use of a high degree of force (see *Sturley v Commissioner of Police* (1984), discussed in para 5.64, post). Third, the use of excessive or unnecessary force, though unlawful and likely to form the basis of an action for assault (or possibly a prosecution), will not necessarily affect the lawfulness of the power being exercised. Thus, for example, excessive force used to effect a lawful arrest will not render the arrest unlawful (*Simpson v Chief Constable of South Yorkshire* (1991) discussed in para 5.64, post). Similarly the use of excessive or unnecessary force in order to gain entry to premises in order to carry out a search under ss 17, 18 or 32(2)(b) (Arts 19, 20 or 34(2)(b)) will not render the entry a trespass, but will expose the constable to an action for assault and/or damages.

Compliance with the law

2.34 A variety of methods exists to encourage compliance with the law and is conveniently dealt with at this point.

(a) *Police training*

The far-reaching effect of the PACE Act on police practices meant that a thorough programme of retraining was necessary for all ranks. At the end of the day, the quality of that training and of police officers is the surest method of securing compliance with the law and proper practice. Supervision by senior officers plays an important part in this process. Two ranks have particular prominence — the custody officer and the superintendent. The former makes the initial decision to detain a person after arrest, with or without a charge. He is also responsible for the welfare of all detained persons at a police station (s 39), and Parts IV and V of the Act and frequent references in the Codes of Practice require his participation before many actions may be taken. The superintendent has a wider role. He must authorise detention without charge beyond the initial 24 hours up to 36 hours and must give permission before more sensitive civil liberties of the suspect at the police station can be infringed (eg denial of legal advice (s 58)). He also has a wider operational role (eg in the deployment of road blocks). Compared to pre-PACE days, he comes into closer contact with junior officers and into more decision-making involving detainees. Both the custody officer and superintendent are intended to bring an element of independence and seniority to decision-making.

2.35 On the other hand, evidence of previous practice indicated that senior officers may not necessarily have been aware of the Judges' Rules.

For example, In *Houghton* (1978) it was a Commander in the Metropolitan Police who directed that a suspect be held incommunicado in breach of the Judges' Rules. In *R v Confait* (see Report of Inquiry 1977) it was a detective chief superintendent of considerable experience who obtained confessions from mentally retarded youths in breach of the Judges' Rules. It may therefore be unrealistic to place too much reliance upon supervision by senior officers. Much will depend on the depth and regularity of training which they are required to undergo, the attitude they adopt towards compliance with the law and Codes of Practice, and the time they have to become involved with day-to-day operations.

(b) *Documentation*

2.36 The PACE Act places considerable store by the recording in writing of police actions. Two benefits accrue. First, it is a salutary discipline for a decision-maker to have to state his reasons for action in writing, especially if he has tended previously to act instinctively. Second, the written record of an officer's actions can be crucial evidence in subsequent legal proceedings or disciplinary proceedings arising out of those actions, or in criminal proceedings against the person who was the object of those actions. The Act and Codes of Practice are littered with examples of documentary records; for example, stop and search records, road check records, records of seized property, custody records and interview records. Most records have to be retained for 12 months and can be inspected by the citizen. Some (eg for road checks) fulfil a fact-finding purpose and will appear in annual reports of police forces. These reports can in turn be examined by other bodies, notably the police committee and Her Majesty's Inspectors of Constabulary. These data should prove invaluable in assessing police practice.

(c) *Complaints and discipline*

2.37 Part IX of the PACE Act includes the second change to the investigation of complaints against the police which Parliament adopted within ten years. The system edges closer towards an independent system. The punishments which can be meted out to an errant officer remain formidable (from dismissal to, for example, reduction in rank). The length and uncertainty of investigations mean that police officers do not generally face them with equanimity. Proceedings may stem from both complaint from the public and from internal inquiries. Most significantly, a breach of any provision in a Code of Practice is a breach of discipline and can be punished accordingly (s 67(8), Art 66(7)). This method of encouraging compliance with the law is potentially the most powerful of all, but for a number of reasons has not proved so. For the position in N.I., see the Police (N.I.) Order 1987.

(d) *Criminal prosecution*

2.38 Certain actions by a police officer, for example, assault or the giving of false evidence, may give rise to criminal liability. This may be discovered following the investigation of a complaint and be prosecuted by the police after consulting the Director of Public Prosecutions or, exceptionally, will be the subject of a private prosecution. Difficulties of proof may be experienced whoever prosecutes, particularly in respect of criminal assaults committed in circumstances in which the alleged assailant and the victim are the only witnesses. However, the private prosecutor is faced with an additional financial obstacle. For legal aid is not available to assist him and, whilst prosecution in a magistrates' court is comparatively cheap, trial before a jury is not. Should the private prosecutor fail to prove his allegation, he may find himself burdened with the costs of the police officer as well as his own. Private prosecutions are therefore very infrequent, and rank very much as a weapon of last resort.

2.39 Prosecution as a method of enforcement can also arise negatively. Thus, if the citizen is prosecuted under s 51 of the Police Act 1964 for an offence against a police officer, he may succeed in showing that the officer was not acting in the execution of his duty at the time. Such a decision may well lead to amended standing orders and new practices at the police station. It can thus have an indirect effect on police conduct. Moreover, even if a conviction is secured against the citizen, the trial judge may still comment on police conduct. These comments will be brought to the attention of a senior officer and are also likely to lead to new police practices.

(e) *Civil action*

2.40 A civil action (for trespass, assault, false imprisonment, negligence or breach of statutory duty) against a police officer for the latter's misconduct is increasingly popular. It has several advantages. It has to be proved on the lesser, civil standard of proof. If successful, the plaintiff is compensated directly and occasionally substantially (eg *White v Commissioner of Police* (1982), *George v Commissioner of Police* (1984)). If the individual is not prosecuted, then a civil action may be the only practicable way in which he can bring the police conduct before a court. For example, if D's premises are searched unlawfully but he is not prosecuted, an action for trespass is his only legal redress. A successful civil action benefits not merely the plaintiff, for the court's ruling may well lead to a change in police practice or attitude. The emphasis on documentation (including tape recording) in the 1984 Act encourages civil actions, since records are generally available for 12 months and a court may take account of them in determining civil liability. Finally, a civil action can satisfy the plaintiff's psychological desire 'to have his day in court'.

2.41   On the other hand, the hurdles facing a plaintiff may be considerable. It can be extremely difficult to obtain legal aid. If he does not, the costs of a High Court action (almost certainly at that level if the plaintiff wants sizeable compensation or if the police decide to defend the action) are prohibitive. Since the chief officer is vicariously liable for the actions of his officers (s 48 of the Police Act 1964) and the police fund bears the cost of compensation, the plaintiff may not feel that fault has been properly punished (even though the effect on an officer's career of a civil action may be devastating). Furthermore, much police conduct will not raise civil liability. For example, there is no civil action which can fit the failure to compile a stop and search record or the improper refusal to allow access to a solicitor. (For a full discussion of this area, see Clayton and Tomlinson, *Civil Actions Against the Police*.)

(f)   *Her Majesty's Inspectors*

2.42   A Chief Inspector and five Inspectors are appointed by the Crown as H M Inspectors of Constabulary (in N.I. s 16 of the Police Act (N.I.) 1970 authorises the appointment of inspectors). The office derives from the system of inspectors appointed under the County and Borough Police Act 1856. They are responsible for inspecting and advising police forces on a wide range of matters. They also have a duty under s 95 of the PACE Act to keep themselves informed as to the workings of the complaints system set up under that Act (in N.I. Art.15, Police (N.I.) Order 1987). In the present context, the Inspectorate has a very important role to play in promoting uniformity in police practice and in the training of officers. It played an active role in the period before the Act came into force and in the early years of its operation. In the Metropolitan force a separate scheme exists. A Deputy Assistant Commissioner is appointed as Inspector of the Metropolitan Police with a small group of supporting officers. He has regular contact with H M Inspectorate and fulfils similar functions of inspection and assessment of police efficiency.

(g)   *Lay Visitors*

2.43   Mention can be made here of the 'lay visitor schemes' which have been set up voluntarily and experimentally in some police areas in recent years. The idea is that members of a lay visiting panel (composed of, for example, members of the police committee, magistrates, local religious and community leaders) can at any time and without warning visit police stations to investigate what is happening there and to check on conditions of detention. If extended nationally, the scheme can be a useful adjunct to other enforcement provisions, since it exposes to independent scrutiny what is often the core of any controversy — the police station. However, the quality of these schemes varies widely.

(h) *Exclusion of evidence*

2.44 There are two reasons why the law may exclude from trial evidence which has been improperly obtained. The first stems from the proven or likely unreliability of the evidence. The clearest example of this arises with confessions. It lay behind the previous principle of voluntariness and is now explicitly stated in s 76(2)(b). For example, if the police have offered an inducement, or made a threat, to a suspect in order to obtain a confession from him, there is a strong probability that the confession will be untrue. This reliability principle is discussed in para 8.55, post, but it is important to note that much of the PACE Act (Parts IV and V) and two Codes (on Detention etc and on Identification) are concerned with what happens at the police station. Breaches of many of these provisions can lead to unreliable confessions or to the accused at least raising the issue at his trial and hoping to muddy the waters. Police officers must therefore be made aware of the need to comply with the provisions. The exclusion of unreliable evidence (and quite possibly the collapse of the prosecution case) can act as a deterrent to police misconduct.

2.45 The second reason for excluding evidence rests upon fairness to the accused. The idea is that, if the police break the law, they should not be allowed to profit from their wrong doing by securing a conviction. The evidence which they have obtained unlawfully should be excluded at trial even if the evidence is true. This type of exclusionary rule can be strict (ie all illegally obtained evidence is always excluded) or discretionary (ie exclusion depends upon a variety of factors). The United States has been the clearest exponent of the former, whilst Scotland is an example of the latter. English common law accepted but has rarely enforced a discretionary exclusionary rule and, with one exception, rejected a strict rule. The exception was the breathalyser legislation. Starting with *Scott v Baker* (1968) the courts took the view that the Road Traffic legislation laid down a set of procedures which had to be strictly followed before a conviction could result (eg *Spicer v Holt* (1976), *Walker v Lovell* (1975)). The arrest became a part of the offence in the sense that, if the police exercised their arrest powers wrongly, the rest of the prosecution was vitiated. It is open to the courts to adopt a similar approach in relation to the stop and search provisions in the 1984 Act, but this is unlikely (see the discussion in para 3.51, post).

2.46 As to a discretionary power to exclude evidence, for many years English courts insisted that they had such a discretion. Lord Goddard uttered the classic statement in *Kuruma v R* (1955):

'the judge always has a discretion to disallow evidence if the strict rules of admissibility would operate unfairly against the accused . . . if, for instance, some admission of some piece of evidence, eg, a document, had been obtained from a defendant by a trick, no doubt the judge might properly rule it out.'

His successors, Lords Parker (in *Callis v Gunn* (1964)) and Widgery produced dicta to similar effect. However, with one exception (*R v Payne* (1963)), the courts consistently refused to exercise this discretion so as to reject evidence, even in the face of clearly illegal conduct by the police. Thus, in *Jeffrey v Black* (1978):

'the simple unvarnished fact that evidence was obtained by police officers who had gone in without bothering to get a search warrant is not enough to justify the justices in exercising their discretion to keep the evidence out' (Lord Widgery) (see also *R v Macintosh* (1982), a case involving a blatant disregard for the Judges' Rules).

In reality, the obiter dicta of Lord Goddard in *Kuruma v R* (1955) forged a myth that judges possessed, and would use, a discretion to exclude evidence which had been improperly obtained. Later Lord Chief Justices fostered that myth but were careful not to apply its message. The House of Lords in *R v Sang* (1979) however rejected Lord Goddard's statement. Instead, Lord Diplock observed:

'(1) A trial judge in a criminal trial has always a discretion to refuse to admit evidence if in his opinion its prejudicial effect outweighs its probative value. (2) Save with regard to admissions and confessions and generally with regard to evidence obtained from the accused after commission of the offence, he has no discretion to refuse to admit relevant admissible evidence on the ground that it was obtained by improper or unfair means.'

The first rule is well established. Evidence of disposition, previous convictions and reputation is normally irrelevant and is for that reason inadmissible. However, even when evidence is deemed relevant and prima facie admissible, 'there should be excluded from the jury information about the accused which is likely to have an influence on their minds prejudicial to the accused which is out of proportion to the true probative value of admissible evidence conveying that information' (Lord Diplock). The second rule is also aimed at securing a fair trial for the accused. Thus, confessions, which have been improperly obtained are suspect and should not be given in evidence. The House of Lords refused to accept that the courts had a further role to play in disciplining the police by excluding evidence which has been obtained 'improperly or unfairly'. This ruling accepted the reality that, whilst the courts had frequently agreed with Lord Goddard's statement, they had regularly refused to accept the disciplinary role.

2.47 The first and second versions of the PACE Bill did not mention the exclusion of improperly obtained evidence, save in relation to confessions (see s 76, Art 74 and see para 8.41, post). The second was however amended in the House of Lords by a detailed clause tabled by Lord Scarman, so that a court could exclude evidence because of illegal, improper or deceptive conduct on the part of the police. The Bill was seen as offering insufficient methods of enforcing its provisions and the exclusionary rule was seen as an effective weapon for the courts to possess against errant policing. The Government responded by accepting the need for an exclusionary rule but by watering it down. Thus, the Lords' detailed amendment was replaced by the looser terms of what is now s 78. The former was rejected (1) because it would unnecessarily punish the police; (2) because it would lead to lengthy trials within trials as to the admissibility or otherwise of the evidence; (3) because the Government's proposal was 'simple and clear in form, yet suitably flexible' (Home Secretary, House of Commons Debate, 29 October 1984, col 1014).

Section 78

2.48   In the context of this book, argument (3) is of most relevance, for it is not at all clear what this opaque section means. It reads as follows:

'(1) In any proceedings the court may refuse to allow evidence on which the prosecution proposes to rely to be given if it appears to the court that, having regard to all the circumstances, including the circumstances in which the evidence was obtained, the admission of the evidence would have such an adverse effect on the fairness of the proceedings that the court ought not to admit it.

(2) Nothing in this section shall prejudice any rule of law requiring a court to exclude evidence.'

[Since s 78 has been used mainly in the field of confessions, it is considered in detail in chapter 8. To avoid repetition the main points and the non-confession areas will be mentioned here.]

The following points can be offered as guidance:

(a)   Section 78 is directed *solely at the trial stage*.

'The purpose of excluding evidence should not be disciplinary. It should be to avoid evidence being adduced which if adduced would lead to an unfair trial.' (Home Secretary, House of Commons Debate, 29 October 1984, col 1012)

However, the section has proved to be a mischievous and unpredictable weapon wielded to protect the accused and to assert the authority of the court over its own proceedings. No matter what the judges may say to the contrary, one inevitable consequence is to discipline the police by rejecting evidence which they have improperly obtained and by often acquitting the defendant (occasionally judicial irritation is openly expressed, eg *R v Canale* (1990)).

(b)   The court has a very wide discretion to exclude evidence, ie it can do so 'if it appears to the court . . .' It follows that the accused must adduce sufficient evidence to raise the issue (cf the Lords' amendment to the PACE Bill which placed the onus on the prosecution to persuade the court not to exclude the evidence). This evidential burden is satisfied by the accused on the standard normally falling on him viz the civil standard of a balance of probabilities.

(c)   Section 78 is to be construed widely after considering all the circumstances and the courts have refused to confine it by firm rules. This gives considerable scope for the defence to raise it. Indeed defence counsel should always be alert to it.

(d)   'Including the circumstances in which the evidence was obtained' is sufficiently open-ended to cover breaches of the PACE Act, Codes of Practice and all other laws, the unreasonable exercise of discretionary powers, deception or tricks. The more significant the breach, the more likely it is that s 78 will be exercised. However, the key to s 78 (sometimes, it would appear, overlooked, or glossed over, by the courts) is not the fact of a breach, but the 'adverse effect on the fairness' of the trial. That link has to be established.

(e)   In the confessions area, it is suggested that s 76(2)(a) (dealing with oppression) was intended as a statement of principle and of what kind of police conduct is regarded as beyond the pale; s 76(2)(b) is then concerned with the mainstream of any criminal justice system viz whether the confession is reliable; and s 78 is there to deal mainly with the non-confession area and with police conduct or other circumstances of which a court disapproves (eg unfair identification methods; see (f) below). It is still open to the House of Lords to formulate such an analysis but in the meantime the Court of Appeal has taken a very different path. S 78 has been used as the main weapon in regulating how the police obtain confessions (see further para 8.67).

(f)   Outside confessions, s 78 has been used in the following areas (precise categories cannot be delineated since the section is of a flexible nature and the courts are unwilling to confine it so).

   (i)   *identification issues*
         Since the law places great store by the accurate identification of suspects, it is rightly suspicious of mistakes or improprieties in the identification procedures (see further para 7.66, post). Section 78 can thus be employed to ensure fairness to the accused (see *R v Nagah* (1990), *R v Conway* (1990), *R v Britton and Richards* (1989), *R v Gall* (1989), *R v Grannell* (1989), *R v Ladlow* (1989), *R v Gaynor* (1988), *R v O'Leary* (1988), *R v Quinn* (1990), *R v Brown* (1991), *R v Samms, Elliot and Bartley* (1991)).

   (ii) The section has been argued in the context of alleged entrapment by the police (ie whether D has been tricked or unfairly trapped into committing an offence) — *R v H* (1987), *R v O'Connor* (1987), *R v Marshall and Downes* (1988), *R v Gill* (1989), *R v Harwood* (1989), *R v Katz* (1989), *R v Ali* (1991), *R v Edwards* (1991) and cf the facts of *DPP v Wilson* (1991).

(iii) The failure to conduct a stop and search properly may be unfair, in that if it had been properly done, D might have given an explanation which would have reduced the eventual charges brought against him, *R v Fennelly* (1989).

(iv) Improprieties in the breath-alcohol procedures in road traffic cases may be unfair to the accused at trial (see *Matto v Wolverhampton Crown Court* (1987)).

(v) If D cannot properly challenge the evidence brought against him in court, it may be unfair to admit it — *R v Quinn* (1990).

(vi) In an area which does not concern this book, s 78 has been regularly pleaded — as to whether it is fair for a court to admit evidence of an accused's previous convictions — *R v O'Connor* (1987), *R v Robertson* (1987), *R v Bennett* (1988), *R v Curry* (1988), *R v Lunnon* (1988), *R v Kempster* (1989), *R v Fedrick* (1990), *R v Boyson* (1991), *R v Chapman* (1991), *R v Turner* (1991). Indeed s 78 has a potentially wide role to play in evidential procedures before and during trial (eg *R v Fields and Adams* (1991), use of an alibi notice in the Crown's case), which are the province of guides to the law of evidence.

S 82(3) (Art 70(3))

This preserves the common law discretion to exclude evidence. It retains very much a residual and sparse role, given the courts' marked reluctance in pre-PACE days ever to exercise it (see para 2.46, ante; as for its use with confessions, there is more scope, see para 8.78, post).

Codes of Practice (ss 66, 67; Arts 65, 66)

2.49 In spite of the considerable detail in its sections and Schedules, the PACE Act is largely an outline of the law. For practical implementation, it must be supplemented by Codes of Practice and Regulations (see post). These add some operational flesh to the legislative skeleton. There are five Codes of Practice:

The Exercise of Powers of Stop and Search,
The Searching of Premises and Seizure of Property,
The Detention, Treatment and Questioning of Persons by the Police,
The Identification of Persons Suspected of Crime (1991),
Tape recording (1988).

The Codes have to be approved by the resolution of both Houses of Parliament (s 67(3)–(5)) — the affirmative resolution procedure, and can be updated from time to time (subject to the same Parliamentary procedure) (s 67(7)). The second, revised edition of the first four Codes came into force on 1 April 1991 after much consultation. They seek to be 'clear and workable guidelines for the police, balanced by strong safeguards for the public' (Foreword to the 1991 Codes).

2.50 In part, the Codes paraphrase some of the Act's provisions and in this way the frequently complex provisions in the Act are explained in a lucid fashion. It follows that the language used in the Codes is looser than that used in the statute. It is important therefore to distinguish between parts of a Code which merely repeat the statute and those which supplement it. The former parts are not the authoritative version. As to the latter, the Codes frequently supplement the Act in very important matters. Indeed, one of the issues regularly discussed during passage of the PACE Bill was whether items properly belonged to the Bill or to a Code. In this context the language employed in the Code assumes a greater significance. Since it bestows additional rights on the citizen and imposes extra duties on the police, it ought, it is suggested, to be interpreted more rigorously than the descriptive parts. However, a further distinction can be drawn. There are some parts of the Codes which are both supplementary to the Act and mandatory (see the conditions of detention, para 7.103, post) and those which are supplementary but advisory. The Code of Practice on Stop and Search, is the best example of the latter. By tackling the elusive concept of 'reasonable suspicion' it inevitably contains a larger measure of guidance than instruction.

Scope

2.51 The Codes of Practice are primarily directed to the police but they also extend to those other officials who are similarly charged with the investigation of offences (s 67(9)) eg commercial investigators employed by a company to investigate possible crimes committed by its staff (*R v Twaites* (1990)). However, whether a person is 'charged' with this duty is a matter of fact to be decided in each case. Thus, an inspector employed by the Department of Trade and Industry under the Companies Act 1985 to investigate a company's affairs has been held, surprisingly, not to be a person so charged for s 67(9) purposes (*R v Seelig and Spens* (1991)). In the Home Office's view an immigration officer investigating the status of an entrant is also not 'charged' (though the officers are instructed to abide by the relevant COP procedures and an immigration COP incorporating them has been issued). By section 113 the Secretary of State for Defence may by order direct that any part of the PACE Act, relating to the investigation of offences or to detained persons, shall apply to investigations under the Army Act 1955, the Air Force Act 1955, or the Naval Discipline Act 1957. S 113 required him to issue Codes of Practice to govern those who conduct these enquiries (ie officers charged with the task of investigating offences under those Acts). (See S I 1986 No 307, and 1989 No 2128.) Unlike s 67, breach of a Code will by itself involve legal liability as regards proceedings taken under one of the Forces' Acts, but, like s 67, a breach does not per se involve liability under the general criminal or civil law. A Code is admissible in evidence in all proceedings, and a court-martial, the Courts-Martial Appeal Court and Standing Civilian Court can take account of it.

2.52 Codes of Practice have become popular in recent years as a method of conveying the finer details of the parent Act. Their legal effect is varied. In some areas a breach of it can be used in evidence at legal proceedings, whereas in others it is merely a consultative document. The Codes of Practice passed by Parliament under the 1984 PACE Act are a form of delegated legislation, similar to the Immigration Rules passed under the Immigration Act 1971. But, whereas the latter bind the immigration appellate authorities, the Codes do not bind the courts. Their effect is as follows. Firstly, breach of a Code does not of itself lead to legal liability for the transgressor (s 67(10)). However, a court may take a breach into account in subsequent proceedings; for example, in deciding whether to admit evidence against an accused in criminal proceedings (ss 76 and 78, Arts 74, 76), or in determining the guilt or civil liability of a police officer or of any other person governed by the Code. Like the previous Judges' Rules (see *R v Prager* (1972)), a breach of a Code does not have to be acted upon by the court. Indeed, it is highly unlikely that a court will pay anything more than fleeting attention to breaches of minor aspects of the Codes. On the other hand, the courts regard many Code provisions as important safeguards for the citizen and treat transgressions of them as serious and substantial and as warranting the exclusion of evidence. The principal category here are the procedures in Code C covering the questioning of suspects and the recording of interviews (see further para 8.12). Secondly, and often more importantly, a breach of a Code is a ground for a complaint against the police under Part IX of the Act and may also lead to disciplinary proceedings against the offending officer, for breach of a Code is a disciplinary offence (s 67(8)); unless the principle of 'double jeopardy' applies, which in essence prevents an officer being punished twice for the same conduct. The Codes are divided into sections and at the end of most are Notes for Guidance. The latter (unlike Annexes to the Codes) are not regarded as provisions of a Code (see para 1.2 to each Code). They clearly enjoy an inferior status. However, it is highly arguable that some Notes for Guidance deserve inclusion in the body of the Code and vice versa; see, for example, Code A, Note IE (stop and search of juveniles), Code C, Note 11A (definition of an interview). In other words some Notes will attract stricter judicial attention than others. More generally, it can be noted that the Code C provisions governing the questioning of suspects have often been approached by the courts as if written in tablets of stone. Sometimes this approach may go too far and prompt a reminder that the Code is there for guidance and not necessarily blind obedience. Thus, in the context of interviews, Bingham LJ remarked in *R v Marsh* (1991):

> '[I]t is plainly desirable that these provisions should not become so highly technical and sophisticated in their construction and application that no police officer, however well intentioned and diligent, could reasonably be expected to comply with them. There has to be a reasonable commonsense approach to the matter such that police officers confronted with unexpected situations, and doing their best to be fair and to comply with the Codes, do not fall foul on some technicality of authority or construction.'

Regulations and other rules

2.53 Various sections of the PACE Act and other legislation permit the Home Secretary to promulgate regulations (eg specifying 'recordable offences' for the purpose of fingerprinting under ss 27 and 61, dealing with the police complaints' procedure). The Codes of Practice are supplemented by Home Office Circulars along with Force standing orders and procedural instructions.

Delegation of duties (s 107)

2.54 Throughout the PACE Act there are powers which can only be exercised by, or on the authority of, a superintendent (eg denial of access to legal advice (s 58), intimate searches (s 55)) or an inspector (eg search after arrest (s 18), review of detention (s 40)). To avoid the situation where there are no available officers of the requisite rank, s 107 permits an officer of at least chief superintendent rank to authorise a chief inspector to act as superintendent and to authorise a sergeant to act as inspector. This principle of delegation is applied to this and any other Act. The terms of s 107 are unlimited and could in theory permit the delegation of duties on a casual basis (eg if there are insufficient senior officers available for a particular shift). The section must however be seen in the light of previous police procedures. That context suggests that s 107 is not intended to permit the delegation of powers on a casual basis. Instead, it links up with the procedure for permitting a junior officer to 'act up' during the lengthy absence of a more senior officer (eg when the latter is on annual leave or is attending a training course). Since this 'acting' senior officer is not in fact promoted to the higher rank, he could not exercise the accompanying powers were it not for s 107. It should be noted that s 107 refers only to *powers*. It seems that delegation cannot be permitted where *duties* are involved. Thus, the *duties* of a review officer under s 40 (an inspector) cannot be discharged by a sergeant who is acting as an inspector (cf s 108 which refers to both the powers and duties of a deputy chief constable). There is no time limit on the length of an authorisation under s 107.

Application of the Act (ss 113, 114)

2.55 The PACE Act is predominantly concerned with the powers of *constables*, though in relation to arrest the powers of the citizen are also dealt with. 'Constable' refers to the ancient office of that name which can be traced back to 900 AD. Despite the fact that police forces are creatures of statute, they are, in essence, simply a number of constables, whose status derives from the common law, organised together in the interests of efficiency. Whilst there are different ranks and there is a tendency to refer to the lowest rank as constable, all ranks are constables. Whenever this, or any other Act, refers to a 'constable' it is therefore referring to all police officers. The hallmark of a constable is his attestation as a constable. Every member of a police force maintained for a police area and every special constable appointed for such an area must, on appointment, be attested as a constable by making the appropriate declaration before a justice of the peace. Until he does so, he has no more authority than an ordinary citizen. After attestation, he has all the additional powers and duties of a constable. This applies equally to other statutory police forces, such as the British Transport Police or Ministry of Defence Police, and to any special constables appointed to such forces (though they rarely operate outside the property which they police). There are other bodies sometimes called 'police' which are not constables eg parks' police. They are simply citizens wearing a uniform and do not have the powers of a constable. As a further complication, some governmental agencies such as Customs and Excise and immigration officers are given statutory powers of search and arrest in connection with the investigation of offences within their particular area of duty, but they again are not 'constables'.

Application to armed forces (s 113)

2.56 Section 113(1) allowed the Secretary of State (for Defence) to direct by statutory instrument that any provision of the PACE Act relating to the investigation of offences, or the detention of persons, should apply, with appropriate modifications, to the investigation of offences under the Army and Air Force Acts 1955, and the Naval Discipline Act 1957. Codes of Practice have also been issued.

Application of the Act to Customs and Excise (s 114)

2.57   Customs and Excise officers investigate crime and deal with the public in much the same way as the police, albeit in respect of a limited number of offences created by customs and excise Acts. Their powers derive, in the main, from those Acts. To ensure the thorough and adequate investigation of offences (which may often be serious in terms of the quantity and kind of goods involved and the potential loss to the Exchequer) it was thought right that the police powers provided by the PACE Act and the appropriate constraints on those powers should apply equally to officers of Customs and Excise. Section 114(2) allowed the application, by Treasury Order, of any provision of the PACE Act relating to the investigation of offences, or to the detention of persons, to officers of Customs and Excise, subject to appropriate modification and certain exceptions. However, the application can only relate to matters for which Customs and Excise have statutory responsibility. This was achieved by a series of statutory instruments in 1985.

3 Stop and search powers

3.01   Prior to the Police and Criminal Evidence Act 1984 (PACE), the police had no general power to stop and search persons or vehicles for stolen goods or other unlawful articles. Some areas of the country (notably London under s 66 of the Metropolitan Police Act 1839) offered such a power in relation to stolen goods and there were, and still are, a motley collection of powers covering specific articles such as prohibited drugs, firearms, crossbows, wild plants, badgers and birds' eggs (see the full list in Annex A to the Code of Practice, A, which deals with the Exercise by Police Officers of Statutory Powers of Stop and Search). The absence of a general power meant that the stopping of a person without his consent was technically a false imprisonment and the search was an assault, whilst the search of a vehicle was a trespass — the stopping possibly being permitted under the road traffic legislation (see para 3.08, post). Apart from risking a civil action in such circumstances, the police officer would step outside his duty and could lose the protection of s 51 of the Police Act 1964 (discussed in para 2.15, ante). In practice, these risks were more theoretical than real and did not prevent widespread stopping and searching with the express or tacit consent of the person. Moreover, the few powers available nationally, such as s 23 of the Misuse of Drugs Act 1971, could be stretched to justify a general search of the person, since the courts were prepared to admit relevant evidence even though it was seized during an illegal search. In this context, Part I of PACE introduced no radical change but, in essence, legalised existing police practice.

3.02   The arguments in favour of a general stop and search power were threefold. First, though the success rate may vary, stops and searches inevitably bring to light crime. In London, for example, the power was seen as an immensely valuable method of crime detection (see *The Use, Effectiveness and Impact of Police Stop and Search Powers*, Willis (Home Office 1983)). Second, a successful stop and search detects and clears up crime in one action and may lead to detection of others; for example, a person found with housebreaking tools automatically contravenes s 25 of the Theft Act 1968 (s 24 Theft Act (N.I.) 1969) and may well then admit to having committed burglaries. Such a power of stop and search can, it was argued, be a valuable contributor to the success rate of a police force. For example, a timely study revealed that arrests resulting from stops accounted for between 20 per cent and 59 per cent of all arrests for offences in connection with the possession of stolen or prohibited goods (Willis (1983) p 18). The success rate of these stops in terms of charges and convictions is however much lower (see *Police and People in London*, Smith (P.S.I. 1983)). Third, the possession of prohibited weapons and articles can only be properly detected by a stop and search, since they can be readily concealed about the person or in a vehicle. Yet, under the previous law, a lawful search for them was only possible after an arrest and that arrest in turn was hedged by restrictions. For example, under the Prevention of Crime Act 1953, it was exercisable if the person's name and address was unknown or if it was necessary to prevent the weapon being used to commit crime (this arrest power is now replaced by s 25 of the Act, see chapter 5, post). It was, so the argument ran, not only essential but also far simpler, to concede a stop and search power to the police. If the search discovered prohibited articles, the formalities of an arrest or summons could then follow.

3.03 The Royal Commission accepted these arguments, believing:

> '. . . that people in the street who have committed property offences or have in their possession articles which it is a criminal offence to possess should not be entirely protected from the possibility of being searched.' (Report, para 3.17)

It was satisfied, on the basis of figures suggesting a 12 per cent arrest rate in the Metropolis (Royal Commission, Law and Procedure Volume, para 26 and Appendices 2 and 3), that the availability of stop and search powers was of use in the detection of crime and recommended that a uniform stop and search power be made available for the whole of England and Wales, firmly based upon reasonable suspicion and subject to strict safeguards on the exercise of such power. Part I of PACE (Part II of the N.I.Order) endorsed part of that recommendation. It empowers the police to stop, detain and search persons and vehicles for stolen and prohibited articles (ss 1 and 2 (Art 3)); and to set up road blocks in certain circumstances (s 4 (Art 6)). There are provisions for the written recording of stops and searches and road blocks (ss 3 and 5 (Arts 4 and 5)) and a Code of Practice supplements PACE. Unfortunately for the purposes of exposition and understanding, PACE does not provide the full picture. Although it provides the principal stop and search power, it does not, as the Commission had suggested, provide the sole one. There are other statutory authorities some of which differ in scope from the PACE power. The list of such authorities includes the Firearms Act 1968, Misuse of Drugs Act 1971, and the Prevention of Terrorism (Temporary Provisions) Act 1989 (see COP, A, Annex A for a list) and is enlarged as and when Parliament sees the need to tackle a particular problem. Thus, in 1987 the Government became 'increasingly anxious about the habitual carrying of knives in public' (Home Secretary, Hansard vol 125, col 684) and added clauses to the Criminal Justice Bill making it an offence to carry certain blades and giving the police a power to stop and search for them (Criminal Justice Act 1988, ss 139, 140, see para 3.23 post). Likewise, a similar power is contained in the Crossbows Act 1987. The important point to note is that, apart from two exceptions (see para 3.29), the requirements in sections 2, 3 and 5 of PACE and the Code of Practice apply to *all* stop and search powers. This means, inter alia, that annual police force reports must contain a record of the stop and search powers exercised during the year. The number of recorded stops and searches more than doubled from a modest start of 109,800 in 1986 to 256,900 in 1990 and the arrests correspondingly increased from 18,900 to 39,200. The consequential charge and conviction rates are not known. The reasons for stop and search are fairly evenly divided between stolen property (97,100) and drugs (97,800), the latter sharply catching the former by 1990. It would appear that the police have grown more confident in the exercise of these powers. On the other hand, early indications are that PACE has hardly affected police enforcement patterns in this field but rather replaced local powers and formalised unofficial stop and search practices (see *British Crime Survey of 1988*, Home Office Research Study no 117(1990) by Skogan).

Consent

3.04 An important preliminary point should be noted: a constable may seek to stop, question and search with the *consent* of the citizen (and without reference to the statutory powers and safeguards set out below). The consent of the citizen is viewed as more desirable than the exercise of a power and it avoids the procedural burdens (see below) of a statutory search. Three situations need to be distinguished. First, an officer is under a duty to investigate crime and preserve the peace. He can therefore approach and ask questions of members of the public. Second, a member of the public can agree to a search. This type of search (voluntary or consensual search) is not an alternative to the statutory stop and search powers. In fact it is not the exercise of a power at all, but a consensual search *precisely because* the police lack a statutory power. In other words, a voluntary search arises when the officer lacks the reasonable suspicion to trigger the exercise of a statutory power. It should not be used to circumvent a statutory power. He should make a note of each voluntary search in his pocket book. The difficulty lies in determining whether the citizen's consent is genuine and freely given. Ignorance of police powers and the manner in which a proposed search is put can easily convince him that he has no option but to agree to the search. It is argued elsewhere (see para 2.18, ante) that this is not a freely given and informed consent. Partial recognition of these difficulties is found in the Notes for Guidance in the Code viz. that on a voluntary search of an adult, the 'officer should always make it clear that he is seeking the cooperation of the person concerned' (para 1D(b)). Conversely the person should not be made to feel that he is under compulsion. Further and more important recognition lies in the injunction that 'Juveniles, persons suffering from a mental handicap or mental disorder and others who appear not to be capable of giving an informed consent should not be subject to a voluntary search' (para 1E). It must be remembered that these Notes for Guidance are not part of the Code (para 1.2) and their breach need not incur the penalty of the exclusion of evidence under s 78 of PACE (Art 76). It is one thing for a statutory stop and search power to be improperly exercised and its fruits excluded under s 78 (Art 76) (see *R v Fennelly* (1989)); it is quite another for a court to use s 78(Art 76) where a person has 'agreed' to a search, albeit in ignorance of his rights and of the officer's lack of power. The matter could be different for his civil remedies since a complaint could be lodged, and trespass or false imprisonment could theoretically be sued (though proof could be difficult and, in the absence of injury, damages likely to be slight); and would be different if he were prosecuted for resisting the officer since he can then argue that the officer was acting outside his duty. The third situation is where the officer has the grounds to exercise a statutory stop and search power. This does not of course jettison the aim of trying to gain consensual submission to the power or imply that the officer should exercise it in a heavy handed or authoritarian manner. On the contrary, 'the cooperation of the person to be searched should be sought in every case, even if he initially objects to the search' (COP, para 3.2). In other words if the person objects to a search, further attempts to obtain his consent should be made before resorting to the use of force.

These three stages can be summarised as follows:

investigating crime	–	permits conversation with public but no power to detain
suspicion/curiosity	–	voluntary search if properly explained

reasonable suspicion   –   exercise of statutory
power, congenially if
possible

Reasonable grounds for suspicion (s 1(3)(Art 3(3)), Code of Practice A)

3.05   An essential precondition for the exercise of the stop and search power is that the constable must have 'reasonable grounds for suspecting that he will find stolen or prohibited articles' (s 1(3), PACE Northern Ireland Order 1989, Art 3(3)). A constable does *not* have the power to stop a person in order to *find* such grounds. This concept of reasonable suspicion (more fully discussed in para 2.02-17, ante) is inherently imprecise and will depend upon the facts of each case but, as the Code of Practice puts it (para 1.6) 'there must be some objective basis for it'. It must therefore be more than mere suspicion, a hunch or an instinct. The constable must have some verifiable information emanating from the suspect (e.g. his description matches that of a recently reported thief), his manner (e.g. furtive behaviour such as trying to hide something or loitering in an alley at the back of a shop), the surrounding circumstances (e.g. reports of a planned drugs party or gang fight and the sighting of known youths heading for the supposed venue); or from a third party (e.g. an informant, complainant, or witness); or from the constable's own observations or knowledge. Usually this information will stem from a combination of sources. The Code (para 1.7) makes it clear that reasonable suspicion can never be supported by personal factors *alone* (e.g. knowledge of a person's previous convictions, a person's colour, age, hairstyle or manner of dress) nor by stereotyped images of certain persons as likely offenders (e.g. skinheads). Similarly a refusal to answer questions may well increase a constable's suspicion but alone it cannot amount to reasonable suspicion since a citizen is under no general legal duty to answer police questions (*Rice v Connolly* (1966) and cf *Green v DPP* (1991)). Insufficient information would also include knowledge that persons of a particular ilk have committed offences in an area or that a particular night-club has in the past been the scene of drug-pushing. Some more objectively justified information will be needed to supplement such knowledge before reasonable suspicion can be satisfied vis-à-vis the particular individual. The point was strikingly made in the first version of the Code of Practice (1985) viz the level of suspicion for stop and search must be no less than that required for arrest without warrant. The only difference might be if an officer has reasonable suspicion that a person is *innocently* carrying a prohibited article, for then such innocence may not entitle an arrest, but may entitle a stop and search. The chances of an officer having such detailed knowledge are of course remote. Properly observed, these requirements are a formidable curb on the use of stop and search powers. In practice they are difficult to observe. For example, supporters of certain football clubs have become notorious for carrying and using offensive weapons, yet in order to justify the search of a particular supporter, there must be something more than past experience with such supporters or suspicion by association before the constable can have reasonable grounds to suspect that a particular person is in possession of an offensive weapon. The constable may therefore be tempted to act on a lower threshold of suspicion. If he does so, sanctions lie with the citizen (para 3.49, post; by making a complaint or bringing a civil action) and the court (if it is persuaded to use its power to exclude any evidence discovered by the constable: see further para 3.51 post). Most importantly, the Code of Practice issues a salutary warning that 'misuse of the powers is likely to be harmful to the police effort in the long-term. This can lead to mistrust of the police by the community' (Notes for Guidance, para 1A). The antagonism which can be caused by stop and search encounters, especially amongst the most targetted (i.e. the 16-24 years age group) is well known (see *Police and People in London*, Smith (1983); *British Crime Survey of 1988*, Skogan (1990)). Some examples follow:

(1) Officer P is alerted by radio of a burglary and the suspect is described. P then sees a person fitting the description — reasonable suspicion to stop and search.

(2) Officer P is alerted by radio of a burglary at a sports shop. P then sees a man in the vicinity of the burglary carrying a large sports bag with its price tag on — reasonable suspicion to stop and search.

(3) As in 2 except there is no price tag visible — suspicion which could harden into reasonable suspicion if the suspect behaves furtively or hurries away when P approaches, but probably not if the suspect simply refuses to answer P's questions.

(4) P sees a coloured man who is a known drugs dealer — insufficient reasons for a stop and search (COP, para 1.7).

(5) An informant tells P that D is selling drugs in an adjacent street — suspicion.

(6) As in 5, but D is a known dealer in prohibited drugs — stronger suspicion.

(7) As in 5 and 6, but the informant has been previously reliable and D is

then seen in the specified street — reasonable suspicion for at least a stop and probably a search, depending on D's reaction to P's approach or conversation.

(8) D is seen loitering near the rear loading bay of a store — suspicion.

(9) As in 8, but D runs off when P approaches — stronger suspicion.

(10) As in 8 and 9, but D runs into a blind alley and is recognised as a convicted thief — reasonable suspicion.

(11) D is stopped by P on leaving a disco or cafe notorious for drugs — no reasonable suspicion, only a hunch.

(12) As in 11, but P asks if he has drugs and D abusively refuses to answer — suspicion but not enough for reasonable suspicion.

The power to stop

(a) *Persons*

3.06 The power to stop and search can be directed against persons of any age (except the Crossbows Act 1987 which applies to persons under 17). As originally drafted, the PACE Bill included a specific power to stop persons for the purpose of a search, but this was later omitted as being unnecessary given the power under s 1(2) (Art 3(2)) to detain a person for the purpose of such a search and the power to use reasonable force to do so (see para 3.35, post). This contrasts with the other statutory powers of search (e.g. s 47, Firearms Act 1968; s 23, Misuse of Drugs Act 1971), all of which give a power to stop, some give a power to detain as well, and others leave the detention power to be implied. Therefore, the power to detain arises, expressly or impliedly, whenever the constable proposes to conduct a search under PACE or any other Act which authorises the search of persons without an arrest. If the reasonable grounds to suspect possession of stolen or prohibited articles arise before the person is stopped, the power to detain arises at the time the person is stopped. However, persons are often stopped by the police simply to enquire about their movements or to seek other information. In these circumstances it is clear that, since there is no general power to stop citizens, still less to detain them, for this purpose (see *Donnelly v Jackman* (1970), *Collins v Wilcock* (1984)), there is no obligation on the citizen to stop when requested to do so by a constable *unless* the constable has decided to exercise his power to search. This will be apparent from the information which, under s 2 (Art 4), he must convey to a person before he proceeds to a search.

3.07 Section 1 of PACE (Art 3) creates no offence but merely authorises the search for, and seizure of, stolen or prohibited articles. There is no need to show that the person was aware of the article or of its nature. For the purposes of prosecution, however, it may well be necessary to establish that the person satisfied the complex requirements of 'possession'. For example, 'possession' in the context of the offence of possession of prohibited drugs has been held to include a mental element which requires knowledge that one has the substance. Thus, in *Lockyer v Gibb* (1967), Lord Parker LCJ said:

> 'If something were slipped into your basket and you had not the vaguest notion that it was there at all you could not possibly be said to be in possession of it.'

In *Warner v Metropolitan Police Commissioner* (1969), the House of Lords held that, where a drug is in a container of some kind, D may possess the container knowing there are contents, but not 'possess' the contents where he is mistaken as to the nature of those contents and not merely their quality. The purpose of these decisions is to avoid the conviction of someone upon whose person, or in whose car or premises, prohibited drugs are found but who was unaware of their presence. Since no offence is created by s 1 of PACE (Art 3 of the Order), an offensive weapon slipped into a person's pocket without his knowledge would entitle a stop and search under s 1 (Art 3), but would not necessarily be sufficient 'possession' for the offence under s 1 of the Prevention of Crime Act 1953 or section 139 of the Criminal Justice Act 1988. (See para 3.22 post for a discussion of possession of stolen or prohibited articles). In cases of 'innocent possession' the COP (para 1.5) encourages officers to obtain voluntary production of the article instead of using the search power.

(b) Vehicles

3.08 A constable in uniform already has a power under s 163 of the Road Traffic Act 1988, to require the driver of a vehicle to stop but there is considerable doubt whether that power can legitimately be used for non-road traffic purposes (see *Hoffman v Thomas* (1974)). In *Steel v Goacher* (1983) the Divisional Court held that the stopping of a vehicle may be justified under the general common law duty of the police to prevent criminal activity, subject to there being reasonable grounds to suspect such activity. The power to stop a vehicle may therefore derive from the common law. However, the Government took the view that 'the police have power under the Road Traffic Act to stop a vehicle without qualification as to purpose' (Government Minister, House of Commons Standing Committee E, 13 December 1983, col 339). On this view, s 1(2) (Art 3(2)) of PACE is concerned with the powers to *detain* a stopped vehicle (thereby clarifying *R v Waterfield and Lynn* (1964) and confirming *Lodwick v Sanders* (1985)) and to search it. The alternative and, it is submitted, preferable view is that s 163 is confined to stops for road traffic purposes and that s 1(2) (Art 3(2)) of PACE permits a constable in uniform to detain a vehicle for the purpose of a search and, by implication, to require that the vehicle be stopped. On this latter view, the power under s 163 of the Road Traffic Act 1988 is unaffected by s 1(2) (Art 3(2)) and the powers will often be used in conjunction with each other. If the constable uses s 163 and the motorist fails to stop, an offence is committed. If he uses the s 1 power, a charge of obstruction under s 51 of the Police Act 1964 would be possible (as to which see para 2.15, ante). Whichever view is preferred, the drafting of Part I of the Act remains unclear, for though it is headed as 'Powers to stop and search', remarkably no specific power to stop persons or vehicles is mentioned, save in relation to s 4 (Art 6) (road checks) and s 6 (Art 8) (statutory undertakers). As regards the other statutory powers of search, some bestow an express power to stop a vehicle (Firearms Act 1968, Misuse of Drugs Act 1971, Sporting Events (Control of Alcohol etc) Act 1985), whilst others are silent on the matter and the above discussion is relevant.

3.09 'Vehicle' includes vessels, aircraft and hovercraft (s 2(10), Art 4(11)). A 'vessel' includes 'any ship, boat, raft or other apparatus constructed or adapted for floating on water' (s 118(1), Art 2(2)). No further definition was considered necessary because 'one would know a vehicle when one saw it' (Minister of State, Standing Committee J, 14 December 1982, col 52). As the case law on other Acts illustrates, this is too simplistic a view. Apart, obviously, from motor vehicles (cf s 185 of the Road Traffic Act 1988, s 136 of the Road Traffic Regulation Act 1984) the term includes trams, bicycles, horse-drawn carts, handcarts and perambulators. Significantly, s 185(1) of the Road Traffic Act 1988 defines a 'trailer' as 'a vehicle drawn by a motor vehicle' so that where, for example, a caravan is drawn by a motor vehicle, two vehicles are involved. An empty poultry shed drawn by a tractor is a vehicle (*Garner v Burr* (1950)), as is an office hut towed by a motor vehicle (*Horn v Dobson* (1933)) and a movable stall on wheels (*Boxer v Snelling* (1972)). In *Boxer* it was said that where there is no statutory definition of 'vehicle' the determination of a borderline case depended not only on the construction and nature of the contrivance but also the circumstances of its use. It is thus a question of fact in each case. For horse-drawn vehicles, the horse is likely to be seen as part of the vehicle but, where ridden, the Act (like the Road Traffic Acts but unlike the Wildlife and Countryside Act 1981, s 9(2), makes no reference to 'animal'. In some rural areas a horse might still be regarded as a 'vehicle' in line with *Boxer*'s reference to the individual circumstances; however if 'vehicle' is interpreted, as it was in *Boxer*, according to the Shorter Oxford English Dictionary, as 'a means of conveyance provided with wheels or runners for the carriage of persons or goods', then articles carried on the animal, for example in saddlebags, cannot be the subject of a stop and search. It is suggested that the former view is more persuasive — if an individual uses and regards an animal as a vehicle it should be treated as such.

3.10   A hovercraft is a motor vehicle for some road traffic purposes and if used on a road may be stopped by a uniformed constable. Searching of stationary aircraft is implied by s 2(10), (Art 4(11)) but can only apply to aircraft landing or parked in public places as defined by s 1(1), (4) and (5) (Art 3(1), (4) and (5)). Other statutory powers of stop and search do not define vehicle but clearly an aircraft qualifies and, since most of these powers can be exercised anywhere, the aircraft need not be parked in a public place (e.g. a search under the Misuse of Drugs Act 1971 of a plane landing on a private airstrip or field). A constable or specified airport official has the power to stop and search aircraft at specified aerodromes for firearms, explosives and other dangerous articles (s 13, Aviation Security Act 1982), whilst a constable can board and search aircraft for anything stolen or unlawfully obtained (s 27, 1982 Act). Customs and Excise officials (and constables) have powers to stop and search vehicles and vessels for goods suspected of excise offences (s 163, Customs and Excise Management Act 1979).

3.11   *Vehicles as premises* — The wide definition of a vehicle can include many forms of mobile homes, such as touring or gypsy caravans, caravanettes and houseboats. If such vehicles are travelling or are situated in 'public places' (as defined and explained by s 1(1), (4) and (5) (Art 3(1), (4) and (5)) — see para 3.24, post), e.g. lay-bys and temporary mooring berths, they can be stopped and searched on reasonable suspicion under s 1 (Art 3). It is arguable that caravans, houseboats and the like, which remain on a permanent site, cease to be 'vehicles' for the purposes of s 1 (Art 3) and, in any event, such sites may not fall within the ambit of public place as defined by s 1(1) (Art 3(3)). It should be noted however that vehicles also qualify as 'premises' for the purpose of searches under PACE (s 23, Art 25) e.g. entry and search in order to make an arrest (s 17, Art 19) or after an arrest under ss 18 or 32 (Arts 20 or 34). An important implication of this broad definition of premises is that the wide powers of seizure under s 19, Art 21 (general power of seizure whilst on premises) can be exercised during a lawful stop and search. Thus, when vehicles are searched under s 1 (Art 3), evidence of *any* offence can be seized if it is necessary to prevent its concealment, loss, damage, alteration or destruction (s 19(3), Art 21(3)), even though the power of seizure for s 1 is limited to 'stolen or prohibited' articles (s 1(6), Art 3(6)). If, on the other hand, the stop and search is unlawful, the court may subsequently use s 78, (Art 76) to exclude any evidence obtained thereby (see further para 3.51 post).

3.12 *Unattended vehicles.* — By implication from s 2(6) of PACE (Art 4(7)) a constable may search an unattended vehicle under the PACE or other statutory powers. He can use reasonable force to do so (s 117, Art 88). The vehicle must, of course, be in a 'public place' and, while that is widely defined (s 1(1) Art 3(1)), s 1(5) (Art 3 (5)) excludes the possibility of a person's vehicle being searched while parked on a drive in his garden or in a yard or other premises occupied with, and used for the purpose of, a dwelling. Section 1(5), Art 3(5) only applies however to vehicles belonging to those residing in such premises or parked there with the consent of the resident. If, for example, D, who resides elsewhere, were to park his car on P's driveway without his consent, the vehicle could be searched, assuming that there are reasonable grounds to suspect that it contains stolen or prohibited articles. (As to the procedure to be followed after the search of unattended vehicles, see para 3.43, post).

'Anything which is in or on a vehicle' (s 1(2)(a)(ii); Art 3(2)(a)(ii))

3.13 The stop and search power extends to 'anything in or on a vehicle'. This clearly includes such inanimate items as a toolbox or luggage in the boot or on a roofrack. It does not however include persons who are in the vehicle. If they are to be searched, there must be reasonable grounds to suspect that they, as opposed to the vehicle itself, are in possession of stolen or prohibited articles. The distinction is far from academic. For example, the police may have information that a youth, whose description fits D, has threatened someone with a bayonet which he carried in the boot of his car. Some hours later D is seen driving his car and carrying three passengers. There would be reasonable grounds to search the vehicle and D, but not the three passengers unless there are further grounds for suspicion such as D being seen to pass something to a back seat passenger.

The object of the search

3.14 As already noted (para 3.07, ante) s 1 of PACE (Art 3) does not create an offence. It merely allows the police to search for evidence of offences viz the possession of stolen or prohibited articles or blades.

Reasonable suspicion that the articles are stolen (para 3.15 post) or prohibited (para 3.16) or blades (para 3.23) is sufficient to authorise seizure (s 1(3) and (6), Art 3(3) and (6)). They need not in fact be stolen or prohibited or blades. In many cases, the mere finding of them or the person's response to inquiries will suffice to give rise to reasonable suspicion and an arrest or summons may follow. Prosecution will then depend on the terms of the relevant statute.

Stolen articles

3.15   In the absence of a definition, it must be assumed that 'stolen' bears the same meaning as that given to 'stolen goods' in the Theft Act 1968, since any offence resulting from the possession of a stolen article will be an offence under the 1968 Act. Under s 24 of that Act, stolen goods:

  (i)   need not have been stolen in England or Wales;

 (ii)   cover not only the original property but also any other property representing it either directly or indirectly. Thus, if D1 steals goods and sells or exchanges them to D2, both are in possession of stolen goods;

(iii)   include those obtained by deception or blackmail, and it is inconceivable that the courts would exclude such other forms of dishonesty from the scope of a s 1 stop and search.

Possession will usually be evidence of one of the offences under the Theft Act 1968 (as regards 'unwitting possession', see para 3.22, post). (To similar effect see s 23 of Theft Act (N.I.) 1969.)

Prohibited articles

3.16   These fall into two types — (a) offensive weapons (s 1(7)(a), Art 3(7)(a)) and a person who has with him in a public place any such weapon may be guilty of an offence under s 1 of the Prevention of Crime Act 1953; and (b) articles for theft (s 1(7)(b)), the carrying of which may likewise constitute an offence under s 25 of the Theft Act 1968 (s 24, Theft Act (N.I.) 1969).

(a)   Offensive weapon

3.17   This is defined in s 1(9), Art 3(10) as:

'any article . . . made or adapted for use for causing injury to persons . . . or . . . intended by the person having it with him for such use by him or by some other person.'

The definition is identical to that in s 1(4) of the Prevention of Crime Act 1953 (as amended by the Public Order Act 1986) and reference can be made to caselaw on that Act. There are three categories:

(i)   '*Articles made for causing injury*' — The question here is whether the article is an offensive weapon *per se* i.e. that its purpose (of causing injury) is so patent as to require no elucidation to a court. Examples are a bayonet, cosh, telescopic truncheon, a police officer's truncheon (unless legitimately carried, see *Houghton v Chief Constable of Greater Manchester* (1986)), a knuckleduster (dicta in *R v Petrie* (1961)), a flick knife (*R v Simpson* (1984)), sword stick (*R v Butler* (1988)), and a rice flail (*Copus v DPP* (1989)). They clearly include firearms and there is thus an overlap with the stop and search power under s 47 of the Firearms Act 1968. Unless injury in s 1(9) can be interpreted to include shock and alarm, then a search for imitation firearms must be justified under the 1968 Act. Explosives are not specifically mentioned. They qualify as offensive weapons in this category if made up as a bomb, but otherwise qualify as category (iii) weapons (below). In so far as the article is sharply pointed or has a blade exceeding 3 inches, there is also an overlap with the stop and search power supplied by the Criminal Justice Act 1988 (see para 3.23 post).

(ii)   '*Articles adapted for use for causing injury*' — Again the question is whether the article is offensive per se. They would include a chair leg studded with nails, a peaked-cap with razor blades embedded in the peak, a sharpened comb, a deliberately broken bottle or glass. 'Adapted' implies a deliberate decision to change the character of the article to make it suitable for the purpose of causing injury (cf. *Maddox v Storer* (1963)). If D were to knock over a milk bottle while backing away from a would-be assailant and then picked up the broken bottle he would not, it is submitted, have 'adapted' the bottle for use for causing injury and, whether or not it is an offensive weapon, will depend on the intent with which D has it with him, for it may then fall within the third category.

(iii)   '*Articles intended to cause injury*' — The purpose of category (i) and (ii) weapons is self-evident and the prosecution needs only to prove possession of them in a public place. In this category, however, it must go further and show that the carrier intended to use the weapon to cause injury (e.g. a washing up liquid bottle filled with acid, cf *R v Formosa* (1990) where the bottle could not qualify as a designed or adapted weapon under the Firearms Act 1968, but could fall within the category (iii) under discussion). It is here that the greatest practical difficulties may arise, for almost all articles are capable of becoming an offensive weapon, from a car jack to a drum of pepper. The facts of each case will of course vary and much may depend upon the citizen's explanation to the police. Thus, in *Buckley v DPP* (1988) the police relied upon the facts that a machete (not offensive per se) had been hidden in the car, a newspaper had been used as a scabbard, which also facilitated the concealment, and his story that he used the machete to cut grass (though other garden tools in the car were not hidden) was unbelievable. In contrast in *Southwell v Chadwick* (1987) it was held that a machete in a sheath and a catapult were not offensive weapons per se and the Crown would therefore have to disprove D's excuse that he used them lawfully to kill squirrels to feed to wild birds which he kept. Moreover, for the purposes of the Prevention of Crime Act 1953 the intention must be to cause injury to others and not to oneself (*R v Fleming* (1989)); thus, if the same view is taken of s 1(9) of PACE (Art 3(10)) and the police are told that D has set off to commit suicide and they intercept him, removal of his weapon would have to be justified on the constable's common law duty to preserve the peace (see para 5.33, post) and not the s 1 stop and search power. It follows that if a constable stops a car for the purpose of a search under PACE, assuming reasonable grounds for suspicion, and finds in the boot various tools, car jack, handle, etc, these would not be prohibited articles unless there is some evidence of an intent to use them to cause injury to others. If D were driving to P's house intent on assaulting P with the car jack, and somehow the constable knew this, the car jack would then be a prohibited article, an offensive weapon. But in such a case the constable already has a power to arrest D in order to prevent the commission by him of an offence with that weapon (s 25 of PACE, Art 27). The stop and search power therefore adds nothing to the constable's powers in such a case. Moreover, unless a constable can see the article or has some specific information about the person, vehicle or circumstances, he will not have the necessary reasonable suspicion to employ s 1, (Art 3). The reasonable suspicion must arise beforehand, and justify, the search. The search cannot be justified afterwards when articles are discovered. It is highly likely therefore that in practice persons will be stopped either at random or on a lesser suspicion than 'reasonable grounds to suspect', based on surrounding circumstances and the constable's experience, for example, of football 'hooligans'. Even if such a search is held to be unlawful, the evidence procured may still be admissible (see s 78, Art 76, and para 3.51, post). The victim has the remedies of a civil action or complaint against the police or may, at his peril, resist the constable, who would be acting outside his duty for the purposes of s 51 of the Police Act 1964 (see further para 2.15, ante).

Articles carried for self-defence

3.18 It has been held that it is not a reasonable excuse for carrying an offensive weapon that it is carried for self-defence unless the person shows that there was an 'imminent, particular threat affecting the particular circumstances in which the weapon was carried', (*Evans v Hughes* (1972) and see also *AG's Reference (No 2 of 1983)* (1984)). Thus, in *Malnik v DPP* (1989) D possessed a rice-flail because he feared that X would become violent when asked to return some property. This was held not to be a reasonable excuse. It is the policy of the law to discourage citizens from embarking on such expeditions when the risk of violence is obvious. D should call the police instead. Anti-rape sprays, some of which are offensive weapons within categories (i) and (ii), can never, it seems, be lawfully carried since they are carried with intent to cause injury, even though the intent is conditional upon being attacked. C.S. Gas, Mace Sprays and electric stun guns the size of a cigarette packet which are carried by many American women, are clearly offensive weapons. If the woman is in fact attacked, the use of the spray might be seen as reasonable self-defence under s 3 of the Criminal Law Act 1967. Even security guards employed by the various security firms are not lawfully entitled to carry truncheons or weapons as a matter of routine (*R v Spanner* (1973)), nor are taxi drivers who carry coshes in their cabs (cf *Patterson v Block* (1984)). Similarly, a shopkeeper or store detective can be searched, at least when on the public side of the counter. If he is behind the counter, the power to search will only arise if he is still in a 'public place' as defined in s 1(1), Art 3(1). In *Anderson v Miller* (1976), a firearm placed under the counter was held still to be within a public place for the purposes of the Firearms Act 1968 and a similarly broad interpretation would be possible under the 1984 Act (see further para 3.24, post).

For use by him or by some other person

The phrase 'or by some other person' in s 1(9), Art 3(10) of PACE is clearly intended to authorise the search for and seizure of an offensive weapon which is carried by a person who has no intention to use it himself but which he is carrying for someone who has. If, therefore,

3.18 *Stop and search powers*

(a) D1 and D2 are together, and

(b) D2 knows that D1 has a weapon with him for D2's use for causing injury, and

(c) D2 has immediate control over it in that he can call for it when he wants to use it, then D1 can be searched under PACE and D2 would have the weapon 'with him' for the purpose of prosecution under the Prevention of Crime Act 1953 (as amended by the Public Order Act 1986; prior to this amendment D1 could not be charged jointly with D2 since the offence under the 1953 Act required that the person who had the article with him must have intended to use it for causing injury). Section 1(7)(b)(ii) (Art 3 (7)(b)(ii)) similarly goes further than (Art 24(1) of the Theft Acts 1968 and 1969 (which refer to articles which D 'has with him') by including within the definition of 'prohibited articles' articles carried by D1 for use by D2. As with s 1(9) (Art 3(10)) this permits the searching of D1 when he is reasonably suspected of carrying a prohibited article for someone else's use. In some cases the parties will be jointly engaged in the criminal enterprise so that both may be arrested even though only one carried prohibited articles.

(b) *Housebreaking implements etc*

3.19 Section 1(7) and (8) of PACE (Art 3(7),(8)) combine the words of s 25(1) and (3) of the Theft Act 1968 (Theft Act (N.I) 1969) in defining a prohibited article as an article made or adapted for use in the course of, or in connection with, or intended for use in:

(i) burglary

(ii) theft

(iii) an offence under s 12 of the Theft Act 1968 (Theft Act (N.I.) 1969) (taking motor vehicle or other conveyance without authority) or

(iv) an offence under s 15 of that Act (obtaining property by deception).

Possession of such an article is an offence under s 25 of the Theft Act (s.24 of the 1969 Act) and the stop and search power is intended to facilitate the detection of such an offence. As has been seen (para 3.18), s 1(7)(b)(ii) (Art 3(7)(b)(ii)) go further than the offence under s 25 of the 1968 Act (s.24 of the 1969 Act) by including articles carried by a person with the intention that some other person should use them. (NB. The N.I. Order also refers to s.172 of the Road Traffic (N.I.) Order 1981. This contains the offence of taking a motor vehicle, trailer or pedal cycle without consent. S.12 of the 1969 Act refers only to other conveyances).

3.20 Although s 1(7)(b) of PACE (Art 3(7)(b)) and s 25(3) of the 1968 and 1969 Acts use the phrase 'made or adapted', there are few articles which are made for the criminal purposes set out in the Act. More often, articles which are made for legitimate purposes are used for illegitimate ones, e.g. skeleton keys, picklocks, jemmies. In each case the important question is the use for which the article is intended rather than whether it is made or adapted for a particular purpose. Some articles such as skeleton keys, call 'for explanation by the accused' (Criminal Law Revision Committee, Eighth Report, para 151) and the absence of an explanation together with the circumstances of possession will normally arouse reasonable suspicion and may amount to evidence from which a court or jury can infer the necessary criminal intention (s 25(3) of the Theft Act 1968).

3.21 There are many more articles, however, in daily legitimate use which can be lawfully employed within s 1(7)(b), Art 3(7)(b) but for which the intention to use them unlawfully will be extremely difficult to discern. For example, gloves, credit cards which can be used to open certain locks or obtain property by deception (*R v Lambie* (1981)), sellotape which may be used to prevent noise when glass is broken and sandwiches or bottles of wine which may be used to cheat one's employer by selling one's own goods rather than his (obtaining by deception, *R v Rashid* (1977); *R v Doukas* (1978)). There may be circumstances in which a constable could have reasonable suspicion for s 1 (Art 3) purposes, for example, a person seen wearing gloves on a hot summer's evening in a darkened alleyway. In the more normal course of events, however, the wearing of gloves could not justify such a suspicion. It follows that if the stop and search powers are to be used widely, the police will have to resort to a random selection or to a lesser standard of suspicion, followed by the discovery of an article, arrest and interrogation in order to prove the criminal intention. Again, the initial stop and search may be justified in fact, but not in law.

Possession in the context of the relevant offences

3.22 As was earlier indicated (para 3.07, ante), s 1 of PACE (Art 3) is not dependent upon the person 'possessing' an article but in the context of the particular offence arising from seizure of the stolen or prohibited articles, a narrower and more complex question of proving 'possession' is called for. In particular, possession may be interpreted as requiring knowledge that the article is in one's possession (cf *Lockyer v Gibb* (1967) and *Warner v MPC* (1969)).

(i) *Unwitting possession of stolen goods.* — Section 22 of the Theft Act 1968 states that a person handles stolen goods if, knowing or believing them to be stolen, he dishonestly receives the goods (receiving is the relevant form of handling in this context though there are many other forms). It is for the prosecution to prove knowledge or belief. 'Knowing' requires actual knowledge that the goods are stolen while 'believing' implies that there would be such knowledge unless D deliberately closes his eyes to circumstances which permit of no other conclusion but that the goods are stolen (*R v Hall* (1985)). Suspicion on the other hand is not enough (*R v Pethick* (1980). It follows that in a case of 'unwitting possession' the stolen goods can be the object of a search under the s 1 (Art 3) power and may be seized, but no offence of handling is committed.

(ii) *Possession of a prohibited weapon or blade.* — Section 1 of the Prevention of Crime Act 1953, s 25 of the Theft Act 1968, s 139 of the Criminal Justice Act 1988 (blades) and s 3 of the Crossbows Act 1987, use the phrase 'has with him' rather than 'has in his possession' and it may be that the former bears a narrower meaning than the latter. For 'possession' can include articles which are at home or elsewhere but still in 'possession' of the person, while 'has with him' can relate only to those articles immediately to hand. This is in fact the distinction drawn between the offence under s 16 of the Firearms Act 1968 (Firearms Act (N.I.) 1969) (possessing a firearm with intent to endanger life) and s 18 of that Act (having with him a firearm with intent to commit an indictable offence). Under s 18 mere possession, for example, having the firearm at home intending to commit an indictable offence in the future, is not sufficient, he must have the firearm with him while in the course of committing the offence; whereas under s 16 such possession with intent to kill is sufficient. As for possession under s 1 of the Firearms Act, the strict view in *Warner*, above, has been adopted (see *R v Waller* (1991)). 'Has with him' has also been interpreted as a narrower form of possession requiring knowledge that the person has the article with him (*R v Cugullere* (1961) and see *R v Russell* (1985)). Such an interpretation is, it is submitted, more in keeping with the mischief at which the statutes are aimed. However, in the context of unlawful possession of drugs, the Court of Appeal in *R v Martindale* (1986) has refused to follow this view and has held that a person remains in possession of articles even if he has forgotten about them (e.g. an offensive weapon in a car's glove compartment or boot which the driver knowingly put there some years ago but has now forgotten about). This view has been persuasively challenged (see [1986] Crim LR 737). Certainly unwitting possession (in the sense of an article secretly dropped into a person's handbag or pocket) is insufficient. Whichever view (*Russell* or *Martindale*) is accepted, the important point for the constable is that such questions do not matter for the purposes of stop and search under s 1 of PACE.

Blades and pointed weapons

3.23   This is the third category of article for which the police can stop and search under PACE. By virtue of s 139 of the Criminal Justice Act 1988 it is an offence to carry in a public place any article 'which has a blade or is sharply pointed' (except for a folding pocket knife with a blade of less than 3 inches). Unlike the Prevention of Crime Act 1953, there is no need for the prosecution to establish that the weapon is offensive per se or is intended to cause injury. Instead the burden lies on the defence to show a 'good reason or lawful authority' for carrying the article (e.g. as a sportsman, as part of a national or religious costume, a chef with his knives en route to work, a carpenter). To assist in the detection of this offence, s 140 of the 1988 Act added to PACE a power for a constable to stop and search for such articles (Art 3(2) (a)(iii) and (9) of the N.I. Order). Examples are a Stanley knife, butterfly knife, carving knife, push dagger, handclaw, footclaw, blowpipe, sharpened comb and knitting needle. They obviously overlap with offensive weapons prohibited by the Prevention of Crime Act 1953 (see para. 3.16 ante). The matter is important when it comes to charging the individual since (a) the maximum penalty is higher under the 1953 Act and (b) the prosecution have the easier task in court if it uses the 1988 Act (see above); but at street level the same problem confronts the constable viz he must have *reasonable suspicion* that D has with him an offensive weapon (1953 Act) or prohibited blade (1988 Act) before he can stop and search D. Rarely will there be such clear information as to satisfy that level.

Venue of the stop and search

3.24   Unfortunately for ready understanding, the statutes which bestow a power of stop and search vary in terms of the place where the power can be exercised. The Annex to the Code of Practice usefully notes the differences. Thus, it will be seen that, for example, the Prevention of Terrorism (Temporary Provisions) Act, the Badgers Act and the Misuse of Drugs

Act can be used *anywhere* (e.g. assuming reasonable suspicion, a constable can enter a private wood to investigate badger baiting and search suspected persons for evidence such as badger tongs; a constable lawfully in a house can search the occupants). This second example shows that, even if a stop and search can be exercised anywhere, the constable must be at that place lawfully (having been invited there, present there with implied permission to investigate an offence, lawfully there under another police power, e.g. a warrant). Some of the statutes allow a stop and search at any place other than a dwelling-house and give the constable the right to enter that place (Wildlife and Countryside Act, Deer Act, Crossbows Act) e.g. he could enter outbuildings on reasonable suspicion that unlicensed wild birds are being kept or birds' eggs are being hoarded. The Firearms Act power is confined to a public place, except where a constable reasonably suspects that a person is carrying a firearm with criminal intent or is trespassing with a firearm. In the latter case he has the right to enter any place (s 47(5) (s 39(6)N.I. Act)). Section 1(1) of PACE (Art 3(1)) uses a more general and opaque definition viz a stop and search by a constable is permitted:

'(a)   in any place to which at the time when he proposes to exercise the power the public or any section of the public has access, on payment or otherwise, as of right or by virtue of express or implied permission; or

(b)   in any other place to which people have ready access at the time when he proposes to exercise the power but which is not a dwelling.'

(a) clearly encompasses a public place, as used in the Firearms Act, and simple examples are all roads, footpaths, subways, recreation grounds, supermarket car parks, public transport, civic buildings such as a museum, cinemas, shops, public houses, restaurants, night clubs, banks, public conveniences or lavatories in shops. Section 35(2) of the Highways Act 1980 permits the local highway authority or district council, to enter into agreements with those who own or have an interest in land on which a building is, or is proposed to be situated, for the provision of ways over, through or under such buildings, to be dedicated as public rights of way. These will normally be maintained by the appropriate authority who may make bye-laws governing the conduct of those using the walkways and the times at which they are open to the public. Such walkways, identifiable by the display of such bye-laws and opening times, fall within s 1(1)(a), Art 3(1)(a). Many cities and towns have local Acts giving powers similar to those of the Highways Act 1980. Where, under the provisions of such local Acts, a footway or place is declared to be a walkway, city walkway or pedestrian way, such areas qualify for s 1(1)(a), Art 3(1)(a). Bye-laws may be made in respect of local Act walkways and the display of these, together with opening times where appropriate, may assist in recognition. The definition is similar to that used in the Prevention of Crime Act 1953 and *Knox v Anderton* (1982) suggests that a landing and staircase in a block of flats qualify. It is identical to the definition used in the Public Order Act 1986 and similar to that in the Public Order Act 1936. Cases under the latter are still relevant. Thus, a tennis court at Wimbledon (*Brutus v Cozens* (1973)) or a football ground (*Cawley v Frost* (1976)) are public places, but not a shop's car park when the shop is closed (*Marsh v Arscott* (1982), and cf *Sandy v Martin* (1974) a road traffic case involving a pub's car park). This last case is most questionable in the context of stop and search since many shop car parks today are easily accessible to the public after shop hours and may be used as shortcuts or as meeting places, but they will fall within the next paragraph. Clearly distinguishable is the fenced and locked car park.

3.25 The scope of s 1(1)(b), Art 3(1)(b) is more uncertain. It is aimed at places adjoining those already covered by s 1(1)(a), Art 1(1)(a). For otherwise a person in a public place, for example, a shop, could avoid a stop and search by the simple expedient of moving to a private part of the premises, for example, a courtyard at the rear of the shop. The key to s 1(1)(b), Art 3(1)(b) is whether 'people' as opposed to 'the public or any section of the public' (in s 1(1)(a), Art 3(1)(a)), have 'ready access to the place'. Under the Public Order Act 1936, the speedway track or similar track between a football pitch and the spectator area was held to be a 'public place' even though the public were not permitted access to it. The Divisional Court considered the premises in their entirety. The fact that the public were not permitted access to certain areas did not exclude them from being a 'public place' (*Cawley v Frost* (1976)). Considering an identical definition of 'public place' in the Firearms Act 1968, the Divisional Court held that a shopkeeper who kept a firearm under the counter of his shop had a loaded firearm in a public place for the purposes of s 19 of that Act, notwithstanding that the public were not permitted access to that side of the counter (*Anderson v Miller* (1976)). Both places can qualify under s 1(1)(b), Art 3(1)(b). Indeed, places with 'ready access' to people are capable of extremely broad interpretation. They can cover all areas into which a person can move with little difficulty e.g. unlocked doors leading to storerooms in a shop or to toilets for the staff, or doors marked 'private' but which are unlocked. They could easily include accessible gardens attached to private dwellings. To avoid undue invasion by the police onto such property, s 1(4) and (5), (Art 3(4) and (5)) make it clear that the police can only search persons or vehicles in the curtilage of a dwelling-house if they believe that the person or vehicle is trespassing. The sub-sections do not therefore give a general power to enter what are private premises. But, by authorising a search of trespassers, they ensure that the police will be acting lawfully towards the person searched or the owner of the vehicle searched. It is still possible, however, for a person to evade a search by going onto premises owned by a relative or friend. He can claim to be there with the express or implied consent of the occupier and, since the premises are not a public place and the constable has no power of entry vis-a-vis the occupier, the constable must leave if required to do so by the occupier (unless of course he can claim some other power of entry, see chapter 4). Section 1(4) and (5), (Art 3(4) and (5)) require 'reasonable grounds for believing' that the person or vehicle is not lawfully on the premises. This is a high standard to satisfy and the fact that, for example, the occupier of a house is not the registered owner of a car parked on his drive would be insufficient on its own to justify a search.

Examples

(1) A vehicle is seen parked at an address, other than that of its owner. It is parked in a driveway at the side of a private house. The constable should enquire of the householder whether it is parked with his permission. If it is, the constable cannot search it. If no householder appears, the constable can only search the vehicle if he has

  (a) reasonable grounds to believe it is not lawfully parked there; and

  (b) reasonable grounds to suspect that stolen or prohibited articles may be found in it.

(2) If a vehicle is parked in the drive of a house which has been converted into an office, the building is not a dwelling, s 1(5), (Art 3(5)) is irrelevant and a search may take place.

(3) D is sitting on his front lawn which abuts onto a public footpath. There is no fence and ready access can be gained from the path. He is in possession of a bayonet which he uses for gardening. The police cannot enter and search D.

(4) As in (3) but E, who is carrying a bayonet, steps onto the lawn without D's consent. The police can enter and search E.

(5) D is seen on a country estate, the grounds of which are open to the public. Section 1 (Art 3) may be used.

(6) D is seen in the enclosed and private garden of the country estate. Section 1 (Art 3) may be used if s 1(4) (Art 3(4)) is satisfied.

(7)   A vehicle is seen in the courtyard of a shop, above which is situated a residential flat. The constable should make enquiries to see if s 1(5) (Art 3(5)) applies (whether the vehicle is there with the permission of the flat occupier) before the vehicle can be searched.

NB   These examples presuppose that the constable has reasonable grounds to suspect that stolen or prohibited articles or blades will be found.

Public place in the offence creating Act

3.26   The offence under s 25 of the Theft Act 1968 (s 24 of the N.I. Act 1969) is committed if D has with him a housebreaking implement 'when not at his place of abode'. It follows that possession anywhere other than at his place of abode is an offence. However, the Prevention of Crime Act 1953 contains a narrower definition of 'public place' than that in s 1(1) (Art 3(1)) of PACE. It might be argued that since the 1953 Act definition does not, for example, include walkways, the police may search for and seize an offensive weapon possessed in a walkway but that the possessor commits no offence under the 1953 Act. There are two answers to this argument. First, whether or not a place is a 'public place' within the 1953 Act is a question of fact and it would be open to a court to hold that a walkway is a public place. Second, the court may draw the reasonable inference that if D had the article in a place which is not a public place within the 1953 Act, and is not his home, he must have carried it to or from such a place through public places (*R v Mehmed* (1963)). Thus, by either route an offence is committed. As for unlawful possession of a blade, this offence is committed in a 'public place' (s 139, Criminal Justice Act 1988) and is defined, non-exclusively, in similar terms to s 1(1)(a) (Art 3(1)(a)) of PACE.

Search as a condition of entry to public places

3.27   Football grounds and night clubs, and similar places of public entertainment fall within s 1(1) (Art 3(1)) of PACE and the other statutory powers of stop and search. However, searches of persons entering them need not be carried out under statute, for it is open to the organisers of such events to require those entering the premises to submit to a search as a condition of entry. Such a search may take place inside the premises or at the entrance and may be conducted by employees of the organisation or uniformed constables. In such a case the constables are not then exercising their statutory powers and none of the safeguards or requirements of ss 2 and 3 (Arts 4 and 5) of PACE apply. The sanction for refusal to submit to such a search is refusal of entry. If, however, one does submit and stolen or prohibited articles are found, an offence may be committed and an arrest may follow. Where the search is preceded by the information required by s 2 (Art 4), it will indicate that the constable is exercising a statutory power and a refusal to comply can then result in reasonable force being used to detain the person and conduct the search; resistance to the officer could lead to a charge under s 51 of the Police Act 1964.

Involuntary presence in a public place

3.28   The fact that a person is not aware that he is in a public place or that he is in a public place involuntarily is no bar to a s 1 (Art 3) search and is unlikely to be a defence to a charge of possession of a prohibited article. In *Winzar v Chief Constable of Kent* (1983), D was carried from a hospital and arrested on the forecourt for being found drunk in a highway. Goff LJ held that the fact that his presence on the highway was momentary or involuntary was immaterial, the offence having been created to deal with persons who were drunk in public places. Similarly an unconscious person could be searched for drugs under the Misuse of Drugs Act 1971 or an intoxicated person for an offensive weapon under s 1 (Art 3) of PACE.

Procedure

3.29   The principal safeguard against abuse of the stop and search power should be the requirement for, and strict application of, reasonable suspicion. However, the difficulties of defining reasonable suspicion and the fact that in many circumstances it will not be possible 'reasonably' to suspect possession of prohibited articles (particularly where they only become prohibited articles when possessed with a particular intent) mean that the principal safeguards *in practice* must be the duties imposed by ss 2 and 3 (Arts 4 and 5) of PACE on constables exercising stop and search powers. Section 2 (Art 4) applies before a search and s 3 (Art 5) afterwards. They apply to all stop and search powers, (other than searches of vehicles conducted by statutory undertakers (as to which see para 3.61, post) and searches in Northern Ireland under the Northern Ireland (Emergency Provisions) Act 1978) thus including, for example, the Misuse of Drugs Act 1971.

3.30   It must be emphasised that these duties only arise if a constable intends a stop and search under a statutory power. He can still try to stop a person or vehicle and ask questions and can still conduct a search with the person's *consent*, be it informed consent or otherwise (but see para 3.04 ante). The duties of ss 2 and 3 (Art 4 and 5) arise if he needs to rely on the *statutory* powers.

A constable in uniform

3.31 The stop and search powers can be used by both uniformed and plain-clothed officers. Use by the latter can clearly pose difficulties if the officer does not identify himself quickly and the citizen resists the officer's instructions. It will normally be an offence of wilful obstruction to refuse to stop for a constable who proposes, on reasonable suspicion, to exercise stop and search powers, or an offence of resisting or assaulting the constable if the person physically resists. An honest but mistaken belief that the person seeking to stop you is not a constable is a good defence to a charge of wilful obstruction under s 51(3) of the Police Act 1964 (*Ostler v Elliott* (1980)), but not to a charge of assault (*R v Forbes and Webb* (1865)). There has been some confusion in relation to the use of reasonable force in self-defence when a person mistakenly believes that he is under attack. Until the decision in *R v Williams (Gladstone)* (1984) the belief had to be reasonable but in Williams it was held that the reasonableness of the belief is only relevant to the question of whether that belief was held, and not to the question of guilt or innocence (see further para 5.65, post).

Section 2(1) (Art 4(1))

3.32 Once a person or vehicle has been detained under any stop and search power, the constable need not proceed with the search if he subsequently discovers that (i) no search is required, e..g. his reasonable suspicion is eliminated after a conversation with the suspect, or (ii) a search is impracticable, e.g. a general melee develops and he must turn his attention elsewhere. The COP para 2.3, makes an important point here. Reasonable suspicion must exist *before* the stop. It cannot be retrospectively generated by the person's reaction to preliminary questioning or by his refusal to answer questions, though, of course, the constable's pre-existing reasonable suspicion will often be confirmed and heightened by the person's reaction.

The duty to inform the suspect (s 2(2) and (3)) (Art 4(2) and (4))

3.33 Once a constable has decided to proceed with a search, he must take reasonable steps to bring to the attention of the person to be searched or of the person in charge of the vehicle (s 2(5) Art 4(6)), the matters mentioned below. This duty should reduce the dangers of arbitrary use of s 1 (Art 3) powers for, firstly, the need to articulate one's reasons for action acts as a restraint. Secondly, the person to be searched is less likely to react aggressively if the constable's purpose is explained to him. The duty is thus a statutory elucidation of what is good police practice. 'Reasonable steps' in s 2(2) (Art 4(2)) take account of the situation where the person to be searched is incapable of understanding the constable's instructions e.g. through intoxication or language difficulties. The phrase requires the constable to establish, if practicable, whether a person accompanying the suspect can act as interpreter (see Code, para 2.7). It can also permit the constable to search once he has tried in slow and clear terms to communicate with the person. The importance of compliance with this duty of informing the suspect lies in the possibility that a court will use section 78 (Art 76) of PACE to exclude evidence obtained from a stop and search unless the constable can prove that he supplied the information (*R v Fennelly* (1989)). The duty to inform does not apply in relation to the search of unattended vehicles, or to searches of vehicles by statutory undertakers (s 6, see para 3.61, post; the latter of these are so frequent and well-established as to make such explanations impracticable and unnecessary) and to searches under s 27(2) of the Aviation Security Act 1982 (searches of persons and aircraft at designated airports for certain cargo). Apart from these exceptions, a constable cannot conduct a search until he has taken reasonable steps to inform the citizen of the following matters:

(1) *The duty to furnish documentary evidence that he is a constable.* — This duty only applies to plain-clothed officers who seek to search the person or vehicle. 'Documentary evidence' avoids the confusion which might follow from a hasty and mumbled identification and refers to an officer's warrant card. On the other hand, the speed with which a warrant card and the other duties below can be addressed to a person does not mean that the person will comprehend the information. Good policing and the requirement of 'reasonable steps' in s 2(2) (Art 4(2)) demand that care be taken in the provision of such information and that the citizen be given adequate opportunity to assimilate it before the constable proceeds to the search.

(2) *The duty to give his name and that of the police station to which he is attached.* — Outside Northern Ireland there is no duty to give the number of the constable because different police forces use different numbering systems and this was felt to endanger clarity. Confusion could still arise when a force has officers bearing a common name who are attached to the same police station. The additional requirement to state the number would remove this possibility. When an

officer is investigating terrorism, there is no duty to state his name (COP, para 2.4). Instead he should give his warrant number.

(3) *The duty to state the object of and grounds for undertaking the search.* — Research studies conducted on the exercise of stop and search powers all indicate a high level of antagonism and resentment if the reasons for the stop and search are not explained (Wiley and Hudick (USA) (1980); Brown (Australia) (1980); Butler and Tharme (1981); Manning and Butler (1982) and Willis (1983) (England)). Thus, it is both legally (see *R v Fennelly*, 1989) and socially necessary to comply with these duties. There is, of course, no duty to state with precision the object of the search. Indeed the constable will seldom know this with any precision but he should indicate whether the object is to search for stolen goods, offensive weapons, housebreaking implements, drugs etc. It is submitted that a statement that he is searching for 'stolen or prohibited goods' is too imprecise for compliance with the section. The *grounds* for undertaking the search appear to mean the grounds giving rise to reasonable suspicion and will invariably indicate the object of the search. For example, a constable is informed by the manager of a shop that a youth, who is described, has just attempted to purchase goods with a stolen credit card. The constable sees a youth answering that description in the vicinity soon afterwards. He should then, having stated his name, state that he proposes to carry out a search for a stolen credit card (the *object* of the search) because a youth answering his description has just attempted to purchase goods at a nearby shop with a stolen credit card (the *grounds* for undertaking it). Similarly if reliable information has been received that a youth was seen waving a dagger or selling drugs, that would give rise to reasonable suspicion that the described youth was in possession of an offensive weapon or prohibited drugs. Thus, the two duties go together in that the reasonable suspicion identifies the article to be searched for.

(4) *The duty to inform the person searched, or person using the vehicle searched, that a written record will be made of the search and that the person can obtain a copy of that record.* — This requirement is designed to prevent the arbitrary exercise of stop and search powers, particularly since the falsifying of the reasons for a search is a disciplinary offence. Working against this deterrent is the fact that there is often pressure on constables to exercise stop and search powers either to demonstrate to supervisors that they are doing their job, or to increase 'productivity' by detecting offences or simply to gather 'intelligence' about persons abroad at particular times (Willis (1983) p 15). If this happens, abuse is bound to occur and could lead

to further abuse such as falsifying the reasons for the stop and search. Thus, the surest safeguard against abuse lies in the proper supervision, by senior police officers, of the exercise of the power, both out of concern for the individual, and out of concern for the long-term credibility and effectiveness of the police.

3.34   The duty under s 2(3)(d) (Art 4(4)(d)) does not in fact arise if it appears to the constable that it will not be 'practicable' to compile a record of the stop and search (s 2(4) (Art 4(5)). The most obvious example of this is the stopping of large numbers of people e.g. football crowds, motor cyclists visiting a seaside resort on a Bank Holiday, or potential suspects following a murder or rape. The argument runs that it is not practicable for a constable in the hurly-burly of football supporters to compile a record of each stop and search on the spot and even less so to compile them later at a police station. In any event, it can be argued, it is highly unlikely that the persons searched will be interested in securing a copy of the written record. Three answers may be given to this argument. Firstly, in some cases such as football matches, persons can be searched as a condition of entry, in which event ss 2 and 3 do not arise. Second, the strictures of the Code of Practice on the meaning of 'reasonable suspicion' make it clear that the police cannot search hundreds of people just because of the officer's previous experience with that type of person. Reasonable suspicion must exist against each person before he is searched. On the other hand, the fact that these arguments were put forward on behalf of the police and accepted by the Government illustrates that *in practice* such routine searches may take place and a lower threshold of reasonable suspicion will then operate. Moreover, the circumstances need not be so extreme for a constable to claim impracticability and this again highlights the importance of supervision by senior officers so as to ensure that 'impracticable' is not stretched unreasonably. Third, it may be that the constable is called away urgently to deal with other matters in which case he can still tell the person that he will make a record of the brief search later at the station.

Reasonable force — the constable

3.35   Section 117 (Art 88) of PACE permits a constable to use 'reasonable force if necessary' to detain or search a person or vehicle. Without such a provision the power under s 1 would be useless against the uncooperative citizen. What is 'reasonable force' is a matter of fact and degree depending on the circumstances, in particular the amount of resistance offered by the citizen. In most cases the force used will be little more than the taking hold of an arm to prevent the person running away. As the resistance mounts so the degree of force to meet it will increase and this may merge into an arrest for assaulting, resisting or wilfully obstructing the constable.

Reasonable force — the citizen

3.36 If the constable has no reasonable suspicion, or if he fails to carry out the duties imposed on him by ss 2 and 3, he is acting unlawfully and not within his duty. Unlike French law where the doctrine of *rebellion* makes unlawful any resistance to the police, even if the officer is acting unlawfully, English law permits a citizen to use reasonable force against a constable, or anyone else who is acting unlawfully against him (s 3 of the Criminal Law Act 1967 and Criminal Law Act (Northern Ireland) 1967). The fact that the citizen knows that he is innocent is not a ground for resisting if the constable has reasonable suspicion. Since it is almost impossible to check on the reasonableness of that suspicion at the time, it would be most unwise to assume that the constable is acting unlawfully. Compliance followed by complaint is the best course. If, however, resistance is resorted to, the force used must be reasonable and, whether or not it is, will depend on the degree of force used by the constable (see the cases cited at para 2.16, ante).

Excessive force

3.37 If either the constable or the citizen uses excessive force, a charge of common assault or of some aggravated assault will lie depending on the force used and the injury caused. If the constable is not acting in the execution of his duty, a charge under s 51 of the Police Act 1964 cannot be brought against the citizen, but the fact that the constable is acting unlawfully is not a defence to a charge of assault arising from the use of excessive force by the citizen.

Detention for the purpose of a search

3.38 Section 2(8) (Art 4(9)) provides that a constable may detain a person or vehicle for such time as is reasonably required to permit a search to be carried out either at the place where the person or vehicle is first detained or nearby. How long a period of detention is required depends on what is being searched for and whether the search is of a person or a vehicle. As is implied by the restrictions on the removal of clothes (s 2(9) (Art 4(10)), the search of a person in public is to be confined to a 'pat down' of the body and search of pockets and similarly accessible areas of clothing such as waistbands of trousers and socks. There is no requirement in PACE that females only be searched by females, though a male officer searching a female suspect would be well advised to confine the search to pockets of clothing and handbags, and the Code of Practice, para 3.5, requires a search to be undertaken by an officer of the same sex if it involves more than a superficial examination. In these circumstances, a search of a person for a small article will seldom take more than ten minutes while a search for a larger article will take less time. On the other hand, if the person is carrying a rucksack, bed roll and similar equipment the search may take considerably longer. Similarly a search of a vehicle could take a considerable amount of time, particularly if the article sought is small (e.g. prohibited drugs) and the vehicle, which could include a caravan or houseboat, is large and full of other articles. What is reasonable is then a matter of fact and degree in the particular circumstances. Detention beyond what is reasonable in the circumstances will be unlawful and could result in civil liability or exclusion of evidence (as discussed in para 3.50–51, post).

'There or nearby ' (s 2(8) Art 4(9))

3.39 The search may be carried out either at the place where the person or vehicle is detained or nearby. A similar provision was contained in s 8(1) of the Road Traffic Act 1972 in the context of breath tests. This too was held to be a matter of fact and degree in all the circumstances of the case. Appellate courts will, since it is a question of fact, generally regard themselves as bound by findings of fact by magistrates and in *Arnold v Hull Chief Constable* (1969) the High Court refused to disturb a finding that a police station one and half miles away was not 'there or nearby'. In *Donegani v Ward* (1969) the Divisional Court similarly refused to disturb a finding that 160 yards from the scene of the stop was not 'there or nearby'. In the context of picketing, the word 'near' should be given a meaning according to commonsense and to the intent and purpose of the particular statute (*Rayware Ltd v TGWU* (1989)). The purpose of the stop and search restriction of 'there or nearby' would appear to be twofold. First, to prevent the stop and search power being used as a device to persuade a person to go to a police station, thus creating a form of 'back door' arrest; and second, to permit a limited degree of flexibility so that searches may take place in less public positions such as shop doorways or a police van if close at hand, thus avoiding embarrassment where possible (see also the Code of Practice, para 3.5, post). The ready proximity of such positions means that in practice 'nearby' should mean a very restricted area. If, for example, a person is placed in a police car and driven to a police station, that is clearly unlawful. Also, it is suggested, he should not be taken beyond a place within sight of the venue of the stop for the officer should always be able to point to a place for a less embarrassing search. Above all, the Code of Practice requires (para 3.1) that every reasonable effort be made to reduce embarrassment to the minimum.

Limitations on the extent of the search — persons

3.40   Section 2(9) (Art 4(10)) does not authorise a constable to require a person to remove any part of his clothing in public other than an outercoat, jacket or gloves (or headgear in Northern Ireland). Thus, hats and shoes are excluded (though an officer can feel under a hat or, if it falls off, he can search it). This, together with the 'there or nearby' requirement in s 2(8) (Art 4(9)), emphasises the limited nature of the search under s 1 (Art 3). It is not intended to be a strip or 'intimate' search: intimate searches can only follow arrest for a specific offence and must be justified and authorised in accordance with s 55 (see chapter 7, post). Section 2 (Art 4) applies to the exercise of *any* stop and search power. Two points should be noted however. Firstly, s 2(9)(a) (Art 4 (10)(a)) only applies to a constable who proposes to 'require' the citizen to remove clothing. The latter may of course *consent* to a more thorough search (for the meaning of consent, see para 3.04). Secondly, s 2(9) (Art 4(10)) only refers to the removal of clothing 'in public'. It is therefore arguable that the constable can remove more clothing (e.g. hat, shoes) if a private place can be found nearby such as a police van. However, if an extensive or strip search of the person is needed, and those under section 23 of the Misuse of Drugs Act 1971 frequently require a more intimate search, he should, it is suggested, be arrested and the search conducted under ss 54 or 55 (Arts 55 and 56) (discussed at para 7.11 post; for the rules governing strip searches, see Annex A to the Code of Practice relating to the Detention etc of persons, and for discussion of an identical provision in the context of search on arrest, see para 5.61, post).

Extent of search — vehicles

3.41   There is no limit to the extent of a search of a vehicle other than the limit on the period of detention to 'such time as is reasonably required to permit a search to be carried out' (s 2(8) Art 4(9)). As with search of persons, the search is not intended to be a 'strip' search involving the removal of panels. Such a detailed search would require garage facilities and the virtual 'arrest' of a motor vehicle. It is suggested that this can only be achieved following the arrest of the person in charge of the vehicle and the search of the vehicle under s 32 (Art 34) ('premises' in s 32 (Art 34) include a vehicle, see s 23 (Art 25)).

Seizure

3.42 A constable may seize articles which he has reasonable grounds to suspect are stolen or prohibited (s 1(6) Art 3(6)). As to the seizure of other articles, if he is searching a vehicle, a vehicle qualifies as premises (s 23 Art 25) and thus the wide powers of seizure under s 19 can be invoked (i.e. seizure of evidence of any offence is allowed if the evidence would otherwise be destroyed etc, see para 4.41, post). If he is searching a person, s 19 does not apply. In that case he must arrest the person and can then seize the evidence of other offences under s 32 (Art 34). The provisions relating to the citizen's access to articles seized and held by the police (s 21 Art 23) and to the police powers to retain such articles (s 22 Art 24) apply to all stops and searches (see para 4.44 post).

Duties to be carried out after search

3.43 *Unattended vehicles.* — Where an unattended vehicle or something in it has been searched, the constable must leave a notice containing the information mentioned in s 2(6) (Art 4(7)). This is a sensible requirement for, if duplicate keys are used to enter the vehicle, the owner may have no other indication that it has been searched. A record must be made and a copy made available to the owner if requested (see s 3 Art 5); whereas search of the person or an attended vehicle need not be recorded in certain circumstances (see s 2(4) Art 4(5)) and para 3.34, ante). No record of what has been seized needs to be included. The reference to compensation for any damage caused (e.g. a forced window) serves to alert the owner to the funds set aside by each police force for the compensation of vehicle owners. The notice should, if practicable, be placed inside the vehicle (s 2(7) Art 4(8)). But if, for example, a lorry's trailer is searched and the constable cannot get into the cab to leave the notice without damaging it, the notice must be left outside the vehicle, normally under a windscreen wiper. The Code (para 4.10) and the law of negligence require that a vehicle should be left secure wherever possible.

Records

3.44 Where a constable has carried out a search under s 1 or any other stop and search power, three situations in relation to records may arise:

(1) The general rule is that he shall make a record of the search in writing at once (s 3(1) Art 5(1)). If asked for a copy, the constable should supply one at once.

(2) If it is not practicable to compile a record at all, e.g. during a search of many football supporters or public protesters, or where the officer's presence is urgently required elsewhere, he need not do so (s 3(1) Art 4(5)).

(3) If it is possible to make a record but not at the time of the search, he can do so as soon as is practicable after the search e.g. the person stopped behaves aggressively and it is not possible to compile the record at once; inclement weather prevents a record being compiled on the spot; or the constable is called away to other urgent duties (s 2(2) Art 5(2)).

The record is compiled on a pro-forma document, called the national search record. A separate record must be completed for each search conducted. However, if a person and vehicle are searched for the same reason, one record will suffice (COP, para 4.6). What happens if the vehicle and all its passengers (e.g. a coach, or minibus) are searched? Convenience to the officer argues for one record, whereas the precautionary sway of PACE arguably requires a separate record for each passenger.

Name of person searched

3.45   Section 3(3) (Art 5(3)) provides that the record shall include the name of the person searched if it is known to the constable and of course the constable can ask for the name. But there is no power to require the name nor to detain a person to find out his name; so, where the name is unavailable, the constable must include a description of the person (s 3(3), (4) Art 5(3),(4)). It is, perhaps, indicative of the mistrust of the police that the request for the name and address of a person stopped is liable to antagonise the person more than the stop and search itself. However, names and addresses of persons abroad at night have long been a source of intelligence and when crimes are committed in the area the list of such persons is a useful starting point in the investigation. The police have then to weigh the usefulness of such intelligence against the antagonism likely to result from a request for names and addresses. The record should note the person's ethnic origin. Where the search is of a vehicle the note must include a description of the vehicle (s 3(5) Art 5(5)) including its registration number (Code, para 4.5(iii)) if it has one. The constable can, where motor vehicles are concerned, exercise Road Traffic Act powers to require the name and address of the driver, but not of passengers, and can discover the name and address of the registered keeper via the Police National Computer. In this respect motorists are more vulnerable than pedestrians.

3.46   The record shall additionally:

(a)   state the object of the search; the grounds for making it; the date and time; the place where it was made; details of anything found; details of any injury or damage caused; and

(b)   identify the constable making it and each constable involved in the search, except in relation to terrorism investigations when his warrant number and duty station will suffice (COP, para 4.5(x)).

Obtaining a copy of the record

3.47   The person searched, or the owner or person in charge of the vehicle searched, may obtain a copy of the written record if he asks for one before the end of a period of 12 months beginning with the date on which the search was made (s 3(7), (8), (9)) (Art 5(8),(9),(10)). It should be noted that the constable is under a duty to tell the citizen of his right to a copy if a record is to be made (s 3(3), (4), (6) Art 4 (2),(3),(4)). The phrase 'asks for one' (s 3(7)) includes a written request. It will be seen below that failure to comply with s 3 (Art 4) is much less likely to be visited by any sanction than other breaches of Part I.

3.48   The duty to make a written record does not apply to the detention and search of vehicles under the Aviation Security Act 1982 (searches for cargo) or by constables employed by statutory undertakers, for example, the search of a vehicle leaving the premises of British Rail by a constable of the British Transport police or leaving a port by the port police force. Such a duty was felt to be unduly burdensome given the frequency of such searches.

The effect of a failure to comply with ss 2 and 3 (Arts 4 and 5)

3.49   The Act does not provide an express penalty for a failure to comply with these provisions, but three sanctions may arise. Firstly, the constable will be acting unlawfully and will expose himself to a civil action. Second, the court may exercise its power under s 78 (Art 76) to exclude evidence obtained by an unlawful stop and search. Third, the constable's conduct can be the subject of a complaint which may lead to disciplinary action. These sanctions will be considered in turn.

Civil action

3.50 In *Christie v Leachinsky* (1947) the House of Lords held that where a constable arrests a person on reasonable suspicion of an arrestable offence, or of any other crime which is arrestable without a warrant, he must, in ordinary circumstances, inform the person of the true grounds for arrest. A failure to do so will normally render the constable liable for false imprisonment and/or assault. In the context of arrest, this decision was given statutory force by s 28 (Art 30) of PACE and is discussed more fully in paras 5.38–43, post. In the context of stop and search, *Pedro v Diss* (1981) (see para 5.43, post) equated detention for the purposes of a search under s 66 of the Metropolitan Police Act 1839 with arrest and held that the failure to inform the person of the reasons for the stop and search meant that the constable was not acting in the execution of his duty for the purpose of s 51 of the Police Act 1964. Thus, a charge of assaulting the constable under s 51 failed. It follows that the constable is also liable for false imprisonment and/or assault. Since the duty to state the object of the search and the grounds for undertaking it are statutory duties (s 2(3), Art 4(4)), the courts will clearly adopt a similar stance under PACE. They may perhaps go further by holding that a failure to carry out *any* of the duties in s 2 (Art 4), will render the constable liable for false imprisonment and/or assault. Substantial damages however are unlikely to be forthcoming, if, for example, a constable fails to give his name but carries out his other duties under s 2 (Art 4). As regards s 3 (Art 5), however, there is no civil action available to cater for a failure to compile a record.

Exclusion of evidence

3.51 If the possible unlawfulness or impropriety of a stop and search is raised before the trial court, the court has the power under s 78 (Art 76) to exclude evidence obtained thereby if its reception would adversely affect the fairness of the proceedings (for a detailed discussion of s 78 (Art 76), see para 2.48, ante). Much is likely to depend on the gravity of the impropriety and of the offence. For example, the excessive manhandling of the accused during a stop and search may lead to the exclusion of evidence at a trial for a minor offence, but this is highly improbable if the evidence discovered relates to a serious arrestable offence e.g. a stop and search which catches a multiple rapist. Similarly, a 'technical' breach of the Act or Code of Practice is unlikely to lead to exclusion of evidence. Thus, the failure to compile a record under s 3 (Art 5), or to do so properly is most unlikely to lead to exclusion of the evidence discovered by the search. A more serious breach is the failure to show that the citizen has been informed of the reasons for the stop and search and one Crown Court has registered its disapproval by excluding the subsequent evidence (*R v Fennelly* (1989)).

Complaints against the police

3.52 The operation of stop and search powers should be closely monitored by each police force. Indeed information recorded under s 3 (Art 5) is to be included in the annual reports of chief officers to police committees (s 5, Art 7). Complaints about the legality or manner of the search may be included in such information or the information can at least be requested by police committees. Though of little practical use to the individual, this level of accountability may have some effect on the future exercise of stop and search powers. Mention can also be made of the consultative committees of PACE set up under s 106 (Art 82). They can be a useful channel for directing complaints and comment about the local operation of stop and search powers. From the individual's standpoint, the Code of Practice for stop and search powers is of far greater importance, for a breach of the Code is a breach of discipline and can therefore be the subject of an official complaint under Part IX of PACE.

Road checks

3.53 Under s 163 of the Road Traffic Act 1988 (Art 180, Road Traffic (NI) Order 1981), a constable in uniform can require the driver of a vehicle to stop but uncertainty surrounds the purposes for which this power can be employed (see para 3.08, ante). To clarify matters, s 4 of PACE (Art 6) permits the police to use s 163 in order to set up road checks, or in more conventional parlance, road blocks, in certain, defined circumstances. A 'road check' means the obstruction of a road in order to stop:

    (a)   all vehicles passing along it; or

    (b)   vehicles selected by any criterion (s 4(2), Art 6(2)).

Road checks are set up by all police forces from time to time, and in particular in the event of a major crime in the area or the escape of a prisoner. Under s 4 (Art 6) a police officer of at least the rank of superintendent may authorise in writing a road check if he has:

1)   Reasonable grounds to believe that a person has committed a serious arrestable offence (as defined by s 116 (Art 87), see para s 2.25–31, ante) and reasonable grounds to suspect that he is, or is about to be,

in the area covered by the road check (s 4(1)(a), (4)(a), Art 6(1)(a),(4)(a)). This has proved to be the most used ground for road checks (see figures below). Simple examples are an alert following a murder or bank robbery. The reasonable cause to suspect that the murderer or bank robbers are in the area will, in the first instance, arise from the report of the crime and this may then result in several road checks being set up to cover all exits from the scene of the crime or escape, each being justified by the same reasonable grounds for suspicion. Reports that the car or person wanted has been seen in the area will also often justify road checks in that area. In these circumstances, there will generally be a greater opportunity to assess the credibility of witnesses but even in such cases the dangerousness of the person sought must be a factor to be taken into account in assessing the need for road checks. It follows that in such cases a lower level of reasonable suspicion will be relied upon.

2) Reasonable grounds for believing that witnesses to a serious arrestable offence are likely to be traced (s 4(1)(b), (4)(b), Art 6(1)(b), (4)(b)). For example, at the end of a football match a fan is stabbed to death. Departing vehicles may be stopped in the hope of finding witnesses to the crime. A child is murdered at about 4 pm. On subsequent days motorists are stopped around that time in case regular travellers may have spotted something on the day of the crime. It should be noted that the superintendent's reasonable belief in s 4(4)(b), (Art 6(4)(b)), refers to the nature of the offence, whereas in the other categories it refers to the likelihood that the relevant person will be found. Potentially, therefore, this category may be over-used viz the officer may authorise a check if he thinks that witnesses of serious arrestable offences may be found. Commonsense, resources and adverse publicity (e.g. following the annual reports of chief officers, see para 3.60, post) are the safeguards against random or trawling exercises or checks set up, for example, to 'raise the public's awareness of crime'. If the police wish to seek witnesses to a road accident (not a serious arrestable offence), section 163 of the Road Traffic Act 1988 gives the power to stop vehicles for a road traffic purpose.

3) Reasonable grounds for believing that a person is intending to commit a serious arrestable offence and reasonable grounds for suspecting that he is, or will be, in the area covered by the road check (s 4(1)(c), (4)(c), Art 6(1)(c), (4)(c)). For example, the police have information that a large sale of drugs is to take place in the area but cannot identify the place of the transaction and thus hope to catch the participants beforehand. Cases of such specific advance information will be exceptional. More usual will be the general knowledge that a particular area has a high level of particular crimes e.g.burglary, and the reasonable belief that, by stopping vehicles and possibly

searching them under s 1 (Art 3), a number of criminals are certain to be caught. The potential for misuse of this power is illustrated by:

(a) the broad scope of 'serious arrestable offences' (see para s 2.25–31, ante);

(b) the fact that vehicles may be stopped by 'any criterion' (s 4(2), Art 6(2)) and the propensity on the part of the police to stop old cars or those driven by coloured drivers is well known; and

(c) the fact that 'intending to commit' in s 4(1)(c), Art 6(1)(c) can refer to an earlier stage of preparation than an attempt or conspiracy, the latter already being 'offences'.

The availability of resources and the policy of good policing in what may be a very sensitive area of policing are the real safeguards against misuse. The possibility of civil actions or the lodging of a complaint are more remote sanctions. In fact the statistics (below) indicate that this is not a popular ground for a road check.

4) A person unlawfully at large is reasonably suspected to be, or about to be, in the area (s 4(1)(d), (4)(d), Art 6(1)(d), (4)(d)), e.g. an escaped prisoner or inmate of a mental hospital; X escapes from a prison in county A and is thought likely to try to contact his family in county B. Both police forces can employ s 4(1)(d) (Art 6(1)(d)).

3.54 The following statistics show that the number of road checks has fluctuated since the introduction of the PACE power and that the number of persons arrested for a reason unconnected with the road check's purpose is a high proportion of the successful road checks

Year	*Number of Road checks*	*Reason for them (as above)*				*Number Arrested* connected unconnected with check's purpose	
		(1)	(2)	(3)	(4)		
1986	377	195	148	24	26	34	30
1987	349	178	116	25	54	36	42
1988	294	153	103	19	39	52	27
1989	227	96	84	11	39	32	27
1990	298	167	97	15	22	18	33

(Home Office Statistical Bulletin, no 14/91).

Setting up a road check in an emergency

3.55 Section 4(3) (Art 6(3)) requires that a police officer of at least the rank of superintendent authorise the setting up of road checks (cf the Royal Commission which had recommended the rank of assistant chief constable, Report, para 3.32). However, s 4(5) (Art 6(5)) provides that a police officer below that rank may authorise one if any of the conditions specified in s 4(1) (Art 6(1)), is satisfied, and it appears to him that a road check is required as a matter of urgency. The authorisation need not be in writing. In most police forces it is the officer in charge of the operations' room who will initiate the road check in response to a reported serious crime or escape. That officer may not be of superintendent rank and may not be able to contact a superintendent or above in situations where seconds count. If a road check is authorised in such circumstances, it must be recorded in writing, a superintendent or above must be informed as soon as is practicable (s 4(6), (7), Art 6(6),(7)) and the latter may then authorise in writing its continuance (s 4(8), Art 6(8)) or discontinuance, in which event he must record in writing the fact that the road check was set up, and the purpose of it (s 4(9), Art 6(9)).

The authorisation

3.56 Every authorisation (including an emergency one under s 4(5) (Art 6(5)) must specify the locality in which the vehicles are to be stopped (s 4(10), Art 6(10)). All written authorisations (i.e. those made initially by a superintendent or those emergency ones subsequently approved by a senior officer) must specify:

(a) the name of the authorising officer;
(b) the purpose, including, where relevant, the serious arrestable offence involved (s 4(14), Art 6(14));
(c) the locality where vehicles are to be stopped (s 4(13), Art 6(13)).

The person in charge of the vehicle is entitled to apply, within 12 months, for a written statement of the reasons for the stop (s 4(15), Art 6(15)). Unlike a stop and search under s 1 (Art 3), however, the constable is under no duty to tell the citizen of that entitlement.

Duration

3.57 An emergency road check must be reported to a senior officer as soon as is practicable. It and all others may then continue for up to seven days in the first instance and can be renewed for seven day periods (s 4(11), (12), Art 6(11), (12)). In some cases (e.g. an escaped prisoner) the road check will have to operate continously but in others (e.g. the reconstruction of a crime in the hope of attracting witnesses), it can be confined to particular times. Section 4(11)(b) (Art 6(11(b)) provides accordingly.

Search of vehicles stopped at road checks

3.58 It will be noted that the scheme of s 4 (Art 6) is to enable the power of stopping under s 163 of the Road Traffic Act 1988 (s.180 of the R.T. (N.I) Order 1981) to be used for the purposes set out in s 4 (Art 6). Two consequences follow from this. Firstly, the power is confined to constables in uniform. Second, the power is one to stop a vehicle and not to search it. As to detaining the vehicle, remarkably this power is not explicitly mentioned in either s 4 (Art 6) or s 163 (s.180). It would however be open to the courts to imply a power to detain the vehicle for the purposes mentioned in s 4 (Art 6), viz to communicate with the occupants (see *DPP v Cary* (1970) and *Lodwick v Sanders* (1985)). In cases involving s 4(1)(a)(c) and (d) (Art 6(1)(a)(c) and (d)) the police will be seeking persons in order to arrest them. If they decide to do so, a power to enter and search the vehicle in order to arrest a person for an arrestable offence, or to recapture a person unlawfully at large, is specifically provided by s 17(1)(b) and (d) (Art 19(1)(b) and (d)) respectively (a 'vehicle' being 'premises' for the purpose of s 17 (Art 19) entry powers (see s 23, Art 25)). Once an arrest is made, s 32 (Art 34) authorises a search of the vehicle for evidence of the offence for which the person has been arrested. If the police have insufficient grounds to make an arrest, there may be reasonable suspicion that the vehicle or its occupants are carrying stolen or prohibited goods. In this case, a s 1 (Art 3) search is appropriate, subject to the duties to inform the person of the matters specified in s 2 (Art 4) and compile a record of the search. If the person stopped under s 4 (Art 6) refuses to cooperate with the police, he must be allowed to continue unless the constable has sufficient reason to arrest him, or to search him and/or the vehicle under s 1 (Art 3), or to detain the vehicle for any road traffic inspection. A sharp contrast exists between the various duties which must be observed in a s 1 (Art 3) search and the silence of s 4 (Art 6) as to the way in which the police officer should treat the motorist. This is, in the main, understandable given the usually fleeting nature of a stop under s 4 (Art 6) and the usually cooperative attitude of the motoring public. However, there are circumstances, especially under s 4(1)(c) (Art 6(1)(c)), where a sensitive approach may be crucial to police/community relations and the officers should be briefed to explain to the motorist the precise purpose of the stop.

Other powers to stop vehicles

3.59   Section 4(16) of PACE (Art 6(16)) makes it clear that the purposes of s 4 (Art 6) are without prejudice to other powers to stop vehicles. The basic power is s 163 of the Road Traffic Act 1988 but, as has been indicated, the precise purposes for which it may be used are uncertain. Clearly it can be used for road traffic purposes e.g. to examine a vehicle for roadworthiness or to warn the driver of a flooded road or accident ahead; but it has been suggested (see para 3.08) that it should not be used for non-traffic purposes. Another alternative to PACE is offered by the common law. Thus, prior to the implementation of PACE and during the miners' strike in 1984, the police successfully relied upon their common law duty to preserve the peace as the basis for stopping vehicles, checking them for travelling pickets, persuading them to turn back, and, on refusal, arresting them. The conditions for exercising this common law power are that the police (a) honestly and (b) reasonably consider that there is (c) a real risk of a breach of the peace, in the sense that it is in close proximity both in place and time (*Moss v McLachlan* (1985)). Condition (b) will depend upon a multitide of factors including, as in *Moss v McLachlan*, whether there have been recent, similar events which have resulted in disorder. But this alone is not, it is submitted, enough. For otherwise all travellers in the direction of, for example, an industrial dispute, all night party or a fox hunt are deemed to be troublemakers. The police need instead to investigate further to determine whether the particular people stopped pose a real threat to the peace. Since most of the PACE road check powers are dependent on a serious arrestable offence ((1) to (3) in para 3.53 above), the common law power is a useful adjunct to deal with public order problems (e.g. suspected hunt saboteurs, travelling hippies, travellers to an acid house party). It consists of a power to stop a vehicle, make enquiries of its passengers (if a search is required and consent refused, then PACE or other stop and search powers are needed) and arrest them if a breach of the peace is imminent and the passengers will not retreat: and being a common law power it is not trammelled by the procedural requirements of PACE. Sanctions for misuse of the power are to lodge a complaint or to sue for false imprisonment.

Information in annual reports

3.60   Chief Officers of Police in the provinces and the City of London are required by s 12 of the Police Act 1964 (in Northern Ireland the Police Act (N.I.) 1970) to report annually on the policing of their area to their police committee, and in the Metropolis the Commissioner makes a report to the Home Secretary who is the Police Authority for the

Metropolis. Section 5(1) (Art 7(1)) requires that such annual reports contain information:

(a) about searches recorded under s 3 (Art 5) and carried out in the police force area during the period to which the report relates, and

(b) about road checks set up in that area during that period.

The information about searches must include the number and category of searches and consequential arrests made in each month under s 1 (s 5(2); Arts 3, 7(2)) but not the number of charges which followed. The information about road checks must include the reasons for authorising each road check and the result of each (s 5(3), Art 7(3)) and also gives the number of vehicles stopped and the number of roads obstructed. The report should also, it is suggested, give information about the locality and duration of each road check, and any hostility provoked by the checks. These reports can serve two functions. Firstly, they can form the basis of research into how the powers in PACE are being used. They are collated by the Home Office and published as a Statistical Bulletin. They can be scrutinised by Her Majesty's Inspectors of Constabulary (as the Royal Commission recommended, Report, para 3.26) but, to date, such scrutiny has sadly not been featured in the Inspectors' Annual Reports. Second, they enable a degree of public accountability through the police committee and through any scheme set up under s 106 (Art 82) to obtain the views of the community on policing in the area.

Searches by constables employed by statutory undertakers

3.61 'Statutory undertakers' are defined by s 7(3) as 'persons authorised by any enactment to carry on any railway, light railway, road transport, water transport, canal, inland navigation, dock or harbour undertaking' (Art 9(3) — 'aerodrome, dock or harbour'). Most have their own police force, the best known being the British Transport Police who police the premises of the British Railways Board, London Regional Transport and other transport undertakings, but there are others such as the Port of Liverpool Police, the Dover Harbour Board Police and the Port of London Authority Police. Legislation already existed empowering such constables to stop, detain and search persons employed by or on the premises of those undertakings; for example, s 54(1) of the British Transport Commission Act 1949; s 157 of the Port of London Act 1964; and the Mersey Docks and Harbour (Police) Order 1975 (SI 1975 No 1224) made under s 14 of the Harbours Act 1964, which is identical to s 157 of the Port of London Act 1968. Section 6(1) of PACE (Art 8(1)) gives a constable the power to stop, detain and search vehicles before they leave a goods area on the premises of the statutory undertaker. 'Goods area' is any area used wholly or mainly for the storage or handling of goods, and which is included in the premises of the statutory undertaker (s 6(2), Art 8(2)).

British Nuclear Fuels plc — premises and goods

3.62 Section 6 of the Public Stores Act 1875 created a power to stop and search persons, vehicles or vessels reasonably suspected of conveying any of Her Majesty's stores which are stolen or unlawfully obtained. Originally applied to the Metropolitan Police, it was extended to constables of the Ministry of Defence Police by the Special Constables Act 1923 and to constables of the Atomic Energy Authority Police by Sch 3 of the Atomic Energy Authority Act 1954. Section 6(3) of PACE extended the power to constables appointed under the Special Constables Act 1923 to police premises in the possession, or under the control, of British Nuclear Fuels plc; or, in Northern Ireland, to special constables appointed to police premises controlled by military forces (s 6(4)). They are deemed to be constables deputed by a public department and any goods or chattels in the possession of BNF plc are deemed to be Her Majesty's (and therefore Public) Stores.

3.63 It has been the custom for a pass to be given to the driver of goods' vehicles specifying the goods carried. That pass is then checked against the vehicle's contents on leaving the premises of the statutory undertaker. In the light of this practice and the need for random searches, the aforementioned constables are exonerated from the duties prescribed by ss 1–3 (Arts 3–5) of PACE when engaged in the search of *vehicles*. Thus, since the 'goods areas' of statutory undertakers do not fall within the scope of public place as defined by s 1(1), the s 1 (Art 3) power cannot be used. Instead a power to search vehicles is bestowed by s 6 (Art 8), but without the need for reasonable suspicion and without the need to follow the procedures in ss 2 and 3 (see ss 2(2) and 3(1) Arts 4(2), 5(1)) and the Code of Practice. If, however, the constable proposes to search a *person*, he is not exonerated from the need to satisfy s 1 (eg the requirement of a public place and reasonable suspicion) nor from the various duties specified in ss 2 and 3. For, ss 2 and 3 (Arts 4, 5) only exclude s 6 (Art 8) from their provisions and in turn s 6 only deals with the stopping and searching of *vehicles* by statutory undertakers. At this point it is convenient to note the special provisions made under ss 13 and 13A of the Aviation Security Act 1982 and ss 22 and 23 of the Aviation and Maritime Security Act 1990. The Secretary of State for Transport can direct airport managers and harbour authorities to arrange for the proper searching of vessels, premises and persons in their area of operation. Once a direction has been made, a constable or other specified person (e.g. a person employed by a private security firm) has the power to search the airport/harbour, any aircraft/ship in it, and any person or other property in it, if he has reasonable cause to suspect that firearms, explosives, or other such destructive articles are in, or may be brought into, the area. For this purpose, the constable or specified person can enter premises within the relevant airport/harbour, he may stop, enter and detain an aircraft/ship, and may also stop, detain and search any person in the area. A constable is bound to observe the Code of Practice on Stop and Search (COP para 1.3), but a specified person such as a private security guard is not. A more limited duty to search can be imposed by the Secretary of State (s 13A of the 1982 Act, s 23 of the 1990 Act) on other persons who carry on business in the relevant airport/harbour or who have access to restricted areas for business purposes (e.g. cargo handlers). The duty is limited to those areas in which the person conducts his business. Premises used only as a private dwelling, of which there are many in harbours containing marina developments, may only be searched under the authority of a magistrate's warrant, and by a constable who is a member of a police force maintained under the Police Act 1964 (or the Police Authority for Northern Ireland), or a constabulary, such as the British Transport Police or Port of London Police, which has made an agreement under s.96 of the PACE Act 1984 (Art 16 of the Police (Northern Ireland) Order 1987) under which they accept the same complaints procedure as police forces maintained under the Police Act 1964 and, in effect, accept the codes of practice under the 1984 Act and 1989 Order. It must be emphasised that only dwellings *within* the harbour are subject to such searches.

Sporting Events

3.64   Under the Sporting Events (Control of Alcohol etc) Act 1985 an officer can stop and search a public service vehicle (including a chartered train), or motor vehicle capable of carrying eight or more passengers (and which is carrying two or more), which is en route to or from a designated sporting event if he has reasonable suspicion that alcohol is being, or has been, carried on it (s 7(3)). Under s 7(2) he can also search a person on reasonable suspicion of having committed an offence under the Act. These include the carrying of alcohol on public transport or at a designated sports ground, or of containers which are used to hold drink and which, when empty, are normally discarded or returned to a supplier but which are capable of causing injury (e.g. a crushed beer can), or the offence of supplying alcohol at a designated sporting event without a magistrate's order. Under s 7(1) the officer can enter any part of the designated sports ground (e.g. directors' hospitality lounge) to enforce the Act. These wide powers are still subject to PACE and the COP, in particular the requirement of reasonable suspicion. Thus, for example, the officer must have the requisite degree of suspicion (COP, paras 1.6, 1.7) of a particular individual (e.g. a bulging jacket, clanking of bottles in a carrier bag, sound of an opened can). Routine or random searches can only be justified with the individual's consent (assuming that it is an informed and freely given consent) or as a condition of entry to premises (and that the search is sufficiently proximate to them).

4 Powers of entry, search and seizure

4.01 Part II of the PACE Act (Part III of the PACE (N.I.) Order) deals with the powers and procedures whereby the police may, firstly, enter and search premises and, secondly, seize and retain property discovered during a search of premises. The Act (Order) codifies much of the earlier statutory and common law and implements some of the recommendations of the Royal Commission on Criminal Procedure (1981) (Cmnd 8092). The passage of the Act through Parliament was dominated by discussion of the favourable treatment accorded certain confidential information (eg medical records, journalistic material). The following preliminary points should be noted: (a) Part II of the Act (Part III of the Order) deals only with the powers of a constable. (b) It is in part without prejudice to his earlier powers (eg various statutes permitting the issue of search warrants are preserved). (c) As elsewhere, Part II (Part III of the Order) must be read in conjunction with the Code of Practice, B, for the latter arguably includes items of sufficient importance to have merited inclusion within the former. (d) The broad powers of seizure in s 19 (Art 21) accompany all powers of search contained in this or any other statute and consensual searches, but are dealt with separately at para 4.41, post. (e) Part II (Part III of the Order) deals with powers of entry and search in relation to premises and 'premises' are given an extended meaning, as follows.

The meaning of 'premises' (s 23) (Art 25)

4.02 Throughout the Act (Order), and with particular relevance to this chapter, 'premises' are defined very widely. They include 'any place'. This can be of a private or public nature and open or enclosed, and, somewhat incongruously, vehicles, vessels, aircraft, hovercraft, tents and other movable structures are specifically mentioned as examples in s 23 (Art 25). Thus, a garden, a forecourt, a public registry office, a car in a garage, a bicycle, a houseboat, a caravan and a workmen's tent are included. As to limitations, a Canadian court in *Re Laporte and R* (1972) has held that a person's body cannot fall within the word 'place', and, whilst an English court is likely to follow suit, it is difficult to imagine what else cannot be counted as premises, especially since s 23 (Art 25) does not offer an exhaustive definition. The word 'place' arose for consideration in *Powell v Kempton Park Co* (1899) in the context of the Betting Act 1853 and Lord James suggested that:

> 'There must be a defined area so marked out that it can be found and recognised as the place where the business is carried on and wherein the bettor can be found. Thus, if a person betted on Salisbury Plain, there would be no 'place' within the Act. The whole of Epsom Downs, or any other racecourse, where betting takes place, would not constitute a 'place': but directly a definite localisation of the business of betting is effected, be it under a tent or even a moveable umbrella, it may be well held that a 'place' exists . . .'

The ideas of delineation and localisation are helpful, but his Lordship's opinion was clearly tied to the narrow context of betting and, given the 1984 Act's (1989 Order's) broader context of the detection of crime, it is highly likely that a race course, football ground or private park open to the public will qualify as a 'place' and therefore 'premises'. Where the premises constitute a 'public place', the police do not need any special powers to enter and search (eg Salisbury Plain). However, there may be parts within a public place (eg a tent) which do count as 'premises' and therefore require the special powers of entry in Part II of the Act (Part III of the Order). Moreover, if the police wish to dig up the land itself, whether it is public or private, the consent of the landowner or one of the powers to be discussed below must be available.

Limitation on the definition of premises by ss 17(2)(b) (Art 19(2)(b)) and 32(7) (Art 34(7)).

4.03   These provisions limit the definition of premises where they consist of 'separate dwellings'. This term is well known in housing legislation and in relation to Rent Acts it has been interpreted as follows:

> 'There is a letting of a part of a house as a separate dwelling . . . if, and only if, the accommodation which is shared with others does not comprise any of the rooms which may fairly be described as 'living rooms' or 'dwelling rooms' . . .' *Cole v Harris* (1945).

A kitchen or lounge is fairly described as a 'living room' and thus a person who shares such a room with others in the same building cannot regard his sleeping quarters as a separate dwelling for the purposes of ss 17 and 32 (Arts 19 and 34). The following examples illustrate the meaning of 'separate dwelling', but it must be emphasised that each case will depend upon its particular facts and that the police should consequently investigate the circumstances whenever time permits. If time does not permit, and the police enter separate dwellings, the entry and search will be unlawful (as to sanctions for unlawful conduct, see paras 2.34–48, ante):

(a) D, a student, occupies a house with four other students. He has a study bedroom and shares the kitchen, bathroom and toilet facilities. If D commits an offence, the entire premises are subject to a search for D (s 17) (Art 19) or evidence of his offence (s 32) (Art 34).

(b) Students occupy self-contained flats in a block in which only the bathroom and toilet facilities are shared. Each flat is a separate dwelling and the limitations of s 17(2)(b) (Art 19(2)(b)) and s 32(7) (Art 34(7)) apply. If, therefore, one student commits an offence, only *the dwelling* in which he is, or is reasonably believed to be, or in which he was when arrested, or immediately before arrest, can be entered and searched *together with* the bathroom and toilet, the communal parts. Note, however, that if D is arrested for an arrestable offence under s 18, 'premises' are not so limited, and any premises occupied or controlled by D may be searched if there are reasonable grounds to believe that there is evidence in them.(See further for the meaning of 'separate dwelling', Hill and Redman, *Law of Landlord and Tenant*, (18th Edn, para. C. 309).

The broad scope of s 23 (Art 25) is of particular significance when it is remembered that all the powers of entry and search dealt with in this chapter concern 'premises'. Its generality can be contrasted with the three attempts which the Standing Committee made at defining 'offshore installation' in s 23 (Art 25). Reliance was finally placed on the earlier version in s 1(3)(b) of the Mineral Workings (Offshore Installations) Act 1971, viz, 'any installation which is maintained, or is intended to be established, for underwater exploitation or exploration', eg an oil-drilling platform.

PART A

General powers of entry and search

4.04 These arise under the authority of a search warrant, or on or after an arrest, or when a breach of the peace is involved, or under specific, miscellaneous statutory powers. The renowned cases of *Leach v Money* and *Entick v Carrington* (1765) remain authorities for the proposition that any invasion of property is a trespass unless supported by a legal power. As will be seen, however, the breadth of legal powers contained in Part II of the Act provides the police with ample opportunity to avoid such civil liability. There is in addition to the statutory and common law powers, the ability to search premises with the consent of the owner or occupier. The various powers are now dealt with together with searches carried out with consent. The procedures for searching premises and removing property are dealt with after the discussion of the powers to which they specifically relate and the general procedures are dealt with at para 4.38 post.

Entry and Search under a search warrant

4.05 'There is no mystery about the word 'warrant'; it simply means a document issued by a person in authority under power conferred in that behalf authorising the doing of an act which would otherwise be illegal.' (Lord Wilberforce in *IRC v Rossminster* (1980)).

The common law permitted only one type of search warrant — a justice of the peace could authorise a warrant to search for stolen goods. Over the years Parliament provided specific warrant powers: indeed, s 26 of the Theft Act 1968 (s 25 Theft Act (N.I.) 1969) in practice superseded the solitary common law power. These statutory powers do not conform to a standard formula but ss 15 and 16 of the PACE Act 1984 (Arts 17 and 18 of the N.I. Order) now provide a standard form of application for, and standard execution of, all search warrants whether issued under the authority of an Act passed before or after the 1984 Act (1989 Order). With the exception of a superintendent's power to issue an authority to search under s 26(2) of the Theft Act 1968 (which was repealed by Sch 7 of the PACE Act 1984; s 25(2) of the Theft Act (N.I.) 1969 was repealed by Sch 7 of the 1989 Order), all pre-existing powers survived the 1984 Act (s 8(5)) and the 1989 Order (Art 10(5)). The piecemeal development of statutory warrant powers meant that under the law as it existed before the 1984 Act and the 1989 Order, warrants could be obtained to search for items which it is an offence knowingly to possess, for example, stolen goods, drugs, firearms, explosives (hereinafter prohibited goods) and for evidence of specific offences under the authority of a particular statutory power, for example, illegal gaming under s 43(4) of the Gaming Act 1968. However, there was no general power to issue a warrant to search for *evidence* of an offence which was *not* prohibited goods or not specifically provided for. One could obtain a warrant to search for evidence of fraud under the Hop (Prevention of Fraud) Act 1866 but not for evidence of murder. The law was therefore ripe for reform. The Royal Commission recommended the retention of these existing powers, most of which permitted a magistrate to issue a warrant to search premises, including the premises of someone not himself implicated in the offence or of someone innocently possessing prohibited goods, but recommended a general power to issue a warrant to search for evidence of crime which is reasonably believed to be on premises which are *not* occupied or controlled by the *suspect*. However, it sought to mark the seriousness of the intrusion on innocent citizens, by (a) confining such searches to 'grave offences', and (b) making the issuing authority a circuit judge. The PACE Act

(PACE Order) follows that recommendation but draws a distinction between the *type of material* sought: broadly the distinction is between non-confidential and confidential material. In respect of non-confidential evidence a magistrate may issue a warrant if, but only if, the offence is a 'serious arrestable offence' (defined by s 116 (Art 87) and discussed at para 2.24, ante). In respect of confidential material only a circuit judge can order its production or issue a warrant to search for and seize it if the offence is a serious arrestable offence (ss 9–14 and Sch 1 (Arts 11–16 and Sch 1) deal with the procedure to be adopted and define confidential material, see Part B at para 4.51, post.).

Summary of the law

4.06   The PACE Act (PACE Order) superimposes the warrant for evidence and the special procedure for obtaining confidential material on the existing statutory and common law powers. Since s 8 (Art 10) refers to 'relevant evidence' (defined by s 8(4) Art 10(4) as 'anything that would be admissible in evidence at a trial for the offence') it could be argued that all applications for warrants to search for evidence of a serious arrestable offence, including those for seeking prohibited goods, which will often be evidence of a serious arrestable offence (eg a search warrant for the proceeds of a £1 million bullion robbery), must be made under s 8 (Art 10). The effect of this interpretation would be to confine pre-existing powers to arrestable or general offences. It is submitted that this is not the intended effect of s 8 (Art 10). If, for example, the material sought is £1 million in gold bullion which is the proceeds of a robbery, an application for a warrant should be sought under s 26(1) of the Theft Act 1968 (s 25 Theft Act (N.I.) 1969). If, however, the material sought is other relevant *evidence* of that offence, it is unobtainable under the 1968 Act and if it is likely to be of substantial value to the investigation (for example, the vehicle used in the robbery), application must be made under s 8 (Art 10). If the material sought is documents in the possession of a bullion dealer which are likely to identify persons dealing in the bullion, these are likely to be confidential material (special procedure material under s 14(1)(a)) (Art 16(1)(a)) and subject to the special procedure set out in Sch 1. As a further complication there will be occasions, admittedly rare, when the material is prohibited goods but is also held in confidence by a third party, for example, documents stolen from a government department and passed to a journalist who holds them in confidence. Section 9(2) (Art 11(2)) provides that pre-existing statutory powers to issue a warrant for such material cease to have effect and the material must then be sought via the special procedure in the 1984 Act (1989 Order). (Note that in these rare cases the offence need not be a serious arrestable offence, though it often will be). Ss 15 and 16 (Arts 17, 18) of the Act apply criteria governing the issue of *all* warrants.

4.07   Research into earlier practice revealed that warrants accounted for only one third of all searches (Royal Commission, Law and Procedure Volume, Appendix 7). That survey concentrated on the Metropolitan Police, and a survey of three provincial police forces suggested that only 17% of searches in the provinces were backed by a magistrate's warrant (Lidstone, *Magisterial Review of the Pre-Trial Criminal Process,* Table 5.11). The latter research also showed that warrants under the Theft Act 1968 and Misuse of Drugs Act 1971 predominated (Lidstone, op cit, paras 5.16 and 5.78). In the first edition of this book it was predicted that fewer search warrants would be sought in the future because (a) the wide ranging post arrest powers under ss 18 and 32 of the PACE Act 1984 (Arts 20 and 34 of the N.I. Order) would be used, and (b) the police would continue to persuade the owner or occupier to consent to a search. Research carried out by the authors under the auspices of the Economic and Social Research Council confirms that this is so. The table below sets out the authority, as recorded in the search register, under which searches were carried out in two English cities over separate six month periods.

Authority for search	Number of searches	% of all searches
Magistrates' Warrant	103	12.0
S 18 PACE Act 1984	405	47.0
S 32 PACE Act 1984	16	1.9
S 17 PACE Act 1984	48	5.6
Consent of person in custody or occupier	278	32.3
Not Stated	11	1.2
Total	861	100.00

It will be seen that a magistrates' warrant was relied upon in only 12 per cent of searches. As in previous research searches for stolen goods and prohibited drugs predominated, accounting for 50.0 per cent and 25.0 per cent respectively of warrant searches and 80.0 per cent and 5.0 per cent respectively of non-warrant searches. It was further predicted that the new warrant under s 8 of the PACE Act 1984 would, given that it was directed toward evidence of a serious arrestable offence which is in possession of innocent third parties and is not held under an obligation of confidence, rarely be used. This proved to be the case. In City A no s 8 warrants were issued during the research period, or indeed since the 1984 Act came into force. In City B only 4 of the 61 warrants issued in the six month research period were issued under s 8 and two of these were probably incorrectly issued. The real impact of the PACE Act 1984 is to be seen in the use of the special procedure under s 9 and Schedule 1 of the Act. A survey of provincial police forces revealed that all had made use of these powers to a greater or lesser extent ranging from 2 applications between 1st January 1986, when the Act came into force, and 1st September 1989, the date of the survey, to 150 applications in that period. In total there were over 1500 applications under Schedule 1 in provincial forces, some of which were multiple applications, ie seeking two or more orders or warrants, with the result that 1629 were granted, consisting of 41 warrants and 1588 production orders. Only 7 applications were refused. In addition 469 cases were recorded in which confidential material was obtained with the consent of the person in possession, but it was made clear that consent had been obtained in many more cases and accurate records of consensual obtaining of material were not kept. As one would expect, the Schedule 1 procedure is used much more by the capital's police than by provincial forces. The Metropolitan Police and City Company Fraud Department pioneered the use of this novel and, for them, long overdue power. Unfortunately records were not kept of the number of applications made under Schedule 1 but we would estimate that almost as many were made by the capital's police as were made by the provincial police. These powers will be dealt with in detail in para 4.51 et seq.

Nature of a warrant

4.08 Provided that the applicant for a warrant acts in good faith, sets out his application fully, complies with the terms of the warrant and executes it in accordance with s 16 (Art 18) of the 1984 Act, he is immune from legal action by the occupier even if the warrant has been improperly issued. The occupier's remedy in such a case lies against the issuing authority, but it will be extremely difficult to substantiate the complaint. For, though the magistrate acts judicially in assessing whether there is sufficient ground for issuing a warrant (*Hope v Evered* (1886)), the application is heard ex parte and the governing test is that of reasonable grounds — a test which is readily satisfied in practice. For the occupier's remedies, see further para 2.34–48, ante. The Act (Order) does offer some assistance here, since s 15 (Art 17) and the Code of Practice provide a checklist of criteria which must be satisfied for all search warrants, and s 8 (Art 10) and Sch 1 list those which a magistrate or circuit judge must additionally observe when hearing an application for a warrant or order for production under the Act in relation to a serious arrestable offence involving confidential information. Earlier statutory powers of search gave magistrates a discretion as to whether to issue a warrant even if a prima facie case is made out and s 8 (Art 10) retains this principle — a magistrate 'may' issue such a warrant. The Royal Commission (1981) noted the 'comment that magistrates may exercise insufficient care in ensuring that a warrant is necessary; and that too often they merely rubber stamp police requests' (Report, para 3.37). Indeed, subsequent research indicated that such magisterial discretion is rarely, if ever, exercised so as to refuse a warrant (see Lidstone, op cit paras 5.38–5.48; 94% of magistrates interviewed 'could not recall ever having refused a search warrant to the police', ibid, para 5.40).

Applications for a warrant — summary

4.09

(a)	Warrants for serious arrestable offences	1984 Act, s 8 (1989 Order Art 10) and Code of Practice
(b)	Warrants for material which it is an offence to possess etc	1984 Act, s 15, (1989 Order Art 17) Code of Practice, terms of particular governing statute eg s 26 of the Theft Act 1968
(c)	Any warrant involving confidential information	1984 Act, ss 9–14 Sch 1, (1989 Order Arts 11–16 and Sch 1) Code of Practice
(d)	Manner of execution of all warrants	1984 Act, ss 16, 19 (1989 Order Arts 18, 21) Code of Practice

The following preliminary points should be noted:

(i) Ss 15 and 16 (Arts 17 and 18) govern the application for and execution of search warrants issued under the PACE Act or Order, and any other enactment whether passed before or after the PACE Act and Order. Importantly s 15(1) (Art 17(1)) states that 'an entry on or search of premises under a warrant is unlawful unless it complies with this section and s 16' (Art 18). (It is not clear from the wording of s 15 whether 'it' refers to the 'warrant' or the entry and search. The clearer formulation in Art 17(1) of the PACE (N.I.) Order, which states 'an entry on or search of premises under a warrant is unlawful unless the warrant complies with this Article and is executed in accordance with Article 18', makes it clear that it is the entry on or search of premises which is unlawful if ss 15 and 16 (Arts 17 and 18) are not complied with. (See *R v Longman* (1988) Crim LR 534 and commentary)).

(ii) One distinction between (a) and (b) is that material sought under (a) need not be unlawfully possessed or involve a breach of the law, whilst material under (b) must meet that requirement and must also be governed by a statutory power to issue a warrant. For example, stolen goods, drugs, explosives and obscene publications come under (b), whereas documents indicating the source of, for example, the explosives can only be obtained under s 8 (Art 10) if the offence is a serious arrestable offence (s 116 (Art 87) defines 'serious arrestable offence' and is discussed at para 2.24, ante).

(iii) Warrants under (b) are issued under other legislation and can cover offences which may or may not be serious arrestable offences.

(iv) In all cases the occupier or owner of the premises to be searched need not be suspected of an offence. Indeed, applications for a warrant (particularly under s 8) are likely to be made more often in respect of third parties who are not themselves suspected of involvement.

(v) The complexity of these procedures is intensified by the fact that some of the preconditions for obtaining a search warrant appear in the Act (Order) whilst others are contained in Code of Practice B.

(vi) The issuing authority will usually either be a magistrate or a circuit judge (a county court judge in N.I.) (under the special procedure provisions (see para 4.51, post) or under the terms of certain pre-existing statutes — eg Incitement to Disaffection Act 1934). The 1984 Act did not endorse a recommendation of the Royal Commission (Report, para 3.45) that senior police officers should be allowed to authorise warrants in cases of urgency. However, some statutes, which do permit such authorisation by the police, survive the 1984 Act (eg Explosives Act 1985, s 73; Official Secrets Act 1911, s 9(2); Licensing Act 1964, s 45; but not the Theft Act 1968, s 26(2), which is repealed by Sch 7 of the 1984 Act. The same provision in s 25(2) of the Theft Act (N.I.) Act 1969 is also repealed by Sch 7 of the N.I. Order)). These authorisations are not warrants and are not therefore governed by ss 15 and 16 of the 1984 Act (Arts 17, 18). The powers of seizure under s 19 (Art 21) do however apply.

Application for a warrant — general

4.10 An application for a search warrant can in principle be made by any police officer, but the Code of Practice, B, para 2.4 requires each application to be approved by at least an inspector (or, in an emergency, by the most senior officer on duty). This is a prudent safeguard given the sometimes difficult legal questions which may arise on an application, eg whether the offence is a serious arrestable one or involves confidential information (in which case the special procedure may arise and the approval of at least a superintendent is necessary; see para 4.68, post). If the search may have a significantly adverse effect on police/community relations, the community liaison officer should be consulted (except in an emergency) (COP, B, para 2.5). The local police/community consultative group, where it exists, or its equivalent, should be informed as soon as practicable after a search has taken place where there is reason to believe that it might have an adverse effect on relations between the police and the community (COP, B, Note 2B). This is a welcome recognition of the unease which can be generated, principally amongst ethnic minorities, by insensitive or heavy-handed policing and which has attracted so much publicity in recent years. If such an effect is likely, it will be good police practice for the liaison officer and/or a member of the police/community panel (see s 106) to witness the execution of the warrant. An application is heard ex parte (except under the special procedure, as to which see para 4.51, post). It must be supported by an information in writing (s 15(3), Art 17(3)) and the issuing authority may ask questions of the officer (s 15(4), Art 17(4)). While circuit judges hearing an application for a warrant under Schedule 1 may ask pertinent questions, magistrates rarely do so, indeed they see little scope for doing so. S 15(2) (Art 17(2)) places the applying constable under a duty to state:

   (i)   the grounds for the search;
  (ii)   the empowering statute; and
 (iii)   to specify the premises to be entered and searched; and
 (iv)   to identify, so far as is practicable, the articles or persons to be sought.

The central requirement is (i). Research into the pre-PACE practice indicated that it may be easily satisfied (Lidstone op cit, Ch 5). 'As a result of information received from a previously reliable source' was a standard formula adopted by the police and more recent research into post-PACE practices shows that such generalities still satisfy s 15 (Art 17). Indeed the Code of Practice (B Note 2A) does not require the officer to reveal the identity of an informant though the officer concerned should be prepared to deal with the accuracy of previous information provided by the source. In the study, carried out by the authors, of warrants issued under the Theft Act 1968, the grounds for the search in 61.0 per cent was the above formula or a variant of it. Of these searches the information proved 'reliable', in that the property sought or some other property was seized, in 41.7 per cent, and 'unreliable' in that nothing was found, in 58.3 per cent. The success rate of searches is, however, too crude a measure of reliability. A successful search may be one in which some property was seized, not necessarily the property sought. Such property is often seized on suspicion that it is stolen, which it may or may not be, but the search is deemed to be successful either way. On the other hand the lack of success may not affect the reliability of the informant. In one case studied the informant had access to the premises and saw the stolen goods there. However, they had been removed by the time the police searched. The word 'informant' is often taken by magistrates to mean the sort of person who is himself involved in crime and who may be at risk if his identity is revealed. In this context it is used to describe any person who supplies information, eg the mother of the thief, a barmaid in whose pub the thief tried to sell property stolen from her, or a witness who saw D leave premises which had been burgled, carrying a bulky black plastic sack. In each of these cases the magistrate could be told the source of the information, though it need not, of course, be set out in the information. Questioning which might reveal this is something of a rarity largely because magistrates recognise that there may be a need to protect sources and assume that all 'information received' is from such a source. The Code of Practice B 2.1 and 2.3 require the police (a) to check that information received is accurate, recent and supplied in good faith, not provided maliciously and, if based on an anonymous source, that corroboration has been sought; and (b) to make reasonable enquiries to establish what, if anything, is known about the likely occupier, the nature of the premises and whether they have been previously searched (many forces keep a register of premises searched for this purpose). The Code is a useful checklist for magistrates who should at least establish that these requirements have been satisfied. As to (iii), s 15(2)(b) (Art 17(2)(b)) imposes a statutory duty on the applicant to 'specify the premises which it is desired to enter and search'. COP B 2.6 (ii) runs 2(b) and 2(c) together and says that the application should state:

'as specifically as is reasonably practicable the premises to be searched and the object of the search;'.

This is misleading. While 2(c) allows a degree of flexibility in identifying the articles or persons to be sought by the phrase 'as far as is practicable', 2(b) provides no such flexibility. It is an unqualified duty to specify correctly the premises to be searched. In the pre-PACE case of *R v Atkinson* (1976) it was held that a warrant to enter flat 45 did not authorise the search of flat 30. This was said to be 'not so much a misdescription of premises as a description of other premises'. The words of the statute are clear and the words of the Code should not be taken as permitting laxity in identifying and specifying the premises to be searched. As to (iv) it must be accepted that a certain amount of leeway in the identification of the property sought (though perhaps not of the person) is justified, particularly in respect of stolen goods. Hence the phrase 'as far as is reasonably practicable' in s 15(2)(c) (Art 17(2)(c)). However, the ESRC spon-

sponsored study carried out by the authors revealed that a number of warrant applications used generic descriptions such as 'electrical goods' or 'ladies clothing' which, even allowing for the difficulty in being specific, should not have been accepted as satisfying s 15(2)(c) (Art 17(2)(c)). If s 15 (Art 17) is to be the safeguard which the Act (and Order) intended, magistrates must be conscientious in satisfying themselves that the requirements of s 15 (Art 17) are satisfied, for it is only by their vigilance that compliance with the statutory requirements can be independently ensured. The statutory requirements of the authorising statute must also be complied with. In *Darbo v DPP* (1991) a warrant issued under s 3 of the Obscene Publications Act 1959 was held to be invalid because it authorised a search not only for 'obscene articles' as stated in s 3, but also for 'any other material of a sexually explicit nature' (which may or may not have been obscene) thereby wrongly conferring a search power beyond that authorised by s 3.

Applications to a magistrate for a warrant for evidence of a serious arrestable offence (s 8, Art 10)

4.11 Section 8 (Art 10) applies to serious arrestable offences and fills the many gaps in the previous warrant procedure, for example, in relation to a murder weapon, tools used in a robbery, evidence of kidnapping or commercial fraud. Moreover, it relates to *evidence* of such offences even if the holder is not suspected of complicity in the offence, whereas many earlier statutory powers were confined to the instruments and proceeds of a particular crime held by a suspect. In addition to the requirements of s 15(2) (Art 17(2)) and the Code of Practice (explained in para 4.10, ante), the magistrate must be satisfied of the matters mentioned in s 8(1) (Art 10(1)). 'Satisfied' has been held to import the ordinary civil standard of proof on the balance of probabilities in the context of Schedule 1 of PACE and is likely to be interpreted similarly here (*R v Norwich Crown Court, ex p Chethams* (1990)). The criteria in s 8(1) are as follows:

(i) A serious arrestable offence is involved (for consideration of this concept, see para 2.24, ante). In the authors' study a s 8 warrant referred to stolen copper cable. In order for such a theft to be a 'serious arrestable offence' the thief would have to obtain a substantial financial benefit or the loser suffer a serious financial loss. This could only be so if the amount of copper cable was so large as to fill the high rise flat in which it was said to be. Even if this were so, a warrant under s 26 of the Theft Act 1968 would be much more appropriate.

(ii) The relevant material is on the premises.

(iii) The material is likely to be, not *is*, of substantial value to the investigation, whether on its own or together with other evidence.

The material could thus be the proceeds of a crime; or evidence of its commission eg murder weapons, skeleton keys; or evidence confirming other material already held by the police such as fingerprints or a gun to match up with bullets found at the scene of a murder. This last example illustrates the importance of the phrase 'together with other material' — a gun without more will not prove murder.

NB   Evidence which is the proceeds of a serious arrestable offence may be sought under s 8 (Art 10), but, as suggested earlier, it is more appropriate to seek it under the particular statutory authority which already permits a warrant to search for such evidence. There may be occasions when the proceeds and evidence of the commission of the serious arrestable offence or other confirmatory evidence are all to be found on the same premises. There is then no legal reason why the application for *all* evidence should not be made under s 8 (Art 10), and it will be convenient since the same grounds apply to all three types of evidence. However, there is no necessity to use the s 8 (Art 10) procedure if the evidence sought is the subject of an existing statutory authority to issue a warrant. An example from the authors' study of the use of PACE Act powers may clarify. An armed robbery of a filling station was carried out by a man described as white, 6ft 5ins tall, wearing a trilby hat. Following a press appeal an anonymous caller named one J.B. as the man responsible. J.B. aged 19, fitted the description. Police wished to search his premises for the firearm used, the money stolen and the trilby hat worn. A warrant under the Firearms Act 1968 and the Theft Act 1968 could have been sought to search for the first two items but while the hat could be seized if found in the course of the search (s 19, Art 21), a search for the hat could not continue once the items mentioned in the warrants had been found (COP, B, 5.9). A warrant under s 8 was granted, the robbery being a serious arrestable offence and all the other requirements being satisfied, to search for all three items.

(iv)   The material is likely to be relevant in the sense of being admissible before a court (s 8(1)(c) and (4)) (Art 10(1)(c) and (4)). The reference to likelihood is understandable given the difficulties of predicting the evidential aspects of a trial which may take place many months later. But, taken together, requirements (iii) and (iv) impose a degree of specificity on the police which ought to exclude the presentation of mere background information which is not potentially admissible at a trial.

(v)   The evidence is neither excluded nor special procedure material nor subject to legal privilege (for which, see para 4.51, post). This requirement, set out in s 8(1)(d) (Art 10(1)(d)), raises difficult legal issues and the magistrates' clerk must play an advisory role. Indeed he should vet each application for issues such as arose in the case of *R v Guildhall Magistrates' Court ex parte Primlak Holdings Co (Panama) Ltd* (1989). Warrants under s 8 had been issued to search the offices of two firms of solicitors for documents relating to the sale of vessels by the collapsed bankers Johnson Matthey. The police believed offences of false accounting had been committed and therefore that the documents did not attract legal privilege, being held with the intention of furthering a criminal purpose within s 10(2) of the 1984 Act (Art 12(2) see para 4.57, post). An application for judicial review of the issue of the warrants succeeded, the court holding that there was no material upon which the magistrates could be satisfied that there were reasonable grounds for believing that the correspondence sought did not include items within s 8(1)(d) (Art 10(1)(d)). Even if, as the police alleged, legal privilege had been lost, the material was almost certainly held in confidence and was therefore special procedure material. Magistrates should not entertain an application under s 8 (Art 10) for a warrant to search for material in the possession of a solicitor in his capacity as legal adviser, and should look with suspicion upon such an application in respect of material held by any businessman in relation to that or any other business. Such material will almost certainly fall into one or other of the three categories mentioned in s 8(1)(d) (Art 10(1)(d)). The correct procedure for obtaining it is to make an application under s 9 and Schedule 1 of the 1984 Act (Art 11 and Schedule 1 of the 1989 Order).

(vi) The authority of a warrant is needed because one of the conditions in s 8(3) (Art 10(3)) is satisfied — essentially because the police have already tried to gain entry, or have been refused entry, or are unlikely to obtain permission to enter, or because speed demands a warrant. These conditions emphasise that a warrant is a last resort and that the police should be prepared to answer questions from the issuing authority along these lines. The reference to a search being 'frustrated or seriously prejudiced' in s 8(3)(d) (Art 10(3)(d)) refers to the dangers of concealment or destruction of the evidence through wilful design or the course of nature (eg the deterioration of perishable matter). Section 8(3)(c) (Art 10(3)(c)) commonly covers cases where the police have already tried to gain access to the premises.

(vii) It is implicit in the requirements of s 8(3) (Art 10(3)) that the police seek access to the material with consent unless this is impracticable or likely to frustrate the purposes of the search. However, it is not a condition precedent to the Justice's ability to grant a warrant that other powers to obtain the material have been tried without success, or have not been tried because they were bound to fail. Thus in *R v Billericay Justices ex p Harris Ltd* (1990) the issue of a s 8 warrant to search for and seize falsified tachograph discs and other documents, was upheld even though the police had the power under s 99 of the Transport Act 1968 to require the person to produce and permit the inspection of such documents. This power had been used by the police on other occasions when they suspected that not all the documents were produced and, having no power to search in such circumstances, their inquiries were frustrated. Suspecting similar non-production they quite properly used s 8.

4.12   The Code of Practice B. 2.8, stipulates that, if a warrant is refused, no further application in respect of the same premises can be made unless it is supported by additional grounds. If that happens, however, there is no obligation on the police to reveal the existence of the earlier application and this is believed to have led to 'forum shopping' in those rare cases in which a magistrate has refused an application. This is very unlikely except in relation to out of hours applications. Procedures under which the clerk must be contacted first and he directs the police to a magistrate are designed to ensure that this does not happen. Where such procedures are not in place magistrates, or their clerks, should enquire about this so that each application can be judged in its proper context.

4.13   The Royal Commission suggested (Report para 3.42) a two-stage procedure whereby the police would apply ex parte for an order directed to the occupier to produce the evidence. If he objected, he could appeal to the court against the order. If he then lost, a warrant could be issued. The Act adopts an inter partes procedure for certain types of evidence of a confidential nature (Sch 1, para 4.51, post), but for all other types of warrants the opportunities for a disgruntled occupier to challenge the issue of a warrant are slender. The issuing authority is not obliged to state its reasons and the contents of the warrant (see para 4.14, post) do not disclose anything of the judicial reasoning. As the observations of Lord Wilberforce in *IRC v Rossminster* (1980), a case concerning entry under the Finance Act 1976, make clear, the degree of specificity in a warrant may be very low — 'I can understand very well the perplexity, and indeed the indignation, of those present on the premises, when they were searched. Beyond knowing, as appears in the warrant, that the search was in connection with a 'tax fraud', they were not told what the precise nature of the fraud was, when it was committed, or by whom it was committed. In the case of a concern with numerous clients, eg a bank, without this knowledge the occupier of the premises is totally unable to protect his customer's confidential information from investigation and seizure. I cannot believe that this does not call for a fresh look by Parliament.' The 1984 Act (1989 Order) does not increase the degree of specificity of a search warrant. Though a copy of the warrant must be given to the occupier, or left on the

premises (s 16(5) to (7)) (Art 18(5) to (7)) and the occupier has the right
to inspect a copy of the warrant, endorsed with the result of the search,
which must be deposited at the court of issue (the court in which the
premises searched is situated in Northern Ireland) (s 16(9) to (12) (Art
18(9) to (12)), this will not disclose the reason why those premises were
searched. The notice of powers and rights which COP B 5.7 requires the
officer conducting the search to give to the occupier is equally unin-
formative in this respect. If the occupier seeks to discover the specific
reasons for the warrant from the police, he will be met with a claim to
privilege against disclosure based on public interest and by the principle that the police are protected against tortious action provided that
they apply for a warrant in good faith and observe the terms of its
execution (Constables Protection Act 1750, *Hope v Evered* (1886)).
The occupier's remedy could lie against the magistrate for exceeding
his jurisdiction (Justices of the Peace Act 1979, s 45, *Horsfield v Brown*
(1932)) but, unless he could prove bad faith on the part of the magistrate
(in which case an action for malicious prosecution would be possible),
he would have to seek judicial review of the court's decision. To do so
would require strong evidence to show that the issuing court had no
reasonable grounds on which to act and, even if successful, such an
action does not bring an award of damages. Section 27 of the Administration of Justice Act 1964 provides for an indemnity out of public
funds to be given to magistrates against whom damages have been
awarded provided that they have acted reasonably. For a review of the
liability of magistrates and in particular for a discussion as to whether
an action is still available at common law against magistrates who act in
bad faith but within their jurisdiction, see *In re McC* (1984).

Contents of a warrant

4.14 All search warrants must specify the name of the applicant, the
date of issue, the empowering statute, the premises to be searched and,
where practicable, the articles or persons sought (s 15(6) Art 17(6)); the
time when the search is to take place need not be stated, but under s 16(3)
(Art 18(3)) *all* warrants must be executed within one month. The reference to the empowering statute in s 15(6)(a)(iii) (Art 17(6)(a)(iii)) will
mention the offence suspected and the type of material which is sought,
but beyond this the occupier has no 'right to be informed of the 'reasonable grounds' of which the judge was satisfied' (Lord Wilberforce in *IRC
v Rossminster* (1980)). Some earlier statutes required the officer executing the warrant to be named therein (eg Firearms Act 1968, s 46; see
further Appendix 5 to the Royal Commission's Law and Procedure Volume), but s 16(1) now permits any constable to execute a warrant. S 125
of the Magistrates' Courts Act 1980 provides that certain warrants
including search warrants, may be executed anywhere in England and

Wales by any person to whom it is directed or by any constable acting within his police area. All police areas in England and Wales contain a number of petty sessional areas (Northern Ireland is one police area). S 125 therefore permits a constable in one petty sessional area to seek a search warrant for execution in another petty sessional area within the same police force. If the warrant is directed to a named police officer, that officer can execute it anywhere in England and Wales. The authors' research shows that it is not uncommon for police officers to apply to magistrates in their area for a search warrant in respect of premises in another petty sessional area but within their force area. One warrant was issued by magistrates in a town in Wiltshire in respect of premises in a Midlands town in a different police and petty sessional area. Magistrates make much of their local knowledge in the issue of warrants. Clearly such knowledge can play no part in the issue of a warrant in respect of premises in another area. The citizen is disadvantaged in such a case because s 16(9) to (12) of the PACE Act 1984 (Art 18 (9) to (12) of the Order) require the police to return the executed warrant, duly endorsed, to the court of issue, where the occupier of the premises may inspect it. If issued by a magistrate in another area the occupier will have to travel to that area, assuming he has the wit to examine the copy warrant given to him, which will indicate in which petty sessional area it was issued. In Northern Ireland the duty is to return the endorsed warrant to the court for the area in which the premises searched is situated (Art 18(c)). It would seem that the framers of the 1984 Act did not anticipate that magistrates would be issuing warrants in respect of premises outside their petty sessional area. Despite the fact that a magistrate's jurisdiction to issue search warrants is not limited to his petty sessional area, it would be in the interest of the public, with little if any detriment to the police, if he exercised his undoubted discretion and refrained from doing so (unless there is some pressing reason why he should deal with the application) and referred the police applicant to a justice of the peace for the petty sessional area in which the premises are situated. Code B 7.2 restates the requirement in s 16 (9) (Art 18(9)) that the executed warrant be endorsed to show whether the articles sought were found and whether other articles were seized. In addition the endorsement must include the date and time of execution, the name of the officer executing it (warrant number and duty station only if a terrorism investigation) and whether a copy of the warrant, and the Notice of Powers and Rights (see para 4.49 post) were handed to the occupier, or whether they were left on the premises, and if so where.

Conduct of searches (s 16, (Art 18) Code of Practice B)

4.15 Sections 15 and 16 (Arts 17 and 18) apply to the application for issue, and to the execution, of all warrants to enter and search premises and the Code of Practice supplements these provisions and makes special provision for search warrants for excluded or special procedure material. Considerable cross-reference between the Act and the Code of Practice is necessary. As to searches by consent, the safeguards in the Code are considered in para 4.27, post. The sanction against overzealous police conduct lies in the occupier's withdrawal of consent, but this may be difficult to enforce once the police are inside the premises.

4.16   (a) *Who may enter and search*? — Any constable may exercise the entry and search powers (eg s 16(1) (Art 18(1)) in relation to warrants). 'Constable' in this context refers to the office rather than the rank. So far as the rank of those executing a search warrant is concerned the Home Office Consolidated Circulars (1977) suggested that whenever possible an officer of the rank of inspector or above should be in charge of executing a warrant and the Code of Practice, B 5.13, directs that he must be for warrants issued under Sch 1. It is not, however, the present day practice to require inspectors to be in charge of a search under a warrant. Of 61 warrants executed in 2 cities in only 18 (29.5 per cent) was an inspector or higher rank in charge. In 9 of these the searches were by armed officers seeking firearms and in 2 searches a superintendent was in charge of a search of premises occupied by a person arrested for a terrorist offence in another country. The remaining searches were drug related and the inspector was a member of the Drug Squad. Warrants issued under s 8 (Art 10) and existing or future statutes, are subject to ss 15 and 16 (Arts 17 and 18), and s 16(2) (Art 18(2)) provides that a warrant may authorise persons to accompany any constable who is executing it. This may be a social worker in offences involving children, or a community relations officer or community leader in searches which might have an adverse effect on police/public relations. In the authors' study no warrant authorised anyone else to accompany the police though on one occasion the police took a carpenter along to lift floorboards. One may note in this context s 48(9) of the Children Act 1989 under which the applicant, usually a social worker, may apply for a warrant authorising any constable to assist in the exercise of an emergency protection order (EPO), using reasonable force if necessary. The court may issue the warrant where it appears that the person attempting to exercise the powers under the EPO (that is, a power to enter specified premises and search for the child subject of the order, s 48(3)), has been, or is likely to be, prevented from doing so by being refused entry to the premises, or access to the named child (s 48(9)). The warrant must be addressed to a constable and executed by him. The applicant must be allowed to accompany him if he desires and the court does not direct otherwise (s 48(10)). The court may also direct that the constable be accompanied by a registered medical practitioner, registered nurse or registered health visitor if he so chooses (s 48(11)). The child should be named, or if not named, identified as clearly as possible (s 48(13)).

4.17 (b) *Timing of the search* — All warrants must be executed within one month of issue (s 16(3) Art 18(3)) and can only be used once. In one city studied by the authors 48.0 per cent of the warrants issued were returned unexecuted. All but one of these were warrants issued under the Misuse of Drugs Act 1971. They were obtained as part of a major drugs operation and were, effectively, renewed if not executed within a month. Searches must, if possible, be conducted at 'a reasonable hour' (s 16(4) Art 18(4)), (COP B, 5.2) unless this would frustrate the purpose of the search. COP Note 5A gives some guidance as to what is reasonable. Police are to have regard, among other considerations, to the times of day at which the occupier of the premises is likely to be present. They should not search at a time when he, or any other person on the premises, is likely to be asleep unless not doing so is likely to frustrate the purpose of the search. This permits much flexibility and a late night or early morning search may often be the best time to find the occupier at home. The 'dawn raid' did not occur very often in the authors' research study. Armed raids took place at this time because few people were about, thus reducing the risk of injury if shots were fired.

4.18 (c) *Procedure for entry* — For *all warrants*, the constable must identify himself to the occupier or, in his absence, to any person who 'appears to the constable to be in charge of the premises' (s 16(6)(b) Art 18(6)(b)). The latter condition could include a suspect's girlfriend or a firm's employee or a student who is sharing a house (bearing in mind the broad definition of 'premises' — para 4.02, ante). It could perhaps extend to a caretaker or a workman engaged, in the occupier's absence, on repairs to property or even to a child. But if the constable is not in uniform, it would be most unwise to undertake a search of premises occupied only by children. In such circumstances a neighbour or other responsible person should be called in to take care of the child. If the constable is not in uniform, he must prove his office (s 16(5)(a) Art 18(5)(a)) and production of his warrant card will be the standard method. He must in any event produce the search warrant and give a copy to the occupier or person in charge. Section 16(5) and (6) (Art 18(5) and (6)) do not prevent the police entering the premises without identifying themselves or producing the warrant when it is necessary to maintain the element of surprise eg lest the occupier flush drugs down the lavatory or prepare to meet the police with force. Section 16(5) refers to the time of occupation rather than the time when the duties are to be performed. The Code of Practice indicates the normal procedure when there is no need for surprise and the exceptional circumstances in which there is such a need (COP B, 5.5). This view was upheld in *R v Longman* (1988). There one of the officers posed as an Interflora lady in order to gain entry and only complied with the section and code after entry but before the search. It was argued on behalf of the appellant that the entry and search were unlawful because the mandatory rules set out in ss 15, 16 and the Code of Practice had not been complied with and that s 16(5) indicated the time at which certain events should happen and certain formalities be observed. The Court of Appeal held that the words of the section mean that when search warrants are being executed certain formalities should be observed; whereas the time at which they should be carried out is determined by the Code of Practice. Para B 5.5 makes it clear that the time when those formalities have to be observed when entry is obtained by force or subterfuge is after entry. The officer is required at the earliest opportunity, after entry and before search, to announce his identity, produce the warrant card and search warrant and, at the first reasonable opportunity, give the occupier a copy of the search warrant. The revised Code of Practice requires that the officer conducting a search, whether under a warrant, under a post-arrest power or with consent, also provide the occupier with a Notice of Powers and Rights (COP B, 5.7, discussed at para 4.49, post). When the search is carried out under a warrant the notice should be given together with a copy of the warrant. If the occupier, or person in charge, is not present, copies of the notice and of the warrant should be left in a prominent place on the premises or appropriate part of the premises and endorsed with the name of the officer in charge of the search, the police station to which he is attached and the date and time of the search. The warrant should be endorsed to show that this has been done. If premises have been entered by force, as they usually will be if the occupier or person in charge is not present, as well as in circumstances when the occupier is present, the officer in charge must satisfy himself that the premises are secure on leaving them either by arranging for the occupier or his agent to be present or by any other appropriate means.

4.19   (d) *Extent and method of search* — Sch 1 warrants are dealt with at para 4.76, post; as for other warrants, the search may only extend to the purpose for which the warrant was issued (s 16(8) Art 18(8)). Thus, bulky items such as video recorders would not justify as minute a search as would drugs, cash or jewellery. On the other hand, where documents are being examined, the extent of the search may be considerable. For the police cannot seize every document they come across and examine it at leisure back at the police station (cf *Reynolds v Commissioner of Police of the Metropolis* (1984)). They must have a reason for believing that each document they seize is relevant to the purpose of the search. The search cannot continue by virtue of the warrant once the items are found or it becomes apparent that they are not on the premises (Code of Practice, para 5.9; eg a rapid search for television sets reveals nothing). However, the search could continue under another power, eg if evidence is discovered of another offence, the occupier is arrested and the police wish to search for evidence of that offence (s 32(2)(b) Art 34 (2)(b)).

4.20 (e) *Force* — All powers of entry and search allow the police to use reasonable force if necessary (s 117 (Art 88)). This is discussed generally at para 2.32 ante and in the context of searches at para 4.48 post.

Post-arrest powers of search

Search following arrest for an arrestable offence Section 18 (Art 20) (see figure 1, post)

4.21 Where a person has been arrested away from his home, for example, at a police station, it will often be necessary for the police to enter and search his premises for evidence of the offence. Indeed, limited research for the Royal Commission (1981) revealed that searches after arrest accounted for 28% of all searches in the Metropolitan Police District and 49% in the provincial forces studied (Royal Commission, Law and Procedure Volume, Appendix 7). This finding was confirmed by subsequent research for the Home Office (44% in the provincial forces studied — Lidstone, op cit, Table 5.11). The legality of searches after arrest was, however, open to doubt. As long ago as 1929 the Royal Commission on Police Powers and Procedure voiced such doubts but observed that the police in practice undertook such searches (Report, paras 120–1). Similarly the Home Office Evidence to the 1981 Royal Commission (No III, p 34) pointed to this police practice. In *McLorie v Oxford* (1982) the Divisional Court resolved the doubts and held that, once a person has been arrested away from his premises, the police have no common law power subsequently to search them. Section 18 reversed this decision and restored the position to what the police believed it to be. The summary power of arrest provided by s 24 (Art 26) (discussed at para 5.07 — 16 post) together with the fact that a majority of offences with which the police daily deal are arrestable offences, meant that the s 18 (Art 20) search power would be relied upon most often. Research carried out by the authors confirms this. The following table shows the authority for searches carried out in two cities over a six month period (as recorded in search registers).

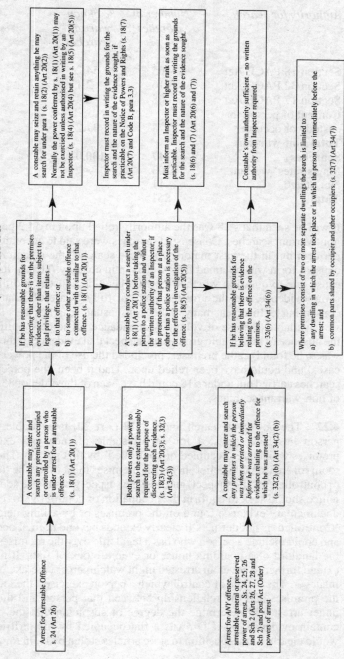

4.21 *Powers of entry, search and seizure*

Authority for search	Number of searches	% of non-warrant searches	% of All searches
Section 18 PACE Act	405	54.2	47.0
Section 32 PACE Act	16	2.1	1.9
Section 17 PACE Act	48	6.4	5.6
Consent of person in custody or occupier	278	37.2	32.3
Total non-warrant Searches	**747**	**100.0**	**86.8**
Magistrates' warrant	103		12.0
Not Stated	11		1.2
Total	**861**		**100.0**

It will be seen that s 18 was the authority relied upon in 54.2 per cent of non-warrant searches. Consensual searches were said to account for 37.2 per cent but in the vast majority of these searches the signature on the consent form was obtained from a person in custody. That in itself may cause one to question whether it was a genuine consent and there was some evidence that the arrestee was not fully aware of what he was consenting to. In a great many of the 'consensual' searches the s 18 power was available (the use of voluntary attendance for some shoplifters and the absence of reasonable grounds to suspect that evidence of the offence was to be found on the premises, precluded the use of the power in some cases) and could have been relied upon. Had it been, the percentage of searches carried out under s 18 could have been of the order of 85 per cent of non-warrant searches.

4.22 The power of search under s 18 (Art 20) is available where a person has been arrested for an arrestable offence and extends to premises which are 'occupied or controlled' by that person. There is no room for 'reasonable belief' here (the premises must in fact be 'occupied or controlled' by the suspect) and, lest the suspect give a false address, the police should seek to confirm the occupation or control by, for example, documentary evidence found on the premises or by asking neighbours. 'Controlled' is not defined. It clearly extends beyond normal occupation and could include a person who has a legal title over the premises such as the landlord of a boarding house or even a block of flats. It may well extend further to cover an arrested night watchman or caretaker or office manager. The degree of control which a person exercises, the location of the premises and the relationship between that person and the person under arrest will determine the degree of suspicion that the premises contain evidence; eg if D owns a flat occupied by his girlfriend, she would clearly be in a position to store articles stolen by D. In *R v Badham*

(1987) (discussed at para 4.26 post) it was held that the search power under s 32(2)(b) (Art 34(2)(b)) was an immediate power, that it had to be exercised at the time of arrest, and that a constable could not return to the premises in which the arrest took place some 4 hours later in order to search them. S 18 (Art 20) is not so limited. Indeed in most cases the search will take place some time after the arrest. It would also seem that the power may be exercised more than once in respect of the same premises. It can clearly be exercised in respect of premises occupied by D and in respect of premises controlled by D, but suppose premises occupied by D are searched with negative results. Later D makes admissions and directs the police to where the property is hidden. There appears to be no reason why another s 18 (Art 20) search should not take place.

Section 18 envisages two types of search:

(a)   Where the person is in police detention at a police station and the police decide to search his premises. The search must be authorised in writing by at least an inspector.

(b)   Where the person is arrested away from a police station and the police wish to search the premises before taking him to the station. Here the constable may act without prior authorisation and need only inform an inspector or more senior officer after the search has taken place (s 18(5), (6) Art 20(5), (6)). This type of search preserves the ideas underlying *Dallison v Caffery* (1965), where Lord Denning permitted a constable a degree of latitude in investigating an offence before taking a person to a police station, provided only that the constable acts reasonably. This principle is preserved in ss 18 and 30 (Arts 20 and 32) and is discussed in detail at para 5.55, post.

Section 18(1) (Art 20(1)) gives the constable the power to enter, s 18(3) contains the element of reasonableness with regard to the extent of the search and s 18(5) (Art 20(5)) demands that the person's presence at the place of search be 'necessary for the effective investigation of the offence'. This last condition is likely to be satisfied in many cases. It would not normally apply to a person caught red-handed since a search of his premises would not assist the investigation of the offence for which he has been arrested. However, s 18(1) (Art 20(1)) allows a search for evidence of 'some other arrestable offence which is connected with or similar to' that offence. Thus, for example, the search of premises of a thief caught red-handed could be authorised for evidence of other stolen property.

4.23   The phrase 'similar to that offence' in s 18(1) (Art 20(1)) is likely to lead to some difficulty. For example, robbery, burglary, obtaining by deception and blackmail are similar to theft, the goods obtained by such offences being regarded as 'stolen' (s 24(4) of the Theft Act 1968).

Criminal damage by destroying property can also be theft of that property and forgery may be similar to deception or be the means of deception. The phrase is clearly not broad enough to cover the facts of *Jeffrey v Black* (1978) where the accused was charged at a police station with theft of a sandwich from a public house and the police subsequently searched his premises for evidence of drug offences. However, it would be permissible in such circumstances to search the premises if there are reasonable grounds to believe that D has committed other offences of theft. It should be noted that, if the accused is arrested at the police station for another offence under s 31 (Art 33), a fresh exercise of the s 18 (Art 20) search power is permissible. Furthermore, the terms of s 19 (Art 21) and the general inclusionary rule of evidence mean that the police may seize and use at trial any evidence (except items subject to legal privilege) of other offences which they discover during the search even if it is dissimilar to, or unconnected with, the offence for which the person has been arrested.

4.24 An inspector (or higher ranking officer) who authorises a search under s 18 (Art 20) or to whom such a search is subsequently reported under s 18(6) (Art 20(6)), must make a written record of the authorisation or that a search under s 18(5) (Art 20(5)) has taken place (s 18(7) Art 20(7)). (This is a record by the supervisory officer and has nothing to do with records which must be made by the officer in charge of the search in search registers (see para 4.50 post)). In *R v Badham* (1987) a Crown Court judge ruled that the authorisation should be in the form of an independent document which the constable should take with him to the premises to be searched. This ruling ignores s 18(8) (Art 20(8)), which requires the record to be in the custody record when the person in occupation or control of the premises is in police detention, and s 18(5) which permits a search without such authorisation. Be that as it may, the Notice of Powers and Rights which COP 5.7 requires officers conducting searches under the s 18 (Art 20) power, or any other power, to serve on the occupier, contains a section for the signature of the person authorising the search and this should satisfy the requirement of *R v Badham*.

Search of premises upon making an arrest ss 18, 32(2)(b) (Arts 20, 34(2)(b))

4.25 Section 32 (Art 34(2)(b)) covers the situation where the police have arrested a person and wish to search those premises on which he has been arrested or in which the person was immediately before the arrest. Section 18 (Art 20) deals with the situation where a person has already been arrested for an arrestable offence away from his own premises and the police now wish to enter and search premises occupied or controlled by him. Section 18 (Art 20) is confined to arrest for arrestable offences while s 32(2)(b) (Art 34(2)(b)) applies to an arrest for *any* offence. The sections can thus overlap but they each offer distinctive features. Taken together they afford the police ample opportunity to search the premises of an arrested person, and have considerably clarified and altered the common law. One may also note that s 17 (Art 19) authorises entry to and search of premises for persons who are to be arrested for an arrestable offence and other offences. The s 18 or the s 32(2)(b) power (Arts 20, 34(2)(b)) may follow such entry and arrest. It must be emphasised that a search of premises for evidence following an entry under s 17 (Art 19) can only follow if an arrest is made. A common reason for seeking a warrant to search premises, rather than use ss 17, 18 or 32(2)(b) (Arts 19, 20 and 34(2)(b)) is that the person sought may not be on the premises. If he is not, the occupiers may be alerted and remove any evidence of that or any other offence. S 19 (Art 21) permits the seizure of such evidence if the constable comes across it in the search for the person but does not authorise a search (see para 4.41 post).

4.26   *Section 32* — The common law allowed the police to search an arrested person and his 'immediate surroundings' (*Dillon v O'Brien* (1887), *Elias v Pasmore* (1934); cf the position in the United States where a search is confined to the 'immediate vicinity' of the arrest — *Chimel v California* (1969)). Section 32 (Art 34) contains no such spatial limitation, except that imposed by s 32(7) (Art 34(7)) in respect of premises consisting of two or more separate dwellings (discussed at 4.03, ante). 'Premises', it will be recalled, (see para 4.02, ante) are given a wide interpretation by s 23 (Art 25). They need not be owned by the arrested person and thus the facts of *Elias v Passmore* (1934) and *McLorie v Oxford* (1982) are encompassed. In the former the plaintiff was arrested on the premises of the National Unemployed Workers Movement, its offices were searched and papers were seized. In contrast, s 18 (Art 20) only covers premises which are 'occupied or controlled' by the arrested person. Consequently, when the police have arrested X on emerging from his house, they can search it under s 32 (Art 34) (because he was there 'immediately before' the arrest) or under s 18 (Art 20). If, however, X has just left someone else's house, they can only use s 32 to search those premises and must use s 18 (Art 20) to enter and search X's house. As regards *McLorie v Oxford*, premises could have been, but were not, searched at the time of arrest and it was held that the common law did not permit the police to return later to search them. Despite the fact that s 32(2)(b) (Art 34(2)(b)) contains no time limit on the exercise of the search power, in *R v Badham* (1987) a Crown Court refused to regard an attempted entry some 4 hours after the arrest as lawful under s 32(2((b), thus perpetuating the common law. The court felt that s 32(2)(b) (and presumably Art 34(2)(b)) was an immediate power, and that it would be wrong to have an open ended right to go back to the premises where an arrest had taken place. That, however, ignores the availability of the s 18 (Art 20) power. When the arrest is for an arrestable offence s 18 (Art 20) is not an immediate power and usually is exercised some time after the arrest. If D is arrested for an arrestable offence in premises occupied or controlled by him it makes no difference which power is used. It may be convenient to search the premises at the time of the arrest (which may then be under s 18 or s 32(2)(b) Arts 20, 34(2)(b)), but there is no reason why the s 18 (Art 20) power may not be exercised then or later. Indeed as suggested in para 4.22 (ante) there appears to be no reason why the s 18 power should not be exercised more than once in respect of the same premises, subject to reasonable cause and authorisation. A search under s 32(2)(b) (Art 34(2)(b)) can only take place if the police have reasonable grounds to believe (s 32(6), Art 34(6)) that the premises contain evidence of the crime for which the person has been arrested, whereas s 18 (Art 20) permits a search if there are reasonable grounds for suspecting not only that there is evidence of the offence for which D was arrested on the premises but also evidence of 'connected or similar offences'. It is a question of fact in every case whether there were such grounds (*R v Beckford* (1991)). In the study carried out by the authors less than 2.0 per cent of searches were carried out under the authority of s 32(2)(b). There was some evidence of under-recording due to a misunderstanding of the recording requirements of the Code of Practice, nevertheless when both powers are available, as usually they are when an arrest takes place on or near premises in which D was, the s 18 (Art 20) power will be relied upon because of the lower threshold of suspicion and the wider range of evidence which can be sought. This is so even though s 19 (Art 21) permits the seizure of evidence of unrelated offences which the police come across during a lawful search under any of the search powers available to the police. If, for example, A is arrested at his house for fraud offences, and during a search the police discover evidence of drug offences, the prosecution may use the evidence in any trial for the latter offences. Only items which a constable has reasonable grounds to suspect are subject to legal privilege cannot be seized under s 18 or s 32 (Arts 20, 34) (s 19(6) Art 21(6)). As to the meaning of 'legal privilege', see para 4.56 post. Material which is 'excluded material' or 'special procedure material' (see para 4.59 post), and for which a warrant under s 8 (Art 10) either cannot be issued (see para 4.11 ante) or which must be sought under the special procedure set out in Schedule 1, may be seized under ss 18, 32 or 19 (Arts 20, 34 and 21) thus by-passing the special procedure. Because s 32(2)(b) (Art 34(2)(b)) authorises the search of premises in which the arrested person was 'immediately before he was arrested' the special procedure may also be by-passed using this power, eg if D, suspected of fraud, is arrested leaving his accountant's office, that office may be searched for evidence of the fraud.

Entry and search with consent

4.27 Research into previous practice indicated that 56% of all searches by the police were conducted before arrest with the consent of the occupier or after arrest with consent or under the uncertain common law power already discussed (Royal Commission Law and Procedure Volume, Appendix 7). That survey was heavily biased toward the Metropolitan Police and in a similar survey involving three provincial police forces 75% of searches were with consent or under common law powers (Lidstone, op cit Table 5.11). Despite the availability of Sections 18 and 32 (Arts 20, 34) following arrest, almost a third of post-arrest searches in the study carried out by the authors were said to have been carried out with the consent of the occupier or the person under arrest. It was anticipated that the police would continue to seek consent. Indeed the Royal Commission pointed out that, 'it is only rarely that the police do not receive consent to enter when looking for evidence, since people are often anxious to cooperate and allow the police every facility' (Report, para 3.41). Nevertheless it was not anticipated that consent would be relied upon in preference to the clear post arrest powers provided. The Code of Practice B, Section 4. requires that:

(a)   the consent be of a person entitled to grant entry to the premises and the officer must make enquiries to satisfy himself that the person is in a position to give such consent;

(b)   the consent must, if practicable, be given in writing on the Notice of Powers and Rights before the search takes place (see para 4.49 post for the Notice of Powers and Rights);

(c)   before seeking consent the officer in charge of the search shall:
    (i)   state the purpose of the proposed search, and if at the time the person is not suspected of an offence, tell him so;
    (ii) inform the person concerned that he is not obliged to consent and that anything seized may be produced in evidence.

The use of the words 'state' and 'inform' in Code B 4.2 suggests that the person should be told orally. It is submitted that it is not sufficient to obtain a signature on a form which contains a written statement of the Code requirements without reading them to the person concerned. The Code B 4.3 makes it clear that an officer cannot enter and search premises under 4.1 if the consent has been given under duress, and he cannot continue if the consent is withdrawn before the search is complete. The above raises a number of questions which must be addressed.

117

Who is entitled to consent?

4.28 The Code of Practice B 4.1 calls for the written consent 'of a person entitled to grant entry to the premises'. In law the consent to enter premises creates, in this context, a bare licence. This may be given expressly or impliedly and the Code requirement of written consent means that an express licence is given. A bare licence can be withdrawn at will. Once it is withdrawn the visitor must leave the premises, and if he does not do so within a reasonable time, he becomes a trespasser. The person who is in exclusive possession or exclusive occupation of the premises can give a licence to enter to anyone he likes. In this context the householder, be he owner, occupier or tenant has exclusive possession and the authority to license entry. However, in the course of ordinary family life other members of the household may invite persons onto the premises. Even a squatter may invite third parties onto the squatted property as licensees (*R v Edwards* (1978)). The householder may revoke the licence so granted (*Robson v Hallett* (1967)). A constable seeking consent to enter premises cannot easily determine who has the right to exclusive possession or exclusive occupation, and the authority to give or refuse a licence, or which members of the household have the actual or ostensible authority to grant a licence to enter. The issue in law is whether the visitor, be he constable or citizen, is entitled to assume that the person granting consent has the authority to do so. In normal circumstances anyone with a right of occupation has the authority to invite others to enter for purposes reasonably related to the purposes of the occupation. In *R v Jones and Smith* (1976) it was held that Smith had entered in excess of the licence granted by his father, which did not include entry to steal, and Smith had no authority to license Jones' entry in order to steal. The householder's spouse who has a right of occupation by virtue of the Matrimonial Homes Act 1983, s 1 is entitled to invite any visitor he or she pleases into the house, and the licence granted is not subject to revocation by the householder. The same applies to a co-habitant, whether he/she has an equitable interest in the property or is a bare licensee but the 'sub-licence' granted by such a bare licensee/co-habitant is subject to revocation by the householder. (*McGowan v Chief Constable of Kingston-upon-Hull* (1968)). Children of the household, with the exception of those of tender years, will have implied authority to invite visitors into the house for ordinary social and business purposes (eg gas meter reader) including police officers carrying out their duties. Children of tender years may have the implied authority to invite friends into the house but it would not be reasonable to assume that they have the authority to invite strangers or police officers. It would in any event be foolish to rely upon the consent of a minor. The occupier, and no doubt the spouse of the occupier, can override or withdraw the consent given by a member of the household who had the authority to grant consent. However, in *R v Thornley* (1980) it was held that once the police enter premises at the invitation of the occupier (the wife in *Thornley*) they can remain there for as long as the invitor so requests, even though a joint occupier (the husband in *Thornley*) orders them to leave. Although there is no English case directly on the point, it would seem that an invitation to enter given by children of the household, be they adults or young persons, can always be overridden by the occupier. The fact that they pay rent or make a contribution to household expenses does not give them an exclusive right to occupy. In this respect they would appear to be in no better position than a lodger who, although he has exclusive occupation of rooms in the house, in the sense that nobody else is entitled to share the use of the rooms with him, is not in exclusive possession. (See Blackburn J in *Allan v Liverpool* (1874), and *Street v Mountford* (1985)). A lodger or sub-tenant will, of course, have the authority to consent to a search of the room occupied by him, but the occupier may be able to override or withdraw that consent depending on the terms of the agreement. One may note at this point that the Code of Practice, B, Notes for Guidance 4A, states that in situations such as lodging houses and similar places where the occupier of a room does not have an exclusive right to occupation as against the landlord, searches should not be made on the basis solely of the landlord's consent unless the tenant is unavailable and the matter is urgent. That is an eminently sensible approach.

Meaning of consent

4.29   'A man cannot be said to be truly willing unless he is in a position to choose freely, and freedom of choice predicates, not only full knowledge of the circumstances on which the exercise of choice is conditional, so that he may be able to choose wisely, but the absence of any feeling of constraint so that nothing shall interfere with the freedom of his will'. (*Bowater v Rowley Regis Corp* (1944), cited with approval by Lord Hodson, in *ICI v Shatwell* (1965)

One cannot doubt that an occupier whose consent to a search is requested after being 'cautioned' in accordance with COP B 4.2 and who then signs the form of consent, has made a free choice and has truly consented. Unfortunately that is not the reality. For example, in the study carried out by the authors the majority of those consenting to a search were in custody following their arrest. At no time were they told that they need not consent, instead they were presented with a printed form which complied with the Code of Practice in that it contained all the requirements of B 4.1–4. They were told their premises were to be searched and told to sign the form. It may be doubted whether in these circumstances the arrested person was 'in a position to choose freely'. Few will have known that they could have refused. COP B 4.3 says 'An officer cannot enter and search premises . . . if the consent has been given under duress'. Threats, violence and illegally used force would clearly exclude consent. The psychologically coercive effect of detention in a police station is well known and the fact that consent was obtained from a person in police custody places a particularly heavy burden on the prosecution to prove that such consent was full and free in the above sense. It should be noted that the revised Code B 4.1 retreats from the position adopted in the first Code which stated 'the consent must be given in writing'. The revised Code says,' . . .the consent must, *if practicable*, be given in writing'. It is submitted that this does not mean that implied consent, as when the occupier remains silent in response to a request, or nods or otherwise signifies consent, will suffice. Express consent is still required but need not be in writing if it is not practicable to obtain written consent. 'Practicable' in this context cannot apply to matters relating to the search, such as the need to make a speedy entry in order to save life. S 17(1)(e) (Art 19(1)(e)) provides for such a situation (see para 4.35, post). It can only apply to circumstances in which the person giving consent is incapable of giving it in writing, eg he is unable to write or has a disability which prevents him doing so. One may further note that the person who gives consent may withdraw it at any time before the search commences, or during the search. A search may not then take place or continue unless, of course, another search power is available, eg the occupier is arrested. The consent may also be a limited consent. Statutory search powers are all limited to a search to the extent that is reasonably required for the purpose of discovering the evidence sought. The person consenting may impose a similar limit, or limit the search to particular areas, eg 'you cannot search the childrens' room'. A search in excess of such limitation will be unlawful. If a constable is lawfully on the premises, as he will be if there with full and free consent, he has the powers of seizure under s 19 (Art 21). If the consent obtained is not a full and free consent, the entry on and search of the premises will be unlawful and the constable will be a trespasser. This may be relevant as to whether or not he is acting in the execution of his duty if he is assaulted in the course of the search (see *Robson v Hallett* (1967)). It may also be relevant to the admissibility of evidence at a subsequent trial (s 78 (Art 76) see para 2.37, ante), to a civil action for trespass and to any disciplinary proceedings resulting from an illegal search and seizure. Failure to observe any provision of the Code of Practice is admissible and relevant in determining any issue raised in such actions (s 67(11), Art 66(10)).

Consent v Power

4.30 Reliance on consent rather than exercising the available s 18 (Art 20) power was justified by senior police officers as follows: 'The spirit, and the intention of the PACE Act 1984 was to cut down on the coercive use of police powers of arrest and search and to enhance the rights of suspects in our care. The police service is complying with these objectives by obtaining consents in place of s 18 authorities on suitable occasions.' By-passing the legal controls on the exercise of powers damages the citizens they were designed to protect. There is no requirement of reasonable suspicion or belief; no limitation on the extent of the search and, though few realise it, s 19 (Art 21) is available, if the consent is genuine, and anything which is reasonably believed to be evidence of a crime, or obtained in consequence of a crime may be seized. If the consent is not a genuine consent the police are operating with unwitting illegality. More damaging is what may be described as `witting illegality' as when official policy urges reliance on consent rather than exercise powers. Constables may then feel justified in using deceptive tactics in order to obtain a signature on a consent form. It is submitted that consent should not be used as a substitute for the exercise of a power. Instead consent must be seen as an adjunct to police powers, and it must be based on a free choice, with full knowledge of the circumstances and in the absence of any feeling of constraint.

Entry and Search without Warrant (s 17 (Art 19))

4.31 S 17 (Art 19) provides a wide ranging power to enter and search premises without a warrant in order to arrest persons or to save life, limb or property. So far as the entry and search for persons is concerned reasonable grounds for believing that the person is on the premises must exist and there is a limitation on search in respect of separate dwellings and, like all search powers, it is a search only to the extent reasonably required for the purpose for which the power was exercised.

(i) *Entry in order to execute a warrant of arrest* (s 17(1)(a), Art 19(1)(a))

4.32 There is a large number of statutes authorising the issue of arrest warrants. However, the wide powers of arrest without warrant under ss 24, 25, Sch 2 (Arts 26, 27, Sch 2) and contained in numerous statutes, mean that arrest warrants are comparatively rare. When they are issued they are usually issued under s 125 of the Magistrates' Courts Act 1980 (Art 20(3) of the Magistrates' Court (N.I.) Order 1981). S 17(1)(a) of the 1984 Act (Art 19(1)(a) of the N.I. Order) makes it clear that a constable may enter and search premises in order to execute such warrants and, if necessary, he can use reasonable force (s 117; Art 88). In *Jones v Kelsey* (1986) it was held that a warrant issued under s 16(1) of the Criminal Courts Act 1973 to arrest for breach of a community order, was a warrant to arrest a person in connection with an offence within s 125(4) of the MCA 1980. It follows that such a warrant is within s 17(1)(a) (Art 19(1)(a)) and the power to enter premises in order to execute it is available. In *R v Peacock* (1989) it was held that a means inquiry warrant issued under s 83(1)(b) of the MCA 1980 for non-payment of a fine was not issued 'in connection with an offence' therefore the s 17 power is not available in respect of such warrants. As to the execution of warrants of arrest, see para 5.70 post. Doubt existed under the earlier law as to whether the police could enter premises in the reasonable belief, as opposed to knowledge, that the person named in the warrant was there. A New Zealand case (*Matthew v Dwan* (1949)) had concluded that there was no such power. Section 17(2)(a) (Art 19(2)(a)) resolves the doubt in the constable's favour: he can enter if he has reasonable grounds for believing that the person is on the premises. To resolve further doubts, warrants of commitment under s 76 of the Magistrates' Courts Act 1980 (Art 92 of the Magistrates' Courts (N.I.) Order 1981) are included in s 17(1)(a)(ii) (Art 19(1)(a)(ii)). These warrants are issued against those who default in paying a magistrates' court order, such as a fine following conviction or an order for maintenance.

(ii) Entry in order to make an arrest without warrant for an arrestable or specified offence (s 17(1)(b) and (c), Art 19(1)(b) and (c))

4.33 At common law there is no general power for the police to enter premises without a warrant to make an arrest. Moreover, the courts will not construe a statutory power of arrest without a warrant as including a power of entry (*Morris v Beardmore* (1980), *Finnigan v Sandiford* (1981)). Parliament must confer the power expressly. (For the power to enter premises in order to require a breath test of the driver of a motor vehicle in an accident involving injury to a third party, or to arrest a person who fails a breath test or refuses to provide a sample of breath, see the Road Traffic Act 1988 s 6(6); Art 145(6) Road Traffic (Amendment) (N.I.) Order 1991). The common law did, however, permit entry in order to arrest a felon, and s 2(6) of the Criminal Law Act 1967 similarly allowed it for the more serious offences. Section 17(1)(b) (Art 19(1)(b)) preserves and extends this power for it applies to arrestable offences, and s 24 (Art 26) (see para 5.07, post) extends that concept to include common law offences and a number of statutory offences. If therefore an offence within this concept has been committed or is reasonably suspected to have been committed, a constable, who knows, or has reasonable grounds for believing (S 17(2)(a) Art 19(2)(a)), that a person known to have committed or reasonably suspected of having committed such an offence is to be found on premises, may enter, by force if necessary (s 117, Art 88), to arrest that person. It is essential that a constable exercising this power (a) has reasonable grounds for suspecting that an arrestable offence has been committed; and (b) reasonable grounds for believing that the person who has committed that offence is on the premises to be entered (see *Kynaston v DPP* (1987), *Chapman v DPP* (1988) and *Riley v DPP* (1990)). The power of entry under s 17(1)(b) (Art 19(1)(b)) is confined to 'arrestable offences' and does not therefore apply to those lesser offences for which s 25 offers a power of arrest (eg *Bailey v Wilson* (1968) — entry to prevent assault; *R v McKenzie and Davies* (1979) — entry to arrest under the Sexual Offences Act 1956). However, s 17(1)(c) (Art 19(1)(c)), which is slightly differently worded extends the power of entry to particular arrest powers mentioned in the subsection, which, though not arrestable offences, are seen as requiring a power to enter premises in order to effect the arrest. These are:

(i) The offence under s 1 of the Public Order Act 1936, the prohibition on the wearing of uniforms in connection with political objects. The power of arrest for this offence under s 7(3) of the 1936 Act is preserved by s 26(2) and Sch 2 of the PACE Act 1984. The other offences to which the section related have been repealed by the Public Order Act 1986. Sch 2, para 7 of the 1986 Act deletes the reference to these offences in s 17(c)(i) and adds the offence under s 4 of the 1986 Act, causing fear or provocation of violence. S 4(3) of the 1986 Act provides the power of arrest and s 17(1)(c) of the 1984 Act the power to enter premises in order to do so. Note that the Public Order Act 1986 creates two arrestable offences, riot (s 1) and violent disorder (s 2) for which there is a power of entry under s 17(1)(b), see para 5.31 post. (In Northern Ireland the offences under Art 9 (threatening words or behaviour) and Art 21 (wearing uniform in public) of the Public Order (N.I.) Order 1987 are arrestable under Art 24 of that Order and Art 19 of the PACE Order provides the power of entry onto premises in order to effect the arrest.)

(ii) The offences of 'squatting' created by ss 6, 7, 8, 9 and 10 of the Criminal Law Act 1977. The 1977 Act had supplied a power of entry. It was repealed by Sch 7, Part 1 and is replaced by s 17(1)(c)(ii). The power is only exercisable by a constable in uniform — s 17(3), since its exercise may be a matter of sensitive policing and a uniform is thought to reduce the possibility of physical resistance by squatters. S 9 of the 1977 Act created an offence of trespass on diplomatic premises and the power of arrest for such offence is preserved by s 26(2) and Sch 2 of the 1984 Act but, for obvious reasons, no power of entry on to such premises is given. (There is no equivalent provision in the Northern Ireland Order). Section 17(1)(c) (Art 19(1)(c)) places the offences mentioned therein on a par with arrestable offences as regards powers of entry to effect an arrest. However, they remain inferior in other respects. The wider investigative powers available on arrest for an arrestable offence under s 24, the powers of entry and search of premises under s 18 *following* an arrest for an arrestable offence, and the extended detention powers if a serious arrestable offence is involved are not available for the s 17(1)(c) offences. On the other hand, it should be noted that s 32 gives the constable power to enter and search the premises where a person has been arrested (or where he was immediately before arrest) and this power extends to a s 17(1)(c) offence. It is understandable that a power to enter is provided for squatting offences by s 17(1)(c). It is less so as regards the public order offences. The arrest and entry powers attached to offences under the Public Order Acts make them formidable weapons.

(iii) Entry in order to recapture a person who is unlawfully at large and whom a constable is pursuing (s 17(1)(d), Art 19(1)(d))

4.34 This power replaces the ancient but uncertain position at common law (see *Genner v Sparkes* (1704)). The reference to 'recapture' covers an escaped prisoner, an escaped mental health patient, an escaped illegal immigrant and an arrested person who has escaped from police custody. 'Pursuing' would clearly cover 'hot pursuit', as it did under the common law (*McLorie v Oxford* (1982)). But it may extend further so as to permit entry some days, months or even years after the escape. This literal reading of the sub-section is to be preferred, for it cannot be supposed that a constable who, for example, receives reliable information while on patrol that an escaped prisoner is hiding in certain premises some weeks after the escape, must seek a warrant or must rely on the consent of the occupier, before entering in order to arrest the person.

(iv) Entry in order to save life or limb, or to prevent serious damage to property (s 17(1)(e) Art 19(1)(e)), or to deal with or prevent a breach of the peace (s 17(6), Art 19(6))

4.35 Section 17(1)(e) (Art 19(1)(e)) seeks to reflect the common law, although the position was for long unclear. Early cases suggested a power of entry to prevent murder (*Handcock v Baker* (1800)) or to terminate an affray (*R v Walker* (1854)). In the only modern authority, the Divisional Court in *Swales v Cox* (1981) summarised, without discussion, the common law as permitting anyone to enter premises without a warrant to prevent murder, to apprehend a felon who had been followed there or to prevent an imminent felony, and as permitting a constable to enter in pursuit of an offender running away from an affray. Section 17(1)(e) (Art 19(1)(e)) adopts the crisp summary of this common law used by the Royal Commission (Report, para 3.38). The policy behind it is sensible, although it should be noted that there is no express requirement that the threat be seen by the constable as serious or urgent. It is, however, strongly arguable that the very nature of the power implies that such requirement be present. Furthermore, unlike the other entry powers in s 17 (Art 19), s 17(1)(e) (Art 19(1)(e)) is not subject to the procedural qualifications of s 17(2). To exempt it from s 17(2)(b) (Art 19(2)(b)) (limitation on search of premises comprised of two or more separate dwellings) is understandable given the sometimes urgent circumstances which may necessitate entry, and to exempt it from s 17(2)(a) (Art 19(2)(a)) (reasonable belief that the person is on the premises) is appropriate when the police are not seeking a person but, for example, a bomb on premises. However, this latter exemption removes from the power any standard of reasonableness and highlights its potentially speculative ambit eg the search of a football coach (being 'premises' under s 23 (Art 25)) when the police suspect offensive weapons but do not suspect any particular person. Furthermore there is no requirement that the threat to life, limb or property should concern the premises in question, eg the police can enter if they believe that the premises contain material such as burglary or arson equipment which may be used against other premises or if a person who has planted a bomb elsewhere is on the premises. The following examples illustrate the scope of s 17(1)(e) (Art 19(1)(e)):

(i) Entry in order to deal with or prevent child or wife-battery.

(ii) Entry into a block of flats where a kidnapper is believed to be. All the flats can be searched since the limiting definition of s 17(2)(b) (Art 19(2)(b)) does not apply.

(iii) Entry into the offices of a trade union or of an extreme political organisation where the police believe offensive weapons are kept, or are being prepared, for use at a picket line or at a political demonstration, though the police need not suspect that any individual culprits are present; vehicles and coaches fall within the definition of premises (s 23) and can thus be entered and searched under s 17(1)(e) (Art 19(1)(e)).

(iv) Where X, a known kidnapper or blackmailer, works for company Y, the latter's premises could be searched for evidence of X's whereabouts or modus operandi.

 (v) Entry to private premises in which a party is being held following a complaint from a guest that a drunken brawl is taking place or is threatened. (A public house, at least while open to the public, is a public place and no special entry powers are needed).
 (vi) Entry to a flat in which youths are believed to be making petrol bombs. A search warrant can be obtained if there are reasonable grounds to believe this is happening but s 17(1)(e) (Art 19(1)(e)) is not limited by that requirement.

This is a most useful power of entry which all police officers would do well to learn by heart. Ostensibly it is not novel since it aims to repeat the common law, but the position at common law was for so long obscure that the statutory elucidation could give impetus to its use. There is, however, no evidence of such use. In the research carried out by the authors only 5.6 per cent of entries were made under s 17 and only 1 of these was justified under s 17(1)(e).

4.36   Whilst s 17(5) (Art 19(4)) abolishes all common law powers to enter premises without a warrant, s 17(6) (Art 19(5)) retains any such power which is designed 'to deal with or prevent a breach of the peace'. Cases in the nineteenth century (*Timothy v Simpson* (1835), *R v Walker* (1854)) established a right of entry for a constable to deal with an actual breach of the peace. *Thomas v Sawkins* (1935) went further. Three police-men had attended a public meeting on private premises, organised to protest against the Incitement to Disaffection Bill and to call for the resignation of the local chief constable. The Divisional Court held that the police have the right to enter and remain on premises where they have reasonable grounds to apprehend that a breach of the peace is imminent or is likely to occur. In *McConnell v Chief Constable of Greater Manchester Police* (1990) the Court of Appeal (Civil Division) confirmed that a breach of the peace can take place on private premises for the purpose of entitling a constable, who genuinely suspected on good grounds that a breach of the peace may occur, to make an arrest. In *Lamb v DPP* (1989) the Divisional court held that a constable has an independent right at common law to remain on premises if he reasonably anticipates a breach of the peace on those premises. The constable, who accompanied a woman to the house in which she had lived with the occupier in order to recover her belongings, was told to leave by the occupier but remained standing in the garden by the kitchen door. The occupier attacked the woman in the kitchen. The constable entered in order to prevent a breach of the peace and was himself attacked. Magistrates, who had found the constable was a trespasser, asked the Divisional Court whether, in those circumstances, he was acting in the execution of his duty in remaining. Answering in the affirmative the Divisional Court appeared to be accepting that the constable was a trespasser, but in stating that he had an independent right to remain they seem to be saying that he was not, the common law right to remain and to enter the premises if the anticipated breach of the peace occurred, making his presence on the premises lawful. This is in line with *Thomas v Sawkins* (above) and confirms the breadth of the common law power. The retention of this power in the Police and Criminal Evidence Act (and also now in the N.I. Order) 'affords the police a desirable degree of flexibility in responding to situations requiring their urgent intervention but which are not readily susceptible to precise statutory definition'. (Notes accompanying the PACE Bill). It should be noted however that there is no common law requirement that the breach of the peace must be imminent or serious. Indeed, it may arise 'whenever harm is actually done or is likely to be done to a person or in his presence to his property or a person is in fear of being so harmed through an assault, an affray, a riot, unlawful assembly or other disturbance' (*R v Howell* (1981)). The Public Order Act 1986 (the Public Order (N.I.) Order 1987) puts into statutory form the common law offences of riot, and unlawful assembly and replaces much of the Public Order Act 1936, in particular the catch all offence in s 5 of the 1936 Act, which is now contained in ss 4 and 5 of the 1986 Act. This Act also leaves the common law unaffected which means that there remains a broad and flexible power, the parameters of which are, unlike the statutory offences, incapable of precise definition.

4.37 The compendium of powers in s 17(1)(c), (e) and (6) (Art 19(1)(c), (e) and (5)) thus arms the police with considerable ability to deal with and prevent breaches of the peace and the powers may well overlap with each other. S 17(1)(e) (Art 19(1)(e)) may be seen as directed towards the most serious and urgent threats to the peace (and it is not, after all, restrained by s 17(2) Art 19(2)) but as regards lesser disturbances it will overlap with the other powers, particularly in England and Wales that in s 4 of the 1986 Act. Since this offence may be committed in public or in private (there is an exception in relation to dwellings contained in s 4(2)) it is likely that greater reliance will be placed on the statutory offence with its concomitant power of entry in order to effect an arrest under s 17(1)(c)). The common law breach of the peace is, however, wider than the s 4 offence. The section 4 offence covers conduct intended to cause a person to believe that immediate unlawful violence will be used, or whereby that person is likely to believe that such violence will be used. The common law covers 'conduct which is itself a breach of the peace and no more' (*Marsh v Ascott* (1982)). Fortunately for the police officer, neither the Act nor Code of Practice requires him to specify to the occupier of the premises which power he is using; he need only claim therefore that he is 'investigating a breach of the peace' so as to justify his entry onto the premises.

These three powers are particularly useful in the preventive context, especially when it is recalled that they can be used against 'premises', as widely defined by s 23 (Art 25) (subject to the qualification in s 17(2) (Art 19(2)) as regards the s 17(1)(e) Art 19(1)(e)) power; see para 4.38(iii), post). Examples of this preventive object would include police attendance at political meetings (wheresoever held), sporting events, night clubs, private domestic disputes and 'blood sports' on private land where the presence of demonstrators is feared.

Procedural requirements for powers (a) to (d)

4.38 Only in relation to entry to arrest for squatting offences under the Criminal Law Act 1977 must the constable act in uniform (s 17(3), repealing s 11 of the 1977 Act). However, the use of uniformed officers may often be desirable under other entry powers as part of a policy of sensitive policing, eg entries and searches in ethnic neighbourhoods, and it is unfortunate that the Code of Practice does not mention the prudence of considering whether to use such officers. Except in relation to his powers under s 17(1)(e) (Art 19(1)(e)), a constable must generally act reasonably. In particular:

 (i) He can only enter and search if he has reasonable grounds to believe that the person sought is on the premises (s 17(2)(a) Art 19(2)(a)). As has been noted (see paras 2.03–04, ante), 'reasonable grounds to believe' is a high standard approaching certainty of belief that the person sought is on the premises to be entered. In practice a constable may then be tempted to rely on a lesser standard, but he should be aware of the fact that in this area he is more likely to be called upon to justify his actions than in many others, especially if force is used in order to gain entry.

 (ii) He can only search to the extent that is reasonably required (s 17(4) Art 19(3)). Since most of the powers in s 17 (Art 19) are directed against persons, a search of, for example, drawers and small cabinets would be unreasonable and therefore unlawful, and the occupier's remedy lies in an official complaint or the launching of a civil action. Any consequential conviction may be prejudiced by an unlawful search if the court decides to exclude the evidence obtained thereby (see para 4.41, post, in relation to the powers of seizure and para 2.44, ante). Section 17(4) (Art 19(3)) does not apply where entry and search are made in accordance with s 17(1)(e) (Art 19(1)(e)). Accordingly, for example, a search under the latter provision for explosives would justify, as well as require, a more detailed examination of the premises.

 (iii) Where the premises consist of separate dwellings eg a boarding house or block of flats, the constable (except in relation to s 17(1)(e) Art 19(1)(e); see para 4.35, ante) can only enter and search that dwelling in which he reasonably believes the person to be and any communal areas on the premises eg a bathroom, cloakroom, garden or leisure/community centre to be shared by the occupiers of a block of flats (s 17(2)(b) Art 19(2)(b)).

(iv) The constable may use reasonable force to enter and search the premises in relation to all the above-mentioned powers (s 117, Art 88). For a fuller discussion of reasonable force, see para 2.32, ante, and in the context of the search of premises para 4.48, post.

(v) Broad powers of seizure accompany the powers in s 17, see para 4.41, post.

Entry without warrant for certain other statutory purposes

4.39   There are some statutes which permit the police and/or other officials to enter premises without a warrant for purposes other than to make an arrest. Many of them are designed to enable the police or such officials to enter and 'keep an eye' on a particular activity, without the pretext of an arrest, and thus supervise an important public policy. For example, s 43(2) of the Gaming Act 1968 allows a constable to enter premises without warrant to examine whether the terms of a gaming licence are being observed. Section 17 of the PACE Act (Art 19 of the Order) is 'without prejudice' to these other enactments and they thus escape the procedural restraints of 17(2) and (4) (Art 19(2) and (3)). Relevant statutes (some have been replaced) are listed in Appendix 4 to the Royal Commission's Law and Procedure Volume. They include powers for the Department of Environment and the Inland Revenue and various sections of the Customs and Excise Acts and, since Parliament regularly adds to the list, there are many others (eg Bees Act 1980, the Licensing (Occasional Permissions) Act 1983, Water Act 1989, Food Safety Act 1990).

Entry and search by other officials and citizens

4.40   It should be remembered that Part II of the Act relates only to constables and therefore does not affect the many statutory powers which have been given to other officials to enter premises. Each continues to be governed by the terms of the empowering statute. Some allow the official to be accompanied by police officers (eg. British Fishing Boats Act 1983), some allow entry to search for and seize evidence (Companies Act 1985, s 448, as amended by the Companies Act 1989) and others are unrelated to search and seizure, for example, warrants reinforcing the power to inspect electricity meters or to cut off power supplies (Rights of Entry (Gas and Electricity Boards) Act 1954). This last example accounts for much of the magistrates' warrant-issuing function (see Lidstone, *Magisterial Review of the Pre-Trial Criminal Process*, ch 6). As to the rights of entry available to members of the public, these are based on old and uncertain common law. *Handcock v Baker* (1800) recognised a right of entry to prevent murder and, obiter, a felony and *Timothy v Simpson* (1835) can be construed as permitting entry to deal with a breach of the peace. The last two rights are, however, unclearly stated in the cases. *Swales v Cox* (1981) on the other hand accepted without argument that a citizen could enter premises without a warrant (1) to prevent murder, (2) to arrest a felon who has been followed to the premises, and (3) to prevent an imminent felony. (Police powers to enter premises to arrest and for the purposes mentioned above, are dealt with in s 17 of the PACE Act 1984 (Art 19 of the 1989 Order) discussed above). It will be seen from s 24(4) and (5) (see para 5.13, post) that the powers of a citizen to make an arrest are tied to the concept of an arrestable offence but they do not coincide precisely with his common law rights of entry.

Powers of seizure

4.41　May the police seize evidence of offences other than that for which they are searching? The common law gives an affirmative answer provided that the evidence implicates the person in a serious offence and the police act reasonably by, for example, not detaining such evidence for longer than is necessary (*Ghani v Jones* (1970)). The Royal Commission agreed that the police should be allowed to seize such additional evidence provided that it was evidence of a grave offence (Report, para 3.49). If it was not or if the police failed to observe the Commission's proposed procedure for searches, the evidence could not be used at trial. Such an exclusionary rule would be a departure for English law and was a controversial suggestion. As the Royal Commission observed, 'We appreciate that the obligatory exclusion of evidence at trial may appear an inflexible restriction, but the right of members of the public to be free from general searches must be respected' (Report, para 3.49). The Government appreciated this 'inflexible restriction' and pointed to:

(i)　the practical difficulties which a constable would face when he is searching for offence X and discovers evidence of offence Y and who must then decide if Y is a grave offence;

(ii)　the controls on police misbehaviour and unreasonable searches which are offered by ss 15, 16 (Arts 17, 18) and the Code of Practice.

The Act (and Order) therefore rejects an automatic exclusionary rule, permits the police to seize evidence of any offence whilst exercising their search powers, and then gives the trial court the power to exclude evidence in certain circumstances (s 78, Art 76).

Scope of seizure

4.42 Section 18(2) (Art 20(2)) allows the police to seize anything for which they are entitled to search under s 18 (Art 20), ie for the primary arrestable offence or some other arrestable offence which is connected with, or similar to, it. Section 8 (Art 10) carries its own seizure power for evidence of the offence mentioned in the warrant (s 8(2) Art 10(2)), as does a special procedure warrant (Sch 1, para 13 (para 10 N.I. Order)). For pre-1984 warrant powers the governing statute specifies what may be seized. Section 19 (Art 21 of the Order) of the 1984 Act is *in addition* to any of these other powers of seizure (s 19(5) Art 21(5)). It applies whenever a constable is lawfully on premises and when he does not already have a power of seizure. A constable need not be aware of the basis for his presence; he may barge in to arrest a person for an arrestable offence in total ignorance of the provisions of s 17(1)(b), (Art 19(1)(b)), but still be lawfully on the premises — see *Foster v Attard* (1985). He may, however, lose his lawfully present status if, for example, he was there with the occupier's consent and that consent is withdrawn. It is also arguable that a failure to comply with the requirements of ss 15 and 16 (Arts 17 and 18) in the application for or execution of a search warrant, renders the constable's presence on the premises unlawful. Thus if, having found the items mentioned in a search warrant, the officer continues with the search in breach of s 16(8) (Art 18(8)), his presence on the premises is no longer lawful. Section 19 is primarily directed towards items which the police discover *adventitiously*, eg the police enter premises by virtue of a search warrant issued under the Theft Act 1968 (Theft Act (N.I.) 1969). They can seize stolen goods (s 26(3)). If they stumble across evidence of a different offence, eg drugs, the evidence can be seized if s 19 (Art 21) is satisfied. It will be seen that s 19(2) and (3) (Arts 21(2) and (3)) supplement the powers of seizure under ss 8, 18 (Arts 10, 20) and other statutes. The only relevant sections of the 1984 Act (1989 Order) which do not carry their own seizure power are ss 17 and 32 (Arts 19, 34). Consequently s 19 (Art 21) applies particularly thereto. The references to 'anything' in the various seizure powers covers not only all forms of property but also an inanimate object such as fingerprints.

Power of search	Power of seizure
s 8 (Art 10)	s 8(2); s 19 (Art 21)
s 18 (Art 20)	s 18(2); s 19 (Art 21)
Schedule 1	Sch 1, para 13; s 19 (para 10; Art 21)
Other statutory warrant powers	Terms of the particular statute; s 19 (Art 21)

Any other power (ss 17, 32,   s 19 (Art 21)
Arts 19,34)

Whenever a constable is lawfully on premises he may, by virtue of s 19 (Art 21), seize anything which on reasonable grounds he believes:

  (i)   to be evidence of the offence which he is investigating (s 19(3)(a) Art 21(3)(a));
 (ii)   to have been obtained in consequence of *any* offence, eg during a search for drugs, he can seize the fruits of a theft such as a television set bought out of stolen money (s 19(2)(a) Art 21(2)(a));
(iii)   to be evidence of *any other offence* eg on searching the premises of a person arrested for theft, he can seize prohibited drugs implicating a person who shares the premises (s 19(3)(a) Art 21(3)(a)).

Section 19 (Art 21) applies to evidence of any offence, serious or minor. Section 8(4) (Art 10(4)) defines 'relevant evidence' as anything that would be admissible at a trial for an offence. The omission of the qualifying adjective 'relevant' in s 19(Art 21) suggests that 'evidence' is used in its popular sense of 'facts in support of' rather than its technical sense of 'admissible evidence'. There are, however, two limitations on the power of seizure. Firstly, the police must believe that seizure is necessary lest the article be 'concealed, lost, altered or destroyed' in relation to (i) and (iii) (s 19(3)(b)). As regards (ii), 'damaged' is added to the criteria (s 19(2)(b) the N.I. Order includes 'damaged' in (2) and (3)(b) suggesting that it was an unintended omission in s 19(3)(b)). This, if a photograph or copy of the article will suffice for the investigation (and copying facilities are available on the premises), that should be done (s 21(5) Art 22(5) gives the police the power to photograph or copy). Secondly, the constable cannot seize any articles which he has reasonable grounds to believe are subject to legal privilege (s 19(6) Art 21(6)). This limitation applies to *all* powers of seizure. An important consequence flows from the fact that legally privileged material is the only category of material exempt from seizure. That is that excluded or special procedure material is not immune from seizure if the police arc lawfully on premises, whether under search powers, or with consent to search or interview, or under a warrant which has not been obtained under the special procedure (Sch 1). The complexities of ss 9–14 (Arts 11–16) and Sch 1 can thus be avoided if one of these other search powers is employed or the constable is otherwise lawfully on the premises and he comes across such material. If the occupier or holder of the information objects to the seizure, he may face a charge of obstructing a constable in the execution of his duty. For example, if the police are searching a social worker's house under the authority of the Misuse of Drugs Act 1971 and come across evidence of the social worker, they can seize it, even though it may qualify as excluded material under s 12 (Art 13). Two further points may be noted:

(i) If the police discover evidence which is held by an innocent purchaser, the police must explain to the holder that he may face civil or criminal proceedings if he tries to part with it (Code of Practice, para 6.3). Such proceedings may take the form of an action for damages or a criminal prosecution for an offence of handling, theft or obtaining by deception, depending on the circumstances of possession and disposal. However, the innocent purchaser for value may in some circumstances obtain a title to the goods which then cease to be stolen (s 24(3) of the Theft Act 1968). He thus commits no offence if he disposes of those goods. Under a Sch 1 search, contempt proceedings can only follow deliberate disobedience of a court order for production (see par 4.75).

(ii) Even if the police search premises unlawfully (eg without a proper consent) and thus seize articles unlawfully, the articles may still be admissible in evidence, subject to s 78 (Art 76) (see para 2.48 ante). The police may also of course face a disciplinary charge or a civil action for their unlawful conduct.

Computers

4.43 Special provision is made for the seizure of information contained in computers. The phrase 'contained in a computer' must be read as including information stored on disc or tape which is not stored in the computer but is only accessible through the medium of a computer. Any other interpretation would exclude so much material as to render the provision virtually useless. It follows that the constable can seize a computer disc or tape or, if he only requires specific information which is on the disc or tape, a print-out of the relevant part (ss 19(4), 20 Art s 21(4), 22). However, the ease with which information can be concealed within a computer (eg by the use of trigger words before access is allowed) and the possibility that the computer on the premises is merely a local terminal for a central database held elsewhere mean that specialist officers will be needed to conduct the search, and that frequently a complete tape must be studied or taken away. Such officers will need to study the operating manual which governs the computer and to interview the computer controller and/or programmer. S 20 (Art 22) extends the s 19(4) (Art 21(4)) provision to all powers of seizure contained in any statutory provision passed or made before or after the 1984 Act (1989 Order) and to the powers of seizure under ss 8 and 18 (Arts 10 and 20) and to the power of seizure when executing a warrant to search for and seize excluded or special procedure material contained in paragraph 13 of Schedule 1 of the

1984 Act (para 10 of Sch 1 of the 1989 Order). Thus, whenever there is a statutory power to seize material, there is a statutory power to require a print-out of computerised information which has been obtained in consequence of an offence or, more usually, which is evidence of an offence, eg a constable executing a warrant under the Obscene Publications Act 1959 may, having seized obscene material, require a print-out of information contained in a computer about the source of the supply of such material.

Post-search and seizure

4.44 The following provisions apply whichever statutory power of seizure is used:

(i) *List of seized articles* (s 21(1), (2) Art 23(1) and (2)). — After seizing any article, the constable must, within a reasonable time, supply the occupier or custodian of the article with a record of what has been seized (cf the common law position, *Arias v Commission of Police of the Metropolis* (1984)). The obligation only arises however if that person requests it. The request may be made at the time of the seizure or subsequently. In searches involving the seizure of many documents, the 'reasonable time' for compiling the record may well be considerable.

(ii) *Owner's access to seized articles.* — The prospect of the police being allowed to seize evidence from innocent third parties and the controversy surrounding police access to confidential information alerted MPs to the disruption which seizure could cause to that party's business. The Government responded with s 21 (Art 23). This applies to all seized articles and permits the person who had custody or control of the article to apply to the police personally or through a representative (eg a lawyer) for (1) supervised access to the article, and/or (2) photographs or copies of the article. For small items the police can usually allow the owner to photograph or copy them under supervision (s 21(4)(a) Art 23(4)(a)); but large numbers of documents they can do so themselves 'within a reasonable time' (s 21(4)(b), (6), (7) Art 23(4)(b), (6), (7)) and can presumably charge the owner for the expense of doing so. However, the obligation to allow access to, or copying of, the articles can be avoided if the officer in charge of the investigation has reasonable grounds to believe that the investigation would be prejudiced thereby (s 21(8) Art 23(8)). There is no reference to 'serious' prejudice and this could tempt the police to deny access on the basis that lengthy documentary evidence is currently being examined and that the inconvenience of copying it or allowing access to it would hamper police investigations. However, the Code of Practice (para 6.9) requires that the grounds for refusal of access be recorded and they could thus be examined in subsequent proceedings under the Police (Property) Act 1897 (or challenged on judicial review, see *Allen v Chief Constable of Cheshire* (1988)). The 'investigation' in s 21(8) (Art 23(8)) which may be prejudiced can include those against other people, eg an investigation into D's alleged fraudulent activities may lead to investigations of his associates.

(iii) *Retention of seized articles.* — Articles may only be retained for as long as is necessary (s 22(2) Art 24(1)). What is 'necessary' will depend on the purposes for which they are held and s 22(2) (Art 24(2)) lists the most common —

    (a) For use as evidence at trial for *any* offence. For example, if the article is subsequently of no use to the police who seized it, it may be retained for the benefit of other agencies. The 'necessity' principle in s 22(1) (Art 24(1)) means that where a photograph or copy will suffice, the article should not be retained (s 22(4) Art 24(4), endorsing *Ghani v Jones* (1970)).

    (b) For forensic examination.

    (c) To establish the article's lawful owner when it is believed to have been obtained unlawfully.

    Other examples include retention for the purpose of an appeal, or where the return of property is against public policy: eg where D is acquitted of, or not prosecuted for, drug offences, it is clearly right for the police not to return the seized drugs. Some items seized for expedient reasons (eg weapons, articles for escape) cannot be retained once the person is released from police detention or custody of a court (s 22(3) (Art 24(3)).

(iv) *Remedies for impropriety.* — The owner's remedies for impropriety by the police consist of a civil action (see para 2.40, ante) and (i) a complaint under the police disciplinary code and procedure; and (ii) recourse to the Police (Property) Act 1897 if he believes that the police are unnecessarily retaining his property. By s 1 of that Act (and see further the Police (Disposal of Property) Regulations 1975, SI 1975 No 1474) he can apply to a magistrates' court for an order to return the property or to force the police to justify its retention. The Code of Practice B(para 6A) instructs the police to advise the owner of this procedure 'where appropriate'. This means where the owner or claimed owner has made it clear to the police that he objects to their retention of the property.

Examples of the various powers in operation

4.45   The following illustrate the operation of the powers thus far discussed and the consensual search. In all these situations the constable will be lawfully on premises for the purposes of s 19 (Art 21) and the powers of seizure provided will be available to the constable. All the examples are subject to the requirement of reasonable cause to suspect or believe as appropriate.

(a)   D, a self-employed businessman, is arrested while driving home from his office for an offence of fraud (an arrestable offence under s 24 (Art 26)). The car (premises within s 23 (Art 25)) may be searched for evidence of that, or a connected or similar offence (s 18 (Art 20)) being premises under his control; or under s 32(2)(b) (premises in which he was when or immediately before being arrested). D's house (premises occupied by him) may be searched (s 18, (Art 20)) as may his office (premises under his control). If during the search of any of these premises the police come across evidence of a totally different offence, eg child sex abuse, that may be seized under s 19 (Art 21). If evidence of the fraud is held by D's accountant it will be held in confidence and will be special procedure material as defined by s 14 (Art 16) (see para 4.63 post). A s 8 (Art 10) warrant cannot be issued to search for and seize the material, instead application must be made under s 9(1) (Art 11(1)) and Schedule 1 (see para 4.51 post). However, if D was arrested in the accountant's office, or immediately on leaving that office, the office may be searched for evidence of the fraud (s 32(2)(b) Art 34(2)(b)) and the material seized even though it is special procedure material.

(b)   D is disturbed while hooking dresses from racks in a clothing store by means of a flexible pole with a hook on the end, which he inserted through the letter box. He is seen to make off with a quantity of clothes and drive off in a car, the registration number of which is noted. The car belongs to a known criminal who lives in the area and who has a caravan in an adjoining police area. A watch is kept on both premises but the car is not at either. S 17(1)(b) (Art 19(1)(b)) is available to authorise entry to either premises to arrest D if, but only if, there are reasonable grounds for believing that D is on the premises. If D is arrested on the premises, s 32(2)(b) (Art 34(2)(b)) authorises the search of those premises for evidence of the offence for which he is arrested. If D is not on the premises, no search for evidence of the offence may be made except with the written consent of a person entitled to consent. If while searching for D the police come across garments which are believed to be those stolen (eg they look in a wardrobe in which a man may hide) they may be seized under s 19(3) (Art 21(3)). If there is reason to believe that D may not be on the premises, s 17 (Art 19) will not be available but a search warrant under s 26 of the Theft Act 1968 (s 25, Theft Act (Northern Ireland) 1969) may be sought if there are reasonable grounds to believe the stolen garments are on the premises. If D is seen driving the car, he may be arrested on reasonable suspicion of theft and his car (premises, s 23 (Art 25)) may be searched under s 18 (Art 20), or s 32(2)(b) (Art 34(2)(b)). D's house and caravan may be searched under s 18. (As an alternative to arresting D immediately, his car may be searched under s 1 PACE Act 1984 (Art 3 PACE (N.I.) Order 1989). If D's unattended car is found, the s 1 (Art 3) power is the only means of lawfully searching the car prior to D's arrest (see para 3.12 ante).

(c) D, who is reasonably suspected of committing a number of burglaries, is arrested while leaving the premises occupied by his girlfriend. Those premises may be searched under s 32(2)(b) (Art 34(2)(b)) and premises occupied by him, eg his home, may be searched under s 18 (Art 20).

(d) D, an unemployed youth, is arrested in the bedroom of a house in which the kitchen and living room are shared with other young persons, for possession of prohibited drugs. All the rooms in the house may be searched for evidence of that offence (s 32(2)(b) and (7), Art 34(2)(b) and (7)). If evidence of other offences is found in rooms occupied by D or the others, it may be seized under s 19 (Art 21).

(e) As in (d) but D occupies a self-contained flat and shares only the bathroom and toilet. Only his rooms and the bathroom and toilet may be searched, since he occupies a 'separate dwelling' (s 32(7) (Art 34(7)); see further para 4.03, ante).

(f) A number of youths are disturbed while in the course of a burglary and make off in several directions. One youth is spotted by a mobile patrol who gave chase. The youth runs into a greengrocer's shop. The police, exercising their s 17 (Art 19) power pursue him into the shop and find him hiding in a backyard toilet. No search of the premises for evidence takes place after the arrest, there being no reasonable belief that evidence of the offence would be found there. However, at the police station it emerges that the arrested youth had been carrying a radio cassette player when he left the scene of the burglary which, it was thought, he might have hidden on the greengrocer's premises. In these circumstances there is no statutory power to enter and search the premises. The s 32(2)(b) (Art 34(2)(b)) power is only available immediately after the arrest (*R v Badham* (1987)) and, since D does not occupy or control the premises, the s 18 (Art 20) power is not available. A search of the premises can therefore only take place with the consent of the occupier, in writing or, if such consent is not forthcoming, with the authority of a magistrates' warrant under s 26 of the Theft Act 1968 (s 25 Theft Act (N.I.) 1989).

(g) Police are called to a house by neighbours who heard screams and sounds of a fight. On arrival the police hear sounds of a fight. Their entry onto the premises is justified by s 17(1)(e) (Art 19(1)(e)). On entry they find a man who has been severely beaten. The occupants, a prostitute and another male, are arrested. The flat is searched under s 32(2)(b) (Art 34(2)(b)) and bloodstained clothing belonging to the occupants and the victim is seized. Some hours later the victim alleges that the woman had invited him to the house for sex. Having entered he was attacked by the male and female and robbed of £150. S 32(2)(b) (Art 34(2)(b)) is no longer available (*R v Badham* (1987)) but s 18 (Art 20) is, robbery being an arrestable offence, and the premises occupied by the arrested persons may be searched for the stolen money.

(h) A police officer investigating burglaries is making house to house inquiries. He is invited into a house by the occupier and while there he sees a video recorder which fits the description of one stolen in the burglaries. The occupier says she bought it off a man who said he had lost his job and was forced to sell some of his belongings. She paid a reasonable price. Even if the occupier is not guilty of handling stolen goods and is not arrested, the video recorder may be seized under s 19(3) (Art 21(3)). In the absence of an arrest no search can take place without written consent. If the occupier is arrested the premises may be searched for evidence related to the offence of handling eg other stolen goods.

Limitation on the extent of non-warrant searches

4.46 Premises may be searched only to the extent necessary to achieve the object of the search, having regard to the size and nature of whatever is sought (ss 17(4), 18(3) and 32(3) Arts 19(3), 20(3) and 34(3), COP, B, para 5.9) A similar provision applies to all warrant searches (s 16(8) Art 18(8)). All searches must therefore be commensurate with the size and nature of the material sought. 'Premises' may bear a narrower meaning in relation to ss 17 and 32 (ss 17(2), 32(7)). All searches 'must be conducted with due consideration for the property and privacy of the occupier . . . and with no more disturbance than necessary' (Code of Practice, para 5.10). The extent of the 'disturbance' will depend on the nature of the material sought, eg vehicles as opposed to cash. An occupier's remedy for an excessive search is to lodge a complaint and, in extreme cases, a civil action can be contemplated. To prevent such incidents, and to avoid allegations that the police have in other respects exceeded their powers or 'planted evidence', it is good police practice to ensure the presence of a third party, especially when the suspect is not present, eg if arrested and detained elsewhere and a search is undertaken under s 18 (Art 20). While there is no provision for a suspect to be present during such a search it is common practice in some police forces to take the suspect who is in custody with them on the search. This serves two purposes; (i) it prevents any allegation of 'planting' of evidence; and (ii) the suspect can save the police time by indicating where the property sought is. (It should be noted that questioning which is confined to the proper and effective conduct of a search is not an interview for the purposes of Code C (COP, C, Note For Guidance 11A)). If the search is conducted under s 18(5) (Art 20(5)) or s 32(2)(b) (Art 34(2)(b)) the suspect will be present. If the occupier wishes to ask a friend, neighbour or other person eg a solicitor, to witness the search he must be allowed to do so. COP, B, para 5.11 goes on to suggest that the occupier may not be allowed to do so if there are reasonable grounds for believing that this would seriously hinder the investigation. If the occupier is not under arrest, the police have no power to refuse to allow a third party to witness the search. If that person does in fact seek to hinder the search he may be committing the offence of obstructing the police in the execution of their duty. This should be sufficient sanction and if the occupier does seek to exercise this right, the Code provides that a search may not be unreasonably delayed for this purpose. There is, unfortunately, no obligation on the police to inform the occupier of this right. The Notice of Powers and Rights, which Code B 5.7 requires to be given to the occupier makes no reference to this right, therefore it will seldom be exercised.

Obtaining entry under ss 17, 18 or 32 (Arts 19, 20 or 34)

4.47   For all the forms of entry and search discussed above, other than entry and search under a warrant and with consent, the constable must attempt to communicate with the occupier or, adopting a tighter test than for warrants (see s 16(6); Art 18(6)), with 'any other person entitled to grant access to the premises' (COP, B, 5.4). (See the discussion of this term in the context of consent at para 4.27 ante). The officer in charge must explain the authority under which he seeks entry and ask the occupier to admit him. However, COP, B, 5.4 does not demand such pleasantries if (i) the premises are known to be unoccupied, or (ii) the occupier or person entitled to grant access are known to be absent; or (iii) there are reasonable grounds for believing that to alert the occupier would frustrate the search or endanger life, eg if the items sought are readily disposable, or the occupier or other person on the premises is believed to be dangerous. When the premises are occupied the officer must identify himself (by warrant number in terrorism cases, otherwise by name) and if not in uniform, show his warrant card, state the purpose of the search and the grounds for undertaking it before a search begins, unless (iii) above applies.

4.48 *Force.* — All the powers of entry and search, but not searches with consent, allow the police to use force if necessary (s 117 (Art 88)). For a fuller discussion of reasonable force, see para 2.32, ante. It can be noted in the present context that it must be shown that force is 'necessary'. Thus, if a constable is met by a householder, he must, even if he holds a warrant for arrest, seek permission to enter, for only if he is refused will force become 'necessary' (cf *Swales v Cox*, post). There are, however, many circumstances in which the constable is absolved from the need for such courtesies eg where the premises are not occupied (apart from the object of the search) by anyone who could give access to them, or where an armed man is pursued onto them. As to the meaning of 'force', the hallowed law of trespass means that 'force' may amount to very little effort. Thus, if a constable 'meets an obstacle, then he uses force if he applies any energy to the obstacle with a view to removing it. It would follow that, where there is a door which is ajar but is insufficiently ajar for someone to go through the opening without moving the door and energy is applied to that door to make it open further, force is being used. *A fortiori* force is used when the door is latched and you turn the handle from the outside and then ease the door open. Similarly, if someone opens any window or increases the opening in any window, or indeed dislodges the window by the application of any energy, he is using force to enter', *Swales v Cox* (1981). As to what is 'reasonable', this will obviously depend on all the circumstances and in particular the type and amount of resistance met. COP, B. 5.6 lists exhaustively the circumstances where force will be necessary:

(i) where access has been refused,
(ii) where it is not possible to communicate with the occupier so as to obtain access,
(iii) where one of the conditions in para 5.4 of the Code applies (see para 4.47 ante) eg the door must be broken down lest evidence be destroyed or lest a dangerous suspect be forewarned.

If force has been used against the premises, the officer in charge must make sure that they are secure before leaving (Code of Practice, para 5.12). On returning to the police station, the officer in charge of the search must make a record of any damage caused in the search register (see para 4.50 post). As to compensation, provided that the entry and use of force have been lawful, whether by warrant or otherwise, the occupier has no right to recompense for any damage caused on his premises.

Notice of powers and rights

4.49   The balancing of powers with safeguards is fine in principle but in practice fails because the citizen against whom the powers are exercised is all too often ignorant of both. COP, B, 5.7 attempts to redress the balance. An officer conducting a search to which the Code applies, that is all the entry and search powers discussed above, including warrant searches, must unless it is impracticable to do so, provide the occupier with a copy of a notice, termed 'A Notice of Powers and Rights'. The notice, which is in standard form comprising an original and a duplicate, must:

   (i) specify whether the search is made under a warrant or under one of the PACE Act (Order) powers. Provision is made on the notice for the signature of the person giving consent to be appended. This suggests that the information required to be given when seeking consent (see COP 4.2) should be given orally and the written authority, if practicable, be given on the notice;

  (ii) summarise the extent of the powers of search and seizure conferred by the PACE Act (Order);

 (iii) explain the rights of the occupier, and of the owner of property seized in accordance with COP, B, 6.1–5 (see s 19 (Art 21)), set out in the Act (Order) and Code;

 (iv) explain that compensation may be payable in appropriate cases for damage caused in entering and searching the premises, and giving the address to which an application for compensation should be directed; and

  (v) state that a copy of the Code of Practice is available for consultation at any police station.

If the occupier is present, the notice should, if practicable, be given to the occupier before the search begins (together with the warrant if a warrant search). While the Act and Code do not require the constable to allow the occupier time to assimilate the contents of the notice (and the warrant), the purpose behind the notice will not be accomplished unless such time is given. Where force or subterfuge is used to gain entry, it may be necessary to secure the premises so as to ensure that the property sought is not disposed of before providing the information required by COP, B, 5.5 and the Notice of Powers and Rights (cf *R v Longman* (1988) discussed at para 4.18 ante), but whenever the occupier is present the information and notice should by analogy to the warrant, be provided before the search begins. If the occupier is not present a copy of the notice (and copy warrant if appropriate) must be endorsed with the name of the officer in charge of the search (warrant number only if a terrorism investigation), the police station to which he is attached and the date and time of the search. (If a warrant search the warrant must be endorsed to show that this has been done). The notice (and warrant if appropriate) must then be left in a prominent place on the premises. The original of the notice should be retained and appended to the Premises Searched Register.

Premises searched register

4.50   Code, B, 8.1 stipulates that a search register be maintained at each sub-divisional police station, in which all records required by the Code are to be entered. Code, B, 7.1 sets out the matters to be included in the register. These include, the address of the premises searched; the time and date of the search; the authority under which the search was made; a list of the articles seized; whether force was used and details of any damage caused. A copy of the warrant or consent where appropriate must be appended to the register or a note made in the register of where they are kept. As indicated in para 4.27, ante, the written consent will normally be contained in the Notice of Powers and Rights. The original of this notice should then, and in all other searches, be appended to the search register.

PART B

B.   Special powers to obtain material or to search premises (s 9 (Art 11) and Sch 1 of the PACE Act and Order)

4.51   Before the PACE Act 1984 the police lacked a general power to obtain material which was likely to be relevant evidence of an offence by A but was in the possession of B who was not himself implicated in the crime. If the material happened to be prohibited articles which it was an offence to possess, such as stolen goods, drugs, firearms etc, a search warrant could be obtained to search for and seize the material even if it was innocently possessed by B. If not within that category there was no general power to obtain access to such material. An exception is provided by the Bankers' Books Evidence Act 1879. Under this Act a High Court Judge may order the inspection of any entries in a banker's books, on application by a party to civil or criminal proceedings. This procedure is, however, of limited use as an investigative tool. First it is confined to banks, second to banker's books (this includes computerised accounts but not bank manager's notes or diary or paid cheques and credit slips) and third, to current legal proceedings, in other words a charge must have been laid or a summons issued (see para 4.121, post). Banks could not consent to requests by the police for access to material not covered by the

Act because to do so would lay them open to an action for breach of confidentiality (a banker's duty of confidentiality being firmly established in *Tournier v National Provincial and Union Bank of England* (1924)). If that duty did not extend to bank manager's notes, banks feared that they might be exposed to an action for defamation if such notes were surrendered voluntarily. Alternatively such cooperation with the police might lead to loss of custom. If legally compelled to disclose information no civil action could follow and, it was thought, customers would understand the necessity to comply with the law. The Royal Commission (1981) recognised this dilemma, which was not confined to banks, when it observed

> 'It is only rarely that the police do not receive consent to enter when looking for evidence . . . However where property or information is held on a confidential basis the holder may be unwilling to disclose it for fear of being sued for breach of duty by the person from whom he received it. Where consent is not immediately forthcoming there may be some temptation for the police to resort to bluff or trickery to obtain the evidence. At present there are few statutory provisions allowing the police to search for evidence during an investigation . . . We consider that there will be rare circumstances where a compulsory power is needed, and should be available to the police before a charge. But . . . we think that it should be a limited power and one subject to stringent safeguards.' (Report, para 3.41.)

4.52 As for other evidence held by third parties, s 8 (Art 10) now gives the police the opportunity to apply for a search warrant if any serious arrestable offence is involved. The confidential basis which might be jeopardised by such searches aroused considerable furore during passage of the 1984 Bill and forced the Government to make concessions so as to protect confidential information. Sections 9 to 14 (Arts 11-16) and Sch 1 were the result of this modification. The attempted balancing of the rights of the citizen and the needs of the police service result in much complexity. In essence three new categories of material were created. The first of these, legally privileged material, is always unavailable to the police unless the client, whose privilege it is, surrenders it and permits the police access to the material. The second category, excluded material, may also be given its literal meaning. In exceptional circumstances a circuit judge (county court judge in Northern Ireland) may make an order for the production to a constable of, or issue a warrant to search for and seize, excluded material. This is rare and will be considered later (para 4.74 post). Subject to this exception excluded material cannot be the subject of a magistrate's warrant or a judicial order permitting police access to it. Access can, however, more readily be obtained to the third category of material, special procedure material. As the name implies the 1984 Act (1989 Order) created a special procedure under which application may be made to a circuit judge (county court judge) for an order requiring the person in possession of the material to produce it to a constable for him to take away, or give him access to it. (These procedures can be circumvented and excluded and special procedure material can be searched for and seized using the powers under s 32(2)(b) (Art 34(2)(b)) and s 19 (Art 21). See para 4.45 example (a).) The complexity of these provisions suggested that little use would be made of them, however, their introduction coincided with an upsurge in offences of fraud much of which resulted from the economic boom of the early 80s. This led to a massive increase in mortgage lending in which banks plunged into a market previously the province of building societies. This provided opportunities for fraud which were seized upon. Government privatisation schemes were similarly seized upon by those who saw the opportunity to make a quick profit regardless of the legality. Much of the responsibility for investigating these offences fell to the Metropolitan Police and City Company Fraud Department which pioneered the use of the power provided by s 9 (Art 11) and Schedule 1 of the 1984 Act (1989 Order) and it is in this area that the real impact of Part II of the PACE Act (Part III of the PACE Order) is to be seen. Similar (but not identical) powers are also provided by the Drug Trafficking Offences Act 1986, the Prevention of Terrorism (Temporary Provisions) Act 1989, and the Criminal Justice Act 1988. The definition of the three categories of material are considered below and the procedure set out in Schedule 1 of the 1984 Act (1989 Order). The similar powers mentioned above will then be considered in Part C. Figure 2 shows in schematic form the routes to be taken to obtain an order or warrant permitting access to, or the search for, material which is evidence of a serious arrestable offence.

4.53 General preliminary points should be borne in mind:

(i) The onus is very much *on the police* to check, *before applying for a warrant*, whether it will involve excluded or special procedure material, for once the police are in possession of a warrant, and have gained access to premises, the occupier of premises cannot prevent them from seizing material under s 19 (Art 21). Only legally privileged material is totally exempt from seizure.

(ii) Where the following provisions apply, the holder of the confidential information may well be placed in an extremely uncomfortable moral position. If he refuses to disclose it, he will probably face the prospect of a hearing before a Crown Court under Sch 1. If he does disclose it, he breaks the confidence owing to his client. However, the latter course may be encouraged in the knowledge that the equitable doctrine of confidence does not protect information which is required by statute to be disclosed or whose non-disclosure is contrary to the public interest such as material relevant to the investigation of a criminal offence, and that disclosure would not therefore expose him to civil liability.

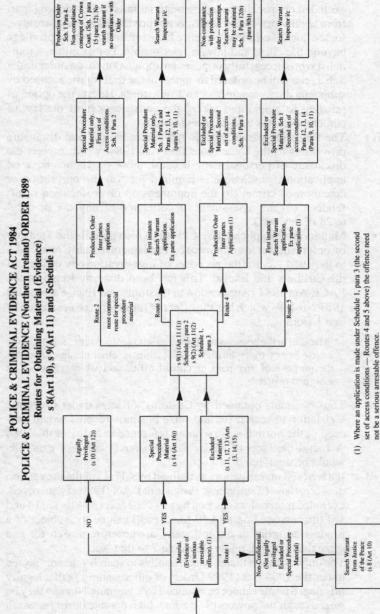

POLICE & CRIMINAL EVIDENCE ACT 1984
POLICE & CRIMINAL EVIDENCE (Northern Ireland) ORDER 1989
Routes for Obtaining Material (Evidence)
s 8(Art 10), s 9(Art 11) and Schedule 1

(1) Where an application is made under Schedule 1, para 3 (the second set of access conditions — Routes 4 and 5 above) the offence need not be a serious arrestable offence.

(iii) Even if an application by the police under Sch 1 to search for excluded or special procedure material fails, the evidence (apart from legally privileged items) is not privileged at the *trial stage*, for the laws of criminal evidence have refused to extend privilege beyond the client and lawyer relationship. For example, a journalist who successfully opposes an application for an order under Sch 1, can still be ordered to appear at the trial for the accused by subpoena duces tecum, as can any witness. He has the option of refusing to attend and taking the consequences of the law of contempt (cf *AG v Mulholland* (1963)).

(iv) The following paragraphs do not contradict the non-disclosure provisions of the Data Protection Act 1984, which protect the disclosure of personal data, because those provisions have no application if disclosure is required for '(a) the prevention or detection of crime; (b) the apprehension or prosecution of offenders; (c) the assessment or collection of any tax or duty' (s 28 of that Act).

(v) Matters are complicated by s 114(2) which permits the Treasury by order (subject to annulment by Parliament) to add a new s 14A to the 1984 Act for the purposes of investigations by officers of the Customs and Excise. This has been done by Reg 6 of the PACE Act 1984 (Application to Customs and Excise Order (SI 1987 No 439) which has the effect of removing the protection of Sch 1 from

> 'Material in the possession of persons who acquired or created it in the course of any trade, business, profession, or other occupation or for the purpose of any paid or unpaid office and which relate to an assigned matter.'

Thus, warrants obtained by Customs' officers under Customs' legislation to search for and seize business records would proceed in the normal way, without reference to Sch 1 of the 1984 Act, and the facts of *IRC v Rossminster* (1980), for example, would be unaffected.

(vi) If a terrorist investigation, as defined by s 17(1) of the Prevention of Terrorism (Temporary Provisions) Act 1989, is involved, excluded material, as defined by ss 11, 12 and 13 (Arts 13, 14 and 15) (discussed at paras 4.59 to 62 post) can be the subject of a production order or exceptionally a warrant to search for and seize the material, under Schedule 7 to that Act.

(vii) The only common factor which applies to search warrants issued under the 1984 Act (1989 Order) or other statutes is that legally privileged items cannot be obtained by a warrant. Nor can they be seized under the powers of seizure which operate during a search of premises (s 19(6) Art 21(6)).

(viii) Material obtained by compulsory powers provided for the investigation and prosecution of crime is held by the police under a duty of confidence and must not be disclosed to third parties unless

(a) a *subpoena duces tecum* is issued against the police requiring the production in court of documents seized; or

(b) the material is in the public domain (for example, documents have been read out in court) when the duty of confidence no longer exists.

Where a *subpoena* has been served the police should not disclose seized documents in advance of the attendance at court without giving the owner of the documents notice of the *subpoena* and a reasonable opportunity to state his objection.

Marcel v Commissioner of the Police of the Metropolis (1991).

In *Tate Access Floors Inc and another v Boswell and Others* (1990) it was held that an Anton Piller order, compelling a defendant to disclose documents and information, could not be made when the civil proceedings involved an allegation of facts which could give rise to a criminal charge, because it would infringe the defendant's privilege against self-incrimination. In *Marcel* (above) it was said that the privilege against self-incrimination was not available to the respondent when the documents were in the possession of the police. If, however, the police exercise their PACE Act (Order) powers, the documents obtained may be available to a party to a civil action by the issue of a *subpoena duces tecum*.

4.54 It is appropriate here to remind the reader that there are five categories of material which need to be distinguished.

(i) Material covered by pre-1984 (1989) statutory warrant powers.

(ii) Material which can be obtained under s 8 of the 1984 Act (Art 10 1989 Order).

(iii) Special procedure material defined by s 14 (Art 16); obtainable only in accordance with Sch I under either set of access conditions set out in the Schedule.

(iv) Excluded material, defined by ss 11, 12 and 13 of the Act (Arts 13, 14 and 15 of the Order); unobtainable unless another statutory warrant power exists and the special procedure is followed.

(v) Legally privileged material, defined by s 10 (Art 12), unobtainable under any statutory power.

The following paragraphs are concerned with (iii) to (v). Schematically, the procedure is as follows:

Material	*Authority*	*Procedure*
Special procedure material not obtainable under pre-existing powers	S 9(1),Sch 1, para 2, 1984 Act (Art 11, 1989 Order)	Application to a circuit judge (county court judge)
Special procedure material obtainable under pre-existing powers	Sch 1, para 3, 1984 Act (Sch 1, para 3, 1989 Order)	Application to a circuit judge (county court judge)
Excluded material not obtainable under pre-existing powers	S 9(1), 1984 Act (Art 11(1) 1989 Order)	Unobtainable*
Excluded material obtainable under pre-existing powers	Sch 1, para 3, 1984 Act (Sch 1, para 3 1989 Order)	Application to a circuit judge (county court judge)
Legally privileged material	Ss 8(1),9(2), 1984 Act (Arts 10, 11(2) 1989 Order)	Unobtainable*
Any material, other than legally privileged material, sought for customs and excise purposes	Customs and Excise legislation	Obtainable by warrant regardless of the 1984 Act's (1989 Order's) provisions on excluded and special procedure material
Excluded or special procedure material relating to a terrorist offence	Sch 7, Prevention of Terrorism (Temporary Provisions) Act 1989	Obtainable by order of a circuit (county court) judge or by warrant of such a judge
Any material, other than legally privileged or excluded material, relating to drug trafficking offences	Ss 27, 28, Drug Trafficking Offences Act 1986	Obtainable by order of a circuit judge or a search warrant issued by by such a judge

*NB While s 9(2) (Art 11(2)) prevents the use of search warrants under statutory provisions existing before the 1984 Act (1989 Order) to search for legally privileged, excluded or special procedure material, search warrants in statutes passed after the 1984 Act (1989 Order) may not do so, eg the Cinemas Act 1985 s 13(3) does include the above prohibition while the Public Order Act 1986, s 24 does not (see para 4.74, note 2, post).

Items subject to legal privilege (s 10 (Art 12))

4.55 Since this material is most often to be found in the possession of members of the legal profession one may expect disputes as to whether the material sought is legally privileged material. If it is *not*, the material is likely to be held in confidence and therefore special procedure material and subject to the procedure outlined below (para 4.67-78, post). If it is, there is no lawful procedure in English law by which a person can be compelled to produce or give access to the material and it cannot be seized during a search of premises. The common law of evidence has long recognised a privilege against the compulsory disclosure of a party's legal advice in both civil and criminal proceedings. The 1984 Act (1989 Order) extends this protection to the pre-trial investigative stage and clarifies the common law which, following the decision in *Frank Truman Export Ltd v MPC* (1977), was unclear. As regards warrants issued by virtue of the 1984 Act (1989 Order), the exemption for legally privileged material is simply stated (s 8(1)(d); Art 10(1)(d)). As regards warrants issued under statutory provisions which pre-date the 1984 Act (1989 Order), the same result is achieved by a more obscure route. S 9(2) (Art 11(2)) nullifies all such provisions as regards legally privileged, excluded and special procedure material. Schedule 1 provides a procedure under which access to special procedure material and, exceptionally, excluded material may be obtained but makes no such provision for legally privileged material. As regards statutory provisions which post-date the 1984 Act (1989 Order) they are not subject to the nullification process of s 9(2) (Art 11(2)) unless the statute providing the warrant power incorporates s 9(2) eg the Cinemas Act 1985 does, the Public Order Act 1986 does not. It is, however, inconceivable that such statutes will be interpreted as permitting entry to premises to search for and seize legally privileged material. The privilege is thus secured. Furthermore, the definition which follows has a wider relevance since the privilege applies to limit the general powers of seizure set out in s 19 (Art 21) (see para 4.41, ante).

Definition of legal privilege

4.56 The definition of legal privilege in s 10 (Art 12) follows that of the

16th Report of the Law Reform Committee (para 17), which in turn sought to reflect the common law. Legal privilege attaches to the following items when in the possession of a person who is entitled to possession of them. First, communications between a professional legal adviser and his client, or any person representing his client, *made in connection with the giving of legal advice to the client.* This advice need not be related to any legal proceedings. Secondly, communications between a professional legal adviser and his client, or any person representing his client or between any of these three and a third person, *made in connection with or in contemplation of and for the purposes of legal proceedings.* Thirdly, privilege attaches to items enclosed with or referred to in either of the above communications, and *made in connection with the giving of legal advice or in connection with or in contemplation of and for the purposes of legal proceedings.* The relationship of lawyer/client may be seen as a closed circle. It is only communications arising within that relationship which are made for the purposes of giving legal advice or which are made in connection with or in contemplation of legal proceedings and for the purposes of those proceedings which are privileged. Similarly items enclosed with such communications are only privileged if they are made within that relationship in connection with the giving of legal advice or in connection with or in contemplation of legal proceedings and for the purposes of those proceedings. Materials which, though made within a solicitor/client relationship but which are not concerned with the giving of legal advice or legal proceedings actual or contemplated, are not privileged. For example, in *R v Inner London Crown Court, ex p Baines and Baines* (1988) it was held that material consisting simply of documents relating to the financing and purchase of a house (conveyancing material) was not legally privileged. Thus what might be described as the commercial activities of a solicitor do not necessarily give rise to legal privilege, though such material will almost always be special procedure material. Material which was in existence before the relationship came into being does not become legally privileged by being brought into the relationship whether by the client or a third party (*Ventouris v Mountain* (1991)). In *R v Guildhall Magistrates, ex parte Primlak Holdings Co (Panama) Ltd* (1989) police obtained warrants under s 8 of the 1984 Act to search for and seize documents in the possession of two firms of solicitors which related to the sale of vessels by the collapsed bankers, Johnson Matthey. The magistrate was persuaded that because offences of false accounting had been committed, the documents did not attract legal privilege because of s 10(2) (see below). A judicial review of the decision to issue the warrants succeeded (see para 4.11 ante). Arguably s 10(2) was of no relevance in this case. Legal privilege probably did not apply to the documents either because they related to commercial rather than legal matters, or because they were original documents not made within the lawyer/client relationship for the purposes of legal advice or legal proceedings.

Thus if D, who has been charged with forgery, passes documents alleged to have been forged to his legal adviser, those documents are not legally privileged. If they are passed to an expert for his opinion, they remain unprivileged but the report made by the expert is privileged being made within the relationship and for the purposes of legal proceedings. The forged documents could but for s 9(2) (Art 11) have been the subject of a search warrant under s 7 of the Forgery and Counterfeiting Act 1981 but the document, though forged, is special procedure material in the hands of the solicitor (see para 4.63, post). Section 9(2) (Art 11(2)) takes away the power of a magistrate to issue a warrant under that Act for special procedure material. Instead application must be made to a circuit judge (county court judge in NI) under Schedule 1, para 3 (the second set of access conditions discussed at para 4.74, post) for an order requiring the solicitor to produce the documents to a constable. If the conditions in Schedule 1, paras 12 and 14 (paras 9 and 11 in N.I.) are satisfied a warrant to enter and search the premises may be issued (see para 4.75, post). The same principle applies to 'items enclosed with or referred to in such communications' (s 10(1)(c); Art 12(1)(c)). For example, D is charged with making a hoax bomb warning call. His solicitor obtains a tape-recording of the call. He requires his client to make another tape using the same words, which he sends to an expert, with the original tape, for comparison. Only the tape made by the client at his solicitor's request is privileged, as is any communication sent with the tape and the expert's report. Should the police wish to obtain the original tape and consent is not forthcoming they may make application under Schedule 1, para 2 (the first set of access conditions discussed at para 4.73, post).

Furthering a criminal purpose (s 10(2); Art 12(2))

4.57 Items held with the intention of furthering a criminal purpose are not items subject to legal privilege. Copies of letters containing legal advice, given in good faith, warning a client of risky conduct which he is contemplating is not within s 10(2) (Art 12(2) (*Butler v Board of Trade* (1971)). In *R v The Central Criminal Court ex p Francis and Francis* (1988) it was held that 'intention' in s 10(2) (Art 12(2)) may include that of a client or third party, reflecting the position at common law as laid down in *R v Cox and Railton* (1884). A production order had been made against a firm of solicitors under s 27 of the Drug Trafficking Offences Act 1986 (the procedure is similar to that under Schedule 1 of the 1984 Act (1989 Order) and the definition of legally privileged, excluded and special procedure material has the same meaning as in the 1984 Act (1989 Order)). The order required the solicitors to give the police access to correspondence and attendance notes in respect of property transactions entered into by a client. Police suspected that the client was being used as the innocent dupe of a relative who was using the client as a a means of salting away the proceeds of drug trafficking. The Divisional Court refused an application for judicial review of the decision to issue the production order holding that the documents were held with the intention of furthering a criminal purpose within s 10(2), even though the criminal intention was not that of the solicitor or client but of a third party. The House of Lords (Lords Bridge and Oliver dissenting) upheld the Divisional Court. In doing so the majority rejected the literal interpretation of s 10(2) by the Divisional Court in *R v Snaresbrook Crown Court, ex parte DPP* (1988) when refusing an order for production of a legal aid application in the possession of the Law Society, which the police believed would support a prosecution of the applicant (who was suing the police for assault) for perverting the course of justice. Glidewell LJ held that the application for legal aid came within s 10(1) even if it contained untrue statements. The 'intention of furthering a criminal purpose', which would deprive the document of its legal privilege must, he held, be that of the person holding the material, the Law Society in that case, which clearly had no such intention. The majority of their Lordships in *Francis* thought that such an interpretation would frustrate the main purpose of Part II of the 1984 Act. The belief that the legislature could not have intended to restrict the effect of s 10(2), and therefore the power of the police to detect crime by confining it to cases where the solicitor had the intention to further a criminal purpose, together with the need to interpret the section so as to reflect the common law, persuaded the majority to 'improve' upon the words of the section and to reflect what was almost certainly the intention of Parliament. The fact that the privilege is that of the client, not of the solicitor, supports their Lordships' view that the client's intention (or that of a third person using the client) to further a criminal purpose should negate the privilege. The majority in rejecting the literal interpretation of the section in *R v Snaresbrook Crown Court* (1988) thought that it did not necessarily undermine that decision. Lord Goff took the view that legal privilege would not be lost under s 10(2) (Art 12(2)) where a communication made by a client to his solicitor contained untrue statements which, if acted upon, could lead to a prosecution for perjury. One may accept this insofar as it refers to the position before trial but the privilege must surely be lost in relation to proceedings for perjury arising out of the evidence given at the trial. The decision in *Dubai Bank Ltd v Galadari and Others (No 6)* (1991), that communications in furtherance of a crime or fraud were not protected from disclosure if they were relevant to an issue in the action, whether or not the plaintiff's claim was founded on that crime or fraud, strongly supports the decision in *Francis* and the view expressed above. One may also note that the court has jurisdiction to give a solicitor directions as to how they should continue to deal with funds and assets held or controlled on behalf of a client against whom there is prima facie evidence that he had obtained them fraudulently. Such directions could include notifying third parties who might have a claim against the client or his assets (and possibly the police investigating the fraud), notwithstanding the solicitors' professional duty of confidentiality toward their client (see *Finers and Others v Miro* (1990)). The Law Society's view is that the decision in Francis is to be narrowly construed as being limited to the situation in which the client is being used as intermediary or an innocent tool by third parties, but the breach made in the wall of legal privilege may be much wider.

4.58 The broad definition of legal privilege in s 10 extends to all searches (including that by consent), since s 19 (Art 21) excludes legally privileged material from the powers of seizure which operate during a search of premises. However, s 19 (Art 21) does not prohibit the use at trial of any legally privileged material which is seized. Moreover, the common law allows evidence, including that subject to legal privilege, to be used at trial howsoever it has been obtained (*Calcraft v Guest* (1898); *Butler v Board of Trade* (1971)). Thus at common law, if the police exceed their search powers and seize legally privileged material, or even steal it, the material can be used in a subsequent prosecution. On the other hand, since the police have no power to seize such material (s 19(6) (Art 21(6)) and hence no power to retain it, it is possible for the owner to take prompt legal action to recover it (see the facts of *Inland Revenue Commissioners v Rossminster* (1980)). The only other safeguard is the court's discretion under s 78 (Art 76) to exclude improperly obtained evidence. As indicated in para 2.48 ante, the courts have, with some exceptions exercised their discretion only in respect of confessional evidence. However, if the police were to seize communications between a client and his solicitor during a search of the client's house and seek to use these at the trial for the offence in respect of which the client consulted the solicitor, it would be tantamount to denying the accused his 'fundamental right' to consult a solicitor and must have 'such an adverse effect on the fairness of the trial' as to justify its exclusion.

Excluded material (ss 11–13; Arts 13–15)

4.59 Ss 11 to 13 (Arts 13 to 15) contain the definition of excluded material. The material covered may, with the exception of 'journalistic material', be described as personal and confidential material. Such material will rarely be of evidential value; but even when it is and even when a most serious crime is under investigation, the legislature decided that the proper balance between the public interest in the detection of crime and the privacy of the individual lay in excluding access to such material, except where a warrant could previously have been issued authorising the search for and seizure of such material (see the discussion of s 9(2) (Art 11(2)) para 4.74, post. Such material is not protected from search and seizure by Customs and Excise — see para 4.53(v), ante.) Excluded material consists of three sub-categories:

(a)   personal records;
(b)   human tissue or tissue fluid taken for the purpose of diagnosis or medical treatment;
(c)   journalistic material (s 11 (Art 13)).

Two preliminary points may be noted:

(i)   There is a degree of overlapping in these provisions. For example, a doctor's records of a patient can fall within s 11(1)(a) or (b); those held by a social worker could fall within any of the categories in s 12.

(ii)   A common theme in s 11 (Art 13) is the element of confidentiality required before material can be regarded as 'excluded'. The law on confidence is uncertain and embryonic. Confidentiality may be express, eg an undertaking signed by a counselling agency before advice is given. More often it will arise by implication, eg a doctor's relationship with a patient imports confidentiality by custom rather than any express undertaking. 'Implication' may mean that a third party can be subject to a confidence if he knows or ought to know that the relevant information is confidential, eg a marriage counsellor or priest who is passed documents by X relating to Y (*Seager v Copydex* (1967), *Coco v Clark* (1969)). The degree to which the general law of confidence applies to s 11 (Art 13) is unclear. If it does, it has been held that a confidence cannot attach to information which is already in the public domain, but it can if the information can only be discovered after considerable research (*Schering Chemicals v Falkman* (1981)). Thus, a journalist who thoroughly researches for an article on the financial operations of a company could claim that his material is held in confidence even though that material could be discovered by any diligent research of published statistics and articles. Again, if the general law of confidence applies, a principle of that law is that there is no 'confidence in iniquity', eg a criminal pursuit, and therefore one party to such a confidence cannot sue if the other discloses it (*Gartside v Outram* (1856), *Initial Services v Putterill* (1968)). This would enable the police to nullify in large measure the scope of s 11 (Art 13) by simply arguing that the relevant material concerns a serious arrestable offence under investigation, is not confidential in the first place, and therefore the material is not protected from search and seizure and may, with the exception of journalistic material, be the subject of a warrant under s 8 (Art 10). Unlike the other material referred to, journalistic material which is not held in confidence, though not excluded material, is special procedure material and is subject to the Sch 1 procedure (see para 4.67, post).

(1) *Personal Records cs 11(1)(a), s 12; Art 13(1)(a), Art 14)*

4.60 This covers personal records which a person has acquired or created in the course of any trade, business, profession or any other occupation or for the purpose of any paid or unpaid office and which he holds in confidence. S 12 (Art 14) defines 'personal records' as documentary and other (eg computerised) records concerning an individual (whether living or dead) who can be identified from them and relating

(a) to his physical or mental health;
(b) to spiritual counselling or assistance given or to be given to him; or
(c) to the counselling or assistance given or to be given to him, for the purposes of his personal welfare, by any voluntary organisation or by any individual who -

    (i) by reason of his office or occupation has responsibility for his personal welfare; or
    (ii) by reason of an order of the court has responsibilities for his supervision.

This is a comprehensive definition. The 'personal records' may be 'acquired' eg by a social worker through dealings with a client; or 'created' eg by a psychiatrist or probation officer during the course of advice to a client. The following points may be noted:

(i) The excluded material consists of 'documents and other records' (s 12 (Art 14)). 'Document' has the same meaning as given in s 10 of the Civil Evidence Act 1968 (s 118(1)) (Part I of the Civil Evidence Act (NI) 1971 (Art 2)) and therefore includes a photograph, disc, tape, film or microfilm. Given this broad non-exclusive definition, the phrase 'other records' as used here and in s 11(c) (Art 13(c)) appears to be superfluous.

(ii) The records need not consist solely of excluded material. For example, a social worker's records may contain much information which is neither confidential nor related to a client's personal welfare, but which is mixed up with information which is. Even if the material sought by the police consists entirely of the non-confidential part of the mix, it remains excluded and unavailable. The wording of s 8 (Art 10) and Schedule 1, para 2 would not seem to permit any severance of the material or an application only for the non-confidential material.

(iii) S 12 (Art 14) significantly cuts down the apparent width of s 11

(Art 13). 'Personal records' must concern an individual (living or dead) who can be identified 'from them'. One possible interpretation of this phrase is that the individual can be identified without recourse to other records; eg if the records contain only a number which refers to an individual who can only be identified by reference to a master list, the record is not a 'personal record' for the purposes of s 12 (Art 14). Such an interpretation would expose many personal records to the risk of seizure where for security reasons the records do not enable the individual to be identified without recourse to another record. A preferable interpretation is that records are 'personal records' if the individual to whom they relate can be identified from the record itself or a related record.

(iv)   The records must relate to one of the three matters mentioned in s 12 (Art 14).

(a)   *Physical or mental health* — This clearly covers records kept by doctors, hospitals, midwives, health visitors and certain social workers such as mental welfare officers and others concerned with the physical and mental health of individuals. The authors' research revealed a case in which access to hospital out-patient records in order to identify a man who had killed another and was himself injured in the struggle, was denied by a circuit judge who rejected the argument that the records were administrative rather than personal. There is no requirement that the holder of the records be professionally qualified. Thus any person who holds himself out as concerned with the physical or mental health of another can benefit, eg physicians not recognised by the British Medical Association such as osteopaths, faith healers and hypnotists.

(b)   *Spiritual counselling or assistance given or to be given* — The key word here is 'spiritual'. It is not qualified in any way and can bear a number of meanings. It clearly covers religious advice and this can extend to unusual, if not dangerous, religious sects such as the Moonies (which sect enjoyed charitable status until 1983). The Government considered and then rejected the possibility of adding 'bona fide' to s 12(b) (Art 14(b)) so as to exclude such organisations from the benefit of claiming protection under the Act. It would, however, be open to a court to use the doctrine of public policy to reject claims to confidentiality by such organisations. In the Oxford English Dictionary 'spiritual' may also mean 'of, pertaining to, affecting or concerning the spirit or higher moral qualities'. This would therefore include the Church of Scientology and other organisations which do not acknowledge a God but purport to promote the greater fulfilment of man's qualities. If this interpretation is adopted, the protection could extend, for example, to Alcoholics Anonymous, and bodies designed to assist the rehabilitation of offenders, for they by publicity or direct action aim to improve moral standards. Finally, the word 'spiritual' can literally include those who claim to communicate with spirits and s 12(c) (Art 14 (c)) could apply to any records kept by a spiritualist.

(c) *Counselling or assistance given or to be given for the purposes of personal welfare* — Records which fall within this category include social work or similar activities, whether professional or not; marriage guidance councils; the NSPCC; the Samaritans; refuges and organisations aimed at assisting alcoholics, drug addicts, the victims of rape or wife-battery; legal advice and records held by unqualified volunteers at advice centres, which do not fall within legal privilege (para 4.56, ante); information held by a personnel officer; homosexual clubs. Again there is no qualification of 'bona fide' and the category could extend in theory to controversial organisations such as the Paedophile Information Exchange; though it would again be open to the courts to invoke public policy to strike out such claims. The Government intended school records to be covered by this category (Standing Committee E, 17 January 1984, col 534) but the courts do not look at Hansard for guidance and the point is debatable. For example, a school record, which includes a pupil's disciplinary offences and which the police would like to examine in relation to a criminal offence under investigation, concerns the pupil's 'personal welfare' but may not involve 'counselling or assistance'. On the other hand, a record of injuries sustained by the pupil, statements that a parent has inflicted them and advice given by the teacher to child and/or parents could fall within 'counselling'. Section 12(c)(ii) (Art 14(c)(ii)) was added at a late Parliamentary stage of the PACE Bill to make clear that protection could extend to agencies responsible for a person because of a court order. This covers the Probation Service, Social Services Departments (responsible for a person in care, eg at a foster home, or under a supervision order), Mental Health Institutions and even the Prison Service. For example, the police may wish to see records held by the Samaritans concerning an arsonist who is known to have contacted such organisations before. If records are kept, they fall within s 12. If no records are kept the excluded material provisions do not of course apply, but the agency's representative can be ordered to appear at the trial and he cannot claim privilege for the conversation. This last point deserves emphasis since it applies to all potential witnesses (save professional legal advisers), even though they may be able to resist the police application to see the evidence before trial. The stark choice facing such witnesses is break your confidence or risk imprisonment for contempt of court (see *A G v Mullholland* (1963)).

(v)   Information held in confidence — s 11(1)(a) (Art 13(1)(a)) stipulates that the personal records must be held in confidence. This is defined by s 11(2) (Art 13(2)) and in relation to personal records the obligation of confidence will normally be implied rather than expressly stated in the relationship.

(2) *Human tissue or tissue fluid (s 11(1)(b); Art 13(1)(b))*

4.61   This is the least problematical of the three categories of excluded material. The tissue will usually be held in confidence by a person connected with a hospital, clinic or laboratory who may well be a non-clinical administrator, rather than a doctor or scientist. The tissue or fluid will usually have been taken from a person who is suspected of a serious arrestable offence. It will not include objects removed from the body such as bullets or packets of drugs secreted or swallowed. These are not human tissue or tissue fluid and can be the subject of a s 8 (Art 10) search warrant if not surrendered voluntarily. Swabs and smears taken from the victim of a crime for forensic comparison with the blood or semen of the suspect are probably not within s 11(2)(b) (Art 13(2)(b)) not being 'taken for the purposes of diagnosis or medical treatment'. If held in confidence such material will be special procedure material but since the obligation of confidence probably relates to the police, rather than to the victim, the forensic scientist will be able to hand the items to the police without fear of a civil action by a victim who seeks to withdraw from a prosecution and prevent the police obtaining access to those samples. Rape units set up in hospitals to provide an alternative source of examination and counselling for victims of rape who are reluctant to complain to the police raise interesting questions. Staff are trained in the collection of forensic evidence which will be stored for one month so as to be available should the victim decide to complain. Material collected may well include human tissue fluid, but it is probably not 'taken for the purposes of diagnosis or medical treatment' and is not then excluded material. It will almost certainly be held in confidence and will be special procedure material, which is potentially available to the police. When a doctor is in possession of human tissue or tissue fluids which are likely to be evidence of a serious arrestable offence, there is no legal process which can oblige him to surrender them but he may do so voluntarily. Guidance issued by the General Medical Council leaves it to the individual's professional judgment as to whether he should break his patient's confidence. If the patient is subsequently convicted, the doctor is protected from a civil action for breach of confidence, there being 'no confidence in iniquity'. If the patient is arrested and not proceeded against or acquitted, the doctor may be at risk of such an action. Doctors can therefore be placed in an invidious position. The development of DNA profiling (genetic fingerprinting) has made the obtaining of human tissue or tissue fluid of greater importance than ever in relation to certain categories of crimes, particularly rape. The fact that an intimate sample (which includes blood, semen and other tissue fluids) can only be taken from a suspect arrested for a serious arrestable offence with his written consent (see s 62 (Art 62) discussed at para 7.97, post) means that there is no legal process under which either the doctor or the suspect can be compelled to provide the evidence which will conclusively prove whether or not the suspect was involved. There is therefore a strong argument for a change in the law either giving the police the power to take an intimate sample without consent, or by making human tissue or tissue fluid in the possession of a doctor, special procedure material which is potentially available, rather than as now, unavailable without consent.

(3) *Journalistic material (ss 11(1)(c), 13; Arts 13 (i)(c), 15)*

4.62   In 1983 the media launched a vociferous campaign to exempt journalists from the search warrant procedures of the PACE Bill. The campaign came in the wake of the House of Lords' decision in *British Steel v Granada* (1980) which refused to recognise a journalist's privilege to protect the confidentiality of his sources, and of s 10 of the Contempt of Court Act 1981 which permits his interests to be weighed in the balance before disclosure is ordered. The campaign was successful, although sections of the media changed their minds and sought to remove the exemption from the Bill. The exemption is found in ss 11(1)(c) and 13 (Arts 13(1)(c) and 15). It is broadly drafted, covering material 'acquired or created' by a person 'for the purposes of journalism' (s 13(1) Art 15(1)). This includes all branches of the media; it is not tied to professional journalists, covering eg the 'amateur' editor of a newsletter; it may arguably cover a letter sent to an editor for publication; it encompasses all the research and background material which a journalist has 'acquired' to write his article eg information from secret sources, or has 'created' for the purpose eg interviews with the subjects of his investigation. 'Document' *includes* 'a map, plan, photograph, disc, tape, film or microfilm' (s 118 (Art 2) which adopts s 10(1) of the Civil Evidence Act 1986 (Part 1 of the Civil Evidence (N.I.) Act 1971)). The phrase 'records other than documents' in s 11(1)(c) (Art 13(1)(c)) would thus appear to be redundant. To cope with unsolicited material, s 13(3) (Art 15(3)) provides that if the supplier intends that it should be used for the purposes of journalism the recipient is to be taken as having received it for that purpose. This intention may be expressed, as where the material is accompanied by a covering letter to that effect, or perhaps more often implied from the fact that it is sent to a newspaper, broadcasting company or a journalist. In order to be excluded material, journalistic material must be held in confidence. There is, however, a separate definition governing such material. S 11(3) (Art 13(3)) includes the definition applied to other forms of excluded material by s 11(2) (Art 13(2)) but adds a requirement that journalistic material be held continuously (by one or more persons) subject to such an undertaking, restriction or obligation since it was first acquired or created for the purposes of journalism. Thus, if a disaffected civil servant passes documents to a journalist, who passes them to another more senior journalist for evaluation, who passes them to his editor, then it is held in confidence so long as each receives it for the purposes of journalism. If this chain of purposes is broken, eg the journalist passes the documents to a non-journalist expert for evaluation, then although the continuity of confidence is maintained the continuity of purpose is not since the expert does not acquire them for the purpose of journalism. If this is correct the documents are no longer excluded material within s 11 (Art 13) but will be special procedure material (s 14(1)(b) Art 16(1)(b)). Similarly if the material is passed to the newspaper's lawyers, it is unlikely that they will receive it 'for the purposes of journalism', rather it will be received, and intended by the sender to be received for the purposes of legal advice. As indicated in the discussion of legal privilege (see para 4.56 ante) an existing document not created within the relationship of lawyer/client does not attract legal privilege. This too will be special procedure material (s 14(1)(b); Art 16(1)(b) discussed at para 4.63 post). Does the material regain its excluded material status if the lawyer returns it to the journalist with his opinion? It will be received for the purposes of journalism and no doubt the lawyer intends that it be received for that purpose but it is doubtful whether the lawyer imposes an obligation of confidence on the journalist. The material may not therefore regain its excluded material status once it is lost. Where material is passed to a journalist for publication it is questionable whether there can be an obligation of confidence in relation to that material. The supplier will no doubt not wish his identity to be revealed but journalists are given protection against the disclosure of sources by the Contempt of Court Act 1981, s 10 — see *In An Inquiry Under the Company Securities (Insider Dealing Act 1985)* (1988). If therefore the material is not held in confidence it is not excluded material but, if it is journalistic material, it will be special procedure under s 14(1)(b) (Art 16(1)(b)). (For a discussion of the limited access to excluded material provided by s 9(2) and Schedule 1, para 3 (Art 11(2) and Schedule 1, para 3) see para 4.74, post.)

Special procedure material (s 14 (Art 16))

4.63 This category of material, as the name implies, is available to the police provided application is made under Schedule 1 and in accordance with that Schedule. In England and Wales, more than 2,000 orders for production of special procedure material, or warrants to search for and seize such material, were granted in the first three years of the PACE Act 1984. These have enabled the police to investigate crimes which they were previously unable to investigate and to obtain evidence in respect of other crimes which they were previously unable to obtain, or were able to obtain only after a charge had been laid under the Bankers' Books Evidence Act 1879. Special procedure material falls into two sub-categories:

(i)   journalistic material which is not excluded material; and
(ii)   material to which s 14(2) (Art 16(2)) applies.

Journalistic material which is not excluded material (s 14(1)(b); Art 16(1)(b))

4.64 Journalistic material is only excluded material if it consists of documents or records other than documents and is continuously held in confidence. A document or record not so held, or any other form of material, whether it is held in confidence or not, which is acquired or created for the purposes of journalism, is special procedure material. Thus, if as argued in para 4.62, ante, material passed to a journalist for publication is not held in confidence, it clearly is journalistic material as defined by s 13 (Art 15) but is not excluded material. It is, however, special procedure material. Photographs taken by press photographers of incidents during a riot were the subject of the first reported case in which an order was made for production of special procedure material which was 'journalistic material' (*R v Bristol Crown Court, ex parte Bristol Press and Picture Agency* (1986)). Though the photographs were 'documents or records other than documents', they were not held in confidence but clearly were 'created for the purposes of journalism' and therefore special procedure material. Video tapes showing members of the Animal Liberation Front held by the BBC have been the subject of a production order. Other film or photographs of demonstrations (eg the 'poll tax' disorder in London in 1990) and of sporting events (involving physical assaults by participants or spectators) have been handed over to the police, either in response to a production order or to the threat of one. Such material created by journalists for the purposes of journalism lacks the requirement that it be held in confidence and is not therefore excluded material but is special procedure material. Articles other than documents or records other than documents, even if held in confidence for journalistic purposes, will not be excluded material but will be special procedure material. Thus if A passes to B, a journalist, a diary belonging to an alleged rapist together with a ski-mask which he wore to hide his face whilst committing the offences, the diary, if held subject to an obligation of confidence, is excluded material and unavailable except with consent of the journalist, while the ski-mask is special procedure material and potentially available under Schedule 1, para 2. If the diary is not held in confidence, being intended for publication, it too is special procedure material and similarly potentially available under Schedule 1, para 2.

Special procedure material to which s 14(2) (Art 16(2)) applies

4.65   Special procedure to which s 14(2) (Art 16(2)) applies is business and financial information which, though held in confidence, is of a less sensitive nature than legally privileged or excluded material. Material is special procedure material if it:

(a)   is not legally privileged or excluded material;

(b)   is in the possession of a person who acquired or created it in the course of any trade, business, profession or other occupation or for the purposes of any paid or unpaid office; and

(c)   is held in confidence, which is defined in exactly the same terms as that in s 11(2) (Art 13(2)) for the purposes of excluded material.

(b)   above covers every form of paid occupation but covers only unpaid activities which involve the holding of an office, eg the treasurer or secretary of a club, trades' union branch or local or national society. To prevent an employer or company creating special procedure material simply by passing it to an employee or associated company under an obligation of confidence, s 14(3), (4) and (5) (Art 16(3), (4) and (5)) provide that

(i)   Where material is acquired by an employee from his employer in the course of his employment, or it is acquired by a company from an associated company, it is only special procedure material if it would have been immediately before its acquisition (s 14(3)(a) and (b); Art 16(3)(a) and (b)). 'Associated company' has the meaning assigned to it by the Income and Corporation Taxes Act 1988 (s 14(6) Art 16(6)).

(ii)   Similarly, if the material is created by an employee in the course of his employment or is created by an associated company, it is only special procedure if it would have been had the employer or associated company created it (s 14(4) and (5) Art 16(4) and (5)).

Banks and building societies will be the main holders of special procedure material which will be of evidential use to the police, followed by eg accountants, solicitors (conveyancing matter and non-legally privileged material), estate agents, financial brokers, insurance brokers, telecommunications companies and journalists in all parts of the media.

4.66   The following examples are given to illustrate the inter-relationship of search warrant powers and the access provisions provided in respect of excluded or special procedure material.

1) Following a gold bullion robbery, a serious arrestable offence (s 116 (Art 87)),

   (i)   the Theft Act 1968, s 26 (Theft Act (N.I.) 1969 s 25) or s 8 of the PACE Act 1984 (Art 10 of the 1989 Order) can be used to search for and seize the stolen bullion.

   (ii)   A bullion dealer has documentary material which may indicate to whom the stolen bullion has been sold. If, as is likely, these documents are held in confidence, they will be special procedure material and may be obtained by application to a circuit (county court) judge under Sch 1, para 2. If not held in confidence, a warrant under s 8 (Art 10) may be obtained.

   (iii)   An investigative journalist has documentary material which purports to identify the man who masterminded the robbery. If held in confidence it is excluded material and not available by any legal process.

   (iv)   An accountant has material which is believed to implicate company X in a 'laundering operation' which converted the stolen bullion into gold coins. This is special procedure material and may be obtained by application under Sch 1.

   (v)   A number of suspects are arrested. They claim they do not know each other. All have portable telephones which, it is believed, they used to contact each other before and during the robbery. The telephone company has computerised records of calls made to and from the telephones owned by the suspects. These are special procedure material and may be obtained by application under Sch 1. The premises of the suspects may be searched under s 18 (Art 20) or s 32(2)(b) (Art 34(2)(b)).

   (vi)   The cars used in the robbery were stolen, resprayed and renumbered. It is believed that garages owned by friends of the suspects were used. A warrant under s 8 (Art 10) may be obtained to search for evidence that the cars were altered in these garages.

   (vii)   Large deposits of money, thought to be the proceeds of the sale of the bullion, are believed to have been made in bank and building society accounts held by the suspects. The records of these accounts are special procedure material and may be obtained by application under Sch 1.

2) A multiple rapist is sought. It is known that he has a disease which he transmitted to his victims.

   (i) A special clinic which a suspect has recently attended for treatment holds blood and other tissue samples taken from the suspect for the purposes of diagnosis. This is excluded material and unobtainable by any legal process.

   (ii) The suspect has visited a psychiatrist. His records are also excluded material and unobtainable.

   (iii) The suspect is a lorry driver. His employer has records of delivery routes on the days on which the rapes were committed which will show that the suspect was in the area of each rape on the day in question. These are special procedure material and may be obtained by application under Sch 1.

   (iv) A journalist has a tape-recording of a telephone conversation with a man who claimed to be the rapist. This is journalistic material in the form of a document but is unlikely to be held in confidence either because there is no confidence in iniquity or because it cannot be implied from the circumstances, which would appear to imply an intention that it be published. The tape is, however, special procedure material (s 14(2)(b); Art 16(2)(b)) and may be obtained by application under Sch 1.

It should be noted that:

(a) the person in possession of excluded or special procedure material may surrender it voluntarily or allow the police access to it; and

(b) excluded and special procedure material may be seized in the course of a search under a warrant or a post-arrest power and in any circumstance in which the police officer is lawfully on the premises (s 19 (Art 21)). This latter power is NOT a power to search for the material. However, s 32(2)(b) (Art 34(2)(b)) permits the search of premises in which the person was when arrested or immediately before being arrested provided there are reasonable grounds to believe that evidence of the offence for which he was arrested is to be found on those premises. Thus if the suspected rapist in 2(i) above is arrested in or on leaving the special clinic, a search of that clinic may be made for the sample of blood and tissue fluid; similarly if he is arrested in or on leaving the psychiatrist's office. If a man suspected of fraud is arrested in or on leaving the office of his accountant, that office may be searched for evidence of the fraud.

(c) Special procedure material as defined by s 14(2) (Art 16(2)) is not protected insofar as it relates to offences within the jurisdiction of Customs and Excise (assigned matters) (see para 4.53(v), ante).

(d) If a 'terrorist investigation', as defined by s 17(1) of the Prevention of Terrorism (Temporary Provisions) Act 1989 is under way, Schedule 7 of that Act provides a procedure, similar to the Schedule 1 procedure, which permits a circuit judge (county court judge in N.I.) to issue an order requiring the production of excluded or special procedure material in circumstances in which the excluded material would not be available in respect of a non-terrorist investigation (see para 4.80, post).

Procedures for obtaining access to excluded or special procedure material — s 9 (Art 11) and Schedule 1

4.67 *Introduction*

Section 9(1) (Art 11(1)) provides that a constable may obtain access to excluded or special procedure material for the purposes of a criminal investigation by making application under Schedule 1 and in accordance with that Schedule. S 9(2) (Art 11(1)) further provides that any statutory provisions existing before the 1984 Act (1989 Order) which authorised the issue of a search warrant to a constable shall cease to have effect so far as it relates to the authorisation of searches

(a)   for items subject to legal privilege;
(b)   for excluded material; or
(c)   for special procedure material consisting of documents or records other than documents.

The effect of s 9(2) (Art 11(2)) is to prevent a magistrate issuing a warrant under a pre-PACE Act (Order) statute when the material sought falls into one of the above categories. Legally privileged material is never obtainable; but as regards excluded material or special procedure material in documentary form, application must be made to a circuit (county court) judge under Schedule 1 either for an order requiring the person in possession of the material to produce it to the police, or for a warrant authorising a constable to enter and search premises for the material. Schedule 1 therefore provides that a circuit (county court) judge may make an order requiring production of the material if either of two sets of access conditions is fulfilled. The first set of access conditions applies when special procedure material (not legally privileged or excluded material) is sought, which would not have been available before criminal proceedings were commenced under any statutory provision existing before the 1984 Act (1989 Order), which may be evidence of a serious arrestable offence, and which is held by a person not himself suspected of involvement in that offence, eg the suspect's bank or building society accounts. The second set of access conditions applies to excluded material and special procedure material in documentary form which, but for s 9(2) (Art 11(2)), could have been the subject of a search warrant under a statutory provision existing before the 1984 Act (1989 Order) eg documents stolen from a government department and passed to a journalist. A warrant under s 26 of the Theft Act 1968 (s 25 of the Theft Act (N.I.) 1969) could have been obtained but for s 9(2) (Art 11(2)). Application can be made to a circuit (county court) judge for a production order or, in certain circumstances, for a warrant to enter and search the premises. Note that there is no requirement in Schedule 1, para 3, that the offence be a serious arrestable offence.

4.68   The procedure under Schedule 1 — No application for a production order or warrant under Schedule 1 can be made without the authority of an officer of at least the rank of superintendent (COP B 2.4). Application for access to, or an order of production of, special procedure material is made to a circuit judge (county court judge in N.I.) and the hearing of the application will take the form of an inter partes hearing at which the person in possession of the material can resist the making of the order (Sch 1, para 7). It was held in *R v Crown Court at Leicester, ex p DPP* (1987) that the only parties to an application for an order under Sch 1, para 4 are the police and the person or institution thought to be in possession of the material. The person to whom the obligation of confidence is owed by that person or institution has no right to be notified of the proceedings or to be present. As with all warrants, an application for a warrant under Sch 1 will be ex parte and will be subject to s 15 of the PACE Act 1984 (Art 17 of the N.I. Order) (see paras 4.13-14 ante).

4.69   Notice of an application — A notice of application for a production order must be served upon the person believed to be in possession of the material sought. Schedule 1 says nothing about the period or form of the notice. In practice at least seven clear days notice is given either by registered post or recorded or personal delivery. If a bank or building society is involved, and particularly if more than one account or branch is involved, the notice should be served on the headquarters with a copy to the branch(es) concerned. If the respondent is an unincorporated association, the notice should name the chairman or secretary (*R v Central Criminal Court ex p Adegbesan* (1986)). Where a company is involved, the notice must be served on the company secretary or clerk or similar officer, and where a partnership is involved, on one of the partners (Sch 1, para 9 — the 1989 Order does not contain an equivalent provision). The proper address for service in the case of a company is the registered or principal office, and in the case of a partnership the principal office of the firm. In all other cases it will be the last known address of the person to be served (Sch 1, para 10). The notice must accurately describe the respondent and all the material sought. Since to conceal, destroy, alter or dispose of the material after service of the notice may be contempt unless any of these are done with the leave of a judge or the written permission of a constable (Sch 1, para 11 (Art 8)), it is only fair that the respondent be made aware of exactly what material is sought. In the *Adegbesan* case the notice gave no clue as to the material sought and as Watkin LJ observed (at p.117):

'It would be impossible for a person who was a recipient of such a notice . . . to know whether he was complying with the clear provisions of para 11 of Schedule 1 unless he was informed precisely of what it was he was called upon to preserve.'

The most satisfactory method of conveying this detail is in writing but there may be occasions when oral communication (by the investigating or supervisory officer) will suffice *(R v Manchester Crown Court, ex p Taylor* (1988)). The crucial requirement is that the respondent be informed. In *R v Central Criminal Court ex p Carr* (1987), Glidewell LJ suggested that the notice ought to indicate the general nature of the offence or offences under investigation (eg 'fraud', 'robbery') and the address of the premises where the material is alleged to be. Further details such as may be included in the information and which will be given to the judge need not be included in the notice to the holder of the material. However, any material given to the judge must be served upon the party against whom the notice is served before the application is heard *(R v Inner London Crown Court, ex p Baines and Baines* (1988). Note that Sch 1, para 11 (Art 8) does not state that concealment etc after receipt of a notice is contempt of court. The Prevention of Terrorism (Temporary Provisions) Act 1989 creates a specific offence in respect of material which is the subject of an application for an order or warrant (s 17(2)). A similar requirement operates under s 2(16) of the Criminal Justice Act 1987 in respect of documents when it is known or suspected that an investigation into serious fraud is being or is likely to be carried out. The facts that the PACE Act and Order do not create a specific offence and that the notice of an application is not an order of a court, suggest that the only offence involved in such concealment etc is that of obstructing the police (s 51(3) of the Police Act 1964). If the police have grounds to suspect that the respondent will conceal etc the material sought, they should seek a warrant (Sch 1, paras 12 and 14 (paras 9 and 11)).

4.70 The recipient of the notice will be holding the material subject to an undertaking of confidence given to the customer or client who is the subject of the police investigation. Is he therefore under a duty to inform the customer or client of the application? In *Barclays Bank plc v Taylor* (1989) the Court of Appeal upheld the striking out of an action by Mr Taylor against the bank for breach of duty in failing to inform him of applications made under the 1984 Act and in failing to contest them. The decision makes it clear that the banks are under no duty to inform a client or to contest an application, however, the question whether the recipient of a notice was under a legal duty *not to inform* the client was less than satisfactorily answered. Lord Donaldson thought that the banks were 'no doubt free to ignore a request [by the police] that [the client] not be informed of the application'. However, his Lordship went on to say that 'he would have been surprised and disappointed if they had done so in the context of a criminal investigation unless they were under a legal obligation to do so'. No doubt banks and reputable organisations will not disappoint the Court of Appeal but in the absence of a legal obligation not to inform the client the less reputable may well feel that their loyalty lies with the client in this matter. S 17(2)(a) of the Prevention of Terrorism (Temporary Provisions) Act 1989 makes it an offence to make a disclosure likely to prejudice the investigation, knowing or having reasonable cause to suspect that a warrant or order has been issued, made or applied for under Sch 7 to that Act. A similar provision in relation to orders or warrants sought under the 1984 Act (1989 Order) would be appropriate, but applicable only if such a requirement is contained in the notice. The form of notice used by the Metropolitan Police sets out para 11 of Schedule 1 (which states that the recipient must not conceal etc the material sought) and specifically requests that the customer/client not be informed. This serves to put the recipient on notice that to do so may hinder the investigation. Should that request be ignored, there is the possibility of an offence under s 51(3) of the Police Act 1964, obstruction of a police officer.

4.71 Hearing the application — The notice is followed by a hearing inter partes, though increasingly banks and similar institutions are not contesting such applications. This trend was boosted by the decision in *Barclays Bank plc v Taylor* (1989) that they are under no duty to do so. It is for the police to satisfy the judge that the access conditions contained in Schedule 1, para 2 or 3 are fulfilled. In *R v Norwich Crown Court ex p Chethams* (1991) the Divisional Court rejected the argument that 'satisfied' as used in para 1 of Schedule 1 meant 'satisfied so as to be sure' (the criminal standard of proof), holding that the ordinary standard of judicial satisfaction is satisfaction on the balance of probabilities (the civil standard of proof). In the absence of an express provision to the contrary it was this latter standard which is to be employed by the judge hearing an application under Schedule 1. The practice is to prepare an information which sets out all the relevant details of the offence under investigation and in so doing seek to establish that the access conditions are satisfied. The constable will then take the oath and either state the facts as set out in the information or, in an uncontested case where the judge has already read the information, answer any questions the judge may ask. There must be evidence that all the first or second set of access conditions have been fulfilled. Any statements which have no substance and which are to the prejudice of the party against whom the order is sought, will be excluded by the judge (*R v Inner London Crown Court, ex p Baines and Baines* (1988)).

The first set of access conditions

4.72   The first set of access conditions is fulfilled if

(a)   there are reasonable grounds for believing -

  (i)   that a serious arrestable offence has been committed;

  (ii)   that there is material which consists of or includes special procedure material and does not also include excluded material on premises specified in the application;

  (iii)   that the material is likely to be of substantial value (whether by itself or together with other material) to the investigation in connection with which the application is made; and

  (iv)   that the material is likely to be relevant evidence;

(b)   other methods of obtaining the material -

  (i)   have been tried without success, or

  (ii)   have not been tried because it appeared that they were bound to fail, and

(c)   it is in the public interest, having regard -

  (i)   to the benefit likely to accrue to the investigation if the material is obtained; and

  (ii)   to the circumstances under which the person in possession of the material holds it,

that the material should be produced or that access to it should be given.

The conditions set out in para 2(a) and (b) are factual and are similar to those in s 8(1) (Art 10(1)). If the serious arrestable offence is specified in Schedule 5, Part I or II, there will be no difficulty in satisfying the judge. If, however, the offence is a serious arrestable offence because of the consequences set out in s 116(6) (Art 87(6)), an explanation will be necessary. It will, of course, be necessary to show that the material sought consists of or includes special procedure material but it may in some cases be more important to show that it does not include excluded material. This will seldom be the case when financial institutions such as banks and building societies are involved, but could be problematic if journalistic material is sought given that this material can be either excluded or special procedure material. A possible interpretation of Schedule 1 para 2(a)(ii) is that an order under para 4 cannot be made if there is excluded material on the premises as well as special procedure material even if the material is separate and identifiable as such. In order to satisfy the judge that the material 'is likely to be of substantial value (whether by itself or together with other material) to the investigation' it will be necessary to describe the offence under investigation, what other evidence there is and how the material sought relates to the investigation. Such material may be only a small part of a much larger pattern of evidence but still be 'of substantial value'. 'Relevant evidence' in relation to an offence means anything that would be admissible in evidence at a trial for the offence (s 8(4) Art 10(4)). The requirement in para 2(b) emphasises the need to approach either the person under investigation, or the holder of the material, in an attempt to obtain the material with their consent or attempt to use other practicable methods of obtaining the material. Only rarely will the police wish to alert the person to the fact that he is under investigation and the fact that the person holding the material may lay himself open to a civil action if he allows access without a court order means that few will do so. Nevertheless it is often necessary to approach the holder of the material to establish that he has the material and possibly to obtain a clear description of the material which is to be subject of an application under Schedule 1. For example, a bank may confirm that they hold an account in the suspect's name, or more than one account, but will require a court order before giving access to it or them. Under an agreement made in 1969 between the Metropolitan Police and the London clearing banks, the latter agreed only to divulge to the police the non-existence of an account or the closure of an account. All other information required the customer's consent or a court order. This agreement is under review. In *R v Lewes Crown Court ex p Hill* (1991) a police officer obtained an order under the Bankers' Books Evidence Act 1879 to inspect bank records in respect of H. He later obtained an order under s 9 and Sch 1 of the PACE Act giving him access to the same bank records but failed to make it clear to the judge that opportunities arising from the order under the 1879 Act had not been fully exploited. On an application for judicial review of the decision to issue the order under the PACE Act, it was held that in the absence of such information the judge could not have been satisfied as to the requirements of para 2(b) and the order should not have been made. The Divisional Court further stated that the applicant for a production order was under an obligation to ensure that all relevant material, even if it was adverse to his case, was before the court. This is not to say that the 1879 Act must be used before the 1984 Act procedure, but where the 1879 Act is used, it must be fully exploited and the 1984 procedure used only when the 1879 Act proves ineffective or insufficient.

4.73 *The public interest requirement* — Schedule 1, para 2(c) requires that the judge be satisfied that it is in the public interest that the material be produced or access to it be given, having regard
(i) to the benefit likely to accrue to the investigation if the material is obtained; and
(ii) to the circumstances under which the person in possession of the material holds it.

The first of these requirements suggests that the more important the material is to the investigation the greater the public interest is in allowing the police to obtain it. In every case the offence must be a serious arrestable offence and once it is established that the material is of substantial value to the investigation there seems to be little to put into the scales which would outweigh this public interest. The circumstances in which the material is held can only refer to the fact that the holder owes a duty of confidence to a third party. A banker, for example, can point to his duty of confidentiality and the possible damage to his relationship with other clients if that duty is breached. However, the purpose of the production order under Schedule 1 is to enable him to breach that duty without incurring legal liability and, since the vast majority of clients will accept that he must comply with a judicial order, the banker/client relationship is unlikely to be damaged. In *R v Central Criminal Court, ex p Carr* (1987) Glidewell LJ appeared to disregard para 2(c)(ii) in taking the view that once it is shown that the documents are in the premises and that they are likely to be of substantial value to the investigation and relevant evidence, it followed that it was in the public interest that they be produced. This approach was confirmed by the Queen's Bench Divisional Court in *R v Northampton Magistrates' Court, ex p DPP* (1991). Granting judicial review of a judge's refusal to issue an order under s 9 and Sch 1 against a firm of solicitors, Taylor LJ held that once a judge had concluded under para 2(a)(i) of Schedule 1 that a serious arrestable offence had been committed, it was hardly consistent to find anything other than that it was an offence for which there was a public interest in bringing the matter to justice. In *R v Bristol Crown Court, ex p Bristol Press and Picture Agency* (1986) unpublished photographs taken by press photographers of a riot were sought by the police. The newspapers raised two issues under para 2(c)(ii); first, that allowing police access to the photographs would compromise the impartiality of the press, and second, that it would increase the risk of injury to photographers. On the first issue the judge took the view that the impartiality of the press would not be compromised if they were compelled to produce them under a court order. As to the second issue, he took the view that photographers were at greater risk when taking photographs for publication than in disclosing unpublished photographs. The public interest therefore lay in making the order for production. Since then some protesters have been seen carrying placards and wearing badges which target press photographers.

The second set of access conditions

4.74 S 9(2) (Art 11(2) provides that any Act (including a local Act) passed before the PACE Act 1984 (or 1989 Order) under which a search of premises for the purposes of a criminal investigation could be authorised by the issue of a warrant to a constable shall cease to have effect so far as it relates to the authorisation of searches:

(a) for items subject to legal privilege; or
(b) for excluded material; or
(c) for special procedure material consisting of documents or records other than documents.

The effect of s 9(2) (Art 11(2)), is to prevent a magistrate issuing a warrant under a pre-existing statutory authority if the material sought falls within the definition of legally privileged, excluded or special procedure material in documentary form. Legally privileged material is never obtainable; but as regards excluded material and special procedure material in documentary form, instead of making an application to a magistrate for a warrant under the particular statute, application must now be made to a circuit (county court) judge under para 3 of Schedule 1, the second set of access conditions. These conditions are fairly easily satisfied, the rationale being that since the material would, but for s 9(2) (Art 11(2)), have been obtainable under a magistrate's warrant, there is no need to adopt the more restrictive conditions which apply in relation to material which can never be the subject of such warrants. The access conditions are:

(a) there are reasonable grounds for believing that there is material which consists of or includes excluded or special procedure material on premises specified in the application;
(b) but for s 9(2) (Art 11(2)) a search of the specified premises could have been authorised by the issue of a warrant to a constable under a statutory provision other than Schedule 1 of the 1984 Act (1989 Order); and
(c) the issue of such a warrant would have been appropriate.

If these conditions are fulfilled the judge may make an order requiring the person who appears to him to be in possession of the material to produce it to a constable or give him access to it. The following points may be noted.

1) Excluded material and special procedure material, if in documentary form, are obtainable under para 3 of Schedule 1,. For example, a government official passes secret documents to a journalist with a view to exposing alleged malpractice by government ministers. Assuming they are held in confidence, they are excluded material under ss 11(1)(c) and 13 (Arts 13(1)(c) and 15). But for s 9(2) (Art 11(2)) the documents could be the subject of a search warrant under the Theft Act if stolen, or under the Official Secrets Act. A magistrate cannot now issue a warrant in respect of the documents under either Act, instead application must be made under Schedule 1, para 3, (the

second set of access conditions) for an order for production of the documents. If the order is not complied with, a warrant may be issued. If any of the conditions in para 14 of Schedule 1 (para 11 of the 1989 Order) are satisfied, a warrant may be sought in the first instance rather than an order (see para 4.76, post). Note that there is no requirement that the offence be a serious arrestable offence.

2) S 9(2) (Art 11(2)) does not apply to statutory powers of search created after the 1984 Act (1989 Order) unless the creating statute applies it. This has been done by the Cinemas Act 1985. S 13(3) authorises a magistrate to issue a warrant to enter premises reasonably suspected of being used as a cinema without a licence (an offence under s 10(1) of the Act) and to search for and seize apparatus or things subject to forfeiture. S 13(8) applies s 9(2) of the 1984 Act to this search power. This may be contrasted with s 24 of the Public Order Act 1986 which authorises a magistrate to issue a warrant to search premises for racially inflammatory material, possession of which is an offence under s 23 of the Act. S 9(2) does not apply to this search power, therefore legally privileged, excluded or special procedure material may be searched for and seized if it is racially inflammatory as defined by s 23. It is difficult to imagine legally privileged material falling within this definition but, in the absence of a definition of journalist or journalism, one can imagine circumstances in which such material is in possession of a newspaper published by an extreme fascist group which could be either excluded or special procedure material. (In Northern Ireland, Art 14 of the Public Order (NI) Order 1987, which provides a power to issue a warrant to search for material which is evidence of an offence under Art 13 of that Order (stirring up racial hatred), is subject to Art 11(2) of the PACE Order 1989. Such evidence in possession of a newspaper will be either excluded or special procedure material and obtainable only by application under Schedule 1.)

The Order

4.75 An order under Schedule 1 is an order that the person who appears to the circuit (county court) judge to be in possession of the material to which the application relates shall -

(a) produce it to a constable for him to take away; or

(b) give him access to it,

not later than the end of a period of seven days from the date of the order or the end of such longer period as the order may specify (Schedule 1 para 4). Where the material consists of information contained in a computer, it must be produced in a visible and legible form in which it can be taken away or the constable given access to it — eg a printout (Schedule 1 para 5). Most orders will require that the material be produced for a constable to take away. Such material is to be treated as material seized by a constable for the purposes of ss 21 and 22 (Arts 23 and 24) (see para 4.44, ante). One may note that there is no power to question the person about the material produced, which may often need explanation. Failure to comply with an order is a contempt of court (Schedule 1, para 12). There is no provision for a warrant to be issued following the failure to comply with an order based on the first set of access conditions being fulfilled, though there is when an order is made following the fulfilment of the second set of access conditions.

Warrant to search for excluded and special procedure material

4.76 The 1984 Act (1989 Order) envisages that an application for the production of or access to documents at an inter partes hearing will be the normal procedure. It should be noted that s 15 (Art 17) of the PACE Act and Order applies to an application for a warrant under Schedule 1, in particular the judge is empowered to question the constable on oath (see para 4.10, ante). Applications for a warrant under Schedule 1, paras 12–14 (para 9–11 of the Order), which are held ex parte, are very much the exception accounting for only 2.5 per cent of applications granted in the first thirty three months of the 1984 Act's operation. Applications for warrants should never become a matter of routine (*R v Maidstone Crown Court, ex p Waitt* (1988)). The Schedule envisages two situations in which a warrant may be issued —

(i) In the first of these the judge must be satisfied that either the first (para 2) or the second (para 3) set of access conditions are fulfilled and, in addition, any of the further conditions set out in para 14 (para 11 of the Order) (para 12(a)(i) and (ii); para 9(a)(i) and (ii) of the Order). The additional conditions relate to the practicability of communicating with the person entitled to grant access to the premises or the material sought; to the likely disclosure of official secrets contained in the material sought if a warrant is not issued; and, perhaps most commonly in this first situation, the likelihood that service of a notice of application for an order of production may seriously prejudice the investigation for the purposes of which the application is sought, or another investigation (para 14(a) to (d); para 10(a) to (d) of the Order). In relation to this last condition Code B, para 2.7 requires that an application for a warrant under para 12 (para 9) shall, where appropriate, indicate why it is believed that service of notice of an application for a production order may seriously prejudice the investigation. If the reason is that the person in possession is implicated in the serious arrestable offence under investigation, it may be more appropriate to arrest him and search the premises for the material (excluded or special procedure) under post arrest powers of search, ss 18 or 32(2)(b) (Arts 20 or 34(2)(b)).

(ii) The second situation envisages a warrant being issued when the second set of access conditions has been fulfilled and an order has been made under para 4, but it has not been complied with. This applies only in those cases in which the material sought (which unlike the first set of access conditions, may be excluded or special procedure material) could, but for s 9(2) (Art 11(2)), have been the subject of a magistrate's warrant but, in compliance with the Act (Order) has been the subject of an order for production under para 4 of Schedule 1. If the person in possession of the material fails to comply with the order a circuit (county court) judge may issue a warrant to enter premises and search for and seize the material. Failure to comply with an order is contempt of court; but the person in possession may decide to defy the court and refuse to deliver up the material, hence the warrant procedure. Strangely, there is no jurisdiction to issue a warrant to search for and seize material which was the subject of an order issued under the first set of access conditions when the order has not been complied with.

The application for a warrant under Schedule 1 must comply with s 15 of the PACE Act (Art 17 of the PACE Order) (para 4.14, ante). Once a circuit (county court) judge has made an ex parte order issuing a warrant under para 12 of Schedule 1, he has no power to entertain an inter partes application to review his order. If it is believed that the warrant was erroneously issued, application should be made to the Queen's Bench Divisional Court for judicial review of the decision (*R v Liverpool Crown Court and Another, ex p Wimpey plc* (1991)).

Executing a warrant issued under Schedule 1

4.77 In addition to the requirements of s 16 (Art 18) (considered at paras 4.15 to 19) which apply to the execution of all warrants, the Code of Practice, B para 5.13, stipulates that an officer of the rank of inspector or above take charge of and be present at a search made under a warrant issued under Schedule 1. He is responsible for ensuring that the search is carried out with discretion and with as little disruption as possible to business or other activities carried on in the premises. After securing the premises to ensure that no material leaves the premises without his knowledge, he should ask for the documents or other records to be produced. He may also, if necessary, ask to see the index (if there is one) to files held on the premises; an inspection may be made of any files which, according to the index, contain any of the material sought. A more extensive search of the premises may only be made if the person refuses to produce the material or to allow access to an index, or if it appears that the index is incomplete, or if the officer in charge has reasonable grounds to believe that such a search is necessary in order to find the material sought. Since constables executing such a warrant are lawfully on premises, the general power of seizure contained in s 19 (Art 21) and the access provisions in s 21 (Art 23) apply (see para 4.41–44, ante). It should be emphasised that material seized is held by the police under a duty of confidence (*Marcel v Commissioner of the Police of the Metropolis* (1991) — see para 4.53(viii), ante). In *R v Leeds Crown Court ex p Switalski* (1990), on an application for judicial review of a decision to grant search warrants under s 9 and Schedule 1 in respect of a solicitor's office, Leonard J pointed out that the circuit judge has to balance two conflicting public interests — the interest in the prevention of crime and the interest in maintaining the confidentiality of communications between clients and their legal advisers. He continued:

> 'I regard this second interest . . . as of the greatest importance and indeed vital for the maintenance of confidence in the legal system. Therefore, the police who have obtained warrants, such as the present, have a very special responsibility to ensure that any information obtained, however inadvertently, is not misused. I would anticipate that in some cases it may well be thought right that the police would be required to give an express undertaking as to the way in which the information will be used so as to emphasise the gravity of the matter.'

Legally privileged material cannot, of course, be lawfully seized under a warrant or under s 19 (Art 21) seizure powers. If such material is inadvertently seized it should be returned to the original holder. Any attempt to use it in evidence is likely to be met with its exclusion under s 78 (Art 76) of the PACE Act (Order) (see para 4.58, ante).

4.78 The following examples illustrate the operation of s 9 (Art 11) and Schedule 1 and its relationship to the s 8 (Art 10) warrant.

Councillors and local government officials are the subject of an investigation into allegations of fraud and corruption involving local and national companies, these are serious arrestable offences (s 116 (Art 87)).

(a)   Councillors and officials are believed to have received large sums of money from a national building contractor. Their bank and building society accounts can be the subject of an application for a production order under Schedule 1, para 2 (the first set of access conditions).

(b)   A former councillor is believed to have acted as the 'go-between' and to have received monies from local and national companies for his consultancy services. His bank and building society accounts can be the subject of an application for a production order under Schedule 1, para 2 (the first set of access conditions). His home and office may be searched under a s 8 (Art 10) warrant for evidence of his involvement and of the companies' involvement with him.

(Alternatively he may be arrested and both premises searched under ss 18 and 32(2)(b) (Arts 20 and 34(2)(b))).

(c)   Documents belonging to the former councillor are held by his accountant. These are special procedure material and may be the subject of an application for a production order under Schedule 1, para 2 (the first set of access conditions).

(d)   The national building contractor has been approached by the police but their officers refuse to co-operate on the advice of their solicitor. There are grounds to believe that service of a notice of an application for an order under para 4 of Schedule 1 would lead to shredding of the material sought. An application may be made for a warrant to search for and seize the material (special procedure material) under paras 12 and 14 of Schedule 1 (paras 9 and 11 of the Order).

(e)   A national newspaper has been conducting its own investigation into the allegations of corruption. They have a great deal of evidence including taped interviews with colleagues of the former councillor in which they detail their involvement in various frauds and implicate the former councillor. These are excluded material if held in confidence and cannot be the subject of an application under Schedule 1, para 2 (the first set of access conditions), nor can they be the subject of an application under para 3 (the second set of access conditions). Reliance must be placed on the co-operation of the newspaper.

(f)   A local newspaper has received a file of invoices and receipts stolen from a local building firm which prove fraud and corruption by a number of local councillors. This is excluded material if held in confidence, special procedure material if not. In either event the material could have been the subject of a warrant under the Theft Act 1968, s 26 (Theft Act (N.I.) 1967, s 25). Such a warrant cannot now be issued (s 9(2); Art 11(2)) but an application can be made for a production order under Schedule 1, para 3, (the second set of access conditions) or a warrant, if the conditions discussed in para 4.76, ante apply.

(g)   A local councillor, reasonably suspected of fraud and corruption, is arrested on leaving the registered office of a building company which it is believed has been paying him to enable them to obtain building contracts. The office can be searched for material which may be evidence of the offence (s 32(2)(b); Art 34(2)(b)) and such material may be seized even if it is special procedure material. The home of the councillor may be searched under s 18 (Art 20).

(h)   A firm of solicitors acted for the building company in negotiating contracts and in the purchase of land from the local authority. The documents relating to the sale of land are not legally privileged (*R v Inner London Crown Court, ex p Baines and Baines* (1987)) and, applying the same principle, nor are the documents relating to negotiation of contracts. They are, however, special procedure material and may be the subject of an application under Schedule 1, para 2 (the first set of access conditions). In no circumstances can they be the subject of a s 8 (Art 10) warrant.

PART C

Particular powers to issue a search warrant or to obtain access to material

4.79 The powers to obtain material considered in this section are powers which are available only in respect of particular offences, or in order to trace the proceeds of crime which are subject to confiscation, and powers to search for or obtain materials which are relevant to an investigation carried out by police forces in other jurisdictions. The powers are contained in —

(a) The Prevention of Terrorism (Temporary Provisions) Act 1989;
(b) The Security Service Act 1989;
(c) The Official Secrets Act 1989 and 1911;
(d) The Drug Trafficking Offences Act 1986;
(e) The Criminal Justice (Confiscation) (Northern Ireland) Order 1990;
(f) The Criminal Justice Act 1987;
(g) The Criminal Justice (International Co-operation) Act 1990 (Criminal Justice Act 1988, s 29)
(h) The Bankers' Books Evidence Act 1879;
(i) The Interception of Communications Act 1985.
(j) In addition the guidelines on the use of equipment in police surveillance operations will be considered.

The relevant parts of the statutes (a) to (i) are set out in the Appendix.

(A) Terrorism investigations

4.80 The Prevention of Terrorism (Temporary Provisions) Act 1989 (POT 89) gives the police wide-ranging powers to obtain materials which are relevant to a terrorist investigation. It is this concept, rather than 'a serious arrestable offence', which governs the issue of warrants or orders. A 'terrorism investigation' is defined by s 17 of the POT Act 1989 as

(a) Investigations into
    (i) the commission, preparation or instigation of acts of terrorism

connected with affairs in Northern Ireland or acts of terrorism of any other description except acts connected solely with the affairs of the United Kingdom or any part of the United Kingdom other than Northern Ireland (s (1)(a)(i) and s 14(2)(a) and (b));

(ii) any other act which appears to have been done in furtherance of or in connection with such acts of terrorism which includes any act which appears to constitute an offence under the following sections of the POT Act 1989 —

section 2 (belonging etc to proscribed organisations);

section 9 (soliciting or receiving money or other property intending etc that it be used for the commission of terrorism offences);

section 10 (soliciting etc contributions to a proscribed organisation); or

section 11 (assisting in the retention or control of terrorist funds); or

section 21 of the Northern Ireland (Emergency Provisions) Act 1978; or

(iii) without prejudice to (ii) above, the resources of a proscribed organisation within the meaning of the POT Act 1989 or the Northern Ireland (Emergency Provisions) Act 1978; and

(b) Investigations into whether there are grounds justifying the making of a proscription order under s 1(2)(a) of the POT Act 1989 or s 21(4) of the Northern Ireland (Emergency Provisions) Act 1978.

It will be noted that s 14(2) and s 17(1)(a) only apply to acts of terrorism connected with the affairs of Northern Ireland and what may be termed international terrorism. The sections do not apply to acts of terrorism connected solely with the affairs of the United Kingdom other than Northern Ireland. Thus an investigation into the planting of bombs by the IRA in London's railway stations, is 'connected with the affairs of Northern Ireland' and is a 'terrorism investigation' for the purposes of s 17. However, acts of terrorism by Welsh Nationalists or Animal Liberationists, being concerned solely with the affairs of the United Kingdom, are not.

4.81 Legally privileged, excluded and special procedure material — Search warrants under the Explosives Act 1875, s 73, the Offences Against the Person Act, 1861, s 65 or the Firearms Act 1968, s 46 are obviously available to police investigating terrorism offences but these are subject to s 9(2) of the PACE Act 1984 (Art 11(2) of the 1989 Order) which removes the jurisdiction of magistrates to issue such warrants when legally privileged, excluded or special procedure material is involved. Schedule 7 of the POT Act 1989 makes provision —

(i) for magistrates to issue a search warrant authorising the entry to and search of premises for evidence relevant to a terrorism investigation which does not include legally privileged, excluded or special procedure material, all of which are defined as in the PACE Act 1984 (PACE Order 1989) (para 4.82, post);

(ii) for a circuit (county court) judge to issue an order for the production of or access to excluded or special procedure material (but not legally privileged material) (para 4.83, post), required for the purposes of a terrorism investigation;

(iii) for a circuit (county court) judge to issue a warrant to enter and search premises and to seize excluded or special procedure material (but not legally privileged material) which is required for the purposes of a terrorism investigation (para 4.84, post);

(iv) in a case of great emergency a superintendent or above may, by written order, give a constable the power to search which a magistrate could give under (i) above, or which a judge could give under (iii) above (para 4.87, post);

(v) where a terrorist investigation in Northern Ireland involves offences of financial assistance for terrorism, the Secretary of State may issue an order giving a constable in Northern Ireland the authority which a warrant under Schedule 7 of the POT Act 1989 would give him or which an order for access to or the production of material under that Schedule would give him (para 4.88, post).

Para 9 of Schedule 1 to the POT Act 1989 made provision to obtain details of a person's interest in land as recorded in the Land Register created by the Land Registration Act 1925. This was a temporary provision which has been repealed on the coming into force of the Land Registration Act 1988. The above provisions will now be considered in more detail.

4.82 (i) **The warrant to search for material other than legally privileged, excluded or special procedure material** — Schedule 7, para 2, provides that a magistrate may issue a warrant, which is similar to the s 8 (Art 10) warrant in the PACE Act and Order. The magistrate must be satisfied that a terrorism investigation is being carried out and that there are reasonable grounds for believing —

(a) that there is material on the specified premises which is likely to be of substantial value (whether by itself or together with other material) to the investigation;

(b) that the material does not consist of or include items subject to legal privilege, excluded material or special procedure material; and

(c) that —

(i)   it is not practicable to communicate with the person entitled to grant entry to the premises; or

(ii)   it is not practicable to communicate with any person entitled to grant access to the material; or

(iii)   entry to the premises will not be granted without a warrant; or

(iv)   the purpose of a search may be frustrated or prejudiced unless immediate entry to the premises is secured (para 2(1) and (2)).

A warrant issued under para 2 authorises the constable to enter the premises, to search them and any person found there, and to seize and retain anything found there or on any person, other than legally privileged material, if there are reasonable grounds for believing —

(a)   that it is likely to be of substantial value (whether by itself or together with other material) to the investigation; and

(b)   that it is necessary to seize it in order to prevent it being concealed, lost, damaged, altered or destroyed (para 3).

Para 3 would appear to contradict para 2(1)(b) which authorises the issue of a warrant only if it does not include legally privileged, excluded or special procedure material, by stating that the warrant authorises the search of the premises and persons found there and the seizure of anything found except legally privileged material. However, this warrant is subject to ss 15 and 16 of the PACE Act 1984 (Arts 17 and 18 of the 1989 Order). S 15(2)(c) (Art 17(2)(c)) requires that the warrant identify (so far as is practicable) the articles (material) to be sought while s 16(8) (Art 18(8)) confines the search to the extent required for the purpose for which the warrant was issued. It follows that para 3 rather clumsily incorporates s 19(3) of the PACE Act 1984 (Art 21(3) of the 1989 Order) which permits the seizure of anything found in premises which is evidence of an offence, and similarly permits the seizure and retention of anything found on the premises (and persons), including excluded or special procedure material, but does not authorise the search of the premises for such material. Para 10 of Schedule 7 states that powers of seizure conferred by Schedule 7 are without prejudice to the powers conferred by s 19 of the PACE Act 1984. Therefore apart from the power to seize material found on persons, para 2(3) adds nothing to police powers, indeed para 2(3)(a) is more restrictive than s 19(3). (It may be argued that since Sch 7, para 10 does not refer to Art 21 of the 1989 Order it gives a limited power of seizure which is otherwise not available in Northern Ireland. However, the simpler explanation is that the POT Act 1989 was passed before the PACE Order 1989, therefore Art 21 (and Arts 22 and 23) applies to Schedule 7 searches.)

4.83   (ii) **Order for production of excluded or special procedure material** — Schedule 7, paras 3 and 4 provide a procedure under which a constable can make application to a circuit judge (county court judge in N.I.) for an order requiring the production to a constable of material consisting of excluded or special procedure material (but not legally privileged material) for him to take away, or to give a constable access to it. The procedure is based on Schedule 1 of the PACE Act 1984 (PACE Order 1989) but there are significant differences. They are:

(i)   the material must be sought for the purposes of a terrorist investigation not a serious arrestable offence, though such an offence may often have been committed by terrorists (para 3(1));

(ii)   an order may apply to excluded or special procedure material, but not to legally privileged material (para 3(1)). It may also apply to government departments and to material held subject to the Official Secrets Acts (para 4(5) and (6));

(iii)   an order may apply to material which is not yet in existence or in the possession of the person concerned, but is expected to come into existence or become available to the person within 28 days of the date of the order. Such an order will require the person concerned to inform the police as soon as possible after it comes into existence or becomes available to him (para 3(3));

(iv)   the conditions of which a judge must be satisfied are simply (a) that a terrorist investigation is being carried out and that there are reasonable grounds for believing that the material is likely to be of substantial value (whether by itself or together with other material) to that investigation; and (b) that it is in the public interest that the material be produced or that access be given to it, having regard —

(a)   to the benefit likely to accrue to the investigation; and

(b)   to the circumstances under which the person in possession holds it (para 3(5));

(v)   unlike the Schedule 1 procedure there is no provision for the person in possession of the material to contest the application, which is made ex parte. Instead provision is made (by Crown Court Rules) for the person subject to the order to seek the discharge or variation of the order (para 4(1) and (2));

(vi)   the period within which the material must be produced or access given to it shall be seven days or such longer or *shorter* period as the judge thinks appropriate in the particular circumstances (para 3(4));

(vii)   the order may, on the application of a constable, include an order that the person who appears to be entitled to grant entry to the premises allow a constable to enter to obtain access to the material (para 3(6)).

As with a Schedule 1 order, material held in a computer must be produced in a visible and legible form in which it can be taken away or read (para 4(4)). A para 3 order is to be treated as an order of the Crown Court (para 4(3)) and failure to comply with an order will be contempt of court.

4.84 (iii) **Warrant to search for excluded or special procedure material** — On application by a constable a circuit (county court) judge may issue a warrant if satisfied:

(a) that an order made under para 3 has not been complied with; or

(b) that there are reasonable grounds for believing that there is on the premises material consisting of or including excluded or special procedure material, that it does not include items subject to legal privilege and that the conditions in para 3(5) are fulfilled and a condition in para 5(3) is fulfilled in respect of that material (para 5(1) and (2)).

(NB para 5(2)(b) and (3) refer to 'the condition' but para 5(3) contains three conditions, any one of which may be fulfilled, 'a condition' is therefore more appropriate.)

The conditions set out in para 3(5) are those which must be fulfilled if an order is to be issued (see para 4.83(iv) above). The conditions in para 5(3) are the same as those set out in Sch 7, para 2(2)(a), (b) and (d) (see para 4.82(c) above) which refer to the practicability of contacting persons entitled to grant access to the premises or the material or the likelihood of serious prejudice to the investigation if immediate access to the material is not secured.

4.85 *Application of the PACE Act 1984 ss 15 and 16 (PACE Order 1989, Arts 17 and 18) and the Code of Practice* — Ss 15 and 16 of the PACE Act 1984 (Arts 17 and 18 of the PACE Order 1989) apply to the issue and execution of search warrants issued under Schedule 7 of the POT Act 1989 (see paras 4.14 et seq, ante). Code of Practice B also applies to Schedule 7 searches (COP 1.3(c)). Of particular relevance to such searches is COP B 2.4, which states that no application for a production order or warrant under Schedule 7 may be made without the authority of an officer of at least the rank of superintendent, and COP 2.7 which requires that an application for a warrant under Schedule 7 must indicate why the issue of a production order may seriously prejudice the investigation. COP B 5.5 states that in a terrorism investigation search there is no need for the officer conducting the search to identify himself by name, the warrant number is sufficient. Similarly COP B 5.8 states that a Notice of Rights and a copy warrant may be endorsed only with the officer's warrant number. COP B 5.13 requires that an officer of at least the rank of inspector take charge of a search under Schedule 7. This also applies to searches under Schedule 1 of the PACE Act and Order and is discussed at para 4.77, ante).

4.86 *Explanation of seized or produced material* — A circuit (county court) judge may, on application by a constable, order any person specified in the order to provide an explanation of any material seized under a warrant issued under paras 3 or 5 or produced under a production order issued under para 3 (para 6(1)). Such an order will not require the disclosure of legally privileged information but a lawyer may be required to disclose the name and address of his client (para 6(2)). Statements made in response to an order may not be used in evidence against the person except for an offence of knowingly or recklessly making a false or misleading statement (para 6(4) and (5)) or on prosecution for some other offence where in giving evidence he makes a statement inconsistent with it (para 6(3)). Failure to comply with such an order will be contempt of court.

4.87 (iv) **Written orders to search in urgent cases** — Schedule 7, para 7 provides that a police officer of at least the rank of superintendent who has reasonable cause to believe that the case is one of great emergency and that in the interests of the State immediate action is necessary, may by written order signed by him give any constable the authority which may be given by a warrant under paras 2 or 5 of Schedule 7. The written order may be accompanied by a notice requiring the person to provide an explanation of any material seized in the same terms and subject to the same conditions as the para 6 requirement considered in para 4.86, above (para 7(4) and (6)). Failure to comply with such a notice without reasonable excuse is a summary offence (para 7(5)).

4.88 (v) **Orders by the Secretary of State in relation to offences involving financial assistance for terrorism** — Where a terrorist investigation concerns acts which appear to the Secretary of State to be an offence under Part III of the POT Act 1989 (offences of contributing toward acts of terrorism (s 9); contributing to the resources of proscribed organisations (s 10); assisting in the retention or control of terrorist funds (s 11)), he may sign an order which gives any constable in Northern Ireland the authority, which a warrant under Schedule 7, paras 2 or 5 gives, to search for material which is not (in the case of para 2) or which is (in the case of para 5) excluded or special procedure material, or which imposes on a person in Northern Ireland the requirement to produce or give access to such material which an order under Schedule 7, para 3 imposes (para 8(2)). He must be satisfied that all the requirements for the issue of a warrant or order set out in paras 2 and 5 and para 3 are fulfilled and that disclosure of information which would be necessary under those provisions would be likely to prejudice the capability of the RUC in relation to the investigation of the offences mentioned above, or would otherwise prejudice the safety of, or persons in, Northern Ireland (para 8(2)(a) and (b)). Disobeying a Secretary of State's production order is an offence (para 8(3)) punishable on conviction on indictment by two years imprisonment or a fine or both; and on summary conviction to up to six months imprisonment or a fine or both. This production order may be varied or revoked and the procedure for such variation or revocation is the same as that in respect of Schedule 7, para 3 orders (para 8(4)) (see para 4.83(v), ante). The Secretary of State may also, by written order signed by him, require the person to provide an explanation of material seized or produced under a written order under para 8(2). This too is in exactly the same terms and subject to the same conditions as the requirement under para 6. Para 7(5) which makes it a summary offence to fail to comply with such a notice also applies to this notice (para 8(5)).

4.89 *Powers of seizure* — the powers of seizure contained in s 19 of the PACE Act 1984 (Art 21 of the 1989 Order) are available whenever a constable is on premises executing a warrant under paras 2 or 5 or a written order under paras 7 or 8 which give the same authority to enter and search premises. A terrorist investigation is to be treated as an investigation of or in connection with an offence, therefore ss 21 and 22 of the PACE Act 1984 (access to and copying of material seized and retention of such material) apply in respect of material seized or obtained under any of the Schedule 7 powers (para 10(1)). This position is the same in Northern Ireland where the Arts 23 and 24 are expressed to apply to any statutory provision, including any passed or made after the making of the 1989 Order. These are discussed at para 4.44, ante. It will be noted that the warrant powers authorise the search of persons. Such a search must be by a person of the same sex (para 10(2)).

4.90 **Access to the Land Register** Para 9 of Schedule 7 which provided for access to the Land Register, a register of property and interests in property in England and Wales created under the Land Registration Act 1925, is repealed by Schedule 9 of the POT Act 1989 on the coming into force of the Land Registration Act 1988. This short measure provides that subject to such conditions as may be prescribed and on payment of a fee, anyone can inspect and make copies of and extracts from (a) entries on the Register and (b) documents referred to in the Register which are in the custody of the Registrar (other than leases or charges or copies of leases and charges). Documents not falling within (b) which are in the custody of the Registrar may be inspected etc (1) as of right, in such cases as may be prescribed and (2) at the discretion of the Registrar in any other case, subject to prescribed conditions and payment of any fee. It follows that the police need no special powers to obtain access to Land Registers hence the repeal of Schedule 9 of the 1989 Act and of a similar provision in s 33 of the Drug Trafficking Offences Act 1986 (see para 4.104, post).

4.91 *Offences in connection with Schedule 7 warrants or orders —* s 17(2) of the POT Act 1989 provides that, when in relation to a terrorist investigation a warrant or order has been issued or made under Schedule 7, a person is guilty of an offence if, knowing or having reasonable cause to suspect that the investigation is taking place, he —

(a) makes any disclosure which is likely to prejudice the investigation; or

(b) falsifies, conceals, or destroys or otherwise disposes of or causes or permits the falsification, concealment, destruction or disposal of, material which is or is likely to be relevant to the investigation. S 17(3) provides that it is a defence for a person charged with an offence under s 17(2)(a) to prove —

    (i) that he did not know and had no reasonable cause to suspect that the disclosure was likely to prejudice the investigation; or

    (ii) that he had lawful authority or reasonable excuse for making the disclosure.

Section 17(4) provides that it is a defence for a person charged with an offence under s 17(2)(b) to prove that he had no intention of concealing any information contained in the material in question from the persons carrying out the investigation. As in all cases where the defendant bears the burden of proof the standard of proof is proof on the balance of probabilities. A person convicted of an offence under s 17(2) may, if convicted on indictment, be sentenced to imprisonment for a term not exceeding five years or a fine or both. On summary conviction six months imprisonment, a fine or both. The offence is therefore an arrestable offence attracting the summary power of arrest under s 24 of the PACE Act 1984 (Art 26 of the 1989 Order).

(B) The Security Service Act 1989

4.92 Before the passing of this Act, the security service (MI5) had no statutory basis for its activities. S 1 of the 1989 Act remedies this and puts MI5 under the authority of the Home Secretary. Its function is the protection of national security and, in particular its protection against threats from espionage, terrorism and sabotage, from the activities of agents of foreign powers and from actions intended to overthrow or undermine parliamentary democracy by political, industrial or violent means and to safeguard the economic well-being of the United Kingdom against threats posed by the actions or intentions of persons outside the British

Islands (s 1(2) and (3)). Examples of threats to the economic well-being were given by the Home Secretary as 'a threat from abroad in respect of a commodity' such as oil or the use by foreign powers of 'covert intelligence methods to obtain scientific and technical secrets' (Hansard, HC, vol 145, col 221). S 2(1) provides for the appointment of a Director General to control the Security Service. He is responsible for the efficiency of the Service and is under a duty to ensure —

> that there are arrangements for securing that no information is obtained by the Service except so far as is necessary for its functions and that such information is not disclosed except for that purpose or the prevention or detection of crime (s 2(a)). He must also ensure that the Service takes no action to further the interest of any political party (s 2(b)). The arrangements under s 2(a) must also ensure that such information is not used for prospective or actual employees except in accordance with provisions approved by the Secretary of State (s 2(3)). Section 2(4) requires an annual report from the Director General.

4.93 Home Secretary's Warrant — To assist in the discharge of their functions the Service can apply to the Home Secretary for a warrant authorising the taking of such action as is specified in the warrant in respect of any property specified (s 3(2)). No entry on or interference with property is unlawful if it is authorised by such a warrant (s 3(1)). The use of the phrase 'or interference with property' makes it clear that a s 3 warrant is more than a search warrant. There is no definition of 'interference', therefore it is capable of covering all tortious or criminal acts against property, not simply trespass. 'Property' is also not defined and must be taken to mean both real and personal property. A s 3 warrant could clearly authorise covert surveillance involving the 'bugging' of premises and similar invasions of privacy which may not involve trespass. It is also wide enough to include 'telephone tapping' but this activity is governed by the Interception of Communications Act 1985 which permits the issue of a warrant authorising the interception of communications if the Home Secretary considers it necessary in the interests of national security (see para 4.123, post).

4.94 Grounds for issue — s 3(2) gives the Secretary of State the authority to issue a warrant authorising the taking of actions specified in it if he:

(a) thinks it necessary to obtain information which —
    (i) is likely to be of substantial value in assisting the Service to discharge any of its functions; and
    (ii) cannot be reasonably obtained by other means; and
(b) is satisfied that satisfactory arrangements are in force under s 2(2)(a) with respect to the disclosure of the information obtained.

The subjective nature of the grounds for issue is only marginally qualified by the requirements of (a)(i) and (ii) and (b).

4.95 *Procedures for the issue of warrants* — Warrants must be issued personally by the Secretary of State or, in urgent cases, by a senior departmental official of Grade 3 or above. In the latter case the Secretary of State must have authorised the issue of the warrant, by telephone or similar means to the official, and a statement of this fact must be endorsed on the warrant (s 3(3)). Warrants issued by the Secretary of State last for six months but may be renewed by him at any time before it expires for a further six months from the date of renewal. An urgent warrant issued by a senior official lasts no more than two working days. It can, of course be replaced by a warrant issued by the Secretary of State but it seems that, assuming the matter is still urgent and the Secretary of State is not available in person, further warrants may be issued by that official (s 3(4) and (5)). The Secretary of State is legally bound to cancel any warrant if satisfied that the action authorised by it is no longer necessary (s 3(6)). Unlike search warrants which may be executed only once, a s 3 warrant stays in force for six months (or two working days if an urgent warrant) and authorises actions throughout that period.

4.96 Section 4 provides for the appointment of a Security Service Commissioner by the Prime Minister. The Commissioner must be, or have been, a judge of the High Court or above, whose functions include the keeping under review of the exercise of the Secretary of State's power to issue warrants under s 3. The present incumbent, Lord Justice Stuart-Smith, in his first annual report under the 1989 Act, declined 'in the public interest' to disclose the number of warrants issued under s 3 in 1990. The 'comparatively small number' of warrants issued were all found to have been properly issued under the 1989 Act.

(C) The Official Secrets Act 1989

4.97 The Official Secrets Act 1989 reforms the law by repealing the controversial 'catch all' provisions of s 2 of the Official Secrets Act 1911. The law now concentrates on the nature of the information disclosed and the damage done by such disclosure. It replaces the broad terms of s 2 with six defined categories of official information and makes the unauthorised disclosure of them an offence. These are:

1) Security and intelligence,
2) Defence,
3) International Relations,

4) Information obtained in confidence from other States or from international organisations,
5) Information likely to result in an offence or other related consequences,
6) Special investigations under statutory warrant issued under the Security Services Act 1989, s 3, or the Interception of Communications Act 1985, s 2.

In (1) to (5) it must be established that specific damage has been caused by the unauthorised disclosure. Where the accused is not a Crown servant or government contractor, it is a defence for him to prove that he did not know, or had no reasonable cause to believe, that the specific damage was likely to be caused. As far as present or former Crown servants or a government contractor are concerned, any unauthorised disclosure of information relating to security or intelligence will be treated as harmful. In (6) the prosecution must prove unauthorised disclosure of information about, or obtained by, action under a warrant under the 1985 or 1989 Acts. Section 11(1) and (2) of the Official Secrets Act 1989 make the offences under the Act arrestable offences by inserting into s 24(2) of the PACE Act 1984 a reference to offences under the 1989 Act (other than offences under s 8(1), (4) or (5)) (see para 5.09, post). Section 11(3) extends the power to issue search warrants under the Official Secrets Act 1911, s 9(1), to these arrestable offences and applies the restriction on the issue of such warrants in respect of legally privileged, excluded or special procedure material, imposed by s 9(2) of the PACE Act 1984 (Art 11(2) of the 1989 Order), to s 9(1) of the 1911 Act. The effect is to require an application under Schedule 1 of the PACE Act (or Order) whenever the material sought could have been obtained under a s 9(1) warrant, had the material not been legally privileged, excluded or special procedure material.

(D) Drug Trafficking Offences Act 1986

4.98   The Drug Trafficking Offences Act 1986 (DTO Act) enables courts in the United Kingdom to recover the proceeds of drug trafficking. These powers apply to all drug trafficking offences for which an offender is to be sentenced in the Crown Court. The Criminal Justice Act 1988 extends confiscation proceedings to all indictable offences, other than drug trafficking offences, and to certain other offences collectively known as 'offences to which Part VI of the Act applies'. Under the 1988 Act, a confiscation order can be made where the offender has benefited from offences within the scope of the Act for which he is to be sentenced, but only if those offences produced aggregate proceeds of at least £10,000. Part VI of the 1988 Act creates no new criminal offence. Some of the offences to which Part VI applies will be serious arrestable offences. In order to determine this the offences must be considered individually — a series of offences with aggregate proceeds of £10,000 will not necessarily be serious arrestable offences. Similarly many drug trafficking offences will be serious arrestable offences. In such cases the power to obtain a search warrant to search for evidence under s 8 of the PACE Act 1984 (Art 10 of the 1989 Order) and the power to apply for an access or production order (and in some circumstances a search warrant) in respect of excluded or special procedure material under Schedule 1 of the PACE Act and Order, will be available. However, because an offence can only be a serious arrestable offence if it is committed within the jurisdiction of the UK courts and the drug trade is international, the DTO Act provides powers to obtain access to or the production of materials (and in certain circumstances a search warrant). Given the extraordinarily wide provisions ('intentionally Draconian', per Lord Lane CJ in *R v Dickens* (1990) and cf *R v Robson* (1990)) available under the DTO Act to trace a person's assets (eg the definition of gift in s 5(9) and (10)), these powers are an indispensable means of enforcing them. They are modelled on the PACE Act 1984, Schedule 1, but are not confined to serious arrestable offences and contain other significant differences. The Act also contains incentives to encourage cooperation in drug trafficking investigations, and to discourage hindrance of such investigations. The 1988 Act similarly has an incentive to encourage cooperation.

4.99 The powers under the Drug Trafficking Offences Act — Sections 27 and 28 of the Act provide powers to obtain access to or the production of material which is likely to be of substantial value to investigations into drug trafficking, and, in limited circumstances, a warrant to enter premises to search for such material. These powers are similar to powers contained in Schedule 1 of the PACE Act 1984. The definitions of legally privileged, excluded and special procedure material are the same but there are significant procedural differences. These are:

(i) An order under s 27 can only be sought for the purposes of an investigation into drug trafficking. Drug trafficking is defined by s 38(1) of the 1986 Act. It means doing or being concerned in acts anywhere in the world which constitute one of a number of offences under the Misuse of Drugs Act 1971 (or the corresponding law of countries other than England and Wales) connected with the supply of controlled drugs. The offences are —

(a) producing or supplying a controlled drug in contravention of the MDA 1971, s 4(1) (or a corresponding law);

(b) transporting or storing a controlled drug in contravention of the MDA 1971, s 5(1) (or a corresponding law);

(c) importing or exporting a controlled drug in contravention of the MDA 1971, s 3(1) (or a corresponding law). Also included are persons who, in England, Wales or elsewhere, enter into or are otherwise concerned in an arrangement whereby —

1) the retention or control by or on behalf of another person of the other person's proceeds of drug trafficking is facilitated, or

2) the proceeds of drug trafficking by another person are used to secure that funds are placed at the other person's disposal or are used for the other person's benefit to acquire property by way of investment.

These are offences under s 24 of the DTO Act 1986 if carried out in England and Wales.

(ii)   Unlike applications under Schedule 1 of the PACE Act and Order, there is no provision for the person in possession of the material sought to contest the issue of the order. The hearing will be ex parte and, as with production orders under the POT Act 1989, provision is made (by Crown Court Rules) for the person subject of the order to seek its discharge or variation (s 27(6)) (Crown Court Rules 1982 r 26B).

(iii)   The conditions which a judge must be satisfied are fulfilled and which are less restrictive than those under the PACE Act 1984, are:

(a)   that there are reasonable grounds for *suspecting* that a person specified in the application has carried on or has benefited from drug trafficking,

(b)   that there are reasonable grounds for *suspecting* that the material to which the application relates —

1) is likely to be of substantial value (whether by itself or together with other material) to the drug trafficking investigation, and

2) does not consist of or include items subject to legal privilege or excluded material; and

(c)   that there are reasonable grounds for *believing* that it is in the public interest that the material be produced or access should be given to it, having regard to the benefit likely to accrue to the investigation and to the circumstances under which the person in possession of the material holds it (s 27(4)(a) to (c)).

It will be noted that conditions (a) and (b) require only the lower threshold of reasonable suspicion, while condition (c) requires reasonable grounds for believing (for a discussion of these concepts see paras 2.02 to 12, ante). All the other production orders require reasonable belief in respect of all the conditions. The application must specify with some particularity what material is sought. This is important not only because the person in possession is not present to contest the application, but also to enable the judge to determine that the material does not consist of or include legally privileged or excluded material (defined in exactly the same terms as Schedule 1 of the PACE Act 1984 discussed at paras 4.55 and 4.59 ante).

(iv) The material which can be obtained under a s 27 Order is anything except legally privileged or excluded material (s 27(4) (b)(ii)). There is no reference to special procedure material. Such material is, however, obtainable under a s 27 order and such an order is not, as Schedule 1, para 3 of the PACE Act and Order is, confined to material within that definition. Thus, while a judge cannot issue a production order under Schedule 1 of the 1984 Act if the material is not special procedure material, he can issue a s 27 order in respect of such material provided it is not legally privileged or excluded material. In addition s 27 overrides any obligation of secrecy or confidentiality imposed on the holder of the material whether statutory or not, and may apply to material in the possession of a government department (s 27(9)). 'Material' is not defined. It clearly includes documents as defined by s 10 of the Civil Evidence Act 1968 but would also include anything in tangible form even if not a document within that definition. Information contained in a computer is included. It must be produced in a visible and legible form so that it can be taken away or read (s 27(8)).

(v) When a judge makes an order for access to material under s 27(2)(b) he may also, on the application of a constable, make an order requiring the person entitled to grant entry to the premises to allow a constable to enter the premises to obtain access to the material (s 27(5)). This is not a power to enter and search but merely facilitates entry to premises in those cases in which the person named in the access order is not the person entitled to grant access to the premises. Such an order is not required when a production order is issued because the material can be brought out of the premises. The entry order should name the person to whom it is directed. On one interpretation of s 27(5) the application for the entry order should accompany the application for an access order. However, a more likely interpretation is that it can be made at the same time or afterwards. If, for example, a constable is refused entry to premises after an access order has been served, it is simpler to permit him to apply for an entry order rather than seek a warrant because the access order has not been complied with.

(vi) Despite the similarity to the PACE Act (and Order) and the POT Act 1989 Order for production of or access to material, Code of

Practice B does not apply to applications for Orders under the DTO Act 1986. However, it will rarely be the case that an officer of the rank of Superintendent does not authorise such an application.

4.100   *Search Warrants* — s 28 of the DTO Act 1986 authorises the issue of a search warrant by a circuit judge in respect of drug trafficking offences as defined by s 38 of that Act (see para 4.99(i) above). The breadth of that definition means that no offence need have been committed within the jurisdiction. A constable or an officer of Customs and Excise may apply. The application for a search warrant under this Act is governed by s 15 of the PACE Act 1984 and their execution by s 16 of that Act and Code of Practice B. A warrant may be issued if the judge is satisfied that any of three sets of conditions are fulfilled.

(i)   The first is the most obvious, that a s 27 order for access to or production of the material has not been complied with (s 28(2)(a)).

(ii)   The second is that the conditions for the issue of a s 27 order are fulfilled but that it would not be appropriate to make an order under that section in relation to the material because —

  (a)   it is not practicable to communicate with any person entitled to produce the material, or

  (b)   it is not practicable to communicate with any person entitled to grant access to the material or entitled to grant entry to the premises on which the material is situated, or

  (c)   the investigation for the purposes of which the application is made might be seriously prejudiced unless a constable could secure immediate access to the material (s28 (2)(b) and (3)).

(iii)   The third is that

  (a)   there are reasonable grounds for suspecting that a specified person has carried on or benefited from drug trafficking, and

  (b)   there are reasonable grounds for suspecting that there is on the premises material relating

    (i)   to the specified person, or

    (ii)   to drug trafficking generally, and

    (iii)   which is likely to be of substantial value (by itself or with other material) to the investigation for which the application is made

but that the material cannot at the time of the application be particularised, and

  (c)   either of the conditions (a) or (c) in the s 28(2)(b) warrant conditions in (ii) above are fulfilled (s 28(2)(c) and (4)).

COP B 2.7 requires that as respects applications for warrants under Sch. 1 of the PACE Act and the POT Act 1989 the reasons why the investigation may be prejudiced must be stated. Though not applicable to applications under s 28 it would be wise to adopt this provision. The issue of a warrant under the conditions set out in s 28(2)(b) and (3) is understandable. Surprise is sometimes essential when there is reason to believe that the material sought might be removed or destroyed if the s 27 procedure were adopted. The s 28(c) and (4) warrant is less easy to justify. The essential requirement that it is not possible to particularise the material sought comes close to authorising a fishing expedition. There is a contradiction between this provision and the requirements of ss 15 and 16 of the PACE Act 1984 (Arts 17 and 18 of the 1989 Order) which apply to s 28 warrants. Section 15(2)(c) states that it is a constable's duty to identify, so far as is practicable, the articles to be sought, while s 15(b) requires that the warrant similarly identify the articles sought. The absence of any particularity in the s 28(2)(c) and (4) conditions of issue suggests that neither of these requirements can be satisfied. Section 16(8) limits the search to the extent required for the purpose for which the warrant was issued. If the purpose is to search for unspecified material such a limitation is of no consequence.

4.101 *Powers of seizure and retention* — s 28(5) provides for a power of seizure and the retention of material sought in the warrant. A warrant under s 28 does not authorise the search for legally privileged or excluded material, therefore such material cannot be seized under the warrant. However, excluded material and any other material not specified in the warrant except legally privileged material, may be seized under the provision of s 19 of the PACE Act 1984 (Act 21 of the 1989 Order) provided the conditions set out in that section are fulfilled (see para 4.42, ante). S 29 provides that a drug trafficking investigation shall be treated as an investigation of or in connection with an offence for the purposes of ss 21 and 22 of the PACE Act 1984 (Arts 23 and 24 of the 1989 Order). It follows that the provisions of those sections apply to material seized under s 28 or produced under a s 27(2)(a) order.

4.102 *Offences of prejudicing an investigation* — s 31 of the DTO Act 1986 provides that where an order under s 27 has been made or applied for and not refused, or a s 28 warrant issued, it is an offence for any person, knowing or suspecting that the investigation is taking place, to make any disclosure which is likely to prejudice the investigation. It is a defence for a person charged with such an offence to prove (on the balance of probabilities):— that he did not know or suspect that the disclosure was likely to prejudice the investigation; or that he had lawful authority or reasonable excuse for making the disclosure. The offence, like the offence under the POT Act 1989, s 17, is punishable by five years imprisonment or a fine or both on conviction on indictment, and to six months imprisonment, a fine or both on summary conviction.

4.103   *Incentives to encourage informants* — s 24(3) of the DTO Act 1986 gives immunity from any civil or criminal liability which might otherwise attach to persons who disclose to a constable any suspicion or belief concerning the proceeds of drug trafficking. This can be of particular importance to banks and other bodies which handle peoples' financial affairs under an obligation of confidence. S 98 of the Criminal Justice Act 1988 creates a similar immunity in respect of such information provided to the police concerning the proceeds of crimes other than drug trafficking.

4.104   *Inspection of Land Register* — s 33 of the DTO Act 1986, which provided a power to require the Land Registrar to disclose information kept by him in the Land Register under the Land Registration Act 1925, was repealed by s 1(2) of the Land Registration Act 1988 which makes provision for access to the Land Register (see para 4.90, ante). A similar power exists in s 100 of the Criminal Justice Act 1988.

4.105   *Disclosure of information held by a government department* — s 30 of the DTO Act 1986 provides a procedure under which a government department can be required to disclose material held by them, in cases where it would be possible for the High Court to make a charging or restraint order in connection with proceedings which have been or are yet to be instituted. The section provides for a two-stage procedure — an application by a prosecutor to the High Court for production to the High Court of material thought likely to facilitate the exercise of the powers of the High Court under ss 8 to 11 of the 1986 Act (restraint, charging and enforcement orders), or the exercise of powers by a receiver appointed under ss 8 to 11, or a charging order. An order for production to the High Court may be made without allowing an officer of the material holding department to appear. When the material has been produced to the High Court, the court may make a further order for the disclosure of the material to a receiver, police officer, member of the Crown Prosecution Service or an officer of Customs and Excise. However, this order cannot be made unless an officer of the material holding department is permitted to make representations. If the disclosure is to a receiver, it must also appear that the material is 'likely to be of substantial value in exercising functions relating to drug trafficking'. Material disclosed to a police officer, crown prosecutor or Customs and Excise officer may be further disclosed for purposes relating to drug trafficking.

(E)   The Criminal Justice (Confiscation) (Northern Ireland) Order 1990

4.106   This Order —

(a)   provides for courts to order the confiscation of assets of offenders convicted of highly profitable crime;

(b)   provides for courts to order the confiscation of proceeds of drug trafficking;

(c)   provides for certain enhancement of court enforcement powers in order to secure payment of confiscation orders; and

(d)   makes further provision in connection with drug trafficking.

In this respect the Order does for Northern Ireland what the Drug Trafficking Offences Act 1986 and the Criminal Justice Act 1988 does for the rest of the United Kingdom. So far as investigative powers are concerned Art 31 of the Order provides for a county court judge to make an order requiring the production of, or access to, material in connection with a drug trafficking investigation in exactly the same terms as s 27 of the Drug Trafficking Offences Act 1986 (see paras 4.98–99, ante). Art 32 authorises the issue of a warrant to search for and seize such material in exactly the same terms as s 28 of the DTO Act 1986 (see para 4.100, ante). Art 33 provides that access and retention requirements imposed in respect of seized material by Arts 23 and 24 of the PACE (N.I) Order 1989, apply to material seized under Arts 31 and 32 of the 1990 Order. The powers of seizure when a constable is lawfully on premises provided by Art 21 of the 1989 Order are available when a constable is lawfully on premises enforcing an order or executing a warrant under the 1990 Order. 'Items subject to legal privilege', 'excluded material' and 'premises' are defined as in the 1989 Order. As in the DTO Act 1986 'items subject to legal privilege' and 'excluded material' cannot be the subject of an order or warrant under the 1990 Order. Art 35 creates offences of prejudicing an investigation into drug trafficking by disclosing information about orders or warrants applied for or issued, which equate with those under s 31 of the DTO Act (see para 4.102, ante). Art 36 provides the incentive to assist drug trafficking investigations by providing immunity from civil or criminal liability to persons who disclose such information, in the same terms as s 24(3) of the DTO Act 1986 (see para 4.103, ante). Art 34 of the 1990 Order provides a procedure under which government departments may be required to disclose material held by them, which is exactly the same as that provided by s 30 of the DTO Act 1986 (see para 4.105, ante).

(F) The Criminal Justice Act 1987

4.107   Section 1 of this Act establishes a Serious Fraud Office, presided over by a Director under the superintendence of the Attorney-General, to investigate and prosecute serious or complex frauds. The SFO is unique in that it comprises lawyers and police officers operating as an investigative team assisted by accountants. Section 2 provides the investigatory powers. They are based on the powers given to inspectors of the Department of Trade and Industry by the Companies Act 1985 and the Financial Services Act 1986. The powers of the Director under s 2 are only exercisable for the purposes of an investigation of a serious or complex fraud (currently a minimum of £2 million) under s 1, 'in any case in which it appears to him that there is good reason to do so'. However, the powers are exercisable not only in relation to a person suspected of such fraud, but also to 'the affairs, or aspects of the affairs of any person'.

4.108   Procedure — The Director may by notice in writing to the person whose affairs are to be investigated, ('the person under investigation') or any other person whom he believes has relevant information:

1)   require him to attend at a specified time and place, and answer questions or otherwise furnish *information* with respect to any matter relevant to the investigation (s 2(2); in 1990–1, 765 notices were issued). There is no right to refuse to answer such questions on the grounds that to do so may incriminate the person and there is no right to obtain particulars of the investigation (*Ex p Nadir* (1990)). However, any statement made in response to such questioning cannot be used as evidence in relation to the offence under investigation except as a prior inconsistent statement (s 2(8)). It is an offence knowingly or recklessly to make a false or misleading statement (s 2(14)) and any statement obtained under s 2(2) can be used as evidence of that offence. A person cannot be required to disclose legally privileged information but a lawyer can be required to disclose the name and address of a client (s 2(9)). This overrides the duty not to do so except on the order of a court (see the Professional Conduct of Solicitors (1986), para 10.5 and *Pascall v Galinski* (1969)). There is no protection for information which is otherwise confidential except that a banker can only be required to breach an obligation of confidence if the person to whom it is owed consents or the requirement is made by the Director (or his delegate) personally.

2)   require him to produce at a specified time and place any specified *documents* which appear to the Director to relate to any matter relevant to the investigation or any other document of a specified class which appear to him to so relate (s 2(3)). The Director can require an explanation of any document produced and may take

copies or extracts from them. If they are not produced the person required to produce them may be required to state, to the best of his knowledge, where they are (s 2(3)(a) and (b)). 'Documents' includes information recorded in any form (s 2(18), and, so, for example, requirement to produce a computer print out or a transcript of recorded conversation can be made. The power to require an explanation of documents under s 2(3)(a) means that documents which are not comprehensible to the investigator can be required to be translated into a comprehensible form. As with information, legally privileged documents cannot be the subject of a requirement under s 2(3) (s 2(9)) and bankers cannot be required to produce documents in breach of their obligation of confidence except with the consent of the person to whom it is owed or if the Director (or his delegate) personally makes the requirement. Otherwise there is no protection for excluded or special procedure material as defined by the PACE Act 1984 (PACE Order 1989). It should be noted that the requirement under s 2(2) and (3) (and the search warrant under s 2(4)) is not confined to evidence likely to be of substantial value to an investigation (as is the case with PACE Act and Order production orders and warrants and other orders and warrants considered in this section). Relevance to the investigation is the only criterion.

4.109 *Search Warrant* — s 2(4) authorises a magistrate to issue a warrant to enter and search premises for documents relevant to an investigation if the magistrate is satisfied that there are reasonable grounds for believing:—

(a)   (i)   that a person has failed to comply with an obligation to produce them under s 2(3); or

      (ii)   it is not practicable to serve a notice under s 2(3); or

      (iii)   that the service of a notice might seriously prejudice the investigation; and

(b)   that the documents are on the premises specified in the information (s 2(4)).

The warrant authorises a constable to enter (using such force as is reasonably necessary) and search the premises and to take possession of the documents specified and to take such steps as are necessary to preserve them and prevent interference with them (s 2(5)). This power must be read in conjunction with the powers of seizure, access and retention contained in ss 19–22 of the PACE Act 1984 (Arts 21–24 of the 1989 Order), which apply to this warrant power. It would therefore seem that the power to take possession and steps to preserve them is intended to deal with the situation in which there is a large number of documents which cannot immediately be removed from the premises. Thus a files storage room may be secured and only supervised access, or no access, allowed to it during the course of the search. Ss 15 and 16 of the PACE Act 1984 (Arts 17 and 18 of the PACE Order 1989) (Para 4.14, ante) apply to this warrant as does Code of Practice B (see COP B 1.3(a)). It follows that the application must be by written information (complaint in NI) on oath (see also s 15(4) 1984 Act) which must specify the premises to be entered and to identify, so far as is practicable, the documents sought. Similarly the warrant, which authorises entry on one occasion only (s 15(5), (Art 17(5)), must specify the premises and documents sought. Though Code B 2.7 does not specifically apply to applications for this warrant, the application should indicate why it is believed that service of a notice requiring production of the documents might seriously prejudice the investigation. In addition to the requirements of s 16 (Art 18) s 2(6) and (7) of the 1987 Act require that unless it is not practicable in the circumstances, a constable executing a warrant under s 2(4), must be accompanied by a member of the SFO or a person, though not a member of the SFO, who has been designated by the Director to accompany him. The former will usually be the lawyer supervising the investigation; the latter may well be an accountant who is assisting and advising the investigation. As with the requirement to produce documents, a warrant cannot authorise the seizure of legally privileged documents but there is no protection for excluded or special procedure material. S 2(10), which gives limited protection to bankers, appears to apply only to a requirement under s 2(3).

4.110 *Offences* — It is an offence knowingly or recklessly to make a false or misleading statement in response to a requirement under s 2 (s 2(14) and (15)). It is also an offence for a person who knows or suspects that an investigation by the police or the SFO into serious or complex fraud is being or is likely to be carried out to falsify, dispose of, or to cause or permit the falsification, concealment, destruction or disposal of, documents which he knows or suspects are or would be relevant to an investigation. It is a defence for the person accused to prove that he had no intention of concealing the facts disclosed by the documents (s 2(16) and (17)).

(G) The Criminal Justice (International Co-operation) Act 1990 (in force 1 July 1991)

4.111 The growth of international crime (particularly in the area of drug trafficking) has added impetus to international co-operation between countries. Two international conventions, the 1957 European Convention on Mutual Assistance and the 1988 Vienna Convention against Illicit Traffic in Narcotic Drugs and Psychotic Substances are ratified by the 1990 Act. The Criminal Justice Act 1988 provides, inter alia, for the service of overseas process in the UK and the service of UK process overseas and similarly for the use of overseas evidence in UK courts and for the use of UK evidence in overseas courts. Two provisions are of relevance in respect of this chapter on the obtaining of evidence.

(a) Obtaining evidence from overseas for use in the UK.
(b) Obtaining evidence in the UK for use overseas.

4.112 *Obtaining evidence from overseas* — Section 3 of the 1990 Act provides for the issue of a 'letter of request' requesting the assistance of a foreign jurisdiction in obtaining evidence. This section replaces s 29 of the Criminal Justice Act 1988 which is repealed by Schedule 5 of the 1990 Act. Application must be made to a magistrate (residing magistrate in NI) or a judge (s 3(1)) by a prosecuting authority, or if proceedings have been instituted, by a person charged in those proceedings (s 3(2)). If it appears to the magistrate or judge

(a) that an offence has been committed or that there are reasonable grounds for suspecting that an offence has been committed; and
(b) that proceedings in respect of the offence have been instituted or the offence is being investigated,

he may issue a letter requesting assistance in obtaining outside the United Kingdom the evidence specified in the letter for use in the proceedings or investigation (s 3(1)). 'Evidence' includes documents and other articles and is therefore wide enough to cover all the forms in which information is conveyed or stored. The letter of request must specify the evidence or articles sought and, since it will be the source of the authority to obtain the evidence in the overseas jurisdiction it would seem necessary to particularise the documents or articles required. It will be noted that an application may be made in respect of any offence not simply serious arrestable or even arrestable offences, and that the court is not required to embark on an inquiry as to the relevance of the evidence to the proceedings or investigation. However, the magistrate or judge has a discretion and may not issue a letter of request in respect of a minor offence or evidence of only marginal relevance. In addition the letter of request must normally be passed to the Secretary of State for transmission to the court or tribunal specified in the letter and exercising jurisdiction in the place where the evidence is to be obtained, or to the appropriate authority for receiving such requests recognised by the government of the country in question (s 3(4)(a) and (b)). A 'Central Authority' within the Home Office has been set up to monitor and authorise all requests for assistance. Doubtless this office will act as a filter and weed out such requests. In cases of urgency a letter of request may be sent direct to a court or tribunal (s 4(5)) but where there is a bilateral Agreement or Arrangement they must always go through the Secretary of State.

4.113 Section 3(3) empowers the Secretary of State to designate a prosecuting authority to issue a letter of request without reference to a court. The minimal grounds for the issue of a letter of request by a court means that they are not much of a safeguard against fishing expeditions. The real safeguard, except in urgent cases, is the Central Authority to whom the letter of request must be sent for transmission to the overseas court or authority.

The following agencies have been authorised to make application to the Central Authority:

The Director of Public Prosecutions
The Crown Prosecution Service
The Fraud Investigation Service
The Serious Fraud Office
The Attorney General
The Department of Trade and Industry
H.M. Commissioner of Customs and Excise.

4.114 *Limitations on the use of overseas evidence.* — Evidence once obtained by a letter of request must not be used for any purpose other than that specified in the letter except with the consent of the authority recognised as the appropriate authority for receiving letters of request. When any document or other article obtained by such a letter is no longer required for the purpose for which it was obtained, it must be returned unless that authority indicates that it need not be (s 3(7)). It would seem that this limitation is confined to evidence or articles obtained through the appropriate authority mentioned in s 3(4)(b). Where it is obtained through an overseas court or tribunal, it does not apply but such a limitation may be imposed as a condition of the provision of such evidence.

4.115 Statements obtained by letter of request from overseas must comply with the rules of admissibility under the law of the U.K. The admissibility of documentary evidence is now governed by ss 23 and 24 of the Criminal Justice Act 1988. If the requirements of either section are satisfied, the statement is admissible subject to a judicial discretion not to admit it under s 25 or, if prepared for the purpose of pending or contemplated criminal proceedings or of a criminal investigation, subject to the leave of the court under s 26. Section 3(8) of the 1990 Act requires that, in exercising the discretion not to admit a statement contained in evidence obtained under a letter of request, the court shall have regard (in addition to the matters to which it must have regard by virtue of s 25(2)(a) to (d)) —

(a) to whether it was possible to challenge the statement by questioning the person who made it; and

(b) if proceedings have been instituted, to whether the local law allowed the parties to the proceedings to be legally represented when the evidence was being taken.

4.116 *Obtaining evidence for use overseas.* Section 4 of the 1990 Act authorises the Secretary of State by notice in writing to nominate a court in England, Wales or Northern Ireland to receive evidence requested by a court or tribunal in another country or territory, or by a prosecuting authority or by any other authority in such country or territory which appears to him to have the function of making such requests. The evidence must be required in connection with criminal proceedings instituted, or with a criminal investigation being carried on, in that country or territory. The Secretary of State, if satisfied that

(a) an offence under the law of the country or territory in question has been, or is reasonably suspected of having been, committed; and

(b) proceedings in respect of the offence have been instituted or an investigation is being carried on there,

has an unfettered discretion, 'if he thinks fit', to nominate a court to receive such evidence (defined as including documents or other articles s 4(5) s 4(2)). In order to receive such evidence the court has the power to secure the attendance of witnesses and to take evidence on oath (s 4(6) and Sch 1). Para 4 of Sch 1 prescribes the circumstances in which witnesses may or may not be compelled to give evidence and rules of court may be made under s 10 of the 1990 Act. Where the request relates to a fiscal matter in respect of which proceedings have not been instituted, the Secretary of State cannot exercise the power under s 4(2) unless

(a) the request is from a commonwealth country or one with which the U.K. has a treaty; or

(b) he is satisfied that the conduct constituting an offence would be an offence of the same or similar nature if done in the U.K. (s 4(3)).

4.117 *Orders for the production of or warrants to search for and seize material relevant to an overseas investigation —* S 7(1) of the 1990 Act extends the scope of s 8 and Schedule 1 of the PACE Act 1984 (Art 10 and Sch 1 of the Northern Ireland Order) to cover offences committed abroad provided that they would amount to a serious arrestable offence if committed in the U.K., while s 7(2) provides for a search warrant to search premises in this country occupied or controlled by a person being proceeded against or having been arrested abroad for an offence which would have been an arrestable offence within the meaning of s 24 of the PACE Act 1984 (Art 26 of the Northern Ireland Order) if committed in the U.K. No application for an order or a warrant under s 7(1) or (2) can be made except on the direction of the Secretary of State in response to a request received:

(a)   from a court or tribunal exercising criminal jurisdiction, or a prosecuting authority, in the country or territory in question; or
(b)   from any other authority in that country or territory which appears to have the function of making such requests,

and any evidence seized by a constable by virtue of this section must be passed to the Secretary of State for transmission to that court, tribunal or authority (s 7(4)). The evidence may require verifying documentation (eg an affidavit confirming that the evidence was found and seized from a particular location).

4.118   The application for a s 8 (Art 10) warrant or an order for access to or the production of excluded or special procedure material (or a warrant to search for such material if appropriate), is governed by the PACE Act 1984 (PACE Order in Northern Ireland) and Code of Practice B except for the direction of the Secretary of State mentioned above which will have to be proved to the magistrate or judge. The issue of a warrant to search premises under s 7(2) of the 1990 Act is governed by that subsection. It provides that a magistrate may issue a warrant to enter and search premises and seize evidence found there if he is satisfied

(a)   that criminal proceedings have been instituted against a person in a country or territory outside the U.K. or that a person has been arrested in the course of a criminal investigation carried on there; and
(b)   that the conduct constituting the offence which is subject of the proceedings or the investigation would constitute an arrestable offence within the meaning of the PACE Act 1984 (or PACE (NI) Order 1989) if it had occurred in the UK; and
(c)   that there are reasonable grounds for suspecting that there is on premises in the U.K. occupied or controlled by that person evidence relating to the offence other than items subject to legal privilege within the meaning of the 1984 Act (1989 Order). To satisfy (c), much reliance on police work overseas will usually be inevitable. Sections 15 and 16 of the PACE Act 1984 (Articles 17 and 18 of the NI Order) apply to the application for and execution of this warrant, nevertheless s 7(3) imposes the same limitation as does s 16(8) (Art 18(8)) — that the power to search is only a power to search to the extent reasonably required for the purpose of discovering the evidence specified in the warrant. The evidence seized must be passed to the Secretary of State for transmission to the requesting body (s 7(4)). Where the evidence consists of documents, the original or a copy can be transmitted. If an article, the article itself or a description, photograph or other representation can be transmitted. In either case it will depend on what is necessary in order to comply with the request (s 7(6)) and that will depend upon the law of evidence in the requesting state. The Treasury may by order direct that these powers

be exercised by an officer of Customs and Excise (s 7(7)). The Secretary of State may by order direct that any of these powers may also be exercisable by a person of any other description specified in the Order (s 7(7)).

So, for example, a warrant can be sought to search D's home, D being a British national, for evidence of conspiracy to circulate pornography abroad, of computer crime involving large scale fraud perpetuated abroad but orchestrated from within the UK, and of a wide variety of customs' offences. Similarly if a foreign police force is investigating a person for a serious offence such as drug-trafficking (though most of the 1990 Act is concerned with drugs, these provisions are not tied to such offences), a constable can apply to a circuit judge for a production order to gain access to confidential material held, for example, by a bank in the hope of tracking down the proceeds of the crime. As with the solely internal use of Sch 1, however, there is no statutory prohibition on the holder of the information telling a home or overseas customer of the police investigation.

4.119   *Transfer of UK prisoner to give evidence or assist investigation and transfer of overseas prisoners to give evidence or assist investigation in the U.K.* — Section 5 gives the Secretary of State the power, if he thinks fit, to issue a warrant providing for a prisoner serving a sentence in a prison or other institution in the U.K. to be transferred to a country or territory outside the U.K. in order to give evidence in criminal proceedings there, or be identified or otherwise assist in the proceedings or investigation. However, no warrant may be issued without the prisoner's consent (s 5(2)). Section 6 provides a similar procedure for bringing a prisoner from overseas to assist in proceedings or investigations in the U.K. A witness order or summons must have been made in respect of the prisoner detained abroad or the Secretary of State must consider it desirable for a prisoner to be identified in or otherwise assist such proceedings or the investigation in the U.K. (s 6(1)). This process is also subject to the consent of the prisoner (s 6(3)).

4.120   Section 23 of the 1990 Act amends s 23 of the Misuse of Drugs Act 1971 by adding a new s (3A) which provides that the power of a constable to enter the premises of persons carrying on the business of producer or supplier of controlled drugs and to inspect books, documents etc, under the authority of a general or special order of the Secretary of State, under s 23(1) of the 1971 Act, shall be exercisable also for the purposes of Part II of the 1990 Act (which ratifies the 1988 Vienna Convention). Section 18 provides that anything which would constitute a drug trafficking offence if done on land in the U.K. is an offence if done on a British ship. Section 19 makes it an offence for a person in a British ship, a ship registered in a state other than the U.K. which is a party to the 1988 Vienna Convention, and a ship not registered in any country or territory, to have a controlled drug in his possession; or be in any way knowingly concerned in the carrying or concealing of a controlled drug on the ship, knowing or having reasonable cause to suspect that the drug is intended to be imported or exported contrary to s 3(1) of the Misuse of Drugs Act 1971. Section 20 and Sch 3 provide an enforcement power in respect of such ships. With the authority of the Secretary of State, and subject to the conditions set out in s 20, an enforcement officer, which includes a constable or customs and excise officer, may stop, board and if necessary require a ship to be taken to a port and detained. He may search it and require any person on board to provide information, using reasonable force, if necessary. If the enforcement officer reasonably suspects that an offence under ss 18 or 19 has been committed, he may arrest anyone he reasonably suspects to be guilty of it; and seize and detain anything found on the ship which appears to him to be evidence of the offence. An enforcement officer shall not be liable in civil or criminal proceedings for anything done in the purported performance of his functions under Sch 3 if the court is satisfied that the act was done in good faith and that there were reasonable grounds for doing it (Sch 3, para 8). Under s 14 a person commits an offence if he conceals, disguises, converts, or transfers from the UK any property which represents the proceeds of drug-trafficking; or if he acquires such proceeds for inadequate consideration (eg a nominal sum paid for a luxury flat). Frequently investigations into such offences will involve access to confidentially held information, either to establish the offence directly or to prove that a third party is being used as part of the laundering process. Again this is an ideal area for the PACE Schedule 1 procedure.

(H)   The Bankers' Books Evidence Act 1879 s 7

4.121   The procedure under s 9(2) and Schedule 1 of the PACE Act 1984 (Art 11(2) and Schedule 1 of the N.I. Order), under which a judge may issue an order for access to or the production of special procedure material, has considerably reduced the reliance on s 7 of the Bankers' Books Evidence Act 1879 but this Act remains in force and may be used in those cases in which a serious arrestable offence is not involved. Section 7 provides that:

> On the application of any party to legal proceedings a judge may order that such a party be at liberty to inspect and make copies of any entry in a banker's books for any of the purposes of such proceedings. That order may be made without summoning the bank or other party, and must be served on the bank three clear days before the order is to be obeyed, unless the judge otherwise orders.

It may be noted that:

1) The Act is confined to banks. This is a severe limitation given the increased role of building societies and other financial institutions.
2) It is confined to banker's books. While this includes the computerised accounts, it does not include such things as the bank manager's notes and diary, paid cheques and credit slips for which a witness summons will be required.
3) Legal proceedings (criminal or civil) must have been instituted by charge or summons in criminal cases.
4) Before making the order the judge should satisfy himself that the application is not a 'fishing expedition' to find material on which to hang a charge, but should consider whether the prosecution, who normally make such an application, have in their possession other evidence against the defendant (*Williams v Summerfield* (1972)).
5) The order ought to be limited to a certain specific period and ought not to be oppressive (*R v Marlborough Street Magistrates' Court, ex p Simpson* (1980)).
6) The fact that the defendant has given notice that he intends to plead guilty is not a reason for refusing the order (*Owen v Sambrook* (1981)).
7) Section 7 gives the court power to authorise the inspection of the bank account of a person who is not a party to the proceedings, but this power should only be exercised within narrow limits (see the two-fold test set out by Lord Esher MR in *South Staffordshire Tramways Co v Ebbsmith* (1895)).
8) An order may be made after the conclusion of a trial as well as before trial. This might be useful in criminal confiscation proceedings where the Drug Trafficking Offences Act 1986 or the PACE Act 1984 procedures are not available (see *D B Deniz Nakliyati TAS v Yugopetrol and others* (1991)).

(I)   The Interception of Communications Act 1985

4.122   In 1984 the European Court of Human Rights found that the then current practice of telephone tapping could not be justified under the European Convention on Human Rights and this placed an international obligation on the United Kingdom Government to change it. The response of the Government was the Interception of Communications Act 1985. This Act is not a comprehensive measure dealing with all forms of surveillance but only applies to the interception of communications transmitted by post or sent by public tele-communications systems licensed under the Telecommunications Act 1984. Such a system is defined by s 4(1) of this Act so as to include all public telecommunications systems, including links between British systems and those overseas. All forms of communications, whatsoever their nature, passing through such systems, such as letters, telephone calls, telex messages, telegrams, computer data or facsimile are covered. The system is not confined to messages passed through wires but includes all forms of message transmission such as radio waves between fixed points.

4.123 Under the 1985 Act a warrant to intercept communications may be issued by the appropriate Secretary of State, (for the Home Department, Northern Ireland or Scotland or the Foreign Secretary). The warrant authorises the person to whom it is addressed to intercept post or such communications made by a public telecommunications system as are described in the warrant (s 2). A warrant may only be issued where the Secretary of State considers it necessary to do so

(a)   in the interest of national security;

(b)   for the purpose of preventing or detecting serious crime; or

(c)   for the purpose of safeguarding the economic well-being of the UK (s 2(2)(a)–(c)).

The wording corresponds to Art 8 of the European Convention but apart from the phrase 'serious crime' there is no definition in the Act of the words used. 'Serious crime' is partly defined in s 10(3). The offence must either involve the use of violence or result in substantial financial gain or amount to conduct by a large number of persons in pursuit of a common purpose, or be such as would lead on conviction to a term of at least three years imprisonment for a person with no previous criminal record. The Government refused to adopt the definition of serious arrestable offence under s 116 PACE Act 1984. This would have meant greater precision but would have included more offences. The present definition limits the number of offences but gives the Home Secretary greater flexibility. The interests of national security will be for the Secretary of State to decide without any statutory guidance, as will activities which affect the economic well-being of the country. The Act does limit the scope of this last purpose by stating that a warrant shall not be considered necessary unless the information sought is information relating to the intentions of persons outside the British Islands. It is intended to cover external threats to the supply of commodities upon which the economy is dependent. (Viscount Whitelaw, HL Debates. Vol 464 Col 879 June 6 1985. Apparently he had oil in mind following the earlier damage to the economy caused by OPEC's lowering of production quotas and the consequential rise in price. See the similar wording in the Security Service Act 1989, para 4.91, ante). A warrant may justify intercepts at more than one address but these must be specified in the warrant and must be an address or addresses likely to be used for the transmission of communications to or from one particular person specified in the warrant. For example, D has an office and flat in London but lives in Essex. The warrant may authorise intercepts on communications from all three addresses used by D. In this sense the warrant is specific as to the person and premises subject of the intercept. The warrant may, however, authorise the interception of other communications in order to be able to intercept the communications from or to D. For example, if A, B and D share a flat with a joint telephone line, all telephone calls to or from that number would be intercepted in order to intercept those to or from D even though only D is named in the warrant. It follows that one warrant may authorise the tapping of more than one telephone line. In 1984, 423 warrants resulted in the tapping of 20,065 lines, more than 47 lines per warrant. 522 warrants were authorised in 1989 suggesting the tapping of some 25,000 lines. Warrants must be signed personally by the Secretary of State, or in cases of extreme urgency by an Assistant Under Secretary or above who is authorised by the Secretary of State to do so. Each warrant lasts for two months but is renewable. Warrants not signed by the Home Secretary expire within 2 working days but may be renewed by him for a period of 2 months. On an application for renewal, the Home Secretary must consider whether the warrant is necessary and if at any time he becomes aware that a warrant is no longer necessary he must cancel it. However, there is no requirement for periodic review. Warrants issued in the interests of national security or for safeguarding the economic well-being are renewable for up to six months at a time while warrants for detecting serious crime can only be renewed for one month at a time. There is no limit in the Act on the number of times a warrant may be renewed and no overall maximum period beyond which warrants cannot be renewed.

4.124 Interception of international communications is much easier than interception of internal communications. The warrant is not limited to a single person or premises, but the Secretary of State can issue a certificate stating the categories of material he considers it necessary to intercept on the grounds contained in s 2. The certificate can target a particular address or addresses in the U.K. only if it is necessary to prevent or detect acts of terrorism. Safeguards on what may be done with intercepted material are contained in s 6. Section 6(1) and (2) place a duty on the Secretary of State to make sure that intercepted material is disclosed and copied to the minimum extent necessary. This does not prevent material collected for, say, national security purposes being disclosed to, say, the Inland Revenue if a large scale fraud is revealed which could have been the subject of a warrant but was not. There could therefore be an exchange of material between the police, security services and customs and excise. Section 6(3) states that copies of intercepted material must be destroyed when its retention is no longer necessary for the purposes mentioned in s 2(2). The White Paper (1980) said that the usual practice was to erase tapes of telephone interceptions within a week. Transcripts of conversations were destroyed after 12 months unless needed for the investigation.

4.125 Under the Act there are two types of telephone tapping, authorised and unauthorised. As to authorised tapping the only question is whether it was properly authorised in accordance with the criteria in the Act. Whether this is so or not is investigated by a Tribunal set up under the Act. Unauthorised tapping (which, says the Government, does not take place on behalf of the police or other governmental bodies) is investigated by the police as is any other criminal act. An individual who believes that communications to or from him have been intercepted may apply to a tribunal of five lawyers who must then investigate to determine whether a warrant or certificate has been issued and, if so, whether it has been properly issued in compliance with the Act. If the tribunal concludes that it was not properly issued, they must notify the complainant, report to the Prime Minister and, if they think fit, cancel the warrant or certificate, order the destruction of any material obtained under it and make an order of compensation against the Secretary of State. Since there is no obligation on the Secretary of State to notify the individual before, during or after an interception has taken place, it is not clear how the individual will ever get to know of an intercept (disclosure by a slip up as in *Malone v MPC (No 2)* (1979) should no longer occur; see s 9 below), nor what evidence will satisfy the tribunal and cause them to investigate. The purpose of the tribunal is simply to examine the procedures under which a warrant was issued. Given that all applications to the Secretary of State will be rigorously scrutinised by officials before reaching him, the likelihood of procedural errors is very small. One may therefore conclude that the Tribunal has been created to deal with problems that probably will not exist. For example, Lord Bridge's review in 1985 did not find a single instance of a procedural irregularity. If the tribunal finds, as it will almost always find, that there has been no contravention of the Act, it will simply report this to the complainant who will not know whether there has been an interception of communications to or from him whether authorised or unauthorised. This is to prevent complainants using the tribunal in order to determine whether they have been the subject of an intercept. The Act also provides for a Commissioner who is a present or past holder of high judicial office and whose task it is to keep under review the workings of the Act. He is only concerned to discover whether there have been abuses in authorised interceptions; he cannot consider whether there has been unauthorised interception by anyone. He reports to the Prime Minister who must lay copies of his report before Parliament, subject to deletion of material the publication of which would be prejudicial to national security, to the prevention and detection of serious crime, or to the economic well-being of the U.K. The report must indicate when this has been done. The procedure of the Tribunal appears to be contrary to natural justice but any judicial review of the procedure is excluded by s 7(8) which also excludes any review of decisions as to their jurisdiction. Thus, while the tribunal is required to apply principles of natural justice in reviewing the Secretary of State's procedures, their own procedures are immune from such review. Section 9 prevents any evidence being adduced or questions being asked in any court tending to suggest either the commission of any offence under s 1 or the existence of a warrant. This appears to prevent the introduction of prosecution evidence based on telephone taps but in fact the Crown never relies on the evidence obtained by tele–phone tapping, though it often is the best evidence, possibly because they do not wish to alert others who might be under investigation to the probability that their telephones are being tapped and mail intercepted. The purpose of s 9 appears to be to prevent the kind of situation which arose in *Malone v MPC (No 2)* (1979), in which the fact that there had been a telephone tap was elicited in cross-examination after counsel had spotted an entry in a policeman's notebook. The prosecution will continue to present evidence based on or confirmed by telephone taps but which does not tend to show that an interception has taken place

(J)   Surveillance and surveillance devices

4.126   In the absence of a law of privacy, the legality of surveillance and the use of surveillance devices depends on whether their use involves a trespass to property. The 'bugging' of premises with listening devices clearly involves a trespass unless done with the consent of the owner or occupier. However, modern technology enables surveillance to be undertaken without trespass. In *Entick v Carrington* (1765) Lord Camden said, 'the eye cannot by the law of England be guilty of trespass' and in *Malone v MPC (No 2)* 1979, Megarry V.C. ruled that the ear is also not guilty, in holding that telephone bugging via the telephone exchange was not a trespass. Video surveillance of crowds attending football matches, public demonstrations and similar large gatherings is now common practice. Public car parks are often the subject of such surveillance as are many city centres, and citizens of Liverpool complain of surveillance by helicopter. More contentiously listening devices are available which permit the most private of conversations to be recorded without trespass to property. No statutory authority is needed for such non-trespassory surveillance and such safeguards as there are to be found, in guidelines issued by the Home Office, are based on the principle that that which is not prohibited by law is lawful. This approach has been rejected by the European Court of Human Rights (see *Malone v MPC (No 2)* (1979), above) and it is questionable whether the administrative guidelines governing aural surveillance satisfy the requirements of the European Convention.

4.127 *Use of surveillance equipment* — General. The guidelines issued by the Home Office (HC Debates, 19 December 1984, written Answer No 169) recognise that the use of surveillance equipment may encroach on the privacy of the individual and lay stress on the circumstances in which such equipment is used. Most concern is directed toward the use of equipment in circumstances in which the targets might reasonably assume a high degree of privacy, for example in their home or hotel bedroom. Less privacy can be expected in public places and is, for that reason, less contentious. Careful consideration of all the circumstances of a particular investigation or operation must therefore be given by senior police officers before authorising the use of surveillance equipment (para 1).

4.128 *The covert use of listening devices.* — The authorising officer must satisfy himself that the following criteria are met:

(a) the investigation concerns serious crime or the investigation of malicious or obscene telephone calls;

(b) normal methods of investigation have been tried and failed, or must from the nature of things, be unlikely to succeed if tried;

(c) there must be good reason to think that the use of the equipment would be likely to lead to an arrest and a conviction, or where appropriate, to the prevention of an act of terrorism;

(d) the use of the equipment is operationally feasible (para 4).

The seriousness of the crime under investigation must then be balanced against the degree of intrusion into the privacy of those under surveillance. Listening devices should only be used in respect of the person's home or hotel bedroom when major organised conspiracies and particularly serious offences, especially crimes of violence, are under investigation (para 5). The covert use of listening, recording and transmitting equipment (for example microphones, tape-recorders and tracking equipment) requires the personal authority of the chief officer (Assistant Commissioner in the Metropolitan Police). This authority may be delegated to an Assistant Chief Constable (Assistant Commissioner or Commander para 3) but only in cases where there is a degree of consent as when the equipment is:

(a) knowingly carried by a person other than a police officer who is a party to a conversation to be recorded or transmitted;

(b) carried by a police officer whose identity is known to at least one other non-police party to a conversation which is to be recorded or transmitted;

(c) installed in premises, with the consent of the lawful occupier, to record or transmit a conversation in circumstances where at least one of the parties to the conversation will know of the surveillance;

(d) used, with the consent of one of the parties concerned, to record a telephone conversation. This may include the investigation of crimes which are not serious such as the investigation of malicious or obscene telephone calls.

(e) used, with the consent, in the case of a vehicle, of the owner (not necessarily the driver) to track a vehicle, package or person (para 7).

Telephone tapping is governed by the Interception of Communications Act 1985 (above) and nothing in these guidelines must be taken as granting dispensation from those procedures. However, the use of a surveillance device, as in (d) above, should not be ruled out simply because it may incidentally pick up one end of a telephone conversation. On the other hand, it would not be appropriate to 'bug' a public telephone box where the sole purpose, or only foreseeable result, is to overhear speech transmitted by telephone. A warrant under the 1985 Act should be sought in such cases (para 12).

4.129   Authorisation should be for a maximum period of one month, after which a fresh application must be made if the surveillance is to continue. Material such as a a tape or video recording made as a result of the use of the surveillance equipment, may be retained only for so long as is required by the circumstances of the inquiry or by any subsequent prosecution, but must be destroyed as soon as it is apparent that it is no longer required (paras 8 and 9). The use of such material outside the police service, Crown Prosecution Service and courts, should only be authorised in exceptional circumstances; for example, when it is necessary in the course of a criminal investigation to enlist the aid of the public, with due regard to the provisions of the Contempt of Court Act 1981. Authority for such use must be obtained from the officer who authorised the use of the equipment concerned; if this is not practicable, from another officer of no lesser rank (para 10). A central record must be kept at police headquarters (New Scotland Yard in the Metropolitan Police) of each application for the use of listening devices. This should include:

(a) the nature of the case;
(b) whether the authority was given or refused and by whom;
(c) broadly how the criteria in para 4 were met; and
(d) the final outcome of the investigation. (In addition when equipment is used more than once during a particular investigation, a record should be kept of each occasion, para 8).

These records should be retained for at least two years and made available to HM Inspectors, together with an inventory of the equipment kept by a particular force, where appropriate (para 11).

4.130   *Covert Visual Surveillance* — The general principles applying to the covert use of listening devices also apply where the target individual is to be observed in the place where he resides. Such surveillance must be authorised by the chief constable (Assistant Commissioner in the M.P.D.), who should not delegate that authority except where the equipment is to be:

(a) used knowingly by a person other than a police officer who is party to the events which are to be observed or recorded;

(b) used by a police officer whose presence is known to at least one member of the non-police subjects of the observation or recordings;

(d) installed in premises, with the consent of the lawful occupier, to observe or record events in circumstances where at least one of the participants will know of the surveillance.

In such cases an Assistant Chief Constable (Deputy Assistant Commissioner or Commander in the MPD) may authorise it (paras 14 and 3).

4.131 Where surveillance equipment is to be used for the observation or recording of particular individuals in a public place (eg to catch drug-pushers, kerb-crawlers), authority may be given by a Chief Superintendent who must be satisfied that it will not involve an unwarrantable intrusion of privacy and is fully justified in all the circumstances of the police operation in question (para 15). As to covert observation from private premises, in *R v Johnson* (1989), Watkins LJ decided that the whereabouts of an observation post can be kept secret at trial provided that (1) before observation begins, the officer in charge of the investigation (at least the rank of sergeant) has visited the post and explained to the occupiers that ultimately the court may, in the interests of justice to the accused (eg on an issue of identification), have to reveal the location of the post, and (2) at least a chief inspector has visited the occupiers immediately prior to trial and repeated the explanation.

4.132 *General surveillance of a public place* — The use of equipment such as closed circuit television cameras, video or photographic equipment in connection with crowd control or public order, such as football matches, public processions, or for traffic control purposes (eg speeding, or traffic light infringements), may be authorised by a Chief Superintendent who must be similarly satisfied as above (para 16).

4.133 Non-recording equipment such as binoculars, night vision equipment and telescopes may be authorised by an officer of the rank of inspector or above. He should ensure that officers using such equipment only use it where strictly necessary in the course of police operations and so as not to intrude unjustifiably on the privacy of persons. If such equipment is to be used to observe target individuals in a private place, the procedures and criteria for authorisation of covert surveillance set out in para 14 (para 4.126 above) must be followed and authority given by an Assistant Chief Constable (Assistant Commissioner or Commander in the M.P.D.) (para 17).

4.134   The rules regarding the retention and use of material, such as video tapes or photographs obtained by surveillance under paras 15 and 16, are the same as for material obtained by listening devices, as are the requirements as to the keeping of records (see above para 4.125) (paras 18, 19 and 20).

4.135   *Urgent cases.* — In circumstances of exceptional urgency when it is impracticable to obtain authorisation specified in the guidelines and surveillance equipment is urgently required for the prevention or detection of crime, a Chief Superintendent or his deputy may authorise its use if the following circumstances apply:

1) though the officer concerned believes the principles above to be met, it is impracticable to obtain prior authority as set out in the guidelines; and
2) the circumstances could not reasonably have been foreseen.

The officer who would normally have authorised its use must be informed as soon as practicable and the appropriate record made. That officer should satisfy himself that the use of the equipment was in accordance with the principles set out in the guidelines, and if not so satisfied he should draw this to the attention of the officer who authorised its use. Wilful abuse of this exceptional urgency procedure is a disciplinary matter to be considered by the Chief Officer of the force concerned (para 21).

5   Powers of arrest

Introduction

5.01   According to Blackstone, arrest is 'the apprehending or restraining of one's person in order to be forthcoming to answer an alleged or suspected crime' (Commentaries (1830) p.289). Faced with the changes wrought by the PACE Act 1984 a modern day Blackstone might amend the definition to read:

> 'Arrest is the apprehending or restraining of one's person in order to detain him at a police station while the alleged or suspected crime is investigated and in order that he be forthcoming to answer an alleged or suspected crime.'

The law of arrest is no longer simply machinery for ensuring the appearance of an alleged offender at court to answer the charges laid. It has developed over the years as an investigative tool for getting a suspected person into a police station where he can be questioned about the offence of which he is suspected. Arrest can also be preventive, as where a person is arrested to prevent a breach of the peace; and protective as where mentally ill or inebriated persons are arrested for their own protection. The commission of an offence is not a prerequisite of such arrests but the vast majority of arrests without a warrant are for offences and justifies the above definition. Before 1967 offences were classified as felonies, misdemeanours and summary offences. If the offence was punishable by imprisonment, a warrant of arrest could be obtained from a magistrate, but arrest without warrant was only permitted at common law in the case of an arrest by a citizen if a felony had been committed, or, in the case of a police officer, on reasonable suspicion that a felony had been committed. Arrest without warrant for a misdemeanour, whether by a police officer or a citizen, was permitted when the offence was seen to be committed, and for a summary offence only if statute provided for such a power of arrest and then in accordance with the conditions of that statutory power. Arrest on reasonable suspicion, as indicated in paras 2.02–12, ante, requires no more than a limited degree of suspicion but was subject to the principle that arrest at such an early stage in the investigation was the exception, the general rule being that arrest should take place at the end of the investigation. As the Royal Commission on Police

5.01 *Powers of arrest*

Powers and Procedures (1929) made clear, the law at that time was that where an arrest was necessary, the constable should make it clear that the person was under arrest on a specific charge and:

> 'thereafter he should not question the prisoner . . . although he should make a note of anything he says and should bring him straight to the police station for formal charging' (para 137).

5.02   There was consequently no advantage to the police in arresting a person at an early stage in the investigation for once he was in custody the first of the Judges' Rules (issued in 1912) prohibited any questioning of the suspect in relation to the offence for which he was arrested. This prohibition was seen by the police as an unnecessary constraint on efficient policing. 'Custody' was not defined by the Judges' Rules but was interpreted as meaning custody following a lawful arrest. If therefore a person attended voluntarily at a police station or was detained short of being arrested, the prohibition did not apply. Thus developed the practice of inviting a person to attend at a police station to assist the police in their inquiries. Those who accepted the invitation seldom did so voluntarily, believing that they were under the coercion of a legal authority. Hence the media phrase 'assisting with inquiries' which is apt to cover a lawful arrest, a genuine voluntary attendance or an unlawful detention. The Royal Commission (1929) found that a number of provincial police forces relied upon unlawful detention short of arrest so as to facilitate the questioning of suspects. The Metropolitan Police sought to justify the practice as 'essential in the interests of justice' (para 151). That Royal Commission saw the advantages of detention for questioning to the innocent person who might be eliminated from the inquiry without the stigma of appearing in court, but declined to recommend that the practice be made lawful because it could devise no way of controlling it. Despite this the practice continued, and the courts acquiesced in its continued use by failing to enforce the Judges' Rules, which had by 1960 ceased to exist as a legal constraint on custodial questioning. In 1964 new Judges' Rules were issued which permitted custodial questioning following a lawful arrest, provided the person had not been charged with or informed that he would be prosecuted for the alleged offence (Home Office Circular 89/ 1978 Rule 1). Arrest for questioning was then legally possible but detention short of arrest to facilitate questioning continued, partly because old habits die hard, and partly because the statutory limitations on detention after arrest did not apply to volunteers or persons detained but not arrested. Moreover the common law constraints on arrest without a warrant on reasonable suspicion still applied to limit the occasions when arrest at an early stage in the investigation was possible. In 1967 s 2 of the Criminal Law Act abolished the distinction between felonies and misdemeanours and created the concept of the arrestable offence, an offence for which the sentence was fixed by law or was under any statute punishable by five or more years imprisonment. This included all former felonies and many misdemeanours and, as the law was brought up to date in later years, almost all offences of theft, criminal damage or violence, which account for the great majority of serious offences dealt with by the police, were arrestable on reasonable suspicion. These changes led to arrest on reasonable suspicion becoming the rule rather than the exception, and to arrest for questioning becoming accepted practice.

5.03 The Royal Commission on Criminal Procedure (1981) recognised this change in investigative practice when it said, somewhat naively, that:

> '[T]he period of detention [following arrest on reasonable suspicion] may be used to dispel or confirm that reasonable suspicion by questioning the suspect or seeking further material evidence with his assistance. This has not always been the law or practice but now seems to be well established as one of the primary purposes of detention upon arrest' (para 3.66).

This acknowledges the fact that the primary purpose of arrest in modern times is to get the suspect into a police station where detention, questioning and other forms of investigation will follow (as will be seen in chapter 6, post, the legal controls on police detention proved ineffective and further facilitated this change of purpose). The police station has long been recognised as a psychologically coercive venue in which the pressure to make admissions or confessions can be more effectively applied. The changes in the law since the beginning of this century combined to make the police station the focal point of the investigation of crime. The naivety of the Commission lies in the implication that dispelling the reasonable suspicion is uppermost in the mind of the investigator. On the contrary, the police arrest a presumptively guilty person at a very early stage of the investigation often with little or no substantive evidence of the person's guilt and set out to prove that guilt by custodial questioning. As Lord Devlin observed:

> 'The face of the police officer is not `sicklied o'er with the pale cast of thought', and once he finds a reasonable quantity of pros, he will act decisively without too much anxiety about the cons.' (*The Judge*, 1979)

The changed role of the law of arrest was given the stamp of judicial approval by the House of Lords in *Mohammed-Holgate v Duke* (1984) before the PACE Act 1984 came into force. A constable arrested a person whom he reasonably suspected of burglary, solely because he believed the offence could not be proved without a confession and that such a confession was more likely to be forthcoming if she were questioned in, what is accepted to be, the coercive atmosphere of a police station. The House of Lords held that in exercising his discretion to arrest (under powers similar to those in section 24(5), (6) and (7) of the PACE Act 1984 (Art 26(5), (6) and (7))), the constable was entitled to take that fact into consideration. Thus arrest for questioning was lawful at common law. The PACE Act set the seal on that development by providing a form of summary arrest for all serious crime and by authorising the detention of the arrestee without charge in order to secure or preserve evidence of the offence for which he was arrested or to obtain such evidence by questioning him.

The case for reform

5.04 The concern of those seeking reform was threefold. First was the use of the law of arrest to facilitate questioning coupled with the related practice of detention short of arrest for questioning; second the excessive use of the law of arrest, and third the complexity of the law. Excessive use was indicated by figures suggesting that 76 per cent of persons proceeded against for indictable offences were arrested and only 24 per cent summonsed. Of the latter many were in fact arrested and then reported for summons, so the true rate of arrest was much higher. The fact that of those arrested a majority were released on police bail suggested that it was police procedures and practice, in particular the practice of arresting for questioning, rather than the need to ensure the appearance of the suspect, which governed the exercise of powers of arrest (Royal Commission Report, para 3.71). The complexity of the law arose from a number of factors: the large number of statutory powers of arrest applicable in the main to summary offences, with each power subject to its own conditions; the existence of a statutory power of arrest in respect of arrestable offences which, as defined, did not include serious common law offences and some statutory offences which could be serious eg indecent assault on a female; the continued existence of a common law power to arrest for a breach of the peace; and confusion in the decided cases over the meaning of arrest, a confusion which is not affected by the PACE Act 1984 and which remains unresolved.

Proposals for reform

5.05 The proposals of the Royal Commission on Criminal Procedure had:

'... two main and interrelated objectives: to restrict the circumstances in which the police can exercise the power to deprive a person of his liberty to those in which it is genuinely necessary to enable them to execute their duty to prevent the commission of offences, to investigate crime, and to bring suspected offenders before the courts; and to simplify, clarify and rationalise the existing statutory powers of arrest, confirming the present rationale for the use of those powers.' (Report, para 3.75)

The Royal Commission, while accepting the 'necessity principle' which would have restricted the exercise of powers of arrest to those occasions when it was necessary according to stated criteria, declined to apply it at the point of *arrest*. Instead they proposed that it apply when the question of *detention* following arrest is being considered in the police station. The PACE Act 1984, which is the source of most powers of arrest without warrant, also declined to apply a necessity principle at the point of arrest in respect of serious offences but does so at the point of arrest for minor offences. The principle is also applied when the detention of a person following an arrest without warrant for any offence is being considered.

The present law of arrest

5.06   The simplification of the law intended by the PACE Act 1984 is not entirely achieved. The foundation for simplification was laid down by the repeal of all the statutory powers of arrest, including those in local Acts, which authorised the arrest of a person without warrant for an offence, or to arrest a person otherwise than for an offence without a warrant or an order of the court, which existed before the PACE Act came into force (s 26(1)) (Art 28(1)). The majority of the police powers to arrest without warrant are contained in the PACE Act which broke new ground in providing a potential power of arrest for every criminal offence (ss 24, 25, 26 and Sch.2) (Arts 26, 27, 28 and Sch 2). However, matters are complicated by the creation of two categories of offences and three categories of powers of arrest. The first category offence is the 'arrestable offence' and carries with it a power of summary arrest; that is, a person reasonably suspected of having committed an arrestable offence may be arrested without more. There are also a number of investigative powers attached to an arrest for an arrestable offence and, if it is a serious arrestable offence, further investigative powers are available. This category includes all the serious criminal offences which were previously arrestable offences, the serious common law offences which were not previously within that definition, and a number of other offences which, while not necessarily serious, are included in order to attract to them the additional investigative powers which are available on an arrest for an arrestable offence. The second category of offence may be termed the 'general offence'. This includes all offences which are not arrestable offences or the subject of a power of arrest preserved by Sch 2, and offences against local bye-laws. A person reasonably suspected of having committed a general offence may only be arrested if it appears to the constable that a summons cannot be served or is inappropriate in the circumstances. Conditions, known as 'general arrest conditions', one of which must be satisfied before a constable can arrest for a general offence, are set out in s 25(3) (Art 27(3)) and import the 'necessity principle' in respect of this category of offence. Within this category are all the summary offences, including motoring offences, from depositing litter to driving without lights, and summary offences created after the PACE Act 1984 was passed, eg s.14 of the Cinemas Act 1985. The third category of powers of arrest is the preservation of a number of statutory powers of arrest created before the PACE Act 1984 (PACE Order 1989) in respect of offences which, though not serious enough to be categorised as arrestable offences, require a power of summary arrest and to which the general arrest conditions are inappropriate, or powers of arrest provided in order to detain persons unlawfully at large or in respect of other matters which do not involve the commission of a criminal offence (s 26(2) and Sch 2) (Art 28(2) and Sch 2). As statutes are up-dated this category will be subject to deletion and as new offences are created to which the general arrest conditions are considered to be inappropriate, it will be added to by the creation of new arrest powers in the offence creating statute. The criterion of 'reasonable grounds for suspecting' which applies to the powers of arrest provided by ss 24 and 25 (Arts 26 and 27), is discussed in paras 2.02-12, ante.

Arrestable offences (s 24 PACE Act 1984) (Art 26 PACE Order 1989)

5.07   Section 24(1) provides for a power of summary arrest in respect of arrestable offences as defined in that section. 'Summary' in this context means done with despatch and without formalities. A number of advantages accrue from defining an offence as an arrestable offence, attracting to it a power of arrest unfettered by the formalities which attend an arrest under s 25 (Art 27). There is a discretion to arrest as indicated by the words 'may arrest' in s 24(4) (Art 26(4). The constable may be guided by criteria such as those which govern the power to arrest under s 25 (Art 27) contained in the general arrest conditions and may, in an appropriate case, decide to proceed by way of a summons. He may, however, arrest where there is reasonable cause to suspect an arrestable offence has been committed, even if none of the criteria mentioned in s 25(3) (Art 27(3)) applies. As will be seen in chapter 6, post, criteria for detention without charge after arrest permits such detention, initially for a maximum of 24 hours (s 41(1)), in order to secure or preserve evidence or to obtain it by questioning. Section 18 permits the search of premises without a warrant following arrest for an arrestable offence and it is this power which will enable the police to 'secure or preserve' evidence while the person is being detained without charge. As the decision in *Mohammed-Holgate v Duke* (1984) indicates (a decision on an almost identically worded discretionary power to arrest as is provided by s 24 (Art 26)), it is perfectly proper to take into account the need to question the person in the police station in exercising that discretion, and by analogy it will be equally proper to take into account the need to search premises for evidence of the offence. The availability of these investigative powers explains the need for a power of summary arrest and will be a strong inducement to exercise the powers provided by s 24 (Art 26). If the offence is, or proves to be, a serious arrestable offence additional investigative powers become available. Those relevant to the decision to arrest are:

(a) Continued detention without charge beyond the normal maximum of 24 hours in order to secure or preserve evidence or to obtain it by questioning may be authorised by a superintendent for up to 12 hours beyond the initial 24 hours. A magistrates' court may authorise further detention either from the initial 24 hours or from the period of detention authorised by a superintendent, for up to 36 hours, also in order to secure, preserve or obtain evidence, and that period may be extended for up to a further period of 36 hours but not to exceed 96 hours detention without charge in total (ss 42, 43 and 44) (Arts 43, 44 and 45).

(b) The right of an arrested person to see a solicitor (s 58) (Art 59) and to have someone informed that he has been arrested (s 56) (Art 57) may be delayed for up to 36 hours.

(c) The taking of intimate and non-intimate samples from the person (ss (and Arts) 62 and 63), subject to authorisation by a superintendent and the appropriate consent.

The availability of these additional investigative powers also explains the need for a power of summary arrest, quite apart from the seriousness of the offence, and it will be perfectly proper for a constable to take into account the need to invoke these provisions in deciding whether to exercise his discretion to arrest.

Scope of arrestable offences

5.08 For the purposes of the Act (Order) the following categories of offence are arrestable offences:

(a) Offences for which the sentence is fixed by law (s 24(1)(a)) (Art 26(1)(a)). This category covers murder and treason and made no change to the previous definition of an arrestable offence in s 2(1) of the Criminal Law Act 1967.

(b) Offences punishable by five years' imprisonment (s 24(1)(b)) (Art 26(1)(b)). By omitting the phrase 'under or by virtue of any enactment' from the previous definition in the Criminal Law Act 1967, s 24(1)(b) (Art 26(1)(b)) extended the definition of an arrestable offence to include common law offences, such as kidnapping, conspiracy to defraud or corrupt public morals, attempting to pervert the course of justice and false imprisonment. This category must, however, be considered against the background of the following restrictions on sentencing.

(i) *Persons not previously sentenced to imprisonment.* S 1 of the Criminal Justice Act 1991 restricts the power of a court to impose a custodial sentence on a convicted person unless:

   (a) the sentence for the offence is fixed by law (see (a) above); or

   (b) the offence is triable only on indictment and a sentence of imprisonment has previously been passed on the offender by a UK court.

These restrictions do not mean that an offence committed by such a person is not an arrestable offence in respect of him. Section 24(1(b) refers to *offences* for which a person over 21 (not previously convicted) may be sentenced to five or more years' imprisonment. Therefore such an offence is an arrestable offence whoever commits it and despite any restrictions on sentencing applicable to that person.

(ii) *Magistrates' Courts Act 1980 (s 33) (Art 46(4) Magistrates' Courts (Northern Ireland) Order 1981).* This provision restricts the sentencing power of a magistrates' court in respect of certain offences triable either on indictment or summarily which, if the value involved does not exceed £2000, must be tried summarily and can be punished by no more than three months' imprisonment. This restriction is to be ignored for the purposes of s 24(1)(b) (Art 26(1)(b)). Thus an offence of criminal damage, normally punishable by up to ten years' imprisonment, and therefore an arrestable offence remains one even if the value of the damage is less than £2000.

Arrestable offences under s 24(2) (Art 26(2))

5.09 These are offences which, though not punishable by five years' imprisonment, were either deemed to be arrestable offences by the statute creating the offences or were provided with a power of arrest without warrant by that statute. They were made arrestable offences by the PACE Act 1984 in order to attract to them the powers of entry to premises to effect the arrest (s 17(1)(b)), (Art 19(1)(b)), or to enter and search premises without a warrant following the arrest (s 18) (Art 20). Should they be or prove to be serious arrestable offences (see paras 2.13–18, ante), the additional investigative powers mentioned in para 5.07, ante, are available. The offences under s 24(2) (Art 26(2)) fall within the following categories:

(a) *Customs and Excise Offences (s 24(2)(a)).* Offences defined in s 1(1) of the Customs and Excise Management Act 1979, which include a number of offences under that Act and the Alcoholic Liquor Duties Act 1979, are arrestable offences. Section 138(1) of the former Act provided that a person reasonably suspected of committing any of these offences, may be arrested by a customs and excise officer, a constable, a member of Her Majesty's Armed Forces, or a coastguard, within three years of the commission of the offence. Making these offences arrestable gives to a constable the power of summary arrest without the time limit imposed by s 138(1), and attracts the investigative powers mentioned above. These are considered necessary in order to ensure the thorough and effective investigation of what might be serious offences in terms of the amount of goods involved and the potential loss to the Exchequer from the evasion of duty. The former power of a constable to arrest under s 138(1) has been repealed by the 1984 Act and 1989 Order. Customs and excise officers are not constables and will continue to rely on s 138(1) in order to effect an arrest for one of these offences (section 24(4) and (5) (Art 26(4) and (5)) provide powers of summary arrest which may be exercised by anyone but, as will be seen, they are restricted powers and will rarely be relied upon by customs and excise officers). There is in s 114(2)(a) a means of providing customs and excise officers with investigative powers equivalent to those provided to constables by the PACE Act 1984. An order under this section, the Police and Criminal Evidence Act 1984 (Application to Customs and Excise) Order 1985 SI No 1800 applies 36 provisions of the PACE Act to customs and excise officers but these do not include the power of summary arrest under s 24 (see Art 3 and Schedule 1).

When an arrest is made for one of the offences mentioned in s 1(1) of the Customs and Excise Management Act 1979, whether under s 138(1) of that Act or s 24 of the PACE Act 1984, by a person who is not a customs and excise officer, (eg a constable), the arrest must be notified to the nearest convenient office of customs and excise (Customs and Excise Management Act 1979 as amended by the PACE Act 1984, Sch 6, para 32).

(b) *Official Secrets Act offences (s 24(2)(b)) (Art 26(2)(b) and (c)).* Offences under the Official Secrets Act 1920 are divided into two classes, those attracting a high penalty and which are therefore arrestable offences, and those which attract a lesser penalty and which are not. The power of arrest provided in respect of both classes by the 1911 Act was repealed by s 26(1) of the PACE Act 1984 (Art

223

28(1)) but, since even the lesser offences are considered to be potentially damaging to the national interest, all those offences which are not arrestable offences by virtue of the term of imprisonment for which a person may be sentenced in respect of them, are made arrestable offences so that they attract the investigative powers mentioned above. The Official Secrets Act 1989 repealed the much criticised 'catch all' and ambiguous s 2 of the 1911 Act. It replaced s 2 by six defined categories of official information, the unauthorised disclosure of which is a criminal offence. Sections 1 to 6 define these categories and create the offences which are punishable, on conviction on indictment, by imprisonment for a term not exceeding two years, or six months on summary conviction and/or a fine. The offences are not therefore arrestable offences within the definition in s 24(1)(a) or (b) but are made so by s 24(1)(c) and also attract the investigative powers mentioned above. The offences under s 8(1)(4) and (5), which relate to unlawful retention of, or failure to take care to prevent unauthorised disclosure of, documents to which ss 1 to 6 relate, or the disclosure of official information, documents or other articles which would give access to documents or information protected against disclosure, are only triable summarily and punishable by a maximum of three months' imprisonment and/or a fine. They are general offences and subject to the arrest conditions contained in s 25 of the PACE Act 1984 (Art 27) (considered later).

(c) *Sexual offences (s 24(2)(c)) (Art 26(2)(d))*. Two offences under the Sexual Offences Act 1956 are made arrestable; viz causing prostitution of women (s 21) and procuration of girls (s 23) (offences under s 2 of the Criminal Law Amendment Act 1885 in Northern Ireland). Indecent assault on a woman (s 14) was included in the PACE Act 1984, the offence then being punishable on conviction on indictment by 5 years imprisonment if against a girl under 13 who was stated to be so in the indictment, otherwise 2 years. S 3(3) of the Sexual Offences Act 1985 increased the penalty to 10 years whatever the age of the woman. The offence is now therefore an arrestable offence by virtue of s 24(2)(b).

(d) *Theft Act offences (s 24(2)(d)) (Art 26(2)(e))*. An offence under s 12(1) of the Theft Act 1968 (taking a motor vehicle or other conveyance without authority) was deemed by s 12(3) to be an arrestable offence, as defined in the Criminal Law Act 1967. The offence under s 25(1) of the Theft Act 1968 (going equipped for stealing) was not but it was specifically clothed with a power of arrest by s 25(4) of PACE. Both are frequently committed offences and it is probably this fact, rather than the possible seriousness of the offences, which justifies their inclusion as arrestable offences in the 1984 Act and provides the police with the investigative powers such offences attract, in particular the power to search premises without a warrant. It should also be noted that articles which may be used to commit these offences are 'prohibited articles' under s 1(7) and (8) (Art 3 (7) and (8)) and persons in possession of them are subject to the stop and search powers under s 1(1) (Art 3(1)). The 1984 Act (1989 Order) therefore provides the police with a formidable package of powers to deal with these offences which, though not necessarily serious in themselves, can often be a prelude to more serious offences. (In Northern Ireland the offence of taking a motor vehicle etc falls under Art 172 of the Road Traffic (NI) Order 1981 or s 12(2) of the Theft Act (NI) 1969. The offence of going equipped etc falls under s 24(1) of the latter Act.)

(e) The Football (Offences) Act 1991 makes any offence under that Act an arrestable offence by adding a paragraph (e) to s 24(2) of the PACE Act. Three offences are created by the 1991 Act which refer to things done at a 'designated football match', that is an association football match designated, or of a description designated, for the purposes of the Act by order of the Secretary of State. The offences, which are only triable summarily, are:

   (i) throwing things at or toward (a) the playing area or adjacent area not open to spectators, or (b) any area in which spectators or other persons may be, without lawful authority or excuse (which shall be for him to prove) (s 2);

   (ii) taking part in chanting of an indecent or racist nature (s 3; 'Chanting' and 'of a racist nature' are defined by s 3(2)(a) and (b));

   (iii) going on to the playing area, or an adjacent area to which spectators are not normally admitted, without lawful authority or excuse (which shall be for him to prove (s 4).

In general these offences may be committed in the period two hours before the advertised start of the match and one hour after the end (see s 1(2)).

These offences are also relevant offences for the purpose of restriction orders under the Football Spectators Act 1989.

Conspiracy, attempting, inciting etc (s 24(3))

5.10 (a)   *Arrestable offences under s 24(1)(a) and (b).* It has already been noted that s 24(1)(b) makes common law conspiracy and other common law offences, such as incitement, arrestable offences provided that the conspiracy or offence incited is punishable by 5 or more years' imprisonment. Most conspiracies and attempts are now statutory offences. Section 3 of the Criminal Law Act 1977 and s 4 of the Criminal Attempts Act 1981 (Art 4 of Criminal Attempts and Conspiracy (NI) Order 1983) provide that penalties for respectively a conspiracy or attempt to commit what are now arrestable offences by virtue of s 24(1)(a) and (b), are punishable to the same extent as the full offence. Incitement is still a common law misdemeanour and when tried on indictment it is punishable by imprisonment at the discretion of the court. Incitement to commit an offence which is triable either way or on indictment only is therefore within s 24(1)(b) as an offence for which a person may be sentenced to imprisonment for five years. Aiding, abetting, counselling or procuring is, by the Accessories and Abettors Act 1861, s 8 (as amended by the Criminal Law Act 1977), punishable to the same extent as commission by the principal offender. It follows therefore that such offences are arrestable if the principal offence is arrestable.

(b)   *Arrestable offences by virtue of s 24(1)(c) and (2) (Art 26(1)(c) and (2)) (s 24(3), Art 26(3)).* Since the offences to which s 24(2) applies are not punishable by 5 years' imprisonment, it follows that conspiring or attempting to commit or inciting, aiding, abetting, counselling or procuring the commission of them are not automatically arrestable offences. Special provision needs to be made for them and s 24(3) does so. Schedule 15, para 98, of the Criminal Justice Act 1988 amends s 24(3)(b) of PACE to exclude the offence of attempting to commit an offence under s 12(1) of the Theft Act 1968 (taking and driving away a motor vehicle etc). Conduct which may be preparatory to such an offence is covered by s 9 of the Criminal Attempts Act 1981 (interference with motor vehicles). (NB s 2(1) and (2)(e) of the Criminal Attempts Act 1981 provide that any provision in any enactment (whenever passed) conferring a power of arrest in respect of the offence shall have effect with respect to the offence of attempting to commit that offence. This is apt to provide a power of arrest in respect of attempts to commit an arrestable offence. Section 24(3), which is without prejudice to s 2 of the 1981 Act, applies to conspiracy, aiding, abetting, counselling or procuring and is therefore much wider than s 2 of the 1981 Act but so far as attempts are concerned it is co-extensive).

5.11   The combined effect of s 24(1)(a), (b), (c) and (2) (Art 26(1), (a), (b), (c) and (2)) is to make all the more serious offences and many of the most commonly committed offences, which may be comparatively trivial in the commission, arrestable offences. Thus they cover, for example, murder, manslaughter, offences involving explosives, offences under Part I of the Forgery and Counterfeiting Act 1981, the major offences against the person, all the offences under the Criminal Damage Act 1971, almost all the Theft Act offences, offences of corruption and related inchoate and secondary offences. Many of these were arrestable under the 1967 Act, and, while the actual number of offences added by the 1984 Act (1989 Order) is small, the frequency with which they are likely to be committed adds significantly to the list of arrestable offences.

The powers of arrest for arrestable offences (s 24(4)–(7)) (Art 26(4)–(7))

5.12 Though drafted differently these provisions re-enact the powers of arrest previously contained in s 2(2)–(5) of the Criminal Law Act 1967 (the power of a constable to enter premises without a warrant to arrest a person under these powers was previously contained in s 2(6) of that Act and is now to be found in s 17(1)(b) of the PACE Act (Art 19(1)(b)) (see para 4.33, ante). Section 24(4) and (5) (Art 26(4) and (5)) contain powers of arrest which are available to anyone while those under s 24(6) and (7) (Art 26(6) and (7)) are available only to a constable. 'Constable' refers to the ancient office of constable requiring attestation before a justice of the peace (see para 2.55, ante).

Powers of arrest — arrest by a private citizen (s 24(4) and (5)) (Art 26(4) and (5))

5.13 Section 24(4) and (5) (Art 26(4) and (5)) provide what are often described as 'citizen's arrest powers' but they are available to constables as well. Since constables have wider powers provided by s 24(6) and (7) (Art 26(6) and (7)) they will rarely need to rely on these powers except possibly in the exceptional circumstances considered below.

1) *Section 24(4) (Art 26(4))*
Under s 24(4)(a) (Art 26(4)(a)) any person may arrest without a warrant any person who is in the act of committing an arrestable offence. There is no question of reasonable cause to suspect that the person is committing such an offence. Either he is or he is not. If he is in the act of committing an arrestable offence, the arrest is lawful; if he is not, it is unlawful. Conversely s 24(4)(b) (Art 26(4)(b)) authorises the arrest without warrant by anyone of anyone whom he has reasonable grounds for suspecting to be committing an arrestable offence. It matters not whether the person is in fact committing an arrestable offence so long as the arrester has reasonable grounds for suspecting that he was doing so. The difficulty may lie in determining when the person is in the act of committing an arrestable offence. Store detectives will often rely on this power to arrest persons in the act of shoplifting. The act of appropriation will be complete when a person takes goods from the shelf and conceals them about his person (*R v McPherson* (1973)) or when he switches labels with the intention of offering a lower price for the goods than was on the original label (*R v Morris* (1983)). Such persons will clearly be in the act of committing an arrestable offence (theft) while in the store. If they are permitted to leave the store they are likely to be in the act of committing the offence for some short time after leaving but it is not clear

227

how long after the appropriation they will continue to be in the act of committing theft, if at all. It depends on whether, and to what extent, appropriation is a continuing act. Construing a similar provision in s 22(1) of the Theft Act 1968, which states that a person handles stolen goods if he receives them 'otherwise than in the course of stealing', the Court of Appeal held that where D1 stole P's property by offering it to D2, the appropriation was complete at the instant the offer was made. D2 did not therefore receive the goods in 'the course of stealing'(*R v Pitham and Hehl*) (1977). The court did not exclude the possibility of appropriation continuing in different circumstances but if it does, when does it cease to continue? D is likely to be in the act of committing theft when stopped outside the store or some way down the street and if he runs off during the time he is being pursued. If D is not pursued but is seen in a cafe some fifteen minutes after the theft, he is unlikely to be 'in the act of committing an arrestable offence'. The citizen/store detective must then rely on s 24(5) (Art 26(5)) if an arrestable offence has been committed.

2) *Where an arrestable offence has been committed (s 24(5)) (Art 26(5))*

(a)   It is clear from the opening words of s 24(5) (Art 26(5)) that it is an essential precondition for arrest under this subsection that an arrestable offence has been committed. This provides a trap for the unwary citizen by preserving the rule laid down in respect of arrests for felony in *Walters v W H Smith & Sons Ltd* (1914). P reasonably suspected that D had stolen a particular book from his stall and arrested him under the common law power which is now s 24(5) (Art 26(5)). Other books had been stolen but not the particular book, therefore no felony (arrestable offence) had been committed in respect of it. P was held liable in damages. Little consideration has been given to this aspect of the law of arrest. The Criminal Law Revision Committee (1965 Cmnd 2695) was prepared to protect the citizen who arrests a person who is reasonably suspected of being in the act of committing an arrestable offence but who is not in fact doing so (s 24(4)(b)) (Art 26(4)(b)) or the citizen who arrests a person without any reasonable suspicion who is in fact guilty of having committed an arrestable offence (s 24(5)(a)) (Art 24(5)(a)). The committee was not however prepared to offer protection to the citizen who reasonably suspects that an arrestable offence has been committed when it has not, and arrests a person whom he reasonably believes has committed it. The 1984 Act continues this approach with the following consequences. If a store detective reasonably, but mistakenly, suspects that a person is stealing from the store, he may lawfully arrest that person while in the store or whilst outside, subject to the extent of 'committing' in this context. However, if the store detective is careful and waits until the suspect appears to have committed the offence and is no longer committing it, and seeks to arrest under s 24(5) (Art 26(5)), he is civilly liable if in fact no arrestable offence has been committed. This applies no matter how reasonable his suspicion may have been. The Criminal Law Revision Committee recognised that the rule penalised the prudent, but declined to change it because they doubted 'whether it would be desirable, or acceptable to public opinion, to increase the powers of arrest enjoyed by a private person' (para 15).

(b) Section 24(5)(a) (Art 26(5)(a)) provides that where an arrestable offence has been committed any person may arrest without warrant any person who is guilty of the offence. The subsection makes the arrest lawful not because of facts and circumstances existing and known to the arrester at the time of the arrest but because the arrested person is subsequently proved to be guilty of the offence. It is difficult to imagine a person who was convicted of the offence for which he was arrested subsequently suing the arrester for false arrest because the arrester had no reasonable grounds for suspecting that he had committed the offence. The Criminal Law Revision Committee thought the provision 'unimportant, as even without it we do not believe a person would be held liable' (para 13); but the Committee included it to put the point beyond argument. Children under ten years of age present store detectives and other private individuals with a particular problem. They are conclusively presumed to be incapable of committing a crime. This means that not only can they not be convicted, but also that no crime at all is committed by an infant. It follows that if an eight year old is seen stealing from a shop, no arrestable offence, indeed no offence, is committed and therefore there is no power of arrest. In the absence of such a power the child cannot lawfully be detained even though it is in the child's interest that he be detained and his parents, and/or the Social Services, be informed. The most that can be done is to inform the police and local authority. The police may be able to take the child into police protection (see s. 46 of the Children Act 1989, discussed at para. 6.15, post) and the local authority has a duty under s. 47 of that Act to investigate where there is reasonable cause to suspect that a child is suffering, or is likely to suffer, significant harm. If so they may take care proceedings under s 31 of that Act.

(c) Section 24(5)(b), (Art 26(5)(b)), on the other hand, requires reasonable grounds for suspecting the person to be guilty of the offence. The legality of the arrest is not affected by the fact that the person arrested did not commit the arrestable offence if there were such reasonable grounds, provided that the offence was committed by someone. For example, security officers arrested three men reasonably suspected of theft from their employer. Two were subsequently acquitted, the third was convicted. The conviction made it clear that an arrestable offence had been committed therefore the arrest of those acquitted was lawful under s 24(5)(b) (Art 26(5)(b)). The acquittal of all three would not necessarily render the arrest unlawful unless the acquittals were based on the fact that an arrestable offence was not committed.

Arrest as a step in the criminal process

5.14 Arrest is a step in the criminal process and an arrest by a private person (or a constable) is lawful only if he intends to take the alleged offender to a constable or magistrate as soon as possible, thereby commencing the criminal process. In *R v Brewin* (1976), B purported to arrest a child in order to take him to his father to be dealt with. It was held that the arrest was unlawful and B was liable for false imprisonment. However, provided the arrest is made with the intention of taking the arrested person to the police, it is not invalidated if the arrester changes his mind en route. In *John Lewis & Co Ltd v Tims* (1952) the House of Lords held that it was lawful for a store detective to take a suspected shoplifter to his employer for a decision whether to prosecute. Since it is the employer who takes the decision and the employee is merely his agent, taking the arrested person to the employer is a necessary first step in the criminal process and doubtless the arrest is intended as such. The rule applies to all arrests but as will be seen a constable is permitted greater scope for action prior to taking the arrested person to a police station (s 30(10) (Art 32(13)) discussed in para 5.55, post).

Arrest by a constable (s 24(6) and (7)) (Art 26(6) and (7))

5.15 *Section 24(6) (Art 26(6)).* — Section 24(6) (Art 26(6)) contains the power which will be relied upon by police constables for the majority of arrests for an arrestable offence. This power, like that in subsection (7), is only available to a constable and authorises an arrest without warrant when the constable has reasonable grounds for suspecting that an arrestable offence has been committed, and he has reasonable grounds for suspecting the person to be guilty of the offence. It follows that an arrest is lawful even if (a) no arrestable offence has been committed and (b) such an offence has been committed but not by the arrested person, provided that in each case there were reasonable grounds for suspicion. Had a constable arrested in the case of *Walters v W H Smith and Sons Ltd*, ante, the arrest would have been lawful. The arrest of a child under ten years of age may also be lawful, even though such a child cannot commit a crime and no crime is committed in law, even if committed in fact. The question will be, did the constable reasonably suspect that an arrestable offence had been committed? If the child is not obviously under ten years of age, the constable could reasonably suspect this. However, if the child is obviously under ten years of age he could not and an arrest would then be unlawful. If the constable is in doubt as to the age of the child, he may consider taking the child into police protection under s 46 of the Children Act 1989 (see the discussion at para 6.15, post). It is arguable that a child under ten years of age who is committing what would be an arrestable offence if he was older, is 'likely to suffer significant harm', the threshold requirement for the exercise of the 'police protection' power.

Section 24(7) (Art 26(7)) — Section 24(7)(a) (Art 26(7)(a)) provides a constable with a power to arrest without warrant anyone who is about to commit an arrestable offence. There is no question of reasonable suspicion. Either the person is about to commit such an offence or he is not. If he is, the arrest is lawful; if he is not, it is unlawful. On the other hand, s 24(7)(b) (Art 26(7)(b)) provides the same power subject to reasonable grounds for suspecting the person to be about to commit an arrestable offence. One may note at this point that while s 28 (Art 30) requires persons arresting under ss 24, 25, (Arts 26, 27) or any other power to inform the person arrested of the fact that he has been arrested and the reasons for the arrest, there is no requirement that the arrester specify the particular arrest power he is relying on. He can, therefore, rely on whichever power authorises the arrest in the particular circumstances with the benefit of hindsight. The difficulty with this power is to determine what the purpose of it is. In creating its predecessor (s 2(5) of the Criminal Law Act 1967), the Criminal Law Revision Committee (1965 Cmnd 2695) relied on common law authority which empowered any person to arrest without warrant anyone who was about to commit a felony. If the person was arrested before he had committed or attempted to commit the arrestable offence, the Committee suggested that the constable could 'bring him before a magistrates' court with a view to his being bound over to keep the peace . . .'. Alternatively the constable could release him, when the danger of the arrestable offence being committed or attempted has passed, on the analogy of the power of a constable to detain a person temporarily in order to prevent the commission of a felony or breach of the peace (para 16) (see now *Albert v Lavin* (1982) for a modern statement of the common law power, discussed in para 5.33, post). If the person has committed or attempted to commit an arrestable offence, the constable has a power of arrest under s 24(6) (Art 26(6)). The law of attempts has been changed since the Criminal Law Act 1967 and a person will now be guilty of a criminal attempt when he does an 'act which is more than merely preparatory to the commission of the offence' (Criminal Attempts Act 1981, s 1) (Criminal Attempts and Conspiracy (NI) Order 1983). What is 'a more than merely preparatory act' is a question of fact for the jury and may be an earlier stage than under the common law (see *R v Jones (KH)* (1990)). However, such acts will seldom indicate to the observer that there is an intention to commit an arrestable offence. In practice the s 24(7) (Art 26(7)) power will only be used when a person threatens to commit an offence of violence to persons or property but does not take any steps to put the threat into effect. The power is then exactly the same as the power to arrest for an actual or threatened breach of the peace. In both cases the person can be taken before a court with a view to having the person bound over to keep the peace. At common law a person may be detained short of arrest if he threatens a breach of the peace and released once the threat ceases to exist. Section 30(7) (Art 32(10)) requires the release of a person arrested at a place other than a police station if, before arriving at the police station, the grounds for arrest cease to exist (see para 5.54, post). Applied to an arrest under s 24(7) (Art 26(7)) this makes the power identical with the common law power though it is an arrest rather than detention (see example (5) in para 5.16, post). There are also a number of substantive offences which may be committed by the person who is 'about to commit an arrestable offence'. The most common is that of going equipped for stealing, contrary to the Theft Act 1968, s 25 (Theft Act (NI) Act 1969 s 24(1)), which is an arrestable offence by virtue of s 24(1)(c) and (2)(d) of the 1984 Act (Art 26(1)(c) and (2)(c)). Possessing a firearm with intent to injure, contrary to the Firearms Act 1968, s 16, and possession of explosives, contrary to the Explosive Substances Act 1883, s 4, are substantive offences punishable by more than 5 years' imprisonment and therefore arrestable offences by virtue of S 24(1)(b) (Art 26(1)(b)). A constable who suspects that a person is about to commit an arrestable offence will then wait until the person has passed the stage of attempt, or has actually committed the crime, or, if he has to intervene before the stage of attempt, he will usually find a substantive arrestable offence to justify an arrest or rely on common law powers to arrest for an actual or apprehended breach of the peace.

5.16 The following examples illustrate the operation of the various arrest powers.

1) D is seen by a store detective putting a packet of bacon, which he has not paid for, into an inside pocket of his coat. D may be arrested under s 24(4)(a) or (b) (Art 26(4)(a) or (b)). If a constable sees D in the act of stealing, he may also arrest D under the same powers.

2) D is seen acting furtively in a store by a store detective. He hides

behind a display counter and is seen to put his hand inside his coat. He does this twice more and leaves the store having made no purchases. He is arrested outside the store. The arrest is justified under s 24(4)(b) (Art 26(4)(b)) if, as is likely, the observed conduct is accepted as reasonable grounds for suspecting that D is in the act of committing an arrestable offence even if D was not in fact committing an arrestable offence. A constable may also arrest under that subsection but can also rely on s 24(6) (Art 26(6)). Here too the lawfulness of the arrest depends upon the existence of reasonable suspicion that an arrestable offence has been committed and that D committed it.

3) A valuable ring is stolen from a jeweller. Only two persons were in the shop at the time of the theft, D and X. X left the shop. D remained. P arrested D though he had no reasonable grounds to suspect that he was responsible. It transpires that D and X work as a team and both are convicted of the theft. The arrest is lawful by virtue of that conviction (s 24(5)(a)) (Art 26(5)(a)). P could be the jeweller or a constable for both could rely on s 24(5)(a) (Art 26(5)(a)). However, if P was a constable he could not rely on s 24(6) (Art 26(6)) which requires reasonable grounds for suspecting that D had committed the arrestable offence.

4) D is in a jeweller's shop examining a tray of rings. As he starts to leave the jeweller notices a ring is missing from the tray. D refuses to submit to a search and runs away. The jeweller gives chase and eventually arrests D. The ring is not stolen. It had dropped behind the counter. D ran off because he had previous convictions for theft and was afraid he would be implicated. The arrest is unlawful. Section 24(5) (Art 26(5)) gives a power to arrest only where an arrestable offence has been committed, no matter how reasonable the grounds for suspecting D may be. If a constable made the arrest in these circumstances it would be lawful under s 24(6) (Art 26(6)) since the jeweller's story plus D's conduct would provide reasonable grounds to suspect the commission of an arrestable offence and that D had committed it.

5) D is in the High Street threatening violence to a travel agent who has ceased to trade and deprived D of a holiday he had booked and paid for. He clearly intends to carry out his threat but has taken no steps to do so. A constable may arrest D under s 24(7) (Art 26(7)), and take him before a magistrates' court with a view to having him bound over to keep the peace. Alternatively, he may release D once the threat of an arrestable offence being committed has passed, as it is likely to once D has been arrested. Section 30(7) (Art 32(10)) requires the release of a person arrested at a place other than a police station if the constable is satisfied that there are no grounds for keeping him under arrest. This section would appear to require the release of D if he is

arrested for being about to commit an arrestable offence and the danger of its commission has passed. The constable (or a citizen) may also rely on the common law power to arrest or detain a person who is likely to cause a breach of the peace. If arrested, a magistrates' court may similarly bind him over to keep the peace and, if detained, he may be released once the danger of a breach of the peace has passed.

The general arrest power (s 25) (Art 27)

5.17 Where a constable reasonably suspects that any offence which is not an arrestable offence (or an offence in respect of which a power of arrest is preserved by Sch 2) has been committed or attempted, or is being committed or attempted, he may arrest the person he suspects of having committed etc. the offence (the relevant person (s 25(2) Art 27(2)), *only* if it appears to him that the service of a summons is impracticable or inappropriate because any of the general arrest conditions are satisfied (s 25(1)) (Art 27(1)). It is crucial to distinguish here between the arrestable offence (s 24) (Art 26), the preserved arrest power offence (Sch 2) and the general offence (s 25) (Art 27). Under s 24 (Art 26) and the various powers preserved by Sch 2 (discussed in para 5.31, post) the discretion to arrest is unfettered, whilst in the case of a general offence the discretion is fettered and an arrest is lawful only if the service of a summons is impracticable or inappropriate because any general arrest condition in s 25(3) (Art 27(3)) is satisfied. In theory the constable should apply criteria similar to these general arrest conditions in deciding whether to exercise his discretion to arrest for an arrestable offence. In practice, however, he will be more concerned with other factors such as the need to question the suspect or to exercise powers of search. These are *not* matters which can be considered in relation to an arrest under s 25 (Art 27), nor, given the nature of the general offences, will the constable need to do so very often. (In those rare cases in which a search of premises is required it can only be carried out under s 32(2)(b), (Art 34(2)(b)) (considered at para 4.25) or with consent.) In relation to offences to which the preserved powers of arrest apply they are offences which require a power of summary arrest not because they are serious but because the nature of the offence makes service of a summons impracticable or inappropriate (eg persons unlawfully at large, illegal entrants to the UK). Since the passing of the 1984 Act various laws have been enacted which provide summary powers of arrest for the same reasons as the preserved powers of arrest. A constable must then know which offences are arrestable offences, which offences carry a preserved power of arrest or a power of summary arrest, all three categories being arrestable summarily, and which offences are general offences. Since this latter category will only be arrestable if a general arrest condition is satisfied, it follows that a constable must also know the general arrest conditions. These conditions are designed to confine the arrest for general offences only to those occasions when it is necessary.

The general arrest conditions, as set out in s 25(3) (Art 27(3)), are —

(a) that the name of the relevant person is unknown to, and cannot be readily ascertained by, the constable;
(b) that the constable has reasonable grounds for doubting whether a name furnished by the relevant person as his name is his real name;
(c) that —
  (i) the relevant person has failed to furnish a satisfactory address for service; or
  (ii) the constable has reasonable grounds for doubting whether an address furnished by the relevant person is a satisfactory address for service;
(d) that the constable has reasonable grounds for believing that arrest is necessary to prevent the relevant person —
  (i) causing physical injury to himself or any other person;
  (ii) suffering physical injury;
  (iii) causing loss of or damage to property;
  (iv) committing an offence against public decency; or
  (v) causing an unlawful obstruction of the highway;
(e) that the constable has reasonable grounds for believing that arrest is necessary to protect a child or other vulnerable person from the relevant person.

Arrest is possible 'if it appears to him [the constable] that service of a summons is impracticable or inappropriate' because any of these conditions is satisfied. This suggests a subjective test ie the constable need only act honestly and need not show any reasonable grounds for his decision. However, the requirements in conditions (b), (c)(ii), (d) and (e) all specify reasonable grounds whilst the remaining conditions (a) and (c)(i) are matters of fact. The test is therefore objective. A constable cannot be said reasonably to doubt that the relevant person has given his correct name and address simply because in his experience people who commit offences do not give correct details (*G v DPP* (1989)). Such cynicism has no reasonable basis. It must be emphasised that the arrest is for an offence; the constable must therefore, first tell the suspect what offence he is suspected of. Having done so he should then request the suspect's name and address. In doing so he need not inform a suspect why he wants it, for example, to facilitate service of a summons (*Nicholas v Parsonage* (1987)).

Service of a summons impracticable or inappropriate (s 25(3)(a), (b) and (c)(i) and (ii) (Art 27(3)(a), (b) and (c)(i) and (ii))

5.18   General arrest conditions (a), (b) and (c) are concerned with the likely effectiveness of the summons procedure; (a) and (b) are self-explanatory. The question raised by conditions (c)(i) and (ii) is, 'what is a satisfactory address for service?' and it is partially answered by s 25(4) (Art 27(4)):

> '... an address is a satisfactory address for service if it appears to the constable —
> (a) that the relevant person will be at it for a sufficiently long period for it to be possible to serve him with a summons; or
> (b) that some other person specified by the relevant person will accept service of a summons for the relevant person at it.'

The commission of offences in the UK by foreign nationals created problems for the police. Because process could not be served in the offender's country, s 25, (Art 27) was relied upon to justify the arrest of the foreign national who was then subjected to 'instant' justice. For example, a French lorry driver drives dangerously in the UK and causes an accident. The Criminal Justice (International Co-operation) Act 1990 (which came into force on 1st July 1991), now enables the police to serve process in a foreign state (ss 1 and 2). This means that an arrest under s 25(3), (Art 27(3)) cannot be justified on the basis that service of process is impracticable or inappropriate.

Short term residency

5.19   Section 25(4)(a) (Art 27(4)(a)) envisages the situation in which a person is temporarily residing at a particular address but is likely to have moved on before a summons can be served, eg the itinerant vagrant staying at a charitable hostel, the traveller or gypsy, or simply the holidaymaker staying at a guest house. The average time for the service of a summons is 88 days (Royal Commission Research Study No 9 (1981)) and may be longer in areas in which a seasonal variation in the prosecution workload is experienced. The address of such persons will seldom be a satisfactory address for service. If therefore such a person is unable to offer an alternative address which is a satisfactory address, or to specify someone, who must by implication reside at a satisfactory address, who will accept service of a summons on his behalf, he will be arrested. In the case of the person with no fixed abode, specifying someone willing to accept service of a summons is the only way to avoid arrest.

Verification of name, address or specified person

5.20   A power to detain while the name, address or other details were verified was removed from the PACE Bill at an early stage following protest, but a process of verification must take place and in many cases where it appears to the constable that verification can be obtained in a reasonably short time, he should explain to the relevant person that verification is necessary and should invite him to remain with him, while the verification takes place. He should also explain that the alternative to cooperation is immediate arrest. If the person refuses to remain, then he must be arrested. Indeed, such a refusal will give the constable further reasonable grounds for doubting that the name or address is correct or that the address is satisfactory. Where the verification process appears likely to take some time the person may be arrested. The guiding principle should be that of protecting the dignity of the individual and subjecting him to the least inconvenience or embarrassment. For example, if it will take an hour to convey a person to a police station and a shorter time to verify the details, it may be more convenient for him to remain with the constable while the verification takes place. On the other hand, it may be less embarrassing to arrest him and take him to a police station for verification than invite him to wait in a busy street for 10 minutes or more. Section 25(1) (Art 27(1)) gives a discretion to arrest when a general arrest condition is satisfied. The constable need not do so if the objective of ensuring that a summons can be served may be achieved without arrest. If an arrest is made and the verification process is completed in the relevant person's favour before he arrives at a police station, the constable is under a legal duty to release the person (see s 30(7) (Art 32(10)) discussed in para 5.54, post). At the police station the duty to release, once the grounds for detention (which in the case of an arrest under s 25 are also the grounds for arrest) cease to exist, rests with the custody officer (see s 34(2) discussed in para 6.16, post).

Protective and preventive arrest (s 25(3)(d)(i)–(v) and (e)) *(Art 25(3)(d)(i)–(v) and (e))*

5.21   These general arrest conditions are concerned with the necessity to arrest in order to protect persons or property or in order to put an end to the offence or prevent further offences.

Physical injury to relevant person or another *(s 25(3)(d)(i)) (Art 27(3)(d)(i))*

5.22   As to general arrest condition (d)(i), the most obvious situation is that in which the relevant person has committed or is committing or attempting to commit, a minor assault (ie not a serious assault amounting to an arrestable offence) upon the person of another and is still threatening violence when the police arrive. Service of a summons may well be practicable but totally inappropriate if there are reasonable grounds for believing that he will continue to be violent and to cause injury to others. The other obvious case is where the relevant person threatens to harm himself. Both examples may overlap with other powers of arrest. The first coincides with arrest for a breach of the peace and in the second the relevant person may be mentally disordered and the power to arrest under s 136 of the Mental Health Act 1983 (Mental Health (NI) Order 1986) (preserved by Sch 2 of the 1984 Act and the 1989 Order) may be invoked. In neither of these cases, however, need the person have committed an offence, whereas an offence is an essential prerequisite in the case of an arrest under s 25 (Art 27). General arrest condition (d)(i) is similar to the repealed power of arrest for possession of an offensive weapon under s 1(3) of the Prevention of Crime Act 1953, ie reasonable cause to believe it is necessary to arrest in order to prevent the commission of an offence in which the weapon might be used. Section 25 (Art 27) (3)(d)(i) will now be the condition to be satisfied in such a case. This would permit arrest if the person in possession of an offensive weapon is reasonably believed to be likely to use the weapon to harm himself or another. However, the stop and search powers in s 1 of the 1984 Act (Art 3 of the 1989 Order) (see chapter 3, ante) may be used to justify a search for and seizure of the weapon and if it is in fact seized, general arrest condition (d)(i) will not be satisfied and the person's arrest cannot be justified by reference to it. Similarly, if an arrest is made relying on condition (d)(i) being satisfied, the person is then searched and the weapon seized under s 32(1) and (8) (Art 34(1) and (8)), the ground for arrest under s 25 (Art 27) (3)(d)(i) no longer applies and the constable is then under a duty to release the person if he has not then reached a police station, unless the arrest can be justified on other grounds. For example, D, a well-known local hooligan, is stopped and searched following information that he was on his way to attack a rival gang leader. He is found to be in possession of a machete, which is seized. His name and address is known, therefore a summons in respect of the offence of possession of an offensive weapon can be served. Arrest condition (d)(i) does not apply given the seizure of the weapon and in the absence of any other arrest condition being satisfied D cannot be arrested. If D continues with his intended attack he may be arrested for an apprehended breach of the peace.

Interference with witnesses

5.23 The general arrest conditions do not, unlike the detention conditions after charge in s 38 (Art 39) (1)(a)(iii) (discussed in para 6.29, post), refer to arrest in order to prevent interference with the administration of justice or with the investigation of an offence. However, if such interference takes the form of threats of violence to persons against whom the original offence was committed or who are witnesses to it, then condition (d)(i) is appropriate to deal with the situation. If there are reasonable grounds to believe that the relevant person will interfere with the course of justice or the investigation of the offence by destroying evidence, then condition (d)(iii) would be appropriate.

Arrest to prevent the relevant person suffering physical injury (s 25(3)(d)(ii)) (Art 27(3)(d)(ii))

5.24 General arrest condition (d)(ii) is concerned with the situation where the suspected offender is likely to be physically attacked by others, for example by relatives of the victim. This is particularly likely in cases involving sexual offences against children. It must be appreciated that threats of violence towards a suspected offender may justify the arrest of those uttering those threats and a constable should be slow to arrest D because P threatens to commit an offence against D. However, the arrest of D is often the only practical solution, particularly if a number of persons utter such threats. Arresting them and leaving D at large is likely to exacerbate the situation.

Causing loss of or damage to property (s 25(3)(d)(iii)) (Art 27(3)(d)(iii))

5.25 'Property' is not defined but in this context it is likely to be interpreted as meaning property of a tangible nature, real or personal. There is no need to extend it to include animals as do other statutory definitions, since 12(1) of the Protection of Animals Act 1911, which permits the arrest of a person in order to prevent harm to animals which are the subject of an offence under that Act, is preserved by s 26(2) and Sch 2 to this Act. Where there are reasonable grounds to believe that it is necessary to arrest in order to prevent damage to, or the destruction of, *property belonging to another*, there will be a power to arrest under s 24(6) (Art 25(6)), since causing criminal damage is an arrestable offence. However, general arrest condition (d)(iii) applies to the loss of or damage to *any* property, including property owned by the relevant person. If then D, P's estranged husband, finds P in the domestic home with her boyfriend, attacks the boyfriend and proceeds to break up the home, the property being damaged may well belong to D and such damage is not an offence of criminal damage and the assault may not amount to an arrestable offence. However, D may be arrested for the general offence of assault on the boyfriend because condition (d)(iii) is satisfied. The arrest may have a salutary effect on D and if, before arriving at the police station, the constable is satisfied that there is no longer a threat to property D must be released (s 30(7)) Art 32(10)). An alternative method of dealing with

239

such a situation is to use the common law power to detain a person committing or about to commit a breach of the peace. If D calms down and the threat to the peace disappears, D may be released (see *Albert v Lavin* (1982) and the discussion in para 5.33, post). Note that s 25 (Art 27) (3)(d)(iii) is not qualified and refers to any damage to property. Together with the summary power of arrest under s 24 (Art 26) for the offence of criminal damage the police have ample powers to arrest in order to prevent damage to property.

Evidence relating to the offence

5.26 The property which may be lost or damaged may well be evidence of the offence which D is alleged to have committed. Most property offences are arrestable under s 24 (Art 26) but there may be occasions when the relevant person is in possession of, or will have access to, property which is evidence of the general offence of which he is suspected and it may be reasonable to believe that it will be destroyed if D remains at large. In such a case general arrest condition (d)(iii) will be satisfied. For example, A approached a constable in the street and complained that D had just shown him indecent photographs of children. Possession of such photographs is an offence under s 160 of the Criminal Justice Act 1988 which is triable only summarily. D may well give his correct name and address so that a summons may be served but is likely to destroy the photographs if left at large. D may then be arrested. When D is arrested there is a power to search him or the premises in which he was arrested or in which he was immediately before he was arrested for evidence of the offence (s 32(2)(a)(ii) and (b)) (Art 34(a)(ii) and (b)).

Committing an offence against public decency (s 25(3)(d)(iv)) (Art 27(3)(d)(iv))

5.27 This general arrest condition is qualified by s 25(5) (Art 27(5)) so as to impose the further condition that an arrest for an offence against public decency can only be made if the conduct takes place in circumstances where members of the public going about their normal business cannot reasonably be expected to avoid the person to be arrested. Since the purpose of this general arrest condition is to enable the constable to remove by arrest the offending person in the circumstances mentioned, it is clear that 'offence against public decency' must refer to offences involving public nudity by such a person, rather than those involving indecent advertisements or displays. The most common offences against public decency are those of indecent exposure — wilful etc exposure of the person (penis) with intent to insult a female, contrary to s 4 of the Vagrancy Act 1824 and similarly s 28 of the Town Police Clauses Act 1847. There is also a rarely used common law offence of outraging public decency, usually committed by exposing the body in public or doing lewd acts. The statutory offences can only be committed by a male against a female while the common law offence may also be committed by a female, eg a Lady Godiva. In addition the Indecency with Children Act 1960 created the offence of indecency toward a child (under 14) which, insofar as it requires merely incitement to do an act of gross indecency, is very similar to the offence of indecent exposure. Persons reasonably suspected of committing any of these offences can only be arrested if the offence is committed in the circumstances stated in s 25(5), eg a man indecently exposing himself in a busy shopping precinct can expect to be arrested as may the person sunbathing nude on a busy seaside promenade or bathing nude on a busy public beach not set aside for that purpose (note that s 25 (Art 27) permits arrest for offences against local bye-laws if a general arrest condition is satisfied whereas previously local bye-laws did not normally carry a power of arrest). Female nudity, apart from nude bathing, is not specifically made an offence by statute, though it can be an offence at common law. Thus a woman running bare breasted across a football pitch commits the common law offence of indecent exposure and may be arrested under s 25 (Art 27) (3)(d)(iv). The power to arrest a woman soliciting in a public place for the purposes of prostitution under s 1(3) of the Street Offences Act 1959 is preserved by s 26(2) and Sch 2 of the PACE Act 1984. Therefore the question whether soliciting is an offence against public decency does not arise.

Male importuning and indecency between men

5.28 It is an offence under s 32 of the Sexual Offences Act 1956 for a man persistently (ie more than one invitation or a series of invitations) to solicit or importune in a public place for an immoral purpose. 'Immoral purpose' may include a man soliciting a woman of any age to have inter-course with him even if the sexual intercourse would not be criminal, eg with a consenting female over sixteen (*R v Goddard* (1991)) (see also the Sexual Offences Act 1985 s 1), and importuning men of any age for homosexual purposes. It is doubtful whether the offence can be described as an offence against public decency for the purposes of s 25(3)(d)(iv), in which case arrest for the offence will depend upon another general arrest condition being satisfied. Section 41 of the Sexual Offences Act 1956 permits *anyone* to arrest without warrant anyone found committing an offence under s 32 (and ss 30 and 31). Clearly so far as the citizen is concerned, this power is unaffected by the repeal of constable's statutory powers of arrest by s 26 of the 1984 Act. It is clear that 'anyone' in s 41 of the 1956 Act includes a constable, but Sch 6, para 9 of the 1984 Act amended s 41, adding at the end of the section the words 'but a constable may only do so in accordance with section 25 of the Police and Criminal Evidence Act 1984'. The result is that the citizen has a greater power of arrest than a constable, albeit only in respect of the offences to which s 41 applies (see further the discussion at para 5.32 post). Most offences of buggery or of gross indecency are arrestable offences being punishable by five or more years' imprisonment, but some forms of both offences are general offences being punishable by only two years' imprisonment (see s 3 of the Sexual Offences Act 1967). Few of these offences will be committed in public though gross indecency in the form of, for example, mutual masturbation may take place in public toilets and in such a situation s 25(3)(d)(iv) may permit an arrest.

Obstruction of the highway (s 25(3)(d)(v)) (Art 27(3)(d)(v))

5.29 General arrest condition (d)(v) deals with those situations in which an offence of unlawfully obstructing the highway is committed and the person committing the offence refuses to move. For example, the protester who sits down in the highway. If he refuses to move on request the only way to prevent the offence continuing is to arrest him. The condition would be satisfied if the facts of *Gelberg v Miller* (1961) were repeated. A motorist refused three requests to move his car parked in a restricted street. When the police threatened to move it, he removed the distributor arm. While s 25 does enable a constable to arrest for parking on a double yellow line, it is only in circumstances of non-cooperation that an arrest would be necessary or permissible for such a trivial offence.

Protection of children and other vulnerable persons (s 25(3)(e)) (Art 27(3)(e))

5.30 General arrest condition (e) may overlap with condition (d)(i) in that a child or other vulnerable person may be threatened with physical injury. However condition (e) is wider and would include the reasonable belief that a child or other vulnerable person might suffer psychological damage if the relevant person is left at large. This would require circumstances in which the child or vulnerable person lives in close proximity to the relevant person and will usually involve a close relationship between them. Since most sexual offences against a child are arrestable offences, condition (e) must be directed at lesser offences such as that contained in s 1 of the Indecency with Children Act 1960 which is punishable, on summary conviction, by up to six months' imprisonment or fine of £2,000 or both. If, for example, a stepfather were to commit an act of gross indecency towards his stepdaughter, or incite her to such an act with him, the offence under s 1 is committed. In such circumstances it may be wrong to leave the child in a position of moral danger and possibly at risk of being the victim of a more serious offence. Section 25(3)(e) (Art 27(3)(e)) would enable a constable to arrest the stepfather and s 38(1)(a)(ii) (Art 39(1)(a)(ii)) would permit his detention after charge if the circumstances give rise to a reasonable belief that it is necessary to protect the child from physical harm (not, it should be noted, moral or psychological harm). The reasonable belief that D may commit more serious sexual offences if released would satisfy the latter subsection. While D is detained steps may be taken to protect the child, by alerting social services who may take proceedings under the Children Act 1989 in respect of the child, or a magistrates' court may impose a condition of D's release on bail that he live elsewhere until the case is tried (Bail Act 1976, s 3(6)). Also within condition (3)(e) is the offence of being drunk while in charge of a child under s 2 of the Licensing Act 1902. The domestic situation in which a violent man is threatening his wife or cohabitee would satisfy condition (e) but overlaps with condition (d)(i) if the threat is of physical injury, or (d)(iii) if it is of damage to property. The relevant person must have committed an offence and the conditions do not provide a means of removing a person from the domestic home in the absence of an offence. Where an injunction has been granted under the Domestic Violence and Matrimonial Proceedings Act 1976 to which a power of arrest is attached under s 2(3) of that Act, or an order of a magistrates' court has been made under s 16 of the Domestic Proceedings and Magistrates' Courts Act 1978 prohibiting the person from entering the matrimonial home and a power of arrest is added under s 18 of that Act, a person who enters in breach of the injunction or order or who threatens or uses violence toward the spouse or cohabitee, may be arrested by virtue of the above powers. These powers of arrest were not repealed by s 26(1) (Art 28(1)) since they are orders of a court, not a power of arrest provided by an Act. Where no injunction or order has been granted but an offence has been committed in such a domestic situation, then arrest may be justified because general arrest condition (d)(i) or (e) is satisfied. Where a breach of the peace takes place or is apprehended, common law powers to arrest or detain may be invoked (see para 5.33, post)

Preserved powers of arrest without warrant (s 26(2)) (Art 28(2)) and Sch 2)

(NB Schedule 2 of the PACE (NI) Order 1989 contains a different list of preserved powers of arrest but the categories are not dissimilar)

5.31 Schedule 2 lists 21 statutes which contain powers authorising a constable to arrest without a warrant or court order. Each is preserved because there is, or is thought to be, a need for powers of arrest, unfettered by the general arrest conditions, in respect of offences which are not sufficiently serious to be categorised as arrestable offences, or in order to preserve existing powers of arrest of persons who have not committed criminal offences but must be detained either for their own safety or because they are illegally at large. The powers will be considered according to 7 broad categories into which they fall.

5.31 *Powers of arrest*

1) *Category I* — Persons unlawfully at large, including persons absent
    from places where they were lawfully detained, deserters or absen-
    tees from HM Forces and illegal immigrants. The following powers
    fall into this category:
      Repatriation of Prisoners Act 1984, s 5(5)
      Mental Health Act 1983, ss 18, 35(10), 36(8), 38(7) and 138
      Reserve Forces Act 1980, Sch 5
      Bail Act 1976, s 7 (person in breach of bail condition or likely to
        breach bail)
      Immigration Act 1971, s 24(2) and paras 17, 24 and 33 of Sch 2
        and para 7 of Sch 3
      Children and Young Persons Act 1969, ss 32 and 32(1)(A) as
        substituted by Schedule 12, para 27, of the Children Act 1989
        (child absent without consent from a place of safety or local
        authority accommodation in which he is required to live).
      Naval Discipline Act 1957, ss 104 and 105
      Army Act 1955, ss 186 and 190B
      Air Force Act 1955, ss 186 and 190B
      Visiting Forces Act 1952, s 13
      Prison Act 1952, s 49
2) *Category II* — Terrorism and related offences
      Emergency Powers Act 1920, s 2
        (A power of arrest may be attached to regulations made under
        the Act.)
      Military Lands Act 1892, s 17(2)
      (Power to make bye-laws in respect of military lands and to arrest
      persons in breach of those bye-laws cf Greenham Common.)
    Schedule 2 also preserved some arrest provisions under the Preven-
    tion of Terrorism (Temporary Provisions) Act 1984. That Act was
    repealed and replaced by the Prevention of Terrorism (Temporary
    Provisions) Act 1989. Section 14 of the 1989 Act provides a power
    of arrest without warrant for offences under ss 2, 8, 9, 10 and 11 of the
    Act (s 14(1)(a)). Persons concerned in the commission etc of acts of
    terrorism may also be arrested without warrant (s 14(1)(b)) as may a
    person subject to an exclusion order provided that if the arrest is made
    in Great Britain the exclusion order was made under s 5 of the 1989
    Act; if in Northern Ireland, under s 6 of the Act (s 14(1)(c) and (3)).
3) *Category III* — Protection of animals
      Animal Health Act 1981, ss 60(5) and 61(1)
      Protection of Animals Act 1911, s 12(1)
        (The general arrest conditions in s 25(3) do not permit arrest to
        prevent continuing harm to animals or the spread of disease by
        obstructing or impeding a constable enforcing the provisions of
        the 1981 Act. The power of arrest under s 61(1) of the 1981 Act is
        preserved to prevent the spread of rabies.)

4) *Category IV* — Road traffic offences

Road Traffic Act 1988, ss 4(5), 6(5) and 103(3)

(Arrest of persons driving etc under the influence of drink or drugs, or with excess alcohol in the blood, or driving while disqualified. In all three cases an unfettered power of arrest is required to prevent the person continuing to drive.)

5) *Category V* — Soliciting for the purpose of prostitution

Street Offences Act 1959, s 1(3)

(The section gives a constable a power to arrest without warrant for the offence of soliciting in a public place for the purpose of prostitution. This area of law is currently under review and the power of arrest is preserved pending the final recommendation of the Criminal Law Revision Committee.)

6) *Category VI* — Arrest for protection

Mental Health Act 1983, s 136

(Power to arrest a mentally disordered person to take him to a place of safety.)

Criminal Justice Act 1972, s 34

(Power to take a person arrested for an offence of drunkenness to a de-toxification centre.)

7) *Category VII* — Squatting and public order offences

Criminal Law Act 1977, ss 6(6), 7(11), 8(4), 9(7) and 10(5)

The Criminal Law Act 1977 created a number of offences in connection with the adverse occupation of premises, known colloquially as 'squatting', and gives a uniformed constable a power of arrest in respect of those offences with the exception of the offence created by s 6. That exception (using or threatening violence for the purpose of gaining entry to premises known to be occupied by someone opposed to such entry) is covered by general arrest conditions 25(3)(d)(i) and (iii). However, the general arrest conditions are inappropriate to the other offences under the 1977 Act given the need to arrest in order to put an immediate end to the offence and/or to enable the offenders to be physically removed from the premises. The powers of arrest provided by the sections mentioned above were therefore preserved. S 17(1)(c) of the PACE Act re-stated the power previously contained in s 11 of the 1977 Act to enter premises in order to arrest a person for these offences. This power is discussed at para 4.33 ante.

Public Order Act 1936, s 7(3)

Section 7(3) gives a constable a power to arrest without warrant any person reasonably suspected of committing an offence under s 1 (wearing a uniform signifying association with any political organisation in a public place or at a public meeting). Sections 4 and 5 of the 1936 Act were repealed by the Public Order Act 1986. The offence under s 4, which prohibited a person having with him an offensive weapon at a public meeting or procession, overlapped with the offence under s 1 of the Prevention of Crime Act 1953. The repeal of s 4 means that the 1953 Act must be relied upon where a person has with him at a public meeting or procession, any offensive weapon. The common law offences of riot, rout, unlawful assembly and affray were replaced by the 1986 Act. Ss. 1 and 2 create the offences of riot and violent disorder respectively. On conviction on indictment riot is punishable by 10 years' imprisonment and violent disorder by five years' imprisonment. Therefore both are arrestable offences as defined by s 24(1)(b). The Act also created a number of offences to which are attached summary powers of arrest. The following sections permit a constable to arrest anyone he reasonably suspects is

s 3(6) committing an affray

s 4(3) causing fear or provocation of violence

s 12(7) knowingly failing to comply with conditions imposed on a public procession

s 14(7) knowingly failing to comply with conditions on a public assembly

s 18(4) using threatening etc, words or behaviour

s 32(4) entering football premises in breach of an exclusion order.

Two sections provide a power to arrest a person reasonably suspected of committing an offence but only if the constable is in uniform

s 13(10) taking part in a prohibited procession

s 39(3) two or more persons trespassing on land

There is also a power of arrest for the offence under s 5(4) of causing harassment, alarm or distress

but only if the person —

(a)   engages in offensive conduct which the constable warns him to stop, and

(b)   engages in further offensive conduct immediately or shortly after the warning.

(It should be noted that s 17(1)(c) of the PACE Act provides a power to enter premises in order to effect the arrest of a person for an offence under s 1 of the 1936 Act and s 4 of the 1986 Act. This is discussed at para 4.33 ante.)

The Sporting Events (Control of Alcohol etc) Act 1985, created a number of summary (or general) offences involving the possession of intoxicating liquor and drink containers capable of causing injury eg cans and bottles, in connection with a designated sporting event in a designated sports-ground or on a specified vehicle. Section 7 provides that a constable may arrest a person whom he has reasonable grounds to suspect is committing or has committed an offence under the Act. Section 7 makes no reference to attempting to commit, as does s 25 of the PACE Act 1984. The nature of the offences under the 1985 Act leave little scope for an attempted offence but, if the conduct falls short of the commission of an offence under the 1985 Act, the power to arrest for an attempt to commit an offence under s 25 of the PACE Act 1984 may be used subject to an arrest condition being satisfied. The Football Spectators Act 1989, s 2 created the offence of not being an authorised spectator entering or remaining on premises as a spectator during a period relevant to a designated football match. S 2(4) provides a power to arrest without warrant a person reasonably suspected of committing such an offence.

Powers of arrest of persons who are not constables (s 26(1)) (Art 28(1))

5.32 Section 26(1) (Art 28(1)) repeals only those statutory powers which enable a *constable* to arrest without warrant for an offence or for conduct which is not an offence (eg a mentally disordered person in a public place). 'Constable' refers to the ancient office of constable (see para 2.55, ante). Consequently statutory powers of arrest given to 'any person' (see eg Theft Act 1978, s.3(4); Sexual Offences Act 1967, s.5(3); Criminal Justice Act 1967, s.91; Sexual Offences Act 1956, s.41; Licensing Act 1902, s.1; Prevention of Offences Act 1851, s.11; Vagrancy Act 1824, s.6 (as amended by the Criminal Justice Act 1948), s.68) and others (eg Customs and Excise Officers and Immigration Officers) who are not constables, are unaffected by the repeal. Moreover since a constable comes within the term 'any person', the powers of arrest directed to any person may be exercised by a constable. In *DPP v Kitching* (1990) the Queen's Bench Divisional Court held that s 91 of the Criminal Justice Act 1967, which provides that:

> 'Any person who in a public place is guilty, while drunk, of disorderly behaviour, may be arrested without warrant.'

had not been repealed by s 26 of the PACE Act. Section 26 and Schedule 2 purport to abolish the power of arrest whereas para 21 of Schedule 6 implies that s 91 remains in force. This latter provision made it clear that a constable's power to arrest under s 91 survived by directing that a constable arresting under s 91 take the person to a treatment centre. The Divisional Court held that the power to arrest was unaffected by s 25 by reason of the express provision in s 25(6) that the section shall not prejudice any power of arrest conferred apart from s 25. It follows that other powers which permit 'any person' to arrest without warrant are similarly unaffected by s 25. Therefore a constable exercising such a power of arrest is not under a legal duty to comply with s 25 — except in relation to an arrest under s 41 of the Sexual Offences Act 1956 (power to arrest in cases of soliciting by men), since para 9 of Schedule 6 of the PACE Act amends that section by adding the words, 'but a constable may only do so in accordance with s 25 of the Police and Criminal Evidence Act 1984'. A Home Office Circular on the PACE Act suggests that it may be prudent to use these powers only when a s 25 condition is met. Unlike the preserved powers of arrest set out in Schedule 2, there will seldom be a need for summary arrest in respect of the offences dealt with by the statutes referred to and compliance with s 25 will not therefore be detrimental to the police.

Common law powers of arrest

5.33 Section 25(6) (Art 27(6)) and s 26 (Art 28) repealed only statutory powers of arrest. Consequently the one power of arrest which the common law confers, namely arrest for breach of the peace, was not affected by the Act (*DPP v Orum* (1989)). A breach of the peace was at one time thought to be any breach of the Queen's peace, but in *R v Howell* (1982) the Court of Appeal said:

> 'We are emboldened to say that there is a breach of the peace whenever harm is actually done or is likely to be done to a person or in his presence to his property or a person is in fear of being harmed through an assault, an affray, a riot, unlawful assembly or other disturbance.'

The decision emphasises that violence, actual or apprehended, is an essential ingredient of a breach of the peace. It follows that loud noise and boisterous behaviour is not, without more, a breach. *Any person* may arrest for a breach of the peace committed in his presence, or where he has reasonable cause to believe a breach of the peace will be committed by a person in the immediate future unless he is arrested, or where a breach of the peace has been committed and he has reasonable grounds to believe it will be renewed if he is not arrested (*Howell*). Where a breach is reasonably apprehended a brief detention and restraint may be sufficient to enable the culprit to calm down, and no further action will be necessary. The common law permits such detention. Lord Diplock in *Albert v Lavin* (1982) put it thus:

> 'Any person in whose presence a breach of the peace is being or reasonably appears to be about to be, committed has the right to take reasonable steps to make the person who is breaking or threatening to break the peace refrain from doing so; and those reasonable steps in appropriate cases will include detaining him against his will. At common law it is not only the right of every citizen, it is also his duty, although, except in the case of a citizen who is a constable, it is a duty of imperfect obligation.'

It is then lawful temporarily to detain and restrain a person breaking or threatening to break the peace without arresting him. If he desists or ceases to threaten a breach of the peace, he may be released. If he persists he may be arrested. Resistance to such restraint is unlawful. A breach of the peace is not a substantive offence but a magistrates' court may deal with it by binding over the person to keep the peace. For powers of entry to effect an arrest for, or to prevent or stop, a breach of the peace see para 4.35, ante (one may note the overlap between this common law power and the statutory power under s 24(7) (Art 26(7)) which authorises a constable to arrest a person who is committing, or who is reasonably suspected to be about to commit an arrestable offence, discussed in para 5.15, ante).

Arrest for fingerprinting (s 27) (Art 29)

5.34 A person arrested for a recordable offence (an offence which is listed in the National Police Records (Recordable Offences) Regulations 1985, SI 1985 No 1941, as amended by SI 1989 No 694 made under s 27(4)) who is detained at a police station and is charged with or been informed that he will be reported for such an offence, will have his fingerprints taken without his consent if the circumstances set out in s (Art) 61(3) and (4) apply. He may also have them taken if he is arrested, detained and charged with, or reported for, *any* offence if he consents in writing (s 61(2)) (Art 61(2)). If the person is convicted of a recordable offence his fingerprints may also be taken without his consent (s 61(6)) (Art 61(6)), and if given a custodial sentence they will be taken while in prison service custody. Section 27 (Art 29) is concerned with the comparatively rare situation in which a person has been convicted of a recordable offence, has not been in police detention for that offence, did not have his fingerprints taken in the course of the investigation by the police, or since the conviction, ie he was not given a custodial sentence in respect of that offence. In these circumstances he may at any time not later than one month after the date of the conviction, be required by any constable to attend a police station so that his fingerprints may be taken (s 27(1)) (Art 29(1)). Such a requirement must give the person a period of at least 7 days within which he must attend at the police station, and may direct that he attend at a specified time or between specified times of the day (s 27(2)) (Art 29(2)). If the person fails to comply with a requirement any constable may arrest him without warrant (s 27(3)) (Art 29(3)). 'Month' means a calendar month (Interpretation Act 1978, Sch 1) and in computing the period the date of the conviction will normally be excluded and the date of the requirement included (*Radcliffe v Bartholomew* (1892)). For example if D is convicted on 30th May, a constable has until 30th June (effectively 23rd June since the requirement must give seven days within which to attend a police station) to make the requirement. The power to arrest arises at the end of the seven day period whenever it is made, eg D is convicted on 30th May. P makes the requirement on 4th

June specifying that D attend between five pm and six pm during the next seven days. Assuming the requirement is made in time to enable D to attend between those times, the power of arrest is available from the 11th June. If made after seven pm on the 4th, that day cannot be counted in the seven days. One may note that the power of arrest is not limited to within one month of the conviction — if a requirement is made within that period and is not complied with, D may be arrested at any time thereafter.

Requirements of a valid arrest (s 28) (Art 30)

5.35   Arrest is the assertion of a legal authority. That authority will stem, in the main, from the statutory powers provided by ss 24 and 25 (Arts 26 and 27), the preserved statutory powers, statutory powers of arrest created since the 1984 Act (1989 Order), and the common law powers. The requirements of the powers, principally the existence of reasonable grounds for suspecting that an arrestable or general offence has been committed, and in respect of general offences, that a general arrest condition is satisfied, must be complied with if the arrest is to be lawful. But there were other requirements laid down by the common law which applied to all persons exercising a power of arrest. These were that the arrest be made in a particular way and that particular information be supplied to the arrested person. If either of these requirements were not complied with the arrest was unlawful. Section 28 (Art 30) put these requirements into statutory form for arrest and modified them slightly in respect of arrest by a constable. Since the common law remains the basis of the law, the common law rules will be considered together with s 28 (Art 30) and the modifications that section makes to those rules.

The mechanics of arrest

5.36   Arrest consists in the seizure or touching of a person's body with a view to his restraint and with the intention to subject the person to the criminal process. The intention must be made known to the person arrested. Words alone may amount to an arrest if they:

> '... In the circumstances of the case, were calculated to bring to the accused's notice, and did bring to the accused's notice, that he was under compulsion and thereafter he submitted to that compulsion.' (Lord Parker CJ, *Alderson v Booth* (1969))

Words which brook no misunderstanding are the simple words 'I arrest you' though it was held in *R v Brosch* (1988) that these words are not a prerequisite of a valid arrest. If he then submits to the arrest it is a valid arrest, subject to the duty to inform him of the grounds for arrest. If he does not submit there is no arrest until there has been a touching or seizure of the person (*Genner v Sparks* (1704)). In *Hart v Chief Consta-*

ble of Kent (1983) this ancient case was applied to an arrest under the breathalyser law. D supplied a specimen of breath while standing on his doorstep. The test proved positive and the constable told D of this and that he was under arrest. The constable took hold of D's arm before he pulled back into his house. It was held that D had been arrested outside his house and the constable was then entitled to enter in pursuit of D by virtue of his common law power (see now s 17(1)(d) (Art 19(1)(d)) discussed in para 4.34, ante). Where the person arrested is known or believed to be deaf, or cannot understand English or is otherwise incapable of understanding, eg is drunk, the arrester need only do what is reasonable when he discovers the inability (*Tims v John Lewis Ltd* (1951) reversed on another point by the House of Lords (1952), and *Wheatley v Lodge* (1971)).

5.37 Where the arrest is made by physical seizure of the person, words indicating that the person is under arrest should accompany the seizure in order to make it a valid arrest at common law. There are, of course, circumstances which make it impossible or even unnecessary to tell the person he is under arrest and in the former case the person should be informed as soon as practicable after the arrest. Section 28(1) (Art 30(1)) confirms the common law rule that where the arrest is made by physical seizure the arrest is not lawful unless the person is told of the fact of arrest, and states that where an arrest is made without the person being informed that he is under arrest, the arrest is not lawful unless he is informed as soon as practicable after the arrest. Section 28(2) (Art 30(2)) modifies the common law rule in respect of an arrest by a constable by requiring the constable to inform the person in such a case even when it is obvious that he has been arrested.

Reasons for arrest

5.38 The common law requires not only that it must be made clear to the arrested person that he is under legal compulsion, but also that he must be told the reasons for the arrest. A failure to give the reasons, or the giving of the wrong reasons, renders the arrest unlawful (*Christie v Leachinsky* (1947)). The rule is subject to limited exceptions. There is no duty to inform the arrested person where (i) the circumstances are such that he must know the general nature of the offence for which he is arrested; and (ii) he makes it impossible to inform him by, for example, running off or attacking the arrester, or where the person is a possibly violent criminal who cannot be approached in the normal way, and see s 14 of the Northern Ireland (Emergency Provisions) Act 1978, considered in *Murray v Ministry of Defence* (1988). Technical or precise language need not be used, still less a precise charge formulated at the stage of arrest. However, it has been held that the statement 'I am arresting you on suspicion of burglary' was not sufficient information to enable the person to know what was the burglary of which he was suspected (*R v Telfer* (1976)). The fact that the officer could easily have obtained sufficient detail to make it clear by use of his radio was important in that decision. The need for fuller information is made clear by the purpose of the requirement which, in the words of Viscount Simon in *Christie v Leachinsky* (1947):

> '. . . turns on the elementary proposition that in this country a person is, prima facie, entitled to his freedom and is only required to submit to restraints upon him if he knows in substance the reason why it is claimed that this restraint is imposed.'

As Lord Simonds, in the same case, said:

> 'Blind, unquestioning obedience is the law of tyrants and of slaves: it does not yet flourish on English soil.'

That this legal requirement is supported by common sense is demonstrated by research which shows that people acquiesce more readily in the exercise of coercive powers accompanied by an explanation for their use, but are likely to respond aggressively to the unreasoned use of such powers (Police and People in London, Policy Studies Institute (1983)).

Ambiguous statements and wrong reasons

5.39 In *Gelberg v Miller* (1961) the court took the view that a motorist, who had been told that he was being arrested for obstructing the police (for which no power of arrest existed), had been lawfully arrested for obstruction of the highway (for which a power of arrest did exist). The word 'obstruction' was sufficient to communicate to him 'in substance' why he was being arrested. However, the decision may be explained on the ground that the purpose of the arrest was obvious to the motorist and the exception to the rule in *Christie v Leachinsky* (1947) applied. In *R v Kulynycz* (1970) the wrong reason for the arrest was given originally and the true reason given at the police station later. It was held that the arrest was unlawful in its inception but was made lawful from the moment the true reason was given, there being no need to release and to re-arrest in order to make continued detention lawful. In *Lewis v Chief Constable for South Wales* (1990) the Court of Appeal approved the decision in *Kulynycz* in dismissing an appeal against the award of damages for false imprisonment. This followed the arrest of two women on reasonable suspicion of burglary, who were not told the reasons for the arrest until 10 minutes afterwards in respect of one woman and 23 minutes in respect of the other. The women were then detained for five hours. Upholding the trial judge's ruling that the unlawfulness of the arrest ceased once reasons had been given, the court said that there was nothing in s 28 about the effect of subsequently giving reasons, but while it could not make an earlier period of arrest lawful, it could make the arrest lawful thereafter. These decisions should not be relied upon in order to excuse the giving of inadequate, ambiguous or wrong reasons for the arrest. However, there is, it is submitted, no legal requirement to state the legal authority upon which the arrest is based. If, for example, an arrest is made for an arrestable offence, there is no need to specify the precise statutory authority for the arrest, provided that correct and adequate reasons are given for it. The fact that the officer states that he is acting under a particular statutory power which does not in fact authorise arrest in the particular circumstances, but the arrest is authorised by another statutory or common law power, should not affect the validity of the arrest. This view is supported by the decision of the Supreme Court of South Australia in *Wark v Dairie* (1983) where it was held that an arrest was not vitiated by the fact that the arresting officer thought he was acting under a power which did not authorise the arrest when he had other powers upon which he could rely. The officer did not tell the person which power he was acting under but had he done so it is submitted that it would not have vitiated the arrest. The purpose of the rule in *Christie v Leachinsky* (1947) is to enable the arrested person to challenge the arrester's reasonable suspicion and to inform him in broad terms what it is that he is accused of. It is not intended to enable a legal argument to take place about the authority for the arrest. With the exception of an arrest under s 24(5)(a), (Art 26(5)(a)), the legality of the arrest is judged on the circumstances existing at the time of the arrest. The fact that the arrested person is not charged with the offence for which he was arrested does not vitiate it if he was in fact committing or about to commit an arrestable offence or there were reasonable grounds to suspect that he was committing or was about to commit or had committed such an offence. On the other hand, the fact that the arrested person pleads guilty to the offence for which he was arrested does not of itself render his arrest and detention lawful if he had not been told that he was being arrested and the reasons for it (*Hill v CC of South Yorkshire* (1989)). Section 28(3) (Art 30(3)) confirms the common law rule that no arrest is lawful unless the person arrested is informed of the ground for the arrest at the time of, or as soon as practicable after, the arrest. Of the phrase 'at the time of . . . arrest' Glidewell LJ said:

> '[it] does not in my view mean simply the precise moment at which the constable lays his hands on the defendant and says `I am arresting you'; it comprehends a short but reasonable period of time around the moment of arrest, both before and, as the statute itself specifically says, after.' (*Nicholas v Parsonage* (1987)

S 28(4) (Art 30(4)) modifies the common law rule in respect of arrest by a constable by requiring that the person be so informed even when the ground for arrest is obvious. As under the former law, however, there is no requirement to inform a person that he is under arrest or of the ground for arrest, if it was not reasonably practicable to do so because the person escaped from arrest before he could be informed (s 28(5)) (Art 30(5)).

5.40 'Practicable' as used in s 28 (Art 30) is not defined. Its meaning will depend on the circumstances. If the reason why he was not informed at the time of arrest is because he was violent, it will be practicable to inform him once he ceases to be so; or if he was drunk, when he is sober. Normally it will be the arresting person who imparts the information but the section simply requires that the person arrested be informed and in those situations in which it is impracticable to inform him at the time of arrest the section will be complied with if he is informed by, for example, the custody officer, once he has sobered up or calmed down at the police station. If it is not practicable to inform the accused of the ground for the arrest at the time of the arrest, the arrest is not invalidated because of a failure to inform when it became practicable to do so (*DPP v Hawkins* (1988)). The limitations of this decision should be noted. The issue was whether the constable was acting in the execution of his duty when he was assaulted by the person he had arrested. Because the person was violent it was not practicable to inform him of the reasons for the arrest. When it became practicable at the police station he was not told, or was given the wrong reason. The decision that the arrest was lawful between these two periods meant the constable was acting in the execution of his duty. However, a civil court hearing an action for false imprisonment, while doubtless agreeing with the Divisional Court that the arrest was lawful from the point when it was not practicable to inform the person up to the point when it became practicable to do so, would be likely to find the arrest unlawful from then on and the resultant detention a false imprisonment.

Interpretation of common law rules and s 28 (Art 30)

5.41 The interpretation of the common law rules applying to arrest is still of relevance in interpreting s 28 (Art 30). Technical or precise language was not required under the rule in *Christie v Leachinsky* and will not be required under s 28. In *Abbassy v Commissioner of Police* (1990), a civil action arising out of an arrest under the pre-PACE Act law, the Court of Appeal took the view that an arrest for 'unlawful possession of a motor car' was apt to describe the offence under s 12 of the Theft Act 1968, taking a motor vehicle without consent. While suggesting that the constable would have been well advised to use more precise language, the Court of Appeal thought it would be wrong to lay down a higher standard than that indicated by the House of Lords in *Christie v Leachinsky*. The advice to use 'more precise language' should be heeded. A constable exercising such an important coercive power should be sure that he has a power of arrest and of the grounds upon which he is exercising that power. It is, as suggested earlier, reasonable that an arrest for which true and adequate grounds were given, should not be vitiated by the constable's mistaken reliance on a particular power which does not authorise that arrest, when another power does, but, it is submitted, it is not reasonable to excuse the giving of wrong or inadequate reasons for the exercise of such a power. It is no doubt reasonable not to expect the constable, still less a citizen, to be specific. Dishonestly taking or obtaining property belonging to another may be one of a number of Theft Act offences and determining which it is may be a task for a lawyer. The statement 'I am arresting you for stealing' together with information identifying the property alleged to be stolen, when and from whom, should be sufficient even if the actual charge proves to be robbery, obtaining by deception or handling stolen goods.

Grounds for arrest under s 25 (Art 27)

5.42 In *Nicholas v Parsonage* (1987) the Divisional Court rejected a submission that, when asking for a name and address under s 25, the constable is required to indicate why the name and address is required ie so that a summons might be served. Glidewell LJ, said:

> 'As a general principle, I would hold that at the time of arrest the arresting constable must indicate in some words ... the offence for which the defendant is being arrested. If he goes on and says: `I am arresting you because you have not given your name and address', so much the better. He has then given all the detail that could possibly be required.' (at p 204)

It should be noted that in that case the constable did tell the defendant what the offence was that he had committed and asked him for his name and address. When it was refused he told the defendant that he had the power to arrest him if he did not give his name and address. Only on this being refused did he arrest the defendant. This approach appears to be correct in principle. It is suggested that while the general principle enunciated by Glidewell LJ must be accepted as the maximum required by law — a constable would be well advised to go further. Before arresting under s 25 (Art 27) when general arrest conditions (3)(a) and (b) are satisfied, a constable might adopt the following procedure.

(a) Inform the relevant person of the offence he is alleged to have committed, using non-technical language;
(b) request the relevant person's name and address;
(c) if refused, warn the relevant person that he will be arrested unless his name and address is given;
(d) if still refused, arrest and if practicable tell the relevant person that he is being arrested for the offence he is alleged to have committed.

In respect of other arrest conditions it may be necessary to explain the legal significance of a failure to satisfy the conditions. For example, if a holidaymaker living at a temporary address in a holiday resort gives the constable his name and the temporary address, which the constable with his local knowledge believes to be a temporary address, eg a guest house, it would be reasonable and within the spirit of the Act, to explain that the address given is not a satisfactory address for the service of a summons and that unless such an address is forthcoming he will be arrested. Only if no such address is forthcoming should he be arrested. The simple principle underlying conditions 25(3)(a) to (c) (Art 27(3)(a) to (c)) is the avoidance of arrest if a summons will suffice. The relevant person should then be given a reasonable opportunity to avoid arrest by supplying the information which would enable him to do so. So far as the other arrest conditions are concerned it may be impractical to lay down any hard and fast rules but the general principle should also be the avoidance of arrest where possible. Thus a person obstructing the highway should be warned that he will be arrested if he does not move and arrested only when that warning is ignored. If a constable has reasonable grounds for believing that arrest is necessary to prevent the relevant person causing harm to other persons (s 25(3)(d)(1)) (Art 27(3)(d)(1)), and the circumstances permit, the relevant person should be informed of this so that he may seek to persuade the constable that his suspicions are unfounded.

Duty to give reasons for the exercise of other coercive powers

5.43   In *Pedro v Diss* (1981) the power to stop and search under s 66 of the Metropolitan Police Act 1839 was equated with arrest and a duty imposed to give reasons for the stop, detention and search. In *Brazil v Chief Constable of Surrey* (1983) the duty to give reasons was extended to the search of persons following arrest. The former duty is now a statutory one under s 2(2) and (3) of the PACE Act (Art 4(2) and (3) of the PACE Order) but there would appear to be a common law duty to give reasons for the exercise of *any* coercive power if the exercise is to be lawful. In any event, it is common sense to do so and thereby reduce the risk of resistance

Voluntary attendance at a police station or elsewhere

5.44   Section 29 (Art 31) states:

'Where for the purpose of assisting with an investigation a person attends voluntarily at a police station or at any other place where a constable is present or accompanies a constable to a police station or any such other place without having been arrested —
(a) he shall be entitled to leave at will unless he is placed under arrest;
(b) he shall be informed at once that he is under arrest if a decision is taken by a constable to prevent him from leaving at will.'

The police did not always tell the media whether a person was under arrest for an offence or whether he was voluntarily assisting them with their inquiries. The media, therefore, used the phrase 'assisting with inquiries' to cover both possibilities and to avoid defaming a person who had not been arrested. However, the phrase disguised a third possibility, that the person was detained short of arrest against his will. As was seen in para 5.01, ante the police regularly used what was in fact unlawful detention in order to avoid the legal constraints in questioning a suspect who had been arrested, or simply because there was no ground for arrest. Once in the coercive atmosphere of a police station he could be interrogated. In this way the constable's suspicion could be turned into reasonable suspicion and then into a prima facie case, or occasionally the suspicion or reasonable suspicion dispelled. If this practice was permitted to continue, the elaborate procedure under Part IV of the Act to control police detention of suspects and to safeguard them against possible abuse would be useless, since a person is not in police detention for the purpose of that Part of the Act unless he has been arrested for an offence and taken to a police station and detained there, or detained elsewhere in the charge of a constable (s 118(2) (Art 2(3))) (discussed in para 6.07, post). It follows that a person who is voluntarily in a police station assisting with police inquiries is not in police detention, nor is a person taken to a police station against his will without being arrested and who is detained there.

Attends voluntarily or accompanies a constable

5.45 By referring to a person who attends voluntarily and one who accompanies a constable to a police station or other place, s 29 (Art 31) distinguishes between the true volunteer and him who believes he is under legal compulsion but who is not (for a discussion of consent and voluntariness in this context see para 2.18, ante). A constable may say 'I require you to accompany me to the police station' or couch it in the form of a request. The intention may be to arrest or simply to get the person to a police station where inquiries can more conveniently be carried out, but in neither case is the person lawfully arrested, and if he believes he is under compulsion he clearly is not a volunteer either. If the intention was to arrest, this will become clear on arrival at a police station and the suspect should then be informed that he is under arrest and of the reasons for the arrest. If the intention was not to arrest, or if the person is a genuine volunteer, it may emerge during the questioning and investigation that there are reasonable grounds for arrest for an offence, not necessarily the offence under investigation. If the constable then decides that the person is not free to leave, he must be informed at once that he is under arrest. Section 29(b) (Art 31(b)) must be read as referring to a decision by the constable to prevent him from leaving at will because there are reasonable grounds for arrest for an offence, and, if it is a general offence, that a general arrest condition is satisfied, for only then will a constable be empowered to arrest for a general offence.

Attends voluntarily at or accompanies a constable to, a police station or any other such place where a constable is present (s 29) (Art 31)

5.46   In a majority of cases it will be a police station to which the person goes voluntarily or accompanies a constable, but there will be other places. The key words are 'any such other place' and will cover cases where, for example, a constable asks a suspected shoplifter to accompany him to the manager's office while inquiries are made into the allegation, or employees are asked to attend at an office within the workplace where a constable is in order to assist in an investigation of theft from the workplace. Such persons are free to leave at will unless arrested and s 29 (Art 31) seeks to ensure that, if the constable determines that they are no longer free to leave, they will immediately be arrested and told that they are under arrest and of the ground for it, thus making it perfectly clear that their status has changed.

Rights of a volunteer

5.47   The volunteer or person who accompanies a constable to a police station or other place, may be a witness or a suspect against whom there is, as yet, insufficient evidence to arrest. Since both are free men they not only have the right to leave at will, they can also demand that a solicitor or friend be present at any interview. Whilst the constable may seek to persuade the person that that is unnecessary, the latter's request cannot lawfully be denied. Code of Practice C, Detention, Treatment and Questioning (hereinafter COP C) para 3.15 emphasises that the person is free to leave unless arrested and, if it is decided that he is no longer free to leave, he must be informed at once that he is under arrest and brought before the custody officer. He is then treated as any other detained person and should be told of his right to have someone informed of his arrest (s 56 discussed at para 7.33, post) and to consult a solicitor (s 58 discussed at para 7.41, post). If he is not placed under arrest but is suspected of an offence, para 10.1 of COP C requires that he be cautioned in the terms set out in para 10.4 before being questioned in order to obtain evidence of the offence under investigation. The caution is required whenever a person is suspected of an offence, as opposed to reasonably suspected which is the trigger for when he may be arrested. A volunteer or person who accompanies a constable and who is a suspect should therefore be cautioned before being questioned and informed that he is not under arrest, is not obliged to remain and may obtain free legal advice (COP C para 3.15, see further para 7.143, post). It should be noted that para 3.15 applies to volunteers in a police station. Para 10.1 on the other hand applies to persons anywhere, and para 10.2 requires that a person who is not under arrest but who is cautioned before or during an interview be told that he is not under arrest and is not obliged to remain with the officer. This clearly applies to the person who attends voluntarily or accompanies a constable to 'any other place where a constable is present'. The 'fundamental right' to leave (Lord Elton, House of Lords, Hansard, July 5, 1984, col 502) is ever present until the person is arrested. It would appear that much use is still being made of the facility for voluntary attendance by some forces (McKenzie, Morgan and Reiner, 'Helping the Police with their Inquiries: the Necessity Principle and Voluntary Attendance at the Police Station', [1990] Crim LR 23). The authors cite a detective sergeant's explanation of the utility of this practice:

> 'First, suppose there is a crime report showing 'not detected', so why not interview him as a witness to see if he becomes a suspect. Second, most of the cases and the suspects are suitable for summons. Therefore there's no pressure to complete the paperwork [as there is with a charge]. Third, it's convenient because you set the time, and last it avoids the time clock consideration. If arrest is necessary later, it doesn't count.'

The first reason may be given some credence but if the Code of Practice is followed little is in fact gained. The second reason is specious. The arrested suspect can be reported for summons and bailed thus relieving the pressure of paperwork. The third reason is more convincing and is probably the main reason why so much reliance is put on voluntary attendance.

The relevant time for arrest of a volunteer or person who accompanied a constable to a police station

5.48 Detention without charge is limited by s 41 (Art 42), and the time from which the period of detention is to be calculated, 'the relevant time', is determined by reference to that section, which provides for a number of eventualities. Section 41 (Art 42) provides that in the case of a person who attends voluntarily at a police station, or accompanies a constable to a police station without having been arrested, the relevant time is the time of his arrest. The possible disadvantage to the arrested person of this provision is discussed at para 6.40 post. It is clear that voluntary attendance can be used to avoid the constraints on detention imposed by the PACE Act 1984.

Custody officers and volunteers

5.49 Since a volunteer or person who accompanies a constable is not in police detention, the custody officer has no statutory duties in respect of him and the period of his attendance is not subject to supervision or review. However, the custody officer, or person in charge at a non-designated station, would be well advised to ensure (i) that constables, in whose charge volunteers are, are aware of their responsibilities under Code C, discussed above, and, (ii) that supervisory officers are also aware of the presence of volunteers or persons who accompanied a constable to the police station (see COP C, Notes for guidance 1A and further at para 7.143, post).

Persons arrested elsewhere than at a police station (s 30(1) and (2)) (Art 32(1) and (2))

5.50   Section 30(1) and (2) (Art 32(1) and (2)) require that where a constable otherwise than at a police station, arrests a person for an offence, or takes a person into custody after his arrest by some person other than a constable, the person shall be taken to a designated police station or, in the special circumstances set out in s 30(3)–(5) (Art 32(3)–(5)), to a non-designated police station, as soon as practicable after his arrest. A 'designated police station' is a police station designated by the chief officer of police for the area as one to be used for detaining persons arrested and for which one or more custody officers will be appointed (s 35) (Art 37). As will be seen (para 6.11, post), a custody officer at a designated police station must be independent of the investigation, and one of his duties is to supervise detention (ss 36–39) (Arts 37–40). A non-designated police station will not be manned by appointed custody officers and, being small stations, may have no police officer independent of the investigation to act as custody officer, the independence being a key element in the scheme for safeguarding the detainee (see 36(7) (Art 37(7)) discussed in para 6.12, post).

Persons arrested in police area A for an offence in police area B

5.51   In *R v Khan* (1991) officers from the West Midlands Serious Crime Squad arrested Khan in Caernarvon for an offence committed in Birmingham. They appear to have driven him from Caernarvon directly to Birmingham rather than, as s 30 seems to require, taking him to a police station in the area in which he was arrested. The Court of Appeal in quashing Khan's conviction, doubted the authenticity of a confession allegedly obtained from Khan during the car journey. S 30 was not considered but, it is submitted, the requirement that an arrested person be taken to a police station 'as soon as practicable' cannot be interpreted as permitting a delay of what might be several hours in taking the person to a police station in the area in which his arrest was sought, rather than a police station in the area in which he was arrested. During such a journey the arrested person is not in police detention and has none of the protections which the Act and Code of Practice provide to detained persons. (It should be noted that Code C para 11.1 states that following a decision to arrest a suspect he must not be interviewed except at a police station unless the delay would lead to one of the consequences set out in Code C para 11(a)–(c). For a definition of interview see Note 11A. It would seem that the 'casual conversation between suspect and police officer en route from Walsall to Bristol' in *R v Younis and Ahmed* (1990), in which admissions were made, would still not be an interview, while that in *Khan* clearly would be; see further Chapter 8, post.) If no questioning of the arrested person in order to obtain evidence in relation to the offence for which he was arrested takes place in the police station in the area in which he was arrested, the 'detention clock' does not start until the arrested person arrives at the first police station to which he is taken in the area in which his arrest was sought, see s 41(3) discussed in para 6.40 post. There is then no detriment to the police in complying with s 30 and the arrested person is in the same position as he would be had he been arrested in the area in which his arrest was sought. (NB Northern Ireland is one police area. The duty to take a person to a police station should there be interpreted as the nearest designated police station, or non-designated police station, if appropriate.)

Arrest by constables working in the area covered by non-designated stations (s 30(3)) (Art 32(3))

5.52   Section 30(3)–(5) (Art 32(3)–(5))lays down the conditions which must be satisfied before a person arrested for an offence or taken into custody can be taken to a non-designated police station. The former provides that *where an arresting officer is working in an area covered by a non-designated police station* the person may be taken to *any* police station unless it appears to the constable that it may be necessary to keep the arrested person in police detention for more than 6 hours. This will be the case in respect of some 75 per cent of arrests (see Royal Commission, para 3.96), which will either be arrests under s 25 (Art 27) for comparatively minor offences where the purpose of the arrest will be to identify the arrested person or check that the address given is a satisfactory address; or arrests of more serious offences which require little, if any, investigation.

Conditions under which any constable may take arrested persons to non-designated stations (s 30(5)) (Art 32(5))

5.53   Section 30(5) (Art 32(5)) permits *any* constable to take an arrested person to a non-designated police station if either of two conditions in s 30(5)(a) (Art 32(5)(a)) are satisfied *and* the condition in s30(5)(b) (Art 32(5)(b)) is also satisfied. The conditions are:

(a) . . .

    (i)   the constable has arrested him without the assistance of any other constable and no other constable is available to assist him;

    (ii) the constable has taken him into custody from a person other than a constable without the assistance of any other constable and no other constable is available to assist him; *and*

(b) it appears to the constable that he will be unable to take the arrested person to a designated police station without the arrested person injuring himself, the constable or some other person.

Section 30(3) and (5) (Art 32(3) and (5)) are independent of each other, the former applying only to a constable working in the area of a non-designated police station, the latter to any constable whether or not he is working in such an area (as to the use of reasonable force in such circumstances see para 5.64, post). The Northern Ireland Order contains an additional reason for taking an arrested person to a non-designated station. That is that it appears to the constable that he will be unable to take him to a designated station without exposing the arrested person or himself to unjustifiable injury. In the circumstance in which policing takes place in Northern Ireland this is understandable. As to constables at non-designated police stations assuming the functions of a custody officer see s 36(7) and (8) (Art 37(7) and (8)) discussed in para 6.12, post). Section 30(6), (Art 32(7)) requires that where the *first* police station to which an arrested person is taken is not a designated police station, he shall be taken to such a station not more than 6 hours after his arrival there unless he is released previously.

Duty to release when the grounds for arrest no longer exist (s 30(7)) (Art 32(10))

5.54 Section 30(7), (Art 32(10)) re-affirms the common law duty to release a person who has been arrested otherwise than at a police station if, before arriving at a police station, the constable becomes aware that the grounds upon which the arrest was made no longer exist (s 30 pre-supposes that there was a lawful arrest for which grounds existed. If there were no grounds the detention of the person is unlawful from the start and is not in law an arrest). A central purpose of the requirement that a person arrested be informed of the grounds for the arrest, laid down by *Christie v Leachinsky* (1947) and now by s 28(3) (Art 30(3)), is to enable a person to show that there are no grounds for his arrest. If he can do so or show that the reasonable grounds relied upon for the arrest are not in fact reasonable, the arrester is then bound to release him and any detention beyond that point is unlawful (*Wiltshire v Barrett* (1966)). The police rarely, if ever, complied with this duty believing that such a release would expose them to an action for false imprisonment. However, the reverse is true. The creation by s 25 (Art 27) of a category of arrest based on the requirement therein that a general arrest condition be satisfied before an arrest is permitted, adds a new dimension to the statutory duty to release when the constable is satisfied that there are no grounds for keeping the person under arrest. Where, for example, a person is arrested under s 25 (Art 27) because general arrest condition (3)(b) (belief that the name is not his real name) is satisfied, but before reaching a police station the constable is satisfied that the name given is his real name, the person must be released. The requirement that the constable must be 'satisfied' that there are no grounds for keeping the person under arrest is clearly subjective and will result in the cautious constable continuing with the arrest in borderline cases while the bolder constable releases. That is permissible, but in a clear case it will not be permissible to use the subjective nature of the test in order to continue with an arrest which should be ended. Where a person is released under s 30(7) (Art 32(10)), the releasing constable must record the fact that he has done so as soon as practicable after the release (s 30(8) and (9)), (Art 32(11) and (12)), presumably in his pocket book unless his own force instructions direct otherwise (the duty to release in the circumstances of s 30(7) (Art 32(10)) after the person arrives at the police station falls on the custody officer; see s 37 (Art 38), discussed in paras 6.16–27, post).

Delay in taking a person to a police station (s 30(10)) (Art 32(13))

5.55 Section 30(10), (Art 32(10) provides that nothing in s 30(1) (Art 32(1)) shall prevent a constable delaying taking a person who has been arrested to a police station if the presence of that person elsewhere is required for such investigations as it is reasonable to carry out immediately. An earlier contradiction in the common law (see Lord Porter in *John Lewis & Co Ltd v Tims* (1952) and Lord Denning in *Dallison v Caffery* (1965)) is resolved. Section 30(10) thus links up with (a) the duty to release under s 30(7) (Art 32(10)), in that it permits the reasonable investigation of matters which might confirm or deny the reasonable suspicion upon which the arrest was made, and (b) the duty under s 28(3) (Art 30(3)) to inform the person of the grounds for arrest. If, for example, D is arrested on reasonable suspicion of burglary on a particular date and time but claims on being arrested that X can prove conclusively that he was elsewhere at that time, it may be reasonable to investigate that alibi immediately, particularly if X is to be found reasonably close to the point of arrest, and consequently necessary that D accompany the constable. Similarly, it may be reasonable to take D to his home to search for the proceeds of the burglary, for example, if the arrest is made in public and it is possible that word of his arrest may reach relatives or friends who may then dispose of the evidence before the constable can return to search his premises (see s 18(5) of the PACE Act 1984 (Art 20(5) 1989 Order) discussed at para 4.21, ante). What is 'reasonable' is a question of fact. In *Dallison v Caffery* it was held that a constable had acted reasonably in taking D to a house where he claimed to have been working at the time of the offence. In *McCarrick v Oxford* (1982), a constable who had arrested D reasonably suspecting that he was driving whilst disqualified, was also held to have acted reasonably in refusing to take D to his house where he had a letter from the Crown Court stating that the disqualification was suspended pending an appeal. The constable tried to confirm the suspension by radio but failed to do so, there being no record of it at any criminal records' office. It was, therefore, reasonable for the constable to assume that police records were correct. A relevant consideration is whether the period of detention of D is likely to be reduced by taking the action which was in fact taken or requested. In *Dallison v Caffery* the detention would have been shorter if D's alibi was verified. In *McCarrick v Oxford* it would not have been, given the constable's belief in the accuracy of police records. Section 30(11) (Art 32(14)) provides that where there is delay in taking the arrested person to a police station, the reasons for it shall be recorded when he first arrives at a police station (persons detained under para 16 of Sch 2 of the Immigration Act 1971 may under para 18 of that Schedule be taken to and from their place of detention in order to ascertain their nationality or citizenship, or for making arrangements for their admission to another country. Section 30(13), (Art 32(16)) provides that nothing in s 30(10), (Art 32(13)) shall be taken to affect this power).

Exemptions

5.56 Section 30(12) (Art 32(15)) exempts from the provisions of s 30(1) (Art 32(1)) a number of powers of arrest in respect of which the duty to take a person to a police station is inappropriate. These are:

(a) Arrest and detention of a would be immigrant who is refused leave to enter and who may be detained on board the ship or aircraft or elsewhere (paras 16(3) and 18(1) of Sch 2, Immigration Act 1971) (s 30(12)(a) Art 32(15)(a)).

(b) Persons arrested for being drunk and disorderly or drunk and incapable who may under s 34(1) of the Criminal Justice Act 1972 be taken to a de-toxification centre (a treatment centre for alcoholics approved by the Secretary of State), where they exist (s 30(12)(b) Art 32(15)(b)).

(c) Persons arrested and detained under s 15(6) or (9) of the Prevention of Terrorism (Temporary Provisions) Act 1989 who may be detained on board the ship or aircraft which brought them, if they are excluded persons, or at such place as the Secretary of State may direct (s 30(12)(c) Art 32(15)(c)).

Arrest for a further offence (s 31) (Art 33)

5.57 Part IV of the Act (Part V of the Order) limits the period of detention without charge following an arrest and s 41(2) (Art 42(2)) provides a formula for determining the time from which the period of detention is to be calculated (the relevant time). In the usual case this will be the time at which the arrested person arrives at the first police station to which he is taken. Where a person has committed more than one offence it would be possible to obtain extended periods of detention by the simple expedient of arresting on offence A, obtaining the maximum period of detention for that offence, then on the release of the person, arresting him for offence B thus commencing a new period of detention. This process could be repeated through as many offences as can be discovered. Section 31 (Art 33), in conjunction with s 41(4) (Art 42(3)), excludes this possibility by requiring that where a person has been arrested for offence A and is at a police station in consequence of that offence, and it appears to a constable that, if he were released from that arrest he would be liable to arrest for some other offence B, he shall be arrested for that offence. Section 41(4) then provides that the time from which the period of detention in respect of that other offence B is to be calculated, shall be the time from which detention in respect of the 'original' offence A was calculated. For example:

> D is arrested for taking and driving away a motor vehicle. He arrives at the first police station to which he is taken at 10 am, that is the time from which the period of detention in respect of that offence is to be calculated (the relevant time). If during questioning the arrested person admits to a number of burglaries which the constable is satisfied he did commit, he must be arrested for those other offences. The 'relevant time' in respect of those offences is also 10 am (ss 31 and 41(4)) (Arts 33 and 42(3)).

The phrase 'and it appears to a constable that . . . he would be liable to arrest . . .' would seem to mean that there are reasonable grounds for suspecting that the person has committed the other offences (and if it is a general offence that a general arrest condition is satisfied), for only then would it appear to a constable that the person is liable to arrest. The former practice in some police forces of arresting on a minor (holding) charge in order to question the suspect on a more serious charge is not entirely precluded by this section. However, when combined with the custody officer's duty to charge or release a person without charge when there is sufficient evidence to do so in respect of the offence for which he was arrested (s 37(7)(a) and (b)) (Art 38(7)(a) and (b)), and the review of detention of persons detained without charge or after charge under s 40 (Art 41), the provisions of s 31 (Art 33) are likely to end the practice.

Search of person on arrest (s 32) (Art 34)

5.58   Where an arrest is made at a place other than a police station, s 32 (Art 34) authorises the search of the person arrested and of the premises in which he was when arrested or immediately before arrest (as for search of premises under this section see paras 4.25–26, ante). It should be stressed that (a) this power is available to a constable whenever he arrests outside a police station whether under s 24, s 25 (Art 26 or 27), a preserved statutory power of arrest, a statutory power of arrest created since the passing of the 1984 Act (1989 Order) or under a common law power of arrest (but not detention under the common law power) and (b) is complementary to the power under s 18 (Art 20) (which permits search of premises occupied or controlled by a person arrested for an arrestable offence). Search of *persons* arrested other than at a police station is the concern of this section. Search of persons arrested at a police station and of persons detained following arrest is governed by ss 54 and 55 (Arts 54 and 55) and is discussed in para 7.11, post.

Dangerous persons

5.59   Section 32(1) (Art 34(1)) provides that a constable may search a person arrested other than at a police station if he has *reasonable grounds for believing that he may present a danger* to himself or others. The search will be for articles which he might use to cause physical injury to himself or others, but there is no requirement that the constable has reasonable grounds for believing that any such article is in his possession, merely that he has reasonable grounds for believing the arrested person may present a danger to himself or others. Such a belief will be present when a person is arrested for an arrestable offence involving violence or threats of violence or for an offence where general arrest condition 25(3)(d)(i) (Art 27(3)(d)(i) and possibly (d)(iii) and (e) apply. In such cases the violent nature of the offence alleged to have been committed or the reasonable belief that it is necessary to arrest to prevent physical injury to the arrested person or others, will provide the reasonable belief that he may present a danger to himself or others. Where the arrest is necessary to prevent damage to property or to protect a child or other vulnerable person, the circumstances of the likely damage and the nature of the threat to the child or other vulnerable person may similarly give grounds for the reasonable belief that he may present such a danger. Where the arrested person appears to be mentally deranged or suicidal he may present a danger to himself or to others and in such a case drugs or pills which might be taken by the arrested person may be the articles to be searched for as well as any weapon of offence.

Search for articles of escape or evidence

5.60 Section 32(2)(a) (Art 34(2)(a)) provides a power to search the arrested person for anything:

(i) which he might use to assist him to escape from lawful custody; or

(ii) which might be evidence relating to an offence.

However, the power may not be exercised unless the constable has reasonable grounds for believing that the arrested person may have something concealed on him for which such search is permitted (s 32(5) Art 34(5)). The police argued strongly for the removal of this requirement on the basis that a person in respect of whom there was not the slightest suspicion has, nevertheless, been known to become violent, produce a weapon and attack the policeman conveying him to a police station. The more obviously dangerous person will have been searched under s 32(1), (Art 34 (1)) since he 'may present a danger' to the constable. Where articles are found in consequence of such a search, they may also be evidence of an offence; for example, D is arrested for robbery in which a knife was used to threaten the victim. Those circumstances give rise to the reasonable belief justifying a search under s 32(1), (Art 34(1)) and s 32(2)(a)(i) and (ii), (Art 34(2)(a)(i) and (ii)) and the knife may be seized under s 32(8) or (9) (Art 34(8) or (9)). Where there are reasonable grounds for believing evidential articles are concealed on the person, which there will be in many more cases than there will be in respect of articles of escape, a search may reveal both kinds of articles. The position is, then, that the risk of harm to an arresting constable or the risk of escape, is not as great as may be suggested by the police, since there will usually be a lawful justification for a search. Nevertheless, there will be arrests in which there are no reasonable grounds for search under s 32(1), (Art 34(1)) or (2)(a)(i) and (ii). In some of these cases search will be with, and in others without, consent. In the latter circumstances the constable runs the risk of a civil action and/or disciplinary proceedings, but the risk of complaint by the arrested person is probably less than the risk of harm to the constable. In such circumstances a constable will proceed to search.

Limitation on the extent of search of the person

5.61 Section 32(3) (Art 34(3)) states that the power to search conferred by s 32(2) (Art 34(2)) is only a power to search to the extent that is reasonably required for the purpose of discovering any such thing or any such evidence. That can be an important limitation in the context of a search of premises under s 32(2)(b) (Art 34(2)(b)), but is of limited value in the context of the search of persons under s 32(2)(a) (Art 34(2)(a)). More so since s 32(3) (Art 34(3)) does not apply to searches under s 32(1) (Art 34(1)) (the search of a dangerous person). The article sought in a search of the person under either subsection may be quite small and only discoverable by a strip or intimate search. Neither form of search is feasible in most arrest situations and this is recognised by s 32(4) (Art 34(4)) which limits the clothing which a constable may require to be removed *in public* to an outer coat, jacket or gloves. (The NI Order includes 'headgear'. In England and Wales we understand that headgear often falls off during a search!) If such clothing is removed the search in public will be limited to a 'pat down' of the body over remaining clothing and a search of pockets, waist bands or stocking tops where articles may be concealed. More thorough searching of clothing by, for example, opening seams, is not appropriate in an arrest situation. Since s 32(4) (Art 34(4)) refers to removal of clothing *in public* there will be a temptation to construe the provision as permitting the removal of other garments in private, for example, in the back of a police van, particularly in an arrest for possession of drugs which might easily be disposed of. However, it is clear from the provisions for search of persons in police detention that strip searching is an exceptional procedure to be carried out only at a police station (see ss 54 and 55 and COP C para 4.1 and Annex A discussed in para 7.15, post). A search of the person can, of course, take place with the consent of the person to be searched. It must, however, be a genuine consent and not obtained by duress. In the context of an arrest it may be difficult to persuade a court that the arrestee consented to a strip search and, if the court is not so persuaded, the constable's actions will be seen as unlawful resulting in the possible exclusion of any evidence found, a finding that the constable was not 'acting in the execution of his duty' if the arrestee is prosecuted for assaulting the constable, or in a civil case, a finding that the constable assaulted the arrestee (see the discussion at para 2.38, ante). If there is a reasonable belief that anything may be concealed which requires a more thorough search than is permitted by s 32 and that it may be used to escape from custody, then resort may be had to the use of handcuffs (see para 5.67, post). Search of the person extends to bags etc carried by the person. However, in an arrest situation it may not be possible to do so. If this is the case the arresting constable should ensure that the arrested person is not permitted access to it and it can then be searched at the police station.

Seizure and retention of articles found

5.62 Section 32(8) (Art 34(8)) provides that a constable searching a person under s 32(1) (Art 34(1)) may seize and retain anything he finds, if he has reasonable grounds for believing that the person searched might use it to cause physical injury to himself or to any other person, eg D is arrested for an offence of violence and is found to be in possession of a knife. It may be seized under s 32(8) (Art 34(8)). Section 32(9) (Art 34(9)) provides that where a constable searches a person under s 32(2)(a) (Art 34(2)(a)) he:

> may seize and retain anything he finds, other than an item subject to legal privilege, if he has reasonable grounds for believing —
> (a)   that he might use it to assist him to escape from lawful custody: or
> (b)   that it is evidence of *an* offence or has been obtained in consequence of the commission of *an* offence.

What are reasonable grounds for a particular belief is a question of fact in each case. The mere fact that a person carries a penknife is not enough, but if the person is violent and has resisted arrest that may be grounds for the reasonable belief that he may use the penknife to escape. Whether there are reasonable grounds to believe the item is evidence of an offence (not necessarily *the* offence for which the person was arrested) will depend upon the nature of the item and the offence. If the offence is theft of money then any monies found on the person may be evidence of the offence and any goods carried may have been obtained in consequence of that offence ie purchased with the stolen money. However, one cannot reasonably believe this to be so unless there are objective facts pointing to such a purchase. Since s 32(9)(b) (Art 34(9)(b)) permits the seizure of evidence of *an* offence or things obtained in consequence of the commission of *an* offence, this creates the same wide power to seize evidence etc in respect of the search of persons as is provided by s 19 (Art 21) in respect of the search of premises. Sections 19–22 (Arts 21–24) govern the process of seizure, the retention by the police of items seized and access to those items while they are in the possession of the police (see further para 4.41, ante). Section 32(10) (Art 34(10)) does not affect the power provided by section 15(3), (4) and (5) of the Prevention of Terrorism (Temporary Provisions) Act 1989 which authorises the stop and search of a person liable to arrest under s 14 of that Act for evidence that he is liable to arrest (3); and to search for such evidence when arrested under s 14, other than for a criminal offence (4). Subsection (5) requires that such searches of persons be carried out by persons of the same sex.

Search to preserve property

5.63   The decision in *R v Churchill* (1989) exposed a further limitation on the power conferred by s 32(2) (Art 34(2)). C was arrested on reasonable suspicion of burglary. The police requested the keys of his car, which was unlocked, in order to take the car to the police station to be searched and where it would be safe rather than left unlocked in a public place. C refused to hand them over and, during a struggle, he struck a police officer. At his trial for assault occasioning bodily harm, it was submitted on C's behalf that the keys were not 'evidence relating to an offence' within s 32(2)(ii) (Art 34 (2)(ii)), therefore the police had no power to search C and the force used to do so was unlawful. The trial judge rejected this submission and held that the car might have contained evidence and the keys could be equated with the car. C's appeal against conviction was allowed, the trial judge being wrong in equating the keys with the car; accordingly the prosecution had failed to establish that the police were acting lawfully in requiring the keys.

The Court of Appeal suggested that the case could have been argued on the basis of the duty of the police to preserve property, citing *Rice v Connolly* (1966). There Lord Parker CJ said:

> 'It is . . . in my judgement clear that it is part of the obligations and duties of a police constable to take all steps which appear to him to be necessary for keeping the peace, for preventing crime or for protecting property from criminal injury . . . and they would further include the duty to detect crime and to bring an offender to justice.'

As a statement of law this is defective. There are many duties imposed on a constable but not all carry a power to enable him to carry them out. As *Rice v Connolly* makes clear, the police, as part of their duty to prevent and detect crime, have a duty to ask questions but no power to require answers. In *R v Waterfield* (1964) it was said that the police had a duty to preserve for use in court evidence of a crime, but that they had no power to detain a car for examination in relation to an offence of dangerous driving (see now powers of search and seizure under ss 18 and 32 and powers of seizure under s 19 (Arts 20, 34 and 21) and powers of retention under ss 20–22 (Arts 22–24) discussed in para 4.41 ante). In *Waterfield*, Ashworth J suggested that:

> 'in most cases it is probably more convenient to consider what the police constable was actually doing and in particular whether such conduct was prima facie an unlawful interference with a person's liberty or property. If so, it is then relevant to consider
> (a) whether such conduct falls within the general scope of any duty imposed by statute or recognised at common law; and
> (b) whether such conduct, albeit within the general scope of such duty, involved an unjustifiable use of powers associated with the duty' (ibid pp 170–171)

(see [1975] Crim LR 617 for a discussion of this 'formula'). Applying this test the constable's conduct in searching for the keys to lock the car fell within this general duty to preserve the property of an arrested person and to prevent crime against that property. The search for the keys would not, it is submitted, involve an unjustifiable use of powers associated with that duty. As such the police would be acting lawfully. Had the car been locked the police would have had the power to search it for evidence of the burglary. A car is 'premises' within s 23 (Art 25) and s 18 or s 32(2)(b) (Art 20 or Art 34(2)(b)) authorises a search of the car. Section 117 (Art 88) permits the use of reasonable force in the exercise of these powers. Searching for and seizing the keys could be described as 'a necessary ancillary action' (see commentary 1989 Crim LR 228) to that search. Alternatively one could point out to the owner that 'reasonable force' includes breaking a window to gain entry. That may produce the keys more quickly than a resisted search of the person.

The use of force to effect an arrest

5.64   The use of reasonable force to effect an arrest or in the prevention of crime is permitted by s 3 of the Criminal Law Act 1967 (Criminal Law Act (NI) 1967). There is, in s 117 of the 1984 Act (Art 88 of the 1989 Order), a general power permitting a police officer to use reasonable force, if necessary, in the exercise of powers conferred by the Act and which do not depend for their exercise on the consent of some person. There is, then, an overlap between the two provisions, but the intention would appear to be to provide the police with a power to use reasonable force in the exercise of all other powers without affecting the power under s 3 of the 1967 Acts. Section 3 states:

> 'A person may use such force as is reasonable in the circumstances in the prevention of crime, or in effecting or assisting in the lawful arrest of offenders or suspected offenders or of persons unlawfully at large.'

The use of reasonable force is not confined to arrests for serious crimes which are arrestable offences but is available in all arrests, even an arrest for a minor offence. However, the important words are 'such force as is reasonable in the circumstances'. The circumstances of an arrest for a minor offence, eg violent resistance, may justify the use of considerable force which would not be justified where the arrest is for a serious arrestable offence in which no resistance is offered (see *Reed v Wastie* (1972)). In *Sturley v Commissioner of Police for the Metropolis* (1984) a police woman lawfully arrested a middle-aged lady for assaulting her. Another constable was present, but the policewoman sought to restrain the lady by putting her left arm behind her back and twisting the wrist. In doing so the wrist was broken. Mars-Jones J, in awarding damages against the police, held that it was not a proper form of restraint in the circumstances. Two police officers should have been able to restrain her by holding both her hands by her sides. One officer on her own could use a hammerlock and bar. The arresting officer must, then, take account of the kind of person he is arresting. Obviously, what may be reasonable force in respect of a muscular man may not be reasonable when applied to a woman of small stature. One constable alone may use greater force than two or more, but when assistance is readily available which will reduce the amount of force necessary to restrain the arrested person it must be called for and used. That much is commonsense, but there is no clear answer to the question, 'how much force can be used in particular circumstances?', simply because circumstances vary so greatly. The arrester is expected to employ balancing criteria when no such criteria have been clearly articulated and in circumstances which do not permit of mature reflection but often demand an immediate response to what could be, or appear to be, a dangerous situation. The law's answer to the question would appear to be, as much force as is believed to be reasonably necessary in order to effect the arrest in the circumstances reasonably believed to exist. This is drawn from the decision of the House of Lords in *Attorney-General for Northern Ireland's Reference (No.1 of 1975)* (1977) where their Lordships considered the Northern Ireland equivalent of s 3 in a case in which a soldier shot and killed a fleeing suspect whom he mistakenly believed to be a terrorist. Lord Diplock made it clear that the test of reasonableness should be applied realistically:

'The jury should remind themselves that the postulated balancing of risk against risk, harm against harm, by the reasonable man is not undertaken in the calm analytical atmosphere of the court room . . .' (ibid p 138)

In evaluating the arrester's conduct the question for the jury is:

'Are we satisfied that no reasonable man (a) with the knowledge of such facts as were known to the accused or reasonably believed by him to exist, (b) in the circumstances and time available to him for reflection, (c) could be of opinion that the prevention of the risk of harm to which others might be exposed if the suspect were allowed to escape justified exposing the suspect to the risk of harm to him that might result from the kind of force that the accused contemplated using.' (Per Lord Diplock, ibid p 137)

In *Simpson v Chief Constable of South Yorkshire* (1991) S, who had been arrested, charged with and convicted of malicious wounding and threatening behaviour, sought to sue the police for false imprisonment, alleging that the use of excessive force in effecting the arrest made the arrest unlawful. Holding that the conviction was not a bar to an action for assault, the Court of Appeal, rejected this argument. Fox LJ had said:

'The circumstances of many arrests were such that errors of judgement might be made. If the arrest was itself justified in law, such errors in the mode of conducting it, although they might be the basis for other remedies, did not seem to be a good basis for invalidating the arrest itself which was necessary in the public interest'.

Mistaken belief that the use of force is justified

5.65   As is clear from the above question for the jury, where a person mistakenly believes the use of force is necessary and the force used would have been reasonable and justified if the facts had been as he believed them to be, then the arrester will be acquitted of any offence if evidence is adduced of reasonable grounds for the belief and that evidence is not disproved. This is in line with the decision of the Divisional Court in *Albert v Lavin* (1982) which, reluctantly, followed earlier dicta in holding that a mistake of fact cannot found a defence of self-defence unless it is based on reasonable grounds. However, the Court of Appeal (Criminal Division) in *R v Williams (Gladstone)* (1984) stated that the reasonableness of the defendant's belief was relevant only to the question whether the belief was in fact held. If it was held, its unreasonableness is *irrelevant* on the question of guilt or innocence. The jury should be directed that the prosecution has the burden of proving the unlawfulness of the appellant's actions; secondly, that if he might have been labouring under a mistake as to the facts he must be judged according to that mistaken view; thirdly this was so whether, on an objective view, the mistake was reasonable or not. This clarifies the law in relation to a mistake of fact in the use of reasonable force in self-defence and the law is now as the Criminal Law Revision Committee (14th Report, Cmnd 7844 (1980) para 283) recommended that it should be, and as the Draft Criminal Code proposes that it should be (see Law Commission 177 (1989) — A Draft Criminal Code for England and Wales, Vol 1 clause 44). At present there is a contradiction between mistake of fact in self-defence and the use of force in order to effect an arrest. However, one must agree with the learned authors of Smith and Hogan — Criminal Law 6th edition (1988) at page 243, footnote 5, that in the light of *Gladstone Williams* and the cases following it Lord Diplock's remarks quoted at the end of para 5.64 above, should be read as if the italicised 'reasonably' were omitted. Thus if a constable sought to arrest D whom he wrongly believed was armed with a weapon, he is to be judged on the facts as he believed them to be, the reasonableness, or otherwise, of that belief going to the question whether the belief was actually held

The use of force after arrest

5.66   The Code of Practice, C para 8.9, states:

> Reasonable force may be used if necessary for the following purposes:
> (i) to secure compliance with reasonable instructions, including instructions given in pursuance of the provisions of a code of practice; or
> (ii) to prevent escape, injury, damage to property or the destruction of evidence.

Once the arrest has been effected and the suspect, if he was violent or resisted arrest, has been subdued or has ceased to be violent, he is in police custody and thereafter the use of force, which must always be reasonable force, is only justified for the purposes mentioned in the COP C para 8.9. The use of force for other purposes, or the use of excessive force for the Code's purposes, invites the sanctions of the criminal law, the civil law and the Discipline Code, and any constable using gratuitous or excessive force against a person in custody can expect to be subjected to all three (see further Ch 2, ante).

The use of handcuffs

5.67 The use of handcuffs in order to restrain an arrested person is not covered by the Act but may be considered under the head of the use of reasonable force, and to some extent links up with the criteria justifying an arrest or search on arrest. For example, if the arrest is justified because the suspected offender is violent and may cause harm to himself or others, a search for articles which might be used to cause physical injury or assist an escape may be justified and also the use of handcuffs. Their use would not, however, be justified when the offence is not one of violence and there are no reasonable grounds for believing the person will become violent or attempt to escape. Home Office guidance to chief officers of police makes it clear that their use is the exception rather than the rule. Thus para 4.65 of the Consolidated Circular to the Police on Crime and Kindred Matters (1977) states:

'Whether a prisoner should be handcuffed must depend on the particular circumstances, as for instance the nature of the charge and the conduct of the person in custody. Handcuffing should not be resorted to unless there is fair ground for supposing that violence may be used or an escape attempted. Handcuffing cannot be justified unless there are special reasons for resorting to it.'

Use of force to resist lawful arrest

5.68 The use of force to resist lawful arrest or detention is not permitted, and may result in a charge of assault with intent to resist lawful arrest by anyone under s 38 of the Offences Against the Person Act 1861, or a charge of assaulting or obstructing a constable in the execution of his duty under s 51 of the Police Act 1964. It is no defence that the arrest was honestly and reasonably believed to be unlawful, ie a mistake of law, not a mistake of fact (*R v Fennell* (1970), *Albert v Lavin* (1982)). Nor is it a defence to a charge of assault on a constable that he was not known to be a constable (*R v Forbes and Webb* (1865), *Kenlin v Gardner* (1967)). The same applies where force is used to prevent the arrest of another person or to assist in his escape (*Albert v Lavin*). In *Hills v Ellis* (1983) D intervened in the arrest of a person believing that the constable had the wrong man. The arrest was, nevertheless, lawful and D was convicted of obstructing the constable in the execution of his duty despite his good motive. In *R v Mark* (1961) D said he thought a constable was a robber and intervened in order to protect the supposed victim. The jury was directed that, if D acted under an honest and reasonable belief that the constable was a robber, they should acquit. That decision has now been overtaken by *R v Williams (Gladstone)* (1984) discussed earlier, so that D will now be judged on the facts as he believed them to be, the reasonableness, or otherwise, of that belief going only to the question of whether he actually held it. However, the mistake in *Mark* was one of fact and not a mistake as to the legal basis of the arrest, a mistake of law as in *R v Fennell* (1970).

Use of force to resist an unlawful arrest

5.69   An unlawful arrest is a crime and reasonable force may be used in self-defence or in the prevention of crime. In *Fennell* the Court of Appeal, per Widgery LJ, said:

> 'It was accepted in the court below that if the arrest had been, in fact, unlawful the appellant would have been justified in using reasonable force to secure the release of his son. This proposition has not been argued before us and we will assume, without deciding it, that it is correct ... Where a person honestly [and reasonably] believes that he or his child is in imminent danger of injury it would be unjust if he were deprived of the right to use reasonable force by way of defence merely because he had made some genuine mistake of fact. On the other hand if the child is in police custody and not in imminent danger of injury there is no urgency of the kind which requires an immediate decision and a father who forcibly releases the child does so at his peril.'

Here too the decision of the Court of Appeal in *R v Williams (Gladstone)* (1984) (see para 5.65, ante) now applies so that the bracketed words should be deleted. A person is to be judged on the facts as he believed them to be and the reasonableness of the belief is relevant *only* to the question whether such a belief was in fact held. If the arrest is, or is believed to be, unlawful, the force used to resist it must be reasonable and not excessive. If the force used is excessive, the person using such force can be arrested and charged with assault. See, for example, *R v Ball* (1989) where B resisted the arrest of his brother in the belief that it was unlawful. At his trial for assault occasioning actual bodily harm, it was assumed the arrest was unlawful and the sole issue for the jury was whether B had used too much force. The jury decided he had and convicted him, the conviction being upheld by the Court of Appeal (Criminal Division). The citizen would be well advised not to interfere with or resist an arrest, but to make a complaint after the event, unless there is the danger of injury or urgency referred to by Widgery LJ, above.

Arrest with a warrant

5.70 Section 1(1) of the Magistrates' Courts Act 1980 (hereinafter MCA 1980) provides that:

'upon an information being laid before a justice of the peace . . . that any person *has, or is suspected of having, committed* an offence the justices may . . .

(a) issue a summons directed to that person requiring him to appear before a magistrates' court for the area to answer the information, or

(b) issue a warrant to arrest that person and bring him before a magistrates' court for the area . . .'

Section 1(4) limits the issue of an arrest warrant in respect of persons aged 17 and over to indictable offences punishable by imprisonment, or where the defendant's address is not sufficiently established for a summons to be served on him. Even before the PACE Act 1984 came into force the police seldom sought warrants to arrest for an offence in the first instance. Since the police have a power of summary arrest for arrestable offences (s 24 PACE Act 1984, Art 26 of PACE Order 1989) and for all other offences when the service of a summons is impractical or inappropriate (s 25, s 26(2) and Sch 2 of the PACE Act 1984 (Arts 27, 28(2) and Sch 2 of the PACE Order 1989) and other statutory powers), there is likely to be even less reliance on the arrest warrant. Prior to the PACE Act 1984 an arrest warrant might have been sought when a person's address was not sufficiently established for a summons to be served on him, a circumstance anticipated by s 1(4) MCA 1980. Section 25(3)(c) of the PACE Act 1984 provides a power to arrest without a warrant in such circumstances and that power of arrest is not confined to the time at which the offence was committed. Section 25(1), (Art 27(1)) refers to the past and the present — 'has been committed or attempted, or is being committed'. Suppose, for example D, who is reasonably suspected of committing an offence is stopped by a constable and required to give his name and address. He persuades the constable that the address given is a satisfactory address for service of a summons when it is not. D is permitted to go on his way having been told he will be reported for the question of a prosecution to be considered. Some days later the constable sees D in the street. He is then aware that the address given is not a satisfactory address. D is still reasonably suspected of having committed an offence and may be arrested under s 25 (Art 27) if a general arrest condition is satisfied, as it is unless D can persuade the constable otherwise. It should be noted that if a summons is served and the accused fails to appear the court may be able to proceed in his absence (ss 11 and 12 MCA 1980) and if this is not possible the court may issue a warrant for his arrest, sometimes referred to as a 'bench warrant' (s 13 MCA 1980). There are two possible reasons, the practicability of a summons apart, why a warrant of arrest under s 1 MCA 1980 should be sought post the PACE Act 1984. The first, and most likely, is for the protection of the constable. Suppose D, who is reasonably suspected of having committed an arrestable offence, is known to be in certain premises. He, and his family, are known to the police and likely violently to resist entry in order to arrest. Though s 17(1)(b) of the PACE Act 1984 (Art 19 of the 1989 Order) authorises the entry into premises in order to arrest a person for an arrestable offence, and s 117 of that Act (Art 88 of the Order) authorises the use of force, a warrant of arrest under s 1 MCA 1980 may be sought in order to obtain the protection of the Constables Protection Act 1750, under which a constable has a complete defence to a civil action if, in good faith, he executes a warrant strictly according to its terms. Section 17(1)(a) of the PACE Act 1984 gives a power to enter premises in order to execute such a warrant. The warrant authorises the use of force but s 117 of the PACE Act 1984 (Art 88 of the 1989 Order) is also available where the s 17 (Art 19) power is exercised. The second possible reason for reliance on an arrest warrant rather than the PACE Act powers to arrest without warrant is that an arrest warrant can be issued when the information alleges that a person:

> 'has, or is suspected of having committed an offence.' (s 1 MCA 1980)

This would appear to permit the issue of a warrant on suspicion alone, unsupported by objectively reasonable grounds. However, the criterion of reasonable suspicion as the threshold for arrest without warrant is pitched so low that the difference, if there is one, is hardly perceptible (see para 2.02–17, ante).

Execution of a warrant of arrest etc — s 33

5.71 Section 125 of the Magistrates' Courts Act 1980 provides that a warrant of arrest issued by a justice of the peace shall remain in force until it is executed or withdrawn; and that such a warrant, together with warrants of commitment or distress (other than for non-payment of rates) or a search warrant, may be executed anywhere in England and Wales by any person to whom it is directed or by any constable acting within his police area. Formerly a warrant to arrest a person 'charged with an offence' could be executed by a constable notwithstanding that he did not have it in his possession at the time, provided it was shown to the person arrested, if he demanded to see it, as soon as practicable. Since this only applied to warrants to arrest a person 'charged with an offence' it meant that it was unlawful to arrest a person for whom a warrant of committal or distress, and in particular a warrant to arrest for non-payment of a fine, had been issued, unless the constable had the warrant in his possession at the time (*De Costa Small v Kirkpatrick* (1979)). Section 33 of the PACE Act 1984 removed this fetter and amended s 125(3) of the Magistrates' Courts Act 1980 to read:

> (3) A warrant to which this subsection applies may be executed by a constable notwithstanding that it is not in his possession at the time; but the warrant shall, on the demand of the person arrested, be shown to him as soon as practicable. (The law in Northern Ireland was amended by Art 156 of the Magistrates' Courts (Northern Ireland) Order 1981.)

The warrants to which this rule applies include a warrant to arrest a person in connection with an offence, warrants to arrest for desertion from HM Forces, warrants of committal or distress and warrants issued under the Domestic Proceedings and Magistrates' Courts Act 1978. (Magistrates' Courts Act 1980, s 125(4) as amended by the 1984 Act, s 33). In *Jones v Kelsey* (1987) it was held that a warrant issued under s 16(1) of the Powers of Criminal Courts Act 1973 to arrest for breach of a community service order was 'a warrant to arrest a person in connection with an offence' within the meaning of s 125(4), the offence either being an offence under s 16 of the 1973 Act or the original offence for which the order was made. See also *R v Peacock* (1988).

278

6 Detention

Introduction

6.01 As was indicated in the introduction to Chapter 5, there was a time when arrest without warrant was generally not possible unless the police were in a position to charge the person with the offence for which he was to be arrested. The arrest then came at the end of the investigation and there was no problem of detention without charge in a police station for long periods before the person was charged and appeared before a court. In Scotland, subject to certain exceptions, the general rule is still that an arrest without warrant must be accompanied by a charge (*Chalmers v Advocate* (HM) (1954)), but south of the border the law has moved on to permit arrest at an early stage in the investigation, often long before there is sufficient evidence to charge the suspect. Scotland is moving in this direction but, instead of arrest on reasonable suspicion, detention on reasonable suspicion is permitted but that period is limited to six hours (s 2(2) of the Criminal Justice (Scotland) Act 1980). Both systems are changing but it may be the volume of crime in England and Wales which has produced the more rapid change in these countries. Be that as it may, change there has been with the result that the investigation of crime now tends to take place in the police station and arrest on reasonable suspicion, which is often arrest for questioning (cf *Mohammed-Holgate v Duke* (1984)), is now the norm.

6.02 This changed use of the law of arrest created difficulties in a legal system whose machinery refused to recognise the change of use. Once a person is charged there is no difficulty; he may be bailed to appear before a court or taken before a court which can decide whether to bail or remand in custody. The investigation of that offence is over and the police have no reason, other than the investigation of other offences, or the belief that he will not appear for his trial or may interfere with witnesses (for which provision is made), to keep the person in custody. It is the period in custody before charge, when the investigation is being actively pursued, that creates difficulty.

Arrest on reasonable suspicion

6.03   Arrest on reasonable suspicion was permitted in the belief that there were legal controls over the period of detention following arrest (*Hussien (Shaabin Bin) v Kam (Chong Fook)* (1970)), but in practice those controls were ineffective. The primary control was intended to be s 43 of the Magistrates' Courts Act 1980 (a consolidation of previous measures) which was a masterpiece of statutory ambiguity. Though 24 hours was mentioned, it was never the maximum period of permitted detention, despite popular belief that it was. The real control lay in s 43(4), which required that a person arrested without warrant and detained in custody should be taken before a magistrates' court 'as soon as practicable'. However, it was only after the Royal Commission of 1981 had aired the concern felt by many at the lack of any legal control over police detention of suspects that the Court of Appeal was able to put a limit on the period represented by that phrase, and even then it was only able to state an upper limit of 'at the very least within 48 hours' (*R v Hudson* (1981)).

6.04   The problem from a police viewpoint was that the arrest was often made at a very early stage in the investigation and, in complex cases, 48 hours were seldom enough to build up sufficient evidence to enable them to charge the suspect. In minor cases the suspect could be bailed to return to a police station under s 43(2) of the Magistrates' Courts Act 1980, but in serious and complex cases that was not possible. The previous law did not actually require that the police prefer a charge before bringing the arrested person before a court, and there was no legal impediment to prevent magistrates deciding whether to bail the suspect or remand him in custody without a charge. Section 128 of the Magistrates' Courts Act 1980 permitted such a remand in police custody for up to 72 hours. A survey carried out for the Royal Commission by the Metropolitan Police showed that of 48,343 persons arrested in a three months period in 1979:

36,257 (75 per cent) were dealt with within 6 hours,
9,668 (20 per cent) within 24 hours,
2,206 (4.6 per cent) within 72 hours.
and 212 (0.4 per cent) were held for 72 hours or more. (Report para 3.96).

It followed that 99.6 per cent of suspects could have been dealt with within the pre-existing legal framework but the police, supported by magistrates' clerks, some lawyers and academics, did not accept that they could take a person before a court without a charge, still less that he could be remanded in custody. This was a convenient interpretation of the law since it gave to the police an apparently valid reason for detaining persons beyond any period permitted by s 43 of the Magistrates' Courts Act 1980 and made them masters of their own, and the suspect's fate; whereas the alternative interpretation gave magistrates some control over the post-arrest detention period. The result was that the police for a long time had a virtually unfettered discretion to detain a suspect in custody and their purposes in doing so were to secure or preserve evidence or to obtain it by questioning the suspect.

New law — summary

6.05   The PACE Act 1984 (PACE Order 1989) recognises that the police station is the venue for the investigation of most serious offences by providing that detention without charge may only be authorised if it is necessary to secure or preserve evidence or to obtain it by questioning. This is identical to the criteria for such detention recommended by the Royal Commission. The Act (Order) also follows the Commission's recommendation that 24 hours from the time the arrested person arrives at the police station should be the maximum period of ordinary detention without charge. However, while the Commission recommended that detention beyond 24 hours should be permissible only in respect of 'grave offences' and with the authority of a magistrates' court, the Act (Order) departs from that recommendation in a significant way. Detention beyond 24 hours is only possible in respect of 'serious arrestable offences' rather than 'grave offences', but a superintendent or more senior police officer may authorise *continued detention* for up to 12 hours beyond the initial 24 hours, if there are reasonable grounds for believing such detention to be necessary to secure or preserve evidence, or to obtain it by questioning and if certain other conditions are satisfied. Thus the police may authorise up to 36 hours of detention without charge. A magistrates' court may issue a warrant of *further detention* authorising detention without charge for up to 36 hours relying on the basic criteria of the necessity to secure, preserve or obtain evidence and other conditions to be discussed. That warrant can again be extended by a magistrates' court for up to 36 hours but in no case can the overall detention period exceed 96 hours. An application for a warrant of further detention can be made at any time during the 36 hours of detention authorised by the police and can therefore be applied for during the initial period of 24 hours detention when it is clear from the outset that more than 36 hours will be required. In such a case there will be no need to seek authority from a superintendent for continued detention, for the period authorised by the warrant will commence on the expiry of the initial 24 hours of detention without charge. There are two reasons for this departure from the recommendation of the Royal Commission, one administrative, one practical. The administrative reason is that applications to a magistrates' court for warrants of detention after 24 hours would create a significant workload. By permitting the police to authorise detention up to 36 hours that workload is significantly reduced. The practical reason is that there will be cases in which the police will consider it necessary to deny the detainee access to a solicitor. As we shall see in Chapter 7, such denial is possible for up to 36 hours, though in practice such denial has been severely limited by the decision in *R v Samuel* (1988). The Act requires the attendance of a detainee before a court on an application for a warrant of further detention and permits the detainee to be legally represented. Permitting the police to authorise detention for up to 36 hours thus postpones the possibility of legal representation of the detainee.

6.06 Reviews of detention, before and after charge, must be carried out 6 hours after detention is authorised and thereafter at intervals of 9 hours. If the grounds for detention cease to exist, or if continued or further detention is not authorised, the person must be (a) released, conditionally or unconditionally, or (b) charged and released on bail to appear before a court, or (c) charged and taken before the next available court. Grounds for detention after charge are clearly stated and there is a Code of Practice for the Detention, Treatment and Questioning of Persons by the Police, (in this Chapter referred to as 'COP C'), breach of which is a disciplinary offence and which governs the treatment of persons detained (Fig 1, post, summarises the detention provisions in schematic form.) The detention procedures are supervised by an officer who is given the title of 'custody officer'. This officer authorises the initial detention without charge and detention after charge and the release of persons from detention can only be authorised by a custody officer. Certain police stations are designated as stations which are to be used for the purpose of detaining arrested persons and it is at these stations that custody officers perform their duties. 'The institution of the custody officer is a major development in the ethos of policing' (junior Home Office minister, House of Lords Debates, 9 July 1984, col 571) and provides an element of direct personal accountability for ensuring that persons detained are properly treated and their rights safeguarded. The importance of this relatively junior police officer (he will normally be a sergeant) cannot be over emphasised. The discussion of Part IV of the PACE Act (Part V of the Order) will consider first some definitions; then the institution of the custody officer; detention without charge and the various duties of the custody officer and others in relation to such detention; detention after charge and the duties relating thereto; and bail and remands in police custody. These provisions apply to adults and arrested juveniles.

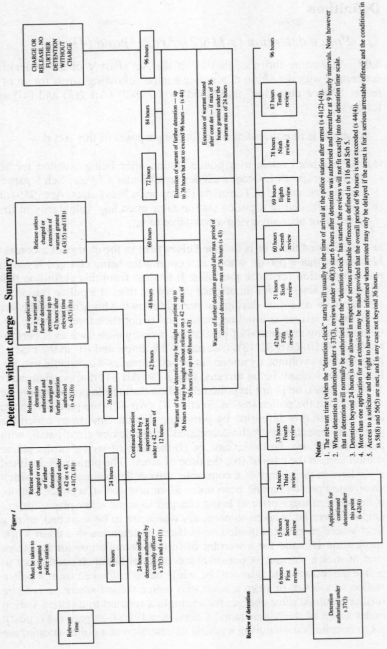

Detention without charge — Summary

Figure 1

Relevant time → Must be taken to a designated police station

6 hours

24 hours ordinary detention authorised by a custody officer — s 37(3) and s 41(1)

24 hours → Release unless charged or cont or further detention authorised under s 42 or s 43 (s 41(7), (8))

Continued detention authorised by a superintendent under s 42 — max of 12 hours

36 hours → Release if cont detention authorised and not charged or further detention authorised (s 42(10))

42 hours → Late application for a warrant of further detention permitted up to 42 hours after relevant time (s 43(5)(b))

Warrant of further detention may be sought at anytime up to 36 hours and may be sought without reliance on s 42 — max of 36 hours (ie) up to 60 hours (s 43)

60 hours → Release unless charged or extension of warrant granted (s 43(15) and (18))

Warrant of further detention granted after max period of continued detention — max of 36 hours (s 43)

Extension of warrant of further detention — up to 36 hours but not to exceed 96 hours — (s 44)

Extension of warrant issued after cont det — if max of 36 hours granted under the warrant max of 24 hours

96 hours → CHARGE OR RELEASE. NO FURTHER DETENTION WITHOUT CHARGE

Review of detention

Detention authorised under s 37(3)

6 hours First review

15 hours Second review

Application for continued detention after this point (s 42(4))

24 hours Third review

33 hours Fourth review

42 hours Fifth review

51 hours Sixth review

60 hours Seventh review

69 hours Eighth review

78 hours Ninth review

87 hours Tenth review

96 hours

Notes

1. The relevant time (when the "detention clock" starts) will usually be the time of arrival at the police station after arrest (s 41(2)-(4)).
2. Where detention is authorised under s 37(3), reviews under s 40(3) start 6 hours after detention was authorised and thereafter at 9 hourly intervals. Note however that as detention will normally be authorised after the "detention clock" has started, the reviews will not fit exactly into the detention time scale.
3. Detention beyond 24 hours is only allowed in respect of serious arrestable offences as defined in s 116 and Sch 5.
4. More than one application for an extension may be made provided that the overall period of 96 hours is not exceeded (s 44(4)).
5. Access to a solicitor and the right to have someone informed when arrested may only be delayed if the arrest is for a serious arrestable offence and the conditions in ss 58(8) and 56(5) are met, and in any case not beyond 36 hours.

Definitions

1)   Police detention (s 118(2), Art 2(3) and (4))

6.07   The entire thrust of Part IV of the Act (Part V of the Order) is concerned with detention at a police station following arrest for an offence. 'Police detention' is defined by s 118(2) (Art 2(3) and (4)) as follows:

A person is in police detention for the purposes of this Act if —

(a) he has been taken to a police station after being arrested for an offence; (the N.I. Order includes arrest under s 14 and Sch 5 para 6 of the Prevention of Terrorism (Temporary Provisions) Act 1989) or
(b) he is arrested at a police station after attending voluntarily at the station or accompanying a constable to it,

and is detained there or is detained elsewhere in the charge of a constable, except that a person who is at a court after being charged is not in police detention for those purposes. It is clear from this definition that (i) a person arrested for an offence otherwise than at a police station, is not in police detention during the period following his arrest and before he actually arrives at a police station and is not therefore in police detention during any period of post-arrest investigation such as is permitted by s 30(10) (Art 32(13)) (see para 5.55, ante); and (ii) in the case of a person who voluntarily attends at or accompanies a constable to a police station without being arrested (see s 29 (Art 31) discussed at paras 5.44-48, ante), he is not in police detention during the period before he is arrested at the police station. Section 41 (Art 42) (see para 6.40 post) links up with this definition by providing that the time from which the period of detention is to be calculated ('the relevant time') will, with minor exceptions, be in the case of (i) the time of arrival at the police station and, in the case of (ii), the time of arrest. The phrase 'is detained elsewhere in the charge of a constable' covers those situations in which an arrested person having been taken to, or arrested at, a police station, is taken from there prior to being charged to some other place; for example, where he is taken to premises which are to be searched, or to a field where property is hidden, or is taken in detention to a court while application is made for a warrant of further detention or for an extension of such a warrant. A person at a court after being charged is not in police detention though he will be while being conveyed from a police station to a court, or from a court to a police station where he is to be further detained after charge; for example a remand to a police station under s 128 of the Magistrates' Courts Act 1980 (see para 6.81, post). As to hospitalisation during a period of detention at a police station, see s 41(6) (Art 42(4)) discussed at para 6.42, post. As to hospitalisation following arrest before being taken to a police station, see para 6.44, post. As to hospitalisation after charge, see s 46(9) (Art 47(5)) discussed at para 6.36, post. Persons who are not arrested for an offence, e.g. a person arrested under s 136 of the Mental Health Act 1983, persons in custody awaiting extradition proceedings or persons in custody awaiting deportation, are not in police detention for the purposes of the PACE Act 1984. However, Code C (para 1.10), directs that its provisions apply to persons in custody at a police station whether or not they have been arrested for an offence, except COP C, Section 15 (reviews and extension of detention) which applies solely to persons in police detention. For conditions of detention, see the COP C, sections 1 to 9, and Chapter 7, post.

2) *Designated police stations (s 35) (Art 36)*

6.08 The separation of the custodial and the investigative powers of the police is an important safeguard for the detained person. Someone who is independent of the investigation is much more likely to take an objective view, hence the introduction of the custody officer. Ideally every police station would have officers appointed to carry out such duties but that is impracticable given first, the large number of police stations, ranging from the two-man rural station to the city centre station staffed by large numbers of police, and second, the small number of personnel able to carry out the duties of custody officer. It would be equally impracticable to require policemen in rural areas to take every arrested person to the city centre station which has a custody officer when it might involve travelling a considerable distance. The chief officer of police for each area must therefore designate a number of police stations which are, subject to s 30(3) and (4) (Art 32(3) and (4)) (see para 5.52, ante), to be used for the purpose of detaining arrested persons (s 35(1) Art 36(1)). The duty is to designate sufficient stations to provide enough accommodation for that purpose (s 35(2)) (Art 36(2)). But within that duty a chief officer may designate a station which has not previously been designated, and may direct that a designation of a station previously made shall cease to operate (s 35(3), Art 36(3)). This provides the necessary flexibility to enable a chief officer to take account of seasonal or other factors which affect the arrest rate and create a temporary need for more accommodation. For example, the opening up of a seaside resort for its summer season or large scale picketing during an industrial dispute may call for police stations in the area to be designated or mobile police stations and cell blocks to be designated for the period of the season or the dispute. 'Designated police station' therefore means a police station for the time being designated under this section (s 35(4)) (Art 36(4)).

3) Times to be treated as approximate only (s 45(2)) (Art 46)

6.09 Whereas previously there were no firm time limits within which arrested persons could be detained, under this part of the Act there are. Section 45(2) (Art 46) provides that a period of time or a time of day is to be treated as approximate only. This is not intended to undermine the safeguards which the Act provides. Perhaps the best explanation of the section's purpose is provided by the Australian Law Reform Commission, who said of a similar scheme:

> 'Perhaps it will not be taken amiss if we say that we trust that common sense will prevail in the application of these provisions in the courts, and that justices, magistrates and judges will not require police officers to go about like rally drivers armed with stop-watches and minute-by-minute log books. The time limit we recommend is merely a statutory guide to reasonable conduct. It should be viewed in that perspective.' (Para 97).

Section 45(2), (Art 46) must be subject to an overriding requirement of reasonableness and good faith. For example, if a review of D's detention is due at 10.15 pm and the inspector or custody officer goes off duty at 10.00 pm, it would be permissible, and make good sense, to review the detention at 9.45 pm rather than leave it for the relief inspector or custody officer who might find it difficult to review the detention with so little time to acquaint himself with the case. Alternatively the review may be delayed for 30 minutes to allow such time. On the other hand, to delay a review for an hour because the interviewing officer believes the suspect 'is about to crack' would be an abuse of s 45(2) (Art 46) (cf para 6.67, post).

4) Custody officers at police station (s 36) (Art 37)

6.10 Section 36(1) (Art 37(1)) provides that one or more custody officers *shall* be appointed for each designated station. The custody officer, who must be of at least the rank of sergeant (s 36(3)) (Art 37(3)), must be appointed by the chief officer of police for the area in which the designated police station is, or by such other officer as he may direct (s 36(2)) (Art 37(2)). Where an appointed custody officer is not readily available to perform the functions of a custody officer, an officer of any rank may perform them (s 36(4)) (Art 37(4)). This provision is intended for a 'real emergency' (Lord Edmund Davies, House of Lords Debates, 18 October 1984 col 112) but that is not what sub-s (4) says. Even in such an emergency it is suggested that only a senior constable, preferably one who has qualified for the rank of sergeant and is therefore aware of the duties involved, should be permitted to perform those duties. (A survey suggests that 16 forces use acting sergeants, constables who are qualified for promotion to that rank, as custody officers on a regular basis — see Police Review, May 25 1990 p 1033). The Minister of State told the House of Lords that 'the Association of Chief Police Officers agrees that, apart from exceptional circumstances, a probationary constable should not be called upon to act as custody officer but, like us, they feel it prudent to allow for exceptional circumstances' (House of Lords Debates, 19 October 1984 col 1113). It is difficult to imagine a probationary constable performing the duties of a custody officer except perhaps in a non-designated station — see para 6.12, post.

6.11 *An independent officer* — Given that the custody officer is the equivalent of a judicial officer with a duty to look after the interests of both police and suspect, a clear separation between the investigative and custodial functions is essential. Section 36(5) and (6) (Art 37(5) and (6)) seek to provide for such independence whenever possible within the operational limits which apply. Section 36(5) states the general rule that none of the functions of a custody officer should be performed by an officer who, *at the time when they fall to be performed*, is involved in the investigation of an offence for which the person is in police detention at that time. If an officer has been involved in the investigation of the offence at some earlier time, he is not debarred. Unless that involvement was deep it should not affect his ability to perform the functions of a custody officer impartially. Where the involvement was deep but not immediate, it would be wise (though not a statutory requirement) for the officer to declare it to a supervisory officer (cf s 36(7) (Art 37(7)) which requires that arresting officers who perform such functions at non-designated police stations do so). Such involvement may prove an embarrassment if at trial the defence seeks to raise his involvement and conduct. Section 36(5) (Art 37(5)) is subject to s 39(2), (Art 40(2)) which relieves the custody officer of his duties in relation to an arrested person when the person is transferred to the custody of an officer investigating the offence, e.g. if the person is taken from the police station to the scene of the crime. That officer is then under a duty to ensure that the person is treated in accordance with the Act and Code of Practice and is therefore temporarily in the position of a custody officer. He is not then independent, but, since he makes no decisions concerning detention, he does not breach the principle of separation between the two functions.

6.12 *Arrested persons at non-designated stations* — Section 30(3) and (4) (Art 32(3) and (4)) permit an arrested person to be taken to a non-designated police station. Where those circumstances apply the functions of a custody officer are performed by an officer who is not involved in the investigation of the offence for which the person is in detention, if such an officer is readily available (s 36(7)(a)) (Art 37(7)(a)). If he is not, the officer who took him to the police station, usually, but not invariably, the arresting officer, or any other officer, may perform these functions (s 36(7)(b)) (Art 37(7)(b)). References to 'custody officer' therefore include these officers (s 36(8)) (Art 37(8)). However, whenever the officer who took the person to a police station is to perform the functions of a custody officer, he shall, as soon as practicable (s 36(10)) (Art 37(10)), inform an officer of at least the rank of inspector who is attached to a designated police station, that he is to do so (s 36(9)) (Art 37(9)). That supervisory officer should then ensure that the detention at a non-designated police station is permitted in the circumstances and that the officer complies with the Act (Order) and Code of Practice in dealing with the person detained. It is important that supervision is provided for the following reasons. Pre-PACE Act research suggested that 75 per cent of suspects are dealt with within six hours. Section 30(3) (Art 32(3)) permits that category of suspect to be taken to a non-designated police station when the arresting officer is working in the area covered by that station, while s 30(4) (Art 32(4)) permits potentially violent persons who have been arrested single-handedly by any constable, to be taken to such a police station. Taken together those provisions could permit a very large number of persons to be taken to non-designated police stations. Though most will be minor offenders and the purpose of detention will often be identification of the person or verification of an address following arrest under s 25 (Art 27), some will be more serious offenders. It is the latter who require the protection offered by the institution of the custody officer and it is possible that s 30(3) and (4) (Art 32(3) and (4)) and s 36(7) (Art 37(7)) provide a means of undermining that protection and also of depriving the suspect of other forms of protection provided by designated police stations. For it is at such police stations that duty solicitors attend and the lay visitor scheme operates. It is therefore incumbent upon supervisory officers who wish to comply with the spirit of the Act, rather than simply the letter, to ensure that non-designated police stations are used only in an emergency or for minor cases which involve identification or verification of names and addresses.

6.13 *Other duties performed by a custody officer (s 36(6) (Art 37(6))* — Interpreted strictly s 36(5) (Art 37(5)) would prevent a custody officer performing routine administrative or procedural duties which may have an investigative function as well; for example, searching the person, taking fingerprints or identifying the arrested person. In order to clarify the position s 36(6) (Art 37(6)) states that nothing in s 36(5) (Art 37(5)) is to be taken to prevent a custody officer from —

(a) performing any function assigned to custody officers by this Act or a code of practice issued under it;

(b) carrying out the duties imposed on custody officers under s 39 of this Act (Art 40) (duty to ensure that detainees are treated in accordance with the Act and codes of practice);

(c) doing anything in connection with the identification of a suspect (this does not include identity parades which, under the Code of Practice governing parades, must be supervised by a uniformed inspector); or

(d) doing anything under ss 7 and 8 of the Road Traffic Act 1988 (taking samples of breath etc). (Arts 144, 146 and 147 of the Road Traffic (Northern Ireland) Order 1981).

Detention of juveniles and children

6.14 Section 52 of the PACE Act 1984, which stated that the detention provisions did not apply to a child under 10 years of age who is arrested without a warrant for an offence other than homicide, was repealed by Sch 15 of the Children Act 1989 (in force October 1991). The same provision deleted the reference to s 52 in the definition of 'arrested juvenile' in s 37(15) of the PACE Act. An 'arrested juvenile' for the purposes of the detention provisions in England and Wales now means:

'A person arrested with or without a warrant who appears to be under the age of 17'.

The result is that the detention provisions apply to children under 10 years of age and to those over 10 years of age but who appear to be under the age of 17 (see Code C 1.5), who are arrested for an offence with or without a warrant. S 28 of the Children and Young Persons Act 1969, which dealt with the detention of children under 10, was repealed by Sch 15 of the Children Act 1989. S 29 of the Children and Young Persons Act 1969, as replaced by Sch 6 of the PACE Act and as amended by Sch 15 of the Criminal Justice Act 1988, deals with the arrest of a child or young person *under a warrant* and his release on the parent or guardian entering into a recognisance, but in other cases the PACE Act 1984 provisions apply. At this point it is convenient to refer to duties which were to be imposed on a custody officer by subss (11) to (14) of s 37 of the PACE Act 1984 if and when s 5 of the Children and Young Persons Act 1969 was implemented. Section 5 was never implemented and so the Criminal Justice Act 1991 repeals both it and section 37(11) to (14). In NI the detention provisions do not apply to a child apparently under the age of 14 who is arrested for an offence other than homicide. The detention of such a child is governed by s 150 of the Children and Young Persons Act (NI) 1968 (Art 52). The detention provisions of the 1989 Order apply therefore to a child apparently under 14 arrested without warrant for an offence of homicide, to a person arrested *with warrant* for any offence who appears to be under the age of 17, and to a person who appears to be over 14 and under 17 years of age arrested *without warrant* for any offence (Art 38(14) and Art 52). Art 38(11)–(13) of the 1989 Order impose a duty on the custody officer to inform the arrested juvenile, parent or guardian and supervisor if subject to a supervision order, of the fact of the arrest and the grounds for detention, similar to the requirement in s 34(2) of the Children and Young Persons Act 1933 as amended by s 57 of the PACE Act 1984, discussed in para 6.15 and para 6.27 below. Section 57 of the 1984 Act substituted subsections for s 34(2) of the Children and Young Persons Act 1933. They require that:

(a) the parent or guardian of the child or young person be informed of the fact that he has been arrested, the reason for the detention and the place of the detention;

(b) if at the time of arrest he is the subject of a supervision order, the supervisor be informed as in (a).

'Parent or Guardian' in s 34(2) includes a local authority if the child is in its care. S 118 of the 1984 Act similarly defines 'parent or guardian' for the purposes of the 1984 Act. (See also COP C, para 1.7 and Notes of Guidance 1C and 1D, and paras 3.7, 3.8 and 3.9 and Notes of Guidance 3C.) Section 57 and the Code of Practice ensure that the adult responsible for the care of the arrested child is informed of the arrest, why he has been arrested and where he is being detained. If the arrested juvenile is in local authority care but is living with his parents, they, as well as the local authority, should normally be contacted unless they are suspected of involvement in the offence (COP C, Notes of Guidance 3C,). An arrested juvenile should not be placed in a police cell except in the circumstances mentioned in COP C para 8.8, and may not in any circumstances be placed in a cell with a detained adult (COP C 8.8) (See also s 31 of the Children and Young Persons Act 1933 which further requires that a girl be detained in the care of a woman). For discussion of the treatment of juveniles, see para 7.112, post.

Non-criminal detention of children (England and Wales)

6.15 The power of a constable to take a child to a place of safety, previously contained in the Children and Young Persons Act 1969, s 28, is replaced by the power to take a child into 'police protection'. Where a constable has reasonable cause to believe that a child (defined as a person under the age of 18) would otherwise be likely to suffer significant harm, he may:

(a) remove the child to suitable accommodation and keep him there; or

(b) take such steps as are reasonable to ensure that the child's removal from any hospital or other place in which he is then being accommodated is prevented (s 46, Children Act 1989).

When a constable has exercised this power the child is referred to as having been taken into 'police protection' rather than police custody or detention. No child may be kept for more than 72 hours (under the previous law the maximum was eight days). As soon as practicable after taking the child into police protection, the constable must ensure that the case is inquired into by the officer designated by the chief officer of the police area concerned. Having completed the inquiry, that officer must release the child from police protection unless there is still reasonable cause to believe that he would still be likely to suffer significant harm. In addition he must as soon as possible:

(a) inform the local authority in the area in which the child was found, of the steps taken or to be taken;
(b) tell the local authority (the appropriate authority) within whose area the child is ordinarily resident, where the child is being accommodated;
(c) inform the child, if capable of understanding, of the steps taken with respect to him and the reasons for taking them and any further steps which may be taken;
(d) take such steps as are reasonably practicable to discover the wishes and feelings of the child;
(e) where the child was taken into police protection by being removed to accommodation which is not provided by a local authority or as a refuge, secure that he is moved to accommodation which is so provided;
(f) he must also take such steps as are reasonably practicable to inform
   (i) the child's parents;
   (ii) a person who is not a parent but who has parental responsibility for him; and
   (iii) any other person with whom he was living immediately before being taken into police protection,
   of the steps taken with respect to the child and the reasons for taking them (s 46(3) and (4)).

While the child is in police protection, the designated officer may apply on behalf of the appropriate authority for an emergency protection order to be made under s 44 of the Children Act 1989. If he does so, the period of the order (maximum of eight days) runs from the time when the child was taken into police protection under s 46(s 45(3)). The police do not assume parental responsibility for Children Act purposes whilst the child is in their protection. Instead there is a general duty to safeguard the child's welfare. In particular parents, those with parental responsibility, any person with whom he was living before being taken into police protection or a person in whose favour a contact order has been made (or a person acting on their behalf) should be permitted such contact as the designated officer considers is both reasonable and in the child's best interest.

General limitation on police detention (s 34) (Art 35)

6.16 Section 34 introduced the scheme for ensuring that a person is detained after arrest only when necessary. Section 34(1) lays down the important principle that a person arrested for an offence (not a person arrested under s 27 (Art 29) (fingerprinting) or under other powers to arrest other than for an offence eg under the Mental Health Act 1983) shall not be kept in police detention except in accordance with the provisions of Part IV of the Act (Part V of the Order). This general principle is followed by a general duty imposed upon the custody officer (subject to an exception to be mentioned), to order the immediate release of a person in police detention if at any time:

(a) he becomes aware that the grounds for detention of that person have ceased to apply; and

(b) he is not aware of any other grounds on which the continued detention of that person could be justified under the provisions of this Part of the Act (s 34(2)) (Art 35(2)).

The grounds for detention without charge are set out in s 37(2) (Art 38(2)) and those for detention after charge in s 38(1) (Art 39(1)) and it is these grounds to which s 34(2) (Art 35(2)) refers. Section 40 (Art 41) provides for periodic reviews of a person's detention which will assist in making the custody officer aware of whether the grounds for detention have ceased to exist. It will be seen later that there are a number of provisions which require the release of a person in police detention upon the expiry of a time limit (s 41(7), (Art 42(5)) expiry of 24 hours detention; s 42(10), (Art 43(9)), release following continued detention; s 43(15) and (18), (Art 44(14) and (17)) release upon refusal of an application for, or upon the expiry of, a warrant for further detention; s 44(7), (Art 45(7)), release on refusal of an extension of a warrant of further detention). The duty to release under s 34(2), (Art 35(2)) is thus confined to:

(a) release of a person on his arrival at a police station because the grounds for his arrest have ceased to exist and there is no other ground to detain him;

(b) release of a person who has been previously detained at a police station under s 37(3) (Art 38(3)) (ie to secure or preserve evidence or to obtain it by questioning), but in respect of whom the grounds for detention no longer exist;

(c) release of a person charged and detained under s 38(2), (Art 39(2)) (for example, to ascertain his name and address), when the reasons for that detention no longer exist;

(d) release of a person who was arrested for an offence, who was released on bail subject to a duty to attend at a police station (s 47), and who so attends but there is insufficient evidence to charge him and no reasonable grounds to detain him under s 47(5).

The following examples illustrate the operation of the duty to release under s 34(2) (Art 35(2)):

1) D is brought to a police station under arrest for an offence. The custody officer determines that there is insufficient evidence to charge him with that offence and that there are no grounds for detention without charge under s 37(2) (Art 38(2)). He must order the immediate release of D.

2) As in (1) above but the custody officer reasonably believes that there are grounds for detention without charge under s 37(2) (Art 38(2)), it being necessary to question D. He authorises the detention under s 37(3) (Art 38(3)). A review officer conducting a review of that detention, (whether at a first or subsequent review, or on a review following the authorisation of continued detention under s 42 (Art 43) or under a warrant of further detention under s 43 (Art 44), or an extension of that warrant under s 44 (Art 45)) determines that the grounds for such detention have ceased to exist and so informs the custody officer. The latter is now aware that the grounds for the person's detention no longer exist and, unless there are other grounds, he must order the immediate release of D. Similarly if the investigating officer reports that, following an interview with D, there is not enough evidence to detain him further.

3) D has been detained in custody as in (2) above and is charged after 6 hours of detention. The custody officer decides that his release is not required by s 38(1) (Art 39(1)) and authorises his detention on one of the grounds set out in s 38(1) (Art 39(1)). The custody officer himself reviews this case and this makes him aware that the grounds for detention no longer apply. He must order the immediate release of D.

4) D is arrested for a general offence because his name and address are not known (general arrest conditions (a) and (c) of s 25(3)) (Art 27(3)). He is charged with the offence, detained in custody after charge under s 38(3) (Art 39(3)) and two hours later his name and address are determined and verified. The custody officer must order the immediate release of D.

The operation of s 34(2)(b) is illustrated by the following example:

5) D is arrested in police area A for a minor offence but the grounds for detention cease to exist. D is wanted in police area B for murder. If there are grounds for D's arrest on that charge, he should then be arrested, the reasonable grounds for suspicion coming from police in area B. The custody officer is not then under a duty to release D but may authorise his detention under s 37(3) (Art 38(3)). (As to the relevant time in such a case see s 41(4) discussed at para 6.40, post.)

Note that Northern Ireland is one police area for the purposes of Art 42.

6)   D is arrested on suspicion of fraud, interviewed and then bailed to attend a police station. When he returns to answer his bail the police investigation has still not produced sufficient evidence to charge him. He may be released on bail or without bail if it is felt that such evidence will not be forthcoming.

If D in the above example is merely wanted for questioning by the other police force, there being no grounds for arrest, he cannot be kept in police detention but can only be requested to assist by remaining at a police station voluntarily.

(NB in *R v McKenzie* (1971) it was doubted whether an arrest under what is now s 6(5) of the Road Traffic Act 1988 (Art 146(3)(b) of the Road Traffic (N.I.) Order 1981) (driving with excess alcohol in the blood) was an arrest for an offence. Section 34(6) (Art 35(7)) resolved any doubt by stating that it is. A custody officer may therefore release a motorist arrested for such an offence on bail to return to a police station after a forensic examination of blood or urine, or to a court after he is charged; but see para 6.30, post.)

6.17   The exception to the duty to release under s 34(2) is provided by s 34(4) (Art 35(4)). There is no duty to release if it appears to the custody officer that the person arrested for an offence was unlawfully at large when arrested, eg where he was an absconder from a remand home or had escaped from prison. Section 34(3) (Art 35(3)) provides that no person in police detention may be released except on the authority of a custody officer at the police station where his detention was authorised, or, if authorised at more than one station, a custody officer at the station where it was last authorised.

Release on bail or without bail

6.18   If D is to be released, the question of whether he should be released unconditionally or subject to bail arises. Section 34(5) (Art 35(6)) requires that a person released under s 34(2) (Art 35(2)) *shall* be released without bail unless it appears to the custody officer that (a) there is need for further investigation of any matter in connection with which he was detained, or (b) proceedings may be taken against him in respect of any such matter. If (a) or (b) apply he *shall* be released on bail. Section 34(5), (Art 35(6)) represents the pre-PACE practice of releasing a person to return to a police station when there is a need for further inquiries into the offence or matters connected with it, eg the investigation of an alibi or forensic examination of some material. When a person is released under s 34(2) (Art 35(2)) and there is such a need, there is a duty to release on bail to return to a police station. The duty to release on bail when proceedings *may* be taken against the person (s 34(5)(b)), (Art 35(6)(b)) is, however, an innovation. Previously the person had to be released unconditionally and informed that he might be prosecuted and would receive a summons in due course if a decision to prosecute was taken. (Section 43(3) of the Magistrates' Courts Act 1980 only permitted bail to a police station when there was a need for further inquiries). Under s 47(3) of the 1984 Act (Art 48(1)) bail is duly defined as a duty to appear at a magistrates' court or to attend at a police station. So it is possible for the custody officer to bail a person to return to a police station in the circumstances envisaged by s 34(5)(b) (Art 35(6)(b)). (Art 35(6) is drafted differently to s 34(5) but the effect is the same). (See further the discussion at paras 6.75-79, post). It should be noted that the duty to release on bail under s 34(5) is applicable only to a release under s 34(2), ie when grounds for detention cease to apply. Release on the expiry of time limits or authorised periods of detention (see post) is a release under the various provisions imposing those limits or authorising the period of detention and all those provisions give the custody officer a discretion to release *on bail* or *without bail.*

Re-arrest following release under s 34(2)

6.19 The release provisions on the expiry of a time limit on police detention, or of an authorised period of detention, prohibit re-arrest for the same offence for which the person was arrested and detained unless new evidence comes to light justifying such a re-arrest. However, there is no similar provision in respect of release under s 34(2). Given that the release must be on bail to return to a police station if there is a need for further investigation and that in many cases the grounds for detention which cease to apply will be the grounds justifying the original arrest under s 25, there is no need for such a provision. If the release is on the basis that there is not sufficient evidence to charge, that there are no grounds for further detention and no need for further investigation, any re-arrest of that person must be based on new evidence which has come to light since the release.

Duties of a custody officer before charge (s 37) (Art 38)

6.20 Where (a) a person is arrested for an offence without warrant, or under a warrant not endorsed for bail (see s 117(2) of the Magistrates' Courts Act 1980), or (b) a person returns to a police station to answer to bail, the custody officer at each police station where he is detained shall, as soon as practicable after the person arrives at the police station, or if arrested at the police station, as soon as practicable after that arrest (s 37(10), Art 38(10), COP C, para 1.1.) determine whether he has before him sufficient evidence to charge that person with the offence for which he was arrested. He may detain the person at the police station for such period as is necessary to enable him to do so (s 37(1)), (Art 38(1)). A person may be arrested for more than one offence and under s 31 (Art 33) for further offences which come to light after the person's arrival at the police station under arrest for the initial offence. Clearly the duty under s 37(1) (Art 38(1)) must be carried out in respect of each offence and, as the COP C, para 1.1, emphasises, as expeditiously as possible. It will be seen (paras 6.39–40, post) that police detention starts, in a majority of cases, on the arrival of the arrested person at the police station (s 41(2)) (Art 42(2). The 'detention clock' will then have started in all cases, and in the case of arrests under s 31 (Art 33) will be well advanced, before a decision to authorise detention without charge is made. It follows that review of detention under s 40, (Art 41), which starts 6 hours after detention is *authorised* (s 40(3)(a)), (Art 41(3)(a)), may well commence some time after the 'detention clock' has started. Research by McKenzie et al, Helping Police with their Inquiries 1990 Crim LR 22, showed a range of 'waiting time' of between 0 minutes to two hours 06 minutes in a sample of observed receptions and 0 minutes to one hour 57 minutes in a sample of custody records (p 26 fn 15).

Insufficient evidence to charge

6.21　If the custody officer determines that there is not sufficient evidence to charge the arrested person, he must release him either on bail (to return to a police station) or without bail, *unless the custody officer has reasonable grounds for believing that his detention without charge is necessary to secure or preserve evidence relating to the offence for which he is under arrest or to obtain such evidence by questioning him* (s 37(2)) (Art 38(2)). These are the only grounds for detention, continued detention under s 42 (Art 43), further detention under s 43 (Art 44), or detention on attendance at a police station following release on bail subject to a duty to attend there (s 47(5)) (although in relation to continued or further detention other conditions must also be satisfied, see paras 6.46 and 6.55, post). There is no prohibition on re-arrest for the same offence following release under s 37(2) (Art 38(2)) as there is in respect of re-arrest following release from detention under s 41(7) (Art 42(5)), s 42(10) (Art 43(9)) and s 43(18) (Art 44(17))(ss 41(9), 42(11) and 43(19)) (Arts 42(7), 43(10) and 44(18))) (as to re-arrest after release from detention see para 6.45, post).

Where there is sufficient evidence to charge

6.22　If the custody officer determines that there is sufficient evidence to charge the person with the offence for which he was arrested, the person shall either,

(a) be charged (s 37(7)(a)) (Art 38(7)(a)). (For the position where more than one offence is involved, see para 6.25, post.) In this case the question whether the person is released on bail or detained in custody is governed by s 38 (Art 39) (see para 6.28, post) and, if he is detained, his detention in custody is subject to review under s 40 (Art 41) (see para 6.65, post) and the duty to bring him before a magistrates' court is governed by s 46, (Art 47) (see para 6.33, post), or

(b) be released without charge either on bail or without bail (s 37(7)(b)) (Art 38(7)(b)). This will arise because the police have decided, or may decide, not to prosecute, or simply to caution the person. Section 37(8) (Art 38(8)) provides that where a decision on prosecution has not yet been taken, the custody officer has a duty to inform the person of this. Thus, if a person is to be prosecuted, he will not have his hopes raised by a release without charge. Section 37(8) (Art 38(8)) also presents the custody officer with another option, that is to inform the person in an appropriate case that he is not to be prosecuted or that he will be cautioned. In future the custody officer may find that he is in a position to exercise this option more often. The decision not to prosecute, or to caution, often has to be made or ratified by higher ranks than custody officers and sometimes requires consultation with other agencies. However, the provision of uniform prosecution and cautioning criteria (see HO Circular 59/1990) means that some decisions can be made by custody officers or inspectors. A number of police forces have already adopted 'instant' cautioning schemes which enable decisions to be made by these ranks and permit the caution to be given within a matter of hours of the offender being arrested. Not only does this save time by reducing the administrative procedure, it also reduces considerably the anxiety associated with waiting for a decision.

Bail of a person released without charge

6.23 Under the previous law bail to return to a police station was only possible when inquiries had to be made before sufficient evidence to charge was available. Under the 1984 Act (1989 Order) (s 47(3)) (Art 48(1)), references to 'bail' are references to bail subject to a duty to appear before a magistrates' court, or to attend at a police station. If, therefore, there is sufficient evidence to charge but there is some doubt as to the appropriate charge, or it is a case in which the person may not be charged or in which he may be cautioned, the person may be released on bail subject to a duty to attend at such police station at such time as the custody officer may appoint. The person must then attend and may be charged or cautioned, the recognisance entered into being enforceable as if it were a recognisance to attend a magistrates' court (s 43(2) of the Magistrates' Courts Act 1980 as amended by s 47(8)), (Arts 48 and 49 of the Magistrates' Courts (N.I.) Order 1981 (Art 48(5)). Should the person's attendance not be required, the custody officer may notify the person in writing of that decision (s 47(4)) (Art 48(7)) (see further, para 6.75, post).

Person unfit to be charged (s 37(9)) (Art 38(9))

6.24 If a person under arrest is unfit to be charged or to be released without charge, he may be kept in police detention until he is. The commonest cause of such unfitness will be intoxication due to alcohol or drugs. Custody officers should be aware that 'Many infirmities are known to mimic alcohol and/or drug intoxication' (Home Affairs Committee, Deaths in Police Custody, p 93). Consequently COP C, para 9.2, places a duty on the custody officer to call the police surgeon, or, in urgent cases, send the person to a hospital, or call another medical practitioner, if it appears that a person brought to a police station is suffering from physical illness or a mental disorder, or is injured, or does not show signs of sensibility and awareness; or fails to respond normally to questions or conversation (other than through drunkenness alone); or otherwise appears to need medical attention. This applies whether or not the person complains and whether or not he has had medical treatment elsewhere (see further paras 7.103-132).

Arrest for more than one offence

6.25 Where the arrest is for more than one offence, or where there is an arrest for a further offence, there may be different determinations in respect of each offence; eg there may be sufficient evidence to charge an offence A but insufficient evidence in respect of offence B. COP C 16.1 provides that in such a case it is permissible to delay bringing the person before a custody officer for charging on offence A until there is sufficient evidence on offence B (see para 6.28, post). However, if the person is brought before a custody officer on offence A the person must be charged with offence A but will not be released if the custody officer authorises detention without charge in respect of offence B.

Detention without charge

6.26 The custody officer may authorise detention without charge, if having determined there is not sufficient evidence to charge the person, he has reasonable grounds for believing such detention is necessary on the grounds stated in s 37(2) (s 37(3)), (Art 38(2) and (3)). The purpose of detention is clearly to enable the police to obtain the evidence necessary to sustain a charge. To 'secure' means to obtain or get, usually by search of the suspect's premises or other premises. To 'preserve' means to keep safe from harm (including the photographing of the scene), which requires a belief that the suspect will, if released, remove, destroy or tamper with the evidence which the police have not yet been able to secure. This clearly does not cover the situation where the suspect is reasonably believed to be likely to interfere with witnesses or otherwise obstruct the course of justice. In such a case the evidence will be available, the suspect must then be charged and his detention after charge will be permissible under s 38(1)(a)(iii), (Art 39(1)(a)(iii)). 'Obtain such evidence by questioning him' clearly refers to interrogation of the suspect. Arrest for questioning then becomes detention for questioning.

Written records and informing the detained person

6.27   Where a custody officer authorises a person who has not been charged to be kept in police detention, he shall, as soon as is practicable, make a written record, in the presence of the person arrested, and at that time inform the person orally of the grounds for his detention (s 37(4) and (5)) (Art 38(4) and (5)). Section 34(2) of the Children and Young Persons Act 1933, as amended by s 57 of the PACE Act 1984, requires that the parent or guardian of an arrested juvenile be informed of the fact that the juvenile has been arrested and detained and the place of detention. If at the time of the arrest the juvenile is subject to a supervision order, the supervisor must be informed (see para 6.14 ante). (Art 38(11) to (13) of the PACE (N.I.) Order requires the custody officer (a) to inform a juvenile arrested without warrant and detained without charge under Art 38(2) that he has reasonable grounds for believing that his detention is necessary in connection with an offence, and to state the offence, (b) to take such steps as are practicable to identify the person responsible for the juvenile's welfare, and (c) if the person is identified and it is practicable to do so, to inform the person of the arrest and the offence alleged to have been committed by the juvenile. The persons who may be responsible for the juvenile's welfare are the parent or guardian, or any other person who for the time being has assumed such responsibility. If a supervision order under the CYP Act (N.I.) 1968, or a probation order under s 1 of the Probation Act (Northern Ireland) 1950, is in force the superviser or probation officer is also to be informed, in every case, 'as soon as it is practicable'.) The duty to inform shall not apply where the person is, at the time the written record is made,

(a) incapable of understanding what is said to him;

(b) violent or likely to become violent; or

(c) in urgent need of medical attention (s 37(6) (Art 38(6)).

(b) and (c) are self-explanatory. (a) would include incapacity by reason of not understanding the language or deafness as well as the more usual incapacity by reason of drink or drugs. Code C, para 1.8, provides that where the information is not given for any of these reasons, he must be given it as soon as is practicable. If the incapacity is due to an inability to understand English or deafness, Code C para 3.6 requires that the custody officer call an interpreter as soon as is practicable, and ask him to provide the information. (See the COP C, Section 13 on interpreters and detained persons generally and para 7.142 post). COP C (para 3.4) repeats the duty under s 37(5) to inform the detainee of the grounds for detention. It is a summary of the statutory duties and should not be taken to detract from them. The Code (para 3.1) also requires the custody officer at the same time to inform the detainee of his statutory rights under s 56 (Art 57) to have someone informed of his detention, and under s 58 (Art 59) to consult with a solicitor and to consult the Code of Practice governing detention or any other Code of Practice. In addition to the oral information, the COP C, para 3.2, requires a written statement of these three rights and a signed acknowledgment of receipt on the custody record. Interpreters may also be required to impart this information (COP C, para 3.6). If the detainee waives his right to consult with a solicitor he should also be asked to sign a waiver on the custody sheet at this time. For further discussion of these procedures, see chapter 7.

Duties of custody officer after charge (s 38) (Art 39)

6.28 Once a person has been charged with an offence there are no investigative reasons for detaining him further. COP C, para 16.1 requires that when an officer considers that there is sufficient evidence to prosecute successfully a detained person, and that the person has said all that he wishes to say about the offence, he should without delay bring him before the custody officer who shall be responsible for considering whether or not he should be charged. If, however, the detained person is suspected of more than one offence, it is permissible to delay bringing him before the custody officer until the above condition is satisfied in respect of all the offences. One should note the restriction on continued questioning in respect of an offence when the officer believes that there is sufficient evidence for a successful prosecution and the person indicates that he has nothing more to say, imposed by COP C, para 11.4 discussed at para 8.38, post. This applies to enquiries made of a person who is detained under s 37(2) and (3) (Art 38(2) and (3)) in order to obtain evidence by questioning the person, and also to enquiries made of persons not yet in police detention, being either those who are not yet arrested or those who are arrested and taken somewhere for investigation before being taken to a police station as permitted by s 30(10) (Art 32(13)) (discussed at para 5.55, ante). One may further note that when other offences are revealed during the period when a person is in police detention, he must be arrested for those offences (s 31) and the relevant time for the purposes of calculating the period of detention is the time of arrival at the police station on his arrest for the original offence (s 41(4)) (Art 42(2)(c)). Thus whilst it is permissible to delay charging until there is sufficient evidence to prosecute all offences successfully, regard must be had to the detention clock which may not permit much delay. If no extension is possible, the person should be charged with the offences for which there is sufficient evidence and a remand in police custody sought to continue the investigation into the remaining offences (see s 128(7) of the Magistrates' Courts Act 1980 as amended by s 48 of the PACE Act 1984, discussed at para 6.81, post). If the custody officer determines that there is sufficient evidence to charge the person, he must either do so or release the person without charge (see s 37(7)(b), (Art 38(7)) discussed in paras 6.20–22, ante). Where the person is charged, s 38(1) (Art 39(1)) imposes a duty on the custody officer to release, either on bail or without bail, unless, in the case of *an adult offender*, one or more of the conditions discussed in para 6.29, post, is satisfied, in which event he may authorise that person's detention after charge. In *R v Samuel* (1988) QB 615 it was held that a suspect could not continue to be denied access to a solicitor under Annex B of COP C once he was charged with an offence, even though questioning was to continue in respect of other offences. If the suspect is charged with one offence and a remand in custody is to be sought under s 128(7) of the Magistrates' Courts Act 1980, he must be allowed access to a solicitor for a reasonable time before the hearing (COP C, Annexe B, A(a) 5).

Grounds for detention after charge

6.29 (a) *Section 38(1)(a)(i) (Art 39(1)(a)(i))* — the name or address of the person arrested cannot be ascertained or the custody officer has reasonable grounds for doubting whether a name or address furnished by him is his real name or address. This embodies the general arrest conditions in s 25(3) (Art 27(3)), (a), (b) and (c) (see paras 5.17–20, ante). It will permit detention after the person has been charged if the arrest condition still applies but it is, of course, applicable to all offences, whether arrestable or general.

(b) *Section 38(1)(a)(ii) (Art 39(1)(a)(ii))* — the custody officer has reasonable grounds for believing that the detention of the person arrested is necessary for his own protection or to prevent him from causing physical injury to any other person or from causing loss of, or damage to, property.

  This embodies the general arrest conditions in s 25(3)(d)(i), (ii) and

(iii) and (3)(e) (Art 27(3)(d)(i), (ii) and (iii) and (3)(e)) (see paras 5.21–26, ante), though as with condition (a) it may apply to an arrest for any offence. In both conditions (a) and (b) the custody officer's reasonable belief will often arise because of what the arresting constable tells him and will then be based on the same grounds, though such a belief may equally arise from his own examination of the arrested person. For example, the custody officer is able to detect mental or physical illness which the arresting officer mistook for belligerence, or the arrested person tells him that he will be attacked by youths seeking revenge if he is released.

(c) *Section 38(1)(a)(iii) (Art 39(1)(a)(iii))* — the custody officer has reasonable grounds for believing that the person arrested will fail to appear in court to answer to bail or that his detention is necessary to prevent him from interfering with the administration of justice or with the investigation of offences or of a particular offence. There are two separate and distinct reasons for detention here. The first, that the detainee will fail to appear in court or answer to bail, may be related to the condition in s 38(1)(a)(i) (Art 39(1)(a)(i)) above, but is more apt to apply at one extreme to the minor offender of no fixed abode; and, at the other extreme, to the serious offender who is of a fixed abode and well known but who, because of the seriousness of the offence and perhaps also because of his previous record, is likely to get a custodial sentence if convicted. If released he may then flee the jurisdiction. The second, concerning interference with the administration of justice, may be related to the condition in s 38(i)(a)(ii) (Art 39(1)(a)(ii)) above in that the detained person may threaten physical injury to witnesses or the destruction of evidence. It is, however, much wider in that the interference may not involve threats. The detained person may, for example, have been overheard saying that he will concoct an alibi on his release. It should be noted that both (b) and (c) require the more exacting standard of *reasonable belief* on the part of the custody officer (see further on this concept para 2.02, ante).

Driving with excess alcohol in the body

6.30 An arrest under s 6(5) of the Road Traffic Act 1988 is an arrest for an offence (see s 34(6) discussed at para 6.16, ante). A person arrested for such an offence can therefore be bailed to a court following a charge or, if a blood or urine sample requires forensic analysis, be released without charge and bailed to return to a police station. However, if in either case the person is still unfit to drive, s 10 of the Road Traffic Act 1988 permits his detention until he is fit to drive. There is therefore no need to rely on s 38(1)(b) in such a case. (In Northern Ireland the Road Traffic (Northern Ireland) Order 1981 contains the equivalent provision).

Arrested juvenile — additional ground for detention (s 38(1)(b)(ii), (Art 39(1)(b)(ii))

6.31 If the person charged with an offence is an arrested juvenile, all the grounds for detention after charge under s 38(1)(a) (Art 39(1)(a)) apply, but in addition he may be detained if the custody officer has reasonable grounds for believing that he ought to be detained in his own interests. Section 38(I)(b)(ii) (Art 39(1)(b)(ii)) offers no guidance as to when this will arise. Section 38(1)(a)(ii) (Art 39(1)(a)(ii)) permits a detention 'for his own protection', a phrase which could overlap with 'in his own interests' but which the Minister of State at the Home Office thought implied a threat of specific harm (Standing Committee E, 14th February 1984, col 1127). An example given in Committee was of the truant who boards a train at Carlisle without paying his fare and is arrested in London. His parents cannot come to collect him until the next day. Though he has been charged it would not be in his interests to release him to wander the streets of London. It should be noted that such detention is only permissible after a juvenile has been arrested and charged with an offence. If the custody officer in England and Wales authorises an arrested juvenile to be kept in police detention under s 38(1) (Art 39(1)), he shall, unless he certifies that it is impracticable to do so, secure that the arrested juvenile is moved to local authority accommodation (s 38(6) as substituted by s 108(5) and Sch 13 of the Children Act 1989. See s 21 of the Children Act 1989 for the categories of children for whom local authorities must provide accommodation. These include juveniles they are requested to receive under s 38(6) of the PACE Act). 'Local authority accommodation' and 'local authority' have the same meaning as in the Children Act 1989 (s 38(6)(A) and s 38(8) as added and amended by the Children Act 1989). (In the Northern Ireland PACE Order the duty is to take the juvenile to a place of safety as defined in Section 180(1) of the CYP Act (Northern Ireland) 1968 which does not include a police station Art 39(6), (7) and (8). In *R v Chief Constable of Cambridge ex p Michel* (1990) the Divisional Court held, in a reserved judgment, that a custody officer was not required by s 38 to transfer an arrested juvenile into the care of a local authority where he was dissatisfied with the proposed arrangements for the secure detention of the juvenile. Code C, Notes for Guidance 16B states that neither the juvenile's behaviour nor the nature of the offence with which he is charged provide grounds for keeping him in police custody rather than seek to arrange for his transfer into local authority care. The guidance needs to be reconsidered in the light of the above case. The juvenile's behaviour in continuing to offend while living in a local authority hostel led the custody officer in the Michel case to require secure accommodation. The belief that the juvenile would see another youth suspected of receiving property, the subject of a burglary admitted by the juvenile, provided the grounds for not releasing from police detention under s 38(1)(a)(iii) and reinforced the custody officer's belief in the need for secure accommodation. It follows that both behaviour and the nature of the offence (ie an offence involving property as yet unrecovered) can provide grounds for requiring secure accommodation. The absence of a clear legal power to detain a person in local authority accommodation was a problem which has now been resolved by s 38(6B). This may mean that custody officers will in future have less cause to be dissatisfied with local authority arrangements. Paragraph 27 of Schedule 12 to the Children Act 1989 substitutes a new s 32(1A) of the Children and Young Persons 'Act 1969. This section now permits the arrest, without warrant, of any juvenile who is absent without permission from such accommodation. Once the arrested juvenile is transferred to local authority accommodation the duties of the custody officer in relation to him cease (s 39(4)) (Art 40(4)).

Authorised detention — informing the detained person

6.32 If the release of the person arrested and charged is not required by s 38(1) (Art 39(1)), the custody officer may authorise him to be kept in police detention (s 38(2)) (Art 39(2)). Where he does so, the custody officer is under a duty to record the grounds for detention and to inform the arrested person in precisely the same terms, and subject to the same exceptions, as when he authorises police detention without charge (s 38(3), (4), (5) and (6)) (Art 39(3) to (6)) (see para 6.27, ante).

Duty to release or take a charged person before a court (s 46) (Art 47)

6.33 If the custody officer becomes aware that the detention of a person, who has been charged with an offence and who has been detained under s 38(1) (Art 39(1)), is no longer justified under that subsection, he must release him under s 34(2) (Art 35(2)). However, if the detention after charge continues to be justified and the person remains in police detention, s 46 (Art 47) makes provision for him to be brought before a magistrates' court in the shortest possible time in the four circumstances foreseen by the section. (Note that Art 47 of the NI PACE Order is drafted so as to take account of the fact that there is no first sitting of magistrates' courts in Northern Ireland, therefore there is no need to specify a period in which magistrates' courts will be held). These are:

(a) *The usual circumstances.* These will arise when the police station at which he is charged and the magistrates' court before which he is to be brought are both in the same petty sessions area and the court sits daily or will be sitting on the day the man is charged (the relevant day for the purpose of the section in this circumstance) or the next day.

The duty is to take the charged and detained person before that court as soon as is practicable and in any event not later than the first sitting after he is charged with the offence. In essence this means that the person will appear before a magistrates' court in the usual circumstances on the day he is charged or the next day (s 46(2) and 7(a)) (Art 47(2)).

(b) *The less usual circumstances.* These will arise when the police station and court are in the same petty sessions area but the court is not due to sit on the day the person is charged (the relevant day) or on the next day. In these circumstances the duty under s 46(2) still applies but the custody officer at the police station at which he is charged is under a further duty to inform the clerk to the justices that there is in the area a person who has been charged and to whom s 46(2) applies (s 46(3)). The duty of the clerk is then to arrange for a magistrates' court to sit not later than the day after the 'relevant day'. Since the clerk will be informed of this on the relevant day (the day the person is charged) a court sitting will then be arranged for that day or the following day. For example where the clerk is informed on a Wednesday he must arrange a sitting for that day if practicable or at the latest for the Thursday (s 46(6)).

(c) *The unusual circumstances.* These will arise when the police station and magistrates' court are in different petty sessions areas and the person charged and detained is to be brought before the court in that area which will be sitting on the day on which he arrives in that area (the relevant day in this circumstance) or the next day. The duty of the custody officer is to have the person removed to that area as soon as practicable and brought before that court as soon as practicable and in any event not later than the first sitting of the court after his arrival in the area. This too will normally mean that the person appears before a court on the day he is charged or the next day (s 46(4) and (7)(b)) (Art 47(3)).

(d) *The most unusual circumstances.* These will arise when, as in (c) above, the police station and court are in different areas but the court is not due to sit on the day the detainee arrives in the area or the next day. The custody officer at the receiving station must then inform the clerk to the justices for his area that he has a person in custody to whom s 46(4) applies and the clerk is then under a duty to arrange a sitting of the court on that day or the next day (s 46(5), (6) and (7)(b)).

6.34 *Sundays and Holy Days* — Where the day after that on which the person is charged, or arrives in the other area (the relevant day), is Christmas Day, Good Friday or a Sunday, the duty of the clerk to the justices is to arrange for a court to sit on the first day after the relevant day which is not one of those days. That is the day after Christmas which is not a Sunday, the Saturday after Good Friday or a Monday (s 46(8)) (Art

47(4)). Section 153 of the Magistrates' Courts Act 1980 permits a court to sit on any day of the year and (if the court thinks fit) on these holy days. The court could therefore override the clerk's duty by sitting on one of those days but it is unlikely that any would wish to do so, unless exceptionally, major public disorder has arisen involving multiple arrests on or before these holy days.

6.35 *Saturdays* — Outside cities and large towns few magistrates' courts sit on a Saturday, even where they sit daily from Monday to Friday. If then a person is charged on a Friday, and he cannot be taken before a court on that day and no court is sitting on the Saturday, then the custody officer must (under s 46(3)) inform the clerk to the justices that he has a person in custody to whom s 46(2) (Art 47(2)) applies and the clerk must arrange a Saturday court. The same result is achieved if the court and police station are in different areas (s 46(6)). If, however, the person is charged on a Friday and does not reach the other area until the Saturday and no court is due to sit on that day, the duty of the clerk is to arrange a court sitting not later than the following Monday (Saturday being the relevant day and s 46(8) (Art 47(4)) applies to exclude the Sunday). Depending on the time of arrival in that area the spirit, if not the letter of the law, may require a Saturday court, for example where the person arrives in the early hours of Saturday morning and there is adequate time to arrange a Saturday court. Although the words 'not later than the day next following the relevant day' could be interpreted as justifying delaying a person's appearance before a court until the Monday, nevertheless it is submitted that, since the purpose of the appearance is to enable a court to decide whether the person should be released or detained in custody, the interests of the detainee, rather than the court's convenience, should be uppermost in the mind of the clerk. Since a magistrate has jurisdiction over the whole of the county in which he sits, it is quite permissible for one petty sessional court to sit on a Saturday and deal with offences committed in other sessional areas in the same county (*R v Avon Magistrates' Courts Committee, ex p Bath Law Society* (1988)). In organising a central Saturday sitting the justices' clerk should have regard to the wishes of the justices, the interests of the defendants and the administrative convenience of the police, prosecution and defence (*R v Avon Magistrates' Courts Committee, ex p Broome* (1988)).

6.36 *Arrested person hospitalised* — Finally, s 46(9) (Art 47(5)) makes it clear that nothing in s 46 requires a person who is in hospital to be brought before a court if he is not well enough. This may sound otiose, but the person may still be in 'police detention' in a hospital. It will be rare that the person who has been charged falls ill and has to be taken to hospital, particularly since s 37(9) (Art 38(9)) permits a person, who is not fit to be charged, to be kept in police detention until he is. The detention in hospital is subject to the limits on detention imposed by this Part of the Act (see para 6.42, post).

Responsibilities in relation to persons detained (s 39) (Art 40)

6.37 Section 39(1)(a) (Art 40(1)(a)) provides that, subject to sub-ss (2) and (4), it shall be the duty of the custody officer at a police station to ensure that all persons in police detention at that station are treated in accordance with the Act (Order) and the Code of Practice relating to the treatment of persons in police detention. Section 39(2)(b) (Art 40(2)) places the same duty on police officers investigating offences when the person is transferred to their custody. This dual duty is important since the person in police detention will be in the charge of each officer at some stage during his detention and each is relieved of his statutory duty toward the person while he is in the charge of the other. Thus, s 39(2)(b)(i) (Art 40(2)) relieves the custody officer of his duty under s 39(1) (Art 40(1)) if he transfers, or permits the transfer of a person in police detention to the custody of a police officer investigating an offence, or to an officer who is to take charge of the person outside a police station; for example, an officer who is to take the person to a court or transfer him to another police station. The officer into whose custody the person is transferred assumes the statutory duty under s 39(1), (Art 40(1)) (s 39(2)(a) and (b)), (Art 40(2)). If the person is returned to the charge of the custody officer, the investigating officer is under a further duty to report to the custody officer as to the manner in which that duty has been discharged while the detainee has been in his custody (s 39(3)) (Art 40(3)).

Arrests by ranks senior to the custody officer

6.38 The fact that the custody officer will generally be of the rank of sergeant, or in some cases constable, means that he may sometimes be faced with the difficult situation in which an arrest is made or authorised by an officer senior to him, or the problem of a senior officer from another station trying to pull rank on him. The senior officer may then give directions which are at variance with any decision made or action already taken by the custody officer or which he would have made or taken but for the senior officer's direction. The custody officer should stand firm. It is highly likely that he will know more about daily PACE procedures, and what are the correct procedures in a particular case, than the senior officer. If the senior officer insists on his directions being followed the custody officer must refer the matter at once to an officer of the rank of superintendent or above who is responsible for the police station at which the custody officer acts (s 39(6)) (Art 40(6)). This provision gives to the custody officer the necessary authority to ensure that he is able to carry out his important duties without having rank pulled on him. That would undermine his authority and detract from the performance of his duties. It is, of course, possible that the superintendent or more senior officer in charge of the police station will support the other senior officer rather than the custody officer, or that he is the arresting or authorising officer who makes the initial conflicting decision. In such cases the custody officer discharges his duty by pointing out that there is a conflict between them. The responsibility thereafter is that of the senior officer in charge of the police station. It should, of course, be pointed out to such officers that under the PACE Act (Order) certain actions can only be authorised by a custody officer, eg the authorisation of detention under s 37(3) (Art 38(3)), the release of a person in police detention (s 34(3)) Art 35(3)) and no one, not even the Chief Constable, unless he appoints himself custody officer, can take those actions. The custody officer would, however, be well advised to record the fact that there was a conflict and what the decision was. (See Code C para 2.2, which requires that for action requiring the authority of an officer of a specified rank, his name and rank must be noted in the custody record.)

Limits on period of detention without charge (s 41) (Art 42)

6.39   Section 41(1) (Art 42(1)) lays down the basic rule that a person shall not be kept in police detention without charge for more than 24 hours. Sections 42 and 43 then provide for authorised detention beyond that time, up to a further 12 hours on the authority of a superintendent or above, and further periods for up to an overall maximum of 96 hours on application to a magistrates' court. However, any extension beyond the basic 24 hours can only be in respect of serious arrestable offences (as to which see paras 2.24–31, ante) and subject to other conditions set out in those sections. The time from which the period of detention is to be calculated (the relevant time) is determined by reference to s 41(2) (Art 42(2)). (For the relevant time in relation to arrest, port detention and port examination under the Prevention of Terrorism (Temporary Provisions) Act 1989, see para 7.146(d), post.)

Calculating the relevant time

6.40   In the usual case of an arrest made in a police area for an offence committed in that area, the relevant time will be the time that the person arrested arrives at the first police station to which he is taken after arrest, (s 41(2)(d)) (Art 42(1)), whether it is or is not a designated police station. Five less usual circumstances are then dealt with (Northern Ireland is one police area, therefore only (b) (c) and (d) apply):

(a) an arrest in England and Wales in police area A for an offence committed in police area B;

(b) an arrest outside England and Wales for an offence committed in England or Wales (or an arrest outside Northern Ireland for an offence committed in Northern Ireland);

(c) the arrest while at a police station of a person who voluntarily attends at, or accompanies a constable to, that police station without having been arrested;

(d) the arrest for further offences committed in police area A of a person who is already in police detention for an offence committed in that police area;

(e) the arrest of a person for further offences committed in police area B who is already in police detention in police area A for an offence committed in that area.

As to (a), where the arrest of a person is sought in one police area in England and Wales, he is arrested in another police area, and he is not questioned in the area in which he is arrested in order to obtain evidence in relation to an offence for which he is arrested (s 41(3)(a), (b) and (c)), the relevant time is:

(i) the time at which that person arrives at the first police station to which he is taken in the police area in which his arrest was sought; or

(ii) the time 24 hours after the person's arrest, whichever is the earlier (s 41(2)(a) and (3)(a), (b) and (c)).

Example 1 D's arrest is sought by South Yorkshire Police for burglary in Sheffield. D is arrested for that offence in London at 6 pm on a Tuesday by the Metropolitan Police. He is not questioned in order to obtain evidence of that offence and is transported to Sheffield arriving at a police station there at 10 am on the Wednesday, 10 am is the relevant time. (Note the special restriction on questioning imposed by COP C 14.1, see para 8.15, post).

Example 2 As in *Example 1* but D was arrested at six am on the Tuesday. The relevant time is six am on the Wednesday and by the time D arrives in Sheffield at 10 am the detention clock will already show four hours.

(Note, firstly, that D may be questioned in order to establish whether he is in fact the person wanted in the other area or about offences he may have committed in London, but he must not be questioned in order to obtain evidence of the offence for which he was arrested. If he is, the relevant time is that of his arrival at the police station in London. Secondly, the period of detention in the London police station while awaiting an escort, does not count towards the overall detention period, but D is in 'police detention' and must be treated in accordance with the Act and Codes of Practice. Note particularly COP C 14.1).

The assumption underlying s 41(3) is that the person whose arrest is sought in one police area but who is arrested in another police area, will either be arrested by officers from the area in which he is arrested, or by officers from the area in which his arrest is sought, but in either case that he will be taken to a police station in the area in which he is arrested, as impliedly required by s 30(1) (discussed at para 5.50, ante) and conveyed from there to the area in which his arrest is sought. In *R v Khan* (1991) officers from the West Midlands Serious Crime Squad arrested Khan in Caernarvon and drove him directly back to Birmingham allegedly obtaining a confession en route. The proper procedure in that case would have been to take the arrested person to a police station in the area in which he was arrested. Examples 1 and 2 above then apply, particularly the special restriction on questioning about the offence while he is in transit imposed by COP C 14.1.

As to (b), where a person is arrested outside England and Wales (or outside Northern Ireland), the relevant time is:

(i)   the time at which he arrives at the first police station to which he is taken in the police area in England and Wales (or Northern Ireland) in which the offence for which he is arrested is being investigated; or

(ii)   the time 24 hours after that person's entry into England or Wales (or Northern Ireland) (s 41(2)(b) Art 42(2)(a)), whichever is the earlier.

Example 3 D is arrested in France for an offence committed in Sheffield. Police officers sent to bring him to Sheffield take a channel ferry and arrive back in Dover at 10 pm, Monday. They put up for the night at Dover police station and travel to Sheffield next morning arriving at a Sheffield police station at three pm Tuesday. That is the relevant time.

Example 4 As in *Example 3*, but they arrive at Sheffield at 11 pm on Tuesday. The relevant time is 10 pm on the Tuesday night and the 'detention clock' already shows one hour when D arrives at the Sheffield police station.

(Note there is no direct prohibition on questioning in this case but in most cases the escorting officers, even if they are investigating the offence, are well advised to refrain from questioning the person about his involvement in the offence during the journey in case objection is subsequently taken to any confession obtained). (See COP C para 11.1 and Note of Guidance 11A; see further para 8.07, post).

As to *(c)*, s 41(2)(c) (Art 42(2)(b)(i) and (ii)) provides that in the case of a person who (i) attends voluntarily at a police station; or (ii) accompanies a constable to a police station without having been arrested and is arrested at the police station, the relevant time is the time of his arrest. He gets no credit for the period spent at a police station prior to his arrest (cf s 41(4) below). As was indicated in paras 5.44–49 ante, s 29 (Art 31) seeks to exclude the possibility that this 'voluntary attendance' may be used to undermine the safeguards applicable to a person in police detention. Yet s 41(2)(c) (Art 40(2)(b)), may operate to defeat that intention. For whilst COP C (para 3.15) requires the police to remind the person that he is free to leave the police station at any time, in practice the person, particularly a person who accompanies the constable in the mistaken belief that he is under compulsion, may well feel constrained to remain. From the police point of view the prospect of obtaining periods of detention which are in addition to those provided by the Act, and possibly in circumstances in which 'police detention' would not be permitted under the Act, may be too strong a temptation. If s 41(2)(c) (Art 42(2)(b)) had made the relevant time in such a case the time of arrival at a police station, the temptation would not arise. (Note that COP C para 12.2, provides for a continuous period of eight hours rest in any period of 24 hours. In the case of a volunteer or person who accompanies a constable to a police station, this provision runs from the time of his arrest at the police station and not the time of his arrival).

Example 5 D accompanies a constable to a police station without being arrested. He arrives there at 3 pm on Tuesday and remains there until 10 am on Thursday when he is arrested. That is the relevant time.

As to *(d)*, s 31 (Art 33) (see para 5.57 ante) provides that where a person has been arrested for an offence, is at a police station in consequence of that arrest and the constable becomes aware that he is liable to be arrested for another offence, he must be arrested for the latter as well. Section 41(4) (Art 42(3)) provides that the relevant time in this case is that at which the person arrived at the police station under arrest for the original offence.

Example 6 D is arrested for possession of drugs. He arrives at the first police station to which he is taken at two pm on Monday. He is detained without charge for questioning in relation to that offence. During that questioning he admits committing several burglaries in that police area. He must be arrested for those offences. The relevant time in respect of those latter offences is also two pm on the Monday even though the arrest takes place on the Tuesday morning.

As to *(e)*, s 31 and s 41(4) work well enough when the further offences for which D is arrested are committed in the police area in which he committed the original offence for which he has been arrested. However, if the further offences have been committed in another police area and s 41(4) applied, the maximum permitted period of detention may well have expired before D can be transferred to the other police area. This would leave no time for the investigation of those offences in that police area. Section 41(5) therefore provides that if:

(a) a person is in police detention in police area A for an offence committed in that area, and
(b) his arrest is sought for an offence committed in police area B in England or Wales, and
(c) he is taken to area B for the purpose of investigating that offence without being questioned in police area A to obtain evidence of that offence,

the relevant time in such a case is:

(i) the time 24 hours after he leaves the place where he is detained in police area A; or
(ii) the time of his arrival at the first police station to which he is taken in police area B, whichever is the earlier.

Example 7 D is arrested in London for possession of drugs. He is detained without charge for questioning about the offence. During questioning it is discovered that D's arrest is sought in a Sheffield for burglary. Section 31 requires that he be arrested for that offence but D is not questioned in order to obtain evidence relating to it. D is charged with the drug offence. There are no grounds for detaining him after charge but he may be detained in respect of the burglary (s 34(2) and s 37(2)) pending his transfer to Sheffield. D leaves the London police station at 10 am having been detained there for 20 hours. He arrives at a Sheffield police station at three pm the same day. That is the relevant time in respect of the burglary offence. A fresh period of detention starts from three pm and the 25 hours D has already spent in police detention do not count toward the Sheffield offence.

Section 41(5)(i) is unlikely to apply since there are no police areas in England and Wales which are more than 24 hours travelling time apart. It could only apply in circumstances where delay is caused by inclement weather or mechanical breakdown. If, as in Example 7 above, D is questioned in order to obtain evidence of the offence in Sheffield, then the relevant time is the time of arrival at the London station under arrest for the London offence, ie s 4(2)(d) applies not s 41(5).

6.41 If the offence is a serious arrestable offence, extension of detention beyond the basic 24 hours may be possible. Both s 42 and s 43 permit a superintendent or magistrates' court respectively, to take account of the distance and time involved in transferring a person to another police area when deciding how long a period of continued or further detention should be granted (see paras 6.46 and 6.54, post).

Hospitalisation of persons in police detention

6.42 Where an arrested person is taken to a police station, detained there and later, before the investigation is complete, is removed to a hospital for medical attention, the crucial question is whether the person is then 'in the charge of a constable' (see s 118(2) and Art 2(3) and (4) discussed at para 6.07, ante). Doubtless the hospital authorities would say that he is in their charge and nothing can be done to or in respect of the person without the consent of the doctor in charge of the person's treatment. However, if the person is questioned while in hospital by police officers seeking evidence of D's involvement in an offence, there is little difference between detention there and in a police station. The problem is neatly resolved by s 41(6) (Art 42(4)) which provides that only the time during which he is being questioned at the hospital, or on the way to or from the hospital, for the purpose of obtaining evidence relating to an offence, shall be included in the calculation of the period of detention.

Example 1 D is in police detention following arrest for burglary. After five hours detention he is taken to hospital and remains there for five days before being declared fit to leave. He is still under arrest. The detention clock stops at five hours on the day he was hospitalised and resumes on his return to a police station.

Example 2 As in *Example 1*, but D is questioned for two hours while at the hospital by officers seeking the whereabouts of property stolen in the burglary. On D's release from hospital the detention clock reads seven hours.

6.43 Section 41(6) (and Art 42(4)) refers to questioning by a police officer for the purpose of obtaining evidence of *an* offence, not *the* offence. Therefore, if D is questioned about other burglaries committed in the area but not about the burglary for which he is under arrest and in police detention, that period of questioning counts as police detention. Difficulties may arise about the purpose of questioning in some cases. For instance, D is under arrest for kidnapping and is hospitalised after arrest and after being taken to a police station. The police question him while in hospital in an attempt to discover where the victim is. The purpose of such questioning is to save life and prevent harm to the victim but should it be successful it will also provide evidence of D's involvement in the offence. Any such period of questioning will count towards the detention period. It is an interview for the purposes of COP C (see Note of Guidance 11A) and is permitted by COP C para 11.1.

Arrested person taken directly to hospital

6.44 Section 41(6) (and Art 42(4)) refers to 'a person who is in police detention' and who is removed to hospital. As indicated in the discussion of the meaning of 'police detention' (see para 6.07 ante), a person is only in police detention if he has been arrested and taken to, or arrested at, a police station, for an offence. A person who is arrested and taken *directly* to a hospital is not in police detention within the meaning of that phrase as defined in s 118(2) (Art 2(3)). It follows that s 41(6) does not apply to such a person. In such a case any periods of questioning while he is in hospital do not count since the detention clock has yet to start. COP C, para 14.2, states that if a person *in police detention* is in hospital he may not be questioned without the agreement of a responsible doctor and Note of Guidance 14A states that such periods of questioning count toward the total period, but the Code is silent as to questioning in the situation suggested above. Clearly the agreement of a responsible doctor would be required and even if the period of questioning does not count, the interview must be conducted in accordance with Code C.

Release of detainees on expiry of detention period

6.45 Section 41(7) and (8) (Art 42(5) and (b)) provide that a person who, at the expiry of 24 hours after the relevant time, is in police detention and has not been charged, *shall* be released either on bail or without bail, unless continued or further detention has been authorised under s 42 or 43 (Arts 43 and 44). A person released under s 41(7) (Art 42(5)) shall not be re-arrested without warrant for the same offence for which he was previously arrested unless new evidence justifying a further arrest has come to light since his release (s 41(9)) (Art 42(7)). This important provision is repeated in s 42(11) (Art 43(10)) and s 43(19) (Art 44(18)) in respect of release from continued or further detention. It covers not only re-arrest on the same evidence but also a re-arrest based on evidence which was *known of and available* at the time of the first arrest or which *became available* during the person's detention following the arrest. The evidence must be new and be discovered after the person's release. However, there is no prohibition on arrest for *another offence* for which he was not initially arrested (but see s 31 (Art 33), arrest for further offences) even if it is based on evidence which was available earlier than the person's release. The word 'evidence' must be given its ordinary rather than its legal meaning since arrests are often based on material which is not evidence in the legal sense. The restriction on re-arrest *without a warrant* leaves open the possibility that the person could be re-arrested for the same offence *under a warrant* issued by a magistrate and based on the same evidence as justified the initial arrest. Section 1 of the Magistrates' Courts Act 1980 does not preclude the issue of a warrant to arrest in such circumstances but it is submitted that a magistrate should not issue one if he is aware that the application is in respect of a person who has already been arrested and detained for a period for that offence and to whom s 41(9) (Art 42(7)) or ss 42(11) (Art 43(10)) or 43(19) (Art 44(18)) applies.

Since a warrant of arrest is seldom sought in respect of an offence for which the police normally have a power of arrest without warrant, magistrates and their clerks should inquire whether there is a statutory restriction on the exercise of that power of arrest without warrant and refuse to issue a warrant of arrest if there is.

Authorisation of continued detention (s 42) (Art 43)

6.46 Section 42 (Art 43) provides for the authorisation by a superintendent, or higher rank, of detention beyond 24 hours after the relevant time, up to a maximum period of 36 hours after the relevant time. Such an officer must have reasonable grounds for believing that the three conditions set out in s 42(1) (Art 43(1)) are satisfied. These conditions are:

(a) the detention of that person without charge is necessary to secure or preserve evidence relating to an offence for which he is under arrest or to obtain such evidence by questioning him (these are the basic grounds for detention without charge);

(b) an offence for which he is under arrest is a serious arrestable offence; and

(c) the investigation is being conducted diligently and expeditiously.

It should be noted that s 42(1)(a) (Art 43(1)(a)) refers to 'evidence relating to *an* offence' and s 42(1)(b) (Art 43(1)(b)) requires that '*an* offence for which he is under arrest is a serious arrestable offence' while s 42(1)(c) (Art 43(1)(c)) refers to 'the investigation'. There is no specific requirement that the evidence sought in (a) should be evidence of the serious arrestable offence mentioned in (b), nor that the investigation referred to in s 42(1)(c) (Art 43(1)(c)) should be into that offence. It is therefore open to a superintendent, in what would be the exceptional case, to authorise continued detention in respect of the investigation of an *arrestable* offence where D is also under arrest for a serious arrestable offence. For example, D is arrested for an offence of rape (a serious arrestable offence) and is detained without charge under s 37(2) (Art 38(2)). After 20 hours of detention D admits committing several burglaries (arrestable offences). D must be arrested for these offences (s 31) (Art 33) and the relevant time is the time at which D arrived at the police station under arrest for the offence of rape. The custody officer determines that it is necessary to detain D without charge in respect of the burglaries in order to secure evidence or to obtain it by questioning D. The rape investigation is nearly complete; only the victim's statement is required but she is under sedation and cannot give a statement for some hours. D cannot be charged without that statement. If a superintendent agrees that it is necessary to detain D in order to secure or obtain evidence of the burglaries (arrestable offences), then s 42(1)(a) (Art 43(1)(a)) is satisfied. Section 42(1)(b) (Art 43(1)(b)) is also satisfied since D is under arrest for a serious arrestable offence, and, if the investigation of the burglaries is being conducted diligently and expeditiously, so is s 42(1)(c) (Art 43(1)(c)). It is clear from the Parliamentary debates that this was not Parliament's intention and it would be open to a court to interpret 'offence' in s 42(1) (Art 43(1) as referring to the original serious arrestable one. The correct procedure would then follow. In other words if D can be charged with the offence of rape, he should be taken before a court and an application made under s 128 of the Magistrates' Courts Act 1980 (as amended by s 48 of the PACE Act) for a remand to police detention for enquiries to be made into the other offences (see para 6.81, post). If these conditions apply, the authorising officer may decide that the maximum of 12 hours continued detention is necessary or that some lesser period may be sufficient. If a lesser period is authorised a further period up to the maximum of 12 hours (36 hours after the relevant time) may be authorised provided that the application is made before the expiry of the first period authorised and that the conditions in s 42(1)(a) to (c) (Art 43(1)(a) to (c)) are still satisfied (s 42(2)) (Art 43(2)) (*R v Taylor* (1991)). If the transfer of the person in police detention to another police area is proposed, the authorising officer must have regard to the distance and time the journey would take (s 42(3)).

Time of authorisation

6.47 No authorisation under s 42(1) (Art 43(1)) above may be given more than 24 hours after the relevant time or before the second review of the person's detention under s 40 (Art 41) has been carried out, though if a period of less than 12 hours is authorised an application to extend continued detention for a further period up to the maximum of 12 hours can be made before the expiry of the first period authorised (*R v Taylor* (1991)). The purpose of the review of detention is to determine whether the grounds for detention still apply. The second review will take place at the latest after 15 hours and, only if the review officer determines that the condition for further detention under s 37(2) (Art 38(2)) still applies (which is the same condition as in s 42(1)(a) Art 43(1)(a)) will detention beyond 15 hours continue. The application for continued detention will be refused if any of the conditions in s 42(1)(a) to (c) (Art 43(1)(a) to (c)) do not apply but such refusal will not prevent the detention of the person up to the maximum period of 24 hours, unless the reason for the refusal is that there is no need for detention in order to secure or preserve evidence or to obtain it by questioning, eg there is sufficient evidence to charge the person or that such evidence is unlikely to be forthcoming. In such a case the person must be charged as required by s 37(7) (Art 38(7)) or released as required by s 34(2) (Art 35(2)). However, the refusal may be on the ground that sufficient evidence to charge will be obtained within the 24 hour period of detention permitted by s 41(1) (Art 42(1)), in which case detention may continue as authorised after the second review up to that time.

Duties of the authorising officer

Representations

6.48 When the appropriate officer has to determine whether to authorise continued detention under s 42 (Art 43), he must give the person whose detention is being considered, or any solicitor representing him who is available at that time, an opportunity to make representations to him about the detention (s 42(6)) (Art 43(5)). The requirement under s 42(6) (Art 43(5)) is mandatory and a purported authorisation of further detention without hearing representations on behalf of the detainee is invalid. *(In the Matter of an Application for a Warrant of Further Detention* (1988)). Such representations may be made orally or in writing (s 42(7)) (Art 43(6)) but the authorising officer may refuse to hear an oral representation from the person in detention if he considers he is unfit to make them by reason of his condition or behaviour (s 42(8)) Art 43(7)) 'Behaviour' in this context would seem to mean violent behaviour. 'Condition' is more problematic. Clearly it would include intoxication through drink or drugs rendering the person incoherent. As to sleep, in s 40(12) (Art 41(12)) (representations to a review officer) sleep is expressly referred to as a reason for not giving the detained person the opportunity to make representations. Section 40(14) is identical to s 42(8) (Art 43(7)), implying that sleep is not within the word 'condition'. It is submitted that, whilst not awakening a detained person to permit representations in a review of existing detention can be justified, it cannot be justified in circumstances in which *continued* detention is being considered. Sleep should not therefore be included within 'condition'. COP C, Note for Guidance 15A suggests bringing the review of detention or an authorisation of continued detention, forward if the person is likely to be asleep at the time when it should take place so that representations can be made without having to wake him.

6.49 *Availability of a solicitor* — The wording of s 42(6)(b) (Art 43(5)(b)) suggests that the solicitor need not be available at the police station to make representations. A representation by telephone is within the subsection and written representations could be delivered. The right to consult with a solicitor under s 58(1) (Art 59) is a right to do so at any time and a request to do so can only be denied in the special circumstances set out in s 58 (Art 59). Code of Practice C, para 6.1, provides that a person in police detention may communicate privately in person, in writing or by telephone with a solicitor of his own choice, and, if he has no solicitor, he should be informed of the availability of a duty solicitor unless his right of consultation has been delayed under s 58 (Art 59). A detainee who wishes his solicitor, or a solicitor, to make representations under s 42(6) (Art 43(5)) on his behalf may then telephone his solicitor or ask to see a duty solicitor. (COP C para 15.1, permits other persons having an interest in the person's welfare to make representations at the discretion of the authorising officer).

Duty to inform detainee of his rights (s 42(9)) (Art 43(8))

6.50 Where an officer authorises the keeping of a person in police detention under s 42(1) (Art 43(1)) and at the time of such authorisation the detainee has not exercised his right under s 56 (Art 57) (to have someone informed of his arrest) or under s 58 (Art 59) (to consult a solicitor), the officer shall inform him of those rights and shall decide whether to permit him to exercise them, applying the criteria in those sections which permit delay in the exercise of the rights (s 42(9) Art 43(8)). This pre-supposes that on being told of these rights, the detainee requests them since both rights are available at his request but not otherwise. The decision of the officer must then be recorded in the custody record and, if the rights are refused, the reasons for the refusal shall also be recorded (s 42(9) Art 43(8)).

Duty to inform and record (s 42(5)) (Art 43(4))

6.51 Where an officer authorises continued detention of a person under s 42(1) (Art 43(1)), he has a duty to inform him of the grounds for his continued detention and to record that decision in the person's custody record. The ruling *In the Matter of an Application for a Warrant of Further Detention* (1988) requires that the authorising officer do more than merely recite the terms of s 42(1) (Art 43(1)) in the custody record. This is an important caveat — to have to state and record one's reasons for making a decision concentrates the mind significantly.

Duty to release on expiry of continued detention (s 42(10)) (Art 43(9))

6.52 When the continued detention of a person has been authorised, the person must be released from police detention, with or without bail, not later than 36 hours after the relevant time *unless* (a) he has been charged with an offence (when s 38 (Art 39) applies) or, (b) his continued detention is authorised or otherwise permitted by a magistrates' court under s 43 (Art 44) (s 42(10) (Art 43(9)). If a person is released under this subsection, he shall not be re-arrested without a warrant for the same offence unless new evidence comes to light after his release which justifies a further arrest (s 42(11) (Art 43(10)) (see para 6.45, ante).

By-passing s 42 (Art 43)

6.53   In some cases it will be clear from the outset that detention will be necessary for more than the 36 hours permitted by s 41 and s 42 (Arts 42 and 43); for example, in the case of rape, forensic examination of clothing may not be completed within that period. In such a case an application to a magistrates court for a warrant of further detention may be sought at any time within the initial 24 hours' detention. A magistrates' court may authorise detention for up to 36 hours and extend that by up to a further 36 hours provided that the overall maximum of 96 hours is not exceeded. The full 96 hours detention can therefore be obtained without seeking an authorisation for continued detention from a superintendent under s 42. The application to a magistrates' court for detention beyond 24 hours is what the Royal Commission recommended but there are two reasons why the police have been given the power to authorise continued detention beyond the initial 24 hours up to a maximum of 36 hours and each reason indicates when s 42 will be relied upon. The first is that on an application for a warrant of further detention the detainee has a right to appear before the court and to be legally represented. Sections 56 and 58 (Arts 57 and 59) which, respectively, give the detainee the right to have someone informed of his arrest and the right to consult a solicitor, permit the police to delay those rights for up to 36 hours, the maximum period of police authorised detention. It follows that when the police wish to exercise that power of delay they will seek continued detention under s 42 (Art 43). The detainee may make representations under s 42 (Art 43) but, access to a solicitor having been delayed, there will be no solicitor representing him and a duty solicitor will not be made available to make such representations on his behalf. The second reason is administrative. It would have been possible to require a magistrates' court to hear all applications for detention beyond 24 hours and to make arrangements to deny legal representation in appropriate cases but, while over 95 per cent of detainees are released within 24 hours, the remaining percentage, though small, represents many thousands of persons and a heavy workload for magistrates' courts. Permitting the police to authorise detention beyond 24 hours and up to 36 hours reduces the workload. Magistrates and their clerks will then hope that whenever it is likely that an investigation can be completed within 36 hours, application will be made to a superintendent for continued detention, rather than to a court for a warrant of further detention. Statistics issued by the Home Office (Statistical Bulletin No 14/91) tell us that in 1990 only 542 persons were detained for more than 24 hours and released without charge. 465 of these were released within 36 hours and the remaining 77 were detained for a longer period under a warrant of further detention (the period is not stated) but eventually released without charge. In 1990 there were 405 applications for a warrant of further detention. Of these only 4 were refused. Of the 401 suspects detained under a warrant of further detention 324 were charged and 77 were released without charge. The numbers of warrants issued have fluctuated from a high of 684 in 1986 to a low of 282 in 1989. The 401 issued in 1990 is more consistent with the 468 and 433 issued in 1987 and 1988 respectively. The table below shows the total period of detention under warrants issued in 1990 including any extension.

Period of detention under a warrant of further detention — 1990 (including extensions)

	No	%
Up to 12 hours	10	2.5
Over 12 and up to 24 hours	88	21.9
Over 24 and up to 36 hours	127	31.7
Over 36 and up to 48 hours	57	14.2
Over 48 and up to 96 hours	119	29.7
Total warrants issued	**401**	**100.0**

Warrants of further detention (s 43), (Art 44)

6.54 Section 43(1) (Art 44(1)) provides that a magistrates' court may issue a warrant of further detention if there are reasonable grounds for believing that the detention of the person is justified. 'Magistrates' Court' in relation to s 43 and s 44 (extension of warrants of further detention) means a court consisting of two or more justices sitting otherwise than in open court (s 45(1)). This does not preclude an application being heard by a stipendiary magistrate. Section 16(3) of the Justices of the Peace Act 1979 provides that a stipendiary magistrate can do alone any act which can be done by two justices under any law unless it contains an express provision to the contrary. In Northern Ireland 'magistrates' court' is not defined as in s 45 of the 1984 Act but Art 44(19) states that an application (complaint) under Art 44 shall not be heard in open court. A warrant will authorise the keeping of the person in police detention for such period as the court thinks fit but not exceeding 36 hours (s 43(11) and (12)), (Art 44(11) and (12)). As with continued detention under s 42, if the person is to be transferred to another police area the court must have regard to the distance and time the journey would take in deciding the period of detention (s 43(13)). This does not apply in Northern Ireland which is one police area.

Grounds for further detention

6.55 A person's further detention, for the purposes of s 43 and s 44 (Arts 44 and 45) (extension of a warrant), is only justified if:

(a) his detention without charge is necessary to secure or preserve evidence relating to an offence for which he is under arrest or to obtain such evidence by questioning him;

(b) *an offence* for which he is under arrest is a serious arrestable offence; and

(c) the investigation is being conducted diligently and expeditiously. (s 43(4)).

These are identical grounds to those in s 42(1) (Art 43(1)). As was suggested at para 6.46 ante, in relation to s 42(1) (Art 43(1)), these conditions do not necessarily confine detention without charge to serious arrestable offences. They could permit a magistrates' court to grant a warrant of further detention when the evidence sought under (a) and the investigation in (c) is in respect of an *arrestable* offence provided that one of the offences for which the person is under arrest is a serious arrestable offence. It has been suggested (para 6.46 ante) that these conditions were not intended to permit the issue of a warrant in the circumstances mentioned and, it is submitted, a magistrates' court faced with such an application should exercise the discretion which s 43(1) (Art 44(1)) gives to it, to refuse the application even if the conditions in s 43(4) (Art 44(4)) are all satisfied. In cases where there is sufficient evidence to charge the person with the serious arrestable offence but further inquiries are necessary in respect of an arrestable offence, the person should be charged and application made under s 128 of the Magistrates' Courts Act 1980, as amended by s 47 of the PACE Act, for detention for further inquiries into that other offence (see para 6.81, post). There is no equivalent power in Northern Ireland.

Time of Application

6.56 The application for a warrant of further detention may be made at any time before the expiry of 36 hours after the relevant time (s 43(5)(a), Art 44(5)(a)) and will depend upon a number of factors, not least the availability of a magistrates' court. If continued detention under s 42 (Art 43) has been granted, application to a magistrates' court for a warrant of further detention will be made between the twenty-fourth and the thirty-sixth hours. Where an application to a superintendent under s 42 (Art 43) is refused an application to a court under s 43, (Art 44) is not precluded but is unlikely to be sanctioned and, if sanctioned, to succeed. If a warrant of further detention is sought without reliance on s 42, (Art 43), the application can be at any time during the initial 24 hours of police detention. In all cases governing factors will be the time at which the lawful detention ends and the time of the next sitting of a magistrates' court. Some flexibility is provided by s 43(5)(b), (Art 44(5)(b)). Thus, where it is not practicable for the magistrates' court to sit at the expiry of 36 hours after the relevant time, but the court will sit during the six hours following the end of that period, application may be made before the expiry of that six hours. Thus, if the 36 hour period expires at 7.00 am on a Monday and a court is due to sit at 10.00 am on that day, application may be made to that court up to 40 hours after the relevant time, at 11.00 am. However, if an application is made after the expiry of 36 hours from the relevant time and it appears to the magistrates' court that it would have been reasonable for the police to have made it before the expiry of that period 'the court *shall* dismiss the application' (s 43(7) Art 44(7)). This provision was considered in *R v Slough JJ., ex p Stirling* (1987). There the police approached the clerk to the justices with an application for a warrant of further detention at 12.45 pm, only a few minutes before the expiry of the 36 hours period of police detention. The justices were asked to hear the application but decided not to do so until after lunch. The application was finally made two hours after the expiration of the 36 hours period. The Divisional Court allowed an application for judicial review on the ground that the application could have been made between 10.30 am and 11.30 am and therefore the police had not acted reasonably in making the application after the expiry of the 36 hours period. Section 43(7), (Art 44(7)) is mandatory and the justices were then bound to dismiss the application. The justices can be criticised for not hearing the application before lunch but the police should have foreseen the situation and applied earlier. In *R v Sedgefield Justices, ex p Milne* (1987) the Divisional Court took the view that the police had acted reasonably in contacting the court at 9.00 am when the 36 hour period was due to expire at 10.48 am. The court did not sit until noon and the application, which the Divisional Court held is made when the constable gives evidence on oath as required by s 43(1), (Art 44(1)), was heard at 12.54 pm. The magistrates were criticised for not hearing the application sooner given the precise timescale laid down by the PACE Act 1984. It is clear that both the police and the courts must act reasonably, the police in making the court aware of the application as soon as they become aware of the need for further detention, and the courts in responding to the police by arranging a hearing within the time limit. COP C, Notes for Guidance 15B recommends that applications for a warrant and its extension be made between 10.00 am and 9.00 pm, and if possible during normal court hours. It further suggests that it will not be practicable to arrange for a court to sit outside these hours. Section 43(6)(a), (Art 44(6)(a)) permits the detention of the person to whom the late application under s 43(5)(b), (Art 44(5)(b)) applies for the period in excess of 36 hours until the application is heard, but the custody officer must make a note in the person's custody record of the fact that he was kept in police detention beyond that period, and the reasons for it (s 43(6)(b)), (Art 44(6)(b)) (see para 6.59, post, detention during an adjournment).

The information (complaint)

6.57 An application for a warrant of further detention must be supported by an information in writing which must state:

(a) the nature of the offence for which the person to whom the application relates has been arrested;
(b) the general nature of the evidence on which that person was arrested;
(c) what inquiries relating to the offence have been made by the police and what further inquiries are proposed by them;
(d) the reasons for believing the continued detention of that person to be necessary for the purpose of such inquiries (s 43(14) Art 44(13)).

The fact that s 43(14) (Art 44(13)) does not specifically refer to a 'serious arrestable' offence supports the argument advanced earlier in para 6.55 (and 6.46), that the wording of s 43(4), (Art 44(4)) would permit a warrant of further detention to be issued in respect of an arrestable offence when the arrest is for that offence *and* a serious arrestable offence. It is submitted that s 43(14)(a), (Art 44(13)(a)) should be read as if it said, 'the nature of the offence alleged to be a serious arrestable offence' etc, for the purpose of stating its nature would seem to be to enable the court to determine that it is a serious arrestable offence. Category (b) above would appear to require a resumé of all the matters which collectively led the arresting officer to believe that the person was guilty of the offence or which gave him reasonable grounds for suspecting that he was guilty of it, and would include hearsay, an informant's tip-off etc. This suggests that 'evidence' in s 43(14)(b), (Art 44(13)(b)) should be given its wider, rather than its legal, meaning. As regards category (c), where the ground for the detention up to the application was the need to obtain evidence by questioning, magistrates ought to be aware of the total period of questioning undergone by the suspect during the previous 36 (or 42 hours). Where future inquiries are to be of a similar kind, magistrates may be reluctant to grant a warrant or, if they do, may do so for only a short time, since questioning during the warranted period of detention will almost always be in the presence of a solicitor (36 hours being the maximum period of denial of access) and such questioning is unlikely to be more successful than previous periods when the detainee was denied such access or when the solicitor was also present. What evidence there is suggests that those cases which, before PACE, were said to justify periods of detention of up to or in excess of 96 hours, were cases involving, for example, large conspiracies, or robberies involving several persons which required extensive inquiries of numbers of persons, sometimes some distance away.

Magistrates may well feel constrained to limit authorised detention to such cases and not grant periods of detention simply to permit the police to 'crack' the suspect by long periods of questioning. Section 43(14)(d), (Art 44(13)(d)) requires the reasons to be stated for believing that the continued detention of the person is necessary for the purposes of such further inquiries. This, together with the other material, will enable the court to decide whether the detention is necessary as required by s 43(4)(a), (Art 44(4)(a)). 'Necessary' is an ordinary English word which means that the court must be satisfied that such detention is indispensable to the securing, preserving, or the obtaining of evidence by questioning, and the information provided must be directed to this end.

The standard of proof

6.58 Both s 43(1) and s 44(1), (Arts 44(1) and 45(1)) require that the magistrates' court be *satisfied* that there are *reasonable grounds for believing* that further detention is *justified*. Section 43(4), (Art 44(4)) then lists three specific conditions which must be met by the police in their application (see para 6.55, ante). 'Satisfied' as used in Schedule 1 of the PACE Act 1984 has been held to import the civil standard of proof on the balance of probabilities (*R v Norwich Crown Court, ex p Chethams* (1990)). Given the different context and the fact that the liberty of the individual is concerned there is a strong argument for saying that 'satisfied' as used here should import the criminal standard of proof beyond reasonable doubt.

The application

6.59 The application for a warrant of further detention must be on oath (s 43(1)) (Art 44(1)) and the magistrates' court may not hear such an application unless the person to whom it relates:

(a) has been furnished with a copy of the information (submitted in support of the application); and
(b) has been brought before the court for the hearing. (s 43(2)), (Art 44(2))

The person shall be entitled to be represented at the hearing and, if he is not represented when he is brought before the court, but wishes to be represented, the court shall adjourn the hearing to enable him to obtain representation (s 43(3)(a), Art 44(3)(a)). This must be taken to mean 'adequate representation'. If therefore the solicitor has not had sufficient time to take full instructions the court should consider an adjournment even if the detainee's solicitor is present. Code C para 2.4 states that, when a person leaves police detention *or is taken before a court*, he or his legal representative *shall* be supplied on request with a copy of the custody record as soon as practicable. Solicitors should therefore request a copy of the custody record before a hearing of the application. D may be kept in police detention during the adjournment (s 43(3)(b), Art 44(3)(b)). Such detention (and detention under s 43(6)(a), on a late application) will count towards the overall period of detention and can, it seems, be used by the police for their further inquiries. Where the application is made during an authorised period of detention this may not result in any unfairness to the detainee. For example the application is made after 30 hours of detention, there is a six hours adjournment and the application is refused. D is released or charged more or less on time. If, however, the application is made in the 35th hour, there is a six hours adjournment and the application is refused, D will have been in detention for five hours more than was originally authorised. If then the police use this period for further questioning D, he may feel justifiably aggrieved. On the other hand, if questioning is not permitted during an adjournment and the application is granted, the police investigation may be hampered by such a delay. Where the application is made close to the end of a period of detention the solicitor representing his client will serve his client's interests best by ensuring that any adjournment is as short as possible.

Period of warrant

6.60   If a magistrates' court issues a warrant of further detention it must state the time at which it was issued and it will authorise the keeping in police detention of the person to whom it relates for the period stated in it (s 43(10)), (Art 44(10)). That period may be any period the court thinks fit, having regard to the evidence before it (s 43(11)), (Art 44(11)) but shall not exceed 36 hours (s 43(12)), (Art 44(12)). If it is proposed to transfer the person to another police area the court shall have regard to the distance and the time the journey will take (s 43(13)). In the first edition of this book it was assumed that a warrant of further detention, granted before the expiry of the maximum period of continued detention permitted by s 42, (Art 43), would begin to operate only at the end of that period, that is after 36 hours of police authorised detention. However, it now appears to be accepted that such a warrant begins to operate from the time of issue (see the Home Office Statistical Bulletin 16/89). This does not affect the total period of detention which may be authorised. For example, D has been detained for 24 hours and the maximum period of continued detention under s 42 (Art 43) has been granted. A warrant of further detention is applied for and granted after 30 hours of detention for the maximum period of 36 hours. The warrant takes effect immediately, therefore at its expiry D will have been in police detention for 66 hours. If an extension is sought under s 44, (Art 45) the magistrates' court may extend the warrant up to the maximum permitted period of 96 hours by authorising a further 30 hours. On the expiry of the warrant the person to whom it relates must be charged or released from police detention, either on bail or without bail (s 43(18)), (Art 44(17)), unless an extension of the warrant is granted. A person released under s 43(18), (Art 44(17)) shall not be re-arrested without warrant for the offence for which he was previously arrested unless new evidence justifying a further arrest has come to light since his release (s 43(19), (Art 44(18)) (see also s 41(9), (Art 42(7)) and s 42(11), (Art 43(10)) discussed in para 6.45, ante).

Extension of a warrant of further detention (s 44) (Art 45)

6.61 A warrant of further detention will always expire less than 96 hours after the relevant time (at 60 hours or less if the maximum period is granted to follow the initial 24 hours given that a warrant of further detention takes effect from the time of issue. It will expire after 72 hours, or less, if the maximum period is granted after continued detention under s 42 (Art 43)). A magistrates' court may extend the warrant on application made by a constable. The application must be made in exactly the same way as that under s 43 (Art 44). Thus s 44(6) (Art 45(6)) extends s 43(2), (3) and (14) (Arts 44(2), (3), (13) and (19)) to an application under s 44 (Art 45)). It will be granted if the court is satisfied that there are reasonable grounds for believing that further detention of the person is justified (s 44(1)) (Art 45(1)). Section 43(4) (Art 44(4)) (conditions which must be satisfied before a person's further detention is justified) applies to an application under s 44 (Art 45). An application for an extension can be made to any magistrates' court, as defined in s 45(1), in whose area the person is detained under a warrant of further detention. If, for example, a person so detained is transferred to another police area, a court in that area may hear the application.

Period of extension

6.62 As with the period of a warrant, the period of the extension of a warrant is at the discretion of the court, having regard to the evidence before it (s 44(2)) (Art 45(2)), but it cannot exceed 36 hours or end later than 96 hours after the relevant time (s 44(3)) (Art 45(3)). Where a warrant of further detention has been extended for a period ending before 96 hours after the relevant time, a magistrates' court may extend it again if satisfied that an extension is justified and the conditions in s 43(4) (Art 44(4)) are still satisfied (s 44(4)) (Art 45(4)). Thus, a number of applications for an extension can be made and the court may extend the time so long as it does not exceed 96 hours from the relevant time. For example, 36 hours is granted under the warrant, and on an application for an extension the court grants a further 24 hours. If another application for an extension is made, the court may grant a further period of 12 hours, assuming that no application was made for continued detention under s 42 (ie 24 + 36 + 24 + 12 = 96 hours). No extension of detention without charge is permitted beyond 96 hours from the relevant time. A warrant must be endorsed with a note of the period of any extension (s 44(5)) (Art 45(5)).

Refusal of warrants

Warrant of further detention refused

6.63 If an application for a warrant of further detention is refused, the person to whom the application refers shall forthwith be charged or released, either on bail or without bail (s 43(15)), (Art 44(14)). However, if not charged the person need not be released before the expiry of 24 hours after the relevant time; or before the expiry of any longer period for which his continued detention is or has been authorised under s 42 (s 43(16)), (Art 44(15)) if such detention can be justified by the need to secure, or preserve evidence, or to obtain it by questioning him. The release of the person is then either under s 41(7), (Art 42(5)) (release on the expiry of 24 hours of police detention) and the prohibition on re-arrest for the same offence under s 41(9) (Art 42(7)) applies; or it is under s 42(10), (Art 43(9)) (release on expiry of authorised continued detention) and the prohibition on re-arrest for the same offence under s 42(11), (Art 43(10)) applies. If an application for a warrant of further detention is refused, no further application can be made, unless supported by new evidence which has come to light since the refusal (s 43(17)), (Art 44(16)). The prohibition is clear and specific. A magistrates' court has no discretion to consider a re-application based on evidence which was available before the refusal of the earlier application but which was overlooked. 'Evidence' in this context may also be accorded its wider, ordinary meaning given the nature of the application, which can clearly include matters which may not be admissible as evidence at a trial of the issues.

Extension of a warrant refused

6.64 Section 44(7) (Art 45(7)) requires that where an application for an extension is refused, the person to whom it relates must be charged forthwith or released on bail or without bail. However, as when a warrant of further detention is refused, the person's release is *not* required before the expiry of any period, or any extension of that period, authorised by a warrant of further detention or an earlier application for an extension, which is applicable to him if such detention is still considered necessary to secure, preserve or obtain evidence by questioning (s 44(8)) (Art 45(8)).

Review of police detention (s 40) (Art 41)

6.65 Periodic reviews of the detention of persons in police detention are provided for by s 40 (Art 41) by an officer known as a 'review officer'. (The review officer is also responsible for reviews of detention of suspected terrorists detained under the Prevention of Terrorism (Temporary Provisions) Act 1989, see Sch 3 and para 7.146(d) post). Two types of detention are subject to review, detention before charge and detention after charge. The purpose of the review in both cases is to determine whether the grounds for detention still exist at the time of the review but in each case the grounds for detention are different. To mark the importance of a review of detention without charge, which may be as long as 96 hours, the review officer is an inspector or higher rank not directly involved in the investigation (s 40(1)(b)) (Art 41(1)(b)); in the case of detention after charge it is the custody officer (s 40(1)(a)) (Art 41(1)(a)), though exceptionally such detention may be as long as, or longer than, 96 hours (see para 6.81, post).

Time of reviews

6.66 The first review takes place 6 hours after the detention was first authorised (s 40(3)(a)) (Art 41(3)(a)) in the case of detention without charge, under s 37(3) (Art 38(3)), and in the case of detention after charge, under s 38(2) (Art 39(3)). The second review takes place not later than nine hours after the first (s 40(3)(b)), (Art 41(3)(b)) and subsequent reviews at intervals of not more than nine hours (s 40(3)(c)), (Art 41(3)(c)). In the case of detention before charge, the time from which the period of detention is to be calculated, the relevant time, will be earlier than the time from which the period of six hours for the first review is to be calculated. The former is usually the time of arrival at the first police station to which the arrestee is taken, the latter the time the decision to detain is taken after the evidence has been reviewed. The result is that the first review in the case of a person detained without charge will take place after the person has been in police detention for longer than six hours. For example D arrives at the station at six pm (the relevant time). The evidence is reviewed and his detention is authorised at 7.15 pm. The first review is then due at 1.15 am after 7¼ hours of police detention. The range of 'waiting time' between arrival at a police station and the decision to detain, has been shown to be from 0 minutes to 2 hours 06 minutes in a sample of observed receptions, and from 0 to 57 minutes in a sample of custody records. See McKenzie et al, Helping the Police with their Inquiries [1990] Crim LR 22 at p 26 fn 15.

Postponement of reviews

6.67 A review may be postponed:

(a) if, having regard to all the circumstances prevailing at the latest time (when the review should take place in accordance with s 40(3), (Art 41(3))) it is not practicable to carry out the review at that time; (s 40(4)(a)), (Art 41(4)(a)) or,

(b) without prejudice to the generality of (a), if at that time the person is being questioned by a police officer and the review officer is satisfied that an interruption for the purpose of carrying out the review would prejudice the investigation (s 40(4)(b)(i)), (Art 41(4)(b)(i)) or

(c) if at that time no review officer is readily available (s 40(4)(b)(ii)), (Art 41(4)(b)(ii)).

Section 40(4)(b), (Art 41(4)(b)) gives two specific reasons why it will not be practicable to carry out the review at the stipulated time. The postponement while questioning is going on will not usually be longer than two hours given the Code's provisions requiring breaks normally after two hours or at recognised meal times (COP C, para 12.7). Since a ground for detention without charge is the need to obtain evidence by questioning, a review in the middle of an ongoing interrogation is unlikely to be particularly beneficial to the detainee since the interrogation implies that the ground still exists. Thus from the police viewpoint a review could ruin a period of interrogation by destroying a carefully nurtured psychological atmosphere in which the detainee's belief in his continued detention is an important factor. The provisions of s 76, (Art 74) (admissibility of confessions) and s 78, (Art 76) (exclusion of unfair evidence) must be borne in mind. If a court subsequently decides that the postponement (either alone or with other facts) was unjustified and perhaps used in order to increase the psychological pressure, any confession obtained may be excluded (see further Chapter. 8, post). The duty to record the reasons for postponement (below) could supply evidence for such exclusion. One may note at this point that, while there will normally be little questioning of a person charged and detained, such a person may still be detained under s 128 of the Magistrates' Courts Act 1980, as amended by s 48, for inquiries into other offences and the review requirements under this section apply to such detention (s 128(8)(d). (There is no equivalent power in Northern Ireland). Postponement because there is no review officer available at the time takes account of the possibility that at one extreme the custody officer is at lunch when the review becomes due, to, at the other extreme, an emergency which takes all ranks above inspector out of the police station for a time. Section 30(3), (Art 32(3)) ensures that persons detained for six or more hours will be detained at a designated police station where custody officers must be appointed and which are likely to have a number of senior officers available, thus reducing the likelihood that a review officer will not be available. Numerous examples of more general impracticabilities can arise in a busy police station and in addition the provision in s 45(2), (Art 46) (see para 6.09, ante) that all times are approximate gives a degree of flexibility by, for example, enabling a review to be brought forward before a review officer goes off duty, or to avoid waking a sleeping prisoner (see COP C Note for Guidance 15A).

6.68 If a review is postponed it must be carried out as soon as practicable after the time when it should have been carried out (s 40(5)), (Art 41(5)) and the review officer must record the reason for the postponement in the custody record (s 40(7)), (Art 41(7)). The next review after the postponed review must take place nine hours after the postponed review should have taken place (s 40(6)), (Art 41(6)). Given the range of reviews and entitlement to meals etc, busy police stations may need to use wall charts to monitor each prisoner and delegate one officer whose main task will be to keep an eye on each chart and tell the custody officer or review inspector when action is needed in respect of a particular prisoner.

Purpose of the review

6.69 *(a) Detention of a person not charged* — The duties of a review officer in respect of a person detained without charge are set out in s 37(1) to (6) (Art 38(1) to (6)), (duties of a custody officer before charge) with the substitution of 'review officer' for 'custody officer' and other necessary amendments. The duties are in all respects the same as those of a custody officer under s 37(1) to (6) (Art 38(1) to (6)) when a person first arrives at a police station under arrest (s 40(8)), (Art 41(8)) (see paras 6.20–27, ante). If the review officer determines that there is sufficient evidence to charge the person with the offence for which he is under arrest the custody officer's duty under s 37(7), (Art 38(7)), to charge or release without charge, then arises. Only two reviews will be possible within the first 24 hours and the second review, which must take place before continued detention can be authorised (s 42(4), (Art 43(3)), will often take place closer to the 24 hour deadline than the fifteenth hour of police detention. If the review officer determines that detention must continue after the second review, the custody officer will then have to consider whether an application for continued detention under s 42, (Art 43), or for a warrant of further detention under s 43, (Art 44), should be made. If either application is made and granted, the reviews immediately following such a grant will be somewhat academic but must, nevertheless, take place. The review officer must, of course, be aware of the period of detention authorised and the grounds upon which it was granted.

6.70 *(b) Detention of person not fit to be charged* — The detention of such a person is permitted by s 37(9) (Art 38(9)), and the duty of the review officer (an inspector or above) is to determine whether he is yet in a fit state to be charged (s 40(9)) (Art 41(9)). If the decision is that he is, the custody officer's duty to charge under s 37(7), (Art 38(7)) then arises.

6.71 *(c) Detention of person after charge* — The duties of the review officer (in this case the custody officer) are set out in s 38(1) to (6) (Art 39(1) to (6)) (duties of custody officer after charge) with the substitution of references to the person whose detention is under review for references to 'person arrested' (s 40(10)) (Art 41(10)). Those duties are discussed in paras 6.28–32, ante. If as a result of his review the custody officer determines that the grounds for detention after charge no longer exist, he is then under a duty to order that person's immediate release from custody as required by s 34(2) (Art 35(2)), without bail unless s 34(5)(a) or (b), (Art 35(5)(a) or (b)) apply.

6.72 *Arresting officer senior to the review officer* — Section 40(11) (Art 41(11)) provides for the situation in which the arresting officer is senior to the review officer and he gives instructions which are, or would be, at variance with those of the review officer. The provision is identical with that contained in s 39(6) (Art 40(6)) in respect of custody officers and reference should be made to the discussion in para 6.38, ante where 'review officer' should be substituted for 'custody officer'.

Representations

6.73 The review officer is under the same duty to permit representations to be made to him as is a superintendent who authorises continued detention under s 42 (Art 43). Section 40(12), (13) and (14) (Art 41(12), (13) and (14)) are identical to the duties in s 42(6), (7) and (8) (Art(5), (6) and (7)), discussed in paras 6.48–51, ante, except that there is no duty to give the person such an opportunity if he is asleep. Code C, Note for Guidance 15A states that if the detainee is likely to be asleep when a review or authorisation of continued detention may take place, it should be brought forward so that he may make representations without being woken up. For example, D arrives at a police station at 8.45 am having been arrested for armed robbery (an arrestable offence). His detention without charge is authorised at 9.00 am. The first review takes place at 3.00 pm, the next is due at 12 mn. COP C 12.1 requires that he has eight hours rest, preferably at night, therefore at 12 mn he is likely to be asleep. The review may be brought forward to 10.00 pm to permit an uninterrupted 8 hours sleep. If it is obvious at that time that continued detention beyond the 24 hours permitted by s 41(1) (Art 42(1)) will be required, the authorisation may take place immediately after the second review (assuming it is found that detention without charge is still necessary) (see s 42(4)(b); Art 43(3)(b)). The 24 hour period of detention expires at 8.45 am on the day following D's arrest and the 12 hours (or lesser period) of continued detention commences at that time. A third review is required at the end of the 24 hour period but, in the circumstances, it is something of a formality. Note for Guidance 15C states that if the only practicable way of conducting a review is over the telephone then it is permissible, provided that the requirements of s 40 of the PACE Act 1984 (Art 41 of the PACE (N.I.) Order 1989) and Sch 3 of the Prevention of Terrorism (Temporary Provisions) Act 1989 are complied with. However, a review to decide whether to authorise a person's continued detention under s 42 of the PACE Act must be done in person.

Bail by the police (s 47) (Art 48)

6.74 Where a person is released on bail under this Part of the Act it is to be bail granted in accordance with the Bail Act 1976, except that nothing in that Act shall prevent the re-arrest without warrant of a person, released on bail subject to a duty to attend at a police station, if new evidence justifying a further arrest has come to light since his release (s 47(1), (2)).This exception is necessary since the arrest powers under s 7 of the Bail Act 1976 (preserved by s 26(2) and Sch 2) would not permit re-arrest in such circumstances. (Note that Art 48 is drafted to take account of the provisions of Art 130 of the Magistrates' Courts (Northern Ireland) Order 1981 which deals with bail).

Definition of 'bail'

6.75 'Bail' is defined by s 47(3) (Art 48(1)) as a reference to bail subject to a duty:

(a) to appear before a magistrates' court at such time and such place; or
(b) to attend at such police station at such time, as the custody officer may appoint.

Bail to a court will follow a charge. Bail to return to a police station was under s 43(2) of the Magistrates' Courts Act 1980 (Magistrates' Court (NI) Order 1981), only possible when inquiries into the case could not be completed. Under the 1984 Act (1989 Order) it continues to be possible to bail a person to return to a police station in such circumstances but it is also possible to bail a person to return to a police station when inquiries have been completed and there is sufficient evidence to charge but when there is some doubt either about the particular charge or whether to charge at all (see para 6.18, ante, for a mandatory duty to release on such bail). As suggested in para 6.22, ante, there will be cases which, applying national guidelines, may not be the subject of a prosecution, or which may be dealt with by a caution. Where the decision cannot be made at the time of the person's release, release on bail to return to a police station may be considered appropriate. Where bail has been granted, the custody officer may then give notice in writing to the person that his attendance at the police station is not required (s 47(4)) (Art 48(7)).

Renewed detention of person bailed to return to a police station

6.76 Section 47(5) provides that a person arrested for an offence who is released on bail subject to a duty to appear at a police station, may, when he attends, be detained without charge in connection with that offence only if the custody officer has reasonable grounds for believing that his detention is necessary to secure or preserve evidence relating to that offence, or to obtain such evidence by questioning him. Section 47(5) seeks to provide for the situation in which there is still insufficient evidence to charge the person on his return to the police station in answer to his bail but such evidence may be secured or preserved by his detention, or obtained by questioning during such detention. There is no need to re-arrest the person on his attendance. Section 37(1)(b) requires the custody officer to determine whether there is sufficient evidence to charge a person who returns to a police station to answer to bail. If there is not, the custody officer must release him, or, if there are reasonable grounds for believing that his detention without charge is necessary to secure or preserve evidence relating to the offence or to obtain it by questioning him, the custody officer may authorise his detention without charge (s 37(2) and (3)). Section 47(5) states that where a person released on bail subject to a duty to attend at a police station does so, he may be detained without charge in connection with the offence for which he was arrested and bailed, on grounds which are identical to those contained in s 37(2). Section 47(5) was included in the PACE Bill at a time when s 37(1) did not apply to a person attending at a police station in answer to his bail. Now that it does, s 47(5) would appear to be unnecessary. (It is omitted from Art 48 of the PACE (N.I.) Order 1989). However, s 47(6) states that where a person is detained under s 47(5), any previous period of police detention is to be included in calculating the period of police detention. Since a person attending at a police station to answer to bail may be detained under s 47(5) or s 37(3) and s 47(6) applies only to the former, it would appear possible to deprive such a person of the benefit of s 47(6) by relying on s 37(3) as authority for his detention. That would be clearly contrary to the spirit and intention of the Act. Therefore, all such detentions should be authorised under s 37(3) and s 47(5) or solely under the latter power.

Re-arrest of persons on bail to attend a police station

6.77 Sections 41(9), 42(11) and 43(19) (Arts 42(7), 43(10) and 44(18)) prohibit re-arrest for the offence for which the person was arrested and subsequently released under ss 41(7), 42(10) or 43(18) (Arts 42(5), 43(9) or 44(17)) unless there is new evidence which has come to light since that release. Section 47(2) (Art 48(10)) makes it clear that nothing in the Bail Act 1976 prevents re-arrests. Section 47(7) (Art 48(11)) states that when the re-arrest is of a person who was released on bail subject to a duty to attend at a police station, the provisions of this Part of this Act shall apply to him as they apply to a person arrested for the first time. Thus, if there is new evidence justifying a re-arrest and the person is re-arrested before the date he is to attend the police station, the custody officer must comply with all the duties and requirements relating to detention already considered. He must treat the arrest as any other arrest and determine whether there is sufficient evidence to charge; or, if there is, to charge the person, or release him on bail or without bail, unless there are grounds for detention without charge as set out in s 37(2) (Art 38(2)). Those grounds are identical to those in s 47(5) and if they exist he may authorise detention without charge under s 37(3) (Art 38(3)). All the duties in respect of persons detained then apply. However, unlike a person who attends a police station to answer to bail whose detention is renewed, any previous detention on the first arrest does *not* count toward the period of detention on re-arrest. Since the re-arrest is to be treated as a fresh arrest, the person may be bailed to return to a police station once more if there is still insufficient evidence to charge and no grounds for detention without charge but further inquiries are necessary. On the other hand, there is no provision for further bailing a person who has been bailed to attend a police station and who complies with that duty unless his detention is renewed and he is to be released without charge after that detention.

Re-arrest of a person released without bail

6.78 The provisions for releasing a person arrested or arrested and detained, against whom there is insufficient, or no evidence, to charge, all provide for release on bail (which will be bail to a police station) or without bail. As we have seen, s 47(7) (Art 48(11)) (para 6.77) provides that re-arrest of a person on bail to a police station for the offence for which he is bailed, is to be treated as a fresh arrest. However, there is no similar provision in respect of a person who is released *without* bail, for example, when questioning exonerates him. If new evidence then comes to light which shows that the person was in fact involved in, or responsible for, the offence for which he has been arrested and released, he may be re-arrested. It is not clear whether this is to be considered as a fresh arrest, in which case previous detention does not count, or as a continuation of detention, in which case it does. In principle such previous detention ought to be counted, otherwise it gives the police two bites at the cherry. On the other hand, the same argument applies to the re-arrest of a person on bail and it would therefore appear that such an arrest will be treated as a fresh arrest. This may be justifiable where there is a considerable time gap between arrests but it could result in a person who is detained for, say 36 hours, being released for lack of evidence or because he is exonerated, and within another 36 hours being re-arrested for the same offence on the discovery of new evidence. On this occasion, the full 96 hours detention might be authorised, resulting in 132 hours of police detention in respect of that offence. The unfairness suggested must, however, be balanced by the alternative possibility that a person is arrested for a serious arrestable offence, detained for the full 96 hours and released for lack of evidence. If then new evidence justifying his re-arrest is discovered and the Act provided that previous detention for that offence had to be included in calculating the period of detention, there would be no point in arresting unless there was sufficient evidence to charge. Such a provision could seriously hamper investigations. That alone is sufficient to justifying treating such a re-arrest as a fresh arrest. It is submitted that a senior officer who is asked to authorise continued detention, and a magistrates' court to whom an application for a warrant of further detention is made, should be made aware of any period of police detention in respect of the offence for which the person has been re-arrested and in respect of which authorised detention is sought.

Section 43 of the Magistrates' Courts Act 1980

6.79　Section 43 of the Magistrates' Courts Act 1980 previously governed bail by the police. As we have seen (para 6.74), bail to a court or a police station is now governed by the PACE Act. However, s 47(8) re-enacted those parts of the previous s 43 which are still relevant. Section 43(1) of the 1980 Act (as substituted by s 47(8)) provides that where a person is granted bail under the PACE Act to appear before a magistrates' court, that court may appoint a later date for his appearance and enlarge the recognisances of any sureties for him. Section 43(2) of the 1980 Act, as substituted, provides that a recognisance of a surety in respect of such bail may be enforced as if it were a recognisance in respect of bail to a magistrates' court (see the Bail Act 1976). Art 48(5) of the 1989 Order makes similar provision in N. Ireland.

Warrants endorsed for bail

6.80　Section 117 of the Magistrates' Courts Act 1980 provides that when magistrates issue a warrant of arrest they may grant the person bail by endorsing the warrant. In criminal proceedings the endorsement will state that the person is to be released on bail subject to a duty to appear before a magistrates' court at the specified time, and in non-criminal cases, that he is to be released on entering into a recognisance (with or without sureties) conditioned for his appearance before a magistrates' court at the specified time. Where a warrant is endorsed for bail on the person entering into a recognisance without sureties, it is not necessary to take him to a police station if he agrees to a recognisance. It could be effected literally on the doorstep but the previous law did not permit this sensible approach. Section 47(8) of the PACE Act amended s 117(3) of the 1980 Act to permit 'doorstep bail' by providing that in such a case a person need not be taken to a police station, but, if he is, he shall be released on his entering into the recognisance (s 117(3)(a)). Section 117(3)(b) covers the situation in which the endorsement provides for bail with sureties which requires that the person be taken to a police station. (Art 48(12) amended Article 129 of the Magistrates' Courts (Northern Ireland) Order 1981 to produce the same effect in the province).

Detention for inquiries into other offences

6.81 Section 128(7) of the Magistrates' Courts Act 1980 permitted a magistrates' court which had decided to remand a person in custody, to commit him to the custody of a constable for a period not exceeding three clear days. Though it was legally possible to remand a person arrested but not charged with an offence, the practice was to charge the person with one offence, a 'holding charge', and seek a remand in police custody to enable him to be questioned about more substantive offences. In some areas the remand to police custody was used to permit local solicitors to see their client before he went off to a remand prison many miles away. Both were permissible since no purpose was specified in the section. Section 48 amended s 128(7) to permit a magistrates' court which has decided to remand a person in custody after applying criteria laid down in the Bail Act 1976, to commit him to detention in a police station for a period not exceeding three clear days (ie three days must intervene between the day of the remand and the day the person is due to appear in court again). Section 128(8), then stipulates that:

(a) he shall be detained under sub-s (7) only if there is a need for such detention for the purpose of inquiries into other offences;
(b) he be brought back to the court which committed him as soon as that need ceases;
(c) he is to be treated as in police detention and s 39 of the 1984 Act applies to him; and
(d) his detention is subject to periodic review under s 40 of the 1984 Act.

The first review will take place six hours after the court authorises detention and the second nine hours after that and thereafter at nine hourly intervals. The review officer in this case is the custody officer since the suspect has already been *charged* once (s 40(1)(a) therefore applies, even though he has been detained for inquiries into other offences with which he is not charged). The officer must determine whether the need to detain for further inquiries still exists. If it does not the detainee must be taken back before the magistrates court which committed him (s 128(8)(b)). The practical effect of this section is that, to take an extreme case, a person may be detained for 96 hours without charge, charged and detained in custody after charge under s 38(1) and (2) for 48 hours awaiting appearance before a magistrates' court. He is then committed by that court to police detention for inquiries into other offences and detained for the three clear days, giving an overall total of 216 hours detention. Though s 128(6) of the MCA Act 1980 prohibits, subject to limited exceptions, the remand of a person in custody for more than eight clear days, it appears that repeated remands may be made under s 128(7) which may in total exceed this period. Thus we are aware of a case in which D, having been charged with burglary, was remanded in police custody under s 128(7) three times, resulting in nine clear days detention beyond that permitted by the PACE Act (Order). This led to the admission by D of 130 other burglaries. The requirement under s 31 that the person in police detention be arrested for further offences which come to light during such detention will mean that this provision will be used to clear up offences which the person may have committed in the police area in which he is detained or elsewhere (cf *R v Holmes, ex p Sherman* (1981)). There is no equivalent provision in Northern Ireland.

Police detention to count towards any custodial sentence

6.82 The actual time spent in prison following a sentence of imprisonment is determined by the Home Secretary's power to release prisoners. For these purposes, in computing the length of a sentence, any time spent in custody before trial or sentence is included (s 67(1) of the Criminal Justice Act 1967, s 26 of the Treatment of Offenders Act (Northern Ireland) 1968). Section 49 of the 1984 Act (Art 49) amended s 67(1), (s 26) and extends it to include periods spent in police detention under the 1984 Act (1989 Order) and any detention under s 14 of the Prevention of Terrorism (Temporary Provisions) Act 1989. Art 49 of the 1989 Order makes similar provision in N. Ireland.

Records of detention (s 50) (Art 50)

6.83 Section 50(1) (Art 50(1)) requires that each police force (the Chief Constable of the RUC) keep written records of detention for more than 24 hours resulting in release without charge, and of warrants of further detention applied for, the result, the period spent in detention under each warrant, and the subsequent disposition of the person. Section 50(2), (Art 50(2)) requires that this minimal information be included in the annual report of the chief officer under s 12 of the Police Act 1964 (s 15(1) of the

Police Act (N.I.) 1970) and in the annual report of the Commissioner of Police of the Metropolis. The information is also published in Home Office Statistical Bulletins quarterly and annually.

Savings

6.84   Section 51 (Art 51) provides that the provisions in Part IV of the PACE Act do not affect detention under the statutory authorities listed in that section. These relate to detention of illegal immigrants, persons excluded under terrorism provisions, absentees, deserters and the like (s 51, Art 51(a) (b) and (c)). Section 51(d), (Art 51(d)) emphasises that nothing in Part IV of the Act (Part V of the Order) affects the right of a person *to apply* for a writ of habeas corpus or other prerogative remedy. However, the provisions in Part IV have meant that detention is lawfully permitted for longer periods than previously and those remedies are therefore much less effective in securing the release of persons detained.

7 Treatment and questioning of persons in police detention

7.01 As Part IV of the PACE Act 1984 (Part V of the Order) recognises, the questioning of suspects by the police at police stations plays an important part in the detection of crime. It may produce a confession which then forms the kernel of the prosecution case (Research Study No 5 for the Royal Commission (1981) found that 50 per cent of defendants made a written or oral confession and that in about 20 per cent of cases a confession was regarded as critical to the success of the prosecution); it may lead to the discovery of evidence; it may produce confessions to other crimes and thus improve the detection rate of the police force; and in any event it is likely to save police time. Lest police powers of questioning be misused, the procedure for the treatment of those in detention assumes great importance. Part V of PACE (Part VI, Order) and three Codes of Practice are relevant to the procedures to be followed at police stations. The Code C relating to the Detention, Treatment and Questioning of Persons by Police Officers is the most important and, unless otherwise indicated, **references to the Code in this chapter are to that one.** Code D deals with the Identification of Persons by Police Officers (see para 7.66, post) and Code E with Tape Recording (see para 8.22, post). In addition, there are several Home Office Circulars issued to all police forces as and when the need for guidance arises and each force has its own Standing Orders which supplement the foregoing. This and chapter 8 trace the law and procedures to be applied to a person from the time of his arrival at a police station to the time of his departure or of him being charged. The 'normal' case is considered first before turning to some special categories (eg 'volunteers', the mentally ill, juveniles). This chapter deals predominantly with the treatment of a suspect and chapter 8 with his questioning, although inevitably there are overlaps.

7.02 The following preliminary points should be noted. First, Part V of PACE (Part VI, Order) and the Code of Practice for the Detention, Treatment and Questioning of Persons by the Police, must be read together. Indeed, there are matters contained in the latter which are arguably of sufficient importance to have merited inclusion in the former (eg the duty to *tell* the detainee of his rights). Second, both documents must be read with sections 76 and 78 in mind (Arts 74 and 76). The former directs the trial court to exclude a confession which has been obtained by oppression or which is unreliable (see further chapter 8). The latter empowers the court to exclude evidence if the court believes that its reception would be unfair (see further, para 8.67, post). Caselaw reveals that the courts pay close attention to the Code when considering the sections. Third, the Code in part paraphrases the provisions of the Act, but in part also supplements them. It is thus important for copies of the Code to be readily available to those in detention and for police officers to be fully acquainted with its provisions. Fourth, the 'Annexes' are to be treated as part of the Code, whereas the 'Notes for Guidance' in the Code mean just that (COP, para 1.3). Fifth, in spite of the great importance of the Code, it is important to remember that it does not have the same force as a statute and that, whilst courts must consider it, they need not follow it. Sixth, the Act and the Code require that certain information be conveyed to the suspect (eg the grounds for detention, s 37(5), Art 38(5)). This duty does not arise if it is impossible to perform eg where the suspect is violent or is in urgent need of medical attention. There are two general safeguards designed to protect the citizen's rights and to guarantee good police conduct viz. documentation and the supervisory role of the custody officer.

Documentation

7.03   PACE and the Codes of Practice accepted the opinion of the Royal Commission that strict recording of what takes place between the police officer and citizen is a critical safeguard for both parties. Consequently, frequent provision is made for recording in writing the length and terms of a person's detention. Two records are used: a custody record which deals with the general conditions of detention; and a record which relates solely to the officer's interview of a suspect.

7.04   (a) *Custody records* — As soon as practicable after being detained at a police station (by being arrested there or taken there under arrest), a person must be allotted a custody record and the grounds for his detention must be recorded in it. The custody officer assumes responsibility for completing the record fully, accurately and as soon as practicable (s 39 (Art 40) and COP, paras 2.1 and 2.3). If a senior officer's permission is required for any action (eg for the taking of a non-intimate sample under s 1 Art 63), his name and rank should be recorded. If the suspect is moved to another police station, the custody record (or preferably a copy) goes with him and the time of and reason for the transfer must be recorded in it. This may be very important for calculating the 'relevant time' in relation to the permissible periods of detention, when D is arrested by police force A and held for some time before being transferred to force B (see para 6.40, ante). The time of the suspect's release must be recorded and this may also be crucial in determining whether the detention time limits have been observed. Indeed all entries into the custody record must be timed and signed (or the warrant number of the relevant officer when he is dealing with a suspect detained under the Prevention of Terrorism legislation, COP, paras 2.2, 2.6) and, if the suspect is required to sign the record but refuses, the fact and time of refusal must be recorded (COP, para 2.7). Hence the custody record will be a critical document at trial if a dispute develops over D's treatment (especially if D was unrepresented at the station). A properly completed record will be strong evidence in a s 76 or 78 argument (Arts 74, 76). At the end of detention, when the person is released or taken before a court, he or his lawyer should be given a copy of the custody record 'as soon as practicable', *if he so requests* (COP, para 2.4). Although a custody record must contain a number of items, none is difficult to state and can be completed promptly. Consequently, if a person is taken before a court, there can be no excuse for not supplying a copy before the appearance. Many of those released from detention, on bail or otherwise, will not demand a copy (through ignorance or lack of interest). However, like stop and search records (s 3(7), (9), Art 5(8), (9)), a copy of a custody record is available for 12 months after the person has been released. There may be occasions when the authenticity of the copy or the accuracy of the original record are disputed. Consequently the detained person or his representative must be allowed to inspect the original custody record after giving reasonable notice. The shape and design of custody records vary between police forces but the required content is uniform.

7.05 (b) *Interview records* — Many interviews at police stations with suspects are now tape recorded and there are elaborate procedures governing the security of tapes so that an accurate record is available (see further para 8.22, post). In addition the interviewing officer must note the formal details of the interview (time, date etc) in his notebook (COP, E para 5.1). The notebook and tapes then represent the interview record. Interviews which are not taped must be written down in an interview record. This covers all non-taped interviews with suspects, for example, those conducted at a hospital or in a police car. The record must state the place, time and length of the interview, any breaks in it, the names of those present and, if different, the time when the record was made. For interviews outside a police station, an officer's pocketbook can be used; for those at a station, special record forms are used. The record must be made simultaneously unless:

(a) it is impracticable to do so, eg through violence on the part of the suspect; or

(b) it 'would interfere with the conduct of the interview' (COP, para 11.5(c)), eg the suspect is unlikely to be forthcoming if the officer produces a record form and begins formalities. This may be reasonable for the occasional, urgent interviews in the street but cannot, it is suggested, be a justifiable excuse for interviews in the already formal atmosphere of a police station. The matters to be recorded are straightforward and officers should get into the habit of compiling an interview record simultaneously in all cases, especially since the interview may be challenged subsequently and a trial court asked to exclude a confession obtained during it (see further on interviews at para 8.07, post).

Custody Officer

7.06   The custody officer has already been described (see para 6.10, ante), suffice it to say here that he is responsible for much of the documentation and is in overall charge of the reception, treatment and welfare of a suspect. At a busy station he or a junior officer will spend most of his time with an eye on the 'detention clock' to ensure that statutory procedures are followed in relation to each detainee. Moreover, the categories of persons who may be at the station add to the complexity facing him viz. (1) 'volunteers' (those helping the police but free to leave, see further paras 5.44 to 49, ante), (2) those who have been arrested, detained but not charged, (3) those charged but not bailed, and (4) those in custody but not necessarily arrested for an offence (eg detained under Mental Health Act or Immigration Act powers). Research (Maguire, 1988) suggests that the custody officer can process (eg prepare a custody record, search a person and record his property, arrange for legal advice) between 3 and 4 suspects per hour but that beyond that extra custody officers are needed or a queue will develop. But even this apparently modest suggestion presupposes that the cases are straightforward (eg there are no requirements for interpreters, a strip search, or medical help) and run smoothly (eg a solicitor can be contacted immediately) and that the custody officer is not also the operations sergeant and is called away to deal with those matters. On the other hand, the type of arrests (eg regular vagrants or drunks) can greatly quicken the number of suspects dealt with. In contrast, at non-designated stations the problem is to find a suitable officer to act as a custody officer. Given his position of responsibility, the custody officer must receive the suspect in strict accordance with PACE, and 'play it by the book'. If he records everything with reasons, he cannot go wrong. This does not, however, necessitate heavy handed formality. Indeed such an attitude will be inappropriate for most suspects. For the vulnerable suspect (eg an elderly shoplifter) the answer is for the custody officer to do his job humanely (eg allowing the suspect to sit, explaining why he has to fill in the forms, relying on a brief search of the suspect or no search at all).

Initial Action

7.07 Those who are detained at a designated police station (either by being taken there under arrest or by being arrested there) will appear before an appointed custody officer. A custody record should be opened at once. The first decision for him to make is whether the person should be charged or released or detained with or without charge (see s 37 (Art 38) and para 6.20, ante). If the person is charged, release on bail has to be considered. If he is detained, the custody officer must tell him the grounds for detention as soon as is practicable (see below). The custody officer's decision at this stage will be determined by the information given to him by the arresting/investigating officer. Practice varies as to the extent of this exchange, some police forces strictly limiting conversation, others allowing a full account of the circumstances to be relayed to the custody officer. For him to reach a reasoned decision it is suggested that at least an outline of the circumstances of, and reasons for, the arrest be given him. There is an understandable temptation for the custody officer to ask the suspect questions such as 'did you do it?' or 'what have you got to say for yourself?', and in such ways begin a conversation with him. The danger is that he then begins to assume the role of an investigator and his proper role as supervisor of the suspect's well-being is compromised. The Code is silent on the subject but it is wise practice for the custody officer to restrict his comments to the tasks which PACE and the Codes require of him and certainly not for him to initiate tangential conversation. For otherwise the conversation becomes an interview for PACE purposes, the caution is not given, the suspect is not read his rights in time, a contemporaneous record of the conversation is not made and a court subsequently uses s 78 (Art 76) of PACE to exclude as unfair any admission which D has made to the custody officer (see *R v Absolam* (1989)). If D volunteers information or makes a relevant remark to the custody officer, it should be noted in the custody record and D asked to read and sign it (COP, para 11.13).

7.08 Either from what another officer tells him or from his own observation, the custody officer will have at this stage to consider whether the person falls into one of the categories for which separate provision is made ie whether an interpreter has to be called because of the person's language difficulties or deafness, or whether an 'appropriate adult' has to be called to witness the interviewing of a juvenile or the mentally ill or handicapped or whether medical assistance has to be summoned (see para 7.106, post for discussion of these groups). The investigating officer may decide instead to question such a person at once and in the absence of the third party. In that case, the permission of a more senior officer (superintendent or above) must be obtained (COP, Annex C; see para 8.21, post). Given the serious evidential

7.08 *Treatment and questioning of persons in police detention*

consequences (see chapter 8) which can flow from a person in one of these special categories being improperly treated, the vigilance of the custody officer in spotting them cannot be overstated.

7.09 If the custody officer decides to detain the suspect in custody, he must tell him (or the 'appropriate adult' where relevant) of the following matters (COP, paras 3.1–4):

   (i)   his right to inform a third party of his detention (see para 7.33);
   (ii)   his right to free legal advice in private (see para 7.41);
   (iii) his right to consult the Codes of Practice;
   (iv)   his right, if a foreigner, to inform his diplomatic representatives (see para 7.133);
   (v)   if the suspect is to be detained, the grounds for the detention. The custody officer may not be in a position to authorise detention until he has heard from the investigating officer. Once he is ready, however, he must inform the suspect as soon as practicable and note the grounds in the custody record (s 37(4), (5), Art 38(4), (5)). So, if, for example, D is arrested and taken in a drunk or violent state to a police station and the custody officer decides to authorise detention, D must be told of the grounds for detention after he comes to his senses and before questioning begins. In any event the grounds must be communicated before a suspect is questioned.

Items (i) to (iii) (and by implication (iv) and (v)) must be conveyed 'clearly' to the suspect (COP, para 3.1). This change to COP in 1991 is aimed at avoiding the mumbled or rapid reading of rights which can mean little to the individual. It also assists the custody officer in gauging whether the suspect falls within one of the special groups (eg a foreign citizen, the deaf). If the suspect is not in a position to comprehend the rights (eg he is drunk, ill, violent, or of foreign tongue), they must be repeated when he is (COP, para 1.8); and it is important for the custody officer to remember this. Under the earlier COP the custody officer had to tell D that he need not exercise his (i)–(iv) rights immediately. This could be a further disincentive to him using them and so the 1991 COP requires the officer to tell him that 'they are continuing rights which may be exercised at any stage during the period in custody' (para 3.1). Whether this subtle modification will alter practice will depend, inter alia, on how encouragingly the custody officer gives the information, on whether D subsequently remembers it and, if he does, how readily an officer responds. As will be seen items (i) and (ii) can be denied to a suspect by a senior officer in certain circumstances for up to 36 hours (see para 7.36, post), but this does not absolve the custody officer from the duty of telling D of his rights at the outset. Quite apart from the foregoing oral notification of his rights, the suspect must be given two written notices by the custody officer which he can then read in the cell. Properly done, the oral and written notifications should be separate. The first repeats items (i) to (iii) above and also sets out D's right to a copy of the custody record, the arrangements for obtaining legal advice (ie that D can seek his own solicitor or use the free duty solicitor scheme) and the caution. The second is a notice of his entitlements under the COP (a prisoners' rights leaflet) such as the physical conditions of his detention and the arrangements for interview. There should be notices in English, Welsh, the principal EEC and the main ethnic languages (the last being dependent on the local demography). A photocopy of the relevant pages from a book of translations can be taken and given to the suspect (but the range of translations can be quite limited). The suspect is asked to acknowledge receipt of these notices by signing the custody record and, if he refuses, the custody officer must note the refusal on the record (COP, para 3.2). If an interpreter is needed, he will be used to convey the foregoing information. If D is blind or unable to read (eg illiterate, dyslexic), the written notices are useless (there is no requirement that copies in braille are available) and the custody officer must instead ensure that a third party is 'available to help in checking any documentation' (COP para 3.14). Liberally interpreted this should require a third party's early presence so as to read the notices to D. The most appropriate person is a solicitor. Indeed, a further and *crucial* matter at this initial stage is for the custody officer to ask D to sign on the custody record whether he wants legal advice (COP, para 3.5). As will be seen, the way in which this question is put can significantly affect D's answer (see further on legal advice, para 7.41).

7.10 The reading of rights and the provision of written notices, if properly done (and this includes allowing D sufficient time to digest the information), offer considerable protection to the suspect. On the other hand, research has frequently shown (eg Sanders et al (1988) in relation to legal advice, see para 7.44, post) that the fact that a person is told of his rights by no means indicates that he will exercise them.

Search of the person at a police station (ss 53–55, (Arts 54–56) COP section 4, Annex A)

7.11 All statutory and common law powers to search a person who has been arrested and who is in detention at a police station were abolished by section 53(1)(a) of PACE (Art 54(1)(a), N.I. Order) and replaced by section 54 (Art 55). All intimate search powers (save for an exception for customs) were abolished by s 53(1)(b) (Art 54(1)(b)) and replaced by s 55 (Art 56). Very occasionally a person who has been stopped under section

1 (Art 3) will be taken to a police station 'nearby' (s 2(8), Art 4(9)) in order to be searched. Since he is not under arrest and therefore not in police detention (s 118(2), Art 2(3)), a non-intimate search cannot be undertaken under s 54 (Art 55) (below). Similarly a strip or intimate search can only be authorised after he has been arrested (S 55, Art 56 and COP, Annex A only apply to detained, ie arrested, persons). The vast majority of searches will be of those arrested. For this purpose a distinction is drawn between intimate and non-intimate searches. The former is defined as a search consisting of 'the physical examination of a person's body orifices' (s 118(1), Art 2(2)), and is governed by s 55 (Art 56) and COP, Annex A. A 'body orifice' covers the ears, mouth, nose, rectum and vagina. A non-intimate search covers all other types of search from a 'pat down' to a strip search and is governed by s 54 (Art 55).

(1)   Non-intimate searches (s 54, Art 55 COP, Annex A)

7.12   Three purposes may lie behind the search of a person detained at a police station:

(a)   to discover evidence of the offence for which the person was arrested or of other offences;

(b)   to compile a written record of the person's possessions so as to avoid any subsequent allegations of planting of evidence by the police or of misappropriation of property;

(c)   to remove articles with which the person may cause injury to others or to himself or with which he may effect an escape. This is a particularly important precaution, given the possibility that a person in detention may seek to take his own life, and the often adverse publicity which such deaths can cause.

Power to search

7.13   Unlike the previous law, s 54 (Art 55) does not refer to the purpose of a search and avoids references to reasonableness. Instead, searches of detained persons at police stations are undertaken *in order to discover what the suspect has with him* both on arrival at the station and during the period of his detention (for search of the person after arrest and *before* arrival at a police station, see s 32 (Art 34) and para 5.58, ante). Articles discovered may then be seized and retained in certain circumstances. Thus, the custody officer is under a duty to ascertain everything which a person in police detention (eg a person who is released on bail but then detained on his return to the station, a person detained under s 135 or 136 of the Mental Health Act 1983) or custody (following a court order) has with him (s 54(1) (Art 55(1)). The power of search is available at any time during D's detention (eg after he has been visited, after he has been in a public area of the station) but he can only be searched a second time for articles with which he can cause harm or his escape (s 54(6A), added by the Criminal Justice Act 1988, Art 55(7) of the N.I. Order). The tasks of seizing and recording articles can be delegated (s 54(1), (3), Art 55(1)(3)), but the section requires the custody officer personally to 'ascertain' the articles. It may seem unrealistic to expect such an officer, who will have many other duties, to ascertain the possessions of each arrested person (eg where a large number of arrested football supporters reach the police station). On the other hand, the custody officer does bring a measure of independence to the investigation and occupies a close supervisory role. Consequently, he decides whether the suspect should be searched and if so, the extent of the search (s 54(6), Art 55(6)); and what articles may be seized and retained (s 54(3), (4), Art 55(3), (4)); and he is responsible for the safe keeping of any seized articles (COP, para 4.1).

7.14 In the majority of cases the detained person will voluntarily turn out his pockets. For those who refuse, reasonable force can be used at the instruction of the custody officer (s 117, Art 88). The custody officer must then decide whether the person should be searched more thoroughly. Since he may know little about the suspect and since it is difficult to predict accurately a person's reaction to custody, for example, the danger he may pose to himself or others unless searched, s 54(6) (Art 55(6)) errs on the side of caution by leaving it to the judgment of the custody officer as to:

(a) whether the person should be searched. Thus, any of the purposes behind a search, mentioned in para 7.12 ante, can be fulfilled.
(b) the extent of a search. This is left to his discretion and can vary from the emptying of pockets to a frisking or to a strip search (but not an intimate search for which s 55 (Art 56) applies and the authorisation of a more senior officer is needed, see para 7.20, post).

This lack of specificity in the statute allows considerable scope for police force standing orders to spell out when the custody officer should act eg that 'all suspects shall be searched' as a matter of routine. But it has been decided that the rationale behind *Brazil v Chief Constable of Surrey* (1983) still applies ie the officer cannot search automatically but has to consider each case on its merits (*Sheehan v Metropolitan Police Commissioner* (1990)). The COP suggests that where D will only be detained for a short time a search may be unnecessary as opposed to the case where it is clear that 'the custody officer will have continuing duties in relation to that person or where that person's behaviour or offence makes an inventory appropriate' (Notes for Guidance, 4A). Whether he searches or not, it is still the statutory duty (s 54(1), Art 55(1)) of the custody officer to ascertain the detainee's possessions, and it is clearly the custody officer's decision in the final analysis as to whether a search is necessary in the particular circumstances. This may arise from the nature of the offence involved and hence the ease of concealment of evidence (eg drugs); the reaction and demeanour of the detained person when asked to empty his pockets (eg a terrified old lady arrested for shoplifting need not be searched); the custody officer's knowledge of the detained person (eg a well known thief specialising in credit cards). Moreover, it can take only one incident of violence at the station for custody officers to honour *Sheehan* more in the breach by ordering routine searches, on a 'seize rather than leave' policy.

Strip searches

7.15 There is a danger that this discretion to search could be used to order a strip search (ie the removal of more than outer clothing, COP Annex A, para 5) so as to humiliate and oppress the detained person. Three safeguards operate. Firstly, Annex A to the COP, makes it clear that a strip search is only allowed if the custody officer believes it to be necessary in order to seize an article which a person is not allowed to keep (eg weapons, evidence of an offence; see the grounds for seizure in s 54(4) Art 55(5), discussed below). Secondly, and more importantly, the custody officer is independent of the investigating officers. Much rests upon his integrity and good sense. Thirdly, his decision, though subjective, must still be taken in good faith. Thus, a strip search undertaken mala fides, for example, 'for the fun of it' or to frighten the suspect, would be unlawful and a trespass to the person. Quite apart from risking a complaint of civil action, such misbehaviour might well persuade a trial judge to exclude evidence under ss 76, 78 (Arts 74, 76). Crucially, the reasons for ordering a strip search and the result of it must be recorded in writing (Code of Practice, Annex A).

The search

7.16 A non-intimate search under s 54 must be carried out by a constable (s 54(8), Art 55(11)) of the same sex as the person to be searched (s 54(9), Art 55(12)). If the suspect is a transvestite, then in order to avoid the exclusion of evidence under ss 76, 78 (Arts 74, 76), it is suggested that D's wishes as to the gender of the officer be respected and noted (preferably signed by D) in the custody record. Reasonable force may be used if necessary (s 117, Art 88), but the custody officer should be alert to the dangers of excessive force being used against the obdurate, but frail, detained person, especially since the issue may later be raised under ss 76 and 78 (Arts 74, 76) and a court asked to exclude evidence which has been improperly obtained (see further para 2.44, ante). Circumstances will vary considerably as to the extent of the search. For a person arrested for theft of radios, a 'pat down' and examination of pockets and wallets should suffice. Indeed, the suspect will often cooperate by producing articles and obviating the need for a search. For a suspected drug pusher, on the other hand, a strip search is likely to be routine and the possibility of an intimate search (see para 7.20, post) should be considered.

Seizure

7.17 Any articles produced by the suspect or discovered during a search may be seized and retained by the custody officer or at his direction (s 54(3), Art 55(3)). The only potential limitation concerns clothing and personal effects. These can only be seized if the custody officer believes that any of the criteria in s 54(4) (Art 55(4)) is satisfied. Thus, they cannot be seized for an ulterior purpose such as to punish the person (for example, by seizure of his glasses). The reasons for any seizure must be explained to D and should be noted in the custody record (COP, para 4.2, 4.5). 'Personal effects' are not defined but may well be delimited by force standing orders. They can include a handkerchief, comb, watch, spectacles, keys and cosmetics. It will be noted that all such items may readily be seized under s 54 eg bootlaces, belts (sub-s (4)(e)(i)); heavy boots, a cigarette lighter (sub-s (4)(a)(ii)); clothing which may be of forensic value (sub-s 4(a)(iii)); keys, sharpened comb (sub-s (4)(e)(iv)); a handkerchief for traces of drugs (sub-s (4)(b)). Although injury may be self-inflicted by the glass component, it is submitted that watches and spectacles ought not in principle to be seized (unless the custody officer has grounds to suspect their misuse). The former are especially important for the detained person in view of the time limits imposed on his detention by Part IV of PACE and the periodic reviews of detention which the police must conduct (see paras 6.65–7.3, ante), whilst the latter enable him to read the notices of rights which he has been given (see COP, para 4.3). The COP (para 4.3) excludes 'cash and other items of value' (eg jewellery) from personal effects, on the basis of self-protection for the police against allegations that such property has been misappropriated. This does not mean that a wedding or other ring or small earrings *have* to be seized. Their existence can simply be noted in the custody record. On the other hand, the volume of suspects may mean that the accurate recording of jewellery is impracticable.

7.18 Two clear qualifications apply to the power of seizure. Firstly, items which the constable has reasonable grounds to believe are subject to legal privilege cannot be seized (s 19(6), Art 21(6)). Secondly, one aspect of the common law (*Brazil v Chief Constable of Surrey* (1983)) is retained by s 54(5) (Art 55(5)) viz a detained person shall be told the reason for the seizure unless this is impracticable because he is violent or unable to understand it. The ratio of *Christie v Leachinsky* (1947), in relation to arrest, is thus relevant for the seizure of property.

Post search

7.19   A custody record must be kept of what the person had with him when he arrived at the police station under arrest or when he was arrested there. This includes the recording of property which has been seized (under s 32, Art 34) by the arresting officer away from the police station (COP para 4.4). The purpose and extent of the search need not be recorded unless a strip search is undertaken. Then, the custody officer must record the reason for it and its results (COP, Annex A, para 8). The detained person 'shall be allowed' to check and sign the record of what has been seized (COP, para 4.4). This implies that he will do so only if he asks to see the record, but it is wise practice for the custody officer always to request the detained person to sign the record. If he refuses, a note of that refusal should be made. Items seized under s 54 (Art 55) can be retained for 'so long as is necessary' (s 22(1), Art 24(1) eg as evidence, for forensic purposes, or to prevent injury (see the illustrations in s 22(2) and (3), Art 24(2), (3)). Details of the property seized must be given to the magistrates' court when the case comes before it (s 48 of the Magistrates' Courts Act 1980). The court may order the return of all or part of the property to the accused if this is in the interests of justice and his safe custody. Ideally the custody record should also note what property was retained by the suspect, what property was kept by the police, and whether property was subsequently taken from, or given to, the suspect during his detention. In other words it should be a complete history of what has happened to the suspect's property during his stay at the station. If another officer has searched him, then the custody record should bear three signatures — the suspect, the searching officer and the custody officer.

(2)   Intimate search (s 55, Art 56 COP, Annex A)

7.20   An intimate search, as opposed to a strip search, means the searching of a 'body orifice' (ie the ears, mouth, nose, rectum and vagina). It was not clear whether the common law permitted the intimate search of a person's body without the person's consent. Such searches did, however, take place, either under the supposed common law or under the general wording of statute, principally the search power in the Misuse of Drugs Act 1971 (s 23(2)). The first version of the Police and Criminal Evidence Bill allowed intimate searches for two purposes — to discover articles which might be used to cause injury (protective purpose) or to discover evidence (investigative purpose). On reflection, the Government felt that the evidential value of such searches was outweighed by their controversial and disagreeable nature and the investigative purpose was omitted in the second version. This meant that in some cases a determined criminal could evade conviction by concealing evidence of a crime (for example, drugs) in a body orifice. Public concern in 1984 at the increasing incidence of heroin addiction and references to a 'drug pushers' charter' led to the reintroduction to the Bill of the investigative purpose of an intimate search. Section 55 (Art 56) placed intimate searches on a firm statutory basis. The preconditions are understandably stricter than those adopted in s 54 (Art 55) for non-intimate searches and the criterion of reasonableness is specifically adopted.

The power

7.21   An officer of at least superintendent rank can authorise an intimate search if he has reasonable grounds to believe that:

(a)   the detained person may have concealed articles which could be used to injure himself or others; or

(b)   the detained person may have concealed Class A drugs with the intention of supplying those drugs to others or of exporting them.

The powers of the Customs and Excise to undertake an intimate search for evidential purposes (s 164 of the Customs and Excise Management Act 1979) are not affected by s 55, but a statutory order (1985) has conferred on Customs the protective power of s 55(1)(a) ie allowed Customs to search additionally for weapons. Intimate searches are not regular occurrences (eg only 62 were recorded in England and Wales in 1988, 50 in 1989 and 51 in 1990). Indeed 29 police forces failed to record a single use in 1990. Their success rate is also very low (only 4 out of 51 searches in 1990).

7.22   The articles in s 55(1)(a) (Art 56(1)(a)) range from a penknife to poison. As to s 55(1)(b) (Art 56(1)(b)), Class A drugs are listed in Sch 2 to the Misuse of Drugs Act 1971. Although heroin is the primary target, the list includes 85 different drugs. Less dangerous drugs in Classes B and C of the 1971 Act cannot therefore be the object of an intimate search. They include amphetamine, cannabis and codeine. A further limitation to s 55(1)(b) is that the officer must believe that the person is carrying the drugs with the intention of supplying them to others and not merely for his own use (s 55(17), Art 56(17)). The target is the drug dealer and courier. At first sight this imposes a stiff burden on the officer, but in reality, if he has sufficient belief that the person is carrying drugs, he should readily and often reasonably be able to infer the necessary intent, even if the person protests that he has drugs but that they are only for his personal use. However, it is conceivable that a court would subsequently exclude evidence if it could be shown that the officer did not reasonably believe that there was the requisite intention. It follows from s 55 (Art 56) that an intimate search for other evidence (eg jewels or money) cannot be authorised. The Government's view was that the repugnant nature of these searches outweighed the evidential value of seized items. However, if the senior officer can find reasonable grounds to believe the presence of weapons or drugs and then authorises a search, any articles which are evidence of a crime and which are discovered by the search can be seized (s 55(12), Art 56(12)).

7.23 The objective standard prior to an intimate search requires material from which an impartial third party would be satisfied that the person has drugs or weapons concealed. There will rarely be any external evidence giving rise to such a belief, though a person's speech may be affected by articles in the mouth or his manner of walking by articles hidden in the rectum. The fact that the person who is arrested for possession of drugs has used such form of concealment previously, together with good information that he is in possession of drugs which have not been found by a normal search, would ground a reasonable belief that an intimate search is necessary. Information from a credible source might also provide the basis for such a belief. For example, D's girlfriend states that she assisted D by inserting drugs into his rectum. A further possibility is that during a strip search body orifices can be visually examined. If an object is seen, that may provide the reasonable grounds to believe that an intimate search is necessary. It must, of course, be borne in mind that during the menstruation period a woman may use tampons, but that these may also be used to conceal drugs or weapons. In such cases, the woman should be asked to remove them and replacements made available to her. An intrusive search would then be necessary only if she refused to do so and if there are reasonable grounds to believe that drugs or weapons are concealed. The high standard required by 'reasonable grounds to believe' suggests that only rarely will such searches of a woman be lawful. On the other hand, the sensitivity which surrounds deaths in police custody argues for searches whenever a doubt exists and hence a lesser standard.

7.24 Further qualifications to the use of intimate searches are that the senior officer must reasonably believe that the article cannot be found without an intimate search (s 55(2), Art 56(2)). In some cases the detained person will produce the article voluntarily. In all cases, the person should be asked to do so, for only on refusal does the coercive power become necessary. Secondly, the person must be told the reason for the intimate search.

Procedure

7.25 Given the intrusive nature of an intimate search, it is suggested that D be reminded of his right to legal advice. If he requests it and a lawyer is readily available, the search should be delayed until he arrives for otherwise the purpose of the reminder is defeated. If the lawyer is delayed the search can proceed but only, it is suggested, where speed is essential. The reminder need not be given in those rare cases where legal advice can be lawfully delayed under s 58(6) (Art 59(8), see para, 7.49, post). The authorisation for an intimate search under s 55 (Art 56) may be given orally (eg by telephone) but it must be confirmed in writing (s 55(3), Art 56(3)). *Drug offence searches* must not take place at a police station (s 55(9), Art 56(9)) but at medical premises and can only be performed by a registered medical practitioner or a registered nurse (some midwives will qualify) (s 55(17), Art 56(17)). *Protective searches* (ie to search for weapons) can take place at a police station and a constable can be authorised by an officer of at least superintendent rank to act if it is impracticable to obtain someone else (s 55(5), (6), Art 56(5), (6)), for example, where no doctor is available and speed is imperative, or the medical practitioner who is called refuses to carry out the search. The reason for such authorisation must be recorded (COP, Annex A, para 9).

7.26 Section 55 (Art 56) allows medical practitioners and nurses to make an intimate search but does not compel them to do so. The British Medical Association has issued guidelines advising the profession that searches can be ethically undertaken for protective purposes and to discover heroin (but other Class A drugs are not mentioned). The Royal College of Midwives, on the other hand, has expressed reservations. Many midwives are also registered nurses and can in principle act. One of the 900 police surgeons is likely to be the first choice when an intimate search is authorised. If this is not practicable, the police will then try a medical practitioner or nurse whom they know to be willing to conduct these searches. Given the availability of these 'suitably qualified persons' (s 55(17), Art 56(17)), it should be rare for a constable to be used (in 1988 all 62 searches were conducted by suitably qualified persons and in 1990 a constable was used in only two out of the 51 recorded searches. Speed in the context of protective searches is the most likely exceptional case. Where it does arise, it would be good police practice for each designated police station to select a number of police officers, of both sexes, to perform these searches and to ensure that they are trained to perform them without causing physical injury to the detained person. This is most important for, whilst reasonable force may be used by a constable (s 117, Art 88), injury can easily be caused during an intimate search and a civil action based on the use of unreasonable force could well follow. It can also be noted that s 117 (Art 88) only applies to a constable who is exercising a coercive power. It can therefore be argued that when, in the majority of cases, 'a suitably qualified person' is conducting the intimate search, neither he nor the accompanying police officers can use force. Only when a constable is performing the search (s 55(6), Art 56(6)) does he have a 'power' which then allows reasonable force. The alternative argument is that the qualified person is exercising the constable's power as his agent and force may therefore be used. Even if this approach is adopted, the use of force is fraught with danger. On the one hand, the attitude of the detained person may well necessitate a number of officers to restrain him, especially if harm to a body orifice is to be prevented or minimised. On the other hand, the use of excessive force or the excessive presence of officers may lead to civil liability or even to a finding of 'oppression' and the exclusion of evidence (see ss 76 and 78; Arts 74, 76). Such difficulties strengthen the need for the special training of officers not only to perform the search but also to assist with it. A possible alternative to the threat of force is to inform D of *R v Smith* (1985), which decided that refusal to supply a sample of hair could in the circumstances be capable of amounting to corroborative evidence. A refusal to agree to an intimate search could be regarded as analogous.

7.27 As to the liability of the 'suitably qualified person' (medical practitioner or nurse), he cannot use force. He need not have considered whether there are reasonable grounds to justify the search. He acts as the agent of the authorising police officer. If he does consider the question and concludes that the grounds do not exist, he must bring his doubts to the attention of the authorising officer, for otherwise he would not be acting as 'innocent agent'. If force is required, he is well advised, even in the exigencies of the situation, to desist from the search.

7.28 The constable and any other person in attendance (eg lawyer or interpreter) should be of the same sex as the detained person and no unnecessary person should be present (COP, Annex A, para 6). The person qualified to carry out the search (except a constable) need not be of the same sex, but the senior officer should be alert to religious and cultural objections which a detained person may have to a search by a doctor of the opposite sex. Moreover, the injunction in the Code may have to be relaxed in the case of juveniles and the mentally disordered, if the only 'appropriate adult' (see para 7.113, post) available to attend the search is of the opposite sex and D specifically requests that adult's presence. The person to be searched must be told beforehand the reason for it (COP, Annex A, para 1). Any person can be searched but intimate searches of juveniles and the mentally disordered can only take place in front of an 'appropriate adult' (unless the detainee requests otherwise). As regards a juvenile, a search can take place in the absence of an appropriate adult but only if the juvenile requests and the adult agrees (COP, Annex A, para 4; the adult's agreement should be sought in writing). No special provision is made for the physically handicapped but the special difficulties which they can create for the detained person and officer argue strongly for the sole use of a medical practitioner.

Seizure

7.29 The types of weapon which may be concealed in a body orifice include a penknife in the mouth, a wrapped razor blade concealed in the vagina, a detonator or radio transmitter designed to detonate explosives elsewhere concealed in the rectum (the objects of physical injury envisaged by s 55, Art 56 need not be the persons in the police station), and a phial of poison concealed in the nose. Whilst the purpose of s 55(1)(a), Art 56(1)(a) is to prevent physical harm, other articles discovered during an intimate search may be seized and retained for other purposes (s 55(12), Art 56(12)), eg as evidence of an offence or to prevent interference with evidence. For example, D threatens violence. He spits out a penknife, and says 'I'll still cut my throat'. It is decided to carry out an intimate search. A razor blade wrapped in foil is discovered and it may be seized. Intimate searches for drugs naturally fall under s 55(1)(b), Art 56(1)(b), but can also fall within s 55(1)(a), Art 56(1)(a) — a packet of heroin concealed in the vagina may come apart and give the carrier a fatal overdose. As with s 55(1)(a), Art 55(1)(a), if Class B or C drugs are discovered during a search for Class A, they can be seized and used at trial.

7.30 If a person is known, or suspected, to have swallowed articles (eg a ring), the police have no power to order an X-ray of the person. Although technically the radiographic examination is not an assault, force, in the absence of consent, would be needed to conduct it and that cannot be justified by PACE. In this situation the only solution for the police is to find a basis for detaining the person and to let 'nature take its course'. The need to secure this evidence would justify detention under PACE (ss 37(2), 42(1), 43(4), Arts 38(2), 43(1), 44(4)).

7.31 The detained person must be told the reason for the seizure of any articles unless violence, likely violence, or incapacity prevent this (s 55(13), Art 56(13)). The phrase 'likely to become violent' appears in other parts of PACE (eg ss 37(6), 38(5); Arts 38(6), 39(5)). It clearly applies when the person has already reacted violently to the police, but in the context of s 55 (Art 56) it may also cover the situation where the person is evidently indignant over the proposed search and further details of it are likely to provoke him to lose patience.

Records

7.32 The custody officer must promptly record the reasons for the intimate search, what parts of the body and why they were searched, who conducted the search, who was present, and its results (s 55(10), Art 56(10), the COP, Annex A, para 7). Moreover, the annual reports of each police force must contain details of intimate searches in accordance with s 55(14)–(16), Art 56(14)–(16). These are collated by the Home Office and form a valuable basis for monitoring the use of the power.

The right to notify the fact of arrest (s 56, Art 57; for brevity the former will be used)

7.33 It is natural for a detained person to want to notify his predicament to his family or close friends. Their worries as to his whereabouts will be allayed and he may be comforted by communicating with them. It is of course possible that he will take the opportunity of alerting his partners in crime. Section 56 of PACE seeks to resolve this dilemma by providing a general right for detained persons to notify third parties of their arrest, subject to the power of the police to delay the exercise of the right in certain circumstances. This scheme follows the pattern of the previous law. Thus, the Administrative Directions (7a) attached to the Judges' Rules allowed a person in custody to telephone his solicitor or friends and to send letters or telegrams, provided that no hindrance was reasonably likely to be caused to the investigation or administration of justice. Section 62 of the Criminal Law Act 1977 then permitted him to inform one 'reasonably named' person of his arrest and whereabouts, subject to a similar power to delay exercise of the right.

The right

7.34 The right to notify applies to a person who is held in 'custody'. In *R v Kerawalla* (1991) the Court of Appeal took the view that this only covers a person whose detention has been *authorised* at a police station or elsewhere. It is respectfully submitted that this interpretation is an unnecessary gloss on the statute and is contrary to the spirit of the PACE Act, opening up the possibility of unnecessary and even lengthy denial of the right. It is suggested that the phrase 'held in custody' is used so as to include a person who is arrested and detained (whether authorised by a custody officer or not) at premises other than a police station (for example, a person arrested for shoplifting and held at the store whilst the owner considers whether to prosecute). The right given by s 56(1) only arises for those held at 'other premises' if the person requests it. For those detained at a police station, however, the COP (para 3.1) supplements s 56(1) by requiring the custody officer to inform the detained person of his right to request notification, and to give him written notice of the right (COP, para 3.2). The right also applies whenever the detained person is moved to another place, for example, from a police station in police force A to one in B. A request and the action taken by the custody officer must be noted in the custody record (COP, para. 5.8). If the request is granted, notification will normally be by telephone since this is the best way of communicating 'as soon as practicable' (s 56(1), COP, para 5.1). However, the argument of police convenience should not exclude the possibility of using an officer to visit the appropriate party. This will be necessary of course if there is no telephone and there may be other circumstances which make the telephone an inappropriate method of communication (e.g. a shared line or publicly situated telephone, the abruptness and coldness of the telephone when news of the arrest is likely to cause distress and shock to a relative). Moreover, the police may be suspicious of the named recipient, not enough to warrant delay of the notification (below) but enough to merit a personal visit by a constable rather than the use of a telephone. Since this will involve some delay in the exercise of s 56, it is important for the visit to be arranged forthwith and advisable for a senior officer (inspector) to approve it. The object of the notification can be a relative, friend or other person who is known to the detained person or who is likely to take an interest in his welfare (s 56(1)). The 'other person' could include a Member of Parliament, clergyman, a community leader or youth club organiser. In some cases D will have no one to contact (e.g. he is a vagrant), whilst in many others he will not want to (see below). However, there may be cases where the custody officer should consider suggesting to D an appropriate person or representative of a social or voluntary organisation (e.g. if D is an overseas visitor, or he is adamant that he does not want his family informed). Only one such person is to be informed. The COP (para 5.1) states that, if the person cannot be contacted, up to *two* alternatives may be tried and that further calls are at the discretion of the custody or investigating officer. This is an improvement on the 1977 Act which spoke only of 'one person reasonably named' but it is still an unnecessary gloss on the clear wording of s 56(1) and of doubtful legality. For the only reasons for denying the notification are set out in s 56(5) and Annex B to the COP. Unless they apply, repeated calls to other persons must be made until successful.

7.35 The initial communication is made at public expense. It consists solely of notifying a third party that D has been arrested and that he is being held at place X. A simple way of satisfying s 62 of the 1977 Act was suggested by the Home Office Circular (74/1978, (v)): where D is arrested at home or otherwise in the company of his family or friends, they can be told immediately of the arrest and where D is being taken. When the arrested person is informed of his right of notification, on arrival at the station, the police can reply that the notification has already taken place and the statute has already been obeyed. A similar interpretation of s 56 is possible since the same wording as s 62 of the 1977 Act is used (D 'has been arrested and is being held in custody'). Indeed, if D is arrested at home and his spouse is told of the arrest, the purpose of s 56 is clearly satisfied. On the other hand, the spirit of s 56 suggests that it may only be satisfied when D, who is actually in custody at a police station, notifies a third party of his arrest. This approach may be needed when for example D is arrested at the premises of friends or in a pub in front of friends and neighbours for there is no guarantee that they will contact D's immediate family after the police have taken D away, or when D decides on arrival at the station that a more appropriate person should be informed.

Denial of the right

7.36   After 36 hours of detention, the right of notification *cannot* be withheld. This period coincides with the time when the police must seek a warrant of further detention from a magistrates' court (s 43, Art 44; see para 6.53, ante). However, until 36 hours have expired, the right may be suspended if the following conditions apply:

(a) The person is in police detention in connection with a serious arrestable offence (s 56(2)).

(b) The delay has been authorised by at least a superintendent. He can do so orally (e.g. by telephone) but it must be confirmed in writing as soon as is practicable (s 56(2),(4)).

(c) The authorising officer has reasonable grounds to believe that the proposed communication will have one or more of the following consequences —

    (i) It will interfere with evidence of a serious arrestable offence or will interfere with, or harm, other persons. So, for example, it may be essential for the safety of a hostage that, when a kidnapper is arrested, other members of the gang are not alerted. Similarly the identity and safety of an informer might be jeopardised unless D's right of notification is delayed. Another example is where D has been arrested prematurely and the police wish to catch the rest of the gang when they attempt the robbery or meet to purchase a supply of prohibited drugs. The offence need not be the same as that for which the person was detained. For example, D is arrested for drug offences. His premises are searched and stolen goods are found. X is suspected of complicity in that and other thefts and the police hope to confront X before he is alerted that D is under arrest and before he disposes of the property.

    (ii) The communication will alert and therefore impede the arrest of others for a serious arrestable offence which has been committed; for example, a robber may be forewarned and avoid a rendez vous if he knows that the driver of the getaway car has been arrested.

    (iii) The recovery of property will be hindered; for example, communication with the suspect's spouse will lead her to destroy or dispose of stolen property or prohibited drugs.

(iv)   The recovery of drug-trafficking proceeds will be hindered by notifying a named person. This was inserted into s 56 of PACE by s 32 of the Drug Trafficking Offences Act 1986 (for Art 57, see similarly the Criminal Justice (Confiscation) (N.I.) Order 1990). D must have been detained for such an offence (as defined in s 38(1) of the 1986 Act; and such offences are deemed to be 'serious arrestable' ones for the purposes of PACE, see s 116(2)(aa) of PACE as inserted by the 1986 Act) and the officer must believe that D has benefited from drug-trafficking (i.e. 'received payment or other reward in connection with drug-trafficking carried on by him or another person', s 1(3) of the 1986 Act). This new provision refers to the 'officer' but must, it is suggested, be interpreted subject to s 56(2) of PACE i.e. to mean a senior officer of at least superintendent rank.

(v)   The recovery of other proceeds by a confiscation order will be hindered. This was added by s 99 of the Criminal Justice Act 1988 (for Art 57, see to identical effect the Order of 1990, above). Under Part VI of that Act the crown court (and to a lesser extent the magistrates' court) can make an order confiscating the benefits which a person has derived from committing an indictable offence. If the police fear that unlawfully obtained property will be disposed of if D notifies someone of his arrest, then (iii) above is available to delay notification, so (v) additionally permits delay where the property has been exchanged into some other form and that other form may be lost unless D's notification is delayed (e.g. shares bought with stolen money will be sold by an accomplice if he is told of D's arrest).

The real difficulty here lies in the superintendent finding sufficient evidence to trigger delay of the notification in respect of *each* person identified by D (he may be able to do so for one but not another; thus, a blanket ban is not allowed. It must be directed against a named person, *R v Quayson* (1989)). He must after all satisfy the more demanding test of 'reasonable grounds to believe', s 56(5) (see further para. 2.02, ante). D wishing to notify a known criminal associate is clear enough but such blatant examples are unusual. Much will depend on the police suspicions about the person to be contacted, the nature of the offence and of D's arrest, and the ease with which (i) to (v) above can be accomplished (e.g. the ready disposal of drugs). On a league table of importance the right of notification is below the right to legal advice and the grounds for delaying it are inevitably more speculative than the narrower basis for denying legal advice (see para. 749). Indeed delay of notification in a particular case may be justifiable when denial of legal advice is not (*R v Quayson* (1989), *R v Parris* (1989)). Consequently, it is suggested that a court is less likely to punish the delay of notification with the exclusion of evidence under ss 76 or 78 (Arts 74, 76) unless in the circumstances it amounts to 'oppression', (s 76(2)(a) Art 74(2)(a)), and even less likely if D has been allowed access to legal advice.

7.37 The detained person must be promptly told the reason for refusing his request and the reason must be included in his custody record. That record can be inspected within 12 months from the person's release. Suspension of the right will in any event cease after 36 hours from the 'relevant time' (usually the time of arrival at the police station, s 41, Art 42; see para 6.40, ante), but it will do so earlier if either the person is charged or the reason for refusing the right ends (COP, Annex B). In the latter event, the custody officer must remind D of the right in clear terms, ask him what he wants to do about it (*R v Cochrane* (1988), *R v Quayson* (1989)) and note the custody record accordingly. The 'review officer' (s 40, Art 41, see para 6.65, ante) who conducts the early reviews of a person's detention is not legally bound to consider the operation of s 56, but, it is suggested, a conscientious officer should do so. Certainly by the time that a senior officer has to consider whether to authorise continued detention (s 42, Art 43; see para 6.46, ante), he must remind the detained person of his right under s 56 and must review any earlier decision to suspend the right (s 42(9), Art 43(8)). If a juvenile is detained, the person responsible for his welfare and, if different, the 'appropriate adult' (see para 7.113, post) *must* be informed of the arrest as soon as is practicable (s 57, Art 58 and COP, paras 3.7, 3.9). The juvenile's right to notify a third party under s 56 is quite *independent* of s 57 (see para 7.116, post). So in theory an older child, for example, may well prefer to use s 56 to contact another adult (e.g. a youth leader, an uncle). The s 56 right can then be suspended just as in the case of adults. However, Brown (1988) reported that use of s 56 by juveniles in addition to s 57 'seldom occurred'. For persons who are mentally ill or handicapped, the 'appropriate adult' must be similarly and unconditionally notified of the arrest (COP, para 3.9). As for foreign citizens, the COP gives them various rights to consult their diplomatic representatives (see para 7.113, post). It also states (para 7A) that these rights cannot be denied or delayed under the criteria of s 56(5). This is a gloss on the statute. Commendable though it is, it should be remembered that a breach of the Notes for Guidance in COP is not necessarily fatal to the admissibility of evidence.

7.38 The grounds for delaying the right of notification under s 56 are more rigidly drawn than those contained in s 62 of the Criminal Law Act 1977. But even under the previous practice, the number of lengthy delays was small (of 1,600,000 arrests in 1982, only 1,353 requests under s 62 were delayed for more than 4 hours and 114 for more than 25 hours —

House of Lords Debate, 26 July 1984, col 498). Research by Brown (1988) revealed that of 5,519 offences recorded, only 111 were categorised as serious arrestable ones (and thereby capable of triggering s 56(5)) but of these delay in notification was authorised in 53 (i.e. less than 1% of all offences, but nearly 50% of serious arrestable offences). On the other hand, research indicates that a large percentage of detained persons do not even choose to exercise the right (Royal Commission (1981) Research Study, No 4; Brown (1988) revealed that only 18% of detainees requested notification). The fact that custody officers must inform each detained person both orally and in writing of s 56 at the start of the detention (COP, paras 3.1, 3.2) should lead to more requests for notification, but the pressures on the suspect in a police station, their frequent willingness to talk to the police, the way in which their rights can be communicated to them, and their embarrassment at having been arrested argue against this. Moreover, it is open to the police to inform the detained person that he will soon be released (with or without bail) and that in the circumstances he may therefore decide not to exercise his right under s 56 (for the application of s 56 to persons detained under the Prevention of Terrorism (Temporary Provisions) Act 1984 (s 56(10), (11)) and other terrorism provisions see para 7.146, post).

Right to communicate

7.39   Section 56 (Art 57) is limited to a right of notification i.e. the right of a detained person to tell a third party of the arrest and of his whereabouts. Normally the police will do so on his behalf. The right to communicate should be distinguished. Under the COP (para 5.6), unless the qualifications in s 56(5) apply, a detained person is allowed to communicate with others by telephone or written message. Unlike the right to notification, telephone calls *may* be charged to him (for example, if a long distance call is involved). Insufficient cash to pay for the communication should not in principle be a reason for denying it. Financial arrangements will usually be feasible. Letters can be read by the police and telephone calls listened to, unless the suspect's lawyer is being contacted (COP, para 5.7). Consequently, the suspect must be warned of this and warned that his communication may be used in evidence (COP, para 5.7). If a telephone call is being abused (either by its content or duration), it can be terminated by the supervisory officer. Also, if an officer of at least inspector rank (cf. the right to notify under s 56 which specifies a superintendent) considers that a letter or telephone call will have one of the consequences listed at para 7.36 above, he can stop or delay if (COP, para 5.6). This applies if D is detained for a serious arrestable or arrestable offence (s 56(5) only applies to the former). A written note on the custody record should be made of any message or call (COP, para 5.8). Particular difficulty may arise for security if an interpreter is used (COP, para 5A) to communicate with someone outside the station.

Visits

7.40   Remarkably little attention is paid to the possibility of visits to the detained person by, for example, his family. If friends or relatives enquire at a police station about D, his whereabouts may be divulged if D agrees and if the reasons for non-communication in s 56(5) (Art 57(5)) do not apply. If D refuses to allow the information to be given, that refusal should be noted and D asked to sign the custody record (COP, para 5.8). If the enquiry about D is received by telephone, the custody officer must be wary of identifying and verifying the caller before responding. As to visits to see D, the custody officer's discretion governs. The availability of officers to supervise the visit and the possible hindrance to the investigation (e.g. a pending interview of D) caused by a visit are obvious reasons for refusing or delaying a visit (COP, para 5B). Once D has been charged, the latter ceases to apply and the former should be overcome whenever possible. Once D has appeared in court and has been remanded in custody by judicial order, he passes into the jurisdiction of the Prison Service and limited access from outsiders is allowed in accordance with the Prison Rules. A note on the custody record should be made of any visit (COP, para 5.8).

Right to legal advice (s 58, Art 59; for brevity the former will be used)

7.41   It can be argued that the right of a detained person to secure legal advice is his most important protection. His motives for wanting it may stem from, inter alia, confusion as to his predicament, a desire for bail or the presence of a friendly face, or a fear of police malpractice. More objectively, he may need advice as to, for example, the substance of the charges against him, or the conditions and length of his detention. The pressures of police interrogation and the technicality of the criminal law mean that the interests of a suspect can only be properly secured after he has received legal advice. Apart from offering legal advice, a lawyer's presence enables him to attend and record the police interview of his client and the various identification procedures which may be used, to make representations to the custody and review officers over the client's proposed detention and to the custody officer on the issue of bail, to check on the physical treatment of the client, and to offer him comfort and support. The Judges' Rules recognised this; 'Every person at any stage of an investigation should be able to communicate and to consult privately with a solicitor.' Research revealed that, for a variety of reasons, relatively few detained persons sought access to legal advice (see the summary of the Royal Commission, paras 4.83–4.85). One of these reasons was undoubtedly the laxity of the law, for there was no obligation on the police to inform the suspect orally of his right of access and the Judges' Rules permitted the withholding of access lest 'unreasonable delay or hindrance is caused to the processes of investigation or the administration of justice.' These broad grounds of denial could be given by any officer and in relation to a person detained for any offence. The Royal Commission (1981) recommended a statutory right to legal advice, subject to more narrowly drawn grounds for denial and then only in relation to grave offences (Report, paras 4.86–4.93). Section 58 of PACE broadly followed the Commission's approach. Of course access to legal advice can only be fully realised if there are enough lawyers and sufficient money to pay for them. This simple proposition hides considerable financial and practical difficulties. For most detained persons the cost of obtaining legal advice is prohibitive. Parliament recognised this and in s 59 of PACE (now replaced) sought to make a reality of legal representation by amending the Legal Aid Act 1982 and extending the duty solicitor scheme at magistrates' courts to include legal advice for persons held in police custody.

The right in outline

7.42 A distinction must be drawn between those persons detained for serious arrestable offences and those held for lesser offences. The latter have an unqualified right, on request, to consult a solicitor privately at any time (s 58(1)). The former have a qualified right since it may be suspended in certain circumstances (s 58(8)). The statutory right for both groups is one of consultation only. This must take place in private (save in relation to terrorism provisions, when the advice may have to be given in the sight and hearing of a uniformed officer, s 58(15); see para 7.146(c), post). The communication may be in person, by writing or by telephone. The Code of Practice, extends the right so that the solicitor may usually remain with his client during the latter's interview (para 6.6). The Act covers persons who have been 'arrested' (s 58(1)) and this applies whether or not an offence has been committed. Thus, it covers a mentally disordered person who is found in a public place, is arrested under s 136 of the Mental Health Act 1983 and is taken temporarily to a police station. The provision arises if the person is 'held in custody' at a police station 'or other premises' (s 56(1)). The latter can cover persons detained on board a ship or aircraft (or other specified place under the Prevention of Terrorism (Temporary Provisions) Act 1989, Sch 2, para 8(4) — detention pending removal from the jurisdiction). The phrase 'held in custody' has been interpreted to mean authorised detention (*R v*

Kerawalla (1991)). It is submitted that the contrary view advanced at para 7.34 ante is preferable and even more so in the context of legal advice (ie s 58 should apply if the person is detained, or held in custody, whether or not a custody officer has authorised it). The Code of Practice again extends the right of access to 'any person' (para 6.1). Persons 'voluntarily' in attendance at a police station have an unrestricted right to contact a solicitor since they are not in police detention and are free unless and until arrested. However, there is no obligation on the police to remind or inform them of that right unless the person is cautioned COP, para 3.15 (though in some forces 'volunteers' are, quite rightly, routinely cautioned).

Notification of the right

7.43 The COP contains several provisions designed to ensure that a detainee is made aware of his right to legal advice. Thus, when a person is arrested at a police station or brought there under arrest, he will appear before a custody officer who must tell him of his right to legal advice and that he may obtain it free (COP, para 3.1). This must be done before any questioning begins and even if it is then decided to delay access to a solicitor (see para 7.49 post). D is asked whether he wants to exercise it. D, or more usually the officer, will then delete the appropriate box on the custody record and D is asked to sign on an adjacent space. He is also asked to sign as to whether he has been told of his rights. It is important that the right be explained clearly and unambiguously (see *R v Beycan* (1990) where the custody officer wrongfully asked 'are you happy to be interviewed in the normal way we conduct these interviews, without a solicitor, friend or representative?'). The custody officer must also hand D a written notice repeating the right and explaining how he can obtain it (COP, paras 3.1–2). A difficulty here is that the right may be read to him discouragingly so that he signs the custody record to refuse legal advice without real understanding; and that he is handed the notice and told to read it in the cell when his emotions, thoughts and even literacy are unreceptive to its message. Each station must prominently display a poster in the charging area advertising the right to legal advice (COP, para 6.3). Whether, in the hurly burly of a charge room, a suspect is able to spot and assimilate the poster is another matter. Although prominently displayed, there is no uniform style of poster. Moreover, illiteracy or a foreign tongue may defeat it. As regards the latter, posters in the main ethnic and E.C. languages should be used 'wherever they are likely to be helpful and it is practicable to do so' (COP, 6H). The nature of the local population, the proximity of the station to a port of entry or tourist resort, and the availability of wallspace in the charge room will influence this. D must also be reminded of the right to free legal advice before an identification procedure takes place, before an officer reviews his detention

(COP, 15.3) or a senior officer authorises his continued detention up to 36 hours under s 42 (Art 43, see para 6.46, ante) and, most importantly, before an interview starts or restarts.

7.44 Simply telling D of his rights, particularly if it is said in an offhand fashion, does not mean that he will try to exercise it. Indeed research prior to PACE indicated that, even when informed, a large majority of suspects did not do so (see Royal Commission, paras 4.83–85, and Baldwin and McConville (1979)). A similar picture has emerged under PACE. Thus, Sanders et al (1989) found that only 24.8% of their sample requested legal advice, and that the reasons for not doing so included the use of at least 21 identifiable ploys or tactics by the police to discourage the right (e.g. reading the right to D too quickly, suggesting that he will not be detained for long, that he will have to wait for a solicitor to attend or that he can have a solicitor later, or that it is normal to interview without a solicitor, see the facts of *R v Beycan* (1990)) and a variety of reasons attributable to the suspect (e.g. a desire to get out of the station as soon as possible, an acceptance of the inevitable, a confidence to survive without a lawyer, the triviality of the offence meant that legal advice was not worth it, dislike of solicitors, the attitude and behaviour of the police). Sanders (1989) concluded that 'suspects have conventional notions of 'worth' and 'triviality' in relation to their alleged offences, and a hatred of detention. These feelings, which discourage requests for advice, are reinforced by police ploys. Confusion about the nature of the 24 hours scheme and whether it is free reinforces this, and again the police tend to add to, or, at least, do not dissipate that confusion. Most worrying of all, perhaps, is that the manner of response by many solicitors in many situations also reinforces these tendencies.' With this background, the strongest inducement for D to exercise his right to free legal advice is the 1991 addition to the COP, which states 'No attempt should be made to dissuade the suspect from obtaining legal advice' (para 6.4). If properly observed, this instruction should greatly increase the use of legal advice. If not, it is certainly a most useful provision for defence lawyers to deploy in seeking to exclude confessional evidence obtained in their absence under sections 76 and 78 (Arts 74, 76).

7.45 It should be noted that the various procedures to alert D of his right to legal advice only apply if he is in custody in the police station. On arrest outside or en route to the station, there is no duty to tell him of the right. Instead there is a general prohibition on questioning an arrested suspect outside the police station (COP, para 11.1; for the exceptional cases where questioning is allowed, see para 8.13, post).

Waiver of the right

7.46 When the custody officer authorises a person's detention, he must tell him of his rights, including the effect of s 58, and that the rights are continuing ones which may be exercised at any time (COP, para 3.1). He is asked whether he wants legal advice and to sign the custody record accordingly (COP, para 3.5; a refusal to sign must also be noted by the custody officer in the record, para 2.7). The brevity of this provision belies its importance and perhaps underestimates the pressures on a suspect at this point to waive legal advice. Such pressures have been well documented (see above and further on the issue of consent, para 2.18, ante). A realistic sanction against an inappropriate waiver is the readiness of the courts to invoke sections 76 and 78 (Arts 74, 76) when a solicitor is not present at an interview (see further chapter 8 post). There will always be a gap between the reading of D's rights and an interview (for the custody officer must complete other procedures) and, when an interview begins (or restarts), the interviewing officer must remind D of his right to free legal advice (COP, para 11.2; the reminder must be noted in the record of interview by the interviewing officer, though D is not required to sign it). The advent of tape-recording may assist in assessing the quality of the reminder and the genuineness of D's consent to be interviewed without legal advice. In those cases where a suspect changes his mind about seeking legal advice and agrees to an interview, the procedure below must be followed. One particular problem of waiver worthy of mention arises when a suspect returns to the station to answer his bail (s 47(3)) and the police propose to question him further. The suspect must be reminded of his right to legal advice (COP, para 11.2), yet the investigating officer may be impatient or hostile at the idea of waiting for legal representation, or may be intent on deterring it, or the legal advice may be difficult to organise, or the suspect may be easily dissuaded from seeking it.

Questioning without legal advice

7.47 The general rule is that a person who asks for legal advice cannot be interviewed until he has obtained it. However, there are four crucial qualifications (COP, para 6.6). If they apply, they should be noted in the record of interview (para 6.17).

(a) Legal advice may be properly denied by a senior officer under s 58(8) of PACE (see para 7.49, post).

(b) A police officer of the rank of at least superintendent can authorise questioning of the suspect if he has reasonable grounds to believe that (i) delay whilst waiting for legal advice will involve an immediate risk of harm to persons or serious loss of, or damage to, property (once this risk has passed, legal advice should proceed unless (a) above, or (ii) and (c) below apply), or (ii) unreasonable delay to the investigation would be caused by having to wait for a lawyer to arrive. There will be the occasional 'seasoned' suspect who will only use one firm of solicitors or one solicitor and for whom the delay in securing his attendance permits the 'detention clock' to run and 'gives him time to think'. The police may have the strongest suspicion that that is his plan but they must still seek the solicitor's attendance. Only then can this provision operate. Examples are where a solicitor may have a long way to travel and, by the time he arrives, the permissible period of detention without judicial warrant may be coming to an end. Questioning can be ordered to begin at once. Similarly, the time for D's rest period under the COP may be fast approaching and there is an urgent need to interview him before the rest period intrudes. Again, the needs of other investigations (eg to discover the whereabouts of accomplices or of a kidnap victim) may demand immediate questioning. Another pertinent example is where the chosen solicitor is already advising another client. Wherever possible the superintendent should discover how long it will take for the solicitor to attend. He may then be able to stall the questioning if the solicitor says he is about to set off. (Brown, 1988, discovered that 51% of suspects requesting legal advice saw a solicitor within an hour, and 65% in 90 minutes). Conversely the solicitor should seek an undertaking (preferably to be noted in the custody record) that questioning will not begin until he arrives (Advising a Suspect, Law Society, para 4.2). If questioning cannot wait, the solicitor should be told so that he can try to organise an agent to appear on his behalf (COP, C, Notes for Guidance 6A). He can also seek to make representations to the custody officer and, if they are written down, they may be useful later when the court considers the admissibility of evidence. To prevent abuse of (b)(ii) it should be noted that under the COP para 6.8 a solicitor who at the time of the interview is present at the station, or who is on his way, or who is easily contactable by telephone, is deemed to be 'available'; therefore the interview should be conducted in his presence and the suspect should not be asked to agree to one without him. If the lawyer arrives after the interview has started, it is imperative that he insists on a private consultation with the client (see COP, para 6.1 which gives that right 'at any time'). He should also ask to see or hear the record of the interview. If legal advice is to be satisfactory and possible exclusion of evidence avoided, it is in the police interests to accommodate such a request.

(c) If a solicitor cannot be obtained (ie the nominated solicitor cannot be contacted or refuses to attend, and/or the duty solicitor cannot attend or the suspect refuses to use the duty solicitor scheme), an officer of at least inspector rank may permit an interview to proceed. Given the importance of legal advice and the court's tendency to exclude a confession if it is improperly denied, it is important for the inspector to verify that all reasonable attempts have been made to secure a lawyer's presence.

(d) If the suspect has changed his mind and no longer wants a lawyer (eg he wants to leave police custody and will not wait for a lawyer to attend), he must either give his agreement to an interview in writing or speak it on to tape, and an officer of at least inspector rank must approve the interview. The danger of improper pressure being brought to bear on the suspect to change his mind is self-evident.

It is suggested that the authorisations in (a) to (d) should be put in writing and attached to the record of interview and read out on the tape. Moreover, the authorising and interviewing officers should be alert to the real possibility that a court will exclude evidence obtained in breach of these provisions.

7.48 It has been decided (*DPP v Billington* (1988), *DPP v Cornell* (1990), *DPP v Skinner* (1990)) that obtaining legal advice cannot delay the breathalyser procedure in road traffic cases. As Lloyd LJ remarked in *Billington,* 'the right to consult a solicitor . . . does not furnish a defendant with a reasonable excuse for not providing a specimen when requested'. This does not mean that a solicitor should not be called — the suspect has after all a right to consult one in private at any time, s 58(1) (Art 59(1)). The police should therefore call one without delay (COP, para 6.2) and, if he arrives very quickly or is readily available (eg he or another available solicitor may be at the station), it is suggested that he be allowed access, albeit brief, to the detainee. He is likely to advise compliance with the police request. The detainee can also ask for a copy of the COP (para 1.2). Whilst this does not entitle him to a leisurely read from cover to cover, it is suggested that it is open for the Court of Appeal to permit him a limited time to read the relevant provisions (eg COP, para 3E!) (but cf the facts of *Skinner*, above, where 10 minutes were held to be too long; on the other hand in *Hudson v DPP* (1991) the defendant was kept at the station for an hour before the breath test procedure was commenced — ample time for a solicitor to be contacted. Hodgson J in *Hudson* wisely suggested that the notice of rights given to D should make it clear that s 58 cannot delay the breath test, for otherwise he may be left, understandably, with the impression that he can delay the process and contact a solicitor at any time).

Denial of legal advice

7.49 At the outset it should be noted first that delaying notification of arrest (s 56) is a quite separate matter from the postponement of legal advice (*R v Parris* (1989)), and second that this is only possible if the suspect has been detained on suspicion of a serious arrestable offence and, in the light of *R v Samuel* (below), will rarely be justifiable. In theory, the denial may last for up to 36 hours (the police must obtain the approval of a magistrates' court if they wish the detention to continue thereafter, see para 6.45, ante), but, since the suspect must be permitted to consult his lawyer for a reasonable time before the court hearing (COP, Annex B, para 5) the full period of denial will not run. For example, D is due to appear in court after 34 hours of detention. His lawyer should be allowed to see him beforehand, perhaps after 33 hours. The circumstances in which legal advice may be withheld for up to 36 hours are the same as those which prevent a third party being notified of the suspect's arrest under s 56 (Art 57) viz:

(a) The person is detained for a serious arrestable offence.
(b) An officer of at least superintendent rank authorises the denial.
(c) He must have a reasonable belief that one of the following facts applies —
   (i) interference with evidence, or harm to other persons will ensue,
   (ii) other suspects will be alerted,
   (iii) recovery of property will be hindered,
   (iv) the recovery of drug trafficking proceeds will be hindered,
   (v) a confiscation order under the Criminal Justice Act 1988 will be frustrated. (s 58(8),(8A), Art 59(8) (8A)).

7.50 If one of these grounds applies, the delay in access to legal advice must cease as soon as the ground ceases. More importantly the suspect must be told (in understandable language, *R v Cochrane* (1988)) that the objection to legal advice no longer applies, asked whether he wants it, and his reply noted (COP, Annex B, para 4; cf the facts of *R v Quayson* (1989) where D was not told). Indeed he must be asked to endorse the custody record. These grounds are much more narrowly drawn than those in the Judges' Rules. But, more significantly, the COP, (Annex B, para 3) contains a qualification which greatly reduces the scope for these grounds. Thus, access to legal advice *cannot* be denied because the lawyer may advise his client not to answer any questions (see the facts of *R v Alladice* (1988)). It follows that:

'the only reason under the [Act] for delaying access to a legal adviser relates to the risk that he would either intentionally or inadvertently, convey information to confederates still at large that would undercut the investigation in progress' (Home Officer Minister, Standing Committee E, 28 February 1984, col 1417).

For example, the suspect may ask the solicitor to pass a message to his wife which sounds innocuous but which is in fact a coded instruction to alert accomplices. This reasoning is an implicit slur on the professional integrity of solicitors and provoked keen discussion between the Law

Society and the Home Office during passage of the PACE Bill. However, in the light of the COP and *R v Samuel* (1988) denial of legal advice under s 58 is extremely difficult for the police to justify. First, the offence must be of a sort for which immediate access to legal advice may have one of the (i) to (v) consequences above (e.g. the ready disposal of drugs, speedy removal of proceeds of crime from the country). Second, the senior officer must have grounds to believe that the suspect will try to pass a message out through his lawyer (thus, he must actually have addressed s 58(8), cf *R v Parris* (1989)). Third, the suspect must have requested a named solicitor. If the police do not know his identity, s 58(8) cannot be triggered since suspicion of solicitors per se will not suffice (see the facts of *R v Davidson* (1988)). Fourth, reliance on s 58(8) must be supported by the facts. Thus, in *R v Guest* (1988) the only other accomplice was dead, so there was no danger of (c)(ii) above; and alternatively the superintendent's fear that the solicitor would alert others was contradicted by the fact that the solicitor already knew of D's arrest before he was denied access! (See also *R v Cochrane* (1988)). Fifth, the emphasis of s 58(8) clearly lies on the character and record of the solicitor. The senior officer must satisfy the relatively high standard (para 2.02, ante) of 'reasonable belief' that the particular solicitor will deliberately or accidentally 'spill the beans'. Evidence of 'deliberate' complicity must be strong for this belief. The officer 'must believe that a solicitor will, if allowed to consult with a detained person, thereafter commit a criminal offence. Solicitors are officers of the court. We think that the number of times that a police officer could genuinely be in that state of belief will be rare' (per Hodgon J in *R v Samuel*). The most obvious offences would be the common law one of perverting the course of justice or impeding the arrest or prosecution of an offender contrary to s 4 of the Criminal Law Act 1967. It is arguable that, if such a belief surrounds a particular solicitor, complaint to the Law Society will have already been made.

7.51 As to solicitors acting as 'innocent postboxes', this possibility could be reduced by a warning from the senior officer to the solicitor about the risks of unwitting participation in the suspect's design. Moreover, 'persons detained by the police are frequently not very clever and the expectation that one of [(i) to (v)] will be brought about in this way seems to contemplate a degree of intelligence and sophistication in persons detained, and perhaps a naivete and lack of common sense in solicitors, which we doubt often occurs. When and if it does, we think it would have to have reference to the specific person detained. The archetype would, we imagine, be the sophisticated criminal who is known or suspected of being a member of a gang of criminals' (per Hodgson J in *R v Samuel*). In many cases it will be the duty solicitor who is called. He will be known to, if not respected by, the police and there will be no reason to deny access (the selection, reselection and training of duty solicitors have been improved significantly under the 'Duty Solicitor Arrangements 1990', issued by the Legal Aid Board). Moreover, if a particular solicitor is distrusted, the simple solution, it is suggested, is for the police to offer D another one (see COP, Annex B, para B4). If that is accepted, then the only reason for the absence of a solicitor will be where the alternative solicitor cannot, or refuses to, attend. Another solution, where it is feared that the solicitor will unwittingly pass coded messages, is to warn the solicitor of the possibility. This is more likely to be feared where one solicitor is representing two suspects and coded messages can be more easily passed. Even so, a considerable degree of sophisticated foresight by the suspects would be needed (it is suggested that *Re Walters* (1987), where vague fears of messages being unwittingly conveyed were upheld, cannot stand in the light of *R v Samuel* (1988)).

7.52   There will be some situations where (i) to (v) do not apply and legal advice has been permitted, but the police do not want certain information passed to the suspect (e.g. that an accomplice has also been arrested, or what an accomplice has said about the suspect's arrest). The decision to comply rests firmly with the solicitor in the light of what he thinks is best for his client.

7.53   The COP rejects one other basis for delaying access. It follows the case of *R v Jones (Sally)* (1984). Thus, if, as often happens, a solicitor is approached by the family or friends of the detained person, is retained on his behalf and attends the police station (since direct access to Healthcall is barred and the duty solicitor names will not be known, the family etc will have to rely on a private rather than duty solicitor), he cannot be refused access just because the detained person has not requested his presence. In fact the suspect must be informed of the solicitor's arrival and asked to sign the custody record indicating whether he wants to see the solicitor (Annex B, para 3). To avoid a wasted journey it is good sense for the solicitor to contact the suspect by telephone before he sets off in case the suspect has already instructed another solicitor.

7.54   The relative unpopularity of criminal work in the legal profession ('Many solicitors will not contemplate it . . . there is an economic necessity to employ persons who have no professional qualifications to attend at the interview of suspects' (per Mann L J in *R v Chief Constable of Avon, ex parte Robinson* (1989)) has led to the despatch of trainee solicitors, legal executives and others to advise suspects. It has even spawned in one district the idea of forming a separate company of advisers within a firm (making the enterprise more profitable for night time duties). It is good practice for the instructed solicitor to arm his representative with a clear letter of authority to act on his behalf. The point is important for an officer of at least inspector rank may exclude a representative if he considers that the representative 'will hinder the investigation of crime' (COP, para 6.12); cf. the arrival of a qualified solicitor, for whose exclusion a superintendent or superior rank must comply with s 58(8), above). The chief constable can issue a force order restricting access to certain types of representatives provided that it is not a blanket ban and that each case is still decided on its merits by the inspector (*R v Chief Constable of Avon, ex parte Robinson* (1989)). He is specifically instructed (COP, para 6.13) to check on the representative's identity, the suitability of his character and anything else contained in the solicitor's letter of authorisation. Clearly a carefully drafted letter explaining the representative's background and experience is very useful. In interpreting this power, Mann L J suggested that just cause for its exercise would be evidence of the representative's inability to act as adviser on behalf of the solicitor, such as 'his appearance, his age, his mental capacity or the police knowledge of him'. Previous convictions would be the clearest evidence of the last but known criminal connections might well suffice. More problematic is the case of a former police officer who appears as a solicitor's representative. Police mistrust (of the 'gamekeeper turned poacher' variety), or previous impressions of him as an officer should not suffice. Instead, it is suggested, there must be clear evidence of instances where the representative has positively hindered an investigation, provided that they extend beyond the range of actions which is quite permissible as part of the giving of legal advice (e.g. telling D of his right of silence). With the recent emphasis on rigorous selection of duty solicitors and their training (see para 7.63, below), the chances of them sending inadequate representatives should be markedly reduced. If a representative is barred, the detainee and solicitor must be informed and the custody record noted (COP, para 6.14; though the reasons given to the solicitor should be carefully drafted in a letter rather than given over the telephone lest defamation be inadvertently risked). If the solicitor in turn cannot attend, the COP is unclear. It is suggested that, to avoid problems of exclusion of evidence at trial, it is prudent, and certainly within the spirit of the COP, for the custody officer either to inform D of the alternative duty solicitor scheme or, if that is the one which has been used, to try to contact the next duty solicitor on the rota or panel.

7.55 If it is decided that a firm of solicitors is persistently sending unsuitable representatives, an officer of at least superintendent rank should be informed with a view to him contacting the local Law Society (COP, para 6F).

7.56 Both s 56 and the COP are silent as to how expeditiously a delay in legal advice should be sought and authorised. Can the police question D in the meantime? In *R v Guest* (1988), a gap of about 110 minutes arose between the request for a solicitor and authorisation for its denial, during which D was interrogated. Ognall J observed,

> 'I entertain no doubt whatever that the police are not entitled, even where written consent of the detained person is obtained, to go on questioning a man for a wholly indefinite period after he has requested a solicitor, while they apparently make up their minds on this fundamentally important matter, namely whether they are going to seek authority to deny him his fundamental right of access to a solicitor. To conclude otherwise would be to drive a coach and horses through the intention behind this Part of the Act and, it must be faced, would be to afford a charter to the police . . . to manipulate the provisions of section 58 so as to divest it of all practical value to the detained person.'

The following points can be made. (1) A superintendent should be physically proximate in most cases. If not, the investigating officer should be able to contact one very quickly. (2) As will be seen in relation to s 78 (see para 8.67, post), it is very unwise for an officer to continue an interview whilst authorisation is sought. Exclusion of any admissions is highly likely. (3) There may be highly exceptional and urgent circumstances (eg life threatening) where an interview is needed but this should be kept to a matter of minutes (not nearly two hours as in *Guest*) and the suspect should agree to it in writing and on tape.

Exclusion of solicitor during interview

7.57 A solicitor can be forced to leave an interview in two situations. First, the client may ask him to withdraw. The only precaution for the solicitor here is to make sure that the client understands the implications of his request. It is suggested that he should ask the client whether he wants another solicitor and, if so, should explain how to obtain one. Second, a solicitor can be asked to leave if his conduct prevents an investigating officer from properly putting his questions to the suspect (COP, para 6.9). Reminding the suspect of his right to silence, requesting that he be allowed to give legal advice in private and objecting to improper questions or improper methods of questioning, do not amount to misconduct for this purpose. The COP C, Notes for Guidance para 6D suggests that 'answering questions on the client's behalf, or providing written replies for the client to quote' might suffice. But there is a fine line between the former example and a solicitor properly assisting an inarticulate suspect. Such a suspect may reasonably require frequent interjections from the solicitor, based on the instructions given to him by the client. Another example could be where the solicitor constantly interrupts the interview by raising legal arguments more suited to the trial and in effect refuses to allow the officer to continue with the questioning. This could be called misconduct in that the lawyer is straying from his limited role of adviser to the suspect. The initial decision to exclude a lawyer is taken by the investigating officer if he 'considers' that questioning is being improperly hindered. However, this subjective element is more than balanced by the following factors:

1) the interviewing officer must consult an officer of at least a superintendent rank (or, if unavailable, at least an inspector, but in that case the inspector must subsequently report the facts to the senior officer);
2) the officer consulted must talk to the solicitor;
3) the officer consulted will make the final decision and he in turn is well advised to consult the contemporaneous interview record (tape or written record) in reaching it;
4) the authorising officer should only act on the clearest evidence of improper conduct by the solicitor since removal of a solicitor is a 'serious step' (COP, para 6.11) and the courts (e.g. *R v Samuel* (1988)) will readily condemn the wrongful denial of legal advice; and
5) if the solicitor is excluded, the suspect must be allowed a replacement and the new solicitor will have the chance to witness the resumed interview (COP, para 6.10, 11).

Any exclusion of a solicitor is likely to be reported to the Law Society (and Legal Aid Board if a duty solicitor is involved, COP, para 6.11).

Securing legal advice

7.58 Once legal advice has been requested, the custody officer must act without delay to secure it (COP, paras 3.5, 6.2). The custody record should help here since it will indicate the time when the right to legal advice was administered and the time when the solicitor was informed. Many suspects will request a named solicitor or firm. The frequency with which named as opposed to duty solicitors are requested by suspects is difficult to gauge (see Brown, 1988; Sanders, 1989). It can vary between regions, depending in part on the quality of the local duty solicitor scheme, and between the times of the day, with for example named solicitors being more available in day time (Sanders, 1989, estimated that one third of legal advice sought comprised the duty scheme but acknowledged the imprecision of this estimate). If the suspect's solicitor cannot be contacted by the custody officer or if the suspect does not know a solicitor, he must be told of the duty solicitor scheme or be given a list of solicitors in the Regional Directory to choose from. If he opts for the latter, the solicitor becomes the suspect's own solicitor and he must claim for legal aid in the normal way. If the suspect cannot obtain a solicitor from the list, he should be allowed to try up to two alternatives and thereafter the custody officer has a discretion to permit further contacts (a discretion which he is well advised to exercise liberally in favour of the detainee). As regards the duty solicitor scheme, this is regulated by the

Legal Aid Board (via its Duty Solicitor Committee), 24 regional committees and over 300 local duty solicitor committees (see the Board's Duty Solicitor Arrangements 1990). There are also two types of provision — a rota, whereby named solicitors are allotted to particular dates, and a panel, whereby all the members of the duty solicitor scheme are available to be called out. In both cases the custody officer will telephone Healthcall which will endeavour to contact the solicitor on duty or one from the panel. The duty solicitor can then give advice up to a limit of £90 in the first instance (at 1991 rates), but this is normally extendible. Nearly 95% of police stations are covered by the duty solicitor scheme (101 out of 1,783 lacked it in 1990) and for the year 1989–90 it cost £31 million to run (an increase of 21.45% over the previous year, reflecting an increase of 20% in the number using it). The average overall cost per suspect was £89.85 (Report of the Legal Aid Board on the Operation and Finance of the Legal Aid Act 1988 for the year 1989–90).

7.59 Three issues arise — whether a solicitor can be contacted, whether (s)he will give advice, and what sort of advice is given. The failure rate in contacting a solicitor is unclear but low (Brown, 1988, suggests 3.5% and Sanders, 1989, 5.4%). Much will depend on the effectiveness of the local duty solicitor scheme. If the suspect's own solicitor is to be contacted outside business hours, there is obviously a greater chance of failure. Whether a solicitor will attend the station to give advice is another matter (one excuse is — 'I've drunk too much to drive; contact the duty solicitor'). Advice over the telephone may suffice or attendance may be pointless since, for example, the police assure the solicitor that they will not deal with the suspect until he has slept or sobered up. Attendance may be summarised as follows:

named solicitor — solicitor's decision whether to attend
duty solicitor — (i) telephone advice mandatory in first instance,
    (ii) attendance mandatory thereafter in certain circumstances,
    (iii) attendance discretionary if the circumstances in (ii) do not apply.

As regards a solicitor named by the suspect, the decision to attend belongs to the solicitor (he is not covered by the arrangements for duty solicitors see below). Clearly if the solicitor no longer practises in the criminal process field, that is the end of the matter (though he can pass him on to a colleague in the same firm and ethically he should surely acquaint or remind the suspect of the duty solicitor scheme). If he does still practise in the area, a serious reason should be required of him before he refuses in principle to attend (e.g. he is already acting for another suspect in the case and there is a likely conflict of interest, or he has experienced insuperable difficulties in representing the particular suspect). There may well be practical reasons why he does not attend (e.g. he is otherwise engaged, he considers that confidential advice over the telephone is possible and will suffice, the suspect is intoxicated or due for sleep and the police have expressed no intention to question him, the suspect has already been charged and the police have expressed no intention to interview him further). Such reasons do not however exclude the option of sending a representative to the station or appointing an agent to act. Moreover, the solicitor may be able to arrange with the custody or investigating officer a future time when he can attend (e.g. the following day when it is proposed to commence an interview). The overriding consideration should be whether the solicitor's presence is needed for the protection of the suspect's interests. At the end of the day, however, if a named solicitor refuses to attend, the suspect has no realistic redress, but the unrealistic option (for his current plight) subsequently to complain to the Law Society.

7.60 As for the attendance of duty solicitors, research indicated that there was a heavy reliance upon telephone advice (see Sanders (1989)). If the offence is trivial and the issues clear, telephone advice may well suffice, but even trivial offences (e.g. kerb crawling) can have serious consequences for an individual and, if he admits to an offence, a legal presence may be needed at least to advise on bail and to explain police procedures. A more pervasive reason for telephone advice may often stem from the strains on the duty solicitor scheme. Another factor used to be that attendance to advise a person arrested for an offence which is not an arrestable one (e.g. assaulting a constable, illegal immigration entry, kerb crawling; see further para 5.07, ante), or a person who is 'voluntarily' assisting the police in connection with such an offence, attracted the lower maximum of remuneration under the legal aid scheme. This differentiation was abolished in 1989 (see Legal Advice and Assistance at Police Stations (Remuneration) Regulations 1989) so that all advice at police stations is governed by the same extendible cost limit.

7.61 In 1989 the Legal Aid Board took over responsibility for the duty solicitor scheme from the Law Society and its Duty Solicitor Committee reviewed the procedures. The resulting Duty Solicitor Arrangements 1990 oblige each duty solicitor who is available on the rota or panel to respond to a call for advice either by attending at the police station, or by speaking to the suspect over the telephone, unless he 'is at or adjacent to the police station and can immediately advise the suspect in person. If the suspect is incapable by reason of drunkenness or violent behaviour of speaking to the duty solicitor, initial advice may be postponed' (para 55(2) of the *Arrangements*). If the latter arises, the duty solicitor should ask the custody officer to call him when the suspect sobers up and certainly before an interview with him takes place. Thus, the solicitor cannot leave a representative (e.g. trainee) to field and deal with requests from Healthcall (e.g. by giving the bleeper to him for the evening). Indeed a representative can only be sent to advise the suspect, if the duty solicitor has already given telephone advice. This requirement of telephone advice says nothing of the quality or extent of the advice and does not, for example, prevent him from giving minimal advice and then sending a representative. Good selection and training of duty solicitors are the keys to sound advice.

7.62 Once telephone advice has been given, the duty solicitor (or his representative) must attend the station only if the suspect so requests and if (a) he has been arrested for an arrestable offence and the police intend to interview him, or (b) the police intend to organise an identification procedure, or (c) the suspect complains to the solicitor of serious maltreatment by the police (para 56(1) of the Arrangements). If the interview with the suspect will not take place until the duty solicitor has finished his period of duty, he must either continue with the case as his own client or arrange for another duty solicitor to take over the case. As for (c), these Arrangements should be viewed as the minimal requirements and arguably *any* complaint of maltreatment should warrant the solicitor's attendance. The precondition of a request from the suspect is partly counterbalanced by the obligation to tell him over the telephone that he 'is entitled to insist' on the solicitor's attendance if (a), (b) or (c) above apply (para 55(2) of the Arrangements); but, as with the notification by the police of the suspect's right to legal advice, much can depend on the manner in which this entitlement is explained or qualified (e.g. 'you have the right for me to be there but frankly there is nothing I can do tonight'). If the suspect requests attendance and there are exceptional circumstances preventing it (e.g. the solicitor's sudden illness), they must be recorded on the legal aid costs claim form (para 56(2)). For those cases outside (a) to (c), the duty solicitor has a discretion as to whether to attend. His guiding light is the interests of the suspect. Two factors are picked out in the Duty Solicitor Arrangements as generally requiring his attendance viz whether he can give satisfactory and confidential advice to the suspect over the telephone, and whether a juvenile or other person at risk is involved. There are many others; for example, whether the suspect is seriously agitated about his detention and needs calming advice, whether he needs advice as to bail, or whether he wants the solicitor to contact other people or make investigations. However, the pressures on the duty solicitor scheme are such that, in some areas of the country, cases outside (a) to (c) are likely to mean frequent non-attendance of solicitors or a heavy reliance upon representatives.

7.63 The success of the Duty Solicitor Arrangements 1990 depends upon (1) the effectiveness of the more rigorous selection and reselection procedures for duty solicitors and their representatives; (2) the increased level of training for participants in the scheme; (3) the overseeing of the National Duty Solicitor Co-ordinator and his five Group Duty Solicitor Managers; (4) the achievement of various performance targets by each local scheme (e.g. availability of a solicitor in 95% of cases collected by Healthcall, 80% of referrals to a rota (75% to a panel) being successful within 30 minutes); (5) the willingness of the central Government to fund this branch of legal aid realistically; and (6) the eagerness of young lawyers entering the profession to undertake this type of work.

Assisting the suspect

7.64 When visiting a client at a police station the solicitor (or representative) should be armed with a copy of PACE, the Codes, the Law Society's Guide to Advising a Suspect, and any other suitable guide. It is not only the police who are tied to record-keeping. The solicitor too must keep notes of when things are done and of what is said. Notes of the former will be crucial if the accuracy of the custody record is questioned. The solicitor's own tape-recorder can easily be used for the latter, though an additional written record/summary is advisable. This function of note-taking will be demanding if the solicitor agrees to represent several suspects. The solicitor or client is entitled to a copy of the custody record as soon as practicable after the suspect leaves police detention, or when he is taken before a court (COP, para 2.4). However, the solicitor has no such entitlement on arrival at the station and before he consults his client. Some custody officers informally permit access and this seems a sensible and quick way of acquainting the solicitor with the background to the case. The officer may be reluctant to reveal the record if it contains remarks made by the suspect but three factors should encourage him to do so. First, a solicitor can only give proper legal advice if he is aware of all the known circumstances. Second, on seeing the record the solicitor may give advice which, from the police point of view, is favourable. If he advises silence from the client, so be it; but very often the advice will, in the face of damaging evidence, produce a formal confession or at least cooperation with the interrogation. Third, the solicitor will see the record in due course anyway and, if the police try to mislead him, by concealing information on the custody record, the spectres of ss 76 and 78 (Arts 74 and 76) will loom large. The solicitor should also attempt to extract the evidential details from the investigating officer. If he is rebuffed because the officer is reluctant to disclose his hand, he should again stress the importance of him giving 'informed' legal advice to his client.

Documentation

7.65 If a suspect requests legal advice, this must be timed and noted in the custody record, along with the steps taken by the police to secure it (COP, para 6.16). If he declines it, he must be asked to sign the record (para 3.5). Similarly if someone else has sent the solicitor, the suspect is asked to sign the custody record and indicate whether he wants the legal advice (COP, Annex B, para 3). If a solicitor is denied access to the suspect or the interview begins in the absence of the solicitor, these should be noted. Needless to say, this documentation or lack of it can have a crucial impact on the subsequent admissibility of evidence under sections 76 and 78 (Arts 74, 76).

Identification

7.66 The police will often wish to conduct various identification procedures in respect of the detained person. A witness may come forward to give visual identification of the offender. Fingerprints and photographs may have to be taken to assist detection or to identify the person with official records. Samples from the person's body may need to be taken for forensic purposes. The following section deals with these procedures. Three general, opening observations should be made. Firstly, this area is governed largely by the Code of Practice for the Identification of Persons by Police Officers (referred to as COP, D in the following paragraphs) rather than by the PACE Act 1984, and, since the whole area of identification is sensitive and controversial, breach of this Code's provisions is likely to have important evidential consequences at trial. The courts have shown themselves willing to use s 78 (Art 76) of PACE to exclude improperly obtained identification evidence (eg *R v Ladlow* (1989), *R v Conway* (1990) and *R v Nagah* (1990)), though disputes over the admissibility of identification evidence should not generally warrant the judge holding a trial within a trial (*R v Beveridge* (1987), *R v Flemming* (1987)). Second, the procedures governing identification apply, with one small exception (see COP, D, para 2A), to police officers who themselves act as identifying witnesses, as well as to witnesses from the general public (see *R v Samms, Elliott and Bartley* (1991)). Third, the following formal identification procedures should be distinguished from an accidental meeting between witness and suspect (eg an off duty police officer recognises a person, who has come to the station on another matter, as a suspect in a crime), see *R v Quinn* (1990), *R v Long* (1991).

7.67 Identification can involve both discovering the identity of the offender per se and testing a suspect's identification in respect of an offence. As regards the former, it is not a criminal offence to refuse to give one's name and personal details (though it is a reason to arrest for a non-arrestable offence, s 25 (Art 27), see para 5.17, ante). In theory this means that D's identity can remain unknown up to and including the trial, though fingerprints and other non-intimate samples (below) can be taken without D's consent and may reveal his identity. If they do not, D must be labelled with a number. A suspect's address can be more of a problem. Again he is under no duty to disclose it. For vagrant adults it is unlikely to raise a problem; but for vagrant juveniles, other police forces and social services should be consulted. As regards the latter (identification of a suspect in order to link him with an offence), detailed provisions (below) exist. However they do not encompass every process. Thus, the simple tasks of taking physical measurements, weighing the person, skin washing and handwriting samples fall outside PACE and depend upon the suspect's consent. Sometimes the observance of ordinary procedures will suffice to obtain these identifications (e.g. D writing his own statement or completing the custody record, or D standing adjacent to a measuring scale in the charge room) but if not, the custody or investigating officer is entitled to point out that D's refusal to cooperate with an identification process (e.g. the washing of skin) can be referred to by the trial judge (see *R v Smith* (1985)). If the police resort to subterfuge, however, they run the real risk of exclusion of evidence under s 78 (Art 76) (e.g. by falsely telling D that forensic evidence will link him with the offence, see *R v Mason* (1987)).

Visual identification

7.68 In 1972 the Criminal Law Revision Committee observed that 'mistaken identification [is] by far the greatest cause of actual or possible wrong convictions' (para 196). A sufficient number of cases are reported to show that the problem remains, but considerable steps have been taken in recent years to alert the courts and the police to the dangers of identification evidence. Thus, a Report by Lord Devlin (1976) HC 338 prompted the Court of Appeal in *R v Turnbull* (1976) to issue guidelines. These stressed the need for the jury to treat identification evidence with special caution and to examine it carefully. The Devlin Report also prompted the Attorney-General to issue guidelines as to how the Director of Public Prosecutions would take special precautions in preparing and prosecuting cases where identification evidence would play a part. The strictures of *Turnbull* are regularly repeated by the courts and, according to the Privy Council, apply to identification evidence by police witnesses as well (*Reid v The Queen* (1989)). They were also responsible for the tightening up of procedures for the use of identification parades and photographs. Thus, Home Office Circulars emphasised the danger of a witness wrongly identifying a suspect and the attendant risks of a wrongful conviction or an unsuccessful prosecution. The various procedures for visual identification of a known suspect are now set out in COP, D. Four can be used — (a) identification parade, (b) group identification, (c) video identification, and (d) confrontation between suspect and witness.

R v Ladlow (1989) decided that there is an order of preference ((a), (b), (c), (d)) and that the police cannot jump from (a) to (d) without considering the intermediate positions (see also *R v Woolls* (1990); thus the police should not release a suspect in the hope of getting an identification by confrontation rather than hold an identification parade, *R v Nagah* (1990)). Likewise the order of preference applies to police officers who are to be identification witnesses (*R v Samms, Elliott and Bartley* (1991)). If the police breach these procedures, there is a real possibility that s 78 (Art 76) will be used to exclude evidence and defeat the prosecution. A precondition for the use of these methods is that there is a dispute over identification i.e. the police have a suspect who challenges the identification evidence of a witness. A useful expedient is for the police to write down the description supplied by the witness and ask him to read and sign it. It can then be used in subsequent court proceedings to refresh his memory. Another precondition is that the identification exercise is likely to have some usefulness. Where, for example, the police know that the suspect has changed his appearance since the offence (e.g. by a different hairstyle), it will be inappropriate (though the fact that the witness has recognised the suspect from an earlier police photograph can be mentioned to the jury, *R v Byrne and Trump* (1987)). It should also be noted that the following procedures do not encompass a chance visual identification (e.g. a witness bumps into a suspect in the street). That is perfectly admissible without more, although the emphasis must clearly be on the fortuitous nature of the encounter.

(a) Identification parade (COP, D, paras 2.3–5, Annex A)

7.69 An identification parade can be held in two situations:

(i) If the suspect requests it and it is practicable to do so, a parade must be held. The latter condition absolves the police from obliging if, for example, the suspect's appearance is so unusual (e.g. his colour, his size) as to rule out the possibility of finding suitable people to attend the parade, or the police station is so congested as to make it impracticable. However, in the latter situation it may be possible to hold a parade at a quieter time. In *R v Ladlow* (1989) there were not only 11 witnesses and 21 defendants, which would have required 221 identification parades, but it was also a Bank Holiday and the procurement of enough volunteers to attend the parade was clearly impracticable. Cases need not be so extreme for the police to face considerable inconvenience in preparing a parade e.g. a Chinese suspect in a mainly non-immigrant area. The impact on police manpower can be severe and in many stations an identification parade is a rarity. However, the onus lies on the police to convince the trial judge of a parade's impracticability (*R v Gaynor* (1988)). An inspector's decision 'must be taken on reasonable grounds and he must take all reasonably practicable steps to investigate the possibility of holding a parade or group identification before holding a confrontation' (*R v Britton and Richards* (1989)). This means that he could consider the possibility of asking the suspect to help to organise a parade; for it may be that he will stand a better chance of finding volunteers (D may belong to a section of the community which will be hostile or apathetic to police requests for help). The onus then passes to D and his solicitor to put forward a realistic proposal (*R v Britton and Richards*). Given the vital importance of accurate identification evidence, a court will not be fobbed off with unsupported claims of impracticability and will not readily accept the alternative of (c) or (d) below (see *R v Gaynor* (1988)). Similarly a court will take a tough stance against any police malpractice or underhand method of obtaining identification in place of the parade provisions (see *R v Nagah* (1990) where D was willing to appear at an identification parade but was released so that identification by confrontation in the street could be made instead of proceeding to a parade). The suspect will clearly consider requesting a parade if he protests his innocence and wishes to discredit the witness. However, the possibility of mistaken identification arising out of a parade is still a real one, especially if the suspect is not used to it and betrays signs of nervousness. It may thus be very important for the suspect to take legal advice before deciding whether to ask for a parade. The Code of Practice, D, (Annex A) allows a solicitor or friend to be present at a parade and allows the suspect to take legal advice before the parade continues. Conversely, if D demands a parade, is not doing so in bad faith, and it is practicable, the COP, D, is unequivocal — it must be held. This applies even if the witnesses have named D and claim to know him, or if a witness has previously identified D in the street. The police may see no point in this (see *R v Conway* (1990), *R v Brown* (1991)) but if D, after legal advice, is determined to put the witnesses to the test, they should be. If they are afraid, it may be possible to put them behind a screen if such a facility is available in the police district.

(ii) If the officer (of any rank) who is in charge of the investigation considers that a parade will be useful and the suspect consents, one may be held. Force would clearly defeat the object. 'Consent' in relation to the mentally ill or handicapped must be given in the presence of the 'appropriate adult'; in relation to juveniles between 14 and 17, the consent of suspect and parent or guardian is needed, for those below 14 the consent of the adult will suffice (COP, D, para 1.11; for the meaning of 'appropriate adult' see para 7.113, post). Again, the suspect may take legal advice before the parade takes place. He may, for example, need to be told that the trial judge can comment on the accused's failure to agree to an identification parade. 'Considers' gives ample discretion to the investigating officer. He should be aware of the procedural preconditions for a parade (below), since some (e.g. as to the showing of photographs to a witness beforehand) may frustrate the holding of a parade and risk the subsequent exclusion of evidence.

(b) *Group identification (COP, D, paras 2.6–9, Annex A)*

7.70 This can be held in the following situations:

(i) If the suspect refuses to participate in an identification parade or a parade is impracticable, the investigating officer must try to organise a group identification i.e. an opportunity for the witness to see the suspect in a group of people.

(ii) In other cases (e.g. where the witness is too nervous to participate in an identification parade, or where the witness is convinced that a group identification is the only reliable method), the investigating officer has a discretion to allow a group identification if he considers it to be more appropriate than a parade.

In both (i) and (ii) D should first be asked to agree and be given the relevant information (see below). But COP, D, paras 2.8 and 2.15(vii), envisage a group identification proceeding without D's consent (e.g. by D being unwittingly surrounded by other persons and secretly observed by the witness). If a group identification is to be tried, an identification officer assumes responsibility. Generally the same safeguards for identification and video parades apply to group identification (see below). The most important is that the procedure must be organised so as to avoid directing the witnesses' attention to one person. The group identification exercise should not usually take place at the police station. It can be organised, for example, at the scene of the crime, an underground station (with the witness placed at the top of an escalator and D asked to ascend it when he is ready), a shopping centre, public house, or even at a court building such as the cafeteria when D returns to answer his bail (*R v Grannell* (1989)) or remand prisoners arriving by bus at court. If it is not practicable (e.g. D is violent, liable to escape, or an alternative venue cannot be arranged realistically), the police station will have to be used. Wherever the venue be, the procedures governing parades (below) should still be followed if at all possible and great care must be taken to ensure that D is not made conspicuous. This last point can effectively defeat many group identifications (see *R v Woolls* (1990)) since it is open to the objection that the random passers-by do not resemble the suspect. From D's point of view, an accurate description of the group noted by his lawyer (perhaps on video if practicable) could be crucial. If the police suspect a person but do not have enough evidence to warrant his detention and if he will not consent to an identification procedure, the police may resort to a 'street identification' i.e. allowing the witness to view the suspect (see para 7.83, post). The COP, D, is vague about this situation but, it is submitted, the general principle applies with even more force viz. that the witness should not be directed or influenced towards the suspect. Thus, in principle, an identification officer (in this context a uniformed officer of experience and unconnected with the case) should supervise the process and record its details in writing and/or tape form and ask the witness to verify the record.

(c) Video identification (COP, D, paras 2.10–12, Annex B)

7.71 The investigating officer can request a video identification (film of the suspect and at least eight non-suspects) if D refuses an identification parade, or group identification, or one cannot be organised, or there is some other reason. An example of the last is where a video is likely to be the most satisfactory way of identifying the suspect (eg a film of D and volunteers in the same position or action, or where a security camera has filmed a suspect entering a room and volunteers are then filmed in identical circumstances). The overriding requirement is that the video be the most satisfactory course of action (COP, D, para 2.10). The COP, D, normally requires D's consent, but permits a video without consent if it is practicable. Since force cannot be used in videotaping D this will be a rare occurrence, for he can simply cover his face. An exception might be where D has already been filmed, e.g. by a security camera, and a comparable tape of volunteers can now be made and shown to a witness.

(d) Confrontation (COP, D, paras 2.13–14, Annex C)

7.72 As a last resort (i.e. if a parade or group or video identification cannot be organised), the suspect can be confronted by the witness. This can arise because the suspect refuses to consent to the other procedures or because these others are impracticable (e.g. because of the suspect's striking appearance, it is not possible to organise an identification parade). The suspect must be forewarned (*R v Ismail* (1990)) but his consent is not essential. Confrontation is the least satisfactory of the identification procedures because of its contrived nature, and all practicable steps should be taken to avoid reliance on it.

Procedure (COP, D, Annex A)

7.73 Since most of the identification parade procedures apply, with appropriate modification, to the other methods of identification, they are mentioned (a) and not repeated in procedures (b) to (d).

(a)   *Identification parade*

7.74   Once an identification parade is agreed upon, it should proceed forthwith (*R v Nagah* (1990)). A uniformed officer who is not involved in the case and who is of at least inspector rank supervises the procedure — the 'identification officer' (COP, D, para 2.2). An officer who is involved must not interfere in any of the arrangements but he can be present in the background. So, for example, the investigating officer should not be present at a confrontation between witness and suspect (*R v Woolls* (1990)), bring the witness into the room for the parade or confrontation, or be seen to talk to the identification officer in the identification room (*R v Gall* (1990)). Likewise great care needs to be taken to avoid the witness seeing the suspect in the environs of the police station prior to the identification process. The whole thrust of these requirements is to ensure that the witness is not unduly influenced in any way about the suspect. The identification officer must pass certain information orally and in writing to the suspect (and the 'appropriate adult' in the case of the mentally ill and juveniles, COP, D, para 1.13). The suspect (or the 'appropriate adult') is then asked to sign his agreement to the arrangements. The COP, D, para 2.15 lists the information which has to be given: the purpose of the exercise, D's entitlement to free legal advice, the procedures (including the presence of an 'appropriate adult' for the mentally ill or a juvenile, or a solicitor or friend for any other suspect), the fact that the suspect is not compelled to participate, but that the fact of refusal can be mentioned at trial, that the police may organise identification covertly without his consent, and whether or not the witness has previously been shown pictures of suspects (though at trial it is not essential for the judge to direct the jury on this, *R v Hinds* (1932)). The identification officer must explain all this and a notice containing the information is also given to D. In particular, he should be asked whether he wishes a solicitor or friend to be present, for whereas a court may forgive a failure to convey some of the other information, a failure to mention legal advice may result in the identification process being improperly conducted or may deprive D of the chance of lodging a legitimate objection to its conduct, and the evidence may subsequently be excluded under s 78 (Art 76). On the other hand, it must be remembered that the test for the operation of s 78 (Art 76) is unfairness and a breach of the COP does not necessarily produce that. The crucial requirement is whether the act of identification was impartially or rigorously performed and a failure to tell D of some matters, though reprehensible, need not affect the accuracy of the witness' identification (*R v Grannell* (1989)). Finally, and immediately before the identification parade, D must be reminded of the procedures to be followed and must be given a caution (COP, D, Annex A, para 5). When he enters the parade room, he is asked whether he objects to any aspect of it. It is here that the advice of an experienced criminal lawyer may be particularly useful in objecting to the physical arrangements for the parade. The duty to tell D whether the witness has been shown pictures or a photofit etc. beforehand, is also useful for the lawyer since at trial that may reduce the weight to be given to the witness' identification on the parade. Above all, the identification officer should do his utmost to satisfy any objections levelled at the proceedings, and, if he cannot, he should explain why. As the preamble to the Home Office Circular (1978) observed:

'Identification parades should be fair and should be seen to be fair. Every precaution should be taken to see that they are so, and in particular to exclude any suspicion of unfairness or risk of erroneous identification through the witnesses' attention being directed specially to the suspected person instead of equally to all persons paraded.'

7.75 In order that the parade 'should be seen to be fair', once it has started, everything relevant to it must take place in the presence and hearing of the suspect and his representative (COP, D, Annex A, para 7). One particular pitfall to be avoided is a conversation between the identification officer and D about the alleged offence. For it will not take much of an interchange before it ranks as an 'interview' for PACE purposes with the attendant duties to caution and record (see para 8.07, post). If D's solicitor or a friend is not present, a colour photograph or preferably a video recording should be taken of the procedure and made available to the defence.

(1)   The parade

7.76 A parade must consist of at least 8 others besides the suspect. They should as far as possible resemble the appearance of the suspect (eg as to height, age, colour, dress, social standing) but the identification officer has a wide discretion (cf *R v Thorne* (1981)). Police officers may be used but their smart grooming etc will often make them inappropriate. A maximum of two suspects may appear in the same parade, provided that they are of 'roughly similar appearance' and that at least 12 other persons participate. If there are more than two suspects, separate parades must be organised and must be composed of different volunteers. This means that multiple parades are rarely feasible. If a prison inmate is to appear in a parade, he can be brought to the police station; if this raises security problems, the parade can be held at the prison and, exceptionally, other inmates can be used to form the parade. Obviously the suspected inmate should only wear prison uniform if the other members of the parade do so. When all the suspects belong to a 'similar group' (eg Army Officers, or police officers accused of assault during a public demonstration), they should be paraded separately, unless two are of similar appearance in which case they can appear along with 12 other persons. If in the example uniformed officers are paraded, their force numbers should be concealed lest the witness be guided by that instead of visual identity. The suspect is allowed to stand where he likes in the line and he can change position after each witness has completed the process.

(2)   Witnesses

7.77   For obvious reasons, if the police already hold a suspect, a witness should not be shown photographs or identikit pictures of him prior to the identity parade or group identification. If he has been shown them prior to D's involvement, then D must be told of this before the identification procedure. Similarly, the witness should be kept in isolation from other witnesses and from members of the parade. The onus on the police (especially the identification officer) is to keep the witness aloof from any personal or visual contact or from any information which might be thought to prejudice his identification. For example, the identification officer must tell the witness that the relevant person *may or may not* be in the parade (see the COP, D, Annex A, paras 12–14, for the various precautions). This quarantine is particularly important when the witness is a police officer. In all cases a witness should never be told whether another witness has already made an identification. That is just the sort of condition, breach of which a court may visit with the exclusion of evidence under s 78 (Art 76). Some police stations are equipped with screens enabling the witness to examine the parade unobserved (some may boast an identification suite, staffed by experienced officers, which can be booked by other divisions in the force). In that case D's lawyer or representative must be present during the parade or the procedure must be recorded on video so that any remarks addressed to, or made by, the witness behind the screen are noted (COP, D, Annex A, para 7; however, it is submitted that a contemporaneous written note would suffice in the absence of a videotape, provided of course that the court is satisfied of its accuracy and this can be achieved by asking D to read and sign it).

(3)   The Identification

7.78   The witness is asked to take his time and to walk along the line at least twice. The identification should be by pointing to, or speaking, the number attached to each person on the parade (there is, quite rightly, no requirement to touch the suspect). If the witness at trial cannot remember which number he selected, the identification officer or other officer present can testify as to the number (*R v Mccay* (1990)), but it is more convenient if the witness is asked to write the number down and sign the identification record. It can then be used to refresh his memory at trial if need be. The witness can ask to see the members of the parade in particular clothing (e.g. wearing a hat) or that they move or gesture in a particular way. The identification officer shall comply, but only after asking the witness whether he can identify anyone without the aid of such a prompt.

The members of the line can also be asked to speak a certain phrase. In that case, the witness should be told that they have been chosen for the parade according to appearance not to voice. In any event, the value of this type of identification is extremely limited. Occasionally the witness will make an identification after the parade has finished (this is permissible if the witness has not acted through an improper motive but through fear of the suspect at the time of the parade — *R v Creamer* (1985)), but in this situation the identification officer should seriously consider a re-run using a different line-up of volunteers or a different order. If he does not, the evidence may be of dubious value with the defence likely to challenge the weight of it at trial — the onus will be on the Crown to establish by examination in chief that the witness genuinely delayed the identification because of fear. At the end of the parade, the identification officer should ask the suspect and, it is suggested, his representative for any comments on the organisation of the parade and he should make a record of them. Any such conversation should be kept within those parameters for otherwise they may qualify as an interview for PACE purposes (see para 8.07, post).

(4)   Documentation

7.79   The prime responsibility for record-keeping falls on the identification officer. He must compile details of the following: the reasons why he considers an identification parade to be impracticable; the suspect's refusal to participate in an identification procedure; whether the suspect wants a lawyer or friend present; the reasons why any member of the identification procedure has been asked to leave; details of those present at the procedure; the circumstances in which prison inmates have been used in the parade. If the suspect is alone during the identification, a photograph or video will be taken of the parade and this is available to the suspect or his solicitor, so that its fairness can be assessed (COP, D, Annex A, para 19).

(b)   Group Identification

7.80   This should follow the procedures governing an identification parade so far as possible (COP, D, para 2.9). Thus, if the suspect agrees to it, his lawyer or representative (e.g. appropriate adult) should be allowed to attend, the procedure should be carefully explained, any objections considered, and the caution given. Whether the suspect consents or not, the members of the group must where possible be chosen for their resemblance to the suspect, no more than two suspects should appear in the group, the witness must be cocooned from improper influence and the identification officer should keep a record of the proceedings including the names of those in the group (though this will usually be impracticable if the procedure takes place in public such as a department store or bus station).

(c)   *Video identification (COP, D. Annex B)*

7.81   Very similar provisions apply to a video parade as they do to an identification parade (e.g. as to the number of participants, the shielding of the witness) but the following are worth mentioning. 1) Video parades will be rare and, if the participants are to do more than stare at the camera, require skill in compilation. It is therefore sensible for each police force to nominate a particular officer or civilian employee to acquire the necessary expertise (e.g. by compiling a databank of witnesses for future use). 2) Because of the detailed and sometimes subtle images which a film can contain, it is highly desirable for the suspect and his representative or friend to see the completed film before it is shown to the witness. If their objections to its objectivity are reasonable and can be accommodated, police and court time and money can be saved at an early stage. 3) Similarly the suspect's representative (but not the suspect) should be given the opportunity of observing the witness viewing the video parade and, if the representative does not attend, a video of the viewing itself must be made. This is particularly important since the witness is allowed to see the videotape as many times as he likes, to repeat sections of it and to freeze individual frames. The apparent certainty or hesitation of a witness' identification may be crucial at trial. 4) If an identification is made, the witness is shown the crucial part of the tape once more for confirmation. 5) If the suspect is not prosecuted or is acquitted, he has the opportunity of witnessing the destruction (i.e. erasing) of the videotape.

(d)   *Confrontation (COP, D, Annex C)*

7.82   Again the identification officer takes charge. The confrontation should take place in front of the suspect's solicitor, interpreter or friend, unless unreasonable delay would be caused by waiting for him. The witness is asked simply whether the suspect is the person in question. Confrontation is perhaps a misnomer for those stations equipped with a screen behind which the witness can see the suspect without being observed. In that case the suspect's lawyer, interpreter or friend should be present or at least the witness' reaction should be recorded on videotape. In this context a bystander does not qualify as a 'friend' (see *R v Woolls* (1990) where the police asked a man, who happened to be at the station on other business and whose niece was married to a policeman, to witness the identification; he was held not to be an appropriate 'friend'). The procedure should be explained to the suspect and an accurate record kept by the identification officer. The witness must be carefully protected from undue influence. A crucial precaution is that he be told that the person he is about to confront may, or may not, be the offender and that, if he cannot identify him, he must say so.

Identification but no arrest

7.83 In those cases where the police suspect a person but do not have enough evidence to arrest him and where he cannot be persuaded to assist in one of the identification methods above, it may be possible to take a witness to the neighbourhood frequented by the suspect to see if it jogs his memory. There are obvious dangers that the police will influence the witness directly or, more probably, indirectly and it is clearly desirable that an officer unconnected with the investigation (depending on available manpower) supervise this covert confrontation. The situation is quite different if a witness suspects someone (e.g. he has seen him in a betting shop, or public house but does not know his name), for he can then be taken to the location and asked to observe (a street identification). If the witness has described a suspect (e.g. D assaults P and runs away), then the suspect should be arrested and, if practicable, one of the identification methods (above) used (rather than D being brought back to the victim for identification in the street).

Photographs and pictures (COP, D, Annex D)

7.84 If the police already suspect a person and an issue of identity arises, then the witness should not be shown any photograph or likeness of him. Instead his identification should be tested by one of the procedures (a) to (d) above. The following section deals with the finding of an offender by photographic means.

7.85 The showing of photographs and identikit and other types of pictures to a witness is a well recognised method of trying to identify offenders (e.g. *R v Palmer* (1914)). The practice was covered in detail by the Home Office Circular 109/1978. Annex D to the COP, D, replaced and largely repeated the instructions of the Circular. As the preamble to the Circular stated:

'The object of showing a group of photographs to a witness is to test his ability to pick out the photograph, if it is there, of the person whom the witness has said that he has seen previously on a specified occasion. Every precaution should be taken to exclude any suspicion of unfairness or erroneous identification.'

Procedure

7.86 An officer of at least sergeant rank (as opposed to inspector in relation to identification parades) supervises the showing of photographs, whilst any officer or police employee can actually show them to a witness. The latter should be kept apart from other witnesses. The fact that he must be given some information (below) means that a juvenile and mentally ill or handicapped witness must be accompanied by an 'appropriate adult' (see para 7.113, post). Obviously the witness must not be prompted when shown the photographs and must be told that the person he saw may not be there. He must be shown at least 12 photographs of, if possible, a similar kind. Thus, a snapshot should not normally be used amongst the regulation-sized photographs held for criminal record purposes. Some searches will involve the witness looking at standard albums. Where, on the other hand, the police have a suspect in mind, his photograph should be mixed in with others of close resemblance. A record must be kept of which photographs were seen by the witness and in which order and they should be available at trial. Similarly, any statement or observation from the witness should be recorded. If the witness identifies a photograph, it shall not be shown to other witnesses (unless the person in the photograph has been cleared by the police). Instead, all the witnesses should, if possible, be asked to attend an identification parade or other identification (see above). In recent years more sophisticated photofit and identikit pictures have been devised to help a witness to reconstruct a suspect's face. They are admissible as evidence (*R v Cook* (1987), *R v Constantinou* (1989)) but it is desirable that a jury be warned as to their accuracy along the lines of *R v Turnbull* (1976) (see the powerful commentary attached to *Constantinou*). If a description of witness X and the resulting picture have led to the arrest of a suspect, then other witnesses Y and Z should not be shown the picture before an identification parade. They may well of course have seen it in the media, if the police have publicised it in an effort to arrest the suspect. If a witness attends a parade, the fact that he has previously been shown a photograph or picture must be revealed to the accused and his lawyer. The reason for this is to alert the defence to the prejudice which may be caused to the accused at trial if it is revealed to the jury that he was identified by police photographs, thus implying that he has a criminal record. The prosecution must handle any such revelation sensitively (*R v Varley* (1914), *R v Hinds* (1932)).

Fingerprints (s and Art 61, PACE)

7.87 Fingerprints can serve two purposes. The first and by far the more frequent usage is to identify the accused so that a record of his antecedents can be prepared for the court. The second is to detect the offender by, for example, comparing prints left at the scene of the crime with national records or with prints taken freshly from the suspect. Research conducted for the Royal Commission indicated that fingerprints were the main source of information to suggest a suspect to the police in about 2% of detected indictable crimes (Report, para 3.125). The law prior to PACE allowed fingerprints to be taken:

  (i)   with consent;
 (ii)   by order of a magistrates' court (s 49 of the Magistrates' Courts Act 1980);
(iii)   on the authority of the police or other authorised persons under the immigration and prevention of terrorism legislation.

The previous practice meant that (i) was used most regularly. In fact the taking of fingerprints was regarded by the police as a matter of routine in much the same way as the emptying of pockets was and still is (see para 7.11, ante). Disputes could then arise occasionally as to whether the person's 'consent' had been freely given. PACE (like the Royal Commission) recognised the slender role for magistrates in this area and placed the emphasis upon the police station. It permits fingerprinting:

 (a)   with the written consent of the individual (s 61(1), Art 61 is identically worded);
 (b)   on the authority of a senior officer in order to detect the offender (s 61(3)(a));
 (c)   as a matter of routine if the suspect is to be prosecuted (s 61(3)(b));
 (d)   after a person has been convicted but where he has not already given his fingerprints under (a) to (c) (s 61(6)).

Two preliminary points should be noted. (1) the expression 'Fingerprints' includes palm prints (s 65, Art 53; for a definition of palm, see *R v Tottenham Justices, ex p M.L. (1986)*). (2) Categories (b)–(d) confer powers on the police. Consequently, if the person resists the taking of the prints, the police can use reasonable force (s 117, Art 88).

(a)   Consent

7.88   Fingerprints can be taken from any person with consent, regardless of the person's age or legal status (e.g. as detainee, or convicted person or member of the public). Three qualifications apply:

  (i)   'the appropriate consent' is needed and this is specially defined by s 65 (Art 53) as the consent of a person over the age of 17, the consent of a person between 14 and 17 and of his parent or guardian, and for a person under 14, the consent of a parent or guardian. A local authority or voluntary organisation may qualify as 'parent or guardian' (s 118, Art 2).
 (ii)   If the consent is given whilst the person is at a police station it must be in writing (s 61(2)).
(iii)   In every case the person must be told the reason for taking the fingerprints and that they will be destroyed (in his presence if he so wishes) if he is not prosecuted or is acquitted (COP, D, para 3.1).

(b) Authority of a senior officer

7.89 This covers persons who are detained (i.e. under arrest) at a police station and who are over the age of 10 (COP, D, para 3.2). An officer of at least superintendent rank can authorise in writing or orally (subject to written confirmation) the taking of fingerprints if he reasonably suspects D of an offence and reasonably believes that the prints 'will tend to confirm or disprove' D's involvement (s 61(3), (4)).

(c) With a view to prosecution

7.90 If a person (over the age of 10) has been charged with, or has been told that he will be reported for, a recordable offence, his prints can be taken whilst he is still in detention at the police station. Crimes which are to be recorded in national police records are 'recordable offences' for fingerprinting purposes (ss 27, 118; Arts 29, 2), and these cover all offences which are punishable by imprisonment (regardless of any curbs on the sentencing of young offenders) and a few other offences (see National Police Records (Recorded Offences) Regulations 1985). The result of these provisions is the routine taking of fingerprints for all those detained at a police station and who may be prosecuted. The fact that a person is reported for prosecution (to the Crown Prosecution Service or the Juvenile Bureau) does not of course mean that proceedings will commence. If they are not, the fingerprints should be destroyed (see below).

(d) After conviction

7.91 For those few whose prints are not taken under (a) to (c) and for the larger number who are prosecuted by way of summons and who have not been held in detention at a police station, s 61(6) permits the taking of fingerprints after conviction. Section 27 (Art 29) provides a power to arrest without warrant in such circumstances (see para 5.34, ante).

Procedure

7.92 In non-consensual cases, reasonable force may be used to obtain the fingerprints (s 117, Art 88) and details must be kept of the circumstances which required force (COP, D, para 3.7). The person must be told the reason for taking the prints and the reason must be recorded (in a custody record if he is in detention, s 61(7), (8)). He must also be told of the possibility that the prints will be destroyed in due course, if he is not prosecuted or not proved to have committed the offence (see further para 7.102, post and s 64 in relation to the destruction of fingerprints, photographs and samples).

Savings

7.93 There are two additional statutory powers to take fingerprints:

(a) under the Immigration Act 1971 (Sch 2, para 18(2)) entrants to the UK may be detained to see if they are entitled to enter and remain. The detention can take place at a port of entry, a police station or a prison. An immigration officer, constable or prison officer has the power to identify the detained person by 'photographing, measuring or otherwise identifying him.' Fingerprints can therefore be taken. The purpose may be to identify the person by checking with records held by the Immigration Service and by the police, or to add that person's prints to police records so as to assist subsequent enforcement of the 1971 Act;

(b) provisions dealing with terrorist offences (Prevention of Terrorism (Temporary Provisions) Act 1989 have adopted and adapted part of the PACE procedure (see para 7.146, post).

Photographs

7.94 Like fingerprints, photographs are primarily used to establish the identity of the person arrested, so as to make sure that the correct person appears in court and, where appropriate, the correct criminal record is produced to the court. The Royal Commission (Report, para 3.133) recommended that the taking of photographs of the accused should be governed by provisions similar to those relating to fingerprints. This approach was adopted by PACE but relegated to a Code of Practice. Thus, photographs of an arrested person may be taken:

(a) with the person's written consent;
(b) if other people are arrested at the same time and photographs are needed to show 'who was arrested, at what time and at what place' (COP, D, para 4.2(i); e.g. at a football match, nightclub or public disorder at a demonstration);
(c) if the person has been charged with, or reported for, a recordable offence (see para 7.90 above);
(d) if the person has been convicted and his photograph has not already been taken (cf s 27 (Art 29) in relation to fingerprints; but unlike that provision there is no power to arrest in order to take a photograph).

The person must be told the reason for the photograph, that it will eventually be destroyed if he is not prosecuted or if he is acquitted, and that he may witness the destruction or obtain a certificate confirming their destruction (see para 7.102, post). In spite of the usefulness of photographs and the minimal intrusion involved, no force can be used to take one (COP, D, para 4.3) (as to the *use* of photographs to assist in the identification of offenders, see para 7.84, ante). A written record must be made of the reasons for (b) to (d) and of the destruction of any photograph taken under (a) to (d) (COP, D, para 4.5).

Taking of samples (ss 62, 63: Arts 62 and 63 of the N.I. Order are mostly identical, so only section references will be used unless they differ)

7.95 It is sometimes necessary for the police to take samples from a person's body in order to check on that person's involvement in an offence. The most obvious instance is the breathalyser in road traffic cases. Sex offences are a less frequent but similarly relevant area (eg swabs taken to detect semen or vaginal traces). The samples under discussion here include blood, saliva (both of which have considerable potential in DNA profiling) urine, hair, semen, scrapings from beneath fingernails and teeth impressions. Prior to PACE, the taking of such samples against the will of the person was an assault. The police had then to rely upon bluff or consent. The road traffic legislation offers one exception — the refusal to supply a sample of breath, blood or urine in drink-driving cases is an offence (s 8 of the Road Traffic Act 1988). PACE considerably extended the power of the police. It followed the Royal Commission (Report, para 3.137) by drawing a distinction between non-intimate samples, which can be taken against the person's will, and intimate samples, which cannot. The sanction against refusal to supply the latter is the power of the court to draw the inference of guilt.

Definitions

7.96 In England and Wales the following terminology is employed:

'intimate sample' means a sample of blood, semen or any other tissue fluid, urine, saliva or pubic hair, or a swab taken from a person's body orifice;
'non-intimate sample' means —
(a) a sample of hair other than pubic hair;
(b) a sample taken from a nail or from under a nail;
(c) a swab taken from any part of a person's body other than a body orifice;
(d) a footprint or a similar impression of any part of a person's body other than a part of his hand (s 65).

As regards (a), this means the pulling of live hair from the skin — garments can be combed for hair following removal of clothing during a search. If clothing is removed in the hope of recovering pubic hair, then this would not appear to be within s 65 and is a way of avoiding it. Item (d) could include a dental impression, but the COP, D, (para 5.1) supplies, it is suggested, a legitimate gloss on the statute by adding it to the 'intimate sample' category. This means, inter alia, that only D's consent and observance of the procedures below will entitle removal of D's dentures. In contrast the definition of non-intimate sample in Northern Ireland is extended to cover a sample of saliva or a swab taken from a person's mouth

(PACE (N.I.) Order 1989, art 53). This means that a mouth sample can be taken, if necessary, by the distasteful use of force (see below).

Intimate samples (s 62)

7.97   These can only be taken if:

(a) The person consents (for the juvenile, aged under 17 but over 14, 'consent' is interpreted as his consent *and* the consent of his parent or guardian; if the juvenile is under 14 then his parent's or guardian's consent will suffice, s 65) and the consent is given in writing. Given the intrusive nature of an intimate sample, it is highly likely that a consent obtained by a trick (e.g. by pretending that the suspect must by law comply) will be met by the subsequent exclusion of the evidence at trial under s 78 (cf. *R v Mason* (1987)).

(b) The person is in police detention i.e. under arrest (s 118, Art 2).

(c) A serious arrestable offence is under investigation.

(d) An officer of at least superintendent rank has reasonable grounds to suspect that the person is involved in the offence.

(e) That officer has reasonable grounds to believe that the taking of an intimate sample 'will tend to confirm or disprove' the person's involvement ('believe' connotes a higher degree of certainty than 'suspect', (see para 2.02, ante), but 'tend to' reduces the effect of this).

The senior officer can give the authorisation orally, for example, over the telephone, but it must be confirmed in writing. He need not be independent of the investigation but the spirit of s 62 demands that considerable effort be made to find an independent officer. Item (e) shows that samples can of course be used to clear a suspect e.g. a genital swab taken from a suspected rapist. Although the person must be in police detention, the sample need not be taken at a police station. D can be taken to a hospital so that a medical practitioner can take the sample.

Procedure

7.98   The suspect must be formally told of the authorisation, the grounds for it, the nature of the offence involved, his entitlement to free legal advice (an important addition in the 1991 COP), that a refusal to consent may be used in evidence (see below) and that the sample will be destroyed if he is not prosecuted or if he is acquitted (s 62(5) (6), COP, D, para 5.2, 5.7). Documentation is very important in the taking of intimate samples. Thus, the suspect's consent, the authorisation and the grounds for it, the fact that consent was given, the giving of the warning on corroboration (below), the reminder of free legal advice, and whether a sample was ultimately destroyed must all be noted in the custody record (or, in the rare cases of a sample taken outside a station, in the officer's notebook). Samples of urine and saliva may be taken by a constable but all others require a registered medical practitioner (s 62(9); cf intimate searches which can be conducted by a nurse or midwife, s 55(5); in Northern Ireland a constable has power to take a sample of saliva on account of it being classified as a non-intimate sample, see below). If, as in most cases, clothing has to be removed and is likely to cause embarrassment, no person of the opposite sex (other than the practitioner or nurse) must attend, nor should there be any unnecessary bystander. Since a sample is taken with consent, there is no need for constables to attend to restrain the person. Consequently only the medical practitioner and one constable (to record what has taken place) need to attend. In the case of a juvenile, he can request an adult of the opposite sex to be present and, unless he specifically objects and the adult agrees, an 'appropriate adult' (see para 7.113, post) must always be present when the clothing is removed (COP, D, para 5.12). As to the subsequent destruction of samples, see para 7.102, post.

Refusal of consent — sanction

7.99 An offender could readily frustrate a police investigation by refusing to sign his consent. He would be confident in the knowledge that the refusal would not prejudice him at trial. One sanction is to make the refusal a criminal offence (cf s 7 of the Road Traffic Act 1988 for refusal to give a sample in drink/driving cases). Another method is to equate refusal with guilt of the offence under investigation. Section 62(10) goes part of this way by the following novelty in criminal law (cf in civil law s 65(2)(b) of the Race Relations Act 1976) — refusal to give a sample without good reason allows the court to draw inferences, including an inference of guilt which is capable of corroborating other evidence. The wording of s 62(10) was taken from the recommendation of the Criminal Law Revision Committee (11th Report) in relation to the refusal of a suspect to answer police questions. There is remarkably no statutory duty on the police to tell the person of this possibility, but the COP, D, (paras 5.2, 5A) quite rightly requires a warning and suggests that the following formula be used — 'You do not have to [provide the sample/allow the swab to be taken], but I must warn you that if you do not do so, a court may treat such a refusal as supporting any relevant evidence against you.' The reason for refusing consent could include, apart from guilt, belligerence (e.g. of a parent at the proposal to take a sample from his child), drunkenness, religious objection (e.g. of a Jehovah's Witness to the taking of a blood sample), physical fear (e.g. of a pregnant suspect at the thought of a genital swab), or simply a belief in innocence coupled with indignation at the police request. Whether the reason amounts to a 'good cause' for the purpose of s 62(10) will be judged by the court or jury. Some assistance can be found in cases dealing with the defence of 'reasonable excuse' for failure to supply a sample of blood or urine under the Road Traffic Act 1988. The value of these cases is however diminished because a wider range of intimate samples can be requested under s 62. The inferences may be drawn at the committal stage and/or at trial. They cannot establish guilt but they are capable of corroborating *any other* evidence against the accused. Thus, an inference is capable of corroborating the complaint of a rape victim. There will be a few cases where the police have only a suspicion against the person and his refusal to give a sample will be incapable of corroborating anything, but it will be recalled that the police need a *reasonable* suspicion and belief before a sample can be lawfully demanded.

The police powers to take intimate samples and to undertake intimate searches may well coincide in relation to the same suspect. The contrast between the powers can be summarised as follows:

	Intimate search	*Intimate sample*
Power	Consent *or* authorisation by the police	Consent *and* authorisation by the police
Object	To find weapons or serious drugs	To find evidence of an offence
Searcher	Medical practitioner, nurse or constable	Medical practitioner

Non-intimate samples (s 63)

7.100 These are exclusively defined by s 65 (see above). Category (c) thereof can include traces of explosives, drugs, blood or semen. In Northern Ireland, the list is extended to cover saliva and a swab from a person's mouth. (As for fingerprints and palm prints, they are covered separately by s 61, see para 7.87, ante). Non-intimate samples may be taken in two situations — with the suspect's consent or without it.

(a) The suspect may give the appropriate written consent ('appropriate' in the context of a juvenile is the same as for the taking of intimate samples, see above). Even if he consents COP, D, adds to s 63 as follows:
    An officer of at least inspector rank must have reasonable grounds to believe that the sample will tend to confirm or disprove the person's involvement in the offence (para 5.4).

(b) The suspect does not consent and an officer of at least superintendent rank authorises a sample to be taken from a person who is in detention (i.e. under arrest) or in custody (following a court order) for what is reasonably *suspected* to be a serious arrestable offence and the officer also has reasonable grounds to *believe* that the sample will tend to confirm or disprove the person's involvement in the offence. Since consent is not needed, reasonable force may be used to obtain the sample (s 117, Art 88). However, if the suspect's resistance is so strong that the use of force will be likely to cause disproportionate injury his refusal can still be used in evidence as corroboration (see *R v Smith* (1985) where the failure to supply a sample of hair, in order to check whether it matched with strands combed from a cap, was held to be capable of corroborating other evidence against the suspect).

7.101 The procedure to be followed (s 63(6)–(9)) is almost identical to that governing intimate samples (s 62(5)–(8)). For example, the suspect must be told the grounds for an authorisation under (b), the nature of the offence, and that the sample will be destroyed if he is acquitted or not prosecuted. However, the COP does not require a reminder about legal advice or any warning about refusal to be given to him. It is suggested that a warning should be given along the lines — that a refusal to consent may be used in evidence against him (*R v Smith* above) and that in any event the police may consider using reasonable force if he does not agree.

Destruction of fingerprints etc (s 64, Art 64)

7.102 Fingerprints, palm prints, photographs including negatives, videotapes and intimate and non-intimate samples taken by the police during the investigation of an offence must be destroyed (along with any copies of prints, photographs or videotapes):

(i) If the person is cleared of the offence (s 64(1)) ie by acquittal or the collapse or withdrawal of the prosecution or by the grant of a royal pardon.

(ii) If no prosecution is brought against the person or he has not been cautioned for the offence (s 64(2)).

(iii) If the records were taken for the purpose of eliminating persons from an investigation (for example, fingerprints or blood samples taken from each person known to have been in the vicinity of the crime) and that purpose has been achieved (s 64(3)).

As regards fingerprints, photographs and videotapes, the person is to be told of his right to witness their destruction and copies are also to be destroyed (s 64(5), (6), COP, D, para 4.1). These welcome provisions do not apply to prints, photographs or samples taken under the Prevention of Terrorism (Temporary Provisions) Act 1989 or prints and photographs taken under the Immigration Act 1971 (s 64(7)). It is felt that the importance of the former to the national interest justifies the retention of what may be useful background information. The difficulty of detecting illegal immigration justifies their retention under the latter. Where a photograph or videotape has been taken of an identification parade, that too must be destroyed if (i) and (ii) above are satisfied (COP, D, Annex A, para 20). As regards *records* of samples, there is no mention in the COP but the spirit of the provisions suggest that they too should be destroyed. On the other hand, data records of fingerprints held on computer must be made secure from access and the citizen can obtain a certificate of compliance with this requirement within three months of requesting it (s 64(5)(b), (6A) as inserted by s 148, Criminal Justice Act 1988; and Art 64(5)(b)). No such statutory requirement exists for other identifying records but again, the spirit and thrust of the aforementioned provisions argue for its general adoption. To complicate matters further, a citizen can obtain a certificate guaranteeing compliance with the duty to destroy photographs (COP, D, 4.1) and data records of fingerprints (above) but not a certificate for other identification methods (e.g. samples, videotapes). The picture is totally confused and this is perhaps an area to which Parliament should pay regular attention.

Physical conditions of detention

7.103 Section 8 of the COP on Detention, Treatment and Questioning (hereafter, COP) sets out the physical arrangements which must be made for the detention of persons at police stations. Some of these provisions (eg adequate heating of a cell in winter, regular meals) will be more important than others when it comes to determining whether oppression or irregularity has been used for the purposes of ss 76, 78 (Arts 74, 76). In designated police stations the facilities should meet Home Office requirements. It is at the smaller non-designated stations that physical conditions are likely to pose most problems, though this is tempered by the limited time a person can be kept there. Each cell must be 'adequately heated, cleaned and ventilated' (para 8.2) and have dimmed night time lighting so that the suspect can sleep and the jailer can check on his condition at the prescribed hourly intervals. Bedding should be clean and of reasonable standard (especially if the person is likely to be detained for a lengthy time e.g. under the prevention of terrorism legislation), and toilet and washing facilities must be available. The cell will not however be comfortable. The risks of damage being caused to fittings and of suicide and self-mutilation mean that the furnishings of cells are spartan. Confinement in a cell will usually suffice for an unruly suspect, but occasionally his violent or unpredictable (e.g. through drugs) behaviour will require handcuffs. If practicable no cell should contain more than one person. An unexpected inrush of arrested persons may make this impracticable, as may congestion at local prisons which forces a police station to accommodate persons on remand and thus cuts down the number of cells available for arrested suspects. As for prisoners on remand, the authority for their detention is the Imprisonment (Temporary Provisions) Act 1980. The Prison Act and Rules apply and not the PACE Code. If double occupancy of a cell is unavoidable, the custody officer should take care to place similar types together (and not, for example, to put an elderly first time shoplifter with an experienced prostitute, or a male homosexual with another man). Occasionally it will be the necessity of placing one suspect on his own (e.g. if he is mentally disturbed or violent, if he is a male transvestite), which will force others to double up in a cell. A juvenile should not be placed in a cell unless there is no other secure accommodation available and he can only be properly supervised in a cell (COP, para 8.8). An interview room nearby might suffice, but placing him in the charge room in view of passing prisoners is unsatisfactory and the absence of a room proximate to the jailer will necessitate a cell. In that case, the door can be left unlocked unless the juvenile's behaviour dictates otherwise. If a juvenile is placed in a cell, the reason must be noted and he must not share it with an adult (though he could with other juveniles). If clothing has to be removed from the detained person (for forensic or other investigative purposes, or for hygiene or health or cleaning purposes) adequate replacements must be supplied, a record made, and, most importantly, the person must not be questioned until they have been offered to him. If thin, standard, disposable clothing is offered, adequate heating of the cell and interview room must be ensured.

7.104 Each detained person should be visited hourly and those who are intoxicated every half an hour (even if asleep, lest for example, they choke on vomit). The Notes to the COP (para 8A) suggest that juveniles, the mentally ill and others whom the police suspect may hurt themselves should be visited even more regularly. Limited police resources and congestion in the charge room will readily prevent this good practice. Occasionally a person's behaviour may be so threatening (eg he has already tried to kill himself) that an officer will have to sit in permanent visual contact with him. Two light meals and one main meal along with drinks should be provided in any 24 hour period, drinks on reasonable request should be offered and special dietary or religious needs (e.g. fasting during Ramadan) should be met as far as practicable. The latter can often be supplied, at their expense, by the suspect's family or friends. The police surgeon may issue, or be approached for, instructions about diet. All meals must be noted. Daily outdoor exercise, especially for those detained to the maximum of 96 hours should be offered, but shortage of supervisory officers or of physical facilities may rule this out. In any 24 hours of detention the detainee must be given 8 uninterrupted hours of rest (COP, para 12.2).

7.105 Once again the importance of accurate documentation as to the person's detention and any complaints he has made must be stressed. For a court may subsequently be called upon to decide whether a confession has been obtained improperly (sections 76 and 78; Arts 74, 76), and the person's surrounding conditions and treatment may, for example, amount to, or contribute to, a finding of oppressive conduct by the police. In this context of record-keeping the custody officer assumes the overall supervision of detained persons. In some designated stations the cell and charging areas are proximate, enabling him to check detainees himself. In others he may also be station sergeant and in charge of an operations room in another part of the building, dividing his time between the two. The regular observation and treatment of detainees are then left very much in the hands of junior officers. Indeed, in busy stations one officer may be delegated mainly to watch the wall charts (ie a board listing the detention, review, meal and other times for each prisoner). Any complaint about the person's treatment (which may come from him or his representative or an officer who is concerned about him) must be passed urgently to an officer of at least inspector rank who is unconnected with the investigation (COP, para 9.1). The implication of this instruction in the COP is that the senior officer will take immediate steps to rectify the situation. Given the implications for the possible exclusion of evidence and the lodging of an official complaint, the complaint should be investigated quickly and as thoroughly as possible in the time available. If physical violence is involved or alleged, the police surgeon must be called (COP, para 9.1). Much will depend on whether the detainee's representations are interpreted by the custody officer as a 'complaint' for COP, para 9.1 purposes. The custody officer may well be able to resolve minor grievances at once (e.g. replace a light bulb, allow D to wash) with no harm to the detainee's interests, especially if the latter's solicitor is consulted and agrees. But even here it behoves the custody officer to make a note, in the custody record, of the problem and of the action taken.

The ill

7.106 The treatment and questioning of persons who are ill should be distinguished from the provisions governing medical examinations in order to determine guilt (see ss 62, 63 and para 7.95, ante). The inevitable controversy which surrounds the death or injury of those in police custody, and problems over the admissibility of evidence which can flow from alleged maltreatment during police custody, mean that medical treatment should be readily sought by the custody or interviewing officer if he has the slightest doubt about the suspect's fitness. Consequently, the provisions of the COP (section 9) err very much on the side of caution in counselling early medical assistance. The moral for the custody officer is to 'play safe' and call a doctor (usually the police surgeon). Thus, if a detained person

'(a) appears to be suffering from physical illness or a mental disorder; or
(b) is injured; or
(c) does not show signs of sensibility and awareness; or
(d) fails to respond normally to questions or conversation (other than through drunkenness alone); or
(e) otherwise appears to need medical attention' (COP, para 9.2),

the custody officer must arrange for medical treatment immediately, *whether or not* the person asks for it and whether or not he has just received non-hospital treatment elsewhere (e.g. he has been given first aid at the scene of the crime, or en route to the station). These last two points are critically important for, if the person's condition deteriorates during police custody or his condition affects his interview, police conduct and the admissibility of a confession are very likely to be challenged. The symptoms of illness may become apparent when the person reaches the station and the custody officer performs the preliminary formalities (see para 7.07, ante). The officer may be helped in divining medical problems by the increasing practice whereby citizens carry documentary evidence of their illness (e.g. an identity card or bracelet specifying it). The custody officer should seek to ensure that the person is fit to be interviewed and that the interviewing officer is aware of any medical conditions affecting the suspect. He may also be able to detect signs of mental illness or mental handicap. The dangers of allowing unsupervised interrogation of these persons are well known (see the Report into the case of *Maxwell Confait* (1977)). Indeed, concern over the interrogation of the mentally handicapped led to the enactment of s 77 of PACE (see para 7.127, post). However, the difficulties of detecting mental disorder and of distinguishing it from intoxication are self-evident and again the message to the custody officer is to be alert to the possibility and to err in favour of summoning medical advice whenever the detained person appears to be mentally disordered or disturbed (unless it is clear that intoxication is the cause of the behaviour). If a person has been taken to a police station under the authority of s 136 of the Mental Health Act 1983 (see further para 7.131, post), a doctor's presence will again by necessary unless it is clear that an assessment of the person under the Act can be made promptly by a doctor and social worker. Special caution is needed in cases of apparent intoxication through drink. On the one hand, a blow to the head, shock, forms of epilepsy or mental illness, the lack of, or taking of, prescribed drugs, or a diabetic condition, may prompt signs of intoxication and conceal the real diagnosis. On the other hand, in cases of genuine intoxication, the custody officer should not allow the person to be left alone for lengthy periods. Indeed, guidance from the Home Office states that, where the person is still incapable of understanding the charge against him after 4 hours of detention, the police surgeon should be called. In cases of doubt the police should always call for medical advice (COP, para 9B). As for drugs, medical advice should be called in all cases. Withdrawal from the drugs may cause harm both to the suspect and to the chances of the court admitting evidence obtained from him in such a situation. If controlled drugs have to be taken, the police surgeon must supervise (COP, para 9.5). This allows him to delegate to the custody officer the task of supplying the medication. If D is asleep when the next dosage is due, the officer should seek the surgeon's instructions as to whether D should be awakened.

7.107 Other cases may arise where the person's health appears to the investigating or custody officer to have deteriorated since his arrival at the police station, or where the person or his representative lodges a complaint about police conduct. If it arises during the person's questioning, the interview should, it is suggested, be terminated at once, the reasons noted on the interview record and the opinion of the custody officer sought. If the symptoms appear to flow from police misconduct (e.g. a physical assault in the cell, or the undue use of force in restraining a suspect), then a police surgeon (COP, para 9.1) or, if unavailable, another doctor or hospital treatment should, it is suggested, be sought. Occasionally the detained person will have drugs with him which he says have been prescribed by a doctor, or he may claim that they have to be collected from his home (e.g. for a heart condition, epilepsy). In both cases a police surgeon should be consulted before the medication is taken (COP, para 9.6).

7.108 Once medical assistance is deemed necessary, it should be obtained without delay, even if this means that the questioning of a person has to be interrupted. The obvious recourse for advice is to the police surgeon. If he is unavailable or cannot attend quickly, a local and readily available general practitioner should be called (each station should therefore have a list of such contacts). In cases of emergency or apparent urgency, hospital treatment is the answer. If an infectious disease appears to be involved, quarantine steps must be taken (COP, para 9.3). The hysteria over AIDS has led to a Home Office Circular on the proper treatment of known or suspected sufferers (no 72 of 1988; and for hepatitis, see 48/89). Whilst sensible precautions are essential (e.g. special care on a search of the person so as to avoid being punctured by a syringe in a coat pocket), victimisation of the suspect or oppressive conduct can have serious implications for the admissibility of evidence under ss 76 and 78 of PACE (Arts 74, 76).

7.109 The Notes for Guidance to the COP (para 9A) suggest that medical advice need not be called for 'minor ailments or injuries which do not need attention'.Certainly a headache cured by the custody officer's offer of an aspirin qualify, but the definition of 'a minor ailment' lies to a large degree in the eye of the beholder and in this context, especially, the accused. Much can be made months later of bruises and scratches which at the time of the detention were self-evidently innocuous. The safest course is for the police surgeon to be called. Whether he is or not, the ailments must be carefully and in detail noted in the custody record.

7.110 When the detained person requests medical treatment or examination, the police surgeon (there are about 21 per police force) should be called in all cases. An independent examination may also be allowed at the person's own expense. Although this provision is couched in discretionary terms (COP, para 9.4), it is clearly in the interests of the police that such examination be permitted. The examination by either police surgeon or other doctor need not be delayed pending the arrival of the other, though ideally both should witness each other's examination. If the detained person has to take medication, the custody officer assumes responsibility for its safe keeping and availability (COP, para 9.5). In keeping with the rest of the Act and Code, written records must be compiled of, inter alia, any request for medical treatment and any medical directions given to the police (COP, paras 9.7–9.9). The custody record can conveniently be used if the person is under arrest. A police surgeon will naturally enter his findings on the custody record, but a general practitioner need not do so (COP, para 9C) because of the confidentiality with his patient. However, the written record must state where his findings are recorded for they may become necessary at subsequent legal proceedings. As to the availability of these records, they qualify as excluded material under s 12 of PACE and, unless the patient consents, can only be used in proceedings with the consent of the patient. Alternatively, the doctor might exceptionally be subpoenaed to give evidence as to his diagnosis.

Special categories

7.111 There are some categories of persons which cannot be dealt with in the normal way, for which PACE has made special provision, and which are conveniently dealt with here. The most critical initial task, both to save time and to avoid subsequent confusion, is to ascertain whether the person falls within one of these special categories. For many the circumstances of the arrest or attendance at the police station, or the comments of the arresting officer will suffice. For some the answer will be obvious (eg the blind; but even here care must be taken in observing the person lest someone with a serious visual handicap — though not blind — is missed). For some a simple test may do the trick (eg the custody officer feigning sign language or lip-reading to see if the person responds or asking simple questions to test his mental ability). For others the chance to write may help (eg to reveal that he cannot speak English, or to communicate his nationality in some written form). The consequences of falling within one of these categories (eg the need for an interpreter, the calling of an appropriate adult, the strict view which a court may take of non-compliance with the COP) yet again illustrate the heavy responsibility lying on the custody officer.

Juveniles

7.112 The largest and most problematic category for which special provision is made is juveniles. It covers any person who appears to be under 17 (s 37(15), Art 38(14)). Thus, if a person refuses to give his age or the officer doubts the one given and the officer assesses the person as a juvenile, he must treat him as such unless and until evidence to the contrary is produced (COP, para 1.5). As for a juvenile under the age of 10, he has by law no criminal liability and so cannot be detained. If he is arrested in the belief that he is older or if he is taken to the station voluntarily or for his well being, it appears to be the practice in some forces for the custody officer to complete the essentials of a custody record, but thereafter the juvenile's return home must normally be arranged. Alerting the local authority's social services should be considered if the custody officer is concerned for the juvenile's physical or moral well being (the authority may decide to exercise its supervisory powers under the Children Act 1989: under that Act 'child' means a person under the age of 18) and, in a clear case of danger to the juvenile, the police themselves have the power under the 1989 Act (s 46) to remove a juvenile and, after liaison with the authority, place him in safe accommodation. If, but for the presumption of *doli vicopox*, a child would have committed a serious offence, such as homicide, the urgency to involve the social services is self-evident. For the ultimate decision may well be not a prosecution but for the local authority to seek a care or supervision order on the basis that the child is beyond parental control (s 31(2)(b)(ii), Children Act 1989).

7.113 If a person in custody is a juvenile, the policy of PACE is to ensure, where practicable, that certain things (eg the taking of an intimate sample) can only be done to him with an 'appropriate consent' and that other things (eg questioning) must be carried out in the presence of an 'appropriate adult'. These terms are defined as follows:

'appropriate consent' for juveniles between 14 and 17 —
> consent of juvenile *and* parent or guardian (including a local authority if the child is in care s 118),

for juveniles below 14 —
> consent of parent or guardian (as defined above), s 65

'appropriate adult' in relation to a juvenile —
   (i)   parent or guardian (including a local authority if the child is in care, s 118)
   (ii)   or a representative of the local social services department,
   (iii)   or a responsible adult aged over 18 (not a police officer or police employee), COP, para 1.7.

7.114 In some cases the parent will be incompetent to act as an appropriate adult because of low intelligence (see *R v Morse* (1991)). In many more he will be incompetent through lack of experience and/or knowledge of police procedures. In others the parent (or guardian) will be implicated in the offence as perpetrator, victim, witness or confidant to the juvenile, or he and the juvenile may be living apart, or they may simply not get on with each other (see *DPP v Blake* (1989)). In these circumstances the parent is clearly an inappropriate adult (COP, para 1C). In other cases the juvenile will be embarrassed or terrified at the prospect of his parent being informed and may beg the custody officer not to do so. This places the latter in a difficult position. The juvenile's fear may be exaggerated or practically it may be impossible to secure a social worker or other adult as a replacement. It is suggested that the custody officer must try to prevail upon the juvenile (unless one of the barring circumstances above apply). The juvenile's fears may be exaggerated or mistaken. The custody officer should however stick to the point and not engage in wider conversation about the alleged offence, for otherwise an interview (see para 8.07, post) will develop, procedural safeguards should apply, the juvenile may make an admission or incriminating comment, and a court may subsequently exclude the conversation under ss 76 and 78. At the end of the day, if the juvenile is adamant (eg he comes from a strictly religious family and fears the repercussions of his parents being informed), he should be asked to nominate some other adult whom he knows or in whom he trusts (eg a religious figure). In many cases the parent will not wish, or be able, to attend (a third of parents according to Research Study No 4 for the Royal Commission) and the custody officer should proceed to seek another appropriate adult. This may prove to be very difficult since a solicitor, an obvious choice, cannot act as one if he is already acting in his professional capacity (COP, para 1F). The Notes for Guidance however are not mandatory and, if no other adult can be found and a solicitor is willing, it is suggested that he can be used. A court is hardly likely to condemn a custody officer for this recourse. The real problem may lie in persuading the lawyer to take on the additional role. He may well be a trainee solicitor and under instructions not to do so. An alternative adult is a social worker but (a) lack of resources (especially at night-time when there may be only one on duty) may exclude him or at least his early presence; and (b) he is not necessarily suited or trained for the role of appropriate adult (see Dixon (1990) at p 121–5). One ready expedient is to throw the ball back into the juvenile's court and ask him to name an individual whom he trusts.

7.115 As for (ii) above, if the juvenile is in local care the authority is the appropriate adult and so, if he is suspected of stealing from the children's home where he lives, a social worker unconnected with the home should ideally be called. Similarly if he has admitted the offence to a social worker, the Notes for Guidance (para 1D) require another social worker in the interests of fairness to act as appropriate adult. This may well be impracticable and the unfairness will be lessened by proper record-keeping by the custody officer and the advent of tape-recording. More generally, the unavailability of social workers, their unwillingness to attend (eg if the juvenile's parent is available but refuses to attend) and even their disposition towards the police mean that the custody officer will have to proceed to category (iii) as the appropriate adult (indeed (ii) and (iii) are not ranked in priority). He may be a person who has looked after the juvenile, or a relative such as an adult sibling, or neighbour or community figure in whom the juvenile can trust. A Home Office Study has reported (Brown, 1989) that the police were successful in 95% of cases in contacting an adult and that of these 77% were parents or relatives, 17% were social workers, and 5% other responsible adults. If an appropriate adult cannot be contacted or cannot attend the station within a reasonable time, the custody officer may have to consider releasing, or charging the juvenile and/or releasing him on bail, for as will be seen, there are many steps in the investigative process which cannot be accomplished without an adult's presence.

Initial Action

7.116 PACE amended s 34 of the Children and Young Persons Act 1933 so that, when a juvenile is arrested, the police must take all practicable steps to identify the parent, guardian, local authority (where relevant) or other person responsible for the juvenile's welfare and tell that person of the arrest, the reasons for it and where the juvenile is being held. This person will usually be the appropriate adult (above) and will also be asked to attend the station in that capacity. He will not always be the appropriate adult (eg the juvenile does not want his parent to be involved, the parent is implicated in the offence, the parent refuses to attend the station) with the result that the custody officer has two duties —

(a) to identify and notify the person responsible for the juvenile's welfare; and

(b) to identify, notify and call the appropriate adult (as defined above).

If the juvenile is in the care of a local authority but is living with his natural or foster parents, the authority is the appropriate adult but the parents or other carers should normally be contacted (COP, para 3C). If he is living in the authority's accommodation, this does not exclude the possibility of calling his natural parents. This will depend on the relationship between them (eg it is inappropriate if the juvenile is in care because of abuse by the parents but not if the parent is temporarily ill or incapacitated). If the juvenile is under local authority supervision, then the supervisor should be informed of his arrest if possible (COP, para 3.8). Even if the conditions for delaying notification of arrest (s 56(5); Art 57(5)) or legal advice (s 58(8); Art 59(8)) apply, this should not stop the custody officer from taking steps to contact the appropriate adult and the person responsible for the juvenile's welfare (COP, Annex B, para B1).

7.117 An important consequence of detention for a juvenile is that he should not be interviewed in the absence of an appropriate adult (COP, para 11.14). This applies to all interviews and not just those in the police station. This does not of course prevent an officer from conversing with a juvenile in the street, but if he suspects him of an offence and questions him about it, an 'interview' will soon develop and the courts may be called upon to exclude any admission unless the proper procedure is followed. (See the cases of *Fogah, Grier, Maguire* in 1989 and para 8.07, post). Given the difficulty of obtaining the adult's presence and the delay in his arrival, urgent interviews are permitted in some circumstances, though in practice they are rarely exercised (see COP, Annex C and para 8.21, post; Brown (1989) found only 2 such cases out of 1,000). Another consequence is that information which must be given to a detained juvenile (see below) must also be given simultaneously to the appropriate adult or repeated when the adult arrives. If it has to be repeated, this must be done in the juvenile's presence (COP, para 3.11). This information consists of the grounds of detention, the right of notification of arrest, the rights to free legal advice and to consult the Codes of Practice, written notices of these rights and the juvenile's other rights in custody, the right to contact diplomatic representatives where relevant, and the caution. The custody officer must explain to the juvenile the function of the appropriate adult (viz. to assist and advise him) and that he can consult privately with the adult at any time (COP, para 3.12). The custody officer does not have to tell the juvenile of these last matters when the adult is present but the spirit of PACE requires that he does, for otherwise any impact it may have will be diluted. An important point to note is that the juvenile must be told of his right to legal advice at the outset. The custody officer should not delay telling him until the appropriate adult arrives, or delay securing legal advice if the juvenile so requests (COP, para, 3G). For otherwise the police could be tempted to question the juvenile in the interim period before the adult attends and only organise a solicitor when the adult confirms the juvenile's request (see the findings of Sanders (1989). Sanders quotes one example where the custody officer 'read D (aged 14) her rights, said 'I will repeat this when your mother comes to the station' and then said 'sign there there and there' without giving D a chance to request a solicitor. When the mother arrived she was told 'When your daughter came to the station she was given her rights and indicated that she didn't want a solicitor. Do you require one now?' She didn't.') If the juvenile wants a solicitor and the adult does not, the former's wishes should be respected.

7.118 The functions of the appropriate adult are: to attend the station as soon as possible, to assimilate D's rights, to witness an intimate search (unless D objects; see para 7.28, ante), to consider calling legal advice (which he can do on behalf of D, COP, para 3.13), to make representations on D's behalf, to witness any interview (unless COP, Annex C, applies), to assess the physical conditions of D (especially whether he is being kept in a police cell since this should generally be avoided, see below), to read and sign an interview record if a solicitor is not present, to observe, to advise D, to help to communicate between the police and D (COP, para 11.16), to receive written notice of any charge (COP, para 16.3), and to receive any statement by a third party which the police wish to put to D (para, 16.4). In addition where an identification procedure (fingerprinting, samples etc) requires the 'appropriate consent', the adult must oblige (but in this case he can *only* be a parent, guardian or local authority, see the definition at para 7.113, above). Whether the adult can adequately perform any of these functions is of course another matter. Research indicates that many parents are so overawed by the criminal process as to be of no use as advisers, whilst others may even side with the interviewing officer (see *Dixon* (1990), *Irving* and *Mackenzie* (1989)).

7.119 A juvenile should not be held in a police cell, unless there is no other way of guaranteeing his security (COP, para 8.8). If he is, the reason must be recorded and he must not be kept there with a detained adult. Few stations possess rooms, other then cells or interview rooms, that can be used to detain juveniles. Often the interview rooms, which could be used for juveniles, are physically apart from the cell area, thus making security impracticable. Occasionally there will be spaces in the secured cell area where a juvenile can be allowed to roam within reason and under the supervision of the jailer but in busy stations this will be impossible, if not dangerous. Much too will depend on the age and character of the juvenile. Very often an ordinary cell will have to be used and perhaps relabelled as a juvenile room. Wherever he is kept, he should be visited more regularly than other detained adults. As for interviews, these must be conducted in the presence of an appropriate adult (unless COP, Annex C applies, see para 8.21, post), and any caution given or repeated in his presence. The adult has to be told (or reminded if he regularly fulfils the role) that his presence is needed to advise the juvenile, observe the fairness of the interview and 'facilitate communication' with the juvenile (COP, para 11.16; to stress the importance of this instruction it was upgraded from the status of Notes for Guidance in the 1986 COP, para 13C). As to the last, the adult can easily become, wittingly or otherwise, the ally or agent of the interviewing officer and increase the pressure on the juvenile. Tape-recording can reduce the risk but may not reflect the pressure of an adult's physical presence. Once charged, the juvenile should normally be transferred to local authority accommodation if he is to be detained (s 38(6), PACE, Art 39(6); the authority being under a duty to provide such accommodation, s 21, Children Act 1989). However, authorities frequently lack secure accommodation in which to keep an unruly juvenile pending his appearance in court and the custody officer has the power to retain him in police custody if he is not satisfied with the authority's arrangements (*R v Chief Constable of Cambridgeshire ex parte Michel* (1990) and further at para 6.31, ante).

7.121 Two further points about juveniles can be noted. First, whenever possible a juvenile should not be interviewed at school without the permission and presence of the headteacher (or nominee) nor arrested at school without that person being informed (COP, paras. 11.15, 11C). Ideally the parents and, if different, the appropriate adult should attend the school. They can sometimes be notified in advance of the police arrival at the school, but these school interviews are by their nature urgent ones and, if the offence is not against the school, a teacher can act as the appropriate adult. If the offence is against the school, the juvenile should be arrested if there is sufficient evidence and questioned elsewhere, or asked to attend the station, or interviewed at home or some other place known to him. Second, if the juvenile is a ward of court and the police wish to question him, they can do so without informing the High Court (*Re R and G* (1990)). The temporary carers of the juvenile will then be under a duty to inform the court if anything significant is likely to occur to the juvenile (eg he is to be prosecuted and a custodial sentence is likely on conviction).

The mentally disordered

7.122 Two situations have to be distinguished. In the first a suspect with mental problems becomes involved in the investigation of a criminal offence. In the second a person who is mentally disordered is brought into a police station by the police under their Mental Health Act powers. The involvement of mentally disordered with the police is likely to increase given the government's policy of keeping such persons within the community as far as possible.

(a)   Treatment of mentally disordered suspects

7.123   The police treatment of those with mental problems is a highly sensitive and occasionally notorious area. Indeed the Report into the death of Maxwell Confait was one of the reasons for the Royal Commission on Criminal Procedure which preceded PACE. The PACE Act has very little to say in the area but the COP contains a number of provisions. Given the context it is likely that the COP's provisions here will be strictly interpreted by the courts. The cardinal requirement of the COP is that, if an officer suspects that a person is mentally disordered, he must treat him as such (COP, para 1.4). Unfortunately it is not possible to define the subject matter precisely and three concepts are used in the police context. 'Mental disorder' is defined in s 1 of the Mental Health Act 1983 as 'mental illness, arrested or incomplete development of mind, psychopathic disorder and any other disorder or disability of mind'. 'Mentally handicapped' means that a person 'is in a state of arrested or incomplete development of mind which includes significant impairment of intelligence and social functioning' (PACE, s 77(3)). The COP (para 1.4) confuses matters further by referring to a person 'mentally incapable of understanding the significance of questions put to him or his replies.' The COP's addition is however useful in putting the police and especially the custody officer on alert. It presumably means someone with such a low i.q. as to make his interrogation of dubious value. For the purposes of exposition the compendious phrase, mental disorder, will be used here as it is in the COP. The arresting officer may be able to spot the mentally disordered from the circumstances of the arrest or the journey to the station, but very often it will be the custody officer who, during the opening formalities, is best placed to detect them. Even so, the decision is a difficult one. Psychiatrists regularly disagree over the meaning of mental disorder, yet police officers have no particular training in its diagnosis. In a fairly common situation, incoherence through drunkenness or drugs could easily mask a mental disability. If there is any suspicion of mental disorders, it is wise to play safe and treat the person as if he does have them, for if such a person is not carefully protected, the police run the real risks of a prosecution floundering through the application of sections 76–78 (Arts 74–6) and of civil and disciplinary action against them.

Treatment during detention

7.124   The policy of PACE towards the mentally disordered is that various procedures can only be performed if 'an appropriate adult' is present. An appropriate adult is defined (COP, para 1.7(b)) as:

(i)   a relative, guardian or other person responsible for the suspect's care or custody;

(ii)   a person experienced in dealing with the mentally disordered or handicapped (eg a specialist social worker or a social worker approved for the purposes of the Mental Health Act 1983, but not a police employee); or

(iii) some other responsible adult aged 18 or more, but not a police employee (eg a neighbour, priest, or schoolteacher).

Category (iii) should only be sought in the absence of (i) and (ii), and, if the suspect prefers (i), that person should be contacted first where practicable. However, as the Notes For Guidance to COP (para 1E) suggest, a person in (i) may be quite inappropriate. He may lack the necessary coolness and independence. A person in category (ii) may therefore be better qualified to handle the particular suspect and may well have some experience of attending a police station and the detention procedures. More practically it may be impossible for D to identify a person in (i), so that category (ii) has to be used.

7.125 If the custody officer decides that D is mentally disordered, (and note that this generic phrase covers the three categories of mental unsoundness mentioned above, COP Notes for Guidance, para 1G), in all cases and whether D requests it or not, the officer must immediately call a police surgeon or, in emergency, send D to hospital or call a medical practitioner (COP, para 9.2). This task takes precedence over the summoning of an appropriate adult (below) since (1) the latter may take some time to contact and (2), if a surgeon is at hand, his immediate diagnosis of no mental disorder may absolve the need to call an adult. Having summoned medical help, the custody officer must identify and contact an appropriate adult as soon as possible, explain the situation and ask him to come to the station (COP, para 3.9) or go to the hospital if D has been sent there. This duty to notify the adult arises even if the general right of notification of arrest (s 56, Art 57) and the right to legal advice (s 58, Art 59) can otherwise be lawfully delayed (COP, Annex B, B1). If the adult is already at the station, the officer must read D his rights (see para 7.117, ante) in front of the adult so that the latter is made aware of them. If he is not there, the rights are read to D in the normal way but must be repeated when the appropriate adult arrives. Similarly any caution must be repeated in the adult's presence (COP, para 10.6). An intimate search (see para 7.23, ante) can only take place in the presence of an appropriate adult of the same sex, unless D otherwise requests (COP, Annex A, para 5; though such a request should be greeted with great caution).

7.126 It may be that D is sufficiently compos mentis to request legal advice, in which case the request must be granted (unless an exception in s 58(8), Art 59(8) applies, see para 7.49, ante) and there is no need for the custody officer to wait until the appropriate adult arrives (unless perhaps the adult will arrive very quickly and D has intimated that the adult knows how to arrange legal advice). If D is unable to request a lawyer, then the appropriate adult can do so on his behalf (COP, para 3.13). This of course presupposes that the adult will appreciate the wisdom of having a lawyer and that he will not be deterred by the police presence and formalities from seeking one. It might make sense for the police to call a lawyer on D's behalf, for it is in their interests that an interview be properly conducted. It is permissible for a solicitor to take instructions from a third party provided that they are confirmed by the client as soon as possible.

Interviews

7.127 Unless an urgent interview can be authorised by a superintendent or higher rank (see para 8.21, post), a mentally disordered person must not be interviewed or asked to sign a statement without an appropriate adult attending (COP para 11.14). Given the evidential dangers, an urgent interview must be regarded as highly exceptional and highly undesirable (COP, Annex C, para. C1). As the Notes for Guidance (para 11B) remark, although mentally disordered persons 'are often capable of providing reliable evidence, they may, without knowing or wishing to do so, be particularly prone in certain circumstances to provide information which is unreliable, misleading or self-incriminating. Special care should therefore always be exercised in questioning such a person and the appropriate adult should be involved . . .' (for examples of how not to interview the mentally disordered, see *R v Delaney* (1988), *R v Lamont* (1989), *R v Moss* (1990)). Indeed the adverse publicity given to the police in recent years following the interrogation of the mentally disordered (principally the Report into the death of Maxwell Confait (1977)) produced a late amendment to the PACE Bill in the form of s 77 (Art 75). It gives greater protection at the trial stage to the mentally *handicapped*. Thus, where the case against D depends wholly or substantially on a confession by him and the judge is satisfied:

(i)   that he is mentally handicapped; and
(ii)   that the confession was not made in the presence of an independent person, (s 77(1)(b))

the judge must warn the jury, that 'there is a special need for caution before convicting the accused in reliance on the confession', and must explain why the need arises. If it is a summary trial, magistrates must treat the case as one in which there is a special need for caution before convicting the accused on his confession (s 77(1), (2)). 'Mentally handicapped' is defined in s 77(3) and should be distinguished from the wider concept of mental disorder. Section 77(3) also defines 'independent person' so as to exclude a police officer or person employed for, or engaged on, 'police purposes'. 'Police purposes' are defined by s 64 of the Police Act 1964 and include special constables, police cadets and civilians employed by the force (eg a telephonist, or a matron employed to look after female prisoners). Section 77 does not require corroborative evidence in support of the confession, but merely a warning as to the special need for caution. As regards a confession obtained from the mentally disordered (as opposed to handicapped), in the absence of an independent party, corroboration is similarly not required but is highly desirable. When combined with the exclusionary terms of ss 76 and 78 (Arts 74, 76) the result is that evidence obtained from the mentally disordered by maltreatment or breaches of PACE and COP will usually be excluded by ss 76 and 78 (*Everett* (1988), *Delaney* (1989)), and s 77 therefore serves a very limited, supporting role for those confessions which are allowed to proceed for the jury's consideration.

7.128 The roles of the appropriate adult during an interview are three-fold viz. (1) to advise D, (2) to observe the fairness of the interview, and (3) to help communicate with D (COP, para 11.16); and the adult should be told of this. The trouble is that the adult may not understand or appreciate the roles. He may be incompetent to perform (1), too ignorant of PACE procedures to do (2) and, in undertaking (3), may unwittingly become a compliant agent of the interviewing officer. The tape-recording of most interviews for indictable offences offers some safeguards and should certainly alert D's lawyer to the option of listening to the tape rather than relying on the interview record (ie a written, police summary of the tape, see para 8.33, post). Once the interview is over, the appropriate adult or solicitor is offered the chance to read and sign any statement taken down by the police or the interview record (COP, para 11.11).

7.129 If the detention of a mentally disordered suspect is to be reviewed, the appropriate adult should be given the opportunity to make representations (COP, para 15.1). This depends on (a) the adult being present — he may not have been contacted yet or he may have gone home, in which case he should, it is suggested, have been forewarned of any pending review; and (b) whether he is able to formulate such representations — a lawyer is likely to have better prospects. If D is to be charged or may be prosecuted, the appropriate adult must be present as the charge is read to him and must also be given a written notice of the particulars of the offence (COP, para 16.3). Once charged or told that a prosecution may follow, the police may wish to confront D with a statement or interview record concerning someone else (eg an accomplice). The COP, para 16.4, requires that a copy of the statement or sight of the record be given to the appropriate adult. It is suggested that he and preferably a lawyer also be present throughout any exchange between D and the police at this stage.

7.130 The physical treatment of mentally disordered suspects calls for caution since their behavioural response to detention is likely to be unpredictable, leading in an extreme case to suicide or an attempt at self-mutilation. If the latter is suspected (something may be known of D's background), D should, if practicable within the station, be kept in a cell within easy sight of the custody or other officer or at least in a cell with ready access for officers, and regular inspections should be made of him.

(b) Persons detained under the Mental Health Act 1983

7.131 Under s 135 of the Mental Health Act 1983 (repeating earlier legislation) (Art 130, Mental Health (NI) Order 1986) a magistrate can issue a warrant authorising the police to remove a mentally disordered person to a place of safety for up to 72 hours. Under s 136 (Art 132 of the Order) a mentally disordered person who is found in a public place to be in immediate need of care or control can be taken by a constable to a place of safety for up to 72 hours, in order that he be examined by a medical practitioner and a social worker who is approved to work in this area, and that arrangements be made for his future treatment and care. Implementation of s 136 is governed by a local policy agreed between the social services, the health authority and the police. As the Code of Practice on the 1983 Act, issued by the Department of Health (1990) under the authority of s 118 of that Act, states, 'the aim of the policy should be to secure the competent and speedy assessment by a doctor and an approved social worker of the person detained' (para 10.2). 'Mental disorder' is defined by section 1 of the 1983 Act (see para 7.123, ante) and must be distinguished from mental handicap. However, it is unrealistic to expect a police officer to make the distinction (unless the person is known to be handicapped or his condition can be quickly discovered by, for example, telephoning a relative). If he can, the handicapped person may well have committed an offence (eg assault on the constable, a public order offence) in which case he must be treated as a suspect under (a) above. In most cases, however, the custody officer should, after hearing the constable, treat the person as a Mental Health Act patient and organise expert advice (below). Although 'place of safety' in ss 135 and 136 includes a police station, ideally it should be used rarely and even then temporarily. As the Department of Health in its Memorandum on the 1983 Act remarked (para 291), '[o]nly in exceptional circumstances should a police station be used as a place of safety'. If it is, the patient 'should remain there for no longer than a few hours while an approved social worker makes the necessary arrangements for his removal elsewhere . . .'. The problem lies in finding a hospital which is physically able to accept the patient and willing to admit him on the recommendation of the intervening constable. Furthermore there is no legal duty on a hospital immediately to accept a person detained under s 136. Hence the police station is a more common first port of call than is desirable, in spite of the likelihood that such a person will have exhibited some bizarre or unusual behaviour in a public place so that mental disorder will be a ready conclusion for the constable and especially the custody officer. Indeed research suggests that the police are very accurate assessors of mental disorder (see Bean, 1979; and Rogers and Faulkener, 1987, who found that 90% of referrals by the police were subsequently supported by psychiatric evidence). Those detained under s 135 are less of a problem since the police are shielded by a magistrates' warrant and provision for treatment at a hospital or other health centre is more likely to have been planned before the warrant was sought.

7.132 A person brought to a police station under s 135 or 136 has not been arrested for an offence but, by virtue of s 137(1), is deemed to be in legal custody. The Mental Health Act is silent as to his treatment there but the COP includes him within its provisions (para 1.10), except those relating to reviews and extensions of detention. Thus, if such a person is questioned about an offence those provisions relating to questioning, cautioning, tape-recording etc are relevant, as are those on the rights to legal advice and to notify an outside person. Furthermore, the Code of Practice on the 1983 Act advises (para 10.6.b) that the local social services and an appropriately qualified doctor should be contacted immediately and that the local policy (above) should have formulated procedures for establishing such contact. That same Code suggests (para 10.11) that the detained person should be given the same information about his Mental Health Act rights and status as if he had been admitted to a hospital. A written notice would suffice from the police point of view, and a clearer explanation could be left for the social worker to impart. As regards the person's physical treatment, the checking of his property and possible removal of clothes (such as a belt, shoelaces) are clearly important lest he try to harm himself or others (COP, section 4, see para 7.17, ante); as are those relating to his conditions of detention and physical comfort (COP, section 8, see para 7.103 ante). If an assessment by a doctor of a s 136 patient can be arranged 'without undue delay' (COP, para 9.2), the custody officer need not call a police surgeon (as he must do for mentally disordered *suspects*, see para 7.125, ante). It is suggested that this 'delay' be interpreted most strictly. The maximum length of detention under the Mental Health Act is 72 hours and, unlike PACE, the purpose is not for questioning about an offence but for medical assessment. Thus, periodic reviews of the patient are not required by statute. However, bearing in mind the DSS instruction above, the encouragement in the COP (para 3.10) to organise the patient's assessment as soon as possible, and the patient's physical and mental well being, it is prudent for a custody officer to organise regular reviews of his custody. Once the patient has been assessed and a decision made about his care, custody at the station ceases since the purpose of s 136 is exhausted, The process may take quite some time since the approved social worker has to explore the patient's family and physchiatric background and may have to arrange for his compulsory admission to hospital (in which case the police have the power to convey him there, s 137, 1983 Act). In practice great efforts are made to persuade the person to enter hospital on a voluntary rather than compulsory basis. Throughout the patient's custody the custody officer should complete the appropriate form (not a custody record since there has been no arrest for an offence) signifying that he is and has been in custody under s 136 so that the person's legal status is clear (Rogers and Faulker, 1987, found that in 36% of referrals to hospital the requisite form was not used, suggesting that there might be a confusion between s 136 cases and 'voluntary' referrals).

Foreign citizens (COP, section 7)

7.133   For the initial treatment of foreign citizens in police detention, two categories must be distinguished.

(a) *Convention Countries.*
     The United Kingdom has signed consular conventions with most countries and, as soon as the suspect, D, has identified his nationality (eg by word or production of a passport), the custody officer can check the list in the COP, Annex F, to see whether it is a convention country. If it is, the relevant consulate *must* be informed of D's detention as soon as practicable. The only exceptions are when D is a political refugee or is seeking asylum. In these cases, D must expressly request the police to inform his diplomatic representative. In order to discover whether these exceptions apply, the police must wait until D's wishes are ascertained (eg via an interpreter, or when D sobers up) and must not go ahead and inform. On the other hand, if D's wishes for not informing the consulate do not concern his political status (eg he is embarrassed, he fears that his country will send him home), the police have no option under the COP — the consulate must be told (however the sanction for failing to do so will be diplomatic rather than legal, since D is hardly likely to complain nor is a court likely to exclude any evidence).

(b) *Non-convention countries*
     Citizens of these countries must be told as soon as practicable of their *right to have* their consulate *informed* of their whereabouts and the grounds for their detention. Again the custody officer must wait until D's wishes are ascertained before contacting the consulate, for D may not wish, for whatever reason, to exercise the right (eg he may have been arrested for demonstrating against his embassy).

The only difference between (a) and (b) is that in (a) the consulate must be told about D's detention (unless the asylum exception applies), whereas in (b) the onus lies on D to ask for it to be told. The following provisions are common to each category.

7.134 Any foreign citizen (including those from the Republic of Ireland) may communicate with his diplomatic representatives at any time (COP, para 7.1). The most convenient, initial method will be by telephone but physical visits to him are clearly included within 'communicate' and consequently this means that there is a right for him to be visited at any time (eg during an interview). This right of communication is unqualified (even if the criteria in s 56(5), Art 57(5) — delay in notification of arrest — are satisfied). Thus, even if the police suspect that communication will alert embassy staff and thereby thwart their investigation, it must be allowed. However, the suspect should only be told of this right of communication 'as soon as practicable'. Delay may be caused by, for example, waiting for an interpreter or for D to sober up, calm down or gain consciousness, or, if large numbers are arrested (eg during a demonstration), by waiting for a custody officer to deal with him. But 'practicability' should not be stretched to cover delays in the investigation, for the test is practicability of the notification procedure and not practicability of the investigating officers.

7.135 As soon as a diplomatic representative arrives at the police station (whether called out by D or not) he must be allowed to talk to D out of the hearing of the police. This applies even if a reason for delaying notification of arrest or legal advice (COP, Annex B) exists — COP, para 7A. On the other hand, the police are not prevented from questioning D whilst the diplomat is being informed or before he arrives at the station.

7.136 The following points should also be noted:

(i) The foregoing provisions only apply to those in police detention (ie under arrest). Those who are at a police station voluntarily have of course the unqualified right to leave and they may demand consular contact as a condition of their cooperation with the police.

(ii) The provisions are independent of the right of notification of arrest (s 56, Art 57) but the latter may be lawfully delayed (see para 7.36, ante).

(iii) In keeping with the general emphasis on documentation, the custody record should state when D was informed of his consular rights and the fact of any communication with his diplomatic representative.

(iv)   If D claims diplomatic immunity, verification will usually be required from a consular official and the Foreign Office.

(v)   If D seeks political asylum or refugee status, the case should be handled sensitively and the Refugee Unit at the Home Office notified. Consular contact should then only be established in the very rare case when D gives his full and informed consent.

Interviews with foreigners

7.137   If the detained person does not understand English and the custody officer is unable to communicate with him, an interpreter will be needed (see further on interpreters, para 7.142, post). Occasionally an officer may be able to oblige. For the more common languages a police force should have a list of appropriate interpreters. For some forces (eg those covering a port) the list should be extensive. If difficulties arise, the local Community Relations Council (though their quality varies) or an ethnic minority or refugee organisation may be able to help or the community liaison officer may have some contacts. It is most important that a list of willing and qualified interpreters be prepared since the need for one may arise urgently (eg a terrorist or kidnapper detained and questioned about the location of a bomb or hostage). The interpreter must be called as soon as practicable (COP, para 3.6), but in the meantime the custody officer should give D a written notice of his rights if one is available in his language. Stations should have a book containing the notices in several languages and the appropriate page can be shown to, or photocopied for, the suspect. This list of languages however is very limited. Exceptionally D may be interviewed before the interpreter arrives (if COP, Annex C is satisfied, see para 8.21, post), but the usefulness will obviously depend on the degree of communication possible (it is here that an officer qualified in the language could be particularly useful).

Immigration cases

7.138   Where the police are involved with the investigation of immigration offences, they may be acting under their own powers (in which case PACE and COP apply) or more normally they will be assisting the Immigration and Nationality Department of the Home Office. If the latter, immigration officers will usually assume responsibility for the detention of an immigrant under the authority of the Immigration Act 1971. When immigration officers are working at a police station, they are instructed to apply the relevant aspects of the PACE Codes of Practice (even though they are not legally bound to, s 67(9) of PACE only applying to a person 'charged with the duty of investigating offences'). To this effect a special COP has been issued by the Immigration Service with the following points. In addition to the usual PACE rights (eg access to legal advice) this COP suggests (para 4.1) that 'consideration should also be given to advising a person that he can contact a representative of an immigrant welfare organisation'. Even if a police officer has already cautioned the detainee, the immigration officer should do so before he conducts an interview (Immigration COP, para 6.3). If the immigration officer wishes to question the detainee after he has been charged, the custody officer should be consulted (para 7.16).

Deafness

7.139 If a suspect is deaf, or so hard of hearing that the custody officer doubts whether an interview will be meaningful, an interpreter must normally be called. It may be possible to interview without an interpreter if either the person agrees in writing or the conditions for an urgent interview in COP, Annex C, apply. If so, the interview can be attempted by shouting, sign language, lip-reading, or written questions and answers; an accurate record of the interview is imperative. If a solicitor is allowed access and cannot communicate, then an interpreter must also be called (COP, para 13.9; and see further on interpreters at para 7.142, post). The biggest problem facing the treatment of a deaf suspect is often the procurement of an interpreter, a task which the custody officer must fulfil as soon as is practicable (COP, para 3.6). Local Social Services Departments may have lists of qualified interpreters but there are not many (only 84 in England and Wales in 1990) who are skilled in both sign language and lip-reading techniques and have experience of police procedures. It is possible that the suspect will be able to recommend one or that a police officer can fill the bill. In the latter case D (or the appropriate adult if relevant) must expressly consent — except that an officer cannot act as interpreter between D and his lawyer, COP, para 13.9. In most cases it is D who will need an interpreter but if the appropriate adult, called to attend the detention of a juvenile or mentally disordered suspect, is hard of hearing, an interview may be impossible without an interpreter. (For the use of tape-recorders in the interviewing of the deaf, see para 8.30, post). If an interpreter has to be called, he should be asked to read the record of interview and sign to confirm its accuracy (COP, para 13.7).

The visually handicapped

7.140 For the blind or those with a serious visual handicap (including a suspect whose glasses have been broken or mislaid), the normal fear of being in a police station is likely to be exacerbated and custody officers should be alert to this. The presence of a third party (eg a solicitor, friend or relative) is most desirable, firstly, to help counter any subsequent allegation of oppression or unreliability (s 76, Art 74) or unfairness (s 78, Art 76), secondly to assist D in the comprehension of documents such as the notice of his rights (there being no requirement in COP for a braille copy to be available), and third, with D's consent, to sign any documents (principally the custody record) on his behalf (COP, para 3.14). The COP (para 1.6) plays safe by requiring the police to treat any person in custody who appears to be blind or seriously visually handicapped as such.

The illiterate

7.141   The illiterate and semi-literate constitute a large category of detained persons for whom the provision of written notices is pointless and to whom the custody officer should therefore pay attention in orally communicating and explaining their rights under para 3.2 of COP. A solicitor, relative, or other third person can fulfil a useful role in explaining documentation (COP, para 3.14). The use of tape-recording helps during interview, but where a statement is taken from D the interviewing officer should read it over carefully and slowly to him (especially if a third party is not present) before asking him to make his mark (COP, para 11.10). If the detainee disagrees with the record, his views must be recorded. Where a person is a regular visitor to the station (eg a vagrant, drunk, prostitute), observance of these precautions may become a ritual, if not a meaningless task, but must nevertheless be performed.

Interpreters

7.142   Interpreters (for the deaf and non-English speakers) pose two particular problems worthy of mention at this stage.

(a)   *Finding an interpreter.* A competent police officer can act (except when the detainee is receiving legal advice) if the detainee expressly agrees (COP, para 13.9). Social Services departments and community and race relations organisations can assist in finding an interpreter. For the more common foreign language, especially at ports and tourist attractions, the police will build up their own list. Indeed some interpreters will become regular employees at a station (they are paid for by the police and this must be explained to the detainee, COP, para 13.8). For the more unusual language a local educational institution or hospital (which will face similar problems of communication and have their own contacts) can be tried.

(b)   *Competence of the interpreter.* Since an interpreter may telephone or write a letter on the detainee's behalf, a problem of security can arise, especially with an untried interpreter. As for security during interview (ie whether the interpreter is conveying the correct information to and from the detainee), the use of tape-recorders is essential. A more frequent problem will be the competence of the interpreter in understanding and conveying technical terms to the detainee (including the notification of his rights under COP, paras 3.1–2). At the end of the interview, the interpreter should be asked to certify the accuracy of the written or taped record (para 13.3, 13.7). For the deaf, a contemporaneous written record should be compiled.

Volunteers

7.143 Special reference to this category must be made since they technically fall outside the documentation provisions of PACE, and may fall into an official, if not legal, limbo. A person who attends a police station voluntarily, or who accompanies a constable to a police station, to help the police with their inquiries is referred to as a volunteer. The accuracy of this word to describe someone who may be under a variety of pressures to help the police with their inquiries is debatable. It is used here partly for convenience and partly because it is used in PACE (s 29, Art 31) and the COP. A volunteer is free to leave at any time unless he is arrested (s 29, Art 31). This may of course be easier said than done in the coercive atmosphere of a police station. Indeed, there is a temptation for the police to preserve the person's status as a volunteer for as long as possible since, once he is arrested, he must be cautioned, official detention begins, periodic reviews of his detention will follow and formal documentation must be completed. Five safeguards against such a practice exist. First, as soon as the police have grounds to believe that the volunteer has committed an offence, he must be cautioned even if he is not at that stage arrested. He must be told that he is not under arrest, that he is not bound to remain at the station and that, if he does so, he can obtain free legal advice (COP, paras 3.15, 10.2). Similarly if the police decide that the person should be prevented from leaving, he should be told that he is being arrested, he must be taken before a custody officer and the latter must tell him of his rights (see para 7.09, ante). Second, although Part V of PACE and most of the COP are directed towards those under arrest, it should be noted that their safeguards apply with greater force to volunteers. For example, the volunteer has an unqualified right to communicate with a lawyer. The COP advises the police to treat volunteers with no less consideration than detainees (para 1A). Thus, for example, refreshments should be provided and the periods of questioning should be interrupted for at least 8 out of 24 hours so as to allow sleep. If a person attends at a police station voluntarily and is then arrested, the aforementioned period of 24 hours begins at the time of his arrest at the station (COP, para 12.2). On the other hand, unlike those in detention (see COP paras 3.1–2), the police are not under a duty to tell the volunteer of his rights unless he is cautioned or arrested (above) or he asks about legal advice in which case he is given written notice of the arrangements. Third, the custody officer plays a crucial role in overseeing the treatment of detained persons in his station. A vigilant and conscientious custody officer will also wish to be kept abreast of developments in all investigations, including those involving volunteers. Such supervision may admittedly be most difficult if the officer dealing with the volunteer is senior to the custody officer. It is perhaps unfortunate that the Code of Practice does not expressly impose supervisory duties on the custody officer in relation to volunteers. Fourth, a written record (a voluntary attendance record) should be kept of the volunteer's personal details and the interview (eg duration, persons present, purpose and result of the interview) and should be handed to the custody officer. Fifth, sections 76 and 78 (Arts 74, 76) are available to deal with the maltreatment or oppressive questioning of a volunteer. On the other hand, minor breaches of the COP are not necessarily fatal in ss 76, 78 terms (Arts 74, 76). If, for example, the facts are such that the volunteer ought to have known that he was a suspect and was being interviewed about an offence, then a mere failure to tell him that he is not bound to remain at the station may not warrant the exclusion of evidence (see *R v Rajakuruna* (1991)).

Questioning of victims

7.144 Much questioning in police stations involves victims and witnesses as well as suspects and three categories merit mention — child victims, victims of sex offences, and adult victims of domestic violence. Evidence of insensitive treatment of all categories, police complacency and notorious examples of the first category have provoked much public interest, media attention and research in recent years. To varying degrees police forces have responded by training officers in the sensitive handling of these victims (often working in a team alongside social workers) and by establishing special units (either alone or in conjunction with other agencies and either in the police station or elsewhere) in which to undertake the questioning of them. For example, in relation to suspected child victims of sexual abuse, an early experiment between the Metropolitan Police and Bexley Social Services (1987) set a trend for many other police/social work projects by illustrating the special interview techniques which can be developed. The matter was given greater urgency by the report into the Cleveland affair (see the Report of the Inquiry into Child Abuse in Cleveland, 1987) which in turn spawned the Advisory Group on Video Evidence (1989, the Pigot Report), Part II of the Criminal Justice Acts 1988 and 1991. These rapid developments have produced both recommendations and changes, some of which impinge on the early interviewing of child victims. In domestic violence, the Home Office Circular (60/1990) was produced in order to treat it more seriously, in particular 'to encourage the development and publicising of force policy statements and strategies to deal with it' (preamble). Thus, each force is urged to issue a policy statement, central features of which should be (Circular 60/1990, para 11) —

— the overriding duty to protect victims, and children, from further attack;
— the need to treat domestic violence as seriously as other forms of violence;
— the dangers of seeking conciliation between assailant and victim;
— the importance of comprehensive record-keeping to allow the chief officer to monitor the effectiveness of the policy in practice.

A detailed discussion of these areas is unfortunately beyond the confines of this book and, because of their regional variations and often embryonic nature, they do not permit of brief exposition.

Prison interviews

7.145 The police may need to interview prison inmates for a variety of reasons eg where he requests it, where it is believed that he has useful information about criminal offences. Liaison with the prison service is essential and the police must bear in mind the pressures on it. A record of prison visits should be kept by the police service and authorised by a senior officer (chief inspector). A distinction needs to be drawn between a compulsory interview (the police have reasonable grounds for suspecting D of an arrestable offence) and a 'voluntary' interview (the police do not suspect D but want information from him). In the latter, D has the right to refuse an interview (though the adjective 'voluntary' may be even less apposite here than for a person in a police station). The Prison Service Circular Instruction (10/1989) states that the spirit of the PACE and COP provisions must be observed and that the prisoner should be treated no less favourably than if he were being interviewed at a police station. A Notice summarising the prisoner's rights must be handed to him before the interview begins and he

'must be allowed ample time to read it thoroughly. If he or she has difficulty in reading it, or appears to have difficulty in understanding it, the notice should be read, and if necessary explained fully. When you are satisfied that the notice is understood, the inmate should be asked to complete the section below to indicate whether or not he or she wishes to consult a solicitor: and then to sign it' preamble to the Notice, issued by the Prison Service).

The benevolence of this instruction is tempered by paragraph 4 of the Notice which explains that, where the police have reasonable grounds for suspecting an arrestable offence, they may put questions to the prisoner and he is 'required to remain in their presence while they do so'. The Notice includes an explanation of the entitlement to legal advice. The temptation may be for the police on the day of the interview to dissuade the prisoner from exercising it on the grounds that contacting a solicitor will cause undue delay. Hence it is important for the interviewing officer to liaise with the prison beforehand to see if the prisoner wants legal advice. However, there is no obligation on the police to do this (advance notice of an interview may jeopardise the usefulness of the interview) and so in practice notice of the right to legal advice will often be given as the interview commences. If the prisoner is to be asked about involvement in offences, it will qualify as an 'interview' for COP, C purposes (see chapter 8) and thus, if facilities exist, an interview should be tape recorded. If not, a contemporaneous written record should be made. The importance of the proper recording of interviews has been regularly emphasised by the courts and failure to do so usually leads to the exclusion of the evidence.

Terrorism provisions

7.146 The rights under s 56 (Art 57), to inform a third party of detention, and under s 58 (Art 59), to legal advice, are qualified if the person is detained under 'terrorism provisions'. This phrase means s 14(1) of the Prevention of Terrorism (Temporary Provisions) Act 1989 (POT Act 1989) and any provision of Schedule 2 or 5 of that Act conferring a power of arrest or detention, and 'terrorism' has the meaning assigned to it by s 20(1) of that Act (s 65 of the PACE Act 1984, as amended by Sch 8, para 6(6) of the POT Act 1989 (Art 2 of the 1989 Order)). It encompasses the detention of

(a) persons who are arrested on suspicion of having committed a variety of 'terrorist' offences; and

(b) persons at a port of entry in order to examine whether they have infringed the terms of the Act.

Detention in both categories is limited to 48 hours but in both categories such detention may be extended on application to the Home Secretary for a further five days (s 14(5), Sch 5, para 6(3)). The previous detention power, under s 12 of the POT Act 1984, was found to be in contravention of the European Convention on Human Rights (*Brogan and Others v UK* (1988)). The Government's response was to derogate under Article 15 of the Convention, such derogation applying to detention under s 14 and Sch 5. As with the 1984 Act, the 1989 Act is not confined to terrorism involving Northern Ireland, but extends to 'international' terrorism (eg Palestinian terrorists detained in the UK). However the 'international' terrorist must be liable to criminal proceedings in the UK or to deportation. The Act is not intended to catch a person involved in terrorism abroad, but who is acting lawfully in this country. (It should be noted that the POT Act 1989 creates two new offences. It is illegal to enter into, or otherwise be concerned in, any arrangement whereby money or other property is made available to a person for terrorist purposes or to a pro-scribed organisation (s 10(1)(c)). It is also illegal to deal with and facilitate the retention or control of terrorist funds (s 11)). The POT Act 1989, in repealing and re-enacting the POT Act 1984 with modifications, is a response to the review of the operation of the 1984 Act by Lord Colville, *Review of the Operation of the Prevention of Terrorism (Temporary Provisions) Act 1984*, Cmnd 264 (1987). The safeguards contained in the PACE Act 1984 applied to persons detained under the POT Act 1984 and now apply to persons detained under the POT Act 1989, as do the same safeguards in the PACE Order 1989 in Northern Ireland. Both the PACE Act (Order) and the Codes of Practice apply to the detained terrorist, for example, documentation must be completed in the ordinary way (but see (d) below), and the taking of intimate samples (s 62 (Art 62)) requires the written consent of the person detained. Some provisions have however been restricted and the following qualifications apply when a person is detained under the terrorism legislation.

(a)   *Search of the person* — S 15(3) of the POT Act 1989 permits a constable who has a power of arrest under s 14 of the Act to stop and search a person for 'any document or other article which may constitute evidence that he is a person liable to arrest' under s 14. The extensive powers of stop and search under s 1 of the PACE Act (Art 3 of the PACE Order) do not permit such a search, though other stop and search powers may apply, eg s 47 of The Firearms Act 1968. The search power under s 15 is not ,as the PACE Act (Order) power is, limited to places where the public have access. It may be exercised anywhere. This power is also wider than that under s 54 of the PACE Act (Art 55 of the PACE Order). The latter powers only apply when a person has been arrested whereas s 15 is a power to search in order to determine whether the person may be arrested.

(b)   *Right to have someone informed when arrested* — The Jellicoe Report (Review of the Operation of the Prevention of Terrorism (Temporary Provisions) Act 1976 (1983)) recommended (para 135) that refusal of the right to communicate the fact of arrest should only arise in the rarest of cases. The European Commission of Human Rights (*Case of McVeigh* (1983)) requires similarly that a special case be made out for refusal, otherwise Article 8(1) of the European Convention is infringed (right to family and private life). In addition to the normal reasons for denying notification of arrest (s 56(5), two further 'special cases' apply to those held under terrorism provisions. They follow the recommendations (nos 24, 25) of the Jellicoe Report. Thus, notification will be refused if:

(i)   it will prejudice the gathering of information about terrorists; or

(ii)   it will alert others and thereby 'make it more difficult' to prevent terrorism and arrest terrorists (s 56(11)(c)). (Nothing in Art 57 of the PACE (N.I.) Order (the equivalent to s 56) applies to a person detained under the terrorism provisions (Art 10)).

The breadth of these additional qualifications is self-evident. Whether their terms stray too far for the European Convention remains to be seen. Refusal of notification may last up to 48 hours from arrival at a police station or any other premises; 'premises' refers to the fact that persons detained under terrorism provisions may be held on board a ship or vessel or other place specified by the Secretary of State (s 30(12)(c)). A crucial qualification to the foregoing is that the Prevention of Terrorism Act applies to 'international' terrorists. Thus, if foreign or Commonwealth nationals are detained, the right to notify their diplomatic representatives arises and this cannot be delayed without a breach of the Code of Practice (see further, para 7.133, ante). For example, X, a foreign national is arrested for murder. His Embassy must be informed at once and its representative must be allowed to see X, though the police may question X until the representative arrives.

(c)   *Right to legal advice* — As with (b), this right may be delayed for a maximum period of 48 hours, as opposed to the general limit of 36 hours. Two further grounds for delaying access to legal advice operate in addition to the general ones in s 58(8). Their terms are identical to those in s 56(b)(i) and (ii) above). The Code of Practice of the Royal Ulster Constabulary included a provision whereby an assistant chief constable can order that access to legal advice will take place in the presence of an officer:

> 'The purpose of the arrangement is not to give the police an extra opportunity to collect information about the detainee but to prevent information being passed out through a solicitor which might make the task of the police more difficult.' (Home Office Minister, Standing Committee E, 28 February 1984, col 1431).

The Jellicoe Report (1983, recommendation 24) proposed that this arrangement be adopted in the PACE ACT. Section 58(14)–(18) gave effect to it. Thus, the rank of at least Commander or Assistant Chief Constable can direct that legal advice must be given in the sight and hearing of a police officer if he has reasonable grounds to believe that any of the prejudicial effects in s 58(8) and (13) will occur. The witnessing officer must be of at least inspector rank, must be in uniform and, in the opinion of the authorising officer, should have no connection with the case (s 58(15), (16)). The subjective nature of the last criterion will enable a realistic interpretation so that, for example, an officer who has merely collated information concerning the case could be employed. Whether he will be able to detect secret messages from the overheard conversation is another matter. He could tape record the conversation for later analysis. The provision has more to do with deterrence than detection (NB for the purposes of ss 56 and 58, certain offences under the terrorism legislation are deemed always to be serious arrestable offences (s 116(5)). (Nothing in Art 59 of the PACE (N.I.) Order 1989 (the equivalent of s 58) applies to a person arrested or detained under the terrorism provisions (Art 59(12)).

(d) *Review of detention* — The detention of a person detained under s 14 must be reviewed as soon as practicable after the beginning of the detention and thereafter at not more than 12 hourly intervals. (The 'relevant time' in relation to an arrest under s 14 of the POT Act 1989 is the time of arrest wherever it takes place in the UK (s 15(6)). The review officer can only authorise continued detention if he is satisfied that one of the conditions set out in para 3 of Sch 3 apply or one of the conditions in paras 4 and 5 of Sch 3 apply. Review of detention pending removal from the territory and of examination without detention must similarly be carried out immediately the detention or examination begins and thereafter at not more than 12 hourly intervals. (The 'relevant time' in relation to port detention or examination is the beginning of the detention or examination (Sch 2, para 8(2) and Sch 5, para 7(4)). The detention or examination can only be continued if the review officer is satisfied that steps taken to remove the person or to complete the examination are being carried out diligently and expeditiously (Sch 3, paras 1 and 2). The review officer in each case must be an officer who has not been directly involved in the matter in connection with which the person is detained or examined. In the case of a review under Sch 3, para 2 (examination without detention) and in the case of a review of detention carried out in the first 24 hours of detention, the review officer must be an officer of at least the rank of inspector. Thereafter he must be an officer of at least the rank of superintendent (Sch 3, para 4). As with review of detention under the PACE Act and Order, provision is made for postponement of a review, for representations about detention, for informing the detainee of his rights under ss 56 or 58 of the PACE Act 1984 (Arts 57 and 59 of the PACE Order), and for recording the outcome of a review (Sch 3, paras 5 to 8). Para 9 contains a provision similar to that contained in s 40(11) of the PACE Act 1984 (Art 41(11) of the PACE (N.I.) Order 1989) to cover the situation where the review officer is of a rank lower than a superintendent and a higher ranking officer then gives directions which are at variance with the duty of the review officer (see para 6.72, ante).

(e) *Other exceptions* — The extended periods of detention permissible under the terrorist legislation were preserved (s 51(b) of PACE Act), as were the powers (1) to search an arrested person who has been arrested not for an offence but for examination (s 32(10)), and (2) to retain fingerprints for the purpose of gathering intelligence (ss 61(9)(b) and 64(7)(b)). The various requirements in the Codes of Practice (eg COP, A para 4.5, COP, C para 2.6) for officers to record their names are replaced in cases of detention under the POT Act by a duty to record the officers' warrant numbers.

8   The Questioning of Suspects

Summary

8.01   The questioning of persons assumes such importance in the detection of crime and the proper conviction of offenders that special provisions govern it in PACE (ss 76–78; Arts 74–76 of the N.I. Order) and have been developed in the Code of Practice, C, (COP). Breach of these provisions is more likely and more regularly to be met with the exclusion of evidence than in any other area of police powers. There are two overriding, but difficult, principles to apply. First, as soon as an officer has grounds to suspect that a person has committed an offence and wishes to question him with a view to prosecution, he must caution that person. Second, an interview with a suspect must be recorded in written or taped form. An investigation, prior to arrest, can be described as having four stages — (1) police suspicion of a person, D, (2) the cautioning of D, (3) the questioning of D, and (4) D's arrest. If D is caught red-handed, all four will coincide. If D is stopped, questioned and arrested in the street (or attends the police station voluntarily, is questioned and then arrested), the sequence will be (1), (3), (2) and (4). Frequently the order will be (1), (4), (2) and (3). The difference between (2) and (3) can be narrow and difficult to distinguish. For example, if a police officer does not suspect D and merely asks him what he saw or knows of an incident, neither (2) nor (3) apply. If anything, D is only a potential witness. If he then asks D whether he was involved in the incident, (3) arises, an 'interview' develops (see below), and it must be recorded. If the officer begins to suspect that D *is* involved, (2) also arises. It will be readily appreciated that such analysis, of what may be a rapidly developing conversation, is far easier to conduct on paper than, for example, in the street. However, the point is important in practice for the COP contains frequent references to both principles, (2) and (3), whilst the courts have been particularly energetic in requiring the proper recording of interviews. Moreover, interviews after arrest attract special procedures, and a distinction needs also to be drawn between the methods of questioning persons inside and outside a police station. In relation to cautioning, a further distinction between Northern Ireland and the rest of the United Kingdom is required. This chapter seeks to deal with these matters.

Cautioning

8.02 In recognition of a person's right to silence (ie the privilege against self-incrimination), once a person charged with the duty of investigating offences (s 67(9), Art 66(8) has grounds to suspect that a person has committed an offence, he must caution him (COP, para 10.1; unless the suspect is too unfit or unruly to be told). This innovation of PACE cast the duty of cautioning a step further back in the investigation process than was required pre-1986 under the Judges' Rules, for they imposed the duty when the officer had *reasonable* grounds to suspect that there was evidence. The trigger for a caution is suspicion and not the weightier term 'belief' (as to the distinction see para 2.02, ante). The caution only arises if the police wish to question the person about the offence *and* in order to obtain evidence to prosecute him. So, questions aimed at, for example, discovering his identity, his whereabouts at the time of the suspected offence, or his relationship with the victim, would not be for that purpose. However, the borderline between these purposes is frequently blurred or overlapping. For example, questions put to discover whether a stop and search should be conducted do not require a caution (COP, para 10.1), but questions about items discovered during a search can easily qualify as an interview (see below) and require a caution. The following points can be mentioned about cautioning. (a) In practice the duty to caution will often coincide with the moment of arrest. (b) The more difficult case is where a person has been answering questions, at a police station or elsewhere, and a stage is reached where the officer begins to suspect him. His natural inclination is to continue the questioning without the interruption of a caution and the deterrent effect which it and (c) below may have on a talkative suspect. In the absence of a contemporaneous record, it may be impossible for a court to judge whether the stage for cautioning was improperly passed — hence the value of recording interviews (see below). (c) A person who is cautioned but not arrested must also be told that he is not under arrest and that he 'is not obliged to remain with the officer' (COP, para 10.2). The latter phrase is not as positive as 'you are free to go' and its tone of delivery may have little or no impact on the suspect. On the other hand, if the instruction is delivered clearly or at least neutrally, it could well encourage a suspect to take the hint and leave. It is thus understandable, but nonetheless indefensible, that officers may try to disguise or blunt the force of the instruction. (d) In the case of a 'volunteer' (ie a person not in police detention) being questioned at a police station, the officer must not only give the caution when the requisite suspicion arises, but must also tell him that he is not under arrest, he is not obliged to stay *and* that, if he does, he can obtain free legal advice (COP, para 3.15). Again the tone and context of delivery are likely to influence the impact of this message, but *if* properly delivered this is a formidable safeguard to the citizen. (e) If a person is arrested, a caution need not be given if it is impracticable (eg D is intoxicated, or violently resists arrest) or if one has already been given immediately prior to the arrest (COP, para 10.3(b)); eg questioning of a person raises sufficient suspicion to warrant a caution at 5.30 pm, a few questions later and there is enough evidence to arrest him at 5.40 pm. A second caution is unnecessary. It is suggested (i) that no harm, and perhaps a little good for the suspect, is done if a second caution is given, even in this example, and (ii) that the word 'immediately' be interpreted strictly, for the circumstances and tension of police questioning can cause a suspect quickly to forget the first caution. (f) If a caution is given to a juvenile or the mentally disordered, it must be given initially in the presence of the appropriate adult or repeated when he arrives (COP, para 10.6). (g) When a person's detention is authorised by a custody officer at a police station, the suspect is given a written notice of his rights and the notice repeats the caution (COP, para 3.2).

8.03   The wording of the caution ('You do not have to say anything unless you wish to do so, but what you say may be given in evidence') seems straightforward but the Notes for Guidance to the COP (paras 10C, 10D) permit the officer to explain it in different words if required. This can be a difficult task for the officer. What he must not do is intimate that a refusal to cooperate and a reliance on his right to silence can be used at trial against the suspect (for the position in Northern Ireland, see below). If he does the opposite and suggests that cooperation will reflect well on the suspect at trial, he runs the risk of s 76(2)(b) being invoked to exclude any admission. The moral must be to stick to the precise words of the caution as closely as possible and if elaboration is unavoidable, to ensure that the suspect's representative or, where relevant, appropriate adult is present. If there is a break in questioning, the interviewing officer must ensure that the suspect remembers the caution on resumption (COP, para 10.5). The simplest way is a reminder that he is still under caution and this will usually suffice if the break is short (eg the officer being called to consult a colleague or to answer a telephone, or the suspect visits the lavatory); but even here an intelligent suspect will benefit from a repetition of the caution, especially if he is unrepresented. After all it does not take long and, with the advent of tape-recording, the length of the break and the suspect's likely awareness of the caution on resumption of questioning may be more accurately assessed and this may affect the subsequent admissibility of the interview (ss 76, 78; Arts 74, 76). Certainly longer breaks warrant repetition of the caution; and re-commencement of an interview will also require a reminder of D's right to free legal advice (COP, para 11.2; cf the importance of this reminder in the U.S. in *Minnick v Mississippi* (1990).

8.04   Three safeguards exist against the careless or deliberate omission of the caution. First, as a breach of the COP, a disciplinary offence is committed. Second, in keeping with PACE's philosophy of requiring documentation, the giving of a caution must be recorded in writing (in a pocketbook, or interview record as appropriate), COP, para 10.7. Third, and most importantly, a complaint as to improper questioning can be raised at trial under ss 76 and 78 (Arts 74 and 76) with a real possibility that a suspect's statement is excluded and the prosecution fails.

Cautioning — Northern Ireland

8.05   The position in Northern Ireland must be distinguished. Under the Criminal Evidence (Northern Ireland) Order 1988, if a suspect fails during interview to mention a fact which he could reasonably have been expected to mention and which he then relies upon at trial, the court may subsequently

(i)   draw such inferences from the failure as appear proper;
(ii)   on the basis of such inferences treat the failure as, or as capable of amounting to, corroboration of any evidence given against the accused in relation to which the failure is material.

Consequently a different caution must be given to the suspect viz.

'You do not have to say anything unless you wish to do so but I must warn you that if you fail to mention any fact which you rely on in your defence in court, your failure to take this opportunity to mention it may be treated in court as supporting any relevant evidence against you. If you do wish to say anything, what you say may be given in evidence.' (Code C, para 10.5)

Moreover, a written notice explaining the effect of the 1988 Order must also be given to the suspect. It should be noted that a person cannot be convicted solely on the basis of an inference drawn from his silence during the police interview (Art 2(4)). However, the possibility of a prosecution being launched solely on that basis is unrealistic. The 1988 Order goes much further than qualifying the right of silence at the interview stage. Under Article 5, if a person is arrested and there is

(i)   on his person; or
(ii)   in or on his clothing or footwear; or
(iii)   otherwise in his possession; or
(iv)   in any place in which he is at the time of his arrest,

any object, substance or mark or there is any mark or any such object: and the officer asks the person to account for the article, then a failure to do so may entitle a court to draw inferences, including an inference capable of amounting to corroboration of other evidence against him. The officer must caution the suspect as follows:

'You do not have to say anything unless you wish to do so but what you say may be given in evidence.

On . . . at . . . a . . . was found on your person/in or on your clothing or footwear/ in your possession/in — where you were at the time/a mark was found on such an object, that is –/ and I have reason to believe that this was attributable to your participation in an offence of . . .'.

Similarly under art 6 a suspect's failure, after an appropriate caution, to tell an officer the reason for his attendance at the venue of an offence can attract such inferences. As for the trial, a similar inference can be drawn from an accused's failure (after proper cautioning of him) to give evidence (art 4).

8.06   As for the rest of the United Kingdom, the recommendations of the Home Office Working Group (on the Right of Silence, 1989), which largely reflect the Criminal Evidence (Northern Ireland) Order, have been put on the shelf for the time being.

Interviews

8.07   Regardless of the venue, any interview between a police officer or person investigating a criminal offence and a suspect must be both recorded, and recorded accurately (COP, para 11.5(a)). Failure to do so has been a regular basis for the exclusion of evidence and for disapproval by the judiciary (see *R v Absolam* (1989), and *R v Matthews* (1990)). It thus becomes crucial to ascertain what is an 'interview'. In the Shorter Oxford Dictionary it is defined as 'a meeting of persons face to face, especially for the purpose of a formal conference on some point'. This broad definition could cover even a chance meeting and conversation in the street and severely hamper police investigations. Clearly the word must be restricted to the context in which it is used — an interview 'with a person suspected of an offence' (COP, para 11.5). In other words the police must suspect a person before any conversation with him ranks as an interview for COP purposes (sometimes this will be obvious eg D is stopped in the street and an offensive weapon is discovered, clearly any questioning will concern a likely offence, see *R v Foster* (1987)). This narrows the term down but still permits a very wide interpretation. Thus, in *Matthews* (1990) the Court of Appeal took the view that 'Normally any discussion or talk between a suspect or prisoner and a police officer about an alleged crime will amount to an 'interview', whether instigated by the suspect, or prisoner or a police officer'.

8.08   The case law on the meaning of 'interview' has established the following — an interview requires a meeting between an officer and a suspect, so that a concealed tape-recording of D's conversations with another person in a police cell will not amount to an interview (though it might be excluded on grounds of unfairness, see *Katz* (1990) and cf *R v H* (1987)); it can take place outside the police station (*Maguire* (1989), *Chung* (1991)); the suspect need not be talking to the investigating officer (*Sparks*

(1991)); it can qualify as an interview even if the officer genuinely believes that he is only having an informal chat, ie the conversation is viewed objectively by the court and, if it decides it is an interview, the officer's belief or motives are irrelevant (*Sparks* (1991)); it should not be given a restricted meaning (*Matthews* (1990), *Sparks* (1991)); it must involve a person whom the police suspect (*Grier* (1989)); it is 'a series of questions directed by the police to a suspect with a view to obtaining admissions on which proceedings [can] be founded', per Bingham LJ in *Absolam* (1989): the 'series of questions' can be quite short (16 in *Fogah* (1989), three in *Manji* (1990), and it is suggested, one will suffice viz 'did you do it?'); the subject matter, not length, of the conversation is the crucial matter (*Foster* (1987)); the questioning must relate to the suspected offence (*Absolam* (1989), *Matthews* (1990), *Pullen* (1991), *Marsh* (1991)); it would appear to require a two-way process (*Younis* (1990)) so that if a suspect 'blurts out' an admission unprompted it is not an interview. This is doubtful since very rarely will a suspect speak without at least a few opening questions from an officer. Moreover, Younis had already been arrested and, it will be suggested, after arrest any conversation *related to the offence* should be an interview. Clearly questions aimed at non-suspects asking for information or explanations are not an interview. In this respect, the decision of the Court of Appeal in *Maguire* (1989) is to be doubted. The suspect there had been arrested and confessed en route to the police station. The Court agreed with the trial judge that questions near the scene of a suspected crime designed to elicit an explanation and legitimate reason for the suspect's conduct did not amount to an interview. Yet *Maguire* had already been arrested and any subsequent questions about the offence could equally as well elicit an explanation of guilt. Indeed the tone of the questions show that the officer was looking for a confession as much as an innocent explanation. However, this interpretation appears to have been accepted in the COP. Its Notes for Guidance (11A) state, 'An interview is the questioning of a person regarding his involvement or suspected involvement in a criminal offence or offences. Questioning a person simply to obtain information or his explanation of the facts or in the ordinary course of the officer's duties, does not constitute an interview.' (The statutory procedure for obtaining a specimen from a motorist for drink-driving offences does not constitute an interview, see *DPP v D* (1991).) Para 11A also excludes 'questioning which is confined to the proper and effective conduct of a search', but this guidance must be treated with caution. If, for example, D is arrested and is taken to his home for a search, accompanying conversation can very easily and quickly qualify as an 'interview'. Given the importance which the courts attach to the proper recording of an interview, it is surprising that the definition of this crucial term is found in the Notes for Guidance. The key to the definition is whether the questioning is directed at D's *involvement* in the offence as opposed to what he saw or knows about the incident. In summary, for an interview

(a) the police must suspect that an offence has been committed;

(b) the police must suspect D of involvement, for otherwise any conversation with a member of the public, eg a witness, would qualify;

(c) the police must ask D questions about his involvement in the offence. So, for example, questions aimed at discovering his identity or conversation on unrelated matters en route to the station such as football do not require a recording. (c) also accommodates the very rare case when the police stumble across an offender and he immediately owns up before any questions can be put to him (any such spontaneous utterances must in any case be noted and D asked to sign the record of them, see COP, para 11.13);

(d) it follows from (a) and (b) that all questioning about the offence after caution and arrest amounts to an interview.

8.09 The foregoing fits in with the caselaw and the purpose of PACE. Among the practical consequences are that the time for cautioning and recording an interview will often coincide; the police may become 'arrest happy' ie arrest at an early stage so as to get D into a station for a proper, recorded interview; they will often have to make the time to compile a written record of an interview outside the station, either contemporaneously or later, COP, para 11.5 (this task may hasten the introduction of taped interviews outside the station, the carrying of recorders by foot or car patrols being quite feasible); they should ask D to read and sign the record so that he adopts it as his own, and if he refuses, note this in the custody record and send a copy of the interview record to D's solicitor (see this suggestion in *Matthews* (1990)); alternatively D should be re-interviewed at the station in the hope that he repeats any admissions. The most difficult practical problem however lies in determining when conditions (a) and (b) above are satisfied. Take the following situation (and cf the facts in *Maguire* (1990)): a police officer hears the sound of breaking glass, approaches the scene and a juvenile runs round the corner into him. (i) the officer, P, asks the juvenile, D, what he has been up to. D replies, 'nothing'. (ii) P 'what's all this broken glass about?' D blushes and says 'I had an accident'. (iii) P, 'what sort of accident?' D explains but (iv) on further questioning D admits to having broken the glass deliberately. (v) P puts the offence of criminal damage to him and asks for clarification. (vi) D elaborates and confirms his admission. On any interpretation stages (v) and (vi) constitute an interview (which must be recorded and, since a juvenile is involved, must take place in the presence of an appropriate adult). On a literal interpretation of the first sentence of the Notes for Guidance para 11A, the interview begins at stage (i) when P has a suspicion (no more) that D has committed an offence. The reality of policing and the need for commonsense require some leeway for the police to make preliminary enquiries without the encumbrance of note-taking and suggest that the interview begins at stage (iv) and D should be cautioned at this point. Since the Notes for Guidance are not binding on the court, it is hoped that a balance along these lines will be adopted. As Bingham LJ was prompted to remark in *R v Marsh* (1991):

'[I]t is plainly desirable that these provisions [the Code] should not become so highly technical and sophisticated in their construction and application that no police officer, however well intentioned and diligent, could reasonably be expected to comply with them. There has to be a reasonable commonsense approach to the matter such that police officers confronted with unexpected situations, and doing their best to be fair and to comply with the Codes, do not fall foul on some technicality of authority or construction.'

Clearly it is a matter of degree and no firm line can be pre-ordained for many cases. Equally, many cases will be clear, eg if D is caught with a jemmy outside, or fleeing from, a broken door, then the time for interview, caution and arrest will arise simultaneously; equally if juvenile D is under arrest and taken by car to a station, any conversation about the offence is an interview and the caution should already have been given. An officer is called to a store after a private detective has seized an alleged shoplifter. The interview should begin if and as soon as, he asks D about the circumstances, since (a) and (b) above are fulfilled. An officer, P, stops D in the street and searches him for an offensive weapon. P is not at the interview stage whilst he explains the reason and powers of the search. If he discovers a knife, then the stage is reached. If he discovers workmens' tools, then questions about them constitute an interview if he suspects an unlawful purpose (for discussion of offensive weapons in the context of stop and search, see para 317, ante). An important point to recall is the status of the COP. Its breach does not necessarily require the exclusion of evidence. That is a matter for ss 76 and 78 of PACE (Arts 74,76). In most cases an unrecorded interview will be fatal (eg the questioning of a juvenile in the example above usually requires stronger protection than that of an adult), whilst in others it may not be 'unfair' (s 78. Art 76) to admit an interview which has otherwise breached the COP.

8.10 The importance of determining when an interview arises lies, firstly, in that an accurate record of it must be compiled (COP, para 11.5), second in that juveniles and the mentally disordered must not usually be interviewed in the absence of an 'appropriate adult' (para 11.14) and, third, in that a person cannot usually be interviewed outside a police station after arrest.

8.11 As a summary the following situations can be distinguished:

1) D is caught red-handed. Arrest and caution apply and any conversation about the offence is an interview.
2) D is stopped and questioned and asked to go to the station. After further questioning he is arrested there. The sequence of events will

be a taped or written interview record, and caution when sufficient suspicion arises (COP, para 10.1), arrest and further caution (COP, para 10.3) and taped (or written) record of any further interview (para 11.5).

3) The same as in (2) except that D is arrested and taken to the station. An interview and caution (based on suspicion) will precede the arrest (reasonable suspicion) and questioning at the station will be recorded.

To a large extent the problems of defining an interview are now reduced by the COP's requirement (para 11.13) that any unsolicited comment by a suspect, outside the interview but relevant to the offence, should be written down and D asked to read and sign the record (see the facts of *R v Younis* (1990) and *R v Scott* (1991)); for example unprompted remarks in the police car or after D has been searched or charged.

Recording of interviews

8.12 As a preliminary to a discussion of the conduct of interviews, it is worthwhile to cite the views of the Lord Chief Justice in 1990 (*R v Canale*):

'the importance of the rules relating to contemporaneous noting of interviews can scarcely be over-emphasised. The object is twofold: not merely to ensure, so far as possible, that the suspect's remarks are accurately recorded and that he has an opportunity when he goes through the contemporaneous record afterwards of checking each answer and initialling each answer, but likewise it is a protection for the police, to ensure, so far as possible, that it cannot be suggested that they induced the suspect to confess by improper approaches or improper promises. If the contemporaneous note is not made, then each of those two laudable objects is apt to be stultified.'

Interviews outside the police station

8.13 If D is arrested outside a police station for *any* offence he must not usually be interviewed *about the offence* until he arrives at the station, COP, para 11.1. Conversations in the police car are to be avoided. There are three exceptions which correspond to three of those justifying delay in the notification of arrest, s 56(5), (Art 54(5)), and in the access to legal advice, s 58(8) (Art 56(8)), viz (a) harm to evidence or persons, (b) the alerting of other suspects, or (c) obstruction in the recovery of property (COP, para 11.1). (a) could include questioning for the sake of a hostage's safety or to try to prevent an accomplice in a brawl from washing or disposing of blood stained clothes; an example of (b) would be to ascertain from D the rendezvous for a gang of shoplifters, who will only proceed to the hoard of property once each member has turned up at a pre-arranged spot; (c) would allow questioning to prevent accomplice robbers from disposing of the proceeds (eg to ascertain the best place for a road check, or the likely ports of entry to alert). The exceptions are both narrow (the police cannot in theory ask a man, found 'with a smoking gun', the question 'what happened?') and flexible for, unlike ss 56 and 58, there is no requirement of authorisation by a senior officer. Operational requirements may mean that it is the arresting officer who decides whether one of the exceptions applies and whether he can continue to question D. As soon as he has enough information to avert, or at least to be in the position to try to avert, one of the aforementioned risks, then questioning must cease until the suspect reaches the station. Apart from risking an official complaint and disciplinary action, an officer who manipulates these exceptions and questions unnecessarily runs the real risk that any statement elicited from D will be excluded at trial. If D is interviewed outside a police station but not arrested, or at least interviewed prior to arrest, the interviewing officer must compile an interview record in his pocketbook or similar report book (COP, para 11.5(a)). This must recount various formalities (eg the place, time, persons present; see COP, para 11.5(b)) and then *either* a verbatim record of the conversation *or* an accurate summary. It must be timed and signed by the officer. All records should be compiled contemporaneously unless (a) the officer thinks this would be impracticable, or (b) it would interfere with the interview (COP, para 11.5(c)). Both are capable of wide interpretation (eg a record is impossible whilst D is dressing and showing the police around his home, or whilst the police fear D may escape, see *R v Parchment* (1989 and 1991) and cf *R v Chung* (1991) where D was handcuffed); or a record would spoil the flow of the interview; and note that there is no requirement in (b) of 'serious' or other extreme 'interference') but there are some limitations. First, in (a) the condition is impracticability not inconvenience, so whereas torrential rain would suffice in the street, the proximate protection of a doorway or police car would not. Second the onus is on the officer to establish (a) or (b) (see *R v Delaney* (1989) where no attempt to prove it seems to have been made). Third, the reason for invoking (a) or (b) must be recorded in his pocketbook (COP, para 11.9) and this reason can then be unhurriedly tested at trial. Fourth, D should normally be asked to read and sign the record (COP, para 11.10 — resolving the *Beycan* (1990), *Brezeanu* (1989), *Parchment* (1989), *Brown* (1989), *Maguire* (1989) disagreement) and he is more likely to do so immediately than some hours later when the officer has produced a summary and when D's thoughts are clearer or his memory of the conversation disagrees with that of the officer. If a summary is to be prepared, it must be done promptly (COP, para 11.7) and must still be offered to D to read and sign. Each interview record should be offered to the suspect for him to sign or indicate where he disagrees, 'unless it is impracticable' (COP, para 11.10). It is suggested that this last phrase is meaningless. A record can always be offered to D however late in the day and whether he chooses to receive it or not is up to him. If D cannot read or refuses to read, the officer should read the record to him (para 11.10) and if an appropriate adult or solicitor or, it is suggested, an interpreter is present during the interview, he too should be asked to read and sign the record.

8.14   Cases on 'oppression' (s 76(2)(a), Art 74(2)(a)) usually revolve around treatment at the police station but it must be remembered that the provisions apply just as well to interviews outside the station. Thus, police conduct on confronting D at his home or in the police car and the things said to him may be highly relevant to ss 76 and 78, especially since D will not have access to legal advice at that stage. Indeed, it can be argued that the need for safeguards for suspects are 'realistically nowadays much greater outside than inside the confines of the police station' (*R v Parchment* (1989); see further on police conduct during interviews at para 8.63, post).

8.15   Three further points can be noted — a juvenile or mentally disordered person cannot normally be interviewed outside a police station without an appropriate adult in attendance (see further para 7.112, ante and for interviews at schools see para 7.121, ante). Properly observed, this is another stringent safeguard for the citizen. Second, a person in police detention at a hospital cannot be questioned without a doctor's approval. If he is, the period counts towards the period of detention (COP, para 14.2, 14A). Third, COP para 14.1 restricts the questioning of suspects in transit between police stations (see para 8.18, post).

Interviews inside the police station

8.16   If a person attends a station in order to answer questions as a potential witness, neither an interview nor record for COP purposes have to be involved, though frequently they are and obviously the police will want to obtain a statement from him. If, on the other hand, he attends to answer questions as a suspect, then the COP is very relevant. As a suspect he will soon have to be cautioned and warned of his rights (COP, para 3.15 and see para 8.02, ante); an 'interview' will be involved and must be recorded. Also if a person is brought to a station under arrest, he will receive a caution and reading of his rights (see COP, para 3.1 and para 7.09, ante). Moreover, each interview or recommencement of an interview at a police station *must* be prefaced by the interviewing officer *reminding* the person of his right to free legal advice (COP, para 11.2; it is suggested that a failure to remind will one day be greeted by the exclusion of evidence under ss 76 and/or 78 (see below)). Although the same reasons for not making a contemporaneous record apply (COP, para 11.5(c), impracticability or interference with the course of the interview), the chief difference from interviews outside the station is that a verbatim record is always practicable in a station either in writing or more commonly on tape. As for the former, this will arise in interviews for summary offences (which do not have to be taped), and interviews for indictable offences which cannot be taped (because of mechanical failure, lack of machines, or wish of the suspect). The record must contain certain formalities (COP, para 11.5). It must be offered to D and his representative (and appropriate adult where relevant) for perusal and signature, and any refusal to sign must be recorded (paras 11.11 and 12). In addition if the suspect makes any relevant comment outside the interview (eg on reception in front of the custody officer), it should be noted on the custody record and he should be asked to acknowledge it by signature (para 11.13). Moreover, any note of D's comments or interview must be disclosed to his solicitor when he arrives (*R v Chung* (1991)). If D insists on an 'off the record' interview, PACE and the COP do not accommodate the possibility. Such a conversation will amount to an 'interview' (*R v Woodall* (1989)) and each interview must be recorded contemporaneously, unless it is impracticable or it would interfere with the conduct of the interview (COP, para 11.5(c)). It is possible to argue that D's insistence can satisfy either exception. However, a summary of the interview must be made (para 11.5(c)) and made as soon as practicable after the interview ends (para 11.7) and then shown to D (para 11.10). This requirement again applies 'unless impracticable' but this is to no avail for, having made the summary, it can hardly be impracticable to *show* it to D. The fact that he does not like it is irrelevant. Thus, it is suggested that the interviewing officer must in turn insist upon a contemporaneous note being made (the presence of a legal adviser may help and it would be quite proper for the interview to be suspended whilst advice is taken). If D is adamant, he has to be told that a record will be subsequently made. D should then be asked to read and sign it, or at least to read it. If he refuses, the document should still be served on the defence (see *R v Matthews* (1990)). It is unlikely to be of great evidential value if D refuses to give evidence at trial. If he does, then it can be used to show consistency or inconsistency (provided that the court admits the statement ie that it is a reliable record of what he said).

Manner of questioning

8.17 The style of questioning which a person faces depends on the circumstances of each case, including whether he has come to the police station voluntarily in order to assist the police or whether he has been arrested and detained for questioning, the personality of the available interviewing officer, and the tactics which the officer decides to adopt. Relatively little attention has been paid in England and Wales to police training in the tactics and psychology of interviewing. Indeed, the Royal Commission suggested that the skills of interviewing should be taught on a 'more systematic basis' (Report, para 4.113). Similarly the law has paid relatively little attention to the way in which interviews are conducted. The

8.17 *The questioning of suspects*

Judges Rules, if observed, would have led to a statement which was admissible within the voluntariness principle. The Administrative Directions supplemented the Rules by specifying certain conditions in which the suspect was to be questioned. Failure to comply with either the Rules or Directions could lead to exclusion of the confession as not being 'voluntary' or as being the product of oppressive questioning. But neither the Rules nor the Directions dealt with the manner of the questioning. The PACE Act (Order) has also eschewed close involvement. The COP offers some guidance on the physical conditions (see below), but leaves the method of questioning to the interviewing officer. Three important considerations operate. First, the advent of tape-recording has exposed deficiencies in the techniques of questioning and persuaded the police to devote more training to the subject. Second, the questioning of suspects is subject to strict time limits. Various reviews of detention and various formalities must be observed at fixed intervals (see the detailed discussion in chapter 6, ante). Furthermore, sleep, refreshments and the suspect's access to his lawyer may naturally interrupt the course of questioning. Third, the evidential requirements for the admissibility of a confession at the trial stage can dictate the style of interrogation. Thus, the questioning of detained persons must not be 'oppressive' or such as otherwise to lead to unreliable evidence (s 76, Art 74) or to an unfair trial (s 78, Art 76). These principles (discussed below) apply to persons under arrest and therefore in detention, but are not confined to the police station. So, for example, questioning in the police car or at the scene of a crime must not be oppressive. 'Oppression' includes 'torture, inhuman or degrading treatment, and the use or threat of violence' (s 76(8)). As to the 'reliability' principle, this essentially excludes a confession made 'in consequence of anything said or done' which was likely to render it unreliable (s 76(2)(b)). As for s 78, the courts have shown a readiness to use it in the context of confessions. It is clear that the ways in which a detained person has been questioned and treated during the questioning will be crucial evidence as to whether the interviewing officer has breached the PACE Act (Order) or Code. Custody officers play an important role in ensuring that officers obey the various procedural rules eg as to the provision of refreshments) and the various statutory duties placed on them as regards documentation.

8.18 Since the custody officer watches over all detained persons, his permission must be obtained before a person is handed over to another police officer for questioning or to accompany him, for example, to the scene of the crime or to check an alibi (COP, para 12.1). Most requests for custody of the person will concern questioning. The custody officer should ask the officer for a report on the state of the investigation and the reason for the questioning. He should be particularly alert lest a person be questioned when there is already sufficient evidence to charge him. If a suspect has been arrested by another police force or outside the country, complex provisions (s 41; see para 6.40 ante) operate to give the police a reasonable time to transport him to the interested police force before the 'detention clock' begins, If he is questioned about the offence by the arresting force, the 'detention clock' begins on his arrival at the police station in that force area, thus reducing the time available for investigation in the other area. Accordingly, the COP (para 14.1) states that no questions may be put to him about the offence while he is in transit between the two police forces, except in order to clarify a voluntary statement he has made.

Physical conditions of the interview

8.19 Whenever possible the interview must take place in interview rooms which are properly heated, lighted and ventilated (COP, para 12.4; the last is especially important to avoid the fog of cigarettes). The person must not be forced to stand. There is no limitation on the number of officers who may attend, but (1) the officer in charge must identify them to the person; (2) he should be aware of the allegation of oppression (see s 76, Art 74) which may subsequently be raised by the defence at trial. The unnecessary presence of officers may be seen as intimidatory and perhaps oppressive. In any 24 hour period, the person must be allowed at least eight hours continuous rest, preferably at night and free from travelling, questioning, or any other interruption. The rest period can be interrupted or delayed if there are reasonable grounds to believe that the normal rest period would:

   (i)   involve a risk of harm to persons or serious loss of, or damage to, property;

   (ii)   delay unnecessarily the person's release from custody; or

   (iii)   otherwise prejudice the outcome of the investigation (para 12.2).

The COP is silent as to who should hold these beliefs but it is suggested that it is consistent with his overall responsibilities for detained persons for the custody officer to reach this decision and for him to record the reasons in the custody record. The first COP stated that for a person arrested at a police station the eight hours' rest period requirement ran from the time of his arrival there. So, for example, if D attended a station voluntarily at 10.00 am and was arrested at 10.00 pm, he had to be permitted eight hours sleep before 10.00 am the following day. The 1991 COP however specifies the time of his arrest as the starting time (para 12.2). This should not, it is suggested, be interpreted as allowing more rigorous questioning of a 'volunteer', for the admissibility of any confession he may make is still governed by the demanding requirements of ss 76 and 78 (see below). Breaks in interviewing will occur at 'recognised meal times' (ie falling within 7–9 am, 12–2 pm, 5–7 pm). Further and shorter breaks will take place every two hours unless the interviewing officer has reasonable grounds to believe that (i)–(iii) above apply. These grounds are sufficiently broad to entitle ready delays of breaks. For example, a person in detention has eaten breakfast by 7.30 am. Lunch is due at 12.30. Breaks from interviewing for coffee or tea at 9.30 and/or 11.30 can be postponed if the officer believes that the suspect is about to confess or that a few more questions will complete the matter and thereby clear up the investigation. The sanctions against improper denial of breaks are (1) the duty to record the grounds for the denial (COP, para 12.11), and (2) the possibility that these grounds may be used to allege 'oppression' under s 76 and to exclude any confession obtained during the questioning (or s 78, see below).

Duties of the interviewing officer

8.20 He is responsible for the detained person's or volunteer's welfare during the interview. He is the officer who approaches a superintendent or higher rank for authorisation to refuse the suspect access to legal advice or to press ahead with questioning even though the person is, for example, drunk or mentally ill. Above all, he must return the person to the custody officer and account for his treatment of the person to him. If a complaint is made against the interviewing officer's conduct, it must be recorded and reported to the custody officer (COP, par 12.8). He in turn reports it to an inspector or higher rank who is unconnected with the investigation (para 9.1). If there is the slightest suggestion of physical injury, the police surgeon must be summoned at once. The interviewing officer must also ensure that the interview is properly recorded, either on tape or by a contemporaneous written record. (The latter may be compiled by him or another officer).

Urgent interviews

8.21 The questioning of the intoxicated, juveniles, the mentally ill or handicapped, foreigners and the deaf is generally prohibited until the detained person sobers up or an appropriate adult or interpreter arrives. However, an officer of at least superintendent rank can authorise questioning to take place if he 'considers that delay will involve an immediate risk of harm to persons or serious loss of or serious damage to property'. (COP, Annex C). For example, D is a suspected terrorist who is believed to have planted a bomb to explode at closing time in a crowded pub or on the route travelled by the Prime Minister. E is believed to be a member of a kidnapping gang, the other members of which are holding a hostage. D and E can be questioned at once about the location of the bomb or the hostage. There are of course dangers that some police officers will use the excuse of urgency to question suspects, who in normal circumstances would not be interrogated without precautions. There are four safeguards against this possibility. First, the questioning is to last only as long as the reason for urgency exists. Thus, the terrorist who reveals the location of a bomb should not without more be questioned. However, he can be if, as is most likely, the police believe that he has knowledge about the whereabouts of accomplices. Second, the grounds for the questioning must be recorded. Third, the interviewing officer should be aware of ss 76 and 78 (Arts 74, 76) and the possible exclusion of confessions at trial if questioning continues unduly. Fourth, the extent and detail of the questioning may inevitably be limited by the nature of the detained person's disability (eg foreign language).

Tape-recording of interviews

8.22 The Criminal Law Revision Committee suggested in 1972 that a study should be made into the tape-recording of suspects. This was duly followed by the Hyde Committee in 1976. The Royal Commission on Criminal Procedure in 1981 agreed with the Hyde Committee that, in order to save the costs and delay of preparing transcripts, a taped summary of police interviews be made. The PACE Act contained a provision (s 60) enabling the Home Secretary to order the taping of interviews and in the meantime field trials in six areas were conducted over a period of two years under the scrutiny of a National Steering Committee (see Willis, Macleod and Naish). These trials proved to be very successful (see Willis et al). The prior implementation of PACE in January 1986 meant that the police had in most cases to make written contemporaneous notes of interviews and this laborious task undoubtably made the police more amenable to the introduction of tape-recording (it also reduces the average length of interviews (Willis et al), but this saving may be more than offset by the time taken in preparing a written record of the taped interview, see para 8.33, post). The routine tape-recording of suspects at police stations was commonplace by 1990 and will be implemented nationally by the end of 1991. Code of Practice E (COP, E hereafter) governs its operation (see also the Home Office Circular 76/1988 but this must always be read subject to Code C). Much of COP, E is devoted to the security of tapes so as to guarantee a complete and accurate record of police interviews. This helps to protect both parties. As the Home Office Circular (para 3) states, it 'will provide an effective safeguard for the rights of suspects. It should also reduce challenges to the admissibility of prosecution evidence based on these interviews'. A by-product of tape-recording has been for police forces to consider and review their training for interviews and for officers to prepare themselves more thoroughly for them. An interview cannot of course be scripted nor can many questions be prepared in advance, but the interviewing officer should at least have planned his approach and have an outline of the more important questions.

Use of tapes

8.23 Once a person has been cautioned for an indictable offence, the general rule is that any interview with him at a police station, including questions and statements put to him after he has been charged, must be tape-recorded (COP, E, para 3.1). There are four exceptions:

(a) interviews with person who have been arrested and therefore cautioned for certain offences involving (i) terrorism and the affairs in Northern Ireland (eg a bomb planted in England by the IRA) or (ii) terrorism and the affairs of countries outside the United Kingdom (eg a bomb planted outside Iberian airways office by Basque separatists). This means that domestic (non-Northern Irish) terrorism *is* covered by tape-recording (eg Welsh nationalists, anti-vivisectionists). For the definition of a terrorism investigation, see para 4.80, ante.

(b) investigations into espionage under section 1 of the Official Secrets Act 1911.

The main reason for picking out (a) and (b) was because of the 'fear that if the full tape was made and its contents became available to terrorist organisations it would compromise national security' (Home Office Junior Minister, H.C. Debates vol 138, col 441). A contemporaneous written record of (a) and (b) has still to be made, but it can be more easily edited for advance disclosure purposes. The police and security services may always tape record if they wish to; it is just that COP, E does not oblige them to and, if they do, its provisions do not apply. In most cases the police will know whether the detention and questioning concern (a) or (b). If they do not but it subsequently becomes apparent (eg a fraud investigation reveals terrorist overtones), the recorder should be switched off. The interviewing officer should then either consult at least a superintendent for permission to continue the interview or, if he believes on reasonable grounds that the interruption would seriously hinder the investigation, he can continue without taping and report the matter at the end to a senior officer (Circular, para 21).

(c) A suitable interview room or tape recorder is unavailable and the custody officer has reasonable grounds to authorise an untaped interview without delay. This is likely to be the most used exception, especially since police force budgets will restrict the number of equipped interview rooms at designated stations and since there will probably be none at non-designated stations. It is suggested that the 'reasonable grounds' justifying a non-taped interview should be the same as those for delaying notification of arrest (s 56(5), Art 57(5)) and denying legal advice (s 58(8), Art 59(8)) ie interference or harm to evidence or persons, the alerting of accomplices or hindrance to the recovery of property. Any lesser grounds could come close to police convenience and, since COP, E has placed the emphasis on taped interviews for indictable offences, such a tendency should be resisted.

(d) It is clear from the outset of the detention that no prosecution will ensue (eg D will be cautioned, D is detained under the Mental Health Act 1983 or Immigration Act 1971 and will be dealt with outside the criminal process). It should be noted that Code of Practice, C, does still apply to all these categories, so that, inter alia, a written record *must* be compiled of any interview.

8.24 The foregoing exceptions are not exclusive and so the police have the option to tape interviews for summary offences. Physical resources will often preclude this in busy stations and most of such offences (eg routine vagrancy or drunkenness offences) are totally unsuited to the paraphernalia of tape recording. However, if the resources are available and the investigation is controversial (eg likely summary offences surrounding public disorder), the police are best advised to play safe and tape-record. Moreover, there are many cases where they cannot be sure at the outset whether the investigation will lead to charges on indictment. Thus, it is suggested that the relatively cool attitude to the taping of summary offences displayed in the Circular (para 16) should be resisted and, wherever the custody officer suspects that the case presents special or potentially contentious aspects, a recording should be made. Another suitable category is the 'volunteer' who agrees to attend for interview in connection with a complicated (eg fraud) or controversial investigation.

8.25 Whether a single or double tape machine is used, the vital task for the interviewing officer is to ensure that a master tape is prepared for the whole of the interview and for the custody and/or the interviewing officer to keep it secure at all time (by storing it at a station or delivering it to the tape librarian of the division). If a tape on a twin deck machine breaks during the interview, it must be sealed at once and the other tape used to continue the interview. The latter should then be copied and then sealed as a master tape. If it cannot be copied, it and the broken tape must be sealed and, according to the Notes for Guidance (para 4M), the interview restarted. Likewise if a tape breaks on a single deck machine and cannot be readily copied, the interview should be restarted (COP, E para 4M). The suspect may baulk at the prospect of beginning a lengthy interview again (and from the police viewpoint, repetition may conflict with the detention clock). Provided that the interviewing officer explains the option of repeating the interview and makes a note to this effect, it is suggested that there is no reason why the original unbroken tape on a twin deck machine and a new one on a single deck cannot be used as long as they are properly sealed, preferably in the presence of a third party, and arrangements are made for a subsequent copying. If the machine itself breaks down and cannot be repaired quickly, the custody officer should be consulted to see if the interview can be moved to another room with a working machine, the tape being, it is suggested, sealed in D's presence and the reason for the gap in the interview written down and also explained by the officer on the new tape. The custody officer should consider giving priority to this request if the offence is more serious than others being investigated at the station. If it is not practicable to change machines, the custody officer must note the circumstances in the custody record and may allow the interview to proceed without taping, but with a written record (COP, E para 4.12).

Conduct of taped interview

8.26 The opening ritual of a taped interview consists of the officer unwrapping and inserting a new blank tape into the recorder in front of the suspect (thus helping to bring home to him the existence and impartiality of the recorder, see COP, E paras 2.1 and 4.1), and reciting a list of information such as his name and rank, the names of everyone present (who should ideally be asked to say a few words for voice identification purposes; this can assist the compilation of the record of interview, below), the date and time of the interview, and most importantly the caution (COP, E para 4.2 and 3) and the reminder of D's entitlement to free legal advice (COP, C para 11.2; if D rejects it, the officer should say 'are you happy for the interview to proceed in the absence of a solicitor?'). Incidents which take place during the interview should be described onto the tape by the interviewing officer (eg 'officer X has just entered the room'). These include the conduct of the accused (eg 'the suspect raised his eyes to the ceiling and sighed', 'I am handing the stolen credit card (exhibit 1) to the suspect', 'the suspect has just punched the palm of his hand to feign a blow'). The interviewing officer should predict how long the interview is likely to last and take the appropriate number of tapes. When the recorder indicates that a tape is about to run out (a warning noise should sound on the tape), he should conclude that part of the interview, replace the tapes in front of the suspect and mark the old one with an identification number. If he forgets to watch the tape counter and the tape suddenly finishes, it must be replaced quickly and the officer should explain on the new one what has happened. This is crucial for otherwise an unexplained gap could lead to allegations of misconduct. Frequently interviews will be interrupted by the officer leaving the room to talk to his colleagues. Provided that the interruption is short and that D *and* a police officer remain in the interviewing room, the tape can be switched off but need not be removed. The time and reason for the break and the time of the restart can be recorded onto the tape. On the other hand, if the provisos do not apply or the suspect leaves the room, the explanation should be spoken onto the tape and the tape removed and sealed. The whole thrust of these provisions is to convince a court that nothing untoward has happened during the gap in the interview process. A simple method on resumption of interview is for the officer to summarise the reason for the interruption and ask D to confirm it. A more delicate problem for the officer is whether to remind D of the caution. To do so may interrupt or stem the flow of D's story. The dangers of exclusion of evidence under ss 76 and 78 (Arts 74, 76) of PACE are real (especially for a suspect in a special category such as a juvenile, see paras 7.111 to 7.114, ante, or if the failure to caution is allied with another breach of the COP or with the absence of a lawyer or other third party) and such that a clear reminder of the caution and its meaning is the wiser course if the break in interview is more than a few minutes. Admittedly 'a few minutes' is like the proverbial 'length of a piece of string', but a precise instruction cannot be given, save to emphasise the potential implications for exclusion of a confession at trial.

8.27 As soon as an interview begins the officer must insert a new tape and state that the interview is to be taped. He must do this even if D has already made it clear that he objects to the recording since the COP requires that D's objections be recorded if possible. Some suspects are likely to be apprehensive at the sight of a tape recorder and the officer reciting the official preliminaries. There is little in the COP but everything in good sense for the officer to explain patiently and clearly to the suspect the wisdom of taping for all concerned. If such persuasion fails, the officer may turn the machine off and must instead make a contemporaneous written record of the interview. He is not bound to do so and there may be occasions where it is reasonable to continue the tape (eg the officer is not convinced of D's objections, or that he really understands the role and relevance of a tape-recorder). The danger lies in ignoring the genuine objections of a suspect with the consequence that the interview is subsequently interpreted as unfair or that the suspect refuses to cooperate and the interview collapses.

8.28 Other objections to recording are likely to arise during the interview eg when a suspect tries to plea bargain or wishes to inform against someone. Again the interviewing officer must try to get the objections on tape. If he fails, he must state this before switching off the tape. The interview does of course continue off tape and he should try to compile a written record, (COP, E para 4.5) though the suspect will probably object to that as well (in which case a written summary will be required subsequently, COP, C para 11.5(c); this also should be explained to the suspect). If the suspects wants to talk about matters unrelated to the current investigation and objects to their recording (eg he is prepared to give information on other offences), the COP (E, par 4.7) instructs that he be allowed to do this after the formal interview is over. There is much sense in this — it avoids a suspect subsequently alleging malpractice during the gap in the tape. But, if the suspect is adamant that he wants to discuss the matter at once, it will have to be dealt with then, the officer giving the appropriate notice on the tape before switching it off. The COP does not prevent, and there is much to be said for, the suspect's lawyer using his own tape recorder during the interview. It may encourage or relax the suspect and reduce conflict over the content of the interview record (below).

8.29 Tape recording may be viewed as a discouragement to informal plea-bargaining or to the acquisition of useful background information, which the suspect is unwilling to give on tape. The police may be tempted to avoid it by interviewing elsewhere (eg in the police car en route to the station, or in the prison cell prior to the taped interview). Two points should be emphasised. First, all interviews with a suspect about a criminal offence must be accurately recorded wherever they take place (COP, C para 11.5) and this includes unsolicited comments outside the context of the interview (para 11.13). Second, a record is only mandatory if the remarks concern an offence.

8.30 If the suspect has hearing difficulties a tape-recording should still be made since it captures the atmosphere and tone of the interview, but a contemporaneous note should also be compiled alongside the tape. If an interpreter is used, that will give the officer a little more time to catch up but it is still a laborious task. It is not enough for him to write down the question and leave the tape to fill in D's answers, since the purpose of the COP here (E, para 4E) is to make available to a deaf suspect a full interview record. Ideally the interpreter should be asked to keep notes of the interview in case there is any dispute as to the accuracy of the record, but if he is using sign language it would be sufficient for the officer to ask the interpreter to read and certify the accuracy of the written record (see Circular, para 17). A videotape for sign language interviews would be ideal and, with falling costs of recorders, a realistic alternative.

8.31 If D (or his representative) complains about his treatment, a custody officer should be called and the tape left running until he arrives. If it has run out, a written note can, and arguably should, then be made of the exchange with the suspect. Once the custody officer has dealt with the complaint, it is up to the interviewing officer whether to resume the interview. It may be that the complaint is clearly vexatious or that it is resolved by the custody officer, in which case an interview may still be appropriate. But if the suspect is still agitated, the officer should bear sections 76 and 78 (Arts 74, 76) of PACE carefully in mind before continuing with the interview. If there is an allegation of physical mistreatment, an inspector and police surgeon should be summoned and resumption of the interview should be left to the decision of the senior officer (COP, C para 9.1, E. paras 4.6, 4H). If D's complaint does not concern his treatment under COP C and E (eg he complains about the circumstances of his stop and search, or arrest), the interviewing officer can continue with the interview and refer the matter to the custody officer at the conclusion of it (COP, E, para 4J).

8.32 At the end of a taped interview, the suspect is offered a chance to add any points and the officer should explain, on tape, what is to happen next (eg 'I will take you to the custody officer who will decide whether to charge you'). If he agrees to make a written statement, the tape remains on until it has been read back to him (though a statement will not often be produced after a taped interview). When the machine is switched off, it is vital for the interviewing officer to make a note in his pocketbook of the details (COP, E para 5.1). A working copy is then taken (either the second tape on a twin deck machine or a separate copy made off a single machine in the presence of the suspect). It is used to produce further copies if needed (these copies could be previously used tapes which have been wiped clean). As for the master tape, it is sealed at the end of the interview and the seal signed by the interviewing officer, the suspect and any third party. If the last two refuse, a senior officer (at least inspector rank) or the custody officer should be called to sign the seal. The master tape must then be stored securely either at the station or, if it is a non-designated station, at a central storeroom (eg with the division's tape librarian). If the suspect is committed for trial, it will be sent to the appropriate Crown Court. Thereafter, the Crown Prosecution Service (or other prosecuting agency) will supervise any use of it. Occasionally access to the master tape will be required whilst it is in police custody; principally to check an allegation that the working copy is inaccurate or to make a further copy if the working tape has been lost or damaged or if the master needs to be edited before trial so as to exclude inadmissible evidence such as previous convictions or allegations against co-defendants. In this case the Crown Prosecution Service must attend the breaking of the seal and the suspect or his solicitor should be invited. If the latter attends, he should be asked to reseal and sign the master copy. If he does not or refuses, the representative of the Crown Prosecution Service should do so (COP, E para 6.2).

Record of interview

8.33 If a case is to be pursued (either by further investigation or referral to the Crown Prosecution Service, CPS) the most difficult, yet crucial, and always time-consuming, task for the investigating officer is to prepare a written record of the interview known as the record of taped interview (ROTI). If a ROTI is accurately and fairly done, it enables the CPS to reach an informed decision whether to prosecute, it is likely to be accepted by the defence and then by the court as admissible evidence (it can be exhibited to the officer's witness statement), and it saves the time and expense of listening to the tape and preparing a full transcript. Its preparation will always take longer than the original interview and for complex enquiries, such as fraud, is a considerable undertaking. The ROTI will require the interviewing officer to find and play back segments of the tape (this can be facilitated if, during the interview, the officer was able unobtrusively to note the tape counter at crucial moments) and decide which parts to summarise and whether any need to be transcribed verbatim. In rooms which have not been properly soundproofed, extraneous noise (such as the inner city building site or heavy traffic) may necessitate frequent hearings of a tape and can even obliterate key words in an interview. Moreover, accents and incoherence can easily lengthen the process. In these circumstances, allied to interruptions for other business, even a short tape of 15 minutes could take 1½ hours for the compilation of a satisfactory ROTI (in practice officers can find it easier in the long run to write the whole interview down). The real sanction against an officer shortcutting this process is that one of the purposes (above) of a record is frustrated and in future the CPS requires a much fuller record. The officer must try to produce (i) a summary of the interview (too long and it will resemble a transcript and defeat the purpose of it), (ii) a balanced account which is fair to the suspect's defence. This is vital if the CPS is to reach a justifiable decision as to prosecution, yet extremely difficult for an officer who may understandably wish to stress the elements of the interview which he believes to be damaging to the suspect. As the Circular (Annex D) puts it, the record must 'reflect any matters to the benefit of the accused including mitigation (such as expressions of remorse or a desire to cooperate or assist in the recovery of property etc)'. (iii) A verbatim account of any admission by the suspect and the question which led to it. This must include:

(a) any questioning of or statements by the suspect on intent, dishonesty, self-defence, consent, the granting of bail or discussions concerning alternative pleas or charges; and

(b) admissions by the suspect to the offence(s) under investigation and any other criminal offences for which he may be prosecuted.

It will be necessary to record verbatim both the question(s) and the answer(s) containing the admissions. Statements such as 'the accused admitted the offence' should never appear in a Record of Taped Interview. Furthermore, where the suspect provides an equivocal response to a question going to the heart of the issue, eg 'I can't remember taking the packet of peas, but as you found it on me I suppose I must have', or where he admits part only of the ingredients necessary to prove the offence, eg 'I took the car but I thought it must have been abandoned', both the question(s) and the answer(s) must be recorded verbatim. Where an earlier admission is retracted or qualified it will again be necessary to record both question and answer verbatim. Similarly where the accused provides a defence to an allegation going beyond a mere denial or guilt, eg 'When I told you earlier that I stabbed him, what really happened was that

I saw the knife on the floor. The man in the red sweater came at me so I picked up the knife and he just sort of ran into it'. The amount of verbatim speech included in the Record of Taped Interview will vary with each interview. The objective is to give an account which accurately reflects the content of the interview with the key parts in direct speech.' (Circular, Annex D).

Moreover, some investigations require a series of precise prepared questions to be put to a suspect and in this situation contemporaneous notes of them can be taken and then inserted into the record of interview. The Notes for Guidance (COP, E para 5B) and Circular (Annex D) further instruct the interviewing officer to send to the CPS a covering note referring to any material on the tape which might be regarded as prejudicial or inadmissible by the court or as unsuitable for advance disclosure to the defence (eg information from an informant). For the latter, the CPS must then abide by the Attorney General's Guidance on Disclosure (1982). This last instruction to the interviewing officer is a tall order given the difficulty, even for experienced lawyers, of predicting what can fall within those categories.

8.34 The task of preparing a record of taped interview (ROTI) is necessary even if the suspect admits the offence. Indeed it will stand as a prima facie admissible confession. The laborious and frequently difficult nature of the task may induce the police to try to persuade suspects to compile and sign a written statement which can then be used as a substitute provided that it accurately reflects the interview.

8.35 At the end of a taped interview, the master copy is sealed in the suspect's presence and securely stored. The second tape is used as a working copy (eg to prepare a record of the interview, to make further copies) and should also be kept securely, for otherwise the master tape will have to be used with all resultant inconvenience. The suspect is given a notice explaining that he or his lawyer can obtain access to, or a copy of, the tape by consulting the CPS. Although the police retain the tapes at this stage, their use in the criminal process, editing, disclosure to the defence etc are at the direction of the CPS.

8.36 A detailed Practice Direction (1989) governs the relationship between the CPS and the defence on such matters as agreeing the ROTI and editing the tape. It is designed to facilitate agreement prior to trial or at least to narrow down the scope of any disagreement, thus avoiding unnecessary adjournments and reducing court time. If the defence wish to challenge the tape, the interviewing officer must be called to prove it in evidence. He should listen to the tape beforehand and he can then testify as to its accuracy (*R v Rampling* (1987)). The tape itself or the agreed ROTI attached to the officer's written statement are the real evidence before the court. By contrast any transcript (see below) is a secondary, administrative matter to help the court and is used at the trial judge's discretion (eg he can allow the jury to take the transcript with them on retiring, or to read after hearing the tape; see *R v Rampling* (1987)).

Transcript

8.37 Expense and time require that the transcription of tapes be kept to a minimum. It may be needed for internal use so as to help the police to pursue an investigation (eg in a complex fraud case where several interviews need to be cross-checked, or where a review of the investigation is necessary, or where the interview is so detailed that the preparation of a transcript is easier than a ROTI); or for external use by the CPS (eg to assess a case, or to prepare it for prosecution) or by the defence. In this last case the police can make the transcript and charge for it. Whether they do so or not, the defence should apply ex parte to the local legal aid committee or, if not aided, to the court clerk to see if the expense of a transcript is a legitimate one for the purposes of costs (Circular, para 33). Whichever side sees fit to require a transcript, it should be made available to the other (unless the defence has prepared one and disclosure would impede proper conduct of the defence), and wherever possible duplication of the preparation of transcripts should be avoided (Circular, paras 34–5).

Charge

8.38 (1)   The general rule is that questioning shall cease when the police believe that there is sufficient evidence to launch a successful prosecution (COP, para 16.1). This means not simply sufficient evidence to charge the person and take him before a court (a prima facie case), but sufficient evidence to ensure a conviction. In most cases the interviewing officer will reach this decision, but in some the custody or more senior officer may decide, for example, on a review of the detention. There are two qualifications to this process. First, the interviewing officer should ascertain whether D 'has said all that he wishes to say about the offence' (COP, para 16.1). Liberally interpreted this could permit the police to coax D into conversation well beyond the spirit of the COP (eg to 'top and tail' a confession). The requirement of contemporaneous recording of the interview (COP, para 11.5) is the crucial safeguard against this (since D will be detained, it will be quite practicable to organise this); and the courts have shown themselves very willing to use ss 76 and 78 (Arts 74, 76) if COP procedures are infringed. Second, if D is detained for more than one offence, he need not be brought before a custody officer until these requirements have been satisfied for each offence (COP, para 16.1). Once the stage has been reached of having sufficient evidence to prosecute, the suspect will be transferred to the custody officer. Thereafter:

(a) The custody officer will, if he agrees, charge the person or administer a formal caution or notify the person of prosecution.

(b) The person will be cautioned again.

(c) If charged, he will be given a written notice specifying particulars of the offence (including its precise legal description), the officer in charge of the case, details of the police station, and a repetition of the caution (COP, para 16.3).

(2) In most cases questioning the suspect will then cease. However:

(a) The suspect may decide to make a written statement (see below).

(b) The police, if they have not done so already, may confront the suspect with a statement or written record or tape of an interview with another person (or read it to him). The suspect must be cautioned again, but must not be prompted in his reaction. The interviewing officer should 'sit back' and wait for the reaction.

(c) Questioning can continue (after a caution has been given) if:

  (i) It is needed to prevent harm. For example, D is charged with kidnapping but has not yet revealed where the hostage is.

  (ii) It is needed to clear up ambiguities in the suspect's earlier statements. For example, whilst D is being charged, the interviewing officer re-reads his answers to the interrogation and spots some inconsistencies.

  (iii) It is in the interests of justice that the accused be confronted with information that has come to light *since* he was charged (or told of possible prosecution). 'Interests of justice' can include the saving of court time and expense. For example, a person who is protesting innocence or who refuses to speak, but who has been charged, can be confronted with the statement of another accused or a witness which prejudices him. (COP, para 16.5).

(3) Details of all charges and the response of the accused to them must be recorded. Similarly, if questioning takes place after charge, the exchanges with the accused must be fully and contemporaneously recorded (COP, paras 16.7–8).

After charge

8.39 Once a person has been charged, the custody officer must decide whether to release him, on or without bail (s 38), or to continue the detention and therefore make arrangements for the accused to appear before a magistrates' court (s 46; for discussion of sections 38 and 46, see paras 6.28 and 6.33, ante). If detained under s 128(7) of the Magistrates' Courts Act 1980 (see para 6.81, ante), D is to be treated in accordance with the PACE Act and Codes and, so far as questioning is concerned, the above applies.

Written statements (Code of Practice, Annex D)

8.40   If a person, detained or otherwise, wishes to make a statement, he may write it himself or the interviewing officer can do so on his behalf. If he writes it himself, he is asked to write first that he is making the statement voluntarily and that he understands the meaning of the caution. He should then be allowed to write freely. Since people are usually unacquainted with the discipline which a narrative requires, the officer can tell the person what matters are relevant and whether what he has written is ambiguous. Since any amendments will appear on the statement as insertions, the officer must take care lest his interruptions be subsequently construed as improper pressure. If the officer is to write the statement, the suspect must similarly be asked to acknowledge his consent and understanding of the caution. The officer must then record every word, including any question and answer designed to clarify the meaning of the statement. On completion, the person is asked to read, amend where necessary, and sign the statement, including a declaration that, inter alia, he has given the statement freely (see the COP, Annex D). If he refuses, for whatever reason, to read and/or sign the statement, that fact shall be recorded after the officer has read the statement to him and asked him to change his mind.

The admissibility of confessions

8.41   One of the most important common law exceptions to the rule against hearsay is the informal admission (ie an incriminating statement made by a party to proceedings). It is admissible as evidence of the truth of its contents on the basis that a person is likely to be telling the truth when he says something against his own interest. At common law when such an admission was made by an accused person before his trial and to a person in authority (usually the police), it was known as a confession. It can range from a full, signed admission of guilt, to an incriminating comment and to a mixed statement containing admissions and exculpations. If this last example occurs, the whole statement should be put in evidence, though the judge may point out to the jury that the incriminating parts are likely to be true, whereas the excuses may not carry the same weight (*R v Sharp* (1988)). The common law stipulated that a confession had to be given voluntarily. As Lord Sumner observed in 1914 in *Ibrahim v R*:

> 'no statement by an accused is admissible in evidence against him unless it is shown by the prosecution to have been a voluntary statement, in the sense that it has not been obtained from him either by fear of prejudice or hope of advantage exercised or held out by a person in authority'.

Similarly a confession must not have been obtained by oppression (*Callis v Gunn* (1964)). This concept of voluntariness was reflected in the Judges'

Rules (preamble, principle (e)). However, uncertainty surrounded the meaning of the concepts (eg 'oppression', 'person in authority') and led to much caselaw. In 1972 the Criminal Law Revision Committee recommended that (a) confessions obtained by oppression should be inadmissible but that (b) those obtained by threats or inducements should only be inadmissible if they were likely to be unreliable (Report, para 65). The Royal Commission (1981) agreed with (a) but would have admitted category (b) subject to a warning to the jury by the judge (or a reminder to the magistrates) as to the danger of unreliability and the need for corroboration (Report, paras 4.132–3). Section 76 of the PACE Act (Art 74, Order) opted for a scheme very similar to that proposed by the CLRC ie the inadmissibility of confessions if obtained by oppression or if likely to be unreliable as a result of anything said or done.

Definition

8.42 'Confession includes any statement wholly or partly adverse to the person who made it, whether made to a person in authority or not and whether made in words or otherwise.' (s 82(1), Art 70(1)). This non-exclusive definition is sufficiently all-embracing to cover even gestures by the accused (eg a nod in answer to police questioning). More doubtful is the case of a person breaking down and crying on hearing a co-accused's confession being read out. The trial judge could decide that such conduct is capable of amounting to a 'statement' and leave it to the jury to assess its genuineness. Or, since s 82(1) uses the word 'includes', it can be argued that a 'statement' is only one form of a confession and that a jury can be left to decide whether the conduct amounts to an acceptance by the accused of the truth of allegations put to him (eg *R v Christie* (1914)). Even more doubtful is the person who blushes or turns pale when an allegation is made. On the other hand, s 82(1) clearly covers an accused who re-enacts a crime on videotape (cf *Li Shu-Ling v R* (1989)). By confining the definition to 'adverse' statements, s 82(1) does not cover exculpatory statements. So if, after being threatened, D makes such a statement in which, for example, he sets up a false alibi and later at his trial puts forward another inconsistent defence, the prosecution can adduce the previous statement and cross-examine D on it since it is not a confession and does not have to satisfy the test of admissibility for confessions. On the other hand, a plea of guilty is within the definition. Thus, if D pleads guilty but is later permitted to change his plea to one of not guilty, the prosecution may have to satisfy the test of admissibility before the previous plea is admitted. Even if it is admissible, the trial judge may exclude it in the exercise of his discretion to ensure a fair trial if the plea was entered when D was unrepresented or on a mistaken view of the law. The definition in s 82(1) abolished the common law rule that a threat or inducement only operated to exclude a confession if it was made or held out by 'a person in authority'. Thus the numerous and complex decisions as to who was a 'person in authority' are of historical interest only. The common law was concerned with the inequality between the accused and the investigators, at one time the middle and higher classes and later the police or similar bodies. It is clear the threats or inducements may emanate from a number of sources other than the police, eg a confession by employee to employer, pupil to teacher, householder to neighbour, or even where a group of vigilantes or the IRA threaten a suspected criminal with violence unless he confesses. The confession may be equally untrue whether the threats are made by the police or some non-police body and s 76 (Art 74) is applicable to both.

Section 76 (Art 74) — Introduction

[To avoid repetition, s 76 in the following discussion is taken to include Article 74 of the PACE Northern Ireland Order 1989].

8.43 The onus lies initially on the defence to 'represent' to the court that the confession is or may be inadmissible. 'Represent' means more than raising a suggestion during cross-examination (*R v Liverpool Juvenile Court, ex parte R* (1988)). It requires the defence to produce sufficient evidence to raise a doubt and convince the court that further investigation into the confession is warranted. This should not be a difficult task. It is not necessary to raise a prima facie case against admissibility. Instead it is sufficient for the defence to suggest that the confession 'was or *may have been* obtained' in breach of s 76. The suggestion may often appear on the face of the custody record (eg by revealing prolonged periods of questioning, an improper denial of entitlements under PACE) or from the content of the interview record. Alternatively it may require the production of witness statements and witnesses (principally the accused). Usually the defence will intimate their intention to the prosecution at the outset and the issue can be dealt with early in the prosecution's case. This means that D is entitled to a ruling on the matter before, or at the end of, the Crown's case and this enables him to organise his defence accordingly (*R v Liverpool Juvenile Court, ex parte R* (1988)). If D does not raise the issue during the prosecution's case, he can do so later, although the damage of letting the jury hear the confession will have been done. Alternatively, and rarely, the court may raise the issue of its own motion and call upon the prosecution to satisfy the court of its admissibility (s 76(3)). If it does so, there is no guarantee that D's counsel, taken unaware, will oppose the admissibility adequately (whereas under s 76(2) it is the defence which raises it) and this may offer some hope for D on appeal.

8.44 The admissibility and relevance of a confession are questions of law to be decided by the judge whereas weight is a question of fact for the jury. In a magistrates' court, the bench is involved in both questions but, if the confession is ruled inadmissible, it must of course perform the difficult task of removing the alleged confession from its mind when deciding guilt. Even if the confession is admitted, the defence may still raise the issue again before the jury by, for example, cross-examining police officers as to the detail of the interrogation which led to the confession. For the jury has to determine the weight, if any, to be given to an admissible confession and it is possible, on hearing how the confession was obtained, that the jury will take a different view of the confession to that of the judge and disregard it or give it little weight.

8.45   Once s 76 is raised, a voir dire, or trial within a trial, must normally be held (*R v Millard* (1987), *R v Liverpool Juvenile Court, ex parte R* (1988)). This includes summary trials. At committal proceedings a voir dire is not usually needed (the matter can be left to the trial judge) unless the confession is the sole evidence against D (*R v Oxford City Justices, ex parte Berry* (1987)). The defence can of course give evidence at the voir dire but D cannot be compelled to testify (*R v Davis* (1990)). On a voir dire the sole issue for the court is the admissibility of the confession. It may be declared inadmissible even if it is true. Thus, evidence led, or cross-examination conducted, by the prosecution designed to show that the confession is true is irrelevant to the issue of admissibility (*R v Davis* (1990), *R v Cox* (1991)). This does not matter at trial on indictment since the jury will be absent when admissibility is determined, but it obviously could at summary trial, so the magistrates must keep the two issues (of admissibility and truth) separate. To complicate matters further, in determining the voir dire it is permissible for the judge to take into account evidence he has already heard in the trial and he is not confined to the voir dire evidence (*R v Tyrer* (1990)). This however runs the risk of the judge deciding on the truth of the confession (as opposed to its admissibility) by believing an earlier witness' evidence given during the trial. There are two stages involved in the admissibility decision — first to discover the facts (eg did the officer hit or bully D), second, to decide whether those facts effect admissibility under s 76 (or s 78).

8.46   A crucial factor in deciding the admissibility of a confession under s 76(2) is the availability of a full record of the suspect's treatment during custody and of his interview. The custody record may be critical evidence of proper procedural compliance (see *R v Trussler* (1988)). Similarly, the absence of a contemporaneous record of the interview deprives the court of the full picture — the court has then to decide (or guess) whether a genuine reason, police convenience, or even deceit has concealed a contemporaneous account from it. Such uncertainty can positively favour the defence or at least thwart the Crown's burden of proof (eg *R v Delaney* (1989)). This raises another general point — once the defence has represented to the court that s 76 may have been infringed, the burden passes to the Crown to satisfy the criminal standard of proof that the confession was not obtained in breach of s 76. It may well be worthwhile for D to raise s 76 even if the evidence does not look strong and consequently his counsel should always be on guard to run it. It may be possible sufficiently to muddy the waters so that the Crown fails to discharge its burden. For example, in *R v Harvey* (1988) D and her lover X were arrested for the murder of Y. X confessed to the crime in front of D and on the next day D also confessed. X died before trial. At D's trial it was established that she was of low intelligence and suffered from a psychopathic disorder. Two psychiatrists testified that D might have confessed 'to protect her lover in a child-like attempt to try to take the blame', the Crown was unable to prove beyond reasonable doubt that D's confession had not been obtained because she had heard X confessing (s 76(2)(b)) and D was acquitted (cf *R v Chung* (1991)).

8.47 In spite of several causes celebres in recent years involving the quashing of convictions based on false or unreliable confessions and calls to emulate the Scottish system, the position remains that an admissible confession does not require corroboration. However, in practice, there have been sufficient examples to caution courts against the ready acceptance of confessional evidence alone and to remind the police and Crown Prosecution Service of the desirability of corroborative evidence. A confession may be admitted if it is 'relevant to any matter in issue in the proceedings' (s 76(1)) (most obviously as regards the offence charged, but also in relation to other conduct, eg as evidence of the accused's disposition where the court has decided to allow such evidence). Subject to the rule of relevance a confession may be used as evidence of *any* matter, including any matter favourable to its maker, though the evidential value of self-serving extracts from a confession may be slight and the judge may well comment on its lack of weight (see *R v Sharp* (1988)). Since an accused is generally neither competent nor compellable for the prosecution, an out-of-court statement by D1 against his co-accused, D2, who is being jointly tried, is inadmissible as evidence against D2 (unless D1 ceases to be a defendant where, for example, the prosecution offers no evidence against D1 or files a nolle prosequi in relation to D1).

8.48 If a confession is excluded because of infringement of s 76, subsequent interviews, in which the confession is repeated, will also be inadmissible if they stem from the original one. For otherwise s 76 can be flouted by subsequent compliance with the rules (*R v Mcgovern* (1991), *R v Blake* (1991), *R v Ismail* (1990)). Occasionally it may be possible for the Crown to prove no connection between them (eg D is oppressed and confesses. He is released on bail but returns to the station with his lawyer and confesses; cf *R v Gillard and Barrett* (1991) in relation to s 78).

Criteria for admissibility

(A)   Oppression (s 76(2)(a); Art 74(2)(a))

8.49   The defence may represent to the court that a confession 'was or may have been obtained by oppression of the person who made it'. This reflects the views of the Criminal Law Revision Committee (11th Report) and of the Royal Commission on Criminal Procedure — that society's abhorrence of methods of investigation amounting to oppression should be signalled by the automatic exclusion of a confession obtained thereby, even if the confession turns out to be true. It also reflects the late development of the common law, which first established oppression as a ground of inadmissibility of confessions in *Callis v Gunn* (1964). This was then incorporated, but not defined, in the revised Judges' Rules of 1964.

8.50   Section 76(8) offers a non-exhaustive definition of the term, based in part on Art 3 of the European Convention on Human Rights:

> '"oppression" includes torture, inhuman or degrading treatment and the use or threat of violence (whether or not amounting to torture).'

'Torture' is the most severe form of oppression and, according to a resolution of the United Nations in 1975, 'constitutes an aggravated and deliberate form of cruel, inhuman or degrading treatment or punishment' (Resolution 3452). It suggests a systematic and premeditated course of action rather than a spontaneous act of violence. The Shorter Oxford English Dictionary defines torture as 'the infliction of excruciating pain, severe or excruciating pain of body, anguish, agony' and, given the courts' predilection for giving words their ordinary dictionary meaning (see *R v Fulling* below), this may be preferred. However, the terms of s 76(8) are well known to international law (eg Article 5, UN Declaration of Human Rights 1948) and it is suggested that guidance can and should be sought from that jurisprudence. Thus, in the 1984 United Nations Convention against Torture and Other Cruel, Inhuman and Degrading Treatment or Punishment, it is defined as 'any act by which severe pain or suffering, whether physical or mental, is intentionally inflicted on a person for such purposes as obtaining from him or a third person information or a confession' (Article 1). 'Inhuman treatment' has been described by the European Commission of Human Rights as covering 'at least such treatment as deliberately causes severe suffering, mental or physical' (*The Greek Case* (1969)). In *Ireland v UK* (1978) the European Court of Human Rights described the interrogation techniques (prolonged wall-standing, hooding, subjection to white (ie high pitched) noise, deprivation of sleep, and rationing of food and drink) employed by the UK Government in Northern Ireland as 'degrading' because they were 'such as to arouse in their victims feelings of fear, anguish and inferiority capable of humiliating and debasing them and possibly breaking their physical or moral resistance' (see also *Soering v UK* (1989)). As to 'violence', it is clear that psychological as well as physical acts are included.

8.51 However, since s 76(8) is not an exhaustive definition, subtle distinctions between its terms are unnecessary and it serves simply to illustrate the type of conduct outlawed by s 76. Indeed the expansive view of oppression taken by the Court of Appeal in *R v Fulling* (1987) has meant that the narrow terms of s 76(8) are virtually redundant. For in *Fulling* the dictionary meaning of oppression was adopted viz

'Exercise of authority or power in a burdensome, harsh, or wrongful manner; unjust or cruel treatment of subjects, inferiors etc; the imposition of unreasonable or unjust burdens'.

Such a wide definition more than embraces s 76(8) and extends oppression well beyond the obvious examples of the rhino whip and knuckleduster. The Lord Chief Justice also added this gloss: 'We find it hard to envisage any circumstances in which such oppression would not entail some impropriety on the part of the interrogator'. He implicitly adopted the trial judges' ruling that 'oppression' means something above and beyond that which is inherently oppressive in police custody and must import some impropriety, some oppression actively applied in an improper manner by the police'. The requirement of impropriety initially focuses the court's attention on what the investigator has done rather than on the effect of his conduct on the suspect (s 76(2)(b) more naturally encompasses the latter, see below). In this sense the approach is an objective one. As to the meaning of impropriety, it is clear that not every breach of PACE or the Code of Practice will qualify. Instead the impropriety or misconduct must be burdensome or unreasonable in the court's view. Thus *R v Davison* (1988) contained a catalogue of improprieties. Not all of them (eg improper denial of a solicitor) amounted to oppression, but failure to release D and to rearrest him as the PACE Act required meant that his detention was unlawful for 9 hours. This then qualified as the exercise of powers in a wrongful manner (per the *Fulling* test) and was *capable* of amounting to oppression. It was certainly enough to pass the burden of proof under s 76(2) to the Crown, which then failed to discharge it. In this way it is suggested that oppression means the employment of techniques (systematic or occasional) designed to break the physical or moral resistance of a person and which do not conform to the court's perception of civilised standards.

8.52 The Code of Practice offers a ready indicator of the sort of standards to which the police must conform and breach of which may amount to oppression. A court may take into account the provisions of the Code (s 67(11), Art 66(10)) and will particularly do so in relation to the admissibility of confessions. Examples of potentially oppressive conduct include: undue and prolonged deprivation of sleep or refreshments; the suspect being required to stand for long periods; prolonged questioning beyond the limits imposed by the Act and denial of breaks in interrogation without reasonable cause (cf the COP,section 12; the extended periods of detention available under Part IV of the Act at first sight appear to deny the possibility that prolonged questioning per se can ever amount to oppression. However, the safeguards open to the suspect, and the procedures to be followed in Part V of the Act and the COP are a clear reminder to the police that certain types of detention and questioning may amount to 'oppression', even though they are not accompanied by the media's stereotype of physical brutality); unnecessary strip or intimate searches or the threat of them by, or in front of, persons of the opposite sex (cf the COP, Annex A); denial of clothes or personal effects without good cause; the treatment of children and the mentally ill in breach of the COP; the deliberate use of dirty cells without adequate washing facilities in the knowledge that the person is being affected by it. Overcrowding in police cells is unlikely to amount to oppression given the fact that it is commonplace in the country; similarly with the lack of exercise, especially since remand prisoners have currently only one hour's exercise per day. But circumstances may vary and what may be commonplace to an 'old lag' may be oppressive to a first offender or suspect with no previous experience of police detention. The improper denial of access to a solicitor is unlikely to suffice (cf the European Court of Human Rights' view in prisoner cases that such denial may be a breach of parts of the Convention but not of Art 3 in respect of inhuman or degrading treatment); but it could well do so if allied to some other activity such as prolonged and unnecessary questioning eg where the police continue to question even though they have sufficient evidence to charge the person. It must be emphasised that much will depend upon the characteristics of the particular person. As Sachs J, observed in 1965, 'What may be oppressive as regards a child, an invalid or an old man or somebody inexperienced in the ways of the world may turn out not to be oppressive when one finds that the accused person is of a tough character and an experienced man of the world'. (*R v Priestley* (1966)). Thus, if a frail D is deliberately placed in a cold interview room and forced to stand (a breach of COP, paras 12.4, 12.5) or a first time shoplifter harshly treated by a store detective, the effect may be oppressive compared to the reaction of a fit young D or an experienced criminal.

8.53 One implication of *R v Fulling* concerns the method of questioning. It is hard to describe lies or tricks practised on a suspect (eg *R v Mason* (1987), where D was falsely told that forensic evidence had been found linking him to the crime) as falling within the dictionary definition of oppression approved in *Fulling*. Moreover, as the very facts of the case indicate (D was told that her lover had been having an affair with another woman for the past three years and that woman just happened to be in the cell next to D), the making of true statements will not often constitute oppression. However, they may exceptionally do so; for example, if D is unaware that her mother is near to death and the police tell her this in order to put pressure on her to confess, this deliberate misuse of the truth could amount to 'harsh' or 'improper' treatment (per *R v Fulling*) and therefore oppression. Certainly persistent, heavyhanded or bullying questioning interspersed with misrepresentations could qualify. For example, in *R v Beales* (1991) a confession extracted during a 35 minute interview was excluded because the officer had invented evidence against D and forcefully confronted him with it, repeatedly misrepresented D's answers and 'hectored and bullied [him] from first to last'. Similarly, threats (eg to inform D's family or employer of his involvement in a police investigation) could qualify. The availability of a tape-recording (as in *Beales*) will be crucial in helping a court to decide whether the questioning has reached a degree of impropriety to be called oppressive, but it is suggested that the circumstances will have to be harsh before it does so and that the style of questioning falls more naturally for consideration under s 76(2)(b) or even s 78. More generally, it should be noted that, despite the broadening of s 76(2)(a) by *R v Fulling*, remarkably little use has been made of it. Instead s 78 has been preferred (it will be suggested, see para 8.67, post that this is a mistaken policy and that s 76(2)(a) should be used more regularly).

8.54   The following additional points on s 76(2)(a) can be noted:

1) The confession must have been obtained by oppression. If D confesses before being subjected to oppressive treatment, s 76(2)(a) does not apply. More realistically, there may be occasions when the police have used oppression but the accused confesses for other reasons unconnected with it (eg after a night in a cell, following oppression, when he decides to get the 'matter off his chest' and save further anxiety to his family). However, the defence will in all probability raise the issue of oppression and it will be extremely difficult for the prosecution to rebut the alleged causal connection between the police conduct and the confession.

2) A confession, which a court decides was, or may have been, obtained by oppression, *must* be excluded, even if it is apparently true. For example, D is severely beaten up by enraged bystanders, neighbours or the police, and confesses to serious sexual offences against young children. His confession will be excluded and, unless supported by other independent evidence or testimony (often unavailable in such cases), the prosecution will fail.

3) A court should be alert to the role which psychological pressure can play upon a person under interrogation.

4) D can be oppressed by the use of threats or violence against others (eg a spouse, children or close friends) of which he is aware. Such psychological pressure can overlap with the question of reliability (see s 76(2)(b) at para 8.55 post) and can be excluded on that basis as well.

5) Since oppression must be the consequence of some improper conduct by the oppressor(s), acts the unintended consequence of which is oppressive are probably not within s 76(2)(a) unless they are improper acts. Proper acts which cause a person to be oppressed are not within s 76(2)(a) but may be within s 76(2)(b).

6) If a confession is obtained by oppression, the things said or done will also render the confession unreliable under s 76(2)(b) (though that subsection need not be relied upon). However, things said or done which do not amount to oppression may nevertheless render the confession unreliable under s 76(2)(b) (ie the greater (2)(a) includes the lesser (2)(b) but the lesser does not necessarily include the greater).

7) Since physical injury is the clearest form of oppression, medical evidence assumes particular importance. Medical examination, preferably by the suspect's own doctor, should be readily allowed at the conclusion of interrogation and to avoid subsequent allegations of brutality, the police should be alert to the need for medical examination before the interrogation, especially if the person arrives at the police station already bearing bruises (see para 7.106, ante).

8) It should be remembered that 'oppression' is not confined to conduct which took place at the police station. Questioning or conduct that occurred at the time of arrest or while the person was being conveyed to a police station may be similarly relevant. In any event, the court will wish to hear an account of the whole proceedings which took place between the police and the accused before deciding whether there has been oppression.

(B)   Reliability (s 76(2)(b), Art 74(2)(b))

8.55 A confession will be inadmissible if it 'was or may have been obtained . . . (b) in consequence of anything said or done which was likely, in the circumstances existing at the time, to render unreliable any confession which might be made [by the person] in consequence thereof, (s 76(2)(b)). The Criminal Law Revision Committee (CLRC) recognised in its 11th Report of 1972 that the common law had developed too strict a rule of voluntariness by requiring that any inducement or threat, no matter how slight or mild, made any resulting confession inadmissible (eg *R v Northam* (1967) — D asked if an offence could be taken into consideration. The officer said there would be no objection — held, an improper inducement; *R v Zaveckas* (1969) — suspect asked 'Will I get bail?', officer answered yes — held, an improper inducement; *R v Smith* (1959) — Sergeant Major threatened to keep troops on parade until the person who had stabbed another soldier owned up — resulting confession inadmissible, though he made a second admissible confession later). The CLRC recommended that the test be relaxed so that a confession obtained by threats or inducements falling short of oppression, should only be inadmissible if the threat or inducement was of a kind likely in the circumstances to produce an unreliable confession. Section 76(2)(b) followed that recommendation being based on Clause 2(2)(b) of the draft Bill annexed to the 11th Report of the CLRC. The phrase in s 76(2)(b) 'anything said or done which was likely' replaced the draft Bill's 'any threat or inducement of a sort likely', thus extending the kinds of conduct which can render a confession unreliable.

8.56   A crucial preliminary point should be noted. The trial judge must initially determine the likelihood of unreliability but, if admitted, the jury will also do so and, in order to avoid the embarrassment of a jury in effect overruling the judge by reaching a different conclusion, the judge is concerned not only with the actual confession but also any confession D *might* have made in consequence of what was said or done. 'On this scheme the judge should imagine that he was present at the interrogation and heard the threat or inducement. In the light of all the evidence given he will consider whether, at the point when the threat was uttered or the inducement offered, any confession which the accused might make as a result of it would be likely to be unreliable.' (CLRC, para 65). This test qualifies the decision of the House of Lords in *DPP v Ping Lin* (1976) which had required a causal connection between the threat or inducement and the resulting confession. Under s 76(2)(b) it is clear that the court may be required to undertake a more speculative journey into considering not only whether the confession was obtained improperly but also whether it *may* have been so obtained. Provided that the accused raises such a possibility in the court's mind, the onus again passes to the prosecution to prove beyond reasonable doubt that the confession was not in fact so obtained.

8.57   The phrase 'anything said or done' in s 76(2)(b) is extremely broad in scope. It can certainly encompass conduct which amounts to oppression under s 76(2)(a), but stretches well beyond that. It can include the fear of prejudice or hope of advantage directed towards the accused which was a key feature of the previous common law. It can also embrace conduct which is directed towards a person other than the accused but which is designed or is likely to make his confession unreliable (for example, a threat or suggestion that official action will be taken against

D's family unless he confesses). It has been held that the phrase does not refer to the accused but must be something external to him which then raises the possibility of unreliability. Thus, self-inflicted drug addiction which could prompt D to agree to anything in order to get bail and to feed the addiction will probably not suffice (*R v Goldenberg* (1989), *R v Crampton* (1991)). This reasoning is questionable since s 76(2)(b) also refers to the 'circumstances existing at the time' and the fact that the police proceed to interview a suspect in circumstances of drug withdrawal is surely something 'said or done' which is likely to render any resulting confession unreliable. It does not matter that the police are unaware of D's difficulties since it has also been held that s 76(2)(b) is tested on an objective basis (see *R v Everett* (1988) where the police thought that D was of average mental age but he was subsequently shown at trial to have a mental age of an eight year old) and the bona fides of the police does not cure unreliability. A less emotive case is where D has been forced by a medical condition to take drugs which (either by taking or not taking them) then affect his mental abilities, or where D is of low intelligence, or suffering side effects from pregnancy (see *R v Mcgovern* (1991)). If the police are aware of this but proceed to interview in an attempt to *trick* D, s 76(2)(b) (and possibly (2)(a)) could certainly apply. If they call the police surgeon (as the COP, para 9B recommends) and he approves the interview, or if they interview unaware of the medical conditions, the *Crampton* and *Goldenberg* cases say that s 76(2)(b) is inapplicable. The argument above suggests that the emphasis of the subsection lies on the objective determination of a confession's reliability, that D's self-inflicted condition is a relevant circumstance to consider, and that D should be allowed to raise the issue. Whether he succeeds is another matter (though he is helped by the burden of proof lying on the prosecution).

8.58 The most obvious external event which is 'said or done' is the conduct of the police. However, this need not emanate from a police officer. Under the previous common law the conduct had to come from a 'person in authority' and complex caselaw built up over the meaning of that phrase. The concept remains under s 76 but it should be remembered that the words or acts may come from *any* person. It is simply that where the words or acts come from 'a person in authority' they are more likely to influence the accused (eg a threat by father to son that the latter had better tell the truth or he will be beaten; cf *R v Cleary* (1963), a promise by employer to employee that, if the latter 'owns up', the former will not sack him, or a threat by headmaster to pupil that unless the latter tells the truth to a police officer, he will be disciplined).

8.59 It can be argued that the phrase 'anything said or done' implies something out of the ordinary, for the proper exercise of normal police powers and procedures, as set out by Parliament, can hardly be allowed to trigger s 76(2)(b). However, in contrast to oppression (see *R v Fulling*, above), the courts have not made s 76(2)(b) dependent on police malpractice. For example, in *R v Harvey* (1988) D's lover confessed in D's presence to murder. The following day D, who had a low intelligence, also confessed and at trial the Crown was unable to discharge the burden of showing that D had not confessed in order to 'protect her lover in a childlike attempt to try to take the blame' (see also *R v Morse* (1991)). It is submitted that this is the correct approach — the emphasis of s 76(2)(b) lies on the reliability or otherwise of the confession and not the propriety of police conduct per se. The absence of bad faith may be of some slight value in tipping the scales in favour of the prosecution and admissibility, since proper conduct is less likely to make the confession unreliable (see *R v Maguire* (1990)). Conversely, even where the police have clearly misbehaved (eg *R v Sparks* (1991) — failures to caution D and to keep a record of interview), that need not affect reliability.

8.60 The value of misbehaviour, from the defence point of view, is that the gravity of any and each breach of PACE and the Codes is more likely to influence the court towards exclusion (eg *DPP v Blake* (1989), *R v Trussler* (1988)), as is the type of breach ie those which are more likely to affect the reliability of a confession. The police conduct can clearly include the physical treatment of D. For example, in *R v Trussler* (1988) the denial of a rest period, as prescribed in the COP (para 12.2), was a crucial factor for the use of s 76(2)(b) (*Quaere*, preventing a chain-smoker from smoking.). To this extent, the category overlaps with oppression in s 76(2)(a) but goes further by covering that conduct which lacks the gravity of oppression but which still has, or is likely to have, an effect on the particular suspect such as to produce an unreliable confession.

8.61 Two other broad categories of police conduct which may attract s 76(2)(b) can be noted —

(a) denial of D's protective rights, and
(b) the method of questioning.

As regards (a), it is not every breach of PACE which may affect the reliability of confessions. Thus in *R v Sparks* (1991) a failure to caution and to record the interview were breaches of the COP (and may be dealt with under s 78, see below), but were held not to be likely, without more, to affect reliability (cf *R v Dooln* (1988)). But there are some provisions in the COP which are designed to protect the accused against himself, especially the vulnerable accused, and breach of which may influence the reliability of what he said. These provisions chiefly concern the physical presence of an adviser for the suspect. The most obvious is a lawyer. So in *R v Mcgovern* (1991) the police conducted a hasty interview at which D became emotionally upset. No lawyer was present to intercede, halt the interview, advise D, and thereby reduce the risk of unreliability. For vulnerable groups of suspects the presence of an effective 'appropriate adult' is crucial (see COP, para 11.14). Thus in *R v Cox* (1991) D's i.q. was lower than 99.6% of the population and he was suggestible. Yet he was questioned, contrary to the COP, in the absence of an appropriate adult. The latter's presence was an essential prerequisite for reliability. Moreover, the presence must be effective and a person called as the appropriate adult may himself be totally incompetent (see *R v Morse* (1991) where the father was of very low intelligence and virtually illiterate; another example is where the appropriate adult cannot understand English). The use of tape-recording goes some way to discovering such cases. Conversely, the absence of a contemporaneous record of the interview will help the defence to raise doubts in the trial judge's mind — another reminder to the police of the necessity of recording confessions.

8.62 In summary, the following degrees of conduct can be identified as falling within s 76(2)(b) in so far as they affect D's protective rights.

1) If the police fail to call a lawyer and/or appropriate adult, D can easily raise s 76(2)(b) on the basis that he was not properly advised and may have said something by pressure/mistake, which makes or might have made the statement unreliable.

2) If the police fail to record the interview or to show him it for approval and D then disagrees with the officer's recollection of the record, he is saying, bluntly, that what was done (or more correctly omitted) led to an unreliable confession (eg *R v Waters* (1989), *R v Doolan* (1988)) ie the police have fabricated or misrepresented the confession. Whether this is so or not, the failure to record deprives the prosecution of evidence which might be used to rebut the allegation.

3) In contrast failure to caution D would not per se trigger s 76(2)(b). D would have to show an extra ingredient which suggests that what he said is unreliable (eg he spoke because of police tricks or pressure and did not really know what he was saying, he simply wanted to escape the station and agreed to anything suggested). It will be seen that this example is more difficult for D to raise successfully under s 76(2)(b), especially if the prosecution can show that D was properly looked after and his other rights were respected. He may be forced to rely on pleading his particular character weaknesses.

8.63 *Method of questioning* — In so far as the questioning becomes burdensome and oppressive s 76(2)(a) comes into play (eg *R v Beales* (1991) where the police repeatedly misrepresented the evidence against D and bullied him), but s 76(2)(b) clearly extends further. It is thus sensible for the defence to plead both (this may encourage a court, cf *R v Beales*, to decide that even if s 76(2)(a) does not apply, the lesser s 76(2)(b) does). How far then does s 76(2)(b) extend? The key lies in deciding whether what was 'said or done' was likely to render a confession 'unreliable'. This requires the court to look carefully at the circumstances of the particular suspect and then for the prosecution to prove beyond reasonable doubt that he spoke in order to give a reliable account and not for other motives. Clearly the method of questioning may produce an unreliable confession in that the suspect may speak for a variety of motives other than that of telling the truth (eg he wants to protect someone; he simply wants to leave the police station and is prepared to say anything, in the hope of retracting it later; he is suggestible and seeks to please his interrogator; he becomes confused and mistakenly incriminates himself; he is persuaded to speak because of promises or threats made to him). In *R v Fulling* (1987), the Lord Chief Justice decided that the following definition of oppression (cited with approval in *R v Prager* (1972)), was insufficient for s 76(2)(a) but suggested that some of it could fall within s 76(2)(b):

> 'questioning which by its nature, duration or other attendant circumstances (including the fact of custody) excites hope (such as the hope of release) or fears, or so affects the mind of the subject that his will crumbles and he speaks when otherwise he would have stayed silent.'

This does of course put the court (and initially the prosecution) in a very difficult position in trying to fathom D's motives for speaking. It is easier if D falls within a group identified by the PACE Act and the COP as 'vulnerable' (eg juveniles). Such persons may be suggestible or readily manipulated, with the consequence that certain styles of questioning are likely to produce unreliable confessions. In relation to the mentally ill or handicapped, the prosecution can face an uphill task. Thus, in *R v Delaney* (1989) the interviewing officer had throughout suggested to D that he really needed psychiatric help, and that if he owned up, people would help him. The officer played down the criminal offence and falsely aroused D's hopes of treatment. As the Lord Chief Justice put it, 'he might, by the same token, be encouraging a false confession.' In a less extreme case, the evidence, or speculation, of psychiatrists or psychologists as to the likely effect of police conduct on D could readily sow sufficient seeds to raise a reasonable doubt (see also, *R v Harvey* (1988)). As for the 'ordinary' suspect, the court must consider all the circumstances of the interrogation and what was said by the police, or any other relevant person (eg parent, friend, co-accused, or even a solicitor who suggests that the evidence is stacked against the accused and that a confession and guilty plea will result in a lesser sentence); and the likely effect of what was said on the mind of the accused taking into account his characteristics. This requires an understanding of the pressures which a police station can engender. As the Lord Chief Justice observed in 1981:

'Very few confessions are inspired solely by remorse. Often the motives of an accused are mixed and include a hope that an early admission may lead to an earlier release or a lighter sentence. If it were the law that the mere presence of such a motive, even if prompted by something said or done by a person in authority, led inexorably to the exclusion of a confession, nearly every confession would be rendered inadmissible. This is not the law. In some cases the hope may be self-generated. If so, it is irrelevant, even if it provides the dominant motive for making the confession. In such a case the confession will not have been obtained by anything said or done by a person in authority. More commonly the presence of such a hope will, in part at least, owe its origin to something said or done by such a person. There can be few prisoners who are being firmly but fairly questioned in a police station to whom it does not occur that they might be able to bring both their interrogation and their detention to an earlier end by confession' (*R v Rennie* (1982) cf *R v Goldenberg* (1989)).

8.64 In some cases the evidence of persistent questioning and misrepresentation by the officer may be clear enough to suggest a state of confusion or hopelessness on the part of the suspect such as is likely to produce unreliable statements (see *R v Beales* (1991)). What about tricks or misrepresentations practised on the suspect? For example, D is told, falsely, that his voice has been recognised on a tape (*R v Blake* (1991)) or that forensic evidence links him to the crime (*R v Mason* (1987), and cf the facts of *R v Kwabena Poku* (1978)). In the right circumstances, this could induce D falsely to confess (eg he hopes to exonerate himself later, he feels there is no option but to concur with the interrogator, he tries to exculpate himself but incidentally incriminates himself). In *Blake* the trial judge used s 76(2)(b), in *Mason* s 78 was used (because the police conduct produced a reliable confession, see para 8.75, post). It is easy enough for the defence to raise s 76(2)(b) in this context, but it is also almost as easy for the prosecution to show that prima facie the suggestion of unreliability is far-fetched. This means that the defence must initially go further when raising s 76(2)(b) in the context of the method of questioning, by painting a realistic scenario (eg of a nervous, inexperienced suspect who 'confesses' in a state of confusion, or a seasoned criminal who is fooled into thinking that a confession, albeit false, is the best way out). A simple example of 'anything said or done' is *R v Zaveckas* (1969) where the accused asked 'if I make a statement, will I be given bail now?' and the police officer replied 'Yes'. The confession was held to be inadmissible and the conviction was quashed. Such facts could easily infringe s 76(2)(b), especially since the trial court is asked to consider the 'likely effect' of such a reply on the reliability of a confession, even if in fact it turns out to be true (see *R v Mcgovern* (1991)). Further examples of conduct the defence can raise under s 76(2)(b) include:

(i) a threat to charge the person with a more serious offence or with more offences unless he makes a statement (see the facts of *R v Howden-Simpson* (1991));

(ii)   a promise to charge him with a less serious offence or not to prosecute at all, if he confesses;

(iii)   a promise to 'put in a good word for him at the trial or before the prosecuting solicitor';

(iv)   a promise to take another offence into consideration at the trial rather than prosecute him separately for that offence (cf *R v Northam* (1967));

(v)   a threat to, or promise not to, prosecute the accused's spouse or mistress or other close relation (cf *R v Middleton* (1974)), the more remote the relationship, the less likely it is that the confession will be unreliable;

(vi)   a threat to inform a third party unless the accused confesses eg to inform his wife of a charge of indecent assault, or his employer of a shoplifting allegation;

(vii)   a threat to prosecute D on a charge unrelated to the one under investigation or to inform another agency about a prosecution (cf *Commissioners of Customs and Excise v Harz and Power* (1967)).

8.65   At common law it was suggested that 'a mere exhortation on religious or moral grounds to tell the truth does not make a resulting confession inadmissible' (CLRC, para 59). For example, 'You had better, as good boys, tell the truth' spoken by a mother to two children in front of a police officer (*R v Reeve and Handcock* (1872)). Indeed, *DPP v Ping Lin* (1976) directed the court to consider whether there was a causal link between such words and the confession. It will be noted, however, that under s 76(2)(b) such words of exhortation *may* lead to exclusion since the court is concerned with the *likelihood* of unreliability in the particular circumstances, and not solely with a causal connection leading to it. Far from clarifying the common law, s 76(2)(b) encourages the defence to raise the issue of 'likely unreliability' in many more circumstances than were possible under the previous law. A narrow dividing line can separate legitimate police responses from illegitimate ones. The commonsense and restraint of the court are the safeguards against abuse of this defence and against simple statements, such as 'I think that it would be better all round if you made a clean breast of it', leading to the exclusion of a confession. Section 76(2)(b) could also include something which is *properly* 'said or done'. The COP (para 11.3) advises:

> 'If the person asks the officer directly what action will be taken in the event of his answering questions, making a statement or refusing to do either, then the officer may inform the person what action the police propose to take in that event provided that that action is itself proper and warranted.'

Such a reply, however 'proper and warranted', may nevertheless be challenged at trial by the defence and be held to exclude a consequential confession if it is considered 'likely' in the circumstances to render the confession unreliable. For example the officer replies to a young woman of a nervous disposition with no previous convictions, 'the ground on which you are being detained is that it is necessary to detain you in order to obtain evidence by questioning. If you provide that evidence, you will be released on bail pending a decision whether or not to prosecute'. If then a confession is seen as the way out of a very unpleasant situation, what was said may lead to exclusion under s 76(2)(b). One answer would be for the court to rule that any reply by a police officer which is 'proper and warranted' is never likely to render a confession unreliable. This is a reasonable interpretation of s 76 if what is said is 'considered in a commonsense way in the light of all the circumstances: and what was said [is] given in a commonsense way the meaning which it would rationally be understood to have by the person to whom it was said' (Lord Morris in *DPP v Ling* (1976)). A police officer faced with the direct question 'what action will you take if I make a statement', should consider carefully his response. If he replies in 'proper and warranted' terms (if necessary after advice from a senior officer) and the interview is taped and/or witnessed by a third party (preferably a solicitor), the prosecution's task of satisfying s 76(2)(b) should be straightforward. As a further safeguard, it should be made clear to the suspect that decisions in respect of his release or detention will be taken by the custody officer and not by the investigating officer. Two further points about s 76(2)(b) can be noted. Firstly, s 76(2)(b) says 'anything said or done'. Does this include an omission? Although the point has not been considered directly, an affirmative answer can be deduced from the cases (eg *R v Mcgovern* (1991) failure to allow access to a solicitor, *R v Cox* (1991) absence of appropriate adult, *R v Doolan* (1988) failure to caution and record interview). Second, something said or done may cease to have effect if there is a significant gap before the confession is made (eg a threat or inducement is made to D but he confesses to another officer two days later). However, the prosecution should find it easy to discharge the burden of proof in the absence of convincing evidence from the defence.

Facts discovered as a result of the confession

8.66 Section 76(4) (Art 74(4)) deals with the admissibility of evidence discovered as a result of an improperly obtained confession:

1) Section 76(4)(5) and (6) (Art 74(5)(6) tackle the following problems. If a confession is declared to be inadmissible, can the prosecution still use evidence discovered as a consequence of that confession and, if so, for what purpose can it be used? For example, if during the investigation of a theft a confession is forced

out of D by oppression and he tells the police where they can find the stolen goods, can the prosecution (a) produce the goods at D's trial and (b) link their discovery to what D told the police? (cf in relation to murder the facts of the Canadian case, *R v Wray* (1970)). The CLRC unanimously recommended an affirmative answer to (a) and, by a majority, to (b). The PACE Act opted for a half-way house. On the one hand, the prosecution can use in evidence 'any facts discovered as a result of the confession' even if the confession is itself inadmissible (s 76(4)(a), Art 74(4)(a)). On the other hand, proof that those facts were discovered as a result of a wholly or partly inadmissible confession is not admissible (s 76(5) and (6), Art 74(5)(6)), *unless the accused himself gives evidence that they were so discovered* (s 76(5), Art 74(5)) endorsing *R v Berriman* (1854)). The policy underlying this latter rule is that it is unfair for the inadmissibility of a confession to be negated by the admissibility of the 'fruits of the crime', unless the accused so chooses. This ended the practice whereby 'it is common for the witness reporting the discovery to say that he made it as a result of 'something which the accused said' (CLRC, para 70(i)). Thus, in the example cited above, the prosecution can produce the stolen goods at trial but cannot show that they were discovered as a result of D's confession, unless D in examination in chief or cross-examination admits that he told the police where to find them. Note that evidence can still be admitted from the admissible part of a partly inadmissible confession (s 76(6)(b), Art 74(6)(b)).

2) Those parts of a confession which are relevant as showing that the accused 'speaks, writes or expresses himself in a particular way' are admissible for that purpose (s 76(4)(b), Art 74(4)(b)). The object of this exception is illustrated by *R v Voisin* (1918) where the body of a murder victim had been found alongside a piece of paper bearing the words 'Bladie Belgiam'. The accused was asked by the police to write 'Bloody Belgian' and he happily wrote 'Bladie Belgiam'. This evidence was held to be admissible. *R v Voisin* did not involve an involuntary confession but it will be noted that s 76(4)(b) (Art 74(4)(b)) can apply even if the confession was improperly obtained and therefore inadmissible. The limitation is that the confession can only be used to identify the characteristics mentioned in the subsection and not to establish the truth of anything said or written or to show that the accused had some special knowledge which only the offender could have had. Apart from misspellings as in *Voisin* (cf misspelt graffiti), examples include catch phrases, handwriting (if the accused has written his own confession) and, if the confession is tape recorded, accent, dialect, stammering and stuttering.

Confessions and s 78 (Art 76: for brevity s 78 will be used)

8.67   It is relatively easy for the defence to raise s 76(2)(b), and it was the CLRC's intention that it be used, in place of the complex common law, to cover cases of inducements, promises etc. Instead the courts have preferred s 78 in this area. For example, in *R v Howden-Simpson* (1991) the interviewing officer told the accused that he would be charged with two offences only if he confessed. If he did not, many charges would be brought. This is precisely the sort of threat or inducement with which s 76(2)(b) was intended to deal. The trial judge considered and rejected it. The Court of Appeal went further and decided that s 78 should have been relied upon to exclude the confession because the officer had indicated what action he would take if D did not confess and therefore the COP had been broken. Similarly in *R v Fogah* (1989), a juvenile was questioned in the absence of an appropriate adult. The latter's presence is required by the COP (para 11.14), inter alia, in order to protect the vulnerable D from making unreliable admissions, yet the court used s 78 to exclude them. The correct vehicle for handling this type of case is, it is submitted, s 76(2)(b). Again in *R v Keenan* (1989), the anti-verballing provisions of the COP (designed to prevent the police manufacturing admissions by D) were clearly broken. The evidence was excluded by s 78 as being unfair to D yet the same result could have been achieved by using s 76(2)(b) viz the failure on the part of the police to make a contemporaneous record of the interview and to show it to D meant that there was no guarantee of its reliability. As will be seen, s 78 has been regularly employed to exclude confessions. It is suggested that it has been overused, particularly as an alternative to s 76(2)(b). After all, that Part of the PACE Act covering s 76 is sub-headed 'Confessions', whereas that dealing with s 78 is 'Miscellaneous'; and s 76 specifically refers to confession, whereas s 78 speaks more broadly of 'evidence'. The background and scheme of the Act (and the gloss of *R v Fulling* (1987) on s 76(2)(a)) suggest the following arrangement:

police impropriety (with or without bad faith)	+	effect on D	=	s 76(2)(a)
lesser police impropriety (with or without bad faith)	+	effect on D	=	s 76(2(b)
police impropriety (with or without bad faith)	+	no real but potential effect on D	=	s 76(2)(b)
no impropriety	+	effect on D	=	s 76(2)(b)
no impropriety	+	no effect on D	=	s 78

8.67 *The questioning of suspects*

In other words s 76 should play a more regular role and s 78 should play the role of sweeper catching police conduct which does not fall within the province of s 76 but which a court finds unacceptable. For example, if a confession is secretly tape-recorded outside the police station, it is hard to describe such a tactic as oppression and, if the speaker has incriminated himself unprompted, the evidence will not be unreliable for s 76(2)(b) purposes. If a court takes the view that such conduct (and cf the deception in *R v Mason* (1987)) is unfair to the trial, it can use s 78 to exclude the confession (cf *R v H* (1987) and *R v Katz* (1990)).

8.68 Section 78 has had a dynamic life. Far from being a legal long stop to catch wayward and obvious examples of injustice, it has been used as a frontline wicketkeeper to discipline the police, protect the accused, and assert the authority of the courts. Sometimes it has been deployed in conjunction with s 76 and sometimes in place of it. Indeed, in reports of some cases on PACE it is difficult to determine which section has been used to exclude a confession (eg *R v Moss* (1990)). It is possible that the House of Lords could swing the pendulum towards the model suggested above, whereby s 78 assumes a residual role mainly in the non-confession area, but the tide looks well set in the Court of Appeal's favour. (For a discussion of s 78 outside the confession area, see para 2.48, ante). When s 78 is raised, the court has a discretion as to whether to hold a voir dire (*Carlisle v DPP* (1987)). How it should exercise that discretion is unclear. If, as it often will be, the confession is the central plank of the prosecution's case, its admissibility should be argued early on in the trial and in a voir dire. Hodgson J in *R v Keenan* (1989) distinguished three situations — (a) where evidence of police irregularity is plain for all to see (eg on the custody record) and the prosecution will concede it and proceed to argue s 78; (b) where there is prima facie evidence of irregularity, the prosecution will then seek to produce evidence in rebuttal and argue s 78; (c) where the defence must produce evidence to raise s 78. Hodgson J also posed the problem that, in determining unfairness under s 78, if objection is taken early on in the trial, the judge is unlikely to know D's likely defence and is in a difficult position to decide whether admissibility of the evidence will affect the fairness of the proceedings. The answer, it is suggested, is to require more from the defence at the voir dire. Indeed, if D's case is thin, the onus lies on him (see below) to establish the unfairness, if necessary by giving evidence (see the commentary in the Criminal Law Review attached to *Rajakuruna* (1991)).

8.69 Unlike s 76 (Art 74), there is no direction in s 78 as to the burden and standard proof. In most cases the defence will raise the issue, though there is nothing to prevent the court doing so of its own motion (cf s 76(3), Art 74(3)). Unless D objects, the prosecution 'proposes to rely' on the evidence (s 78), therefore D must clearly raise s 78 and point to some element of unfairness. Sometimes this will be readily apparent ((a) above), in other cases D will have to produce evidence (eg a witness to police conduct outside the station). But, as will be seen, misconduct by the police is not the criterion for s 78; the defence must go further and suggest to the court that the fairness of the proceedings will be adversely affected if the confession is admitted. Once this evidential burden has been discharged, the task falls then to the prosecution to rebut the allegation of unfairness. As to the overall burden of proof, on a strict reading of s 78 (and in contrast to the express instructions of s 76) it is suggested that the burden of proof lies on the defence — they must convince the court to such an extent 'that it appears to the court' that s 78 is satisfied. If this is correct then the standard is the civil one (partly because of the word 'appears' and partly in line with the general rule of evidence that a burden of proof on the accused is to be discharged to the balance of probabilities). The cases have not yet squarely confronted these issues and there are indications that (see the commentary to *R v Keenan* (1989)) an evidential burden lies initially on D and that, if the legal burden lies anywhere, it is on the prosecution (see also *R v Beveridge* (1987), *Vel v Owen* (1987)). The following preliminary points can be noted.

1) S 78 only applies to the evidence on which the prosecution proposes to rely. This means that it must be argued *before* the evidence is given.
2) The evidence must affect 'proceedings' and these are defined (s 82(1), Art 76) as criminal proceedings (thus including committal and a court-martial).
3) Though the effect is on the proceedings, the whole of the investigatory stage is open to scrutiny.
4) S 78 is quite separate from the common law power to exclude confessions (s 82(3), *Sat-Bhambra* (1989), see further at para 8.78, post).
5) In one of the earliest decisions on PACE it was decided by the Court of Appeal that s 78 applies to confessions and that they are not the sole preserve of s 76 (*R v Mason* (1987)).
6) The relevant confession has usually been made to the police but this is not essential. Section 78 can be used to try to exclude a confession made to others (eg a doctor as in *R v Mcdonald* (1991)).
7) The phrase '*such* an adverse effect in s 78 suggests that a minor adverse effect will not lead to exclusion, whereas a more adverse effect will. In practice it is likely simply to operate as a *de minimis* rule.
8) In reaching its conclusions the court is to consider all the circumstances (eg the amount of other evidence against the accused, the character of the accused) and is specifically referred to the circumstances in which the confession was obtained.

9) The court exercises a discretion and this gives the trial judge some leeway. Provided that he interprets the PACE Act and the COP correctly (no mean achievement) and professes to consider all the circumstances, the chances of a successful appeal are considerably diminished (*R v O'Leary* (1988)). The existence of this discretion means also that it should not be fettered by the erection of rules — each decision rests on its particular facts (cf *R v Canale* (1990) and *R v Gillard and Barrett* (1991)). If an appellate court concludes that the discretion has been wrongly exercised (or not exercised at all), it may be able to put itself in the position of the trial judge and consider whether or how the discretion should have been exercised (*R v Parris* (1989)).

10) Since many of the teething problems of PACE, which necessitated the use of s 78, have now been resolved and revised Codes of Practice have been adopted, it may be that the next few years will see a diminution in the number of cases involving s 78.

11) S 76(4),(5) (see para 8.66, ante) is applicable only to a confession excluded under that section. There is no equivalent in s 78, however it is open to a court to decide that it is unfair to admit evidence found in consequence of a confession which has been unfairly obtained.

12) Occasionally a judge has remarked that it is not the court's function to punish/discipline the police for failure to observe PACE and the COP (*R v Delaney* (1989), *R v Fennelly* (1989)). However, it is suggested that such reasoning is disingenuous for, no matter how the court expresses it, an inevitable consequence of exclusion of evidence is that the police are disciplined by the collapse of a prosecution. Hodgson J, it is submitted, came closer to the mark in *R v Samuel* (1988) when he described police disciplinary procedures as 'a much less secure method of ensuring compliance' with the PACE Act than ss 76 and 78 (cf the trenchant criticism of police conduct by Lord Lane CJ in *R v Canale* (1990)).

8.70 The terse terms of s 78 give little help as to their proper interpretation and the courts have displayed a range of approaches. Three general points can be made. First, the section is to be construed widely (*R v Keenan* (1989)). Second, the test is *fairness* of the proceedings, not fairness to the defence. In other words, fairness to the defence, the prosecution and to the court (that it be able to hear all the relevant evidence) must also be considered (*DPP v Marshall* (1988), *R v Quinn* (1990), *R v Kerawalla* (1991)). Third, it may be, as Auld J remarked in *R v Katz* (1990) that

'The circumstances of each case are almost always different, and judges may well take different views in the proper exercise of their discretion even where the circumstances are similar. This is not an apt field for hard case law and well founded distinctions between cases'.

8.71 These points are a clear encouragement to the defence to use the section. Whilst recognising the unpredictable nature of s 78, it is possible to identify factors which have influenced its use. The commonest trigger for the application of s 78 is where the defence can prove that there has been a breach of PACE or the Codes of Practice. In principle breach of the former should be treated more seriously since the Codes are not binding on the courts (the point was raised but not pursued in *R v Keenan* (1989)), but what should matter is the relevance of the breach to the fairness of the proceedings and, since the COP, C, has far more to say on interrogation procedures than the statute, in practice breaches of the COP are usually of greater relevance for the reception of confessions. It has been clearly established that not every breach of correct procedures will be greeted with exclusion of evidence (eg *R v Keenan* above, *R v Parris* (1989), *R v Waters* (1989), *R v Delaney* (1989)). Much depends on the type and extent of the breach. Thus, exclusion is more likely if the breach is flagrant (*R v Canale* (1990), where the Lord Chief Justice found a cynical disregard of the rules governing the contemporaneous recording of interviews) or wilful (*R v Nagah* (1990) where, although D agreed to an identification parade, he was released so that a street identification could more easily be made), and in bad faith (see the remarks by Lord Lane CJ in *R v Alladice* (1988) that a court might find it easier to employ s 78 if bad faith on the part of the police is proved). Correspondingly mistaken conduct on the part of the police carried out in good faith may tilt against the use of s 78 or at least be a neutral factor in the equation (see *R v Clarke* (1989) where the officers did not realise that D was deaf, but the breach of (now) COP, para 13.5 could still be considered by the court; *R v Younis* (1990) where the suspect 'volunteered' most of the remarks in the police car and there was no evidence of deliberate police prompting; see also *R v Kerawalla* (1991) where the absence of bad faith was a factor). However, unlike s 76(2)(a), impropriety is not essential (*R v O'Leary* (1988), *R v Samuel* (1988)) and good faith does not remedy a significant breach of PACE procedures. If the procedure is regarded by the court as an important one, it does not matter whether lack of adherence to it was wilful or through ignorance, the effect on the proceedings being the same in either case. See, for example, *R v Walsh* (1990) involving, inter alia, denial of legal advice, omitting to note the reason for not recording an interview contemporaneously, and failure to show D the record of interview. These were regarded as significant and substantial breaches which were not cured by good faith. Similarly in *R v Foster* (1987), the officer failed to appreciate that his brief chat with D in the street was an interview for PACE purposes and therefore did not make a contemporaneous record of it (for a similar mistake by an inexperienced officer, see *R v Sparks* (1991)). This then focuses attention on the type of PACE procedure which has been breached. It should be noted that 'the mere fact that there has been a breach of the Codes of Practice does not of itself mean that evidence has to be rejected' (per Lord Lane CJ in *R v Delaney* (1989)). A link between the breach and fairness to the proceedings must be established (eg *R v Hughes* (1988), *R v Dunford* (1990)). If the PACE procedure is an important safeguard for the suspect, an adverse effect on the fairness of the proceedings is more likely and s 78 is more easily invoked. Chief of these are the provisions designed to prevent verballing of the suspect (ie concocted admissions), see *R v Keenan* (1988). Transgression of them often warrants s 78 because (a) it is unfair to deprive D of his rights (especially legal advice), (b) it is unfair to the court since it is deprived of a more accurate record of an interview (eg a contemporaneous record), (c) it is unfair for the criminal process since admission of the confession would allow one side (the prosecution) to win by foul play. These reasons appear throughout the cases, though often they are not articulated, especially (c). Indeed sometimes the courts, having found improprieties, proceed almost automatically to apply s 78 without considering the two stages of s 78 ie how the evidence arose, and whether it will have an adverse effect on the proceedings (*R v Hughes* (1988)). This category of safeguards is essentially twofold — (1) provision of legal or other advice, and (2) the accurate recording of an interview either by a contemporaneous record or by showing D a summary of the interview.

8.72 Provision of legal or other advice — The starting point in category (1) is *R v Samuel* (1988) where D was interviewed after being improperly denied a solicitor (see further para 7.49, ante). Section 76 was not pleaded before the Court of Appeal but s 78 was, and the Court concluded that denial of 'one of the most important and fundamental rights of a citizen' — legal advice — could well have an adverse effect on the proceedings. This conclusion was assisted by the finding that, if the solicitor had been allowed access, he would probably have advised silence. It emphasises that denial of legal advice per se is not enough. It must also be shown that it produced an adverse effect. (For another early case of improper denial of legal advice, see *R v Smith* (1987)). The point was made again in *R v Alladice* (1988) where a solicitor was wrongly denied access (a clear breach of s 58, PACE and the COP); the interview was otherwise conducted properly, the solicitor would probably have reminded D of his right to silence but D, being used to police interviews, already knew that (indeed he exercised it at times during the interview), therefore the solicitor's presence would not have made a difference and there was no unfairness to the proceedings. To the same effect see *R v Dunford* (1990) where the improper denial of legal advice was balanced by D's knowledge of his rights and ability to cope on his own. (For comments on the importance of legal advice, see also *R v Dunn* (1990)). Other cases in which denial of access to legal advice has led to exclusion of the confession include:

R v Vernon (1988), where D was not told of the duty solicitor scheme or that a solicitor was on the way.

R v Absolam (1989) D was not told of his right to legal advice and proceeded to make damaging admissions: and to similar effect, *R v Williams* (1989). A failure to remind D of his right before an interview begins or re-starts (COP, para 11.2) is another potential area for judicial disapproval.

R v Parris (1989), s 58 was wrongly used to deny D legal advice. A solicitor's presence would probably have led D to use his right of silence and at the least would have given the court a witness to the interrogation to help it decide between the police and D's version.

R v Beycan (1990), D was wrongfully denied a solicitor by being told 'we usually interview without a solicitor . . .' This was particularly unfair since he was a foreigner with poor English and therefore vulnerable at the station.

The complexity of the offence under investigation may exacerbate the need for legal advice and the unfairness of its denial (see *R v Guest* (1988), a charge of principal in the second degree to murder; as Ognall J drily observed, an area of law 'not free from difficulty even among experienced criminal lawyers'). The advice need not be that of a lawyer.

R v Fogah (1989), D a juvenile, was improperly interviewed without the protection of an appropriate adult's presence.

Accurate recording

8.73 Examples of a failure to comply with category (2) are:

R v Canale (1990), where interviews were not contemporaneously recorded and the reason given on the subsequent record of interview was *b.w.* (ie 'best way' is not to record an interview contemporaneously). This 'lamentable attitude' (Lord Lane CJ) towards proper police procedures strongly influenced the Court of Appeal's decision to use s 78.

R v Dunn (1990), there had been a failure to record a conversation — prima facie a reason for exclusion of it, but this was balanced by the presence of D's legal adviser during the interview.

cf *R v Matthews* (1990) where D's comments were noted after the interview ended but the note was not shown to her, a clear breach of the COP. The Court of Appeal did not disturb the trial judge's refusal to use s 78, apparently on the basis (or lack of it) that he had considered all the circumstances and his discretion could not be challenged.

R v Scott (1991) D made an incriminating remark, unprompted by the police, which was noted but not shown to D for his immediate denial or confirmation. Instead he was forced to deny it at trial, thus exposing himself to prejudicial cross-examination and this was held to be unfair for s 78 purposes.

R v Maloney and Doherty (1988), interviews outside and inside the station were not contemporaneously recorded, notes of the interviews were not shown to the suspects and, although they could not read, no lawyer or third party was made available to assist them.

8.74 Some cases will involve both categories (1) and (2) — see *R v Walsh* (1990) where legal advice was improperly denied, the interview was not contemporaneously recorded and the eventual record was not shown to D. These were significant and substantial breaches of PACE procedures, fairness had not been satisfied and the good faith of the officers could not prevent the application of s 78 (cf to like effect, *R v Williams* (1989)). In contrast, there are many minor provisions in the COP, breach of which will have no effect on the fairness of the trial (eg failure to supply meals and drink on time; *R v Deacon* (1987) where failures to record the time when an interview finished and to allow eight hours continuous rest were considered by the court but clearly did not weigh heavily); and the courts have frequently remarked that it is not every breach of the COP that will lead to exclusion under s 78 (*Keenan, Parris*). Those provisions that are mandatory are more likely to warrant it than those which are directory (*R v Grier* (1989)). Also, there may a culmination of minor breaches of procedure which in total justify the exercise of the s 78 discretion (eg *R v Moss* (1990)).

8.75 Section 78 has also been used to condemn the tactics and content of police questioning. In fact this was the concern of the first leading case on the section, *R v Mason* (1987). Following an arson attack, D was questioned by the police who, in the absence of other evidence, falsely told him and then his solicitor that D's fingerprints had been found on the bottle used to carry the petrol. D then confessed to his involvement. The Court of Appeal was enraged that D's solicitor had been hoodwinked ('a most reprehensible thing') thereby affecting the advice he gave his client, and used s 78 to exclude D's confession. This does not mean that deceit practised on D alone is legitimate. On the contrary, the court issued a stern rebuke against such deception. This has wider implications and could prevent an interviewing officer from telling D falsely that a co-accused has already confessed or spilled the beans on D. It could be different if the officer truthfully told D that another person or even a lover had already confessed. That might not constitute oppression for s 76(2)(a) (see *R v Fulling* (1987) and para 8.49, ante) and, in the light of *R v Mason*, would not trigger s 78, though it may satisfy s 76(2)(b) depending on the impact it may have on the particular suspect and the likely unreliability of anything he says (see *R v Harvey* (1988) and para 8.59, ante). Another example of s 78 in this context is suggested by *R v Howden-Simpson* (1991) where the interviewing officer had told D that if he confessed he would be charged with only two offences, but if he denied it he would be separately charged on a number of counts. The

Court of Appeal suggested that such an inducement could well fall foul of s 78 (see the powerful commentary to the decision in the Criminal Law Review). In *R v Sparks* (1991) the failure to caution (and to record the interview) was a substantial breach of the COP and warranted exclusion of the conversation under s 78. See also *R v Saunders*(1988) where the key component of a caution (that D need not say anything) was omitted. Again, as in *Sparks*, there was also a breach of the recording provisions for interviews. On the other hand, failure to tell/remind D that he is a 'volunteer' and free to leave (COP para 10.2) is not necessarily a substantial breach (*R v Rajakuruna* (1991), particularly where D ought to have known that he was a suspect in an investigation.

8.76 The suspect's character and the effect of police conduct on him may be important. If he is of stout disposition, versed in criminal procedure and able to look after himself in interviews, s 78 may not be exercised (*R v Canale* where D had served in a paratroop regiment, *R v Alladice* where D was well aware of, and in fact used, his right of silence; see also *R v Osman, R v Dunford* where D had previous convictions and experience of police interviews). Whereas for a frail suspect unused to police procedures, breaches of PACE and COP may have much greater significance for the fairness of the trial (cf *R v Beycan* (1990) where D was a foreign citizen with poor English and no experience of the criminal process). The presence of other evidence against D should not affect the decision whether there is unfairness (that aspect is the preserve of s 2(1) of the Criminal Appeal Act 1968, the proviso to which can counterbalance any exclusion of evidence under s 78), *R v Walsh*. However, where there is enough other evidence to convict D, the court might be more easily persuaded to exclude the peripheral and disputed evidence whilst still allowing the rest to go before the jury (*R v Waters, R v Keenan*). By contrast the absence of other evidence, apart from the disputed area, could be crucial to the fairness of the trial (in *R v Canale* (1990) the disputed interviews were the only effective evidence against D and *R v Cochrane* (1988) where the interviews were the only evidence against D and, since s 58 had been transgressed, it was unfair to use them). That other evidence may even be linked to and infected by the disputed area (*R v Beycan* (1990) where it was held that once s 78 excluded admissions at the station, it was unfair to admit statements made in the car en route there). Indeed, as with s 76 (*R v Ismail* (1990), see further para 8.48 ante) an earlier, improper interview may affect a subsequent, proper one such as to warrant the latter's exclusion as well. This may be because the impropriety still influences the later interview, or because the court is determined not to let the police flagrantly flout the rules and then 'get away with it' by later obeying them (*R v Canale* (1990)). However, the court, in exercising its discretion may find that the later interview is not so tainted and can refrain from using s 78 (see *R v Gillard and Barrett* (1991); the distinction between this case and *Canale*, above, is narrow and seems to depend on the degree of flagrancy of misconduct).

8.77   As has been seen, police misconduct is the most regular pretext for using s 78. This does not mean that fairness to the accused is only criterion for its use. Fairness to the prosecution may also need to be considered. Thus, in *R v Hughes* (1988) it was decided that D had genuinely consented to an interview without a solicitor and that balancing the interests of the prosecution and of D did not require the use of s 78 (cf *R v Smith* (1987)). As the court pointed out in *R v Kerawalla* (1991), the overall fairness of the proceedings has to be judged.

The Common Law

8.78   Common law prohibited confessions which were obtained by oppression or were not voluntarily made, but was not otherwise concerned with how confessional evidence was obtained when it came to decide on its admissibility (eg *Kuruma v The Queen* (1955), *Jeffrey v Black* (1978), *R v Sang* (1979)). What role has the common law, specifically preserved by s 82(3) (Art 70(3)), to play in the light of sections 76 and 78 (Arts 74, 76)? It remains as a separate head for excluding evidence (see the reference by Lord Lane CJ in *R v Delaney* (1989), May LJ in *R v O'Leary* (1988), and *Matto v Wolverhampton Crown Court* (1987)). One use was suggested in *R v Sat-Bhambra* (1989) where it was held that sections 76 and 78 are prospective only ie they can exclude a confession *before* it is given in evidence in court. Section 82(3) thus allows the court to remedy earlier unfairness to the accused by excluding a previously admitted confession (after a voir dire D's confession had been admitted, but on hearing further medical evidence the judge later changed his mind). Another use is where D2 seeks to rely on a confession by D1 which was excluded under s 76 or s 78. Both sections permit only the exclusion of evidence upon which the prosecution seek to rely. The common law discretion is not so limited. Elsewhere it is suggested that the common law has no role to play since sections 76 and 78 have not only supplemented it but have also extended the court's powers to exclude confessions and other evidence. This is not of course to deny the court's overriding discretion to exclude evidence if its prejudicial effect outweighs its probative value (endorsed by the House of Lords in *R v Sang* (1979)).

Northern Ireland

8.79   In Northern Ireland, Articles 74 and 76 of the PACE Order govern the admissibility of most confessions, but where a scheduled offence (ie a terrorist investigation) is involved, s 8 of the Northern Ireland (Emergency Provisions) Act 1978 (as amended in 1987) takes over. If such an offence is to be tried on indictment (the vast majority of cases and they will be conducted without a jury; for the rare, summary trial the PACE Order governs), the prosecution proposes to rely on a statement by D, and

'prima facie evidence is adduced that the accused was subject to torture, to inhuman or degrading treatment, or to any violence or threat of violence (whether or not amounting to torture), in order to induce him to make the statement,

then, unless the prosecution satisfies the court that the statement was not obtained by so subjecting the accused in the manner indicated by that evidence, the court shall do one of the following things, namely —

(i)   in the case of a statement proposed to be given in evidence, exclude the statement;

(ii)   in the case of a statement already received in evidence, continue the trial disregarding the statement; or

(iii) in either case, direct that the trial shall be restarted before a differently constituted court (before which the statement in question shall be inadmissible).' (s 8(2)).

The equivalent provision in the PACE Order (Art 74(2)(a)) is much wider, since its criterion of 'oppression' has been relatively liberally interpreted by *R v Fulling* (1987). The 1978 Act lacks an equivalent to Art 74(2)(b) and, moreover, the Act's equivalent of Art 76 in the PACE Order is expressed differently viz the court has a discretion to do one of (i) to (iii) above in respect of a confession 'if it appears to the court that it is appropriate to do so in order to avoid unfairness to the accused or otherwise in the interests of justice' (s 8(3)). This wording is sufficiently close to that of Art 76 to enable the courts in Northern Ireland to adopt the rulings of other courts in the United Kingdom on that Article (ie s 78 of the PACE Act), whether they will do so is of course another matter.

Appendix 1

Police and Criminal Evidence Act 1984

PART I

POWERS TO STOP AND SEARCH

1 Power of constable to stop and search persons, vehicles, etc.

(1) A constable may exercise any power conferred by this section—

(*a*) in any place to which at the time when he proposes to exercise the power the public or any section of the public has access, on payment or otherwise, as of right or by virtue of express or implied permission; or

(*b*) in any other place to which people have ready access at the time when he proposes to exercise the power but which is not a dwelling.

(2) Subject to subsection (3) to (5) below, a constable—

(*a*) may search—
    (i) any person or vehicle;
    (ii) anything which is in or on a vehicle,

for stolen or prohibited articles or any article to which subsection (8A) below applies; and

(*b*) may detain a person or vehicle for the purpose of such a search.

(3) This section does not give a constable power to search a person or vehicle or anything in or on a vehicle unless he has reasonable grounds for suspecting that he will find stolen or prohibited articles or any article to which subsection (8A) below applies.

(4) If a person is in a garden or yard occupied with and used for the purpose of a dwelling or on other land so occupied and used, a constable may not search him in the exercise of the power conferred by this section unless the constable has reasonable grounds for believing—

(*a*) that he does not reside in the dwelling; and

(*b*) that he is not in the place in question with the express or implied permission of a person who resides in the dwelling.

(5) If a vehicle is in a garden or yard occupied with and used for the purposes of a dwelling or on other land so occupied and used, a constable may not search the vehicle or anything in or on it in the exercise of the power conferred by this section unless he has reasonable grounds for believing—

(*a*) that the person in charge of the vehicle does not reside in the dwelling; and (*b*) that the vehicle is not in the place in question with the express or implied permission of a person who resides in the dwelling.

(6) If in the course of such a search a constable discovers an article which he has reasonable grounds for suspecting to be a stolen or prohibited article or an article to which subsection (8A) below applies, he may seize it.

(7) An article is prohibited for the purposes of this Part of this Act if it is—

(*a*) an offensive weapon; or
(*b*) an article—
    (i) made or adapted for use in the course of or in connection with an offence to which this sub-paragraph applies; or
    (ii) intended by the person having it with him for such use by him or by some other person.

(8) The offences to which subsection (7)(*b*)(i) above applies are—

(*a*) burglary;
(*b*) theft;
(*c*) offences under section 12 of the Theft Act 1968 (taking motor vehicle or other conveyance without authority); and
(*d*) offences under section 15 of that Act (obtaining property by deception).

(8A) This subsection applies to any article in relation to which a person has committed, or is committing or is going to commit an offence under section 139 of the Criminal Justice Act 1988.

(9) In this Part of this Act "offensive weapon" means any article—

(*a*) made or adapted for use for causing injury to persons; or
(*b*) intended by the person having it with him for such use by him or by some other person.

2 Provisions relating to search under section 1 and other powers

(1) A constable who detains a person or vehicle in the exercise—

(*a*) of the power conferred by section 1 above; or
(*b*) of any other power—
    (i) to search a person without first arresting him; or
    (ii) to search a vehicle without making an arrest,
    need not conduct a search if it appears to him subsequently—
    (i) that no search is required; or
    (ii) that a search is impracticable.

(2) If a constable contemplates a search, other than a search of an unattended vehicle, in the exercise—

(*a*) of the power conferred by section 1 above; or
(*b*) of any other power, except the power conferred by section 6 below and the power conferred by section 27(2) of the Aviation Security Act 1982—
    (i) to search a person without first arresting him; or
    (ii) to search a vehicle without making an arrest,

it shall be his duty, subject to subsection (4) below, to take reasonable steps before he commences the search to bring to the attention of the appropriate person—

(i) if the constable is not in uniform, documentary evidence that he is a constable; and

(ii) whether he is in uniform or not, the matters specified in subsection (3) below;

and the constable shall not commence the search until he has performed that duty.

(3) The matters referred to in subsection (2)(ii) above are—

(a) the constable's name and the name of the police station to which he is attached;

(b) the object of the proposed search;

(c) the constable's grounds for proposing to make it; and

(d) the effect of section 3(7) or (8) below, as may be appropriate.

(4) A constable need not bring the effect of section 3(7) or (8) below to the attention of the appropriate person if it appears to the constable that it will not be practicable to make the record in section 3(1) below.

(5) In this section "the appropriate person" means—

(a) if the constable proposes to search a person, that person; and

(b) if he proposes to search a vehicle, or anything in or on a vehicle, the person in charge of the vehicle.

(6) On completing a search of an unattended vehicle or anything in or on such a vehicle in the exercise of any such power as is mentioned in subsection (2) above a constable shall leave a notice—

(a) stating that he has searched it;

(b) giving the name of the police station to which he is attached;

(c) stating that an application for compensation for any damage caused by the search may be made to that police station; and

(d) stating the effect of section 3(8) below.

(7) The constable shall leave the notice inside the vehicle unless it is not reasonably practicable to do so without damaging the vehicle.

(8) The time for which a person or vehicle may be detained for the purposes of such a search is such time as is reasonably required to permit a search to be carried out either at the place where the person or vehicle was first detained or nearby.

(9) Neither the power conferred by section 1 above nor any other power to detain and search a person without first arresting him or to detain and search a vehicle without making an arrest is to be construed—

(a) as authorising a constable to require a person to remove any of his clothing in public other than an outer coat, jacket or gloves; or

(b) as authorising a constable not in uniform to stop a vehicle.

(10) This section and section 1 above apply to vessels, aircraft and hovercraft as they apply to vehicles.

Appendix 1

3 Duty to make records concerning searches

(1) Where a constable has carried out a search in the exercise of any such power as is mentioned in section 2(1) above, other than a search—

(*a*)   under section 6 below; or

(*b*)   under section 27(2) of the Aviation Security Act 1982,
he shall make a record of it in writing unless it is not practicable to do so.

(2) If—

(*a*) a constable is required by subsection (1) above to make a record of a search; but

(*b*) it is not practicable to make the record on the spot,
he shall make it as soon as practicable after the completion of the search.

(3) The record of a search of a person shall include a note of his name, if the constable knows it, but a constable may not detain a person to find out his name.

(4) If a constable does not know the name of the person whom he has searched, the record of the search shall include a note otherwise describing the person.

(5) The record of the search of a vehicle shall include a note describing the vehicle.

(6) The record of a search of a person or a vehicle—

(*a*)   shall state—
  (i)   the object of the search;
  (ii)   the grounds for making it;
  (iii)   the date and time when it was made;
  (iv)   the place where it was made;
  (v)   whether anything, and if so what, was found;
  (vi)   whether any, and if so what, injury to a person or damage to property appears to the constable to have resulted from the search; and

(*b*)   shall identify the constable making it.

(7) If a constable who conducted a search of a person made a record of it, the person who was searched shall be entitled to a copy of the record if he asks for one before the end of the period specified in subsection (9) below.

(8) If—

(*a*)   the owner of a vehicle which has been searched or the person who was in charge of the vehicle at the time when it was searched asks for a copy of the record of the search before the end of the period specified in subsection (9) below; and

(*b*)   the constable who conducted the search made a record of it,
the person who made the request shall be entitled to a copy.

(9) The period mentioned in subsections (7) and (8) above is the period of 12 months beginning with the date on which the search was made.

(10) The requirements imposed by this section with regard to records of searches of vehicles shall apply also to records of searches of vessels, aircraft and hovercraft.

4 Road checks

(1) This section shall have effect in relation to the conduct of road checks by police officers for the purpose of ascertaining whether a vehicle is carrying—

    (*a*) a person who has committed an offence other than a road traffic offence or a vehicle excise offence;

    (*b*) a person who is a witness to such an offence;

    (*c*) a person intending to commit such an offence; or

    (*d*) a person who is unlawfully at large.

(2) For the purposes of this section a road check consists of the exercise in a locality of the power conferred by section 163 of the Road Traffic Act 1988 in such a way as to stop during the period for which its exercise in that way in that locality continues all vehicles or vehicles selected by any criterion.

(3) Subject to subsection (5) below, there may only be such a road check if a police officer of the rank of superintendent or above authorises it in writing.

(4) An officer may only authorise a road check under subsection (3) above—

    (*a*) for the purpose specified in subsection (1)(*a*) above, if he has reasonable grounds—

      (i) for believing that the offence is a serious arrestable offence; and

      (ii) for suspecting that the person is, or is about to be, in the locality in which vehicles would be stopped if the road check were authorised;

    (*b*) for the purpose specified in subsection (1)(*b*) above, if he has reasonable grounds for believing that the offence is a serious arrestable offence;

    (*c*) for the purpose specified in subsection (1)(*c*) above, if he has reasonable grounds—

      (i) for believing that the offence would be a serious arrestable offence; and

      (ii) for suspecting that the person is, or is about to be, in the locality in which vehicles would be stopped if the road check were authorised;

    (*d*) for the purpose specified in subsection (1)(*d*) above, if he has reasonable grounds for suspecting that the person is, or is about to be, in that locality.

(5) An officer below the rank of superintendent may authorise such a road check if it appears to him that it is required as a matter of urgency for one of the purposes specified in subsection (1) above.

(6) If an authorisation is given under subsection (5) above, it shall be the duty of the officer who gives it—

    (*a*) to make a written record of the time at which he gives it; and

    (*b*) to cause an officer of the rank of superintendent or above to be informed that it has been given.

(7) The duties imposed by subsection (6) above shall be performed as soon as it is practicable to do so.

(8) An officer to whom a report is made under subsection (6) above may, in writing, authorise the road check to continue.

(9) If such an officer considers that the road check should not continue, he shall record in writing—

(*a*) the fact that it took place; and
(*b*) the purpose for which it took place.

(10) An officer giving an authorisation under this section shall specify the locality in which vehicles are to be stopped.

(11) An officer giving an authorisation under this section, other than an authorisation under subsection (5) above—

(*a*) shall specify a period, not exceeding seven days, during which the road check may continue; and
(*b*) may direct that the road check—
    (i) shall be continuous; or
    (ii) shall be conducted at specified times, during that period.

(12) If it appears to an officer of the rank of superintendent or above that a road check ought to continue beyond the period for which it has been authorised he may, from time to time, in writing specify a further period, not exceeding seven days, during which it may continue.

(13) Every written authorisation shall specify—

(*a*) the name of the officer giving it;
(*b*) the purpose of the road check; and
(*c*) the locality in which vehicles are to be stopped.

(14) The duties to specify that purposes of a road check imposed by subsection (9) and (13) above include duties to specify any relevant serious arrestable offence.

(15) Where a vehicle is stopped in a road check, the person in charge of the vehicle at the time when it is stopped shall be entitled to obtain a written statement of the purpose of the road check if he applies for such a statement not later than the end of the period of twelve months from the day on which the vehicle was stopped.

(16) Nothing in this section affects the exercise by police officers of any power to stop vehicles for purposes other than those specified in subsection (1) above.

5 Reports of recorded searches and of road checks

(1) Every annual report—

(*a*) under section 12 of the Police Act 1964; or
(*b*) made by the Commissioner of Police of the Metropolis, shall contain

information—

   (i) about searches recorded under section 3 above which have been carried out in the area to which the report relates during the period to which it relates; and

   (ii) about road checks authorised in that area during that period under section 4 above.

(2) The information about searches shall not include information about specific searches but shall include—

   (*a*) the total numbers of searches in each month during the period to which the report relates—

      (i) for stolen articles;

      (ii) for offensive weapons [or articles to which section 1(8A) above applies]; and

      (iii) for other prohibited articles;

   (*b*) the total number of persons arrested in each such month in consequence of searches of each of the descriptions specified in paragraph (*a*)(i) to (iii) above.

(3) The information about road checks shall include information—

   (*a*) about the reason for authorising each road check; and

   (*b*) about the result of each of them.

6 Statutory undertakers, etc.

(1) A constable employed by statutory undertakers may stop, detain and search any vehicle before it leaves a goods area included in the premises of the statutory undertakers.

(2) In this section "goods area" means any area used wholly or mainly for the storage or handling of goods.

(3) For the purposes of section 6 of the Public Stores Act 1875, any person appointed under the Special Constables Act 1923 to be a special constable within any premises which are in the possession or under the control of British Nuclear Fuels Limited shall be deemed to be a constable deputed by a public department and any goods and chattels belonging to or in the possession of British Nuclear Fuels Limited shall be deemed to be Her Majesty's Stores.

(4) In the application of subsection (3) above to Northern Ireland, for the reference to the Special Constables Act 1923 there shall be substituted a reference to paragraph 1(2) of Schedule 2 to the Emergency Laws (Miscellaneous Provisions) Act 1947.

7 Part *I* — *supplementary*

(1) The following enactments shall cease to have effect—

   (*a*) section 8 of the Vagrancy Act 1824;

   (*b*) section 66 of the Metropolitan Police Act 1839;

(*c*) section 11 of the Canals (Offences) Act 1840;

(*d*) section 19 of the Pedlars Act 1871;

(*e*) section 33 of the County of Merseyside Act 1980; and

(*f*) section 42 of the West Midlands County Council Act 1980

(2) There shall also cease to have effect—

(*a*) so much of any enactment contained in an Act passed before 1974, other than—

   (i) an enactment contained in a public general Act; or

   (ii) an enactment relating to statutory undertakers, as confers power on a constable to search for stolen or unlawfully obtained goods; and

(*b*) so much of any enactment relating to statutory undertakers as provides that such a power shall not be exercisable after the end of a specified period.

(3) In this Part of this Act "statutory undertakers" means persons authorised by any enactment to carry on any railway, light railway, road transport, water transport, canal, inland navigation, dock or harbour undertaking.

PART II

Powers of Entry, Search and Seizure

8 Power of justice of the peace to authorise entry and search of premises

(1) If on an application made by a constable a justice of the peace is satisfied that there are reasonable grounds for believing—

(*a*) that a serious arrestable offence has been committed; and

(*b*) that there is material on premises specified in the application which is likely to be of substantial value (whether by itself or together with other material) to the investigation of the offence; and

(*c*) that the material is likely to be relevant evidence; and

(*d*) that it does not consist of or include items subject to legal privilege, excluded material or special procedure material; and

(*e*) that any of the conditions specified in subsection (3) below applies, he may issue a warrant authorising a constable to enter and search the premises.

(2) A constable may seize and retain anything for which a search has been authorised under subsection (1) above.

(3) The conditions mentioned in subsection (1)(*e*) above are—

(*a*) that it is not practicable to communicate with any person entitled to grant entry to the premises;

(*b*) that it is practicable to communicate with a person entitled to grant entry to the premises but it is not practicable to communicate with any person entitled to grant access to the evidence;

(*c*) that entry to the premises will not be granted unless a warrant is produced;

(*d*) that the purpose of a search may be frustrated or seriously prejudiced unless a constable arriving at the premises can secure immediate entry to them.

(4) In this Act "relevant evidence", in relation to an offence, means anything that would be admissible in evidence at a trial for the offence.

(5) The power to issue a warrant conferred by this section is in addition to any such power otherwise conferred.

9 Special provisions as to access

(1) A constable may obtain access to excluded material or special procedure material for the purposes of a criminal investigation by making an application under Schedule 1 below and in accordance with that Schedule.

(2) Any Act (including a local Act) passed before this Act under which a search of premises for the purposes of a criminal investigation could be authorised by the issue of a warrant to a constable shall cease to have effect so far as it relates to the authorisation of searches—

    (*a*) for items subject to legal privilege; or

    (*b*) for excluded material; or

    (*c*) for special procedure material consisting of documents or records other than documents.

10 Meaning of "items subject to legal privilege"

(1) Subject to subsection (2) below, in this Act "items subject to legal privilege" means—

(*a*) communications between a professional legal adviser and his client or any person representing his client made in connection with the giving of legal advice to the client;

(*b*) communications between a professional legal adviser and his client or any person representing his client or between such an adviser or his client or any such representative and any other person made in connection with or in contemplation of legal proceedings and for the purposes of such proceedings; and

(*c*) items enclosed with or referred to in such communications and made—

    (i) in connection with the giving of legal advice; or

    (ii) in connection with or in contemplation of legal proceedings and for the purposes of such proceedings,

when they are in the possession of a person who is entitled to possession of them.

(2) Items held with the intention of furthering a criminal purpose are not items subject to legal privilege.

11 Meaning of "excluded material"

(1) Subject to the following provisions of this section, in this Act "excluded material" means—

(a) personal records which a person has acquired or created in the course of any trade, business, profession or other occupation or for the purposes of any paid or unpaid office and which he holds in confidence;

(b) human tissue or tissue fluid which has been taken for the purposes of diagnosis or medical treatment and which a person holds in confidence;

(c) journalistic material which a person holds in confidence and which consists—

  (i) of documents; or

  (ii) of records other than documents.

(2) A person holds material other than journalistic material in confidence for the purposes of this section if he holds it subject—

(a) to an express or implied undertaking to hold it in confidence; or

(b) to a restriction on disclosure or an obligation of secrecy contained in any enactment, including an enactment contained in an Act passed after this Act.

(3) A person holds journalistic material in confidence for the purposes of this section if—

(a) he holds it subject to such an undertaking, restriction or obligation; and

(b) it has been continuously held (by one or more persons) subject to such an undertaking, restriction or obligation since it was first acquired or created for the purposes of journalism.

12 Meaning of "personal records"

In this Part of this Act "personal records" means documentary and other records concerning an individual (whether living or dead) who can be identified from them and relating—

(a) to his physical or mental health;

(b) to spiritual counselling or assistance given or to be given to him; or

(c) to counselling or assistance given or to be given to him, for the purposes of his personal welfare, by any voluntary organisation or by any individual who—

  (i) by reason of his office or occupation has responsibilities for his personal welfare; or

  (ii) by reason of an order of a court has responsibilities for his supervision.

13 Meaning of "journalistic material"

(1) Subject to subsection (2) below, in this Act "journalistic material" means material acquired or created for the purposes of journalism.

(2) Material is only journalistic material for the purposes of this Act if it is in the possession of a person who acquired or created it for the purposes of journalism..

(3) A person who receives material from someone who intends that the recipi-

ent shall use it for the purposes of journalism is to be taken to have acquired it for those purposes.

14 Meaning of "special procedure material"

(1) In this Act "special procedure material" means —

(*a*) material to which subsection (2) below applies; and
(*b*) journalistic material, other than excluded material.

(2) Subject to the following provisions of this section, this subsection applies to material, other than items subject to legal privilege and excluded material, in the possession of a person who—

(*a*) acquired or created it in the course of any trade, business, profession or other occupation or for the purpose of any paid or unpaid office; and
(*b*) holds it subject—
   (i) to an express or implied undertaking to hold it in confidence; or
   (ii) to a restriction or obligation such as is mentioned in section 11(2)(*b*) above.

(3) Where material is acquired—

(*a*) by an employee from his employer and in the course of his employment; or
(*b*) by a company from an associated company,

it is only special procedure material if it was special procedure material immediately before the acquisition.

(4) Where material is created by an employee in the course of his employment, it is only special procedure material if it would have been special procedure material had his employer created it.

(5) Where material is created by a company on behalf of an associated company, it is only special procedure material if it would have been special procedure material had the associated company created it.

(6) A company is to be treated as another's associated company for the purposes of this section if it would be so treated under section 416 of the Income and Corporation Taxes Act 1988.

15 Search warrants — safeguards

(1) This section and section 16 below have effect in relation to the issue to constables under any enactment, including an enactment contained in an Act passed after this act, of warrants to enter and search premises; and an entry on or search of premises under a warrant is unlawful unless it complies with this section and section 16 below.

(2) Where a constable applies for any such warrant, it shall be his duty—

(*a*) to state—
   (i) the ground on which he makes the application; and
   (ii) the enactment under which the warrant would be issued;

(*b*) to specify the premises which it is desired to enter and search; and

(*c*) to identify, so far as is practicable, the articles or persons to be sought.

(3) An application for such a warrant shall be made ex parte and supported by an information in writing.

(4) The constable shall answer on oath any question that the justice of the peace or judge hearing the application asks him.

(5) A warrant shall authorise an entry on one occasion only.

(6) A warrant—

(*a*) shall specify—
   (i) the name of the person who applies for it;
   (ii) the date on which it is issued;
   (iii) the enactment under which it is issued; and
   (iv) the premises to be searched; and

(*b*) shall identify, so far as is practicable, the articles or persons to be sought.

(7) Two copies shall be made of a warrant.

(8) The copies shall be clearly certified as copies.

16 Execution of warrants

(1) A warrant to enter and search premises may be executed by any constable.

(2) Such a warrant may authorise persons to accompany any constable who is executing it.

(3) Entry and search under a warrant must be within one month from the date of its issue.

(4) Entry and search under a warrant must be at a reasonable hour unless it appears to the constable executing it that the purpose of a search may be frustrated on an entry at a reasonable hour.

(5) Where the occupier of premises which are to be entered and searched is present at the time when a constable seeks to execute a warrant to enter and search them, the constable—

(*a*) shall identify himself to the occupier and, if not in uniform, shall produce to him documentary evidence that he is a constable;

(*b*) shall produce the warrant to him; and

(*c*) shall supply him with a copy of it.

(6) Where—

(*a*) the occupier of such premises is not present at the time when a constable seeks to execute such a warrant; but

(*b*) some other person who appears to the constable to be in charge of the premises is present, subsection (5) above shall have effect as if any reference to the occupier were a reference to that other person.

(7) If there is no person present who appears to the constable to be in charge of the premises, he shall leave a copy of the warrant in a prominent place on the premises.

(8) A search under a warrant may only be a search to the extent required for the purpose for which the warrant was issued.

(9) A constable executing a warrant shall make an endorsement on it stating—

(*a*) whether the articles or persons sought were found; and
(*b*) whether any articles were seized, other than articles which were sought.

(10) A warrant which—

(*a*) has been executed; or
(*b*) has not been executed within the time authorised for its execution,
   shall be returned—
   (i) if it was issued by a justice of the peace, to the clerk to the justices for the petty sessions area for which he acts; and
   (ii) if it was issued by a judge, to the appropriate officer of the court from which he issued it.

(11) A warrant which is returned under subsection (1) above shall be retained for 12 months from its return—

(*a*) by the clerk to the justices, if it was returned under paragraph (i) of that subsection; and
(*b*) by the appropriate officer, if it was returned under paragraph (ii).

(12) If during the period for which a warrant is to be retained the occupier of the premises to which it relates asks to inspect it, he shall be allowed to do so.

17 Entry for purpose of arrest, etc.

(1) Subject to the following provisions of this section, and without prejudice to any other enactment, a constable may enter and search any premises for the purpose—

(*a*) of executing—
   (i) a warrant of arrest issued in connection with or arising out of criminal proceedings; or
   (ii) a warrant of commitment issued under section 76 of the Magistrates' Courts Act 1980;
(*b*) of arresting a person for an arrestable offence;
(*c*) of arresting a person for an offence under—
   (i) section 1 (prohibition of uniforms in connection with political objects), of the Public Order Act 1936;
   (ii) any enactment contained in sections 6 to 8 or 10 of the Criminal Law

Act 1977 (offences relating to entering and remaining on property);
  (iii) section 4 of the Public Order Act 1986 (fear or provocation of violence);
(*d*) of recapturing a person who is unlawfully at large and whom he is pursuing; or
(*e*) of saving life or limb or preventing serious damage to property.

(2) Except for the purpose specified in paragraph (*e*) of subsection (1) above, the powers of entry and search conferred by this section—

(*a*) are only exercisable if the constable has reasonable grounds for believing that the person whom he is seeking is on the premises; and
(*b*) are limited, in relation to premises consisting of two or more separate dwellings, to powers to enter and search—
  (i) any parts of the premises which the occupiers of any dwelling comprised in the premises use in common with the occupiers of any other such dwelling; and
  (ii) any such dwelling in which the constable has reasonable grounds for believing that the person whom he is seeking may be.

(3) The powers of entry and search conferred by this section are only exercisable for the purposes specified in subsection (1)(*c*)(ii) above by a constable in uniform.

(4) The power of search conferred by this section is only a power to search to the extent that is reasonably required for the purpose for which the power of entry is exercised.

(5) Subject to subsection (6) below, all the rules of common law under which a constable has power to enter premises without a warrant are hereby abolished.

(6) Nothing in subsection (5) above affects any power of entry to deal with or prevent a breach of the peace.

18 Entry and search after arrest

(1) Subject to the following provisions of this section, a constable may enter and search any premises occupied or controlled by a person who is under arrest for an arrestable offence, if he has reasonable grounds for suspecting that there is on the premises evidence, other than items subject to legal privilege, that relates—

(*a*) to that offence; or
(*b*) to some other arrestable offence which is connected with or similar to that offence.

(2) A constable may seize and retain anything for which he may search under subsection (1) above.

(3) The power to search conferred by subsection (1) above is only a power to search to the extent that is reasonably required for the purpose of discovering such evidence.

(4) Subject to subsection (5) below, the powers conferred by this section may not be exercised unless an officer of the rank of inspector or above has authorised them in writing.

(5) A constable may conduct a search under subsection (1) above—

(*a*) before taking the person to a police station; and
(*b*) without obtaining an authorisation under subsection (4) above,

if the presence of that person at a place other than a police station is necessary for the effective investigation of the offence.

(6) If a constable conducts a search by virtue of subsection (5)above, he shall inform an officer of the rank of inspector or above that he has made the search as soon as practicable after he has made it.

(7) An officer who—

(*a*) authorises a search; or
(*b*) is informed of a search under subsection (6) above,
    shall make a record in writing—
    (i) of the grounds for the search; and
    (ii) of the nature of the evidence that was sought.

(8) If the person who was in occupation or control of the premises at the time of the search is in police detention at the time the record is to be made, the officer shall make the record as part of his custody record.

19 General power of seizure, etc.

(1) The powers conferred by subsections (2), (3) and (4) below are exercisable by a constable who is lawfully on any premises.

(2) The constable may seize anything which is on the premises if he has reasonable grounds for believing—

(*a*) that it has been obtained in consequence of the commission of an offence; and
(*b*) that it is necessary to seize it in order to prevent it being concealed, lost, damaged, altered or destroyed.

(3) The constable may seize anything which is on the premises if he has reasonable grounds for believing—

(*a*) that it is evidence in relation to an offence which he is investigating or any other offence; and
(*b*) that it is necessary to seize it in order to prevent the evidence being concealed, lost, altered or destroyed.

(4) The constable may require any information which is contained in a computer and is accessible from the premises to be produced in a form in which it can be taken away and in which it is visible and legible if he has reasonable grounds for

believing—

   (*a*) that—

      (i) it is evidence in relation to an offence which he is investigating or any other offence; or

      (ii) it has been obtained in consequence of the commission of an offence; and

   (*b*) that it is necessary to do so in order to prevent it beingconcealed, lost, tampered with or destroyed.

(5) The powers conferred by this section are in addition to any power otherwise conferred.

(6) No power of seizure conferred on a constable under any enactment (including an enactment contained in an Act passed after this Act) is to be taken to authorise the seizure of an item which the constable exercising the power has reasonable grounds for believing to be subject to legal privilege.

20 Extension of powers of seizure to computerised information

(1) Every power of seizure which is conferred by an enactment to which this section applies on a constable who has entered premises in the exercise of a power conferred by an enactment shall be construed as including a power to require any information contained in a computer and accessible from the premises to be produced in a form in which it can be taken away and in which it is visible and legible.

(2) This section applies—

   (*a*) to any enactment contained in an Act passed before this Act;

   (*b*) to sections 8 and 18 above;

   (*c*) to paragraph 13 of Schedule 1 to this Act; and

   (*d*) to any enactment contained in an Act passed after this Act.

21 Access and copying

(1) A constable who seizes anything in the exercise of a power conferred by any enactment, including an enactment contained in an Act passed after this Act, shall, if so requested by a person showing himself—

   (*a*) to be the occupier of premises on which it was seized; or

   (*b*) to have had custody or control of it immediately before the seizure, provide that person with a record of what he seized.

(2) The officer shall provide the record within a reasonable time from the making of the request for it.

(3) Subject to subsection (8) below, if a request for permission to be granted access to anything which—

(*a*) has been seized by a constable; and
(*b*) is retained by the police for the purpose of investigating an offence,

is made to the officer in charge of the investigation by a person who had custody or control of the thing immediately before it was so seized or by someone acting on behalf of such a person, the officer shall allow the person who made the request access to itunder the supervision of a constable.

(4) Subject to subsection (8) below, if a request for a photographor copy of any such thing is made to the officer in charge of the investigation by a person who had custody or control of the thing immediately before it was so seized, or by someone acting on behalf of such a person, the officer shall—

(*a*) allow the person who made the request access to it under the supervision of a constable for the purpose of photographing or copying it; or
(*b*) photograph or copy it, or cause it to be photographed or copied.

(5) A constable may also photograph or copy, or have photographed or copied, anything which he has power to seize, without a request being made under subsection (4) above.

(6) Where anything is photographed or copied under subsection (4)(*b*) above, the photograph or copy shall be supplied to the person who made the request.

(7) The photographor copy shall be so supplied within a reasonable time from the making of the request.

(8) There is no duty under this section to grant access to, or to supply a photograph or copy of, anything if the officer in charge of the investigation for the purposes of which it was seized has reasonable grounds for believing that to do so would prejudice—

(*a*) that investigation;
(*b*) the investigating of an offence other than the offence for the purposes of investigating which the thing was seized; or
(*c*) any criminal proceedings which may be brought as a result of—
    (i) the investigation of which he is in charge; or
    (ii) any such investigation as is mentioned in paragraph (*b*) above.

22 Retention

(1) Subject to subsection (4) below, anything which has been seized by a constable or taken away by a constable following a requirement made by virtue of section 19 or 20 above may be retained so long as is necessary in all the circumstances.

(2) Without prejudice to the generality of subsection (1) above—

(*a*) anything seized for the purpose of a criminal investigation may be retained, except as provided by subsection (4) below,—
    (i) for use as evidence at a trial for an offence; or

      (ii) for forensic examination or for investigation in connection with an offence; and

   (*b*) anything may be retained in order to establish its lawful owner, where there are reasonable grounds for believing that it has been obtained in consequence of the commission of an offence.

(3) Nothing seized on the grounds that it may be used—

   (*a*) to cause physical injury to any person;

   (*b*) to damage property;

   (*c*) to interfere with evidence; or

   (*d*) to assist in escape from police detention or lawful custody,

may be retained when the person from whom it was seized is no longer in police detention or the custody of a court or is in the custody of a court but has been released on bail.

(4) Nothing may be retained for either of the purposes mentioned in subsection (2)(*a*) above if a photograph or copy would be sufficient for that purpose.

(5) Nothing in this section affects any power of a court to make an order under section 1 of the Police (Property) Act 1897.

23 Meaning of "premises", etc.

In this Act—

"premises" includes any place and, in particular, includes—

   (*a*) any vehicle, vessel, aircraft or hovercraft;

   (*b*) any offshore installation; and

   (*c*) any tent or movable structure; and

"offshore installation" has the meaning given to it by section 1 of the Mineral Workings (Offshore Installations) Act 1971.

PART III

Arrest

24 Arrest without warrant for arrestable offences

(1) The powers of summary arrest conferred by the following subsections shall apply—

   (*a*) to offences for which the sentence is fixed by law;

   (*b*) to offences for which a person of 21 years of age or over (not previously convicted) may be sentenced to imprisonment for a term of five years (or might be so sentenced but for the restrictions imposed by section 33 of the Magistrates' Courts Act 1980); and

   (*c*) to the offences to which subsection (2) below applies, and in this Act "arrestable offence" means any such offence.

(2) The offences to which this subsection applies are—

(*a*) offences for which a person may be arrested under the customs and excise Acts, as defined in section 1(1) of the Customs and Excise Management Act 1979;

(*b*) offences under the Official Secrets Act 1920 that are not arrestable offences by virtue of the term of imprisonment for which a person may be sentenced in respect of them;

(*bb*) offences under any provision of the Official Secrets Act 1989 except section 8(1), (4) or (5);

(*c*) offences under section 22 (causing prostitution of women) or 23 (procuration of girl under 21) of the Sexual Offences Act 1956;

(*d*) offences under section 12(1) (taking motor vehicle or other conveyance without authority, etc.) or 25(1) (going equipped for stealing, etc.) of the Theft Act 1968;

(*e*) any offence under the Football (Offences) Act 1991.

(3) Without prejudice to section 2 of the Criminal Attempts Act 1981, the powers of summary arrest conferred by the following subsections shall also apply to the offences of—

(*a*) conspiring to commit any of the offences mentioned in subsection (2) above;

(*b*) attempting to commit any such offence other than an offence under section 12(1) of the Theft Act 1968;

(*c*) inciting, aiding, abetting, counselling or procuring the commission of any such offences;

and such offences are also arrestable offences for the purposes of this Act.

(4) Any person may arrest without a warrant—

(*a*) anyone who is in the act of committing an arrestable offence;

(*b*) anyone whom he has reasonable grounds for suspecting to be committing such an offence.

(5) Where an arrestable offence has been committed, any person may arrest without a warrant—

(*a*) anyone who is guilty of the offence;

(*b*) anyone whom he has reasonable grounds for suspecting to be guilty of it.

(6) Where a constable has reasonable grounds for suspecting that an arrestable offence has been committed, he may arrest without a warrant anyone whom he has reasonable grounds for suspecting to be guilty of the offence.

(7) A constable may arrest without a warrant—

(*a*) anyone who is about to commit an arrestable offence;

(*b*) anyone whom he has reasonable grounds for suspecting to be about to commit an arrestable offence.

25 General arrest conditions

(1) Where a constable has reasonable grounds for suspecting that any offence which is not an arrestable offence has been committed or attempted, or is being committed or attempted, he may arrest the relevant person if it appears to him that service of a summons is impracticable or inappropriate because any of the general arrest conditions is satisfied.

(2) In this section "the relevant person" means any person whom the constable has reasonable grounds to suspect of having committed or having attempted to commit the offence or of being in the course of committing or attempting to commit it.

(3) The general arrest conditions are—

(*a*) that the name of the relevant person is unknown to, and cannot be readily ascertained by, the constable;

(*b*) that the constable has reasonable grounds for doubting whether a name furnished by the relevant person as his name is his real name;

(*c*) that—
  (i) the relevant person has failed to furnish a satisfactory address for service; or
  (ii) the constable has reasonable grounds for doubting whether an address furnished by the relevant person is a satisfactory address for service;

(*b*) that the constable has reasonable grounds for believing that arrest is necessary to prevent the relevant person—
  (i) causing physical injury to himself or any other person;
  (ii) suffering physical injury;
  (iii) causing loss of or damage to property;
  (iv) committing an offence against public decency; or
  (v) causing an unlawful obstruction of the highway;

(*e*) that the constable has reasonable grounds for believing that arrest is necessary to protect a child or other vulnerable person from the relevant person.

(4) For the purposes of subsection (3) above an address is a satisfactory address for service if it appears to the constable—

(*a*) that the relevant person will be at it for a sufficiently long period for it to be possible to serve him with a summons; or

(*b*) that some other person specified by the relevant person will accept service of a summons for the relevant person at it.

(5) Nothing in subsection (3)(*d*) above authorises the arrest of a person under sub-paragraph (iv) of that paragraph except where members of the public going about their normal business cannot reasonably be expected to avoid the person to be arrested.

(6) This section shall not prejudice any power of arrest conferred apart from this section.

26 Repeal of statutory powers of arrest without warrant or order

(1) Subject to subsection (2) below, so much of any Act (including a local Act) passed before this Act as enables a constable—

(*a*) to arrest a person for an offence without a warrant; or

(*b*) to arrest a person otherwise than for an offence without a warrant or an order of a court,

shall cease to have effect.

(2) Nothing in subsection (1) above affects the enactments specified in Schedule 2 to this Act.

27 Fingerprinting of certain offenders

(1) If a person—

(*a*) has been convicted of a recordable offence;

(*b*) has not at any time been in police detention for the offence; and

(*c*) has not had his fingerprints taken—

   (i) in the course of the investigation of the offence by the police; or

   (ii) since the conviction,

any constable may at any time not later than one month after the date of the conviction require him to attend a police station in order that his fingerprints may be taken.

(2) A requirement under subsection (1) above—

(*a*) shall give the person a period of at least 7 days within which he must so attend; and

(*b*) may direct him to so attend at a specified time of day or between specified times of day.

(3) Any constable may arrest without warrant a person who has failed to comply with a requirement under subsection (1) above.

(4) The Secretary of State may by regulations make provision for recording in national police records convictions for such offences as are specified in the regulations.

(5) Regulations under this section shall be made by statutory instrument and shall be subject to annulment in pursuance of a resolution of either House of Parliament.

28 Information to be given on arrest

(1) Subject to subsection (5) below, where a person is arrested, otherwise than by being informed that he is under arrest, the arrest is not lawful unless the person arrested is informed that he is under arrest as soon as is practicable after his arrest.

(2) Where a person is arrested by a constable, subsection (1) above applies regardless of whether the fact of the arrest is obvious.

(3) Subject to subsection (5) below, no arrest is lawful unless the person arrested is informed of the ground for the arrest at the time of, or as soon as is practicable after, the arrest.

(4) Where a person is arrested by a constable, subsection (3) above applies regardless of whether the ground for the arrest is obvious.

(5) Nothing in this section is to be taken to require a person to be informed—

(a) that he is under arrest; or
(b) of the ground for the arrest,

if it was not reasonably practicable for him to be so informed by reason of his having escaped from arrest before the information could be given.

29 Voluntary attendance at police station, etc.

Where for the purpose of assisting with an investigation a person attends voluntarily at a police station or at any other place where a constable is present or accompanies a constable to a police station or any such other place without having been arrested—

(a) he shall be entitled to leave at will unless he is placed under arrest;
(b) he shall be informed at once that he is under arrest if a decision is taken by a constable to prevent him from leaving at will.

30 Arrest elsewhere than at police station

(1) Subject to the following provisions of this section, where a person—

(a) is arrested by a constable for an offence; or
(b) is taken into custody by a constable after being arrested for an offence by a person other than a constable,

at any place other than a police station, he shall be taken to a police station by a constable as soon as practicable after the arrest.

(2) Subject to subsections (3) and (5) below, the police station to which an arrested person is taken under subsection (1) above shall be a designated police station.

(3) A constable to whom this subsection applies may take an arrested person to any police station unless it appears to the constable that it may be necessary to keep the arrested person in police detention for more than six hours.

(4) Subsection (3) above applies—

(a) to a constable who is working in a locality covered by a police station which is not a designated police station; and
(b) to a constable belonging to a body of constables maintained by an authority other than a police authority.

(5) Any constable may take an arrested person to any police station if—

(*a*) either of the following conditions is satisfied—
  (i) the constable has arrested him without the assistance of any other constable and no other constable is available to assist him; and
  (ii) the constable has taken him into custody from a person other than a constable without the assistance of any other constable and no other constable is available to assist him; and
(*b*) it appears to the constable that he will be unable to take the arrested person to a designated police station without the arrested person injuring himself, the constable or some other person.

(6) If the first police station to which an arrested person is taken after his arrest is not a designated police station, he shall be taken to a designated police station not more than six hours after his arrival at the first police station unless he is released previously.

(7) A person arrested by a constable at a place other than a police station shall be released if a constable is satisfied, before the person arrested reaches a police station, that there are no grounds for keeping him under arrest.

(8) A constable who releases a person under subsection (7) above shall record the fact that he has done so.

(9) The constable shall make the record as soon as is practicable after the release.

(10) Nothing in subsection (1) above shall prevent a constable delaying taking a person who has been arrested to a police station if the presence of that person elsewhere is necessary in order to carry out such investigations as it is reasonable to carry out immediately.

(11) Where there is delay in taking a person who has been arrested to a police station after his arrest, the reasons for the delay shall be recorded when he first arrives at a police station.

(12) Nothing in subsection (1) above shall be taken to affect—

(*a*) paragraphs 16(3) or 18(1) of Schedule 2 to the Immigration Act 1971;
(*b*) section 34(1) of the Criminal Justice Act 1972; or
(*c*) section 15(6) and (9) of the Prevention of Terrorism (Temporary Provisions) Act 1989 and paragraphs 7(4) and 8(4) and (5) of Schedule 2 and paragraphs 6(6) and 7(4) and (5) of Schedule 5 to that Act.

(13) Nothing in subsection (1) above shall be taken to affect paragraph 18(3) of Schedule 2 to the Immigration At 1971.

31 Arrest for further offence

Where—

(*a*) a person—
  (i) has been arrested for an offence; and

(ii) is at a police station in consequence of that arrest; and

(b) it appears to a constable that, if he were released from that arrest, he would be liable to arrest for some other offence,

he shall be arrested for that other offence.

32 Search upon arrest

(1) A constable may search an arrested person, in any case where the person to be searched has been arrested at a place other than a police station, if the constable has reasonable grounds for believing that the arrested person may present a danger to himself or others.

(2) Subject to subsections (3) to (5) below, a constable shall also have power in any such case—

(a) to search the arrested person for anything—
  (i) which he might use to assist him to escape from lawful custody; or
  (ii) which might be evidence relating to an offence; and

(b) to enter and search any premises in which he was when arrested or immediately before he was arrested for evidence relating to the offence for which he has been arrested.

(3) The power to search conferred by subsection (2) above is only a power to search to the extent that is reasonably required for the purpose of discovering any such thing or any such evidence.

(4) The powers conferred by this section to search a person are not to be construed as authorising a constable to require a person to remove any of his clothing in public other than an outer coat, jacket or gloves.

(5) A constable may not search a person in the exercise of the power conferred by subsection (2)(a) above unless he has reasonable grounds for believing that the person to be searched may have concealed on him anything for which a search is permitted under that paragraph.

(6) A constable may not search premises in the exercise of the power conferred by subsection (2)(b) above unless he has reasonable grounds for believing that there is evidence for which a search is permitted under that paragraph on the premises.

(7) In so far as the power of search conferred by subsection (2)(b) above relates to premises consisting of two or more separate dwellings, it is limited to a power to search—

(a) any dwelling in which the arrest took place or in which the person arrested was immediately before his arrest; and

(b) any parts of the premises which the occupier of any such dwelling uses in common with the occupiers of any other dwellings comprised in the premises.

(8) A constable searching a person in the exercise of the power conferred by

subsection (1) above may seize and retain anything he finds, if he has reasonable grounds for believing that the person searched might use it to cause physical injury to himself or to any other person.

(9) A constable searching a person in the exercise of the power conferred by subsection (2)(*a*) above may seize and retain anything he finds, other than an item subject to legal privilege, if he has reasonable grounds for believing—

(*a*) that he might use it to assist him to escape from lawful custody; or

(*b*) that it is evidence of an offence or has been obtained in consequence of the commission of an offence.

(10) Nothing in this section shall be taken to affect the power conferred by section 15(3), (4) and (5) of the Prevention of Terrorism (Temporary Provisions) Act 1989.

33 Execution of warrant not in possession of constable

. . . [This section amends the Magistrates' Courts Act 1980, s125].

PART IV DETENTION

DETENTION— CONDITIONS AND DURATION

34 Limitations on police detention

(1) A person arrested for an offence shall not be kept in police detention except in accordance with the provisions of this Part of this Act.

(2) Subject to subsection (3) below, if at any time a custody officer—

(*a*) becomes aware, in relation to any person in police detention, that the grounds for the detention of that person have ceased to apply; and

(*b*) is not aware of any other grounds on which the continued detention of that person could be justified under the provisions of this Part of this Act,

it shall be the duty of the custody officer, subject to subsection (4) below, to order his immediate release from custody.

(3) No person in police detention shall be released except on the authority of a custody officer at the police station where his detention was authorised or, if it was authorised at more than one station, a custody officer at the station where it was last authorised.

(4) A person who appears to the custody officer to have been unlawfully at large when he was arrested is not to be released under subsection (2) above.

(5) A person whose release is ordered under subsection (2) above shall be released without bail unless it appears to the custody officer—

(*a*) that there is need for further investigation of any matter in connection with which he was detained at the time during the period of his detention; or

(*b*) that proceedings may be taken against him in respect of any such matter,

and, if it so appears, he shall be released on bail.

(6) For the purposes of this Part of this Act a person arrested under section 6(5) of the Road Traffic Act 1988 is arrested for an offence.

35 Designated police stations

(1) The chief officer of police for each police area shall designate the police stations in his area which, subject to section 30(3) and (5) above, are to be the stations in that area to be used for the purpose of detaining arrested persons.

(2) A chief officer's duty under subsection (1) above is to designate police stations appearing to him to provide enough accommodation for that purpose.

(3) Without prejudice to section 12 of the Interpretation Act 1978 (continuity of duties) a chief officer—

(*a*) may designate a station which was not previously designated; and

(*b*) may direct that a designation of a station previously made shall cease to operate.

(4) In this Act "designated police station" means a police station designated under this section.

36 Custody officers at police stations

(1) One or more custody officers shall be appointed for each designated police station.

(2) A custody officer for a designated police station shall be appointed—

(*a*) by the chief officer of police for the area in which the designated police station is situated; or

(*b*) by such other police officer as the chief officer of police for that area may direct.

(3) No officer may be appointed a custody officer unless he is of at least the rank of sergeant.

(4) An officer of any rank may perform the functions of a custody officer at a designated police station if a custody officer isnot readily available to perform them.

(5) Subject to the following provisions of this section and to section 39(2) below, none of the functions of a custody officer in relation to a person shall be performed by an officer who at the time when the function falls to be performed

is involved in the investigation of an offence for which that person is in police detention at that time.

(6) Nothing in subsection (5) above is to be taken to prevent a custody officer—

(*a*) performing any function assigned to custody officers—
   (i) by this Act; or
   (ii) by a code of practice issued under this Act;
(*b*) carrying out the duty imposed on custody officers by section 39 below;
(*c*) doing anything in connection with the identification of a suspect; or
(*d*) doing anything under sections 7 and 8 of the Road Traffic Act 1988.

(7) Where an arrested person is taken to a police station which is not a designated police station, the functions in relation to him which at a designated police station would be the functions of a custody officer shall be performed—

(*a*) by an officer who is not involved in the investigation of an offence for which he is in police detention, if such an officer is readily available; and
(*d*) if no such officer is readily available, by the officer who took him to the station or any other officer.

(8) References to a custody officer in the following provisions of this Act include references to an officer other than a custody officer who is performing the functions of a custody officer by virtue of subsection (4) or (7) above.

(9) Where by virtue of subsection (7) above an officer of a force maintained by a police authority who took an arrested person to a police station is to perform the functions of a custody officer in relation to him, the officer shall inform an officer who—

(*a*) is attached to a designated police station; and
(*b*) is of at least the rank of inspector,

that he is to do so.

(10) The duty imposed by subsection (9) above shall be performed as soon as it is practicable to perform it.

37 Duties of custody officer before charge

(1) Where—

(*a*) a person is arrested for an offence—
   (i) without a warrant; or
   (ii) under a warrant not endorsed for bail, or
(*b*) a person returns to a police station to answer to bail,

the custody officer at each police station where he is detained after his arrest shall determine whether he has before him sufficient evidence to charge that person with the offence for which he was arrested and may detain him at the police station for such period as is necessary to enable him to do so.

(2) If the custody officer determines that he does not have such evidence before

him, the person arrested shall be released either on bail or without bail, unless the custody officer has reasonable grounds for believing that his detention without being charged is necessary to secure or preserve evidence relating to an offence for which he is under arrest or to obtain such evidence by questioning him.

(3) If the custody officer has reasonable grounds for so believing, he may authorise the person arrested to be kept in police detention.

(4) Where a custody officer authorises a person who has not been charged to be kept in police detention, he shall, as soon as is practicable, make a written record of the grounds for the detention.

(5) Subject to subsection (6) below, the written record shall be made in the presence of the person arrested who shall at that time by informed by the custody officer of the grounds for his detention.

(6) Subsection (5) above shall not apply where the person arrested is, at the time when the written record is made—

(*a*) incapable of understanding what is said to him;
(*b*) violent or likely to become violent; or
(*c*) in urgent need of medical attention.

(7) Subject to section 41(7) below, if the custody officer determines that he has before him sufficient evidence to charge the person arrested with the offence for which he was arrested, the person arrested—

(*a*) shall be charged; or
(*b*) shall be released without charge, either on bail or without bail.

(8) Where—

(*a*) a person is released under subsection (7)(*b*) above; and
(*b*) at the time of his release a decision whether he should be prosecuted for the offence for which he was arrested has not been taken,

if shall be the duty of the custody officer so to inform him.

(9) If the person arrested is not in a fit state to be dealt with under subsection (7) above, he may be kept in police detention until he is.

(10) The duty imposed on the custody officer under subsection (1) above shall be carried out by him as soon as practicable after the person arrested arrives at the police station or, in the case of a person arrested at the police station, as soon as practicable after the arrest.

(11) [Repealed by Criminal Justice Act 1991.]

(15) In this Part of this Act—

"arrested juvenile" means a person arrested with or without a warrant who appears to be under the age of 17;

"endorsed for bail" means endorsed with a direction for bail in accordance with section 117(2) of the Magistrates' Courts Act 1980.

38 Duties of custody officer after charge

(1) Where a person arrested for an offence otherwise than under a warrant endorsed for bail is charged with an offence, the custody officer shall order his release from police detention, either on bail or without bail, unless—

 (*a*) if the person arrested is not an arrested juvenile—
   (i) his name or address cannot be ascertained or the custody officer has reasonable grounds for doubting whether a name or address furnished by him as his name or address is his real name or address;
   (ii) the custody officer has reasonable grounds for believing that the detention of the person arrested is necessary for his own protection or to prevent him from causing physical injury to any other person or from causing loss of or damage to property; or
   (iii) the custody officer has reasonable grounds for believing that the person arrested will fail to appear in court to answer to bail or that his detention is necessary to prevent him from interfering with the administration of justice or with the investigation of offences or of a particular offence;
 (*b*) if he is an arrested juvenile—
   (i) any of the requirements of paragraph (a) above is satisfied; or
   (ii) the custody officer has reasonable grounds for believing that he ought to be detained in his own interests.

(2) If the release of a person arrested is not required by subsection (1) above, the custody officer may authorise him to be kept in police detention.

(3) Where a custody officer authorises a person who has been charged to be kept in police detention, he shall, as soon as practicable, make a written record of the grounds for the detention.

(4) Subject to subsection (5) below, the written record shall be made in the presence of the person charged who shall at that time be informed by the custody officer of the grounds for his detention.

(5) Subsection (4) above shall not apply where the person charged is, at the time when the written record is made—

 (*a*) incapable of understanding what is said to him;
 (*b*) violent or likely to become violent; or
 (*c*) in urgent need of medical attention.

(6) Where a custody officer authorises an arrested juvenile to be kept in police detention under subsection (1) above, the custody officer shall, unless he certifies —

 (*a*) that, by reason of such circumstances as are specified in the certificate, it is impracticable for him to do so; or (*b*) in the case of an arrested juvenile who has attained the age of 15 years, that no secure accommodation is available and that keeping him in other local authority accommodation would not be adequate to protect the public from serious harm from him,

secure that the arrested juvenile is moved to local authority accommodation.

(6A) In this section —

"local authority accommodation" means accommodation provided by or on behalf of a local authority (within the meaning of the Children Act 1989);
"secure accommodation" means accommodation provided for the purpose of restricting liberty;
"sexual offence" and "violent offence" have the same meanings as in Part I of the Criminal Justice Act 1991;

and any reference, in relation to an arrested juvenile charged with a violent or sexual offence, to protecting the public from serious harm from him shall be construed as a reference to protecting members of the public from death or serious personal injury, whether physical or psychological, occasioned by further such offences committed by him.

(6B) Where an arrested juvenile is moved to local authority accommodation under subsection (6) above, it shall be lawful for any person acting on behalf of the authority to detain him.

(7) A certificate made under subsection (6) above in respect of an arrested juvenile shall be produced to the court before which he is first brought thereafter.

(8) In this Part of this Act "local authority" has the same meaning as in the Children Act 1989.

39 Responsibilities in relation to persons detained

(1) Subject to subsections (2) and (4) below, it shall be the duty of the custody officer at a police station to ensure—

(*a*) that all persons in police detention at that station are treated in accordance with this Act and any code of practice issued under it and relating to the treatment of persons in police detention; and
(*b*) that all matters relating to such persons which are required by this Act or by such codes of practice to be recorded are recorded in the custody records relating to such persons.

(2) If the custody officer, in accordance with any code of practice issued under this Act, transfers or permits the transfer of a person in police detention—

(*a*) to the custody of a police officer investigating an offence for which that person is in police detention; or
(*b*) to the custody of an officer who has charge of that person outside the police station,

the custody officer shall cease in relation to that person to be subject to the duty imposed on him by subsection (1)(*a*) above; and it shall be the duty of the officer to whom the transfer is made to ensure that he is treated in accordance with the provisions of this Act and of any such codes of practice as are mentioned in subsection (1) above.

(3) If the person detained is subsequently returned to the custody of the custody officer, it shall be the duty of the officer investigating the offence to report to the custody officer as to the manner in which this section and the codes of practice have been complied with while that person was in his custody.

(4) If an arrested juvenile is moved to local authority accommodation under section 38(6) above, the custody officer shall cease in relation to that person to be subject to the duty imposed on him by subsection (1) above.

(5) [Repealed by Children Act 1989.]

(6) Where—

(*a*) an officer of higher rank than the custody officer gives directions relating to a person in police detention; and
(*b*) the directions are at variance—
  (i) with any decision made or action taken by the custody officer in the performance of a duty imposed on him under this Part of this Act; or
  (ii) with any decision or action which would but for the directions have been made or taken by him in the performance of such a duty,

the custody officer shall refer the matter at once to an officer of the rank of superintendent or above who is responsible for the police station for which the custody officer is acting as custody officer.

40 Review of police detention

(1) Reviews of the detention of each person in police detention in connection with the investigation of an offence shall be carried out periodically in accordance with the following provisions of this section—

(*a*) in the case of a person who has been arrested and charged, by the custody officer, and
(*b*) in the case of a person who has been arrested but not charged, by an officer of at least the rank of inspector who has not been directly involved in the investigation.

(2) The officer to whom it falls to carry out a review is referred to in this section as a "review officer".

(3) Subject to subsection (4) below—

(*a*) the first review shall be not later than six hours after the detention was first authorised;
(*b*) the second review shall be not later than nine hours after the first;
(*c*) subsequent reviews shall be at intervals of not more than nine hours.

(4) A review may be postponed—

(*a*) if, having regard to all the circumstances prevailing at the latest time for it specified in subsection (3) above, it is not practicable to carry out the review at that time;

(*b*) without prejudice to the generality of paragraph (a) above—

    (i) if at that time the person in detention is being questioned by a police officer and the review is satisfied that an interruption of the questioning for the purpose of carrying out the review would prejudice the investigation in connection with which he is being questioned; or

    (ii) if at that time no review officer is readily available.

(5) If a review is postponed under subsection (4) above it shall be carried out as soon as practicable after the latest time specified for it in subsection (3) above.

(6) If a review is carried out after postponement under subsection (4) above, the fact that it was so carried out shall not affect any requirement of this section as to the time at which any subsequent review is to be carried out.

(7) The review officer shall record the reasons for any postponement of a review in the custody record.

(8) Subject to subsection (9) below, where the person whose detention is under review has not been charged before the time of the review, section 37(1) to (6) above shall have effect in relation to him, but with the substitution—

(*a*) of references to the person whose detention is under review for references to the person arrested; and

(*b*) of references to the review officer for references to the custody officer.

(9) Where a person has been kept in police detention by virtue of section 38(9) above, section 37(1) to (6) shall not have effect in relation to him but it shall be the duty of the review officer to determine whether he is yet in a fit state.

(10) Where the person whose detention is under review has been charged before the time of the review, section 38(1) to (6) above shall have effect in relation to him, with the substitution of references to the person whose detention is under review for references to the person arrested.

(11) Where—

(*a*) an officer of higher rank than the review officer gives directions relating to a person in police detention; and

(*b*) the directions are at variance—

    (i) with any decision made or action taken by the review officer in the performance of a duty imposed on him under this Part of this Act; or

    (ii) with any decision or action which would but for the directions have been made or taken by him in the performance of such a duty,

the review officer shall refer the matter at once to an officer of the rank of superintendent or above who is responsible for the police station for which the review officer is acting as review officer in connection with the detention.

(12) Before determining whether to authorise a person's continued detention the review officer shall give—

(*a*) that person (unless he is asleep); or

(*b*) any solicitor representing him who is available at the time of the review,

an opportunity to make representations to him about the detention.

(13) Subject to subsection (14) below, the person whose detention is under review of his solicitor may make representations under subsection (12) above either orally or in writing.

(14) The review officer may refuse to hear oral representations from the person whose detention is under review if he considers that he is unfit to make such representations by reason of his condition or behaviour.

41 Limits on period of detention without charge

(1) Subject to the following provisions of this section and to sections 42 and 43 below, a person shall not be kept in police detention for more than 24 hours without being charged.

(2) The time from which the period of detention of a person is to be calculated (in this Act referred to as "the relevant time")—

(*a*) in the case of a person to whom this paragraph applies, shall be—
   (i)   the time at which that person arrives at the relevant police station; or
   (ii) the time 24 hours after the time of that persons' arrest, whichever is the earlier;

(*b*) in the case of a person arrested outside England and Wales, shall be—
   (i)   the time at which that person arrives at the first police station to which he is taken in the police area in England or Wales in which the offence for which he was arrested is being investigated; or
   (ii) the time 24 hours after the time of that persons' entry into England and Wales,

whichever is the earlier;

(*c*) in the case of a person who—
   (i)   attends voluntarily at a police station; or
   (ii) accompanies a constable to a police station without having been arrested,

and is arrested at the police station, the time of his arrest;

(*d*) in any other case, except where subsection (5) below applies, shall be the time at which the person arrested arrives at the first police station to which he is taken after his arrest.

(3) Subsection (2)(*a*) above applies to a person if—

(*a*) his arrest is sought in one police area in England and Wales;

(*b*) he is arrested in another police area; and

(*c*) he is not questioned in the area in which he is arrested in order to obtain evidence in relation to an offence for which he is arrested;

and in sub-paragraph (i) of that paragraph "the relevant police station" means the first police station to which he is taken inthe police area in which his arrest was sought.

(4) Subsection (2) above shall have effect inrelation to a person arrested under section 31 above as if every reference in it to his arrest or his being arrested were a reference to his arrest or his being arrested for the offence for which he was originally arrested.

(5) If—

(*a*) a person is in police detention in a police area in England and Wales ("the first area"); and

(*b*) his arrest for an offence is sought in some other police area in England and Wales ("the second area"); and

(*c*) he is taken to the second area for the purposes of investigating that offence, without being questioned in the first area in order to obtain evidence in relation to it,

the relevant time shall be—

  (i) the time 24 hours after he leaves the place where he is detained in the first area; or

  (ii) the time at which he arrives at the first police station to which he is taken in the second area,

whichever is the earlier.

(6) When a person who is in police detention is removed to hospital because he is in need of medical treatment, any time during which he is being questioned in hospital or on the way there or back by a police officer for the purpose of obtaining evidence relating to an offence shall be included in any period which falls to be calculated for the purposes of this Part of this Act, but any other time while he is in hospital or on his way there or back shall not be so included.

(7) Subject to subsection (8) below, a person who at the expiry of 24 hours after the relevant time is in police detention and has not been charged shall be released at that time either on bail or without bail.

(8) Subsection (7) above does not apply to a person whose detention for more than 24 hours after the relevant time has been authorised or is otherwise permitted in accordance with section 42 or 43 below.

(9) A person released under subsection (7) above shall not be re-arrested without a warrant for the offence for which he was previously arrested unless new evidence justifying a further arrest has come to light since his release.

42 Authorisation of continued detention

(1) Where a police officer of the rank of superintendent or above who is re-

sponsible for the police station at which a person isdetained has reasonable grounds for believing that—

    (*a*) the detention of that person without charge is necessary to secure or preserve evidence relating to an offence for which he is under arrest or to obtain such evidence by questioning him;

    (*b*) an offence for which he is under arrest is a serious arrestable offence; and

    (*c*) the investigation is being conducted diligently and expeditiously,

he may authorise the keeping of that person in police detention for a period expiring at or before 36 hours after the relevant time.

(2) Where an officer such as is mentioned in subsection (1) above has authorised the keeping of a person in police detention for a period expiring less than 36 hours after the relevant time, such an officer may authorise the keeping of that person in police detention for a further period expiring not more than 36 hours after that time if the conditions specified in subsection (1) above are still satisfied when he gives the authorisation.

(3) If it is proposed to transfer a person in police detention to another police area, the officer determining whether or not to authorise keeping him in detention under subsection (1) above shall have regard to the distance and the time the journey would take.

(4) No authorisation under subsection (1) above shall be given in respect of any person—

    (*a*) more than 24 hours after the relevant time; or

    (*b*) before the second review of his detention under section 40 above has been carried out.

(5) Where an officer authorises the keeping of a person in police detention under subsection (1) above, it shall be his duty—

    (*a*) to inform that person of the grounds for his continued detention; and

    (*b*) to record the grounds in that person's custody record.

(6) Before determining whether to authorise the keeping of a person in detention under subsection (1) or (2) above, an officer shall give—

    (*a*) that person; or

    (*b*) any solicitor representing him who is available at the time when it falls to the officer to determine whether to give the authorisation,

an opportunity to make representations to him about the detention.

(7) Subject to subsection (8) below, the person in detention or his solicitor may make representations under subsection (6) above either orally or in writing.

(8) The officer to whom it falls to determine whether to give the authorisation may refuse to hear oral representations from the person in detention if he considers that he is unfit to make such representations by reason of his condition or behaviour.

(9) Where—

    (*a*) an officer authorises the keeping of a person in detention under subsection (1) above; and

    (*b*) at the time of the authorisation he has not yet exercised a right conferred on him by section 56 or 58 below,

the officer—

      (i)   shall inform him of that right;

    (ii) shall decide whether he should be permitted to exercise it;

   (iii) shall record the decision in his custody record; and

   (iv) if the decision is to refuse to permit the exercise of the right, shall also record the grounds for the decision in that record.

(10) Where an officer has authorised the keeping of a person who has not been charged in detention under subsection (1) or (2) above, he shall be released from detention, either on bail or without bail, not later than 36 hours after the relevant time, unless—

    (*a*) he has been charged with an offence, or

    (*b*) his continued detention is authorised or otherwise permitted in accordance with section 43 below.

(11) A person released under subsection (10) above shall not be re-arrested without a warrant for the offence for which he was previously arrested unless new evidence justifying a further arrest has come to light since his release.

43 Warrants of further detention

(1) Where, on an application on oath made by a constable and supported by an information, a magistrates' court is satisfied that there are reasonable grounds for believing that the further detention of the person to whom the application relates is justified, it may issue a warrant of further detention authorising the keeping of that person in police detention.

(2) A court may not hear an application for a warrant of further detention unless the person to whom the application relates—

    (*a*) has been furnished with a copy of the information; and

    (*b*) has been brought before the court for the hearing.

(3) The person to whom the application relates shall be entitled to be legally represented at the hearing and, if he is not so represented but wishes to be so represented—

    (*a*) the court shall adjourn the hearing to enable him to obtain representation; and

    (*b*) he may be kept in police detention during the adjournment.

(4) A person's further detention is only justified for the purposes of this section or section 44 below if—

    (*a*) his detention without charge is necessary to secure or preserve evidence relating to an offence for which he is under arrest or to obtain such evidence by questioning him;

(*b*) an offence for which he is under arrest is a serious arrestable offence; and

(*c*) the investigation is being conducted diligently and expeditiously.

(5) Subject to subsection (7) below, an application for a warrant of further detention may be made—

(*a*) at any time before the expiry of 36 hours after the relevant time; or

(*b*) in a case where—

    (i) it is not practicable for the magistrates' court to which the application will be made to sit at the expiry of 36 hours after the relevant time; but

    (ii) the court will sit during the 6 hours following the end of that period, at any time before the expiry of the said 6 hours.

(6) In a case to which subsection (5)(*b*) above applies—

(*a*) the person to whom the application relates may be kept in police detention until the application is heard; and

(*b*) the custody officer shall make a note in that person's custody record—

    (i) of the fact that he was kept in police detention for more than 36 hours after the relevant time; and

    (ii) of the reason why he was so kept.

(7) If—

(*a*) an application for a warrant of further detention is made after the expiry of 36 hours after the relevant time; and

(*b*) it appears to the magistrates' court that it would have been reasonable for the police to make it before the expiry of that period,

the court shall dismiss the application.

(8) Where on an application such as is mentioned in subsection (1) above a magistrates' court is not satisfied that there are reasonable grounds for believing that the further detention of the person to whom the application relates is justified, it shall be its duty—

(*a*) to refuse the application; or

(*b*) to adjourn the hearing of it until a time not later than 36 hours after the relevant time.

(9) The person to whom the application relates may be kept in police detention during the adjournment.

(10) A warrant of further detention shall—

(*a*) state the time at which it is issued;

(*b*) authorise the keeping in police detention of the person to whom it relates for the period stated in it.

(11) Subject to subsection (12)below, the period stated in a warrant of further detention shall be such period as the magistrates' court thinks fit, having regard to the evidence before it.

(12) The period shall not be longer than 36 hours.

(13) If it is proposed to transfer a person in police detention to a police area other than that in which he is detained when the application for a warrant of further detention is made, the court hearing the application shall have regard to the distance and the time of the journey would take.

(14) Any information submitted in support of an application under this section shall state—

(a) the nature of the offence for which the person to whom the application relates has been arrested;

(b) the general nature of the evidence on which that person was arrested;

(c) what inquiries relating to the offence have been made by the police and what further inquiries are proposed by them;

(d) the reasons for believing the continued detention of that person to be necessary for the purposes of such further inquiries.

(15) Where an application under this section is refused, the person to whom the application relates shall forthwith be charged or, subject to subsection (16) below, released, either on bail or without bail.

(16) A person need not be released under subsection (15) above—

(a) before the expiry of 24 hours after the relevant time; or

(b) before the expiry of any longer period for which his continued detention is or has been authorised under section 42 above.

(17) Where an application under this section is refused, no further application shall be made under this section in respect of the person to whom the refusal relates, unless supported by evidence which has come to light since the refusal.

(18) Where a warrant of further detention is issued, the person to whom it relates shall be released from police detention, either on bail or without bail, upon or before the expiry of the warrant unless he is charged.

(19) A person released under subsection (18) above shall not be re-arrested without a warrant for the offence for which he was previously arrested unless new evidence justifying a further arrest has come to light since his release.

44 Extension of warrants of further detention

(1) On an application on oath made by a constable and supported by an information a magistrates' court may extend a warrant of further detention issued under section 43 above if it is satisfied that there are reasonable grounds for believing that the further detention of the person to whom the application relates is justified.

(2) Subject to subsection (3) below, the period for which a warrant of further detention may be extended shall be such period as the court thinks fit, having regard to the evidence before it.

(3) The period shall not—

(*a*) be longer than 36 hours; or
(*b*) end later than 96 hours after the relevant time.

(4) Where a warrant of further detention has been extended under subsection (1) above, or further extended under this subsection, for a period ending before 96 hours after the relevant time, on an application such as is mentioned in that subsection a magistrates' court may further extend the warrant if it is satisfied as there mentioned; and subsections (2) and (3)above apply to such further extensions as they apply to extensions under subsection (1) above.

(5) A warrant of further detention shall, if extended or further extended under this section, be endorsed with a note of the period of the extension.

(6) Subsections (2), (3), and (14) of section 43 above shall apply to an application made under this section as they apply to an application made under that section.

(7) Where an application under this section is refused, the person to whom the application relates shall forthwith be charged or, subject to subsection (8) below, released, either on bail or without bail.

(8) A person need not be released under subsection (7) above before the expiry of any period for which a warrant of further detention issued in relation to him has been extended or further extended on an earlier application made under this section.

45 Detention before charge — supplementary

(1) In sections 43 and 44 of this Act "magistrates' court" means a court consisting of two or more justices of the peace sitting otherwise than in open court.

(2) Any reference in this Part of this Act to a period of time or a time of day is to be treated as approximate only.

46 Detention after charge

(1) Where a person—

(*a*) is charged with an offence; and
(*b*) after being charged—
　　(i) is kept in police detention; or
　　(ii) is detained by a local authority in pursuance of arrangements made under section 38(6) above,

he shall be brought before a magistrates' court in accordance with the provisions of this section.

(2) If he is to be brought before a magistrates' court for the petty sessions area in which the police station at which he was charged is situated, he shall be brought

before such a court as soon as is practicable and in any event not later than the first sitting after he is charged with the offence.

(3) If no magistrates' court for that area is due to sit either on the day on which he is charged or on the next day, the custody officer for the police station at which he was charged shall inform the clerk to the justices for the area that there is a person in the area to whom subsection (2) above applies.

(4) If the person charged is to be brought before a magistrates' court for a petty sessions area other than that in which the police station at which he was charged is situated, he shall be removed to that area as soon as is practicable and brought before such a court as soon as is practicable after his arrival in the area and in any event not later than the first sitting of a magistrates' court for that area after his arrival in the area.

(5) If no magistrates' court for that area is due to sit either on the day on which he arrives in the area or on the next day—

(*a*) he shall be taken to a police station in the area; and

(*b*) the custody officer at that station shall inform the clerk to the justices for the area that there is a person in the area to whom subsection (4) applies.

(6) Subject to subsection (8) below, where a clerk to the justices for a petty sessions area has been informed—

(*a*) under subsection (3) above that there is a person in the area to whom subsection (2) above applies; or

(*b*) under subsection (5) above that there is a person in the area to whom subsection (4) above applies,

the clerk shall arrange for a magistrates' court to sit not later than the day next following the relevant day.

(7) In this section " the relevant day"—

(*a*) in relation to a person who is to be brought before a magistrates' court for the petty sessions area in which the police station at which he was charged is situated, means the day on which he was charged; and

(*b*) in relation to a person who is to be brought before a magistrates' court for any other petty sessions area, means the day on which he arrives in the area.

(8) Where the day next following the relevant day is Christmas Day, Good Friday or a Sunday, the duty of the clerk under subsection (6) above is a duty to arrange for a magistrates' court to sit not later than the first day after the relevant day which is not one of those days.

(9) Nothing in this section requires a person who is in hospital to be brought before a court if he is not well enough.

47 Bail after arrest

(1) Subject to subsection (2) below, a release on bail of a person under this Part of this Act shall be a release on bail granted in accordance with the Bail Act 1976.

(2) Nothing in the Bail Act 1976 shall prevent the re-arrest without warrant of a person released on bail subject to a duty to attend at a police station if new evidence justifying a further arrest has come to light since his release.

(3) Subject to subsection (4) below, in this Part of this Act references to "bail" are references to bail subject to a duty—

(*a*) to appear before a magistrates' court at such time and such place; or
(*b*) to attend at such police station at such time,

as the custody officer may appoint.

(4) Where a custody officer has granted bail to a person subject to a duty to appear at a police station, the custody officer may give notice in writing to that person that his attendance at the police station is not required.

(5) Where a person arrested for an offence who was released on bail subject to a duty to attend at a police station so attends, he may be detained without charge in connection with that offence only if the custody officer at the police station has reasonable grounds for believing that his detention is necessary—

(*a*) to secure or preserve evidence relating to the offence; or
(*b*) to obtain such evidence by questioning him.

(6) Where a person is detained under subsection (5) above, any time during which he was in police detention prior to being granted bail shall be included as part of any period which falls to be calculated under this Part of this Act.

(7) Where a person who was released on bail subject to a duty to attend at a police station is re-arrested, the provisions of this Part of this Act shall apply to him as they apply to a person arrested for the first time.

(8) . . . [amends the Magistrates' Courts Act 1980, ss43, 117].

48 Remands to police detention

. . . [amends the Magistrates' Courts, Act 1980, s128].

49 Police detention to count towards custodial sentence

. . . [amends the Criminal Justice Act 1967, s67].

50 Records of detention

(1) Each police force shall keep written records showing on an annual basis—

(*a*) the number of persons kept in police detention for more than 24 hours and subsequently released without charge;
(*b*) the number of applications for warrants of further detention and the results of the applications; and
(*c*) in relation to each warrant of further detention—
(i) the period of further detention authorised by it;

(ii) the period which the person named in it spent in police detention on its authority; and

(iii) whether he was charged or released without charge.

(2) Every annual report—

(*a*) under section 12 of the Police Act 1964; or

(*b*) made by the Commissioner of Police of the Metropolis,

shall contain information about the matters mentioned in subsection (1) above in respect of the period to which the report relates.

51 Savings

Nothing in this Part of this Act shall affect—

(*a*) the powers conferred on immigration officers by section 4 of and Schedule 2 to the Immigration Act 1971 (administrative provisions as to control on entry etc.);

(*b*) the powers conferred by or by virtue of section 14 of the Prevention of Terrorism (Temporary Provisions) Act 1989 or Schedule 2 or 5 to that Act (powers of arrest and detention and control of entry and procedure for removal);

(*c*) any duty of a police officer under—

(i) section 129, 190 or 202 of the Army Act 1955 (duties of governors of prisons and others to receive prisoners, deserters, absentees and persons under escort);

(ii) section 129, 190 or 202 of the Air Force Act 1955 (duties of governors of prisons and others to receive prisoners, deserters, absentees and persons under escort);

(iii) section 107 of the Naval Discipline Act 1957 (duties of governors of civil prisons, etc.); or

(iv) paragraph 5 of Schedule 5 to the Reserve Forces Act 1980 (duties of governors of civil prisons); or

(*d*) any right of a person in police detention to apply for a writ of habeas corpus or other prerogative remedy.

52 Children

[Repealed by Children Act 1989.]

PART V

QUESTIONING AND TREATMENT OF PERSONS BY POLICE

53 Abolition of certain powers of constables to search persons

(1) Subject to subsection (2) below, there shall cease to have effect any Act (including a local Act) passed before this Act in so far as it authorises—

(*a*) any search by a constable of a person in police detention at a police station;

or

(*b*) an intimate search of a person by a constable;

and any rule of common law which authorises a search such as is mentioned in paragraph (*a*) or (*b*) above is abolished.

(2) . . . [repealed].

54 Searches of detained persons

(1) The custody officer at a police station shall ascertain and record or cause to be recorded everything which a person has with him when he is—

(*a*) brought to the station after being arrested elsewhere or after being committed to custody by an order or sentence of a court; or

(*b*) arrested at the station or detained there under section 47(5) above.

(2) In the case of an arrested person the record shall be made as part of his custody record.

(3) Subject to subsection (4) below, a custody officer may seize and retain any such thing or cause any such thing to be seized and retained.

(4) Clothes and personal effects may only be seized if the custody officer—

(*a*) believes that the person from whom they are seized may use them—
   (i) to cause physical injury to himself or any other person;
   (ii) to damage property;
   (iii) to interfere with evidence; or
   (iv) to assist him to escape; or

(*b*) has reasonable grounds for believing that they may be evidence relating to an offence.

(5) Where anything is seized, the person from whom it is seized shall be told the reason for the seizure unless he is—

(*a*) violent or likely to become violent; or

(*b*) incapable of understanding what is said to him.

(6) Subject to subsection (7) below, a person may be searched if the custody officer considers it necessary to enable him to carry out his duty under subsection (1) above and to the extent that the custody officer considers necessary for that purpose.

(6A) A person who is in custody at a police station or is in police detention otherwise than at a police station may at any time be searched in order to ascertain whether he has with him anything which he could use for any of the purposes specified in subsection (4)(*a*) above.

(6B) Subject to subsection (6C) below, a constable may seize and retain, or cause to be seized and retained, anything found on such a search.

(6C) A constable may only seize clothes and person effects in the circumstances specified in subsection (4) above.

(7) An intimate search may not be conducted under this section.

(8) A search under this section shall be carried out by a constable.

(9) The constable carrying out a search shall be of the same sex as the person searched.

55 Intimate searches

(1) Subject to the following provisions of this section, if an officer of at least the rank of superintendent has reasonable grounds for believing—

    (*a*) that a person who has been arrested and is in police detention may have concealed on him anything which—
        (i) he could use to cause physical injury to himself or others; and
        (ii) he might so use while he is in police detention or in the custody of a court; or

    (*b*) that such person—
        (i) may have a Class A drug concealed on him;and
        (ii) was in possession of it with the appropriate criminal intent before his arrest,

he may authorise an intimate search of that person.

(2) An officer may not authorise an intimate search of a person for anything unless he has reasonable grounds for believing that it cannot be found without his being intimately searched.

(3) An officer may give an authorisation under subsection (1) above orally or in writing, but if he gives it orally, he shall confirm it in writing as soon as is practicable.

(4) An intimate search which is only a drug offence search shall be by way of examination by a suitably qualified person.

(5) Except as provided by subsection (4) above, an intimate search shall be by way of examination by a suitably qualified person unless an officer of at least the rank of superintendent considers that this is not practicable.

(6) An intimate search which is not carried out as mentioned in subsection (5) above shall be carried out by a constable.

(7) A constable may not carry out an intimate search of a person of the opposite sex.

(8) No intimate search may be carried out except—

    (*a*) at a police station;
    (*b*) at a hospital;
    (*c*) at a registered medical practitioner's surgery; or
    (*d*) at some other place used for medical purposes.

(9) An intimate search which is only a drug offence search may not be carried out at a police station.

(10) If an intimate search of a person is carried out, the custody record relating to him shall state—

(a) which parts of his body were searched; and

(b) why they were searched.

(11) The information required to be recorded by subsection (10) above shall be recorded as soon as practicable after the completion of the search.

(12) The custody officer at a police station may seize and retain anything which is found on an intimate search of a person, or cause any such thing to be seized and retained—

(a) if he believes that the person from whom it is seized may use it—

   (i)   to cause physical injury to himself or any other person;

   (ii) to damage property;

   (iii) to interfere with evidence; or

   (iv) to assist him to escape; or

(b)   if he has reasonable grounds for believing that it may be evidence relating to an offence.

(13) Where anything is seized under this section, the person from whom it is seized shall be told the reason for the seizure unless he is—

(a) violent or likely to become violent; or

(b) incapable of understanding what is said to him.

(14) Every annual report—

(a) under section 12 of the Police Act 1964; or

(b) made by the Commissioner of Police of the Metropolis,

shall contain information about searches under this section which have been carried out in the area to which the report relates during the period to which it relates.

(15) The information about such searches shall include—

(a) the total number of searches;

(b) the number of searches conducted by way of examination by a suitably qualified person;

(c) the number of searches not so conducted but conducted in the presence of such a person; and

(d) the result of the searches carried out.

(16) The information shall also include, as separate items—

(a) the total number of drug offence searches; and

(b) the result of those searches.

(17) In this section—

"the appropriate criminal intent" means an intent to commit an offence under—

  (a) section 5(3) of the Misuse of Drugs Act 1971 (possession of controlled drug with intent to supply to another); or
  (b) section 68(2) of the Customs and Excise Management Act 1979 (exportation etc. with intent to evade a prohibition or restriction);

"Class A drug" has the meaning assigned to it by section 2(1)(b) of the Misuse of Drugs Act 1971;

"drug offence search" means an intimate search for a Class A drugwhich an officer has authorised by virtue of subsection (1)(b) above;and

"suitable qualified person" means—

  (a) a registered medical practitioner, or
  (b) a registered nurse.

56 Right to have someone informed when arrested

(1) Where a person has been arrested and is being held in custody in a police station or other premises, he shall be entitled, if he so requests, to have one friend or relative or other person who is known to him or who is likely to take an interest in his welfare told, as soon as is practicable except to the extent that delay is permitted by this section, that he has been arrested and is being detained there.

(2) Delay is only permitted—

  (a) in the case of a person who is in police detention for a serious arrestable offence; and
  (b) if an officer of at least the rank of superintendent authorises it.

(3) In any case the person in custody must be permitted to exercise the right conferred by subsection (1) above within 36 hours from the relevant time, as defined in section 41(2) above.

(4) An officer may give an authorisation under subsection (2) above orally or in writing but, if he gives it orally, he shall confirm it in writing as soon as is practicable.

(5) Subject to sub-section (5A) below an officer may only authorise delay where he has reasonable grounds for believing that telling the named person of the arrest—

  (a) will lead to interference with or harm to evidence connected with a serious arrestable offence or interference with or physical injury to other persons; or
  (b) will lead to the alerting of other persons suspected of having committed such an offence but not yet arrested for it; or
  (c) will hinder the recovery of any property obtained as a result of such an offence.

(5A) An officer may also authorise delay where the serious arrestable offence is a drug trafficking offence or an offence to which Part VI of the Criminal Justice Act 1988 applies (offences in respect of which confiscation orders under that Part may be made) and the officer has reasonable grounds for believing—

(*a*) where the offence is a drug trafficking offence, that the detained person has benefited from drug trafficking and that the recovery of the value of that person's proceeds of drug trafficking will be hindered by the exercise of the right conferred by subsection (1) above; and

(*b*) where the offence is one to which Part VI of the Criminal Justice Act 1988 applies, that the detained person has benefited from the offence and that the recovery of the value of the property obtained by that person from or in connection with the offence or of the pecuniary advantage derived by him from or in connection with it will be hindered by the exercise of the right conferred by subsection (1) above.

(6) If a delay is authorised—

(*a*) the detained person shall be told the reason for it; and

(*b*) the reason shall be noted on his custody record.

(7) The duties imposed by subsection (6) above shall be performed as soon as is practicable.

(8) The rights conferred by this section on a person detained at a police station or other premises are exercisable whenever he is transferred from one place to another; and this section applies to each subsequent occasion on which they are exercisable as it applies to the first such occasion.

(9) There may be no further delay in permitting the exercise of the right conferred by subsection (1) above once the reason for authorising delay ceases to subsist.

(10) In the foregoing provisions of this section references to a person who has been arrested include references to a person who has been detained under the terrorism provisions and "arrest" includes detention under those provisions.

(11) In its application to a person who has been arrested or detained under the terrorism provisions—

(*a*) subsection (2)(*a*) above shall have effect as if for the words "for a serious arrestable offence" there were substituted the words "under the terrorism provisions";

(*b*) subsection (3) above shall have effect as if for the words from "within" onwards there were substituted the words "before the end of the period beyond which he may no longer be detained without the authority of the Secretary of State"; and

(*c*) subsection (5) above shall have effect as if at the end there were added "or

(*d*) will lead to interference with the gathering of information about the commission, preparation or instigation of acts of terrorism; or

(*e*) by alerting any person, will make it more difficult—

    (i) to prevent an act of terrorism; or

(ii) to secure the apprehension, prosecution or conviction of any person in connection with the commission, preparation or instigation of an act of terrorism.".

57 Additional rights of children and young persons

. . . [amends the Children and Young Persons Act 1933, s34].

58 Access to legal advice

(1) A person arrested and held in custody in a police station or other premises shall be entitled, if he so requests, to consult a solicitor privately at any time.

(2) Subject to subsection (3) below, a request under subsection (1) above and the time at which it was made shall be recorded in the custody record.

(3) Such a request need not be recorded in the custody record of a person who makes it at a time while he is at a court after being charged with an offence.

(4) If a person makes such a request, he must be permitted to consult a solicitor as soon as is practicable except to the extent that delay is permitted by this section.

(5) In any case he must be permitted to consult a solicitor within 36 hours from the relevant time, as defined in section 41(2) above.

(6) Delay in compliance with a request is only permitted—

(*a*) in the case of a person who is in police detention for a serious arrestable offence; and

(*b*) if an officer of at least the rank of superintendent authorises it.

(7) An officer may give an authorisation under subsection (6) above orally or in writing but, if he gives it orally, he shall confirm it in writing as soon as is practicable.

(8) Subject to sub-section (8A) below an officer may only authorise delay where he has reasonable grounds for believing that the exercise of the right conferred by subsection (1) above at the time when the person detained desires to exercise it—

(*a*) will lead to interference with or harm to evidence connected with a serious arrestable offence or interference with or physical injury to other persons; or

(*b*) will lead to the alerting of other persons suspected of having committed such an offence but not yet arrested for it; or

(*c*) will hinder the recovery of any property obtained as a result of such an offence.

(8A) An officer may also authorise delay where the serious arrestable offence is a drug trafficking offence or an offence to which Part VI of the Criminal Justice

Act 1988 applies and the officer has reasonable grounds for believing—

(*a*) where the offence is a drug trafficking offence, that the detained person has benefited from drug trafficking and that the recovery of the value of that person's proceeds of drug trafficking will be hindered by the exercise of the right conferred by subsection (1) above; and

(*b*) where the offence is one to which Part VI of the Criminal Justice Act 1988 applies, that the detained person has benefited from the offence and that the recovery of the value of the property obtained by that person from or in connection with the offence or of the pecuniary advantage derived by him from or in connection with it will be hindered by the exercise of the right conferred by subsection (1) above.

(9) If delay is authorised—

(*a*) the detained person shall be told the reason for it; and

(*b*) the reason shall be noted on his custody record.

(10) The duties imposed by subsection (9) above shall be performed as soon as is practicable.

(11) There may be no further delay in permitting the exercise of the right conferred by subsection (1) above once the reason for authorising delay ceases to subsist.

(12) The reference in subsection (1) above to a person arrested includes a reference to a person who has been detained under the terrorism provisions.

(13) In the application of this section to a person who has been arrested or detained under the terrorism provisions—

(*a*) subsection (5) above shall have effect as if for the words from "within" onwards there were substituted the words "before the end of the period beyond which he may no longer be detained without the authority of the Secretary of State";

(*b*) subsection (6)(*a*) above shall have effect as if for the words "for a serious arrestable offence" there were substituted the words "under the terrorism provisions"; and

(*c*) subsection (8) above shall have effect as if at the end there were added "or

(*d*) will lead to interference with the gathering of information about the commission, preparation or instigation of acts of terrorism; or

(*e*) by alerting any person, will make it more difficult—

(i) to prevent an act of terrorism; or

(ii) to secure the apprehension, prosecution or conviction of any person in connection with the commission, preparation or instigation of an act of terrorism.".

(14) If an officer of appropriate rank has reasonable grounds for believing that, unless he gives a direction under subsection (15) below, the exercise by a person arrested or detained under the terrorism provisions of the right conferred by subsection (1) above will have any of the consequences specified in subsection (8) above (as it has effect by virtue of subsection (13) above), he may give a direction under that subsection.

(15) A direction under this subsection is a direction that a person desiring to exercise the right conferred by subsection (1) above may only consult a solicitor in the sight and hearing of a qualified officer of the uniformed branch of the force of which the officer giving the direction is a member.

(16) An officer is qualified for the purpose of subsection (15) above if—

(*a*) he is of at least the rank of inspector; and

(*b*) in the opinion of the officer giving the direction he has no connection with the case.

(17) An officer is of appropriate rank to give a direction under subsection (15) above if he is of at least the rank of Commander or Assistant Chief Constable.

(18) A direction under subsection (15) above shall cease to have effect once the reason for giving it ceases to subsist.

59 Legal Aid

[Repealed]

60 Tape-recording of interviews

(1) It shall be the duty of the Secretary of State—

(*a*) to issue a code of practice in connection with the tape-recording of interviews of persons suspected of the commission of criminal offences which are held by police officers at police stations; and

(*b*) to make an order requiring the tape-recording of interviews of persons suspected of the commission of criminal offences, or of such descriptions of criminal offences as may be specified in the order, which are so held, in accordance with the code as it has effect for the time being.

(2) An order under subsection (1) above shall be made by statutory instrument and shall be subject to annulment in pursuance of a resolution of either House of Parliament.

61 Fingerprinting

(1) Except as provided by this section no person's fingerprints may be taken without the appropriate consent.

(2) Consent to the taking of a person's fingerprints must be in writing if it is given at a time when he is at a police station.

(3) The fingerprints of a person detained at a police station may be taken without the appropriate consent—

(*a*) if an officer of at least the rank of superintendent authorises them to be taken; or

(*b*) if—

(i) he has been charged with a recordable offence or informed that he will be reported for such an offence; and

(ii) he has not had his fingerprints taken in the course of the investigation of the offence by the police.

(4) An officer may only give an authorisation under subsection (3)(*a*) above if he has reasonable grounds—

(*a*) for suspecting the involvement of the person whose fingerprints are to be taken in a criminal offence; and

(*b*) for believing that his fingerprints will tend to confirm or disprove his involvement.

(5) An officer may give an authorisation under subsection (3)(*a*) above orally or in writing but, if he gives it orally, he shall confirm it in writing as soon as is practicable.

(6) Any person's fingerprints may be taken without the appropriate consent if he has been convicted of a recordable offence.

(7) In a case where by virtue of subsection (3) or (6) above a person's fingerprints are taken without the appropriate consent—

(*a*) he shall be told the reason before his fingerprints are taken; and

(*b*) the reason shall be recorded as soon as is practicable after the fingerprints are taken.

(8) If he is detained at a police station when the fingerprints are taken, the reason for taking them shall be recorded on his custody record.

(9) Nothing in this section—

(*a*) affects any power conferred by paragraph 18(2) of Schedule 2 to the Immigration Act 1971; or

(*b*) except as provided in section 15(10) of, and paragraph 7(6) of Schedule 5 to, the Prevention of Terrorism (Temporary Provisions) Act 1989, applies to a person arrested or detained under the terrorism provisions.

62 Intimate samples

(1) An intimate sample may be taken from a person in police detention only—

(*a*) if a police officer of at least the rank of superintendent authorises it to be taken; and

(*b*) if the appropriate consent is given.

(2) An officer may only give an authorisation if he has reasonable grounds—

(*a*) for suspecting the involvement of the person from whom the sample is to be taken in a serious arrestable offence; and

(*b*) for believing that the sample will tend to confirm or disprove his involvement.

(3) An officer may give an authorisation under subsection (1) above orally or in writing but, if he gives it orally, he shall confirm it in writing as soon as is practicable.

(4) The appropriate consent must be given in writing.

(5) Where—

(*a*) an authorisation has been given; and

(*b*) it is proposed that an intimate sample shall be taken in pursuance of the authorisation,

an officer shall inform the person from whom the sample is to be taken—

(i) of the giving of the authorisation; and

(ii) of the grounds for giving it.

(6) The duty imposed by subsection (5)(ii) above includes a duty to state the nature of the offence in which it is suspected that the person from whom the sample is to be taken has been involved.

(7) If an intimate sample is taken from a person—

(*a*) the authorisation by virtue of which it was taken;

(*b*) the grounds for giving the authorisation; and

(*c*) the fact that the appropriate consent was given,

shall be recorded as soon as is practicable after the sample is taken.

(8) If an intimate sample is taken from a person detained at a police station, the matters required to be recorded by subsection (7) above shall be recorded in his custody record.

(9) An intimate sample, other than a sample of urine or saliva, may only be taken from a person by a registered medical practitioner.

(10) Where the appropriate consent to the taking of an intimate sample from a person was refused without good cause, in any proceedings against that person for an offence—

(*a*) the court, in determining—

(i) whether to commit that person for trial; or

(ii) whether there is a case to answer; and

(*b*) the court or jury, in determining whether that person is guilty of the offence charged,

may draw such inferences from the refusal as appear proper; and the refusal may, on the basis of such inferences, be treated as, or as capable of amounting to, corroboration of any evidence against the person in relation to which the refusal is material.

(11) Nothing in this section affects sections 4 to 11 of the Road Traffic Act 1988.

63 Other samples

(1) Except as provided by this section, a non-intimate sample may not be taken from a person without the appropriate consent.

(2) Consent to the taking of a non-intimate sample must be given in writing.

(3) A non-intimate sample may be taken from a person without the appropriate consent if —

(a) he is in police detention or is being held in custody by the police on the authority of a court; and

(b) an officer of at least the rank of superintendent authorises it to be taken without the appropriate consent.

(4) An officer may only give an authorisation under subsection (3) above if he has reasonable grounds—

(a) for suspecting the involvement of the person from whom the sample is to be taken in a serious arrestable offence; and

(b) for believing that the sample will tend to confirm or disprove his involvement.

(5) An officer may give an authorisation under subsection (3) above orally or in writing but, if he gives it orally, he shall confirm it in writing as soon as is practicable.

(6) Where—

(a) an authorisation has been given; and

(b) it is proposed that a non-intimate sample shall be taken in pursuance of the authorisation,

an officer shall inform the person from whom the sample is to be taken—

(i) of the giving of the authorisation; and

(ii) of the grounds for giving it.

(7) The duty imposed by subsection (6)(ii) above includes a duty to state the nature of the offence in which it is suspected that the person from whom the sample is to be taken has been involved.

(8) If a non-intimate sample is taken from a person by virtue of subsection (3) above—

(a) the authorisation by virtue of which it was taken; and

(b) the grounds for giving the authorisation,

shall be recorded as soon as is practicable after the sample is taken.

(9) If a non-intimate sample is taken from a person detained at a police station, the matters required to be recorded by subsection (8) above shall be recorded in his custody record.

64 Destruction of fingerprints and samples

(1) If—

(a) fingerprints or samples are taken from a person in connection with the investigation of an offence; and

(b) he is cleared of that offence,

they must be destroyed as soon as is practicable after the conclusion of the proceedings.

(2) If—

(*a*) fingerprints or samples are taken from a person in connection with such an investigation; and

(*b*) it is decided that he shall not be prosecuted for the offence and he has not admitted it and been dealt with by way of being cautioned by a constable,

they must be destroyed as soon as is practicable after that decision is taken.

(3) If—

(*a*) fingerprints or samples are taken from a person in connection with the investigation of an offence; and

(*b*) that person is not suspected of having committed the offence,

they must be destroyed as soon as they have fulfilled the purpose for which they were taken.

(4) Proceedings which are discontinued are to be treated as concluded for the purposes of this section.

(5) If fingerprints are destroyed—

(*a*) any copies of the fingerprints shall also be destroyed; and

(*b*) any chief officer of police controlling access to computer data relating to the fingerprints shall make access to the data impossible, as soon as it is practicable to do so.

(6) A person who asks to be allowed to witness the destruction of his fingerprints or copies of them shall have a right to witness it.

(6A) If—

(*a*) subsection (5)(*b*) above falls to be complied with; and

(*b*) the person to whose fingerprints the data relate asks for a certificate that it has been complied with,

such a certificate shall be issued to him not later than the end of the period of three months beginning with the day on which he asks for it, by the responsible chief officer of police or a person authorised by him or on his behalf for the purposes of this section.

(6B) In this section—

"chief officer of police" means the chief officer of police for an area mentioned in Schedule 8 to the Police Act 1964; and

"the responsible chief officer of police" means the chief officer of police in whose area the computer data were put on to the computer.

(7) Nothing in this section—

(*a*) affects any power conferred by paragraph 18(2) of Schedule 2 to the Immigration At 1971; or

(*b*) applies to a person arrested or detained under the terrorism provisions.

65 Part V — supplementary

In this Part of this Act—

"appropriate consent" means—

   (*a*) in relation to a person who has attained the age of 17 years, the consent of that person;

   (*b*) in relation to a person who has not attained that age but has attained the age of 14 years, the consent of that person and his parent or guardian; and

   (*c*) in relation to a person who has not attained the age of 14 years, the consent of his parent or guardian;

"drug trafficking" and "drug trafficking offence" have the same meaning as in the Drug Trafficking Offences Act 1986

"fingerprints" includes palm prints;

"intimate sample" means a sample of blood, semen or any other tissue fluid, urine, saliva or pubic hair, or a swab taken from a person's body orifices;

"non-intimate sample" means—

   (*a*) a sample of hair other than pubic hair;

   (*b*) a sample taken from a nail or from under a nail;

   (*c*) a swab taken from any part of a person's body other than a body orifice;

   (*d*) a footprint or a similar impression of any part of a person's body other than a part of his hand;

"the terrorism provisions" means section 14(1) of the Prevention of Terrorism (Temporary Provisions) Act 1989 and any provision of Schedule 2 or 5 to that Act conferring a power of arrest or detention; and

"terrorism" has the meaning assigned to it by section 20(1) of that Act.

and references in this Part to any person's proceeds of drug trafficking are to be construed in accordance with the Drug Trafficking Offences Act 1986.

PART VI

CODES OF PRACTICE — GENERAL

66 Codes of practice

The Secretary of State shall issue codes of practice in connection with—

   (*a*) the exercise by police officers of statutory powers—

      (i) to search a person without first arresting him; or

      (ii) to search a vehicle without making an arrest;

   (*b*) the detention, treatment, questioning and identification of persons by police officers;

(*c*) searches of premises by police officers; and

(*d*) the seizure of property found by police officers on persons or premises.

67 Codes of practice — supplementary

(1) When the Secretary of State proposes to issue a code of practice to which this section applies, he shall prepare and publish a draft of that code, shall consider any representations made to him about the draft and may modify the draft accordingly.

(2) This section applies to a code of practice under section 60 or 66 above.

(3) This Secretary of State shall lay before both Houses of Parliament a draft of any code of practice prepared by him under this section.

(4) When the Secretary of State has laid the draft of a code before Parliament, he may bring the code into operation by order made by statutory instrument.

(5) No order under subsection (4) above shall have effect until approved by a resolution of each House of Parliament.

(6) An order bringing a code of practice into operation may contain such transitional provisions or savings as appear to the Secretary of State to be necessary or expedient in connection with the code of practice thereby brought into operation.

(7) The Secretary of State may from time to time revise the whole or any part of a code of practice to which this section applies and issue that revised code; and the foregoing provisions of this section shall apply (with appropriate modifications) to such a revised code as they apply to the first issue of a code.

(8) A police officer shall be liable to disciplinary proceedings for a failure to comply with any provision of such a code, unless such proceedings are precluded by section 104 below.

(9) Persons other than police officers who are charged with the duty of investigating offences or charging offenders shall in the discharge of that duty have regard to any relevant provision of such a code.

(10) A failure on the part—

(*a*) of a police officer to comply with any provision of such a code; or

(*b*) of a person other than a police officer who is charged with the duty of investigating offences or charging offenders to have regard to any relevant provisions of such a code in the discharge of that duty, shall not of itself render him liable to any criminal or civil proceedings.

(11) In all criminal and civil proceedings any such code shall be admissible in evidence; and if any provision of such a code appears to the court or tribunal conducting the proceedings to be relevant to any question arising in the proceedings it shall be taken into account in determining that question.

(12) In this section "criminal proceedings" includes—

(a) proceedings in the United Kingdom or elsewhere before a court-martial constituted under the Army Act 1955, the Air Force Act 1955 or the Naval Discipline Act 1957 or a disciplinary court constituted under section 50 of the said Act of 1957;

(b) proceedings before the Courts-Martial Appeal Court; and

(c) proceedings before a Standing Civilian Court.

PART VIII

EVIDENCE IN CRIMINAL PROCEEDINGS —

GENERAL: CONVICTIONS AND ACQUITTALS

73 Proof of convictions and acquittals

(1) Where in any proceedings the fact that a person has in the United Kingdom been convicted or acquitted of an offence otherwise than by a Service court is admissible in evidence, it may be proved by producing a certificate of conviction or, as the case may be, of acquittal relating to that offence, and proving that the person name in the certificate as having been convicted or acquitted of the offence is the person whose conviction or acquittal of the offence is to be proved.

(2) For the purposes of this section a certificate of conviction or of acquittal—

(a) shall, as regards a conviction or acquittal on indictment, consist of a certificate, signed by the clerk of the court where the conviction or acquittal took place, giving the substance and effect (omitting the formal parts) of the indictment and of the conviction or acquittal; and

(b) shall, as regards a conviction or acquittal on a summary trial, consist of a copy of the conviction or of the dismissal of the information, signed by the clerk of the court where the conviction or acquittal took place or by the clerk of the court, if any, to which a memorandum of the conviction or acquittal was sent;

and a document purporting to be a duly signed certificate of conviction or acquittal under this section shall be taken to be such a certificate unless the contrary is proved.

(3) References in this section to the clerk of a court include references to his deputy and to any other person having the custody of the court record.

(4) The method of proving a conviction or acquittal authorised by this section shall be in addition to and not to the exclusion of any other authorised manner of proving a conviction or acquittal.

74 Conviction as evidence of commission of offence

(1) In any proceedings the fact that a person other than the accused has been

convicted of an offence by or before any court in the United Kingdom or by a Service court outside the United Kingdom shall be admissible in evidence for the purpose of proving, where to do so is relevant to any issue in those proceedings, that that person committed that offence, whether or not any other evidence of his having committed that offence is given.

(2) In any proceedings in which by virtue of this section a person other than the accused is proved to have been convicted of an offence by or before any court in the United Kingdom or by a Service court outside the United Kingdom, he shall be taken to have committed that offence unless the contrary is proved.

(3) In any proceedings where evidence is admissible of the fact that the accused has committed an offence, in so far as that evidence is relevant to any matter in issue in the proceedings for a reason other than a tendency to show in the accused a disposition to commit the kind of offence with which he is charged, if the accused is proved to have been convicted of the offence—

(*a*) by or before any court in the United Kingdom; or
(*b*) by a Service court outside the United Kingdom,
he shall be taken to have committed that offence unless the contrary is proved.

(4) Nothing in this section shall prejudice—

(*a*) the admissibility in evidence of any conviction which would be admissible apart from this section; or
(*b*) the operation of any enactment whereby a conviction or a finding of fact in any proceedings is for the purposes of any other proceedings made conclusive evidence of any fact.

75 Provisions supplementary to section 74

(1) Where evidence that a person has been convicted of an offence is admissible by virtue of section 74 above, then without prejudice to the reception of any other admissible evidence for the purpose of identifying the facts on which the conviction was based—

(*a*) the contents of any document which is admissible as evidence of the conviction; and
(*b*) the contents of the information, complaint, indictment or charge-sheet on which the person in question was convicted,

shall be admissible in evidence for that purpose.

(2) Where in any proceedings the contents of any document are admissible in evidence by virtue of subsection (1) above, a copy of that document, or of the material part of it, purporting to be certified or otherwise authenticated by or on behalf of the court or authority having custody of that document shall be admissible in evidence and shall be taken to be a true copy of that document or part unless the contrary is shown.

(3) Nothing in any of the following—

(*a*) section 13 of the Powers of Criminal Courts Act 1973 (under which a conviction leading to probation or discharge is to be disregarded except as mentioned in that section);

(*b*) section 392 of the Criminal Procedure (Scotland) Act 1975 (which makes similar provision in respect of convictions on indictment in Scotland); and

(*c*) section 8 of the Probation Act (Northern Ireland) 1950 (which corresponds to section 13 of the Powers of Criminal Courts Act 1973) or any legislation which is in force in Northern Ireland for the time being and corresponds to that section,

shall affect the operation of section 74 above; and for the purposes of that section any order made by a court of summary jurisdiction in Scotland under section 182 or section 183 of the said Act of 1975 shall be treated as a conviction.

(4) Nothing in section 74 above shall be construed as rendering admissible in any proceedings evidence of any conviction other than a subsisting one.

CONFESSIONS

76 Confessions

(1) In any proceedings a confession made by an accused person may be given in evidence against him in so far as it is relevant to any matter in issue in the proceedings and is not excluded by the court in pursuance of this section.

(2) If, in any proceedings where the prosecution proposes to give in evidence a confession made by an accused person, it is represented to the court that the confession was or may have been obtained—

(*a*) by oppression of the person who made it; or

(*b*) in consequence of anything said or done which was likely, in the circumstances existing at the time, to render unreliable any confession which might be made by him in consequence thereof,

the court shall not allow the confession to be given in evidence against him except in so far as the prosecution proves to the court beyond reasonable doubt that the confession (notwithstanding that it may be true) was not obtained as aforesaid.

(3) In any proceedings where the prosecution proposes to give in evidence a confession made by an accused person, the court may of its own motion require the prosecution, as a condition of allowing it to do so, to prove that the confession was not obtained as mentioned in subsection (2) above.

(4) The fact that a confession is wholly or partly excluded in pursuance of this section shall not affect the admissibility in evidence—

(*a*) of any facts discovered as a result of the confession; or

(*b*) where the confession is relevant as showing that the accused speaks, writes or expresses himself in a particular way, of so much of the confession as is necessary to show that he does so.

(5) Evidence that a fact to which this subsection applies was discovered as a result of a statement made by an accused person shall not be admissible unless evidence of how it was discovered is given by him or on his behalf.

(6) Subsection (5) above applies—

(a) to any fact discovered as a result of a confession which is wholly excluded in pursuance of this section; and

(b) to any fact discovered as a result of a confession which is partly so excluded, if the fact is discovered as a result of the excluded part of the confession.

(7) Nothing in Part VII of this Act shall prejudice the admissibility of a confession made by an accused person.

(8) In this section "oppression" includes torture, inhuman or degrading treatment, and the use or threat of violence (whether or not amounting to torture).

77 Confessions by mentally handicapped persons

(1) Without prejudice to the general duty of the court at a trial on indictment to direct the jury on any matter on which it appears to the court appropriate to do so, where at such a trial—

(a) the case against the accused depends wholly or substantially on a confession by him; and

(b) the court is satisfied—

(i) that he is mentally handicapped; and

(ii) that the confession was not made in the presence of an independent person,

the court shall warn the jury that there is special need for caution before convicting the accused in reliance on the confession, and shall explain that the need arises because of the circumstances mentioned in paragraphs (a) and (b) above.

(2) In any case where at the summary trial of a person for an offence it appears to the court that a warning under subsection (1) above would be required if the trial were on indictment, the court shall treat the case as one in which there is a special need for caution before convicting the accused on his confession.

(3) In this section—

"independent person" does not include a police officer or a person employed for, or engaged on, police purposes;

"mentally handicapped", in relation to a person, means that he is in a state of arrested or incomplete development of mind which includes significant impairment of intelligence and social functioning; and

"police purposes" has the meaning assigned to it by section 64 of the Police Act 1964.

78 Exclusion of unfair evidence

(1) In any proceedings the court may refuse to allow evidence on which the prosecution proposes to rely to be given if it appears to the court that, having regard to all the circumstances, including the circumstances in which the evidence was obtained, the admission of the evidence would have such an adverse effect on the fairness of the proceedings that the court ought not to admit it.

(2) Nothing in this section shall prejudice any rule of law requiring a court to exclude evidence.

PART VIII — Supplementary

82 Interpretation

(1) In this Part of this Act—

"confession" includes any statement wholly or partly adverse to the person who made it, whether made to a person in authority or not and whether made in words or otherwise;

"court-martial" means a court-martial constituted under the Army Act 1955, the Air Force Act 1955 or the Naval Discipline Act 1957 or a disciplinary court constituted under section 50 of the said Act of 1957;

"proceedings" means criminal proceedings, including—

(a) proceedings in the United Kingdom or elsewhere before a court-martial constituted under the Army Act 1955 or the Air Force Act 1955;
(b) proceedings in the United Kingdom or elsewhere before the Courts-Martial Appeal Court—
   (i) on the appeal from a court-martial so constituted or from a court-martial constituted under the Naval Discipline Act 1957; or
   (ii) on a reference under section 34 of the Courts-Martial (Appeals) Act 1968; and
(c) proceedings before a Standing Civilian Court; and

"Service court" means a court-martial or a Standing Civilian Court.

(2) In this Part of this Act references to conviction before a Service court are references—

(a) as regards a court-martial constituted under the Army Act 1955 or the Air Force Act 1955, to a finding of guilty which is, or falls to be treated as, a finding of the court duly confirmed;
(b) as regards —
   (i) a court-martial; or
   (ii) a disciplinary court,

constituted under the Naval Discipline Act 1957, to a finding of guilty which is, or falls to be treated as, the finding of the court;

and "convicted" shall be construed accordingly.

(3) Nothing in this Part of this Act shall prejudice any power of a court to exclude evidence (whether by preventing questions from being put or otherwise) at is discretion.

PART X

Police-general

106 Arrangements for obtaining the views of the community on policing

(1) Arrangements shall be made in each police area for obtaining the views of people in that area about matters concerning the policing of the area and for obtaining their co-operation with the police in preventing crime in the area.

(2) Except as provided by subsections (3) to (7) below, arrangements for each police area shall be made by the police authority after consulting the chief constable as to the arrangements that would be appropriate.

(3) The Secretary of State shall issue guidance to the Commissioner of Police of the Metropolis concerning arrangements for the Metropolitan Police district; and the Commissioner shall make such arrangements after taking account of that guidance.

(4) The Commissioner shall make separate arrangements—

(*a*) for each London borough;
(*b*) for each district which falls wholly within the Metropolitan Police District; and
(*c*) for each part of a district which falls partly within that District.

(5) The Commissioner shall consult the council of each London borough as to the arrangements that would be appropriate for the borough.

(6) The Commissioner shall consult the council of each such district as is mentioned in subsection (4)(*b*) above as to the arrangements that would be appropriate for the district.

(7) The Commissioner shall consult the council of each such district as is mentioned in subsection (4)(*c*) above as to the arrangements that would be appropriate for the part of the district for which it falls to him to make arrangements.

(8) The Common Council of the City of London shall issue guidance to the Commissioner of Police for the City of London concerning arrangements for the City; and the Commissioner shall make such arrangements after taking account of that guidance.

(9) A body or person whose duty it is to make arrangements under this section shall review the arrangements so made from time to time.

(10) If it appears to the Secretary of State that arrangements in a police area are not adequate for the purposes set out in subsection (1) above, he may require the body or person whose duty it is to make arrangements in that area to submit a report to him concerning the arrangements.

(11) After considering the report the Secretary of State may require the body or person who submitted it to review the arrangements and submit a further report to him concerning them.

(12) A body or person whose duty it is to make arrangements shall be under the same duties to consult when reviewing arrangements as when making them.

107 Police officers performing duties of higher rank

(1) For the purpose of any provision of this Act or any other Act under which a power in respect of the investigation of offences or the treatment of persons in police custody is exercisable only by or with the authority of a police officer of at least the rank of superintendent, an officer of the rank of chief inspector shall be treated as holding the rank of superintendent if he has been authorised by an officer of at least the rank of chief superintendent to exercise the power or, as the case may be, to give his authority for its exercise.

(2) For the purpose of any provision of this Act or any other Act under which such a power is exercisable only by or with the authority of an officer of at least the rank of inspector, an officer of the rank of sergeant shall be treated as holding the rank of inspector if he has been authorised by an officer of at least the rank of chief superintendent to exercise the power of, as the case may be, to give his authority for its exercise.

PART XI

MISCELLANEOUS AND SUPPLEMENTARY

113 Application of Act to Armed Forces

(1) The Secretary of State may by order direct that any provision of this Act which relates to investigations of offences conducted by police officers or to persons detained by the police shall apply, subject to such modifications as he may specify, to investigations of offences conducted under the Army Act 1955, the Air Force Act 1955 or the Naval Discipline Act 1957 or to persons under arrest under any of those Acts.

(2) Section 67(9) above shall not have effect in relation to investigations of offences conducted under the Army Act 1955, the Air Force Act 1955 or the Naval Discipline Act 1957.

(3) The Secretary of State shall issue a code of practice, or a number of such codes, for persons other than police officers who are concerned with enquiries into offences under the Army Act 1955, the Air Force Act 1955 or the Naval Discipline Act 1957.

(4) Without prejudice to the generality of subsection (3) above, a code issued under that subsection may contain provisions, in connection with enquiries into such offences, as to the following matters—

    (*a*) the tape-recording of interviews;

    (*b*) searches of persons and premises; and

    (*c*) the seizure of things found on searches.

(5) If the Secretary of State lays before both Houses of Parliament a draft of a code of practice under this section, he may by order bring the code into operation.

(6) An order bringing a code of practice into operation may contain such transitional provisions or savings as appear to the Secretary of State to be necessary or expedient in connection with the code of practice thereby brought into operation.

(7) The Secretary of State may from time to time revise the whole or any part of a code of practice issued under this section and issue that revised code, and the foregoing provisions of this section shall apply (with appropriate modifications) to such a revised code as they apply to the first issue of a code.

(8) A failure on the part of any person to comply with any provision of a code of practice issued under this section shall not of itself render him liable to any criminal or civil proceedings except those to which this subsection applies.

(9) Subsection (18) above applies—

    (*a*) to proceedings under any provision orf the Army Act 1955 or the Air Force Act 1955 other than section 70; and

    (*b*) to proceedings under any provision of the Naval Discipline Act 1957 other than section 42.

(10) In all criminal and civil proceedings any such code shall be admissible in evidence and if any provision of such a code appears to the court or tribunal conducting the proceedings to be relevant to any question arising in the proceedings it shall be taken into account in determining that question.

(11) In subsection (10) above "criminal proceedings" includes—

    (*a*) proceedings in the United Kingdom or elsewhere before a court-martial constituted under the Army Act 1955, the Air Force Act 1955 or the Naval Discipline Act 1957 or a disciplinary court constituted under section 50 of the said Act of 1957;

    (*b*) proceedings before the Courts-Martial Appeal Court; and

    (*c*) proceedings before a Standing Civilian Court.

(12) Parts VII and VIII of this Act have effect for the purposes of proceedings—

(*a*) before a court-martial constituted under the Army Act 1955 or the Air Force Act 1955;

(*b*) before the Courts-Martial Appeal Court; and

(*c*) before a Standing Civilian Court,

subject to any modifications which the Secretary of State may by order specify.

(13) An order under this section shall be made by statutory instrument and shall be subject to annulment in pursuance of a resolution of either House of Parliament.

114 Application of Act to Customs and Excise

(1) "Arrested", "arresting", "arrest" and "to arrest" shall respectively be substituted for "detained", "detaining", "detention" and "to detain" wherever in the customs and excise Acts, as defined in section 1(1) of the Customs and Excise Management Act 1979, those words are used in relation to persons.

(2) The Treasury may by order direct—

(*a*) that any provision of this Act which relates to investigations of offences conducted by police officers or to persons detained by the police shall apply, subject to such modifications as the order may specify, to investigations conducted by officers of Customs and Excise of offences which relate to assigned matters, as defined in section 1 of the Customs and Excise Management Act 1979, or to persons detained by officers of Customs and Excise; and

(*b*) that, in relation to investigations of offences conducted by officers of Customs and Excise—

    (i) this Act shall have effect as if the following section were inserted after section 14—

"Exception for Customs and Excise.

14A. Material in the possession of a person who acquired or created it in the course of any trade, business, profession or other occupation or for the purpose of any paid or unpaid office and which relates to an assigned matter, as defined in section 1 of the Customs and Excise Management Act 1979, is neither excluded material nor special procedure material for the purposes of any enactment such as is mentioned in section 9(2) above."; and

    (ii) sections 55 above shall have effect as if it related only to things such as are mentioned in subsection (1)(*a*) of that section and

(*c*) that in relation to customs detention (as defined in any order made under this subsection) the Bail Act 1976 shall have effect as if references in it to a constable were references to an officer of Customs and Excise of such grade as may be specified in the order.

(3) Nothing in any order under subsection (2) above shall be taken to limit any powers exercisable under section 164 of the Customs and Excise Management Act 1979.

(4) In this section "officers of Customs and Excise" means officers commissioned by the Commissioners of Customs and Excise under section 6(3) of the Customs and Excise Management Act 1979.

(5) An order under this section shall be made by statutory instrument and shall be subject to annulment in pursuance of a resolution of either House of Parliament.

115 Expenses

Any expenses of a Minister of the Crown incurred in consequence of the provisions of this Act, including any increase attributable to those provisions in sums payable under any other Act, shall be defrayed out of money provided by Parliament.

116 Meaning of "serious arrestable offence"

(1) This section has effect for determining whether an offence is a serious arrestable offence for the purposes of this Act.

(2) The following arrestable offences are always serious—

(*a*) an offence (whether at common law or under any enactment) specified in Part I of Schedule 5 to this act; and

(*aa*) any of the offences mentioned in paragraphs (*a*) to (*d*) of the definition of "drug trafficking offence" in section 38(1) of the Drug Trafficking Offences Act 1986;

(*b*) an offence under an enactment specified in Part II of that Schedule.

(3) Subject to subsections (4) and (5) below, any other arrestable offence is serious only if its commission—

(*a*) has led to any of the consequences specified in subsection (6) below; or
(*b*) is intended or is likely to lead to any of those consequences.

(4) An arrestable offence which consists of making a threat is serious if carrying out the threat would be likely to lead to any of the consequences specified in subsection (6) below.

(5) An offence under section 2, 8, 9, 10 or 11 of the Prevention of Terrorism (Temporary Provisions) Act 1989 is always a serious arrestable offence for the purposes of section 56 or 58 above, and an attempt or conspiracy to commit any such offence is also always a serious arrestable offence for those purposes.

(6) The consequences mentioned in subsections (3) and (4) above are

(*a*) serious harm to the security of the State or to public order;
(*b*) serious interference with the administration of justice or with the investigation of offences or of a particular offence;
(*c*) the death of any person;
(*d*) serious injury to any person;
(*e*) substantial financial gain to any person; and
(*f*) serious financial loss to any person.

(7) Loss is serious for the purposes of this section if, having regard to all the circumstances, it is serious for the person who suffers it.

(8) In this section "injury" includes any disease and any impairment of a person's physical or mental condition.

117 Power of constable to use reasonable force

Where any provision of this act—

(*a*) confers a power on a constable; and

(*b*) does not provide that the power may only be exercised with the consent of some person, other than a police officer,

the officer may use reasonable force, if necessary, in the exercise of the power.

118 General interpretation

(1) In this Act—

"arrestable offence" has the meaning assigned to it by section 24 above; "designated police station" has the meaning assigned to it by section 35 above;

"document" has the same meaning as in Part I of the Civil Evidence Act 1968;

"intimate search" means a search which consists of the physical examination of a person's body orifices;

"item subject to legal privilege" has the meaning assigned to it by section 10 above;

"parent or guardian" means—

(*a*) in the case of a child or young person in the care of a local authority, that authority;

(*b*) [Repealed by Children Act 1989.]

"premises" has the meaning assigned to it by section 23 above;

"recordable offence" means any offence to which regulations under section 27 above apply;

"vessel" includes any ship, boat, raft or other apparatus constructed or adapted for floating on water.

(2) A person is in police detention for the purposes of this Act if—

(*a*) he has been taken to a police station after being arrested for an offence or after being arrested under section 14 of the Prevention of Terrorism (Temporary Provisions) Act 1989 or under paragraph 6 of Schedule 5 to that Act by an examining officer who is a constable; or (*b*) he is arrested at a police station after attending voluntarily at the station or accompanying a constable to it,

and is detained there or is detained elsewhere in the charge of a constable, except that a person who is at a court after being charged is not in police detention for those purposes.

119 Amendments and repeals

(1) The enactments mentioned in Schedule 6 to this Act shall have effect with the amendments there specified.

(2) the enactments mentioned in Schedule 7 to this Act (which include enactments already obsolete or unnecessary) are repealed to the extent specified in the third column of that Schedule.

(3) The repeals in Parts II and IV of Schedule 7 to this Act have effect only in relation to criminal proceedings.

120 Extent

(1) Subject to the following provisions of this section, this Act extends to England and Wales only.

(2) The following extend to Scotland only—

section 108(4) and (5);

section 110;

section 111;

section 112(1); and

section 119(2), so far as it relates to the provisions of the Pedlars Act 1871 repealed by Part VI of Schedule 7.

(3) The following extend to Northern ireland only—

section 6(4), and

section 112(2).

(4) The following extend to England and Wales and Scotland—

section 6(1) and (2);

section 7;

section 83(2), so far as it relates to paragraph 8 of Schedule 4;

section 108(1) and (6);

section 109; and

section 119(2), so far as it relates to section 19 of the Pedlars Act 1871.

(5) The following extend to England and Wales, Scotland and Northern Ireland—

section 6(3);

section 83(2), so far as it relates to paragraph 7(1) of Schedule 4; and section 114(1).

(6) So far as they relate to proceedings before courts-martial and Standing Civilian Courts, the relevant provisions extend to any place at which such proceedings may be held.

(7) So far as they relate to proceedings before the Courts-Martial Appeal Court, the relevant provisions extend to any place at which such proceedings may be held.

(8) In this section "the relevant provisions" means—

   (a) subsection (11) of section 67 above;
   (b) subsection (12) of that section so far as it relates to subsection (11);
   (c) Parts VII and VIII of this Act, except paragraph 10 of Schedule 3;
   (d) subsections (2) and (8) to (12) of section 113 above; and
   (e) subsection (13) of that section, so far as it relates to an order under subsection (12).

(9) Except as provided by the foregoing provisions of this section, section 113 above extends to any place to which the Army Act 1955, the Air Force Act 1955, or the Naval Discipline Act 1957 extends.

(9A) Section 119(1), so far as it relates to any provision amended by Part II of Schedule 6, extends to any place to which that provision extends.

(10) Section 119(2), so far as it relates—

   (a) to any provision contained in—

the Army Act 1955;

the Air Force Act 1955;

the Armed Forces Act 1981; or

the Value Added Tax Act 1983;

   (b) to any provision mentioned in Part VI of Schedule 7, other than section 18 of the Pedlars Act 1871,

extends to any place to which that provision extends.

(11) so far as any of the following—

section 115;

in section 118, the definition of "document";

this section;

section 121; and

section 122,

has effect in relation to any other provision of this Act, it extends to any place to which that provision extends.

121 Commencement

(1) This Act, except section 120 above, this section and section 122 below, shall come into operation on such day as the Secretary of State may by order made by statutory instrument appoint, and different days may be so appointed for different provisions and for different purposes.

(2) Different days may be appointed under this section for the coming into force of section 60 above in different areas.

(3) When an order under this section provides by virtue of subsection (2) above that section 60 above shall come into force in an area specified in the order, the duty imposed on the Secretary of State by that section shall be construed as a duty to make an order under it in relation to interviews in that area.

(4) An order under this section may make such transitional provision as appears to the Secretary of State to be necessary or expedient in connection with the provisions thereby brought into operation.

122 Short title

This Act may be cited as the Police and Criminal Evidence Act 1984.

SCHEDULE 1

SPECIAL PROCEDURE

(section 9)

Making of orders by circuit judge

1. If on an application made byt a constable a circuit judge is satisfied that one or other of the sets of access conditions is fulfilled, he may make an order under paragraph 4 below.

2. The first set of access conditions is fulfilled if—

(a) there are reasonable grounds for believing—
    (i) that a serious arrestable offence has been committed;
    (ii) that there is material which consists of special procedure material or also includes special procedure material and does not also include excluded material on premises specified in the application;
    (iii) that the material is likely to be of substantial value (whether by itself or together with other material) to the investigation in connection with which the application is made; and
    (iv) that the material is likely to be relevant evidence;

(b) other methods of obtaining the material—
    (i) have been tried without success; or
    (ii) have not been tried because it appeared that they were bound to fail; and

(c) it is in the public interest, having regard—
    (i) to the benefit likely to accrue to the investigation if the material is obtained; and
    (ii) to the circumstances under which the person in possession of the material holds it,
    that the material should be produced or that access to it should be given.

3. The second set of access conditions is fulfilled if—

(a) there are reasonable grounds for believing that there is material which consists of or includes excluded material or special procedure material on premises specified in the application;

(b) but for section 9(2) above a search of the premises for that material could have been authorised by the issue of a warrant to a constable under an enactment other than this Schedule; and

(c) the issue of such a warrant would have been appropriate.

4. An order under this paragraph is an order that the person who appears to the circuit judge to be in possession of the material to which the application relates shall—

(a) produce it to a constable for him to take away; or

(b) give a constable access to it,

not later than the end of the period of seven days from the date of the order or the end of such longer period as the order may specify.

5. Where the material consists of information contained in a computer—

(a) an order under paragraph 4(a) above shall have effect as an order to produce the material in a form in which it can be taken away and in which it is visible and legible; and

(b) an order under paragraph 4(b) above shall have effect as an order to give a constable access to the material in a form in which it is visible and legible.

6. For the purpose of sections 21 and 22 above material produced in pursuance of an order under paragraph 4(a) above shall be treated as if it were material seized by a constable.

Appendix 1

Notices of applications for orders

7. An application for an order under paragraph 4 above shall be made inter partes.

8. Notice of an application for such an order may be served on a person either by delivering it to him or by leaving it at his proper address or by sending it by post to him in a registered letter or by the recorded delivery service.

9. Such a notice may be served—

(*a*) on a body corporate, by serving it on the body's secretary of clerk or other similar officer;and

(*b*) on a partnership, by serving it on one of the partners.

10. For the purposes of this Schedule, and of section 7 of the Interpretation Act 1978 in its application to this Schedule, the proper address of a person, in the case of secretary or clerk or other similar officer of a body corporate, shall be that of the registered or principal office of that body, in the case of a partner of a firm shall be that of the principal office of the firm, and in any other case shall be the last known address of the person to be served.

11. Where notice of an application for an order under paragraph 4 above has been served on a person, he shall not conceal, destroy, alter or dispose of the material to which the application relates except—

(*a*) with the leave of a judge; or

(*b*) with the written permission of a constable,

until—

(i) the application is dismissed or abandoned; or

(ii) he has complied with an order under paragraph 4 above made on the application.

Issue of warrants by circuit judge

12. If on an application made by a constable a circuit judge—

(*a*) is satisfied—

(i) that either set of access conditions is fulfilled; and

(ii) that any of the further conditions set out in paragraph 14 below is also fulfilled; or

(*b*) is satisfied—

(i) that the second set of access conditions is fulfilled; and

(ii) that an order under paragraph 4 above relating to the material has not been complied with,

he may issue a warrant authorising a constable to enter and search the premises.

13. A constable may seize and retain anything for which a search has been authorised under paragraph 12 above.

14. The further conditions mentioned in paragraph 12(*a*)(ii) above are—

(a) that it is not practicable to communicate with any person
entitled to grant entry to the premises to which the application relates;
(b) that it is practicable to communicate with a person entitled to grant entry to
the premises but it is not practicable to communicate with any person
entitled to grant access to the material;
(c) that the material contains information which—
(i) is subject to a restriction or obligation such as is mentioned in section
11(2)(b) above; and
(ii) is likely to be disclosed in breach of it if a warrant is not issued;
(d) that service of notice of an application for an order under paragraph 4
above may seriously prejudice the investigation.

15. —(1) If a person fails to comply with an order under paragraph 4 above, a
circuit judge may deal with him as if he had committed a contempt of the Crown
Court.

(2) Any enactment relating to contempt of the Crown Court shall have effect in
relation to such a failure as if it were such a contempt.

Costs

16. The costs of any application under this Schedule and of anything done or to
be done in pursuance of an order made under it shall be in the discretion of the
judge.

SCHEDULE 2

Preserved Powers of Arrest

(section 26)

1892 c. 43.	Section 17(2) of the Military Lands Act 1892.
1911 c. 27.	Section 12(1) of the Protection of Animals Act 1911.
1920 c. 55.	Section 2 of the Emergency Powers Act 1920.
1936 c. 6.	Section 7(3) of the Public Order Act 1936.
1952 c. 52.	Section 49 of the Prison Act 1952.
1952 c. 67.	Section 13 of the Visiting Forces Act 1952.
1955 c. 18.	Sections 186 and 190B of the Army Act 1955.
1955 c. 19.	Sections 186 and 190B of the Air Force Act 1955.
1957 c. 53.	Sections 104 and 105 of the Naval Discipline Act 1957.
1959 c. 37.	Section 1(3) of the Street Offences Act 1959.

1969 c. 54.	Section 32 of the Children and Young Persons Act 1969.
1971 c. 77.	Section 24(2) of the Immigration Act 1971 and paragraphs 17, 24 and 33 of the Schedule 2 and paragraph 7 of Schedule 3 to that Act.
1976 c. 63.	Section 7 of the Bail Act 1976.
1977 c. 45.	Sections 6(6), 7(11), 8(4), 9(7) and 10(5) of the Criminal Law Act 1977.
1980 c. 9.	Schedule 5 to the Reserve Forces Act 1980.
1981 c. 22.	Sections 60 (5) and 61(1) of the Animal Health Act 1981.
1983 c. 2.	Rule 36 in Schedule 1 to the Representatin of the People Act 1983.
1983 c. 20	Sections 18, 35(10), 36(8), 38(7), 136(1) and 138 of the Mental Health Act 1983.
1984 c. 47.	Section 5(5) of the Repatriation of Prisoners Act 1984.

SCHEDULE 5

SERIOUS ARRESTABLE OFFENCES

(section 116)

PART I

OFFENCES MENTIONED IN SECTION 116(2)(A)

1. Treason.

2. Murder.

3. Manslaughter.

4. Rape.

5. Kidnapping.

6. Incest with a girl under the age of 13.

7. Buggery with
   (a) a boy under the age of 16; or
   (b) a person who has not consented.

8. Indecent assault which constitutes an act of gross indecency.

PART II

Explosive Substances Act 1883 *(c.3)*

1. Section 2 (causing explosion likely to endanger life or property).

Sexual Offences Act 1956 (c. 69)

2. Section 5 (intercourse with a girl under the age of 13).

Firearms Act 1968 (c. 27)

3. Section 16 (possession of firearms with intent to injure).

4. Section 17(1) (use of firearms and immitation firearms to resist arrest).

5. Section 18 (carrying firearms with criminal intent).

... [repealed]

6. ... [repealed]

Taking of Hostages Act 1982 (c. 28)

7. Section 1 (hostage-taking).

Aviation Security Act 1982 (c. 36)

8. Section 1 (hijacking).

Criminal Justice Act 1988 (c. 33)

9. Section 134 (Torture).

The Road Traffic Act 1988 (c. 52)

10. Section 1 (causing death by reckless driving).

Aviation and Maritime Security Act 1990 (c. 31)

11. Section 1 (endangering safety at aerodromes).

12. Section 9 (hijacking of ships).

13. Section 10 (seizing or exercising control of fixed platforms).

Appendix 2

Code of practice for the exercise by police officers of statutory powers of stop and search

1 General

1.1 This code of practice must be readily available at all police stations for consultation by police officers, detained persons and members of the public.

1.2 The notes for guidance included are not provisions of this code, but are guidance to police officers and others about its application and interpretation. Provisions in the annexes to the code are provisions of this code.

1.3 This code governs the exercise by police officers of statutory powers to search a person without first arresting him or to search a vehicle without making an arrest. The main stop and search powers in existence at the time when this code was prepared are set out in the Annex, but that list should not be regarded as definitive.

1.4 This code does not apply to the following powers of stop and search:

    (i) Aviation Security Act 1982, s27(2);
    (ii) Police and Criminal Evidence Act 1984, s6(1) (which relates specifically to powers of constables employed by statutory undertakers on the premises of the statutory undertakers).

1.5 The exercise of the powers to which this code applies requires reasonable grounds for suspicion that articles unlawfully obtained or possessed are being carried. Where a police officer has reasonable grounds to suspect that a person is in innocent possession of a stolen or prohibited article, the power of stop and search exists notwithstanding that there would be no power of arrest. However, every effort should be made to secure the voluntary production of the article before the power is resorted to.

1.6 Whether reasonable grounds for suspicion exist will depend on the circumstances in each case, but there must be some objective basis for it. An officer will need to consider the nature of the article suspected of being carried in the context of other factors such as the time and the place, and the behaviour of the person concerned or those with him. Reasonable suspicion may exist, for example, where information has been received such as a description of an article being carried or of a suspected offender; a person is seen acting covertly or warily or attempting to hide something; or a person is carrying a certain type of article at an unusual time or in a place where a number of burglaries or thefts are known to have taken place recently. But the decision to stop and search must be based on all the facts which bear on the likelihood that an article of a certain kind will be found.

1.7 Reasonable suspicion can never be supported on the basis of personal factors alone. For example, a person's colour, age, hairstyle or manner of dress, or the fact that he is known to have a previous conviction for possession of an unlawful article, cannot be used alone or in combination with each other as the sole basis on which to search that person. Nor may it be founded on the basis of stereotyped images of certain persons or groups as more likely to be committing offences.

Notes for guidance

1A   It is important to ensure that powers of stop and search are used responsibly. An officer should bear in mind that he may be required to justify the use of the powers to a senior officer and in court, and also that misuse of the powers is likely to be harmful to the police effort in the long term. This can lead to mistrust of the police by the community. It is also particularly important to ensure that any person searched is treated courteously and considerately.

1B   This code does not affect the ability of an officer to speak to or question a person in the ordinary course of his duties (and in the absence of reasonable suspicion) without detaining him or exercising any element of compulsion. It is not the purpose of the code to prohibit such encounters between the police and the community with the co-operation of the person concerned and neither does it affect the principle that all citizens have a duty to help police officers to prevent crime and discover offenders.

1C   The power of search under paragraph 4(2) of Schedule 5 to the Prevention of Terrorism (Temporary Provisions) Act 1989 which does not require reasonable grounds for suspicion is not a power of stop and search as defined in paragraph 1.3 and is not covered by this code, but searches carried out under paragraph 4(2) should follow the procedures laid down in this code as far as practicable.

1D   Nothing in this code affects

(a)   the routine searching of persons entering sports grounds or other premises with their consent, or as a condition of entry; or
(b)   the ability of an officer to search a person in the street on a voluntary basis. In these circumstances, an officer should always make it clear that he is seeking the co-operation of the person concerned.

1E   If an officer acts in an improper manner this will invalidate a voluntary search. Juveniles, persons suffering from a mental handicap or mental disorder and others who appear not to be capable of giving an informed consent should not be subject to a voluntary search.

2 Action before a search is carried out

2.1 Where an officer has the reasonable grounds for suspicion necessary to exercise a power of stop and search he may detain the person concerned for the purposes of and with a view to searching him. There is no power to stop or detain a person against his will in order to find grounds for a search.

2.2 Before carrying out a search the officer may question the person about his behaviour or his presence in circumstances which gave rise to the suspicion, since he may have a satisfactory explanation which will make a search unnecessary. If, as a result of any questioning preparatory to a search, or other circumstances which come to the attention of the officer, there cease to be reasonable grounds for suspecting that an article is being carried of a kind for which there is a power of stop and search, no search may take place.

2.3 The reasonable grounds for suspicion which are necessary for the exercise of the initial power to detain may be confirmed or eliminated as a result of the questioning of a person detained for the purposes of a search (or such questioning may reveal reasonable grounds to suspect the possession of a different kind of unlawful article from that originally suspected); but the reasonable grounds for suspicion without which any search or detention for the purposes of a search is unlawful cannot be retrospectively provided by such questioning during his detention or by his refusal to answer any question put to him.

2.4 Before any search of a detained person or attended vehicle takes place the officer must take reasonable steps to give the person to be searched or in charge of the vehicle the following information:

   (i) his name (except in the case of enquiries linked to the investigation of terrorism, in which case he shall give his warrant number) and the name of the police station to which he is attached;

   (ii) the object of the search; and

   (iii) his grounds for undertaking it.

2.5 If the officer is not in uniform he must show his warrant card. In doing so in the case of enquiries linked to the investigation of terrorism, the officer need not reveal his name.

2.6 Unless it appears to the officer that it will not be practicable to make a record of the search, he must also inform the person to be searched (or the owner or person in charge of a vehicle that is to be searched, as the case may be) that he is entitled to a copy of the record of the search if he asks for it within a year. If the person wishes to have a copy and is not given one on the spot, he should be advised to which police station he should apply.

2.7 If the person to be searched, or in charge of a vehicle to be searched, does not understand what is being said, the officer must take reasonable steps to bring the information in paragraphs 2.4 to 2.6 to his attention. If the person has someone with him then the officer must try to establish whether that person can interpret.

Appendix 2

Note for Guidance

2A In some circumstances preparatory questioning may be unnecessary, but in general a brief conversation or exchange will be desirable as a means of avoiding unsuccessful searches. Where a person is lawfully detained for the purpose of a search, but no search in the event takes place, the detention will not thereby have been rendered unlawful.

3 Conduct of the search

3.1 Every reasonable effort must be made to reduce to the minimum the embarrassment that a person being searched may experience.

3.2 The co-operation of the person to be searched should be sought in every case, even if he initially objects to the search. A forcible search may be made only if it has been established that the person is unwilling to co-operate (e.g. by opening a bag) or resists. Although force may only be used as a last resort, reasonable force may be used if necessary to conduct a search or to detain a person or vehicle for the purposes of a search.

3.3 The length of time for which a person or vehicle may be detained will depend on the circumstances, but must in all circumstances be reasonable and not extend beyond the time taken for the search. The thoroughness and extent of a search must depend on what is suspected of being carried, and by whom. If the suspicion relates to a particular article which is seen to be slipped into a person's pocket, then, in the absence of other grounds for suspicion or an opportunity for the article to be moved elsewhere, the search must be confined to that pocket. In the case of a small article which can readily be concealed, such as a drug, and which might be concealed anywhere on the person, a more extensive search may be necessary. [See *Note 3B*]

3.4 The search must be conducted at or nearby the place where the person or vehicle was first detained.

3.5 Searches in public must be restricted to superficial examination of outer clothing. There is no power to require a person to remove any clothing in public other than an outer coat, jacket or gloves. Where on reasonable grounds it is considered necessary to conduct a more thorough search (e.g. by requiring a person to take off a T-shirt or headgear), this should be done out of public view (e.g. in a police van or nearby police station if there is one). Any search involving the removal of more than an outer coat, jacket, gloves, headgear or footwear may only be made by an officer of the same sex as the person searched and may not be made in the presence of anyone of the opposite sex unless the person being searched specifically requests it. [See *Note 3A*]

Notes for Guidance

3A A search in the street itself should be regarded as being in public for the purposes of paragraph 3.5 above, even though it may be empty at the time a search begins. Although there is no power to require a person to do so, there is nothing to prevent an officer from asking a person to voluntarily remove more than an outer coat, jacket or gloves in public.

3B As a search of a person in public should be a superficial examination of outer clothing, such searches should be completed as soon as possible.

4 Action after a search is carried out

(a) General

4.1 An officer who has carried out a search must make a written record unless it is not practicable to do so, on account of the numbers to be searched or for some other operational reason, e.g. in situations involving public disorder.

4.2 The record must be completed as soon as practicable — on the spot unless circumstances (e.g. other immediate duties or very bad weather) make this impracticable.

4.3 The record must be made on the form provided for this purpose (the national search record).

4.4 In order to complete the search record the officer should normally seek the name, address and date of birth of the person searched, but under the search procedures there is no obligation on a person to provide these details and no power to detain him if he is unwilling to do so.

4.5 The following information should always be included in the record of a search even if the person does not wish to identify himself or give his date of birth;

   (i)   the name of the person searched, or (if he withholds it) a description of him;
   (ii) a note of the person's ethnic origin;
   (iii) when a vehicle is searched, a description of it, including its registration number; [See *Note 4B*]
   (iv) the object of the search;
   (v) the grounds for making it;
   (vi) the date and time it was made;
  (vii) the place where it was made;
 (viii) its results;
   (ix) a note of any injury or damage to property resulting from it;
   (x) the identify of the officer making it (except in the case of enquiries linked to the investigation of terrorism, in which case the record shall state the officer's warrant number and duty station). [See *Note 4A*]

4.6 A record is required for each person and each vehicle searched. However, if a person is in a vehicle and both are searched, and the object and grounds of the search are the same, only one record need be completed.

Appendix 2

4.7 The record of the grounds for making a search must, briefly but informatively, explain the reason for suspecting the person concerned, whether by reference to his behaviour or other circumstances.

(b) Unattended vehicles

4.8 After searching an unattended vehicle, or anything in or on it, an officer must leave a notice in it (or on it, if things in or on it have been searched without opening it) recording the fact that it has been searched.

4.9 The notice should include the name of the police station to which the officer concerned is attached and state where a copy of the record of the search may be obtained and where any application for compensation should be directed.

4.10 The vehicle must if practicable be left secure.

Notes for Guidance

4A Where a search is conducted by more than one officer the identity of all the officers engaged in the search must be recorded on the search record.

4B Where a vehicle has not been allocated a registration number (e.g. a rally car or a trials motorbike) that part of the requirement under 4.5(iii) does not apply.

SUMMARY OF MAIN STOP AND SEARCH POWERS [See paragraph 1.3]   ANNEX

POWER	OBJECT OF SEARCH	EXTENT OF SEARCH	WHERE EXCERCISABLE
Unlawful articles general			
1. Public Stores Act 1875, s6	HM Stores stolen or unlawfully obtained	Persons, vehicles and vessels	Anywhere where the constabulary powers are exercisable*
2. Firearms Act 1968, s47	Firearms	Persons and vehicles	A public place**
3. Misuse of Drugs Act 1971, s23	Controlled drugs	Persons and vehicles	Anywhere
4. Customs and Excise Management Act 1979, s163	Goods: (a) on which duty has not been paid; (b) being unlawfully removed, imported or exported; (c) otherwise liable to forfeiture to HM Customs and Excise	Vehicles and vessels only	Anywhere*
5. Aviation Security Act 1982, s27(1)	Stolen or unlawfully obtained goods	Airport employees and vehicles carrying airport employees or aircraft or any vehicle in a cargo area whether or not carrying an employee	Any designated airport
6. Police and Criminal Evidence Act 1984, s1	Stolen goods; articles for use in certain Theft Act offences; offensive weapons, including bladed or sharply-pointed articles (except folding pocket knives with a bladed cutting edge not exceeding 3 inches)	Persons and vehicles	Where there is public access***
Police and Criminal Evidence Act 1984, s6(3) (by a constable of the United Kingdom Atomic Energy Authority Constabulary in respect of property owned or controlled by British Nuclear Fuels plc)	HM Stores (in the form of goods and chattels belonging to British Nuclear Fuels plc)	Persons, vehicles and vessels	Anywhere where the constabulary powers are exercisable*

569

SUMMARY OF MAIN STOP AND SEARCH POWERS [See paragraph 1.3] ANNEX *continued*

POWER	OBJECT OF SEARCH	EXTENT OF SEARCH	WHERE EXCERCISABLE
Unlawful articles general			
7. Sporting Events (Control of Alcohol etc) Act 1985, s7	Intoxicating liquor	Persons, coaches and trains	Designated sports grounds or coaches and trains travelling to or from a designated sporting event
8. Crossbows Act 1987, s4	Crossbows or parts of crossbows (except crossbows with a draw weight of less than 1.4 kilograms)	Persons and vehicles	Anywhere except dwellings
Evidence of game and wildlife offences			
9. Poaching Prevention Act 1862, s2	Game or poaching equipment	Persons and vehicles	A public place
10. Deer Acts 1963, s5 and 1980, s4****	Evidence of offences under the Act	Persons and Vehicles	Anywhere except dwellings
11. Conservation of Seals Act 1970, s4	Seals or hunting equipment	Vehicles only	Anywhere
12. Badgers Act 1973, s10****	Evidence of offences under the Act	Persons and vehicles	Anywhere except dwellings
13. Wildlife and Countryside Act 1981, s19	Evidence of wildlife offences	Persons and vehicles	Anywhere except dwellings
Other			
14. Prevention of Terrorism (Temporary Provisions) Act 1989, s 15(3)	Evidence of liability to arrest under section 14 of the Act	Persons and vehicles	Anywhere

* Including, in the case of a vessel, territorial waters.

** Anywhere in the case of reasonable suspicion of offences of carrying firearms with criminal intent or trespassing with firearms.

*** Any place where the public is at the time entitled to go or places other than dwellings where people have ready access at the time (unless land attached to a dwelling where the person or vehicle is permitted to be).

**** Now 1991.

Appendix 3

Code of practice for the searching of premises by police officers and the seizure of property found by police officers on persons or premises

1 General

1.1 This code of practice must be readily available at all police stations for consultation by police officers, detained persons and members of the public.

1.2 The notes for guidance included are not provisions of this code, but are guidance to police officers and others about its application and interpretation.

1.3 This code applies to the following searches of premises:

(a) searches of premises undertaken for the purposes of an investigation into an alleged offence, with the occupier's consent, other than routine scenes of crime searches and searches following the activation of fire or burglar alarms or bomb threat calls;

(b) searches of premises under powers conferred by sections 17, 18 and 32 of the Police and Criminal Evidence Act 1984;

(c) searches of premises undertaken in pursuance of a search warrant issued in accordance with section 15 of, or Schedule 1 to, that Act, or Schedule 7 to the Prevention of Terrorism (Temporary Provisions) Act 1989.

'Premises' for the purpose of this code is defined in section 23 of the Police and Criminal Evidence Act 1984. It includes any place and, in particular, any vehicle, vessel, aircraft, hovercraft, tent or movable structure. It also includes any off-shore installation as defined in section 1 of the Mineral Workings (Offshore Installations) Act 1971.

2 Search warrants and production orders

(a) Action to be taken before an application is made

2.1 Where information is received which appears to justify an application, the officer concerned must take reasonable steps to check that the information is accurate, recent and has not been provided maliciously or irresponsibly. An application may not be made on the basis of information from an anonymous source where corroboration has not been sought.

2.2 The officer shall ascertain as specifically as is possible in the circumstances the nature of the articles concerned and their location.

2.3 The officer shall also make reasonable enquiries to establish what, if anything, is known about the likely occupier of the premises and the nature of the premises themselves; and whether they have been previously searched and if so how recently; and to obtain any other information relevant to the application.

2.4 No application for a search warrant may be made without the authority of an officer of at least the rank of inspector (or, in a case of urgency where no officer of this rank is readily available, the senior officer on duty). No application for a production order or warrant under Schedule 1 to the Police and Criminal Evidence Act 1984, or under Schedule 7 to the Prevention of Terrorism (Temporary Provisions) Act 1989, may be made without the authority of an officer of at least the rank of superintendent.

2.5 Except in a case of urgency, if there is reason to believe that a search might have an adverse effect on relations between the police and the community then the local police/community liaison officer shall be consulted before it takes place. In urgent cases, the local police/community liaison officer should be informed of the search as soon as practicable after it has been made. [See *Note 2B*]

(b) Making an application

2.6 An application for a search warrant must be supported by an information in writing, stating:

    (i)   the enactment under which the application is made;
    (ii) as specifically as is reasonably practicable the premises to be searched and the object of the search;
    (iii) the grounds on which the application is made (including, where the purpose of the proposed search is to find evidence of an alleged offence, an indication of how the evidence relates to the investigation).

2.7 An application for a search warrant under paragraph 12(a) of Schedule 1 to the Police and Criminal Evidence Act 1984, or under Schedule 7 to the Prevention of Terrorism (Temporary Provisions) Act 1989, shall also, where appropriate, indicate why it is believed that service of notice of an application for a production order may seriously prejudice the investigation.

2.8 If an application is refused, no further application may be made for a warrant to search those premises unless supported by additional grounds.

Notes for Guidance

2A *The identity of an informant need not be disclosed when making an application, but the officer concerned should be prepared to deal with any questions the magistrate or judge may have about the accuracy of previous information provided by that source or other related matters.*

2B The local police/community consultative group, where it exists, or its equivalent, should be informed as soon as practicable after a search has taken place where there is reason to believe that it might have had an adverse effect on relations between the police and the community.

3 Entry without warrant

(a) Making an arrest etc

3.1 The conditions under which an officer may enter and search premises without a warrant are set out in section 17 of the Police and Criminal Evidence Act 1984.

(b) Search after arrest of premises in which arrest takes place or in which the arrested person was present immediately prior to arrest

3.2 The powers of an officer to search premises in which he has arrested a person or where the person was immediately before he was arrested are as set out in section 32 of the Police and Criminal Evidence Act 1984.

(c) Search after arrest of premises other than those in which arrest takes place

3.3 The specific powers of an officer to search premises occupied or controlled by a person who has been arrested for an arrestable offence are as set out in section 18 of the Police and Criminal Evidence Act 1984. They may not (unless subsection 5 of section 18 applies) be exercised unless an officer of the rank of inspector or above has given authority in writing. That authority should (unless wholly impracticable) be given on the Notice of Powers and Rights (see paragraph 5.7(i)). The record of the search required by section 18(7) of the Act shall be made in the custody record, where there is one.

4 Search with consent

4.1 Subject to paragraph 4.4 below, if it is proposed to search premises with the consent of a person entitled to grant entry to the premises the consent must, if practicable, be given in writing on the Notice of Powers and Rights before the search takes place. The officer must make enquiries to satisfy himself that the person is in a position to give such consent. [See *Note 4B* and *paragraph 5.7(i)*]

4.2 Before seeking consent the officer in charge of the search shall state the purpose of the proposed search and inform the person concerned that he is not obliged to consent and that anything seized may be produced in evidence. If at the time the person is not suspected of an offence, the officer shall tell him so when stating the purpose of the search.

4.3 An officer cannot enter and search premises or continue to search premises under 4.1 above if the consent has been given under duress or is withdrawn before the search is completed.

4.4 It is unnecessary to seek consent under paragraphs 4.1 and 4.2 above where in the circumstances this would cause disproportionate inconvenience to the person concerned. [See *Note 4C*]

Notes for Guidance

4A   In the case of a lodging house or similar accommodation a search should not be made on the basis solely of the landlord's consent unless the tenant is unavailable and the matter is urgent.

4B   Where it is intended to search premises under the authority of a warrant or a power of entry and search without warrant, and the co-operation of the occupier of the premises is obtained in accordance with paragraph 5.4 below, there is no additional requirement to obtain written consent as at paragraph 4.1 above.

4C   Paragraph 4.4 is intended in particular to apply, for example, to circumstances where police have arrested someone in the night after a pursuit and it is necessary to make a brief check of gardens along the route of the pursuit to see whether stolen or incriminating articles have been discarded.

5 Searching of premises: general considerations

(a) Time of searches

5.1 Searches made under warrant must be made within one calendar month from the date of issue of the warrant.

5.2 Searches must be made at a reasonable hour unless this might frustrate the purpose of the search. [See *Note 5A*]

5.3 A warrant authorises an entry on one occasion only.

(b) Entry other than with consent

5.4 The officer in charge shall first attempt to communicate with the occupier or any other person entitled to grant access to the premises by explaining the authority under which he seeks entry to the premises and ask the occupier to allow him to do so, unless:

    (i) the premises to be searched are known to be unoccupied;
    (ii) the occupier and any other person entitled to grant access are known to be absent; or
    (iii) there are reasonable grounds for believing that to alert the occupier or

any other person entitled to grant access by attempting to communicate with him would frustrate the object of the search or endanger the officers concerned or other persons.

5.5 Where the premises are occupied the officer shall identify himself (by warrant number in the case of enquiries linked to the investigation of terrorism) and, if not in uniform, show his warrant card (but in so doing in the case of enquiries linked to the investigation of terrorism, the officer need not reveal his name); and state the purpose of the search and the grounds for undertaking it, before a search begins, unless sub-paragraph 5.4(iii) applies.

5.6 Reasonable force may be used if necessary to enter premises if the officer in charge is satisfied that the premises are those specified in any warrant, or in exercise of the powers described in 3.1 to 3.3 above, and where:

   (i)   the occupier or any other person entitled to grant access has refused a request to allow entry to his premises;

  (ii)   it is impossible to communicate with the occupier or any other person entitled to grant access; or

 (iii)   any of the provisions of 5.4 (i) to (iii) apply.

(c) Notice of Powers and Rights

5.7 If an officer conducts a search to which this code applies he shall, unless it is impracticable to do so, provide the occupier with a copy of a notice in a standard format:

   (i)   specifying whether the search is made under warrant, or with consent, or in the exercise of the powers described in 3.1 to 3.3 above (the format of the notice shall provide for authority or consent to be indicated where appropriate — see 3.3 and 4.1 above);

  (ii)   summarising the extent of the powers of search and seizure conferred in the Act;

 (iii)   explaining the rights of the occupier, and of the owner of property seized in accordance with the provisions of 6.1 to 6.5 below, set out in the Act and in this code;

 (iv)   explaining that compensation may be payable in appropriate cases for damage caused in entering and searching premises, and giving the address to which an application for compensation should be directed; and

  (v)   stating that a copy of this code is available to be consulted at any police station.

5.8 If the occupier is present, copies of the notice mentioned above, and of the warrant (if the search is made under warrant) should if practicable be given to the occupier before the search begins, unless the officer in charge of the search reasonably believes that to do so would frustrate the object of the search or endanger the officers concerned or other persons. If the occupier is not present, copies of the notice, and of the warrant where appropriate, should be left in a prominent place on the premises or appropriate part of the premises and endorsed with the name of the officer in charge of the search (except in the case of enquiries linked to the investigation of terrorism, in which case the officer's warrant number should be given), the name of the police station to which he is attached and the date and time of the search. The warrant itself should be endorsed to show that this has been done.

(d) Conduct of searches

5.9 Premises may be searched only to the extent necessary to achieve the object of the search, having regard to the size and nature of whatever is sought. A search under warrant may not continue under the authority of that warrant once all the things specified in it have been found, or the officer in charge of the search is satisfied that they are not on the premises.

5.10 Searches must be conducted with due consideration for the property and privacy of the occupier of the premises searched, and with no more disturbance than necessary. Reasonable force may be used only where this is necessary because the co-operation of the occupier cannot be obtained or is insufficient for the purpose.

5.11 If the occupier wishes to ask a friend, neighbour or other person to witness the search then he must be allowed to do so, unless the officer in charge has reasonable grounds for believing that this would seriously hinder the investigation. A search need not be unreasonably delayed for this purpose.

(e) Leaving premises

5.12 If premises have been entered by force the officer in charge shall, before leaving them, satisfy himself that they are secure either by arranging for the occupier or his agent to be present or by any other appropriate means.

(f) Search under Schedule 1 to the Police and Criminal Evidence Act 1984

5.13 An officer of the rank of inspector or above shall take charge of and be present at any search made under a warrant issued under Schedule 1 to the Police and Criminal Evidence Act 1984 or under Schedule 7 to the Prevention of Terrorism (Temporary Provisions) Act 1989. He is responsible for ensuring that the search is conducted with discretion and in such a manner as to cause the least possible disruption to any business or other activities carried on in the premises.

5.14 After satisfying himself that material may not be taken from the premises without his knowledge, the officer in charge of the search shall ask for the documents or other records concerned to be produced. He may also, if he considers it to be necessary, ask to see the index to files held on the premises, if there is one; and the officers conducting the search may inspect any files which, according to the index, appear to contain any of the material sought. A more extensive search of the premises may be made only if the person responsible for them refuses to produce the material sought, or to allow access to the index; if it appears that the index is inaccurate or incomplete; or if for any other reason the officer in charge has reasonable grounds for believing that such a search is necessary in order to find the material sought. [See *Note 5B*]

Notes for Guidance

5A In determining at what time to make a search, the officer in charge should have regard, among other considerations, to the times of day at which the occupier of the premises is likely to be present, and should not search at a time when he, or any other person on the premises, is likely to be asleep unless not doing so is likely to frustrate the purpose of the search.

5B In asking for documents to be produced in accordance with paragraph 5.14 above, officers should direct the request to a person in authority and with responsibility for the documents.

5C If the wrong premises are searched by mistake, everything possible should be done at the earliest opportunity to allay any sense of grievance. In appropriate cases assistance should be given to obtain compensation.

6 Seizure and retention of property

(a) Seizure

6.1 Subject to paragraph 6.2 below, an officer who is searching any premises under any statutory power or with the consent of the occupier may seize:

(a) anything covered by a warrant; and
(b) anything which he has reasonable grounds for believing is evidence of an offence or has been obtained in consequence of the commission of an offence.

Items under (b) may only be seized where this is necessary to prevent their concealment, alteration, loss, damage or destruction.

6.2 No item may be seized which is subject to legal privilege (as defined in section 10 of the Police and Criminal Evidence Act 1984).

6.3 An officer who decides that it is not appropriate to seize property because of an explanation given by the person holding it, but who has reasonable grounds for believing that it has been obtained in consequence of the commission of an offence by some person, shall inform the holder of his suspicions and shall explain that, if he disposes of the property, he may be liable to civil or criminal proceedings.

6.4 An officer may photograph or copy, or have photographed or copied, any document or other article which he has power to seize in accordance with paragraph 6.1 above.

6.5 Where an officer considers that a computer may contain information that could be used in evidence, he may require the information to be produced in a form that can be taken away and in which it is visible and legible.

(b) Retention

6.6 Subject to paragraph 6.7 below, anything which has been seized in accordance with the above provisions may be retained only for as long as is necessary in the circumstances. It may be retained, among other purposes:

    (i) for use as evidence at a trial for an offence;

   (ii) for forensic examination or for other investigation in connection with an offence; or

  (iii) where there are reasonable grounds for believing that it has been stolen or obtained by the commission of an offence, in order to establish its lawful owner.

6.7 Property shall not be retained in accordance with 6.6(i) and (ii) (i.e. for use as evidence or for the purposes of investigation) if a photograph or copy would suffice for those purposes.

(c) Rights of owners etc

6.8 If property is retained the person who had custody or control of it immediately prior to its seizure must on request be provided with a list or description of the property within a reasonable time.

6.9 He or his representative must be allowed supervised access to the property to examine it or have it photographed or copied, or must be provided with a photograph or copy, in either case within a reasonable time of any request and at his own expense, unless the officer in charge of an investigation has reasonable grounds for believing that this would prejudice the investigation of an offence or any criminal proceedings. In this case a record of the grounds must be made.

Note for Guidance

6A *Any person claiming property seized by the police may apply to a magistrate's court under the Police (Property) Act 1897 for its possession, and should, where appropriate, be advised of this procedure.*

7 Action to be taken after searches

7.1 Where premises have been searched in circumstances to which this code applies, other than in the circumstances covered by paragraph 4.4 above, the officer in charge of the search shall, on arrival at a police station, make or have made a record of the search. The record shall include:

    (i) the address of the premises searched;

   (ii) the date, time and duration of the search;

  (iii) the authority under which the search was made. Where the search was made in the exercise of a statutory power to search premises without warrant, the record shall include the power under which the search was made; and where the search was made under warrant, or with written consent, a copy of the warrant or consent shall be appended to the record or kept in a place identified in the record;

  (iv) the names of all the officers who conducted the search (except in the case of enquiries linked to the investigation of terrorism, in which case the record shall state the warrant number and duty station of each officer concerned);

   (v) the names of any persons on the premises if they are known;

  (vi) either a list of any articles seized or a note of where such a list is kept and, if not covered by a warrant, the reason for their seizure;

 (vii) whether force was used, and, if so, the reason why it was used;

(viii) details of any damage caused during the search, and the circumstances in which it was caused.

7.2 Where premises have been searched under warrant, the warrant shall be endorsed to show:

    (i) whether any articles specified in the warrant were found;

   (ii) whether any other articles were seized;

  (iii) the date and time at which it was executed;

  (iv) the names of the officers who executed it (except in the case of enquiries linked to the investigation of terrorism, in which case the warrant number and duty station of each officer concerned shall be shown);

   (v) whether a copy, together with a copy of the Notice of Powers and Rights was handed to the occupier; or whether it was endorsed as required by paragraph 5.8, and left on the premises together with the copy notice and, if so, where.

7.3 Any warrant which has been executed or which has not been executed within one calendar month of its issue shall be returned, if it was issued by a justice of the peace, to the clerk to the justices for the petty sessions area concerned or, if issued by a judge, to the appropriate officer of the court from which he issued it.

8 Search registers

8.1 A search register shall be maintained at each sub-divisional police station. All records which are required to be made by this code shall be made, copied, or referred to in the register.

Appendix 4

Code of practice for the detention, treatment and questioning of persons by police officers

1 General

1.1 All persons in custody must be dealt with expeditiously, and released as soon as the need for detention has ceased to apply.

1.2 This code of practice must be readily available at all police stations for consultation by police officers, detained persons and members of the public.

1.3 The notes for guidance included are not provisions of this code, but are guidance to police officers and others about its application and interpretation. Provisions in the annexes to this code are provisions of this code.

1.4 If an officer has any suspicion, or is told in good faith, that a person of any age may be mentally disordered or mentally handicapped, or mentally incapable of understanding the significance of questions put to him or his replies, then that person shall be treated as a mentally disordered or mentally handicapped person for the purposes of this code. [See *Note 1G*]

1.5 If anyone appears to be under the age of 17 then he shall be treated as a juvenile for the purposes of this code in the absence of clear evidence to show that he is older.

1.6 If a person appears to be blind or seriously visually handicapped, deaf, unable to read, unable to speak or has difficulty orally because of a speech impediment, he should be treated as such for the purposes of this code in the absence of clear evidence to the contrary.

1.7 In this code 'the appropriate adult' means:

(a) in the case of a juvenile:
  (i) his parent or guardian (or, if he is in care, the care authority or voluntary organisation);
  (ii) a social worker; or
  (iii) failing either of the above, another responsible adult aged 18 or over who is not a police officer or employed by the police.
(b) In the case of a person who is mentally disordered or mentally handicapped:

    (i) a relative, guardian or other person responsible for his care or custody;

    (ii) someone who has experience of dealing with mentally disordered or mentally handicapped persons but is not a police officer or employed by the police (such as an approved social worker as defined by the Mental Health Act 1983 or a specialist social worker); or

    (iii) failing either of the above, some other responsible adult aged 18 or over who is not a police officer or employed by the police. [See *Note 1E*]

1.8 Whenever this code requires a person to be given certain information he does not have to be given it if he is incapable at the time of understanding what is said to him or is violent or likely to become violent or is in urgent need of medical attention, but he must be given it as soon as practicable.

1.9 Any reference to a custody officer in this code includes an officer who is performing the functions of a custody officer.

1.10 This code applies to persons who are in custody at police stations whether or not they have been arrested for an offence and to those who have been removed to a police station as a place of safety under sections 135 and 136 of the Mental Health Act 1983. Section 15, however, applies solely to persons in police detention.

1.11 Persons in police detention include persons taken to a police station after being arrested under section 14 of the Prevention of Terrorism (Temporary Provisions) Act 1989 or under paragraph 6 of Schedule 5 to that Act by an examining officer who is a constable.

Notes for Guidance

1A Although certain sections of this code (e.g. section 9 — treatment of detained persons) apply specifically to persons in custody at police stations, those there voluntarily to assist with an investigation should be treated with no less consideration (e.g. offered refreshments at appropriate times) and enjoy an absolute right to obtain legal advice or communicate with anyone outside the police station.

1B This code does not affect the principle that all citizens have a duty to help police officers to prevent crime and discover offenders. This is a civic rather than a legal duty; but when a police officer is trying to discover whether, or by whom, an offence has been committed he is entitled to question any person from whom he thinks useful information can be obtained, subject to the restrictions imposed by this code. A person's declaration that he is unwilling to reply does not alter this entitlement.

1C The parent or guardian of a juvenile should be the appropriate adult unless he is suspected of involvement in the offence, is the victim, is a witness, is involved in the investigation or has received admissions. In such circumstances it will be desirable for the appropriate adult to be some other person. If the parent of a juvenile is estranged from the juvenile, he should not be asked to act as the appropriate adult if the juvenile expressly and specifically objects to his presence.

1D If a child in care admits an offence to a social worker, another social worker should be the appropriate adult in the interest of fairness.

1E In the case of persons who are mentally disordered or mentally handicapped, it may in certain circumstances be more satisfactory for all concerned if the appropriate adult is someone who has experience or training in their care rather than a relative lacking such qualifications. But if the person himself prefers a relative to a better qualified stranger his wishes should if practicable be respected.

1F A solicitor who is present at the station in a professional capacity may not act as the appropriate adult.

1G The generic term "mental disorder" is used throughout this code. "Mental disorder" is defined by the Mental Health Act 1983 as "mental illness, arrested or incomplete development of mind, psychopathic disorder and any other disorder or disability of mind." It should be noted that "mental disorder" is different to "mental handicap" although the two forms of disorder are dealt with similarly throughout this code.

2 Custody records

2.1 A separate custody record must be opened as soon as practicable for each person who is brought to a police station under arrest or is arrested at the police station having attended there voluntarily. All information which has to be recorded under this code must be recorded as soon as practicable, in the custody record unless otherwise specified.

2.2 In the case of any action requiring the authority of an officer of a specified rank, his name and rank must be noted in the custody record. The recording of names does not apply to officers dealing with persons detained under the Prevention of Terrorism (Temporary Provisions) Act 1989. Instead the record shall state the warrant number and duty station of such officers.

2.3 The custody officer is responsible for the accuracy and completeness of the custody record and for ensuring that the record or a copy of the record accompanies a detained person if he is transferred to another police station. The record shall show the time of and reason for transfer and the time a person is released from detention.

2.4 When a person leaves police detention or is taken before a court he or his legal representative or his appropriate adult shall be supplied on request with a copy of the custody record as soon as practicable. This entitlement lasts for 12 months after his release.

2.5 The person who has been detained, the appropriate adult, or legal representative who gives reasonable notice of a request to inspect the original custody record after the person has left police detention should be allowed to do so. A note of any such inspection should be made in the custody record.

2.6 All entries in custody records must be timed and signed by the maker. In the case of a record entered on a computer this should be timed and contain the operator's identification. Warrant numbers should be used rather than names in the case of detention under the Prevention of Terrorism (Temporary Provisions) Act 1989.

2.7 The fact and time of any refusal by a person to sign a custody record when asked to do so in accordance with the provisions of this code must itself be recorded.

3 Initial action

(a) Detained persons: normal procedure

3.1 When a person is brought to a police station under arrest or is arrested at the police station having attended there voluntarily the custody officer must inform him clearly of the following rights and of the fact that they are continuing rights which may be exercised at any stage during the period in custody.

- (i) the right to have someone informed of his arrest in accordance with section 5 below;
- (ii) the right to consult privately with a solicitor in accordance with section 6 below, and the fact that independent legal advice is available free of charge; and
- (iii) the right to consult this and the other codes of practice. [See *Note 3E*]

3.2 The custody officer must give the person a written notice setting out the above three rights, the right to a copy of the custody record in accordance with paragraph 2.4 above and the caution in the terms prescribed in section 10 below. The notice must also explain the arrangements for obtaining legal advice. The custody officer must also give the person an additional written notice briefly setting out his entitlements while in custody. [See *Notes 3A* and *3B*] The custody officer shall ask the person to sign the custody record to acknowledge receipt of these notices and any refusal to sign must be recorded on the custody record.

3.3 A citizen of an independent Commonwealth country or a national of a foreign country (including the Republic of Ireland) must be informed as soon as practicable of his rights of communication with his High Commission, Embassy or Consulate. [See *Section 7*]

3.4 If the custody officer authorises a person's detention he must inform him of the grounds as soon as practicable and in any case before that person is then questioned about any offence.

3.5 The person shall be asked to sign on the custody record to signify whether or not he wants legal advice at this point. The custody officer is responsible for ensuring that the person signs the custody record in the correct place to give effect to his decision. Where legal advice is requested (and unless Annex B applies) the custody officer must act without delay to secure the provision of such advice to the person concerned.

(b) Detained persons: special groups

3.6 If the person appears to be *deaf* or there is doubt about his *hearing* or speaking ability or ability to understand English, and the custody officer cannot establish effective communication, the custody officer must as soon as practicable call an interpreter and ask him to provide the information required above. [See *Section 13*]

3.7 If the person is a juvenile, the custody officer must, if it is practicable, ascertain the identity of a person responsible for his welfare. That person may be his parent or guardian (or, if he is in care, the care authority or voluntary organisation) or any other person who has, for the time being, assumed responsibility for his welfare. That person must be informed as soon as practicable that the juvenile has been arrested, why he has been arrested and where he is detained. This right is in addition to the juvenile's right in section 5 of the code not to be held incommunicado. [See *Note 3C*]

3.8 In the case of a juvenile who is known to be subject to a supervision order, reasonable steps must also be taken to notify the person supervising him.

3.9 If the person is a juvenile, is mentally handicapped or is suffering from a mental disorder, then the custody officer must, as soon as practicable, inform the appropriate adult (who in the case of a juvenile may or may not be a person responsible for his welfare, in accordance with paragraph 3.7 above) of the grounds for his detention and his whereabouts, and ask the adult to come to the police station to see the person.

3.10 It is imperative that a mentally disordered or mentally handicapped person who has been detained under section 136 of the Mental Health Act 1983 should be assessed as soon as possible. If that assessment is to take place at the police station, an approved social worker and a registered medical practitioner should be called to the police station as soon as possible in order to interview and examine the person. Once the person has been interviewed and examined and suitable arrangements have been made for his treatment or care, he can no longer be detained under section 136. The person should not be released until he has been seen by both the approved social worker and the registered medical practitioner.

3.11 If the appropriate adult is already at the police station when information is given to the person as required in paragraphs 3.1 to 3.4 above then the information must be given to the detained person in his presence. If the appropriate adult is not at the police station when the information is given then the information must be given to the detained person again in the presence of the appropriate adult once that person arrives.

3.12 The person should be advised by the custody officer that the appropriate adult (where applicable) is there to assist and advise him and that he can consult privately with the appropriate adult at any time.

3.13 If, having been informed of the right to legal advice under paragraph 3.11 above, the appropriate adult considers that legal advice should be taken, then the provisions of section 6 of this code apply. [See *Note 3G*]

3.14 If the person is blind or seriously visually handicapped or is unable to read, the custody officer should ensure that his solicitor, relative, the appropriate adult or some other person likely to take an interest in him (and not involved in the investigation) is available to help in checking any documentation. Where this code requires written consent or signification, then the person who is assisting may be asked to sign instead if the detained person so wishes. [See *Note 3F*]

(c) Persons attending a police station voluntarily

3.15 Any person attending a police station voluntarily for the purpose of assisting with an investigation may leave at will unless placed under arrest. If it is decided that he should not be allowed to do so then he must be informed at once that he is under arrest and brought before the custody officer, who is responsible for ensuring that he is notified of his rights in the same way as other detained persons. If he is not placed under arrest but is cautioned in accordance with section 10 below, the officer who gives the caution must at the same time inform him that he is not under arrest, that he is not obliged to remain at the police station but that if he remains at the police station he may obtain free legal advice if he wishes.

3.16 If a person who is attending the police station voluntarily (in accordance with paragraph 3.15) asks about his entitlement to legal advice, he should be given a copy of the notice explaining the arrangements for obtaining legal advice. [See *paragraph 3.2*]

(d) Documentation

3.17 The grounds for a person's detention shall be recorded, in his presence if practicable.

3.18 Action taken under paragraphs 3.6 to 3.14 shall be recorded.

Notes for Guidance

3A The notice of entitlements is intended to provide detained persons with brief details of their entitlements over and above the statutory rights which are set out in the notice of rights. The notice of entitlements should list the entitlements contained in this code, including visits and contact with outside parties (including special provisions for Commonwealth citizens and foreign nationals), reasonable standards of physical comfort, adequate food and drink, access to toilets and washing facilities, clothing, medical attention, and exercise where practicable. It should also mention the provisions relating to the conduct of interviews, the circumstances in which an appropriate adult should be available to assist the detained person and his statutory rights to make representation whenever the period of his detention is reviewed.

3B In addition to the notices in English, translations into Welsh, the main ethnic minority languages and the principal EC languages should be available whenever they are likely to be helpful.

3C If the juvenile is in the care of a local authority or voluntary organisation but is living with his parents or other adults responsible for his welfare then, although there is no legal obligation on the police to inform them, they as well as the authority or organisation should normally be contacted unless suspected of involvement in the offence concerned. Even if a juvenile in care is not living with his parents, consideration should be given to informing them as well.

3D Most local authority Social Services Departments can supply a list of interpreters who have the necessary skills and experience to interpret for the deaf at police interviews. The local Community Relations Council may be able to provide similar information in cases where the person concerned does not understand English. [See section 13]

3E The right to consult the codes of practice under paragraph 3.1 above does not entitle the person concerned to delay unreasonably any necessary investigative or administrative action while he does so. Procedures requiring the provision of breath, blood or urine specimens under the terms of the Road Traffic Act 1988 need not be delayed.

3F Blind or seriously visually handicapped persons may be unwilling to sign police documents. The alternative of their representative signing on their behalf seeks to protect the interests of both police and suspects.

3G The purpose of paragraph 3.13 is to protect the rights of a juvenile, mentally disordered or mentally handicapped person who may not understand the significance of what is being said to him. If such a person wishes to exercise the right to legal advice the appropriate action should be taken straightaway and not delayed until the appropriate adult arrives.

4 Detained persons' property

(a) Action

4.1 The custody officer is responsible for:

(a) ascertaining:
  (i) what property a detained person has with him when he comes to the police station (whether on arrest, re-detention on answering to bail, commitment to prison custody on the order or sentence of a court, lodgement at the police station with a view to his production in court from such custody, arrival at a police station on transfer from detention at another station or from hospital or on detention under section 135 or 136 of the Mental Health Act 1983);
  (ii) what property he might have acquired for an unlawful or harmful purpose while in custody.
(b) the safekeeping of any property which is taken from him and which remains at the police station.

To these ends the custody officer may search him or authorise his being searched to the extent that he considers necessary (provided that a search of intimate parts of the body or involving the removal of more than outer clothing may only be made in accordance with Annex A to this code). A search may only be carried out by an officer of the same sex as the person searched. [See *Note 4A*]

4.2 A detained person may retain clothing and personal effects at his own risk unless the custody officer considers that he may use them to cause harm to himself or others, interfere with evidence, damage property or effect an escape or they are needed as evidence. In this event the custody officer may withhold such articles as he considers necessary. If he does so he must tell the person why.

4.3 Personal effects are those items which a person may lawfully need or use or refer to while in detention but do not include cash and other items of value.

(b) Documentation

4.4 The custody officer is responsible for recording all property brought to the police station that a detained person had with him, or had taken from him on arrest. The detained person shall be allowed to check and sign the record of property as correct. Any refusal to sign should be recorded.

4.5 If a detained person is not allowed to keep any article of clothing or personal effects the reason must be recorded.

Notes for Guidance

4A Section 54(1) of PACE and paragraph 4.1 require a detained person to be searched where it is clear that the custody officer will have continuing duties in relation to that person or where that person's behaviour or offence makes an inventory appropriate. They do not require every detained person to be searched. Where, for example, it is clear that a person will only be detained for a short period and is not to be placed in a cell, the custody officer may decide not to search him. In such a case the custody record will be endorsed "not searched", paragraph 4.4 will not apply, and the person will be invited to sign the entry.

Where the person detained refuses to sign, the custody officer will be obliged to ascertain what property he has on him in accordance with paragraph 4.1

4B Paragraph 4.4 does not require the custody officer to record on the custody record property in the possession of the person on arrest, if by virtue of its nature, quantity or size, it is not practicable to remove it to the police station.

4C Paragraph 4.4 above is not to be taken as requiring that items of clothing worn by the person be recorded unless withheld by the custody officer in accordance with paragraph 4.2.

5 Right not to be held incommunicado

(a) Action

5.1 Any person arrested and held in custody at a police station or other premises may on request have one person known to him or who is likely to take an interest in his welfare informed at public expense as soon as practicable of his whereabouts. If the person cannot be contacted the person who has made the request may chose up to two alternatives. If they too cannot be contacted the person in charge of detention or of the investigation has discretion to allow further attempts until the information has been conveyed. [See *Notes 5C* and *5D*]

5.2 The exercise of the above right in respect of each of the persons nominated may be delayed only in accordance with Annex B to this code.

5.3 The above right may be exercised on each occasion that a person is taken to another police station.

5.4 The person may receive visits at the custody officer's discretion. [See *Note 5B*]

5.5 Where an enquiry as to the whereabouts of the person is made by a friend, relative or person with an interest in his welfare, this information shall be given, if he agrees and if Annex B does not apply. [See *Note 5D*]

5.6 Subject to the following condition, the person should be supplied with writing materials on request and allowed to speak on the telephone for a reasonable time to one person [See *Note 5E*]. Where an officer of the rank of Inspector or above considers that the sending of a letter or the making of a telephone call may result in:

(a) any of the consequences set out in the first and second paragraphs of Annex B and the person is detained in connection with an arrestable or a serious arrestable offence; or
(b) either of the consequences set out in paragraph 8 of Annex B and the person is detained under the Prevention of Terrorism (Temporary Provisions) Act 1989,

that officer can deny or delay the exercise of either or both these privileges.

However, nothing in this section permits the restriction or denial of the rights set out in sections 5.1 and 6.1.

5.7 Before any letter or message is sent, or telephone call made, the person shall be informed that what he says in any letter, call or message (other than in the case of a communication to a solicitor) may be read or listened to as appropriate and may be given in evidence. A telephone call may be terminated if it is being abused. The costs can be at public expense at the discretion of the custody officer.

(b) Documentation

5.8 A record must be kept of:

(a) any request made under this section and the action taken on it;
(b) any letters, messages or telephone calls made or received or visits received; and
(c) any refusal on the part of the person to have information about himself or his whereabouts given to an outside enquirer. The person must be asked to countersign the record accordingly and any refusal to sign should be recorded.

Notes for Guidance

5A An interpreter may make a telephone call or write a letter on a person's behalf.

5B In the exercise of his discretion the custody officer should allow visits where possible in the light of the availability of sufficient manpower to supervise a visit and any possible hindrance to the investigation.

5C If the person does not know of anyone to contact for advice or support or cannot contact a friend or relative, the custody officer should bear in mind any local voluntary bodies or other organisations who might be able to offer help in such cases. But if it is specifically legal advice that is wanted, then paragraph 6.1 below will apply.

5D In some circumstances it may not be appropriate to use the telephone to disclose information under paragraphs 5.1 and 5.5 above.

5E The telephone call at paragraph 5.6 is in addition to any communication under paragraphs 5.1 and 6.1.

6 Right to legal advice

(a) Action

6.1 Subject to paragraph 6.2, any person may at any time consult and communicate privately, whether in person, in writing or on the telephone with a solicitor. [See *Note 6B*]

6.2 The exercise of the above right may be delayed only in accordance with Annex B to this code. Whenever legal advice is requested (and unless Annex B applies) the custody officer must act without delay to secure the provision of such advice to the person concerned.

6.3 A poster advertising the right to have legal advice must be prominently displayed in the charging area of every police station. [See *Note 6H*]

6.4 No attempt should be made to dissuade the suspect from obtaining legal advice.

6.5 Reminders of the right to free legal advice must be given in accordance with paragraphs 11.2, 15.3 and paragraphs 2.15(ii) and 5.2 of code of practice D.

6.6 A person who wants legal advice may not be interviewed or continue to be interviewed until he has received it unless:

(a) Annex B applies; or
(b) an officer of the rank of superintendent or above has reasonable grounds for believing that:
  (i) delay will involve an immediate risk of harm to persons or serious loss of, or damage to, property; or
  (ii) where a solicitor, including a duty solicitor, has been contacted and has agreed to attend, awaiting his arrival would cause unreasonable delay to the process of investigation; or
(c) The solicitor nominated by the person, or selected by him from a list:
  (i) cannot be contacted; or
  (ii) has previously indicated that he does not wish to be contacted; or
  (iii) having been contacted, has declined to attend;

  and the person has been advised of the Duty Solicitor Scheme (where one is in operation) but has declined to ask for the duty solicitor, or the duty solicitor is unavailable. (In these circumstances the interview may be started or continued without further delay provided that an officer of the rank of Inspector or above has given agreement for the interview to proceed in those circumstances — see *Note 6b*).

(d) The person who wanted legal advice changes his mind. In these circumstances the interview may be started or continued without further delay provided that the person has given his agreement in writing or on tape to being interviewed without receiving legal advice and that an officer of the rank of Inspector or above has given agreement for the interview to proceed in those circumstances.

6.7 Where 6.6(b)(i) applies, once sufficient information to avert the risk has been obtained, questioning must cease until the person has received legal advice or 6.6(a), (b)(ii), (c) or (d) apply.

6.8 Where a person has been permitted to consult a solicitor and the solicitor is available (i.e. present at the station or on his way to the station or easily contactable by telephone) at the time the interview begins or is in progress, he must be allowed to have his solicitor present while he is interviewed.

6.9 The solicitor may only be required to leave the interview if his conduct is such that the investigating officer is unable properly to put questions to the suspect. [See *Notes 6D* and *6E*]

6.10 If the investigating officer considers that a solicitor is acting in such a way, he will stop the interview and consult an officer not below the rank of superintendent, if one is readily available, and otherwise an officer not below the rank of inspector who is not connected with the investigation. After speaking to the solicitor, the officer who has been consulted will decide whether or not the interview should continue in the presence of that solicitor. If he decides that it should not, the suspect will be given the opportunity to consult another solicitor before the interview continues and that solicitor will be given an opportunity to be present at the interview.

6.11 The removal of a solicitor from an interview is a serious step and, if it occurs, the officer of superintendent rank or above who took the decision will consider whether the incident should be reported to the Law Society. If the decision to remove the solicitor has been taken by an officer below the rank of superintendent, the facts must be reported to an officer of superintendent rank or above who will similarly consider whether a report to the Law Society would be appropriate. Where the solicitor concerned is a duty solicitor, the report should be both to the Law Society and to the Legal Aid Board.

6.12 In this code 'solicitor' means a solicitor qualified to practise in accordance with the Solicitors Act 1974. If a solicitor wishes to send a clerk or legal executive to provide advice on his behalf, then the clerk or legal executive shall be admitted to the police station for this purpose unless an officer of the rank of inspector or above considers that such a visit will hinder the investigation of crime and directs otherwise. Once admitted to the police station, the provisions of paragraphs 6.6 to 6.10 apply.

6.13 In exercising his discretion under paragraph 6.12, the officer should take into account in particular whether the identity and status of the clerk or legal executive have been satisfactorily established; whether he is of suitable character to provide legal advice (a person with a criminal record is unlikely to be suitable unless the conviction was for a minor offence and is not of recent date); and any other matters in any written letter of authorisation provided by the solicitor on whose behalf the clerk or legal executive is attending the police station. [See *Note 6F*]

6.14 If the inspector refuses access to a clerk or legal executive or a decision is taken that such a person should not be permitted to remain at an interview, he must forthwith notify a solicitor on whose behalf the clerk or legal executive was to have acted or was acting, and give him an opportunity of making alternative arrangements. The detained person must also be informed and the custody record noted.

6.15 If a solicitor arrives at the station to see a particular person, that person must (unless Annex B applies) be informed of the solicitor's arrival and asked whether he would like to see him. This applies even if the person concerned has already declined legal advice. The solicitor's attendance and the detained person's decision must be noted in the custody record.

(b) Documentation

6.16 Any request for legal advice and the action taken on it shall be recorded.

6.17 If a person has asked for legal advice and an interview is begun in the absence of a solicitor or his representative (or the solicitor or his representative has been required to leave an interview), a record shall be made in the interview record.

Notes for Guidance

6A In considering whether paragraph 6.6(b) applies, the officer should where practicable ask the solicitor for an estimate of the time that he is likely to take in coming to the station, and relate this information to the time for which detention is permitted, the time of day (i.e. whether the period of rest required by paragraph 12.2 is imminent) and the requirements of other investigations in progress. If the solicitor says that he is on his way to the station or that he will set off immediately, it will not normally be appropriate to begin an interview before he arrives. If it appears that it will be necessary to begin an interview before the solicitor's arrival he should be given an indication of how long police would be able to wait before paragraph 6.6(b) applies so that he has an opportunity to make arrangements for legal advice to be provided by someone else.

6B A person who asks for legal advice should be given an opportunity to consult a specific solicitor (for example, his own solicitor or one known to him) or the duty solicitor where a Duty Solicitor Scheme is in operation. If advice is not available by these means, or he does not wish to consult the duty solicitor, the person should be given an opportunity to choose a solicitor from a list of those willing to provide legal advice. If this solicitor is unavailable, he may choose up to two alternatives. If these attempts to secure legal advice are unsuccessful, the custody officer has discretion to allow further attempts until a solicitor has been contacted and agrees to provide legal advice.

6C Procedures undertaken under section 7 of the Road Traffic Act 1988 do not constitute interviewing for the purposes of this code.

6D In considering whether paragraph 6.9 applies, a solicitor is not guilty of misconduct if he seeks to challenge an improper question to his client or the manner in which it is put or if he advises his client not to reply to particular questions or if he wishes to give his client further legal advice. It is the duty of a solicitor to look after the interests of his client and to advise him without obstructing the interview. He should not be required to leave an interview unless his interference with its conduct clearly goes beyond this. Examples of misconduct may include answering questions on the client's behalf, or providing written replies for the client to quote.

6E In a case where an officer takes the decision to exclude a solicitor, he must be in a position to satisfy the court that the decision was properly made. In order to do this he may need to witness what is happening himself.

6F If an officer of at least the rank of inspector considers that a particular solicitor or firm of solicitors is persistently sending as clerks or legal executives persons who are unsuited to provide legal advice, he should inform an officer of at least the rank of superintendent, who may wish to take the matter up with the Law Society.

6G Subject to the constraints of Annex B, a solicitor may advise more than one client in an investigation if he wishes. Any question of a conflict of interest is for the solicitor under his professional code of conduct. If, however, waiting for a solicitor to give advice to one client may lead to unreasonable delay to the interview with another, the provisions of paragraph 6.6(b) may apply.

6H In addition to the poster in English, a poster or posters containing translations into Welsh, the main ethnic minority languages and the principal EC languages should be displayed wherever they are likely to be helpful and it is practicable to do so.

7 Citizens of independent Commonwealth countries or foreign nationals

(a) Action

7.1 A citizen of an independent Commonwealth country or a national of a foreign country (including the Republic of Ireland) may communicate at any time with his High Commission, Embassy or Consulate. He must be informed of this right as soon as practicable. He must also be informed as soon as practicable of his right to have his High Commission, Embassy or Consulate told of his whereabouts and the grounds for his detention.

7.2 If a citizen of an independent Commonwealth country or a national of a foreign country with which a consular convention is in force is detained, the appropriate High Commission, Embassy or Consulate shall be informed as soon as practicable, subject to paragraph 7.4 below. The countries to which this applies as at 20 April 1990 are listed in Annex F.

7.3 Consular officers may visit one of their nationals who is in police detention to talk to him and, if required, to arrange for legal advice. Such visits shall take place out of the hearing of a police officer.

7.4 Notwithstanding the provisions of consular conventions, where the person is a political refugee (whether for reasons of race, nationality, political opinion or religion) or is seeking political asylum, a consular officer shall not be informed of the arrest of one of his nationals or given access to or information about him except at the person's express request.

(b) Documentation

7.5 A record shall be made when a person is informed of his rights under this section and of any communications with a High Commission, Embassy or Consulate.

Note for Guidance

7A *The exercise of the rights in this section may not be interfered with even though Annex B applies.*

8 Conditions of Detention

(a) Action

8.1 So far as is practicable, not more than one person shall be detained in each cell.

8.2 Cells in use must be adequately heated, cleaned and ventilated. They must be adequately lit, subject to such dimming as is compatible with safety and security to allow persons detained overnight to sleep. No additional restraints should be used within a locked cell unless absolutely necessary, and then only suitable handcuffs.

8.3 Blankets, mattresses, pillows and other bedding supplied should be of a reasonable standard and in a clean and sanitary condition. [See *Note 8B*]

8.4 Access to toilet and washing facilities must be provided.

8.5 If it is necessary to remove a person's clothes for the purposes of investigation, for hygiene or health reasons or for cleaning, replacement clothing of a reasonable standard of comfort and cleanliness shall be provided. A person may not be interviewed unless adequate clothing has been offered to him.

8.6 At least two light meals and one main meal shall be offered in any period of 24 hours. Drinks should be provided at mealtimes and upon reasonable request between mealtimes. Whenever necessary, advice shall be sought from the police surgeon on medical or dietary matters. As far as practicable, meals provided shall offer a varied diet and meet any special dietary needs or religious beliefs that the person may have; he may also have meals supplied by his family or friends at his or their own expense. [See *Note 8B*]

8.7 Brief outdoor exercise shall be offered daily if practicable.

8.8 A juvenile shall not be placed in a police cell unless no other secure accommodation is available and the custody officer considers that it is not practicable to supervise him if he is not placed in a cell. He may not be placed in a cell with a detained adult.

8.9 Reasonable force may be used if necessary for the following purposes:

(i) to secure compliance with reasonable instructions, including instructions given in pursuance of the provisions of a code of practice; or

(ii) to prevent escape, injury, damage to property or the destruction of evidence.

8.10 Persons detained should be visited every hour, and those who are drunk, every half hour. [See *Note 8A*]

(b) Documentation

8.11 A record must be kept of replacement clothing and meals offered.

8.12 If a juvenile is placed in a cell, the reason must be recorded.

Notes for Guidance

8A Whenever possible juveniles and other persons at risk should be visited more regularly.

8B The provisions in paragraphs 8.3 and 8.6 respectively regarding bedding and varied diet are of particular importance in the case of a person detained under the Prevention of Terrorism (Temporary Provisions) Act 1989. This is because such a person may well remain in police custody for some time.

9 Treatment of Detained Persons

(a) General

9.1 If a complaint is made by or on behalf of a detained person about his treatment since his arrest, or it comes to the notice of any officer that he may have been treated improperly, a report must be made as soon as practicable to an officer of the rank of inspector or above who is not connected with the investigation. If the matter concerns a possible assault or the possibility of the unnecessary or unreasonable use of force then the police surgeon must also be called as soon as practicable.

(b) Medical Treatment

9.2 The custody officer must immediately call the police surgeon (or, in urgent cases, send the person to hospital or call the nearest available medical practitioner) if a person brought to a police station or already detained there:

(a) appears to be suffering from physical illness or a mental disorder; or
(b) is injured; or
(c) does not show signs of sensibility and awareness; or
(d) fails to respond normally to questions or conversation (other than through drunkenness alone); or
(e) otherwise appears to need medical attention.

This applies even if the person makes no request for medical attention and whether or not he has recently had medical treatment elsewhere (unless brought to the police station direct from hospital). It is not intended that the contents of this paragraph should delay the transfer of a person to a place of safety under section 136 of the Mental Health Act 1983 where that is applicable. Where an assessment under that Act is to take place at the police station, the custody officer has discretion not to call the police surgeon so long as he believes that the assessment by a registered medical practitioner can be undertaken without undue delay. [See *Note 9A*]

9.3 If it appears to the custody officer, or he is told, that a person brought to the police station under arrest may be suffering from an infectious disease of any significance he must take steps to isolate the person and his property until he has obtained medical directions as to where the person should be taken, whether fumigation should take place and what precautions should be taken by officers who have been or will be in contact with him.

9.4 If a detained person requests a medical examination the police surgeon must be called as soon as practicable. He may in addition be examined by a medical practitioner of his own choice at his own expense.

9.5 If a person is required to take or apply any medication in compliance with medical directions, the custody officer is responsible for its safekeeping and for ensuring that he is given the opportunity to take or apply it at the appropriate time. No police officer may administer controlled drugs subject to the Misuse of Drugs Act 1971 for this purpose. A person may administer such drugs to himself only under the personal supervision of the police surgeon.

9.6 If a detained person has in his possession or claims to need medication relating to a heart condition, diabetes, epilepsy or a condition of comparable potential seriousness then, even though paragraph 9.2 may not apply, the advice of the police surgeon must be obtained.

(c) Documentation

9.7 A record must be made of any arrangements made for an examination by a police surgeon under paragraph 9.1 above and of any complaint reported under that paragraph together with any relevant remarks by the custody officer.

9.8 A record must be kept of any request for a medical examination under paragraph 9.4, of the arrangements for any examinations made, and of any medical directions to the police.

9.9 Subject to the requirements of section 4 above the custody record shall include not only a record of all medication that a detained person has in his possession on arrival at the police station but also a note of any such medication he claims he needs but does not have with him.

Notes for Guidance

9A The need to call a police surgeon need not apply to minor ailments or injuries which do not need attention. However, all such ailments or injuries must be recorded in the custody record and any doubt must be resolved in favour of calling the police surgeon.

9B It is important to remember that a person who appears to be drunk or behaving abnormally may be suffering from illness or the effects of drugs or may have sustained injury (particularly head injury) which is not apparent, and that someone needing or addicted to certain drugs may experience harmful effects within a short time of being deprived of their supply. Police should therefore always call the police surgeon when in any doubt, and act with all due speed.

9C If a medical practitioner does not record his clinical findings in the custody record, the record must show where they are recorded.

10 Cautions

(a) When a caution must be given

10.1 A person whom there are grounds to suspect of an offence must be cautioned before any questions about it (or further questions if it is his answers to previous questions that provide grounds for suspicion) are put to him for the purpose of obtaining evidence which may be given to a court in a prosecution. He therefore need not be cautioned if questions are put for any other purposes, for example, to establish his identity or his ownership of any vehicle or the need to search him in the exercise of powers of stop and search.

10.2 Whenever a person who is not under arrest is initially cautioned before or during an interview he must at the same time be told that he is not under arrest and is not obliged to remain with the officer (see paragraph 3.15).

10.3 A person must be cautioned upon arrest for an offence unless:

(a) it is impracticable to do so by reason of his condition or behaviour at the time; or
(b) he has already been cautioned immediately prior to arrest in accordance with paragraph 10.1 above.

(b) Action: general

10.4 The caution shall be in the following terms:

"You do not have to say anything unless you wish to do so, but what you say may be given in evidence."

Minor deviations do not constitute a breach of this requirement provided that the sense of the caution is preserved. [See *Notes 10C* and *10D*]

10.5 When there is a break in questioning under caution the interviewing officer must ensure that the person being questioned is aware that he remains under caution. If there is any doubt the caution should be given again in full when the interview resumes. [See *Note 10A*]

(c) Juveniles, the mentally disordered and the mentally handicapped

10.6 If a juvenile or a person who is mentally disordered or mentally handicapped is cautioned in the absence of the appropriate adult, the caution must be repeated in the adult's presence.

(d) Documentation

10.7 A record shall be made when a caution is given under this section, either in the officer's pocket book or in the interview record as appropriate.

Notes for Guidance

10A In considering whether or not to caution again after a break, the officer should bear in mind that he may have to satisfy a court that the person understood that he was still under caution when the interview resumed.

10B It is not necessary to give or repeat a caution when informing a person who is not under arrest that he may be prosecuted for an offence.

10C If it appears that a person does not understand what the caution means, the officer who has given it should go on to explain it in his own words.

10D In case anyone who is given a caution is unclear about its significance, the officer concerned should explain that the caution is given in pursuance of the general principle of English law that a person need not answer any questions or provide any information which might tend to incriminate him, and that no adverse inferences from this silence may be drawn at any trial that takes place. The person should not, however, be left with a false impression that non-cooperation will have no effect on his immediate treatment as, for example, his refusal to provide his name and address when charged with an offence may render him liable to detention.

Appendix 4

11 Interviews: general

(a) Action

11.1 Following a decision to arrest a suspect he must not be interviewed about the relevant offence except at a police station (or other authorised place of detention) unless the consequent delay would be likely:

(a) to lead to interference with or harm to evidence connected with an offence or interference with or physical harm to other persons; or
(b) to lead to the alerting of other persons suspected of having committed an offence but not yet arrested for it; or
(c) to hinder the recovery of property obtained in consequence of the commission of an offence.

Interviewing in any of these circumstances should cease once the relevant risk has been averted or the necessary questions have been put in order to attempt to avert that risk. For the definition of an interview see *Note 11A*.

11.2 Immediately prior to the commencement or re-commencement of any interview at a police station or other authorised place of detention, the interviewing officer should remind the suspect of his entitlement to free legal advice. It is the responsibility of the interviewing officer to ensure that all such reminders are noted in the record of interview.

11.3 No police officer may try to obtain answers to questions or to elicit a statement by the use of oppression or shall indicate, except in answer to a direct question, what action will be taken on the part of the police if the person being interviewed answers questions, makes a statement or refuses to do either. If the person asks the officer directly what action will be taken in the event of his answering questions, making a statement or refusing to do either, then the officer may inform the person what action the police propose to take in that event provided that that action is itself proper and warranted.

11.4 As soon as a police officer who is making enquiries of any person about an offence believes that a prosecution should be brought against him and that there is sufficient evidence for it to succeed, he should ask the person if he has anything further to say. If the person indicates that he has nothing more to say the officer shall without delay cease to question him about that offence. This should not, however, be taken to prevent officers in revenue cases or acting under the confiscation provisions of the Criminal Justice Act 1988 or the Drug Trafficking Offences Act 1986 from inviting suspects to complete a formal question and answer record after the interview is concluded.

(b) Interview records

11.5(a) An accurate record must be made of each interview with a person suspected of an offence, whether or not the interview takes place at a police station.

(b) The record must state the place of the interview, the time it begins and ends, the time the record is made (if different), any breaks in the interview and the names of all those present; and must be made on the forms provided for this purpose or in the officer's pocket-book or in accordance with the code of practice for the tape-recording of police interviews with suspects.

(c) The record must be made during the course of the interview, unless in the investigating officer's view this would not be practicable or would interfere with the conduct of the interview, and must constitute either a verbatim record of what has been said or, failing this, an account of the interview which adequately and accurately summarises it.

11.6 The requirement to record the names of all those present at an interview does not apply to police officers interviewing persons detained under the Prevention of Terrorism (Temporary Provisions) Act 1989. Instead the record shall state the warrant number and duty station of such officers.

11.7 If an interview record is not made during the course of the interview it must be made as soon as practicable after its completion.

11.8 Written interview records must be timed and signed by the maker.

11.9 If an interview record is not completed in the course of the interview the reason must be recorded in the officer's pocket book.

11.10 Unless it is impracticable the person interviewed shall be given the opportunity to read the interview record and to sign it as correct or to indicate the respects in which he considers it inaccurate. If the interview is tape-recorded the arrangements set out in the relevant code of practice apply. If the person concerned cannot read or refuses to read the record or to sign it, the senior police officer present shall read it over to him and ask him whether he would like to sign it as correct (or make his mark) or to indicate the respects in which he considers it inaccurate. The police officer shall then certify on the interview record itself what has occurred.

11.11 If the appropriate adult or the person's solicitor is present during the interview, he should also be given an opportunity to read and sign the interview record (or any written statement taken down by a police officer).

11.12 Any refusal by a person to sign an interview record when asked to do so in accordance with the provisions of the code must itself be recorded.

11.13 A written record should also be made of any comments made by a suspected person, including unsolicited comments, which are outside the context of an interview but which might be relevant to the offence. Any such record must be timed and signed by the maker. Where practicable the person shall be given the opportunity to read that record and to sign it as correct or to indicate the respects in which he considers it inaccurate. Any refusal to sign should be recorded.

Appendix 4

(c) Juveniles, the mentally disordered and the mentally handicapped

11.14 A juvenile or a person who is mentally disordered or mentally handi-capped, whether suspected or not, must not be interviewed or asked to provide or sign a written statement in the absence of the appropriate adult unless Annex C applies.

11.15 Juveniles may only be interviewed at their places of education in excep-tional circumstances and then only where the principal or his nominee agrees. Every effort should be made to notify both the parent(s) or other person respon-sible for the juvenile's welfare and the appropriate adult (if this is a different person) that the police want to interview the juvenile and reasonable time should be allowed to enable the appropriate adult to be present at the interview. Where awaiting the appropriate adult would cause unreasonable delay and unless the interviewee is suspected of an offence against the educational establishment, the principal or his nominee can act as the appropriate adult for the purposes of the interview.

11.16 Where the appropriate adult is present at an interview, he should be informed that he is not expected to act simply as an observer; and also that the purposes of his presence are, first, to advise the person being questioned and to observe whether or not the interview is being conducted properly and fairly, and secondly, to facilitate communication with the person being inter-viewed.

Notes for Guidance

11A An interview is the questioning of a person regarding his involvement or suspected involvement in a criminal offence or offences. Questioning a person only to obtain information or his explanation of the facts or in the ordinary course of the officer's duties does not constitute an interview for the purpose of this code. Neither does questioning which is confined to the proper and effective conduct of a search.

11B It is important to bear in mind that, although juveniles or persons who are mentally disordered or mentally handicapped are often capable of providing reliable evidence, they may, without knowing or wishing to do so, be particularly prone in certain circumstances to provide information which is unreliable, mis-leading or self-incriminating. Special care should therefore always be exercised in questioning such a person, and the appropriate adult should be involved, if there is any doubt about a person's age, mental state or capacity. Because of the risk of unreliable evidence it is also important to obtain corroboration of any facts admitted whenever possible.

11C A juvenile should not be arrested at his place of education unless this is unavoidable. In this case the principal or his nominee must be informed.

12 Interviews in police stations

(a) Action

12.1 If a police officer wishes to interview, or conduct enquiries which require the presence of, a detained person the custody officer is responsible for deciding whether to deliver him into his custody.

12.2 In any period of 24 hours a detained person must be allowed a continuous period of at least 8 hours of rest, free from questioning, travel or any interruption arising out of the investigation concerned. This period should normally be at night. The period of rest may not be interrupted or delayed unless there are reasonable grounds for believing that it would:

    (i) involve a risk of harm to persons or serious loss of, or damage to, property;

    (ii) delay unnecessarily the person's release from custody; or

    (iii) otherwise prejudice the outcome of the investigation.

If a person is arrested at a police station after going there voluntarily, the period of 24 hours runs from the time of his arrest and not the time of arrival at the police station.

12.3 A detained person may not be supplied with intoxicating liquor except on medical directions. No person who is unfit through drink or drugs to the extent that he is unable to appreciate the significance of questions put to him and his answers may be questioned about an alleged offence in that condition except in accordance with Annex C. [See *Note 12B*]

12.4 As far as practicable interviews shall take place in interview rooms which must be adequately heated, lit and ventilated.

12.5 Persons being questioned or making statements shall not be required to stand.

12.6 Before the commencement of an interview each interviewing officer shall identify himself and any other officers present by name and rank to the person being interviewed, except in the case of persons detained under the Prevention of Terrorism (Temporary Provisions) Act 1989 when each officer shall identify himself by his warrant number and rank rather than his name.

12.7 Breaks from interviewing shall be made at recognised meal times. Short breaks for refreshment shall also be provided at intervals of approximately two hours, subject to the interviewing officer's discretion to delay a break if there are reasonable grounds for believing that it would:

    (i) involve a risk of harm to persons or serious loss of, or damage to, property;

    (ii) delay unnecessarily the person's release from custody; or

    (iii) otherwise prejudice the outcome of the investigation.

12.8 If in the course of the interview a complaint is made by the person being questioned or on his behalf concerning the provisions of this code then the interviewing officer shall:

    (i)   record it in the interview record; and
    (ii) inform the custody officer, who is then responsible for dealing with it in accordance with section 9 of this code.

(b) Documentation

12.9 A record must be made of the times at which a detained person is not in the custody of the custody officer, and why; and of the reason for any refusal to deliver him out of that custody.

12.10 A record must be made of any intoxicating liquor supplied to a detained person, in accordance with paragraph 12.3 above.

12.11 Any decision to delay a break in an interview must be recorded, with grounds, in the interview record.

12.12 All written statements made at police stations under caution shall be written on the forms provided for the purpose.

12.13 All written statements made under caution shall be taken in accordance with Annex D to this code.

Notes for Guidance

12A If the interview has been contemporaneously recorded and the record signed by the person interviewed in accordance with paragraph 11.10 above, or has been tape recorded, it is normally unnecessary to ask for a written statement. Statements under caution should normally be taken in these circumstances only at the person's express wish. An officer may, however, ask him whether or not he wants to make a statement.

12B The police surgeon can give advice about whether or not a person is fit to be interviewed in accordance with paragraph 12.3 above.

13 Interpreters

(a) General

13.1 Information on obtaining the services of a suitably qualified interpreter for the deaf or for persons who do not understand English is given in Note for Guidance 3D.

(b) Foreign languages

13.2 Unless Annex C applies, a person must not be interviewed in the absence of a person capable of acting as interpreter if:

(a) he has difficulty in understanding English;

(b) the interviewing officer cannot himself speak the person's own language; and

(c) the person wishes an interpreter to be present.

13.3 The interviewing officer shall ensure that the interpreter makes a note of the interview at the time in the language of the person being interviewed for use in the event of his being called to give evidence, and certifies its accuracy. He shall allow sufficient time for the interpreter to make a note of each question and answer after each has been put or given and interpreted. The person shall be given an opportunity to read it or have it read to him and sign it as correct or to indicate the respects in which he considers it inaccurate. If the interview is tape-recorded the arrangements set out in the relevant code of practice apply.

13.4 In the case of a person making a statement in a language other than English:

(a) the interpreter shall take down the statement in the language in which it is made;

(b) the person making the statement shall be invited to sign it; and

(c) an official English translation shall be made in due course.

(c) The deaf and speech handicapped

13.5 If a person appears to be deaf or there is doubt about his hearing or speaking ability, he must not be interviewed in the absence of an interpreter unless he agrees in writing to be interviewed without one or Annex C applies.

13.6 An interpreter should also be called if a juvenile is interviewed and the parent or guardian present as the appropriate adult appears to be deaf or there is doubt about his hearing or speaking ability, unless he agrees in writing that the interview should proceed without one or Annex C applies.

13.7 The interviewing officer shall ensure that the interpreter is given an opportunity to read the record of the interview and to certify its accuracy in the event of his being called to give evidence.

(d) Additional rules for detained persons

13.8 All reasonable attempts should be made to make clear to the detained person that interpreters will be provided at public expense.

13.9 Where paragraph 6.1 applies and the person concerned cannot communicate with the solicitor, whether because of language hearing or speech difficulties, an interpreter must be called. The interpreter may not be a police officer when interpretation is needed for the purposes of obtaining legal advice. In all other cases a police officer may only interpret if he first obtains the detained person's (or the appropriate adult's) agreement in writing or if the interview is tape-recorded in accordance with the relevant code of practice.

13.10 When a person is charged with an offence who appears to be deaf or there is doubt about his hearing or speaking ability or ability to understand English, and the custody officer cannot establish effective communication, arrangements must be made for an interpreter to explain as soon as practicable the offence concerned and any other information given by the custody officer.

(e) Documentation

13.11 Action taken to call an interpreter under this section and any agreement to be interviewed in the absence of an interpreter must be recorded.

Note for Guidance

13A If the interpreter is needed as a prosecution witness at the person's trial, a second interpreter must act as the court interpreter.

14 Questioning: special restrictions

14.1 If a person has been arrested by one police force on behalf of another and the lawful period of detention in respect of that offence has not yet commenced in accordance with section 41 of the Police and Criminal Evidence Act 1984 no questions may be put to him about the offence while he is in transit between the forces except in order to clarify any voluntary statement made by him.

14.2 If a person is in police detention at a hospital he may not be questioned without the agreement of a responsible doctor. [See *Note 14A*]

Note for Guidance

14A If questioning takes place at a hospital under paragraph 14.2 (or on the way to or from a hospital) the period concerned counts towards the total period of detention permitted.

15 Reviews and extensions of detention

(a) Action

15.1 The review officer is responsible under section 40 of the Police and Criminal Evidence Act 1984 (or, in terrorist cases, under Schedule 3 to the Prevention of Terrorism (Temporary Provisions) Act 1989) for determining whether or not a person's detention continues to be necessary. In reaching a decision he shall provide an opportunity to the detained person himself to make representations (unless he is unfit to do so because of his condition or behaviour) or to his solicitor or the appropriate adult if available at the time. Other persons having an interest in the person's welfare may make representations at the review officer's discretion.

15.2 The same persons may make representations to the officer determining whether further detention should be authorised under section 42 of the Act or under Schedule 3 to the 1989 Act. [See *Note 15A*]

(b) Documentation

15.3 Before conducting a review the review officer must ensure that the detained person is reminded of his entitlement to free legal advice. It is the responsibility of the review officer to ensure that all such reminders are noted in the custody record.

15.4 The grounds for and extent of any delay in conducting a review shall be recorded.

15.5 Any written representations shall be retained.

15.6 A record shall be made as soon as practicable of the outcome of each review and application for a warrant of further detention or its extension.

Notes for Guidance

15A If the detained person is likely to be asleep at the latest time when a review of detention or an authorisation of continued detention may take place, the appropriate officer should bring it forward so that the detained person may make representations without being woken up.

15B An application for a warrant of further detention or its extension should be made between 10am and 9pm, and if possible during normal court hours. It will not be practicable to arrange for a court to sit specially outside the hours of 10am to 9pm. If it appears possible that a special sitting may be needed (either at a weekend, Bank/Public Holiday or on a weekday outside normal court hours but between 10am and 9pm) then the clerk to the justices should be given notice and informed of this possibility, while the court is sitting if possible.

15C If in the circumstances the only practicable way of conducting a review is over the telephone then this is permissible, provided that the requirements of section 40 of the Police and Criminal Evidence Act 1984 or of Schedule 3 to the Prevention of Terrorism (Temporary Provisions) Act 1989 are observed. However, a review to decide whether to authorise a person's continued detention under section 42 of the Act must be done in person rather over the telephone.

16 Charging of detained persons

(a) Action

16.1 When an officer considers that there is sufficient evidence to prosecute a detained person, and that there is sufficient evidence for a prosecution to succeed, and that the person has said all that he wishes to say about the offence, he should without delay (and subject to the following qualification) bring him before the custody officer who shall then be responsible for considering whether or not he should be charged. When a person is detained in respect of more than one offence it is permissible to delay bringing him before the custody officer until the above conditions are satisfied in respect of all the offences (but see paragraph 11.4). Any resulting action should be taken in the presence of the appropriate adult if the person is a juvenile or mentally disordered or mentally handicapped.

16.2 When a detained person is charged with or informed that he may be prosecuted for an offence he shall be cautioned in the terms of paragraph 10.4 above.

16.3 At the time a person is charged he shall be given a written notice showing particulars of the offence with which he is charged and including the name of the officer in the case (in terrorist cases, the officer's warrant number instead), his police station and the reference number for the case. So far as possible the particulars of the charge shall be stated in simple terms, but they shall also show the precise offence in law with which he is charged. The notice shall begin with the following words:

"You are charged with the offence(s) shown below. You do not have to say anything unless you wish to do so, but what you say may be given in evidence."

If the person is a juvenile or is mentally disordered or mentally handicapped the notice shall be given to the appropriate adult.

16.4 If at any time after a person has been charged with or informed he may be prosecuted for an offence a police officer wishes to bring to the notice of that person any written statement made by another person or the content of an interview with another person, he shall hand to that person a true copy of any such written statement or bring to his attention the content of the interview record, but shall say or do nothing to invite any reply or comment save to caution him in the terms of paragraph 10.4 above. If the person cannot read then the officer may read it to him. If the person is a juvenile or mentally disordered or mentally handicapped the copy shall also be given to, or the interview record brought to the attention of, the appropriate adult.

16.5 Questions relating to an offence may not be put to a person after he has been charged with that offence, or informed that he may be prosecuted for it, unless they are necessary for the purpose of preventing or minimising harm or loss to some other person or to the public or for clearing up an ambiguity in a previous answer or statement, or where it is in the interests of justice that the person should have put to him and have an opportunity to comment on information concerning the offence which has come to light since he was charged or informed that he might be prosecuted. Before any such questions are put he shall be cautioned in the terms of paragraph 10.4 above. [See *Note 16A*]

16.6 Where a juvenile is charged with an offence and the custody officer authorises his continuing detention he must try to make arrangements for the juvenile to be taken into the care of a local authority to be detained pending appearance in court unless he certifies that it is impracticable to do so in accordance with section 38(6) of the Police and Criminal Evidence Act 1984. [See *Note 16B*]

(b) Documentation

16.7 A record shall be made of anything a detained person says when charged.

16.8 Any questions put after charge and answers given relating to the offence shall be contemporaneously recorded in full on the forms provided and the record signed by that person or, if he refuses, by the interviewing officer and any third parties present. If the questions are tape-recorded the arrangements set out in the relevant code of practice apply.

16.9 If it is not practicable to make arrangements for the transfer of a juvenile into local authority care in accordance with paragraph 16.6 above the custody officer must record the reasons and make out a certificate to be produced before the court together with the juvenile.

Notes for Guidance

16A The service of the Notice of Intended Prosecution under sections 1 and 2 of the Road Traffic Offenders Act 1988 does not amount to informing a person that he may be prosecuted for an offence and so does not preclude further questioning in relation to that offence.

16B Neither a juvenile's behaviour nor the nature of the offence with which he is charged provides grounds for the custody officer to retain him in police custody rather than seek to arrange for his transfer to the care of the local authority.

ANNEX A

INTIMATE AND STRIP SEARCHES [See paragraph 4.1]

(a) Action

1. Body orifices may be searched only if an officer of the rank of superintendent or above has reasonable grounds for believing:

(a) that an article which could cause physical injury to a detained person or others at the police station has been concealed; or

(b) that the person has concealed a Class A drug which he intended to supply to another or to export; and

(c) that in either case an intimate search is the only practicable means of removing it.

The reasons why an intimate search is considered necessary shall be explained to the person before the search takes place.

2. An intimate search may only be carried out by a registered medical practitioner or registered nurse, unless an officer of at least the rank of superintendent considers that this is not practicable and the search is to take place under sub-paragraph 1(a) above.

3. An intimate search under sub-paragraph 1(a) above may take place only at a hospital, surgery, other medical premises or police station. A search under sub-paragraph 1(b) may take place only at a hospital, surgery or other medical premises.

4. An intimate search at a police station of a juvenile or a mentally disordered or mentally handicapped person may take place only in the presence of the appropriate adult of the same sex (unless the person specifically requests the presence of a particular adult of the opposite sex who is readily available). In the case of a juvenile the search may take place in the absence of the appropriate adult only if the juvenile signifies in the presence of the appropriate adult that he prefers the search to be done in his absence and the appropriate adult agrees. A record should be made of the juvenile's decision and signed by the appropriate adult.

5. A strip search (that is a search involving the removal of more than outer clothing) may take place only if the custody officer considers it to be necessary to remove an article which the detained person would not be allowed to keep.

6. Where an intimate search under sub-paragraph 1(a) above or a strip search is carried out by a police officer, the officer must be of the same sex as the person searched. Subject to paragraph 4 above, no person of the opposite sex who is not a medical practitioner or nurse shall be present, nor shall anyone whose presence is unnecessary.

(b) Documentation

7. In the case of an intimate search the custody officer shall as soon as practicable record which parts of the person's body were searched, who carried out the search, who was present, the reasons for the search and its result.

8. In the case of a strip search he shall record the reasons for the search and its result.

9. If an intimate search is carried out by a police officer, the reason why it is impracticable for a suitably qualified person to conduct it must be recorded.

ANNEX B

DELAY IN NOTIFYING ARREST OR ALLOWING ACCESS TO LEGAL ADVICE

A. Persons detained under the Police and Criminal Evidence Act 1984

(a) Action

1. The rights set out in sections 5 or 6 of the code or both may be delayed if the person is in police detention in connection with a serious arrestable offence, has not yet been charged with an offence and an officer of the rank of superintendent or above has reasonable grounds for believing that the exercise of either right:

    (i)   will lead to interference with or harm to evidence connected with a serious arrestable offence or interference with or physical injury to other persons; or

    (ii) will lead to the alerting of other persons suspected of having committed such an offence but not yet arrested for it; or

    (iii) will hinder the recovery of property obtained as a result of such an offence.

    [See *Note B3*]

2. These rights may also be delayed where the serious arrestable offence is either:

    (i)   a drug trafficking offence and the officer has reasonable grounds for believing that the detained person has benefited from drug trafficking, and that the recovery of the value of that person's proceeds of drug trafficking will be hindered by the exercise of either right or;

    (ii) an offence to which Part VI of the Criminal Justice Act 1988 (covering confiscation orders) applies and the officer has reasonable grounds for believing that the detained person has benefited from the offence, and that the recovery of the value of the property obtained by that person from or in connection with the offence or if the pecuniary advantage derived by him from or in connection with it will be hindered by the exercise of either right.

3. Access to a solicitor may not be delayed on the grounds that he might advise the person not to answer any questions or that the solicitor was initially asked to attend the police station by someone else, provided that the person himself then wishes to see the solicitor. In the latter case the detained person must be told that the solicitor has come to the police station at another person's request, and must be asked to sign the custody record to signify whether or not he wishes to see the solicitor.

4. These rights may be delayed only for as long as is necessary and, subject to paragraph 9 below, in no case beyond 36 hours after the relevant time as defined in section 41 of the Police and Criminal Evidence Act 1984. If the above grounds

611

cease to apply within this time, the person must as soon as practicable be asked if he wishes to exercise either right, the custody record must be noted accordingly, and action must be taken in accordance with the relevant section of the code.

5. A detained person must be permitted to consult a solicitor for a reasonable time before any court hearing.

(b) Documentation

6. The grounds for action under this Annex shall be recorded and the person informed of them as soon as practicable.

7. Any reply given by a person under paragraphs 4 or 9 must be recorded and the person asked to endorse the record in relation to whether he wishes to receive legal advice at this point.

B. Persons detained under the Prevention of Terrorism (Temporary Provisions) Act 1989

(a) Action

8. The rights set out in sections 5 or 6 of this code or both may be delayed if paragraph 1 above applies or if an officer of the rank of superintendent or above has reasonable grounds for believing that the exercise of either right:

   (a) will lead to interference with the gathering of information about the com-mission, preparation or instigation of acts of terrorism; or
   (b) by alerting any person, will make it more difficult to prevent an act of terrorism or to secure the apprehension, prosecution or conviction of any person in connection with the commission, preparation or instigation of an act of terrorism.

9. These rights may be delayed only for as long as is necessary and in no case beyond 48 hours from the time of arrest. If the above grounds cease to apply within this time, the person must as soon as practicable be asked if he wishes to exercise either right, the custody record must be noted accordingly, and action must be taken in accordance with the relevant section of this code.

10. Paragraphs 3 and 5 above apply.

(b) Documentation

11 Paragraphs 6 and 7 above apply.

Notes for Guidance

B1 Even if Annex B applies in the case of a juvenile, or a person who is mentally disordered or mentally handicapped, action to inform the appropriate adult (and the person responsible for a juvenile's welfare, if that is a different person) must nevertheless be taken in accordance with paragraph 3.7 and 3.9 of this code.

B2 In the case of Commonwealth citizens and foreign nationals see Note 7A.

B3 Police detention is defined in section 118(2) of the Police and Criminal Evidence Act 1984.

B4 The effect of paragraph 1 above is that the officer may authorise delaying access to a specific solicitor only if he has reasonable grounds to believe that that specific solicitor will, inadvertently or otherwise, pass on a message from the detained person or act in some other way which will lead to any of the three results in paragraph 1 coming about. In these circumstances the officer should offer the detained person access to a solicitor (who is not the specific solicitor referred to above) on the Duty Solicitor Scheme.

B5 The fact that the grounds for delaying notification of arrest under paragraph 1 above may be satisfied does not automatically mean that the grounds for delaying access to legal advice will also be satisfied.

ANNEX C

URGENT INTERVIEWS

1. If, and only if, an officer of the rank of superintendent or above considers that delay will involve an immediate risk of harm to persons or serious loss of or serious damage to property:

   (a) a person heavily under the influence of drink or drugs may be interviewed in that state; or
   (b) an arrested juvenile or a person who is mentally disordered or mentally handicapped may be interviewed in the absence of the appropriate adult; or
   (c) a person who has difficulty in understanding English or who has a hearing disability may be interviewed in the absence of an interpreter.

2. Questioning in these circumstances may not continue once sufficient information to avert the immediate risk has been obtained.

3. A record shall be made of the grounds for any decision to interview a person under paragraph 1 above.

Note for Guidance

C1 The special groups referred to in Annex C are all particularly vulnerable. The provisions of the annex, which override safeguards designed to protect them and to minimise the risk of interviews producing unreliable evidence, should be applied only in exceptional cases of need.

ANNEX D

WRITTEN STATEMENTS UNDER CAUTION (See paragraph 12.13)

(a) Written by a person under caution

1. A person shall always be invited to write down himself what he wants to say.

2. Where the person wishes to write it himself, he shall be asked to write out and sign before writing what he wants to say, the following:

"I make this statement of my own free will. I understand that I need not say anything unless I wish to do so and that what I say may be given in evidence."

3. Any person writing his own statement shall be allowed to do so without any prompting except that a police officer may indicate to him which matters are material or question any ambiguity in the statement.

(b) Written by a police officer

4. If a person says that he would like someone to write it for him, a police officer shall write the statement, but, before starting, he must ask him to sign, or make his mark, to the following:

"I, ..., wish to make a statement. I want someone to write down what I say. I understand that I need not say anything unless I wish to do so and that what I say may be given in evidence."

5. Where a police officer writes the statement, he must take down the exact words spoken by the person making it and he must not edit or paraphrase it. Any questions that are necessary (e.g. to make it more intelligible) and the answers given must be recorded contemporaneously on the statement form.

6. When the writing of a statement by a police officer is finished the person making it shall be asked to read it and to make any corrections, alterations or additions he wishes. When he has finished reading it he shall be asked to write and sign or make his mark on the following certificate at the end of the statement:

"I have read the above statement, and I have been able to correct, alter or add anything I wish. This statement is true. I have made it of my own free will."

7. If the person making the statement cannot read, or refuses to read it, or to write the above mentioned certificate at the end of it or to sign it, the senior police officer present shall read it over to him and ask him whether he would like to correct, alter or add anything and to put his signature or make his mark at the end. The police officer shall then certify on the statement itself what has occurred.

ANNEX E

SUMMARY OF PROVISIONS RELATING TO MENTALLY DISORDERED AND MENTALLY HANDICAPPED PERSONS

1. If an officer has any suspicion or is told in good faith that a person of any age, whether or not in custody, may be suffering from mental disorder or mentally handicapped, or cannot understand the significance of questions put to him or his replies, then he shall be treated as a mentally disordered or mentally handicapped person. [See *paragraph 1.4*]

2. In the case of a person who is mentally disordered or mentally handicapped, 'the appropriate adult' means:

(a) a relative, guardian or some other person responsible for his care or custody;
(b) someone who has experience of dealing with mentally disordered or mentally handicapped persons but is not a police officer or employed by the police; or
(c) failing either of the above, some other responsible adult aged 18 or over who is not a police officer or employed by the police. [See *paragraph 1.7(b)*]

3. If the custody officer authorises the detention of a person who is mentally handicapped or is suffering from a mental disorder he must as soon as practicable inform the appropriate adult of the grounds for the person's detention and his whereabouts, and ask the adult to come to the police station to see the person. If the appropriate adult is already at the police station when information is given as required in paragraphs 3.1 to 3.4 the information must be given to the detained person in his presence. If the appropriate adult is not at the police station when the information is given then the information must be given to the detained person again in the presence of the appropriate adult once that person arrives. [See *paragraphs 3.9* and *3.11*]

4. If the appropriate adult, having been informed of the right to legal advice, considers that legal advice should be taken, the provisions of section 6 of the code apply as if the mentally disordered or mentally handicapped person had requested access to legal advice. [See *paragraph 3.13*]

5. If a person brought to a police station appears to be suffering from mental disorder or is incoherent other than through drunkenness alone, or if a detained person subsequently appears to be mentally disordered, the custody officer must immediately call the police surgeon or, in urgent cases, send the person to hospital or call the nearest available medical practitioner. It is not intended that these provisions should delay the transfer of a person to a place of safety under section 136 of the Mental Health Act 1983 where that is applicable. Where an assessment under that Act is to take place at the police station, the custody officer has discretion not to call the police surgeon so long as he believes that the assessment by a registered medical practitioner can be undertaken without undue delay. [See *paragraph 9.2*]

6. It is imperative that a mentally disordered or mentally handicapped person who has been detained under section 136 of the Mental Health Act 1983 should be assessed as soon as possible. If that assessment is to take place at the police station, an approved social worker and a registered medical practitioner should be called to the police station as soon as possible in order to interview and examine the person. Once the person has been interviewed and examined and suitable arrangements have been made for his treatment or care, he can no longer be detained under section 136. The person should not be released until he has been seen by both the approved social worker and the registered medical practitioner. [See *paragraph 3.10*]

7. If a mentally disordered or mentally handicapped person is cautioned in the absence of the appropriate adult, the caution must be repeated in the adult's presence. [See *paragraph 10.6*]

8. A mentally disordered or mentally handicapped person must not be interviewed or asked to provide or sign a written statement in the absence of the appropriate adult unless an officer of the rank of superintendent or above considers that delay will involve an immediate risk of harm to persons or serious loss of or serious damage to property. Questioning in these circumstances may not continue in the absence of the appropriate adult once sufficient information to avert the risk has been obtained. A record shall be made of the grounds for any decision to begin an interview in these circumstances. [See *paragraphs 11.14* and *Annex C*]

9. Where the appropriate adult is present at an interview, he should be informed that he is not expected to act simply as an observer; and also that the purposes of his presence are, first, to advise the person being interviewed and to observe whether or not the interview is being conducted properly and fairly, and, secondly, to facilitate communication with the person being interviewed. [See *paragraph 11.16*]

10. If the detention of a mentally disordered or mentally handicapped person is reviewed by a review officer or a superintendent, the appropriate adult must, if available at the time be given opportunity to make representations to the officer about the need for continuing detention. [See *paragraphs 15.1* and *15.2*]

11. If the custody officer charges a mentally disordered or mentally handicapped person with an offence or takes such other action as is appropriate when there is sufficient evidence for a prosecution this must be done in the presence of the appropriate adult. The written notice embodying any charge must be given to the appropriate adult. [See *paragraphs 16.1* and *16.3*]

12. An intimate search of a mentally disordered or mentally handicapped person may take place only in the presence of the appropriate adult of the same sex, unless the person specifically requests the presence of a particular adult of the opposite sex. [See *Annex A, paragraph 4*]

Notes for Guidance

E1 In the case of persons who are mentally disordered or mentally handicapped, it may in certain circumstances be more satisfactory for all concerned if the appropriate adult is someone who has experience or training in their care rather than a relative lacking such qualifications. But if the person himself prefers a relative to a better qualified stranger his wishes should if practicable be respected. [See Note 1E]

E2 The purpose of the provision at paragraph 3.13 is to protect the rights of a mentally disordered or mentally handicapped person who does not understand the significance of what is being said to him. It is not intended that, if such a person wishes to exercise the right to legal advice, no action should be taken until the appropriate adult arrives. [See Note 3G]

E3 It is important to bear in mind that although persons who are mentally disordered or mentally handicapped are often capable of providing reliable evidence, they may, without knowing or wishing to do so, be particularly prone in certain circumstances to provide information which is unreliable, misleading or self-incriminating. Special care should therefore always be exercised in questioning such a person, and the appropriate adult involved, if there is any doubt about a person's mental state or capacity. Because of the risk of unreliable evidence, it is important to obtain corroboration of any facts admitted whenever possible. [See Note 11B]

E4 Because of the risks referred to in Note E3, which the presence of the appropriate adult is intended to minimise, officers of superintendent rank or above should exercise their discretion to authorise the commencement of an interview in the adult's absence only in exceptional cases, where it is necessary to avert an immediate risk of serious harm. [See Annex C, sub-paragraph 1(b) and Note C1]

ANNEX F

COUNTRIES WITH WHICH CONSULAR CONVENTIONS ARE IN FORCE AS AT 20 APRIL 1990

Algeria
Antigua and Barbuda
Argentina
Australia
Austria
Bahamas
Bangladesh
Belgium
Benin
Bhutan
Bolivia
Brazil

Bulgaria
Burkina Faso
Bylorussian SSR
Cameroon
Canada
Cape Verde
Central African Republic
Chile
China
Colombia
Congo
Costa Rica

Appendix 4

Côte d'Ivoire
Cuba
Cyprus
Czechoslovakia
Democratic People's Republic of
  Korea
Denmark
Djibouti
Dominica
Dominican Republic
Ecuador
Egypt
El Salvador
Equatorial Guinea
Fiji
Finland
France
Gabon
German Democratic Republic
Germany, Federal Republic of
Ghana
Greece
Guatemala
Guinea
Guyana
Haiti
Holy See
Honduras
Hungary
Iceland
India
Indonesia
Iran (Islamic Republic of)
Iraq
Ireland
Israel
Italy
Jamaica
Japan
Jordan
Kenya
Kiribati
Lao People's Democratic Republic
Lebanon
Lesotho
Liberia
Liechtenstein
Luxembourg
Madagascar

Malawi
Mali
Mauritius
Mexico
Mongolia
Morocco
Mozambique
Nepal
Netherlands
New Zealand
Nicaragua
Niger
Nigeria
Norway
Oman
Pakistan
Panama
Papua New Guinea
Paraguay
Peru
Philippines
Poland
Portugal
Republic of Korea
Republic of South Vietnam
Romania
Rwanda
Saint Lucia
Samoa
Sao Tome and Principe
Saudi Arabia
Senegal
Seychelles
Somalia
South Africa
Soviet Union
Spain
Suriname
Sweden
Switzerland
Syrian Arab Republic
Togo
Tonga
Trinidad and Tobago
Tunisia
Turkey
Tuvalu
Ukrainian SSR
United Arab Emirates

United Kingdom
United Republic of Tanzania
United States of America
Uruguay
Vanuatu

Venezuela
Yemen
Yugoslavia
Zaire

Appendix 5

Code of practice for the identification of persons by police officers

1 General

1.1 This code of practice must be readily available at all police stations for consultation by police officers, detained persons and members of the public.

1.2 The notes for guidance included are not provisions of this code, but are guidance to police officers and others about its application and interpretation. Provisions in the Annexes to the code are provisions of this code.

1.3 If an officer has any suspicion, or is told in good faith, that a person of any age may be suffering from mental disorder or mentally handicapped, or mentally incapable of understanding the significance of questions put to him or his replies, then that person shall be treated as a mentally disordered or mentally handicapped person for the purposes of this code.

1.4 If anyone appears to be under the age of 17 then he shall be treated as a juvenile for the purposes of this code in the absence of clear evidence to show that he is older.

1.5 If a person appears to be blind or seriously visually handicapped, deaf, unable to read, unable to speak or has difficulty orally because of a speech impediment, he should be treated as such for the purposes of this code in the absence of clear evidence to the contrary.

1.6 In this code 'the appropriate adult' means:

(a) in the case of a juvenile:
   (i) his parent or guardian (or, if he is in care, the care authority or voluntary organisation); or
   (ii) a social worker; or
   (iii) failing either of the above, another responsible adult aged 18 or over who is not a police officer or employed by the police;
(b) in the case of a person who is mentally disordered or mentally handicapped:
   (i) a relative, guardian or some other person responsible for his care or custody; or
   (ii) someone who has experience of dealing with mentally disordered or mentally handicapped persons but is not a police officer or employed

by the police (such as an approved social worker as defined by the Mental Health Act 1983 or a specialist social worker); or

(iii) failing either of the above, some other responsible adult aged 18 or over who is not a police officer or employed by the police.

1.7 Any reference to a custody officer in this code includes an officer who is performing the functions of a custody officer. Any reference to a solicitor in this code includes a clerk or legal executive except in Annex D, paragraph 7.

1.8 Where a record is made under this code of any action requiring the authority of an officer of a specified rank, his name (except in the case of enquiries linked to the investigation of terrorism, in which case the officer's warrant number should be given) and rank must be included in the record.

1.9 All records must be timed and signed by the maker. Warrant numbers should be used rather than names in the case of detention under the Prevention of Terrorism (Temporary Provisions) Act 1989.

1.10 In the case of a detained person records are to be made in his custody record unless otherwise specified.

1.11 In the case of any procedure requiring a suspect's consent, the consent of a person who is mentally disordered or mentally handicapped is only valid if given in the presence of the appropriate adult; and in the case of a juvenile the consent of his parent or guardian is required as well as his own (unless he is under 14, in which case the consent of his parent or guardian is sufficient in its own right). [See *Note 1E*]

1.12 In the case of a person who is blind or seriously visually handicapped or unable to read, the custody officer should ensure that his solicitor, relative, the appropriate adult or some other person likely to take an interest in him (and not involved in the investigation) is available to help in checking any documentation. Where this code requires written consent or signification, then the person who is assisting may be asked to sign instead if the detained person so wishes. [See *Note 1F*]

1.13 In the case of any procedure requiring information to be given to or sought from a suspect, it must be given or sought in the presence of the appropriate adult if the suspect is mentally disordered, mentally handicapped or a juvenile. If the appropriate adult is not present when the information is first given or sought, the procedure must be repeated in his presence when he arrives. If the suspect appears to be deaf or there is doubt about his hearing or speaking ability or ability to understand English, and the officer cannot establish effective communication, the information must be given or sought through an interpreter.

1.14 Any procedure in this code involving the participation of a person (whether as a suspect or a witness) who is mentally disordered, mentally handicapped or a juvenile must take place in the presence of the appropriate adult; but the adult must not be allowed to prompt any identification of a suspect by a witness.

1.15 Subject to paragraph 1.16 below, nothing in this code affects any procedure under:

    (i) Sections 4 to 11 of the Road Traffic Act 1988 or sections 15 and 16 of the Road Traffic Offenders Act 1988; or

    (ii) paragraph 18 of Schedule 2 to the Immigration Act 1971; or

    (iii) the Prevention of Terrorism (Temporary Provisions) Act 1989: section 15(9), paragraph 8(5) of Schedule 2, and paragraph 7(5) of Schedule 5.

1.16 Notwithstanding paragraph 1.15, the provisions of section 3 below on the taking of fingerprints, and of section 5 below on the taking of body samples, do apply to persons detained under section 14 of, or paragraph 6 of Schedule 5 to, the Prevention of Terrorism (Temporary Provisions) Act 1989. (In the case of fingerprints, section 61 of PACE is modified by section 15(10) of, and paragraph 7(6) of Schedule 5 to, the 1989 Act.) There is, however, no statutory requirement (and, therefore, no requirement under paragraph 3.4 below) to destroy fingerprints or body samples taken in terrorist cases, no requirement to tell the persons from whom these were taken that they will be destroyed, and no statutory requirement to offer such persons an opportunity to witness the destruction of their fingerprints.

1.17 In this code, references to photographs include references to optical disc computer printouts.

Notes for Guidance

1A The parent or guardian of a juvenile should be the appropriate adult unless he is suspected of involvement in the offence concerned, is the victim, is a witness, is involved in the investigation or has received admissions. In such circumstances it will be desirable for the appropriate adult to be some other person. The estranged parent of a juvenile should not be asked to act as the appropriate adult if the juvenile expressly and specifically objects to his presence.

1B If a child in care admits an offence to a social worker, another social worker should be the appropriate adult in the interest of fairness.

1C In the case of persons who are mentally disordered or mentally handicapped, it may in certain circumstances be more satisfactory for all concerned if the appropriate adult is someone who has experience or training in their care rather than a relative lacking such qualifications. But if the person himself prefers a relative to a better-qualified stranger his wishes should if practicable be respected.

1D A solicitor who is present in a professional capacity may not act as the appropriate adult.

1E For the purposes of paragraph 1.11 above, the consent required to be given by a parent or guardian may be given, in the case of a juvenile in the care of a local authority or voluntary organisation, by that authority or organisation.

Appendix 5

1F Persons who are blind, seriously visually handicapped or unable to read may be unwilling to sign police documents. The alternative of their representative signing on their behalf seeks to protect the interests of both police and suspects.

1G Further guidance about fingerprints and body samples is given in Home Office circular 27/1989.

1H The generic term "mental disorder" is used throughout this code. "Mental disorder" is defined by the Mental Health Act 1983 as "mental illness, arrested or incomplete development of mind, psychopathic disorder and any other disorder or disability of mind". It should be noted that "mental disorder" is different to "mental handicap" although the two forms of disorder are dealt with similarly throughout this code.

2 Identification by witnesses

(a) Cases where the suspect is known

2.1 In a case which involves disputed identification evidence, and where the identity of the suspect is known to the police, the methods of identification by witnesses which may be used are:

    (i)   a parade;
    (ii) a group identification;
    (iii) a video film
    (iv) a confrontation.

2.2 The arrangements for, and conduct of, these types of identification shall be the responsibility of an officer in uniform not below the rank of inspector who is not involved with the investigation ("the identification officer"). No officer involved with the investigation of the case against the suspect may take any part in these procedures.

Identification Parade

2.3 In a case which involves disputed identification evidence a parade must be held if the suspect asks for one and it is practicable to hold one. A parade may also be held if the officer in charge of the investigation considers that it would be useful, and the suspect consents.

2.4 A parade need not be held if the identification officer considers that, whether by reason of the unusual appearance of the suspect or for some other reason, it would not be practicable to assemble sufficient people who resembled him to make a parade fair.

2.5 Any parade must be carried out in accordance with Annex A.

Group Identification

2.6 If a suspect refuses or, having agreed, fails to attend an identification parade or the holding of a parade is impracticable, arrangements must if practicable be made to allow the witness an opportunity of seeing him in a group of people.

2.7 A group identification may also be arranged if the officer in charge of the investigation considers, whether because of fear on the part of the witness or for some other reason, that it is, in the circumstances, more satisfactory than a parade.

2.8 The suspect should be asked for his consent to a group identification and advised in accordance with paragraphs 2.15 and 2.16. However, where consent is refused the identification officer has the discretion to proceed with a group identification if it is practicable to do so.

2.9 A group identification should, if practicable, be held in a place other than a police station (for example, in an underground station or a shopping centre). It may be held in a police station if the identification officer considers, whether for security reasons or on other grounds, that it would not be practicable to hold it elsewhere. In either case the group identification should, as far as possible, follow the principles and procedures for a parade as set out in Annex A.

Video Film Identification

2.10 The identification officer may show a witness a video film of a suspect if the investigating officer considers, whether because of the refusal of the suspect to take part in an identification parade or group identification or other reasons, that this would in the circumstances be the most satisfactory course of action.

2.11 The suspect should be asked for his consent to a video identification and advised in accordance with paragraphs 2.15 and 2.16. However, where such consent is refused the identification officer has the discretion to proceed with a video identification if it is practicable to do so.

2.12 A video identification must be carried out in accordance with Annex B.

Confrontation

2.13 If neither a parade, a group identification nor a video identification procedure is arranged, the suspect may be confronted by the witness. Such a confrontation does not require the suspect's consent, but may not take place unless none of the other procedures are practicable.

2.14 A confrontation must be carried out in accordance with Annex C.

Notice to Suspect

2.15 Before a parade takes place or a group identification or video identification is arranged, the identification officer shall explain to the suspect:

    (i) the purposes of the parade or group identification or video identification;

(ii)   the fact that he is entitled to free legal advice;

(iii) the procedures for holding it (including his right to have a solicitor or friend present);

(iv) where appropriate the special arrangements for juveniles;

(v)   where appropriate the special arrangements for mentally disordered and mentally handicapped persons;

(vi) the fact that he does not have to take part in a parade, or co-operate in a group identification, or with the making of a video film and, if it is proposed to hold a group identification or video identification, his entitlement to a parade if this can practicably be arranged;

(vii) the fact that, if he does not consent to take part in a parade or co-operate in a group identification or with the making of a video film, his refusal may be given in evidence in any subsequent trial and police may proceed covertly without his consent or make other arrangements to test whether a witness identifies him;

(viii) whether the witness had been shown photographs, photofit, identikit or similar pictures by the police during the investigation before the identity of the suspect became known. [See *Note 2B*]

2.16 This information must also be contained in a written notice which must be handed to the suspect. The identification officer shall give the suspect a reasonable opportunity to read the notice, after which he shall be asked to sign a second copy of the notice to indicate whether or not he is willing to take part in the parade or group identification or co-operate with the making of a video film. The signed copy shall be retained by the identification officer.

(b) Cases where the identity of the suspect is not known

2.17 A police officer may take a witness to a particular neighbourhood or place to see whether he can identify the person whom he said he saw on the relevant occasion. Care should be taken however not to direct the witness's attention to any individual.

2.18 A witness must not be shown photographs or photofit, identikit or similar pictures if the identity of the suspect is known to the police and he is available to stand on an identification parade. If the identity of the suspect is not known, the showing of such pictures to a witness must be done in accordance with Annex D. [See *paragraph 2.15(viii)*]

(c) Documentation

2.19 The identification officer shall make a record of the parade, group identification or video identification on the forms provided.

2.20 If the identification officer considers that it is not practicable to hold a parade, he shall tell the suspect why and record the reason.

2.21 A record shall be made of a person's refusal to co-operate in a parade, group identification or video identification.

Notes for Guidance

2A *Except for the provisions of Annex D para 1, a police officer who is a witness for the purposes of this part of the code is subject to the same principles and procedures as a civilian witness.*

2B *Where a witness attending an identification parade has previously been shown photographs or photofit; identikit or similar pictures, it is the responsibility of the officer in charge of the investigation to make the identification officer aware that this is the case.*

3 Identification by fingerprints

(a) Action

3.1 A person's fingerprints may be taken only with his consent or if paragraph 3.2 applies. If he is at a police station consent must be in writing. In either case the person must be informed of the reason before they are taken and that they will be destroyed as soon as practicable if paragraph 3.4 applies. He must be told that he may witness their destruction if he asks to do so within five days of being cleared or informed that he will not be prosecuted.

3.2 Powers to take fingerprints without consent from any person over the age of ten years are provided by section 61 of the Police and Criminal Evidence Act 1984. Reasonable force may be used if necessary.

3.3 Section 27 of the Police and Criminal Evidence Act 1984 describes the circumstances in which a constable may require a person convicted of a recordable offence to attend at a police station in order that fingerprints may be taken. [See *Note 3A*]

3.4 The fingerprints of a person and all copies of them taken in that case must be destroyed as soon as practicable if:

(a) he is prosecuted for the offence concerned and cleared; or
(b) he is not prosecuted (unless he admits the offence and is cautioned for it).

An opportunity of witnessing the destruction must be given to him if he wishes and if, in accordance with paragraph 3.1, he applies within five days of being cleared or informed that he will not be prosecuted.

3.5 When fingerprints are destroyed, access to relevant computer data shall be made impossible as soon as it is practicable to do so.

3.6 References to fingerprints include palm prints.

(b) Documentation

3.7 A record must be made as soon as possible of the reason for taking a person's fingerprints without consent and of their destruction. If force is used a record shall be made of the circumstances and those present.

Appendix 5

Note for Guidance

    3A References to recordable offences in this code relate to those offences for which convictions are recorded in national police records. (See section 27(4) of the Police and Criminal Evidence Act 1984.)

4 Identification by photographs

(a) Action

    4.1 The photograph of a person who has been arrested may be taken at a police station only with his written consent or if paragraph 4.2 applies. In either case he must be informed of the reason for taking it and that the photograph will be destroyed if paragraph 4.4 applies. He must be told that he may witness the destruction of the photograph or be provided with a certificate confirming its destruction if he applies within five days of being cleared or informed that he will not be prosecuted.

    4.2 The photograph of a person who has been arrested may be taken without consent if:

      (i) he is arrested at the same time as other persons, or at a time when it is likely that other persons will be arrested, and a photograph is necessary to establish who was arrested, at what time and at what place; or

     (ii) he has been charged with, or reported for a recordable offence and has not yet been released or brought before a court [see *Note 3A*]; or

   (iii) he is convicted of such an offence and his photograph is not already on record as a result of (i) or (ii). There is no power of arrest to take a photograph in pursuance of this provision which applies only where the person is in custody as a result of the exercise of another power (e.g. arrest for fingerprinting under section 27 of the Police and Criminal Evidence Act 1984).

    4.3 Force may not be used to take a photograph.

    4.4 Where a person's photograph has been taken in accordance with this section, the photograph, negatives and all copies taken in that particular case must be destroyed if:

    (a) he is prosecuted for the offence and cleared; or

    (b) he is not prosecuted (unless he admits the offence and is cautioned for it).

    An opportunity of witnessing the destruction or a certificate confirming the destruction must be given to him if he so requests, provided that, in accordance with paragraph 4.1, he applies within five days of being cleared or informed that he will not be prosecuted. [See *Note 4B*]

(b) Documentation

    4.5 A record must be made as soon as possible of the reason for taking a person's photograph under this section without consent and of the destruction of any photographs.

Notes for Guidance

4A All references to photographs include computer images.

4B This paragraph is not intended to require the destruction of copies of a police gazette in cases where, for example, a remand prisoner has escaped from custody, or a person in custody is suspected of having committed offences in other force areas, and a photograph of the person concerned is circulated in a police gazette for information.

5 Identification by body samples, swabs and impressions

(a) Action

5.1 Dental impressions and intimate samples may be taken from a person in police detention only:

> (i) if an officer of the rank of superintendent or above considers that the offence concerned is a serious arrestable offence; and
>
> (ii) if that officer has reasonable grounds to believe that such an impression or sample will tend to confirm or disprove the suspect's involvement in it; and
>
> (iii) with the suspect's written consent.

5.2 Before a person is asked to provide an intimate sample he must be warned that a refusal may be treated, in any proceedings against him, as corroborating relevant prosecution evidence. [See *Note 5A*] He must also be reminded of his entitlement to have free legal advice and the reminder must be noted in the custody record.

5.3 Except for samples of urine or saliva, intimate samples may be taken only by a registered medical or dental practitioner as appropriate.

5.4 A non-intimate sample, as defined in paragraph 5.11, may be taken from a detained suspect only with his written consent or if paragraph 5.5 applies. Even if he consents, an officer of the rank of inspector or above must have reasonable grounds for believing that such a sample will tend to confirm or disprove the suspect's involvement in a particular offence.

5.5 A non-intimate sample may be taken without consent if an officer of the rank of superintendent or above has reasonable grounds for suspecting that the offence in connection with which the suspect is detained is a serious arrestable offence and for believing that the sample will tend to confirm or disprove his involvement in it.

5.6 Where paragraph 5.5 applies, reasonable force may be used if necessary to take non-intimate samples.

5.7 The suspect must be informed, before the intimate or non-intimate sample or dental impression is taken, of the grounds on which the relevant authority has been given, including the nature of the suspected offence, and that the sample will be destroyed if paragraph 5.8 applies.

5.8 Where a sample or impression has been taken in accordance with this section, it and all copies of it taken in the particular case must be destroyed as soon as practicable if:

(a) the suspect is prosecuted for the offence concerned and cleared; or
(b) he is not prosecuted (unless he admits the offence and is cautioned for it).

(b) Documentation

5.9 A record must be made as soon as practicable of the reasons for taking a sample or impression and of its destruction. If force is used a record shall be made of the circumstances and those present. If written consent is given to the taking of a sample or impression, the fact must be recorded in writing.

5.10 A record must be made of the giving of a warning required by paragraph 5.2 above.

(c) General

5.11 The following terms are defined in section 65 of the Police and Criminal Evidence Act 1984 as follows:

(a) 'intimate sample' means a sample of blood, semen or any other tissue fluid, urine, saliva or pubic hair, or a swab taken from a person's body orifice;
(b) 'non-intimate sample' means:
  (i) a sample of hair other than pubic hair;
  (ii) a sample taken from a nail or from under a nail;
  (iii) a swab taken from any part of a person's body other than a body orifice;
  (iv) a footprint or similar impression of any part of a person's body other than a part of his hand.

5.12 Where clothing needs to be removed in circumstances likely to cause embarrassment to the person, no person of the opposite sex who is not a medical practitioner or nurse shall be present, (unless in the case of a juvenile, that juvenile specifically requests the presence of a particular adult of the opposite sex who is readily available) nor shall anyone whose presence is unnecessary. However, in the case of a juvenile this is subject to the overriding proviso that such a removal of clothing may take place in the absence of the appropriate adult only if the juvenile signifies in the presence of the appropriate adult that he prefers the search to be done in his absence and the appropriate adult agrees.

Notes for Guidance

5A In warning a person who refuses to provide an intimate sample or swab in accordance with paragraph 5.2, the following form of words may be helpful:

'You do not have to [provide this sample] [allow this swab to be taken], but I

must warn you that if you do not do so, a court may treat such a refusal as supporting any relevant evidence against you.'

ANNEX A

IDENTIFICATION PARADES

(a) General

1. A suspect must be given a reasonable opportunity to have a solicitor or friend present, and the identification officer shall ask him to indicate on a second copy of the notice whether or not he so wishes.

2. A parade may take place either in a normal room or in one equipped with a screen permitting witnesses to see members of the parade without being seen. The procedures for the composition and conduct of the parade are the same in both cases, subject to paragraph 7 below (except that a parade involving a screen may take place only when the suspect's solicitor, friend or appropriate adult is present or the parade is recorded on video).

(b) Parades involving prison inmates

3. If an inmate is required for identification, and there are no security problems about his leaving the establishment, he may be asked to participate in a parade or video identification. (A group identification, however, may not be arranged other than in the establishment or inside a police station.)

4. A parade may be held in a Prison Department establishment, but shall be conducted as far as practicable under normal parade rules. Members of the public shall make up the parade unless there are serious security or control objections to their admission to the establishment. In such cases, or if a group or video identification is arranged within the establishment, other inmates may participate. If an inmate is the suspect, he should not be required to wear prison uniform for the parade unless the other persons taking part are other inmates in uniform or are members of the public who are prepared to wear prison uniform for the occasion.

(c) Conduct of the parade

5. Immediately before the parade, the identification officer must remind the suspect of the procedures governing its conduct and caution him in the terms of paragraph 10.4 of the code of practice for the detention, treatment and questioning of persons by police officers.

6. All unauthorised persons must be excluded from the place where the parade is held.

7. Once the parade has been formed, everything afterwards in respect of it

Appendix 5

shall take place in the presence and hearing of the suspect and of any interpreter, solicitor, friend or appropriate adult who is present (unless the parade involves a screen, in which case everything said to or by any witness at the place where the parade is held must be said in the hearing and presence of the suspect's solicitor, friend or appropriate adult or be recorded on video).

8. The parade shall consist of at least eight persons (in addition to the suspect) who so far as possible resemble the suspect in age, height, general appearance and position in life. One suspect only shall be included in a parade unless there are two suspects of roughly similar appearance in which case they may be paraded together with at least twelve other persons. In no circumstances shall more than two suspects be included in one parade and where there are separate parades they shall be made up of different persons.

9. Where all members of a similar group are possible suspects, separate parades shall be held for each member of the group unless there are two suspects of similar appearance when they may appear on the same parade with at least twelve other members of the group who are not suspects. Where police officers in uniform form an identification parade, any numerals or other identifying badges shall be concealed.

10. When the suspect is brought to the place where the parade is to be held, he shall be asked by the identification officer whether he has any objection to the arrangements for the parade or to any of the other participants in it. The suspect may obtain advice from his solicitor or friend, if present, before the parade proceeds. Where practicable, steps shall be taken to remove the grounds for objection. Where it is not practicable to do so, the officer shall explain to the suspect why his objections cannot be met.

11. The suspect may select his own position in the line. Where there is more than one witness, the identification officer must tell the suspect, after each witness has left the room, that he can if he wishes change position in the line. Each position in the line must be clearly numbered, whether by means of a numeral laid on the floor in front of each parade member or by other means.

12. The identification officer is responsible for ensuring that, before they attend the parade, witnesses are not able to:

    (i)   communicate with each other about the case or overhear a witness who has already seen the parade;
    (ii) see any member of the parade;
    (iii) on that occasion see or be reminded of any photograph or description of the suspect or be given any other indication of his identity; or
    (iv) see the suspect either before or after the parade.

13. The officer conducting a witness to a parade must not discuss with him the composition of the parade, and in particular he must not disclose whether a previous witness has made any identification.

14. Witnesses shall be brought in one at a time. Immediately before the witness inspects the parade, the identification officer shall tell him that the person he

saw may or may not be on the parade and if he cannot make a positive identification he should say so. The officer shall then ask him to walk along the parade at least twice, taking as much care and time as he wishes. When he has done so the officer shall ask him whether the person he saw in person on an earlier relevant occasion is on the parade.

15. The witness should make an identification by indicating the number of the person concerned.

16. If the witness makes an identification after the parade has ended the suspect and, if present, his solicitor, interpreter or friend shall be informed. Where this occurs, consideration should be given to allowing the witness a second opportunity to identify the suspect.

17. If a witness wishes to hear any parade member speak, adopt any specified posture or see him move, the identification officer shall first ask whether he can identify any persons on the parade on the basis of appearance only. When the request is to hear members of the parade speak, the witness shall be reminded that the participants in the parade have been chosen on the basis of physical appearance only. Members of the parade may then be asked to comply with the witness's request to hear them speak, to see them move or to adopt any specified posture.

18. When the last witness has left, the identification officer shall ask the suspect whether he wishes to make any comments on the conduct of the parade.

(d) Documentation

19. If a parade is held without a solicitor or a friend of the suspect being present, a colour photograph or a video film of the parade shall be taken. A copy of the photograph or video film shall be supplied on request to the suspect or his solicitor within a reasonable time.

20. Where a photograph or video film is taken in accordance with paragraph 19, it shall be destroyed or wiped clean at the conclusion of the proceedings unless the person concerned is convicted or admits the offence and is cautioned for it.

21. If the identification officer asks any person to leave a parade because he is interfering with its conduct the circumstances shall be recorded.

22. A record must be made of all those present at a parade or group identification whose names are known to the police.

23. If prison inmates make up a parade the circumstances must be recorded.

24. A record of the conduct of any parade must be made on the forms provided.

Appendix 5

ANNEX B

VIDEO IDENTIFICATION

(a) General

1. Where a video parade is to be arranged the following procedures must be followed.

2. Arranging, supervising and directing the making and showing of a video film to be used in a video identification must be the responsibility of an identification officer or identification officers who have no direct involvement with the relevant case.

3. The film must include the suspect and at least eight other people who so far as possible resemble the suspect in age, height, general appearance and position in life. Only one suspect shall appear on any film unless there are two suspects of roughly similar appearance in which case they may be shown together with at least twelve other persons.

4. The suspect and other persons shall as far as possible be filmed in the same positions or carrying out the same activity and under identical conditions.

5. Provision must be made for each person filmed to be identified by number.

6. If police officers are filmed, any numerals or other identifying badges must be concealed. If a prison inmate is filmed either as a suspect or not, then either all or none of the persons filmed should be in prison uniform.

7. The suspect and his solicitor, friend, or appropriate adult must be given a reasonable opportunity to see the completed film before it is shown to witnesses. If he has a reasonable objection to the video film or any of its participants, steps should, if practicable be taken to remove the grounds for objection. If this is not practicable the identification officer shall explain to the suspect and/or his representative why his objections cannot be met and record both the objection and the reason on the forms provided.

8. The suspect's solicitor, or where one is not instructed the suspect himself, where practicable should be given reasonable notification of the time and place that it is intended to conduct the video identification in order that a representative may attend on behalf of the suspect. The suspect himself may not be present when the film is shown to the witness(es). In the absence of a person representing the suspect the viewing itself shall be recorded on video. No unauthorised persons may be present.

(b) Conducting the Video Identification

9. The identification officer is responsible for ensuring that, before they see the film, witnesses are not able to communicate with each other about the case or overhear a witness who has seen the film. He must not discuss with the witness

the composition of the film and must not disclose whether a previous witness has made any identification.

10. Only one witness may see the film at a time. Immediately before the video identification takes place the identification officer shall tell the witness that the person he saw may or may not be on the video film. The witness should be advised that at any point he may ask to see a particular part of the tape again or to have a particular picture frozen for him to study. Furthermore, it should be pointed out that there is no limit on how many times he can view the whole tape or any part of it. However, he should be asked to refrain from making a positive identification or saying that he cannot make a positive identification until he has seen the entire film at least twice.

11. Once the witness has seen the whole film at least twice and has indicated that he does not want to view it or any part of it again, the identification officer shall ask the witness to say whether the individual he saw in person on an earlier occasion has been shown on the film and, if so, to identify him by number. The identification officer will then show the film of the person identified again to confirm the identification with the witness.

12. The identification officer must take care not to direct the witness's attention to any one individual on the video film, or give any other indication of the suspect's identity. Where a witness has previously made an identification by photographs, or a photofit, identikit or similar picture has been made, the witness must not be reminded of such a photograph or picture once a suspect is available for identification by other means in accordance with this code. Neither must he be reminded of any description of the suspect.

(c) Tape Security and Destruction

13. It shall be the responsibility of the identification officer to ensure that all relevant tapes are kept securely and their movements accounted for. In particular, no officer involved in the investigation against the suspect shall be permitted to view the video film prior to it being shown to any witness.

14. Where a video film has been made in accordance with this section all copies of it must be destroyed if the suspect:

(a) is prosecuted for the offence and cleared; or
(b) is not prosecuted (unless he admits the offence and is cautioned for it).

An opportunity of witnessing the destruction must be given to him if he so requests within five days of being cleared or informed that he will not be prosecuted.

(d) Documentation

15. A record must be made of all those participating in or seeing the video whose names are known to the police.

16. A record of the conduct of the video identification must be made on the forms provided.

ANNEX C

CONFRONTATION BY A WITNESS

1. The identification officer is responsible for the conduct of any confrontation of a suspect by a witness.

2. Before the confrontation takes place, the identification officer must tell the witness that the person he saw may or may not be the person he is to confront and that if he cannot make a positive identification he should say so.

3. The suspect shall be confronted independently by each witness, who shall be asked "Is this the person?" Confrontation must take place in the presence of the suspect's solicitor, interpreter or friend, unless this would cause unreasonable delay.

4. The confrontation should normally take place in the police station, either in a normal room or in one equipped with a screen permitting a witness to see the suspect without being seen. In both cases the procedures are the same except that a room equipped with a screen may be used only when the suspect's solicitor, friend or appropriate adult is present or the confrontation is recorded on video.

ANNEX D

SHOWING OF PHOTOGRAPHS

(a) Action

1. An officer of the rank of sergeant or above shall be responsible for supervising and directing the showing of photographs. The actual showing may be done by a constable or a civilian police employee.

2. Only one witness shall be shown photographs at any one time. He shall be given as much privacy as practicable and shall not be allowed to communicate with any other witness in the case.

3. The witness shall be shown not less than twelve photographs at a time. These photographs shall either be in an album or loose photographs mounted in a frame or a sequence of not fewer than twelve photographs on optical disc, and shall, as far as possible, all be of a similar type.

4. When the witness is shown the photographs, he shall be told that the photograph of the person he saw may or may not be amongst them. He shall not be

prompted or guided in any way but shall be left to make any selection without help.

5. If a witness makes a positive identification from photographs, then, unless the person identified is otherwise eliminated from enquiries, other witnesses shall not be shown photographs. But both they and the witness who has made the identification shall be asked to attend an identification parade or group or video identification if practicable unless there is no dispute about the identification of the suspect.

6. Where the use of a photofit, identikit or similar picture has led to there being a suspect available who can be asked to appear on a parade, or participate in a group or video identification, the picture shall not be shown to other potential witnesses.

7. Where a witness attending an identification parade has previously been shown photographs or photofit, identikit or similar pictures (and it is the responsibility of the officer in charge of the investigation to make the identification officer aware that this is the case) then the suspect and his solicitor must be informed of this fact before the identity parade takes place.

8. None of the photographs (or optical discs) used shall be destroyed, whether or not an identification is made, since they may be required for production in court. The photographs should be numbered and a separate photograph taken of the frame or part of the album from which the witness made an identification as an aid to reconstituting it.

(b) Documentation

9. Whether or not an identification is made, a record shall be kept of the showing of photographs and of any comment made by the witness.

Appendix 6

Other statutory material

PREVENTION OF TERRORISM (TEMPORARY PROVISIONS) ACT 1989

PART IV

ARREST, DETENTION AND CONTROL OF ENTRY

14 Arrest and detention of suspected persons

(1) Subject to subsection (2) below, a constable may arrest without warrant a person whom he has reasonable grounds for suspecting to be—

(a) a person guilty of an offence under section 2, 8, 9, 10 or 11 above;

(b) a person who is or has been concerned in the commission, preparation or instigation of acts of terrorism to which this section applies; or

(c) a person subject to an exclusion order.

(2) The acts of terrorism to which this section applies are—

(a) acts of terrorism connected with the affairs of Northern Ireland; and

(b) acts of terrorism of any other description except acts connected solely with the affairs of the United Kingdom or any part of the United Kingdom other than Northern Ireland.

(3) The power of arrest conferred by subsection (1)(c) above is exercisable only—

(a) in Great Britain if the exclusion order was made under section 5 above; and

(b) in Northern Ireland if it was made under section 6 above.

(4) Subject to subsection (5) below, a person arrested under this section shall not be detained in right of the arrest for more than forty-eight hours after his arrest.

(5) The Secretary of State may, in any particular case, extend the period of forty-eight hours mentioned in subsection (4) above by a period or periods specified by him, but any such further period or periods shall not exceed five days in all and if an application for such an extension is made the person detained shall as soon as practicable be given written notice of that fact and of the time when the application was made.

639

(6) The exercise of the detention powers conferred by this section shall be subject to supervision in accordance with Schedule 3 to this Act.

(7) The provisions of this section are without prejudice to any power of arrest exercisable apart from this section.

PART V

INFORMATION, PROCEEDINGS AND INTERPRETATION

17 Investigation of terrorist activities

(1) Schedule 7 to this Act shall have effect for conferring powers to obtain information for the purposes of terrorist investigations, that is to say—

    (*a*) investigations into—
- (i) the commission, preparation or instigation of acts of terrorism to which section 14 above applies; or
- (ii) any other act which appears to have been done in furtherance of or in connection with such acts of terrorism, including any act which appears to constitute an offence under section 2, 9, 10 or 11 above or section 21 of the Northern Ireland (Emergency Provisions) Act 1978; or
- (iii) without prejudice to sub-paragraph (ii) above, the resources of a proscribed organisation within the meaning of this Act or a proscribed organisation for the purposes of section 21 of the said Act of 1978; and

    (*b*) investigations into whether there are grounds justifying the making of an order under section 1(2)(*a*) above or section 21(4) of that Act.

(2) Where in relation to a terrorist investigation a warrant or order under Schedule 7 to this Act has been issued or made or has been applied for and not refused, a person is guilty of an offence if, knowing or having reasonable cause to suspect that the investigation is taking place, he—

    (*a*) makes any disclosure which is likely to prejudice the investigation; or

    (*b*) falsifies, conceals or destroys or otherwise disposes of, or causes or permits the falsification, concealment, destruction or disposal of, material which is or is likely to be relevant to the investigation.

(3) In proceedings against a person for an offence under subsection (2)(*a*) above it is a defence to prove—

    (*a*) that he did not know and had no reasonable cause to suspect that the disclosure was likely to prejudice the investigation; or

    (*b*) that he had lawful authority or reasonable excuse for making the disclosure.

(4) In proceedings against a person for an offence under subsection (2)(*b*) above it is a defence to prove that he had no intention of concealing any information contained in the material in question from the persons carrying out the investigation.

(5) A person guilty of an offence under subsection (2) above is liable—

(*a*) on conviction on indictment, to imprisonment for a term not exceeding five years or a fine or both;

(*b*) on summary conviction, to imprisonment for a term not exceeding six months or a fine not exceeding the statutory maximum or both.

SCHEDULE 7

Section 17.

TERRORIST INVESTIGATIONS

PART I

ENGLAND, WALES AND NORTHERN IRELAND

Interpretation

1. In this Part of this Schedule a "terrorist investigation" means any investigation to which section 17(1) of this Act applies and "items subject to legal privilege", "excluded material" and "special procedure material" have the meanings given in sections 10 to 14 of the Police and Criminal Evidence Act 1984.

Search for material other than excluded or special procedure material

2. (1) A justice of the peace may, on an application made by a constable, issue a warrant under this paragraph if satisfied that a terrorist investigation is being carried out and that there are reasonable grounds for believing—

(*a*) that there is material on premises specified in the application which is likely to be of substantial value (whether by itself or together with other material) to the investigation;

(*b*) that the material does not consist of or include items subject to legal privilege, excluded material or special procedure material; and

(*c*) that any of the conditions in sub-paragraph (2) below are fulfilled.

(2) The conditions referred to in sub-paragraph (1)(c) above are—

(*a*) that it is not practicable to communicate with any person entitled to grant entry to the premises;

(*b*) that it is practicable to communicate with a person entitled to grant entry to the premises but it is not practicable to communicate with any person entitled to grant access to the material;

(*c*) that entry to the premises will not be granted unless a warrant is produced;

(*d*) that the purpose of a search may be frustrated or seriously prejudiced unless a constable arriving at the premises can secure immediate entry to them.

(3) A warrant under this paragraph shall authorise a constable to enter the premises specified in the warrant and to search the premises and any person found there and to seize and retain anything found there or on any such person, other

than items subject to legal privilege, if he has reasonable grounds for believing—

  (*a*) that it is likely to be of substantial value (whether by itself or together with other material) to the investigation; and
  (*b*) that it is necessary to seize it in order to prevent it being concealed, lost, damaged, altered or destroyed.

(4) In Northern Ireland an application for a warrant under this paragraph shall be made by a complaint on oath.

Order for production of excluded or special procedure material

3. (1) A constable may, for the purposes of a terrorist investigation, apply to a Circuit judge for an order under sub-paragraph (2) below in relation to particular material or material of a particular description, being material consisting of or including excluded material or special procedure material.

(2) If on such an application the judge is satisfied that the material consists of or includes such material as is mentioned in sub-paragraph (1) above, that it does not include items subject to legal privilege and that the conditions in sub-paragraph (5) below are fulfilled, he may make an order that the person who appears to him to be in possession of the material to which the application relates shall—

  (*a*) produce it to a constable for him to take away; or
  (*b*) give a constable access to it,

within such period as the order may specify and if the material is not in that person's possession (*a*nd will not come into hispossession within that period) to state to the best of his knowledge and belief where it is.

(3) An order under sub-paragraph (2) above may relate to material of a particular description which is expected to come into existence or become available to the person concerned in the period of twenty-eight days beginning with the date of the order; and an order made in relation to such material shall require that person to notify a named constable as soon as possible after the material comes into existence or becomes available to that person.

(4) The period to be specified in an order under sub-paragraph (2) above shall be seven days from the date of the order or, in the case of an order made by virtue of sub-paragraph (3) above, from the notification to the constable unless it appears to the judge that a longer or shorter period would be appropriate in the particular circumstances of the application.

(5) The conditions referred to in sub-paragraph (2) above are—

  (*a*) that a terrorist investigation is being carried out and that there are reasonable grounds for believing that the material is likely to be of substantial value (whether by itself of together with other material) to the investigation for the purposes of which the application is made; and
  (*b*) that there are reasonable grounds for believing that it is in the public interest, having regard—
    (i) to the benefit likely to accrue to the investigation if the material is obtained; and

(ii) to the circumstances under which the person in possession of the material holds it,

that the material should be produced or that access to it should be given.

(6) Where a judge makes an order under sub-paragraph (2)(b) above in relation to material on any premises he may, on the application of a constable, order any person who appears to him to be entitled to grant entry to the premises to allow a constable to enter the premises to obtain access to the material.

(7) In Northern Ireland the power to make an order under this paragraph shall be exercised by a county court judge.

4. (1) Provision may be made by Crown Court Rules as to—

(a) the discharge and variation of orders under paragraph 3 above; and
(b) proceedings relating to such orders.

(2) The following provisions shall have effect pending the coming into force of Crown Court Rules under sub-paragraph (1) above—

(a) an order under paragraph 3 above may be discharged or varied by a Circuit judge on a written application made to the appropriate officer of the Crown Court by any person subject to the order;
(b) unless a Circuit judge otherwise directs on grounds of urgency, the applicant shall, not less than forty-eight hours before making the application, send a copy of it and a notice on writing of the time and place where the application is to be made to the constable on whose application the order to be discharged or varied was made or on any other constable serving in the same police station.

(3) An order of a Circuit judge under paragraph 3 above shall have effect as if it were an order of the Crown Court.

(4) Where the material to which an application under that paragraph relates consists of information contained in a computer—

(a) an order under sub-paragraph (2)(a) of that paragraph shall have effect as an order to produce the material in a form in which it can be taken away and in which it is visible and legible; and
(b) an order under sub-paragraph (2)(b) of that paragraph shall have effect as an order to give access to the material in a form in which t is visible and legible.

(5) An order under paragraph 3 above—

(a) shall not confer any right to production of, or access to, items subject to legal privilege;
(b) shall have effect notwithstanding any obligation as to secrecy or other restriction on the disclosure of information imposed by statute or otherwise.

(6) An order may be made under paragraph 3 above in relation to material in the possession of a government department which is an authorised government

department for the purposes of the Crown Proceedings Act 1947; and any such order (which shall be served as if the proceedings were civil proceedings against the department) may require any officer of the department, whether named in the order or not, who may for the time being be in possession of the material concerned to comply with it.

(7) In the application of this paragraph to Northern Ireland for references to a Circuit judge there shall be substituted references to a county court judge and for references to a government department or authorised government department there shall be substituted references to a Northern Ireland department or authorised Northern Ireland department.

Search for excluded or special procedure material

5. (1) A constable may apply to a Circuit judge for a warrant under this paragraph in relation to specified premises.

(2) On such an application the judge may issue a warrant under this paragraph if satisfied—

(a) that an order made under paragraph 3 above in relation to material on the premises has not been complied with; or

(b) that there are reasonable grounds for believing that there is on the premises material consisting of or including excluded material or special procedure material, that it does not include items subject to legal privilege and that the conditions in sub-paragraph (5) of that paragraph and the condition in sub-paragraph (3) below are fulfilled in respect of that material.

(3) The condition referred to in sub-paragraph (2)(b) above is that it would not be appropriate to make an order under paragraph 3 above in relation to the material because—

(a) it is not practicable to communicate with any person entitled to produce the material; or

(b) it is not practicable to communicate with any person entitled to grant access to the material or entitled to grant entry to the premises on which the material is situated; or

(c) the investigation for the purposes of which the application is made might be seriously prejudiced unless a constable could secure immediate access to the material.

(4) A warrant under this paragraph shall authorise a constable to enter the premises specified in the warrant and to search the premises and any person found there and to seize and retain anything found there or on any such person, other than items subject to legal privilege, if he has reasonable grounds for believing that it is likely to be of substantial value (whether by itself or together with other material) to the investigation for the purposes of which the application was made.

(5) In Northern Ireland the power to issue a warrant under this paragraph shall be exercised by a county court judge.

Explanation of seized or produced material

6. (1) A Circuit judge may, on an application made by a constable, order any person specified in the order to provide an explanation of any material seized in pursuance of a warrant under paragraph 2 or 5 above or produced or made available to a constable under paragraph 3 above.

(2) A person shall not under his paragraph be required to disclose any information which he would be entitled to refuse to disclose on grounds of legal professional privilege in proceedings in the High Court, except that a lawyer may be required to furnish the name and address of his client.

(3) A statement by a person in response to a requirement imposed by virtue of this paragraph may only be used in evidence against him—

(*a*) on a prosecution for an offence under sub-paragraph (4) below; or
(*b*) on a prosecution for some other offence where in giving evidence he makes a statement inconsistent with it.

(4) A person who, in purported compliance with a requirement under this paragraph—

(*a*) makes a statement which he knows to be false or misleading in a material particular; or
(*b*) recklessly makes a statement which is false or misleading in a material particular.

is guilty of an offence.

(5) A person guilty of an offence under sub-paragraph (4) above is liable—

(*a*) on conviction on indictment, to imprisonment for a term not exceeding two years or a fine or both;
(*b*) on summary conviction, to imprisonment for a term not exceeding six months or a fine not exceeding the statutory maximum or both.

(6) In Northern Ireland the power to make an order under this paragraph shall be exercised by a county court judge.

(7) Paragraph 4(1), (2), (3) and (6) above shall apply to orders under this paragraph as they apply to orders under paragraph 3.

Urgent cases

7. (1) If a police officer of at least the rank of superintendent has reasonable grounds for believing that the case is one of great emergency and that in the interests of the State immediate action is necessary, he may by a written order signed by him give to any constable the authority which may be given by a search warrant under paragraph 2 or 5 above.

(2) Where an authority is given under this paragraph particulars of the case shall be notified as soon as may be to the Secretary of State.

(3) An order under this paragraph may not authorise a search for items subject to legal privilege.

(4) If such a police officer as is mentioned in sub-paragraph (1) above has reasonable grounds for believing that the case is such as is there mentioned he may by a notice in writing signed by him require any person specified in the notice to provide an explanation of any material in pursuance of an order under this paragraph.

(5) Any person who without reasonable excuse fails to comply with a notice under sub-paragraph (4) above is guilty of an offence and liable on summary conviction to imprisonment for a term not exceeding six months or a fine not exceeding level 5 on the standard scale or both.

(6) Sub-paragraphs (2) to (5) of paragraph 6 above shall apply to a requirement imposed under sub-paragraph (4) above as they apply to a requirement under that paragraph.

Orders by Secretary of State in relation to certain investigations

8. (1) This paragraph has effect in relation to a terrorist investigation concerning any act which appears to the Secretary of State to constitute an offence under Part II of this Act.

(2) Without prejudice to the foregoing provisions of this Part of this Schedule, the Secretary of State may by a written order signed by him or on his behalf give to any constable in Northern Ireland the authority which may be given by a search warrant under paragraph 2 or 5 above or impose on any person in Northern Ireland any such requirement as may be imposed by an order under paragraph 3 above if—

   (a) he is satisfied as to the matters specified in those paragraphs respectively for the issue of a warrant by a justice of the peace or the making of an order by a country court judge; and
   (b) it appears to him that the disclosure of information that would be necessary for an application under those provisions would be likely to prejudice the capability of members of the Royal Ulster Constabulary in relation to the investigation of offences under Part III of this Act or otherwise prejudice the safety of, or of persons in, Northern Ireland.

(3) A person who disobeys an order under this paragraph which corresponds to an order under paragraph 3 above (a "Secretary of State's production order") is liable—

   (a) on conviction on indictment, to imprisonment for a term not exceeding two years or a fine or both;
   (b) on summary conviction, to imprisonment for a term not exceeding six months or a fine not exceeding the statutory maximum or both.

(4) A Secretary of State's production order may be varied or revoked by the Secretary of State and references in paragraphs 4(4), (5) and (6) and 5 above to an order under paragraph 3 above shall include references to a Secretary of State's production order.

(5) The Secretary of State may by a written order signed by him or on his behalf require any person in Northern Ireland to provide an explanation or any material seized or produced in pursuance of an order under the foregoing provisions of this paragraph; and paragraphs 6(2) to (5) and 7(5) above shall apply to an order under this sub-paragraph as they apply to an order or notice under those paragraphs.

Access to Land Register

9. (1) The Chief Land Registrar shall, on an application made by a police officer of at least the rank of superintendent, in relation to a person specified in the application or to property so specified, provide the applicant with any information kept by the Registrar under the Land Registration Act 1925 which relates to that person or property.

(2) On any such application there shall be given to the Registrar a certificate stating that there are reasonable grounds for suspecting that there is information kept by him which is likely to be of substantial value (whether by itself or together with other information) to a terrorist investigation.

(3) The information to be provided by the Registrar under this paragraph shall be provided in documentary form.

Supplementary

10. (1) Any power of seizure conferred by this Schedule is without prejudice to the powers conferred by section 19 of the Police and Criminal Evidence Act 1984 and for the purposes of sections 21 and 22 of that Act *(*access to, and copying and retention of, seized material)—

  (a) a terrorist investigation shall be treated as an investigation of or in connection with an offence; and
  (b) material produced in pursuance of an order under paragraph 3 or 8 above shall be treated as if it were material seized by a constable.

(2) A search of a person under this Part of this Schedule may only be carried out by a person of the same sex.

PART II

SCOTLAND

Interpretation

11. In this Part of this Schedule a "terrorist investigation" means any investigation to which section 17(1) of this Act applies.

Appendix 6

Order for production of material

12. (11) A procurator fiscal may, for the purpose of a terrorist investigation, apply to a sheriff for an order under sub-paragraph (2) below in relation to particular material or material of a particular description.

(2) If on such an application the sheriff is satisfied that the conditions in sub-paragraph (5) below are fulfilled, he may make an order that the person who appears to him to be in possession of the material to which the application relates shall—

(a) produce it to a constable for him to take away; or
(b) give a constable access to it,

within such period as the order may specify and if the material is not in that person's possession (and will not come into his possession within that period) to state to the best of his knowledge and belief where it is.

(3) An order under sub-paragraph (2) above may relate to material of a particular description which is expected to come into existence or become available to the person concerned in the period of twenty-eight days beginning with the date of the order; and an order made in relation to such material shall require that person to notify a named constable as soon as possible after the material comes into existence or becomes available to that person.

(4) The period to be specified in an order under sub-paragraph (2) above shall be seven days from the date of the order or, in the case of an order made by virtue of sub-paragraph (3) above, from the notification to the constable unless it appears to the sheriff that a longer or shorter period would be appropriate in the particular circumstances of the application.

(5) The conditions referred to in sub-paragraph (2) above are—

(a) that a terrorist investigation is being carried out and that there are reasonable grounds for believing that the material to which the application relates is likely to be of substantial value (whether by itself or together with other material) to the investigation; and
(b) that there are reasonable grounds for believing that it is in the public interest, having regard—
   (i) to the benefit likely to accrue to the investigation if the material is obtained; and
   (ii) to the circumstances under which the person in possession of the material holds it,

that the material should be produced or that access to it should be given.

(6) Where the sheriff makes an order under sub-paragraph (2)(b) above in relation to material on any premises he may, on the application of the procurator fiscal, order any person who appears to him to be entitled to grant entry to the premises to allow a constable to enter the premises to obtain access to the material.

13. (1) Provision made be made by Act of Adjournal as to—

(*a*) the discharge and variation of orders under paragraph 12 above; and

(*b*) proceedings relating to such orders.

(2) The following provisions shall have effect pending the coming into force of an Act of Adjournal under sub-paragraph (1) above—

(*a*) an order under paragraph 12 above may be discharged or varied by a sheriff on a written application made to him by any person subject to the order;

(*b*) unless the sheriff otherwise directs on grounds of urgency, the applicant shall, not less than forty-eight hours before making the application, send a copy of it and a notice in writing of the time and place where the application is to be made to the procurator fiscal on whose application the order to be discharged or varied was made.

(3) Where the material to which an application under paragraph 12 above relates consists of information contained in a computer—

(*a*) an order under sub-paragraph (2)(a) of that paragraph shall have effect as an order to produce the material in a form in which it can be taken away and in which it is visible and legible; and

(*b*) an order under sub-paragraph (2)(b) of that paragraph shall have effect as an order to give access to the material in a form in which it is visible and legible.

(4) Subject to paragraph 17(1)(b) below, an order under paragraph 12 above shall have effect notwithstanding any obligation as to secrecy or other restriction on the disclosure of information imposed by statute or otherwise.

(5) An order may be made under paragraph 12 above in relation to material in the possession of a government department which is an authorised government department for the purposes of the Crown Proceedings Act 1947; and any such order (which shall be served as if the proceedings were civil proceedings against the department) may require any officer of the department, whether named in the order or not, who may for the time being be in possession of the material concerned to comply with such order.

Warrant for search of premises

14. (1) A procurator fiscal may, for the purpose of a terrorist investigation, apply to a sheriff for a warrant under this paragraph in relation to specified premises.

(2) On such application the sheriff may issue a warrant authorising a constable to enter and search the premises if the sheriff is satisfied—

(*a*) that an order made under paragraph 12 above in relation to material on the premises has not been complied with; or

(*b*) that the conditions in sub-paragraph (3) below are fulfilled.

(3) The conditions referred to in sub-paragraph (2)(b) above are—

    (*a*) that there are reasonable grounds for believing that there is material on the premises specified in the application in respect of which the conditions in sub-paragraph (5) of paragraph 12 above are fulfilled; and

    (*b*) that it would not be appropriate to make an order under that paragraph in relation to the material because—

        (i) it is not practicable to communicate with any person entitled to produce the material; or

       (ii) it is not practicable to communicate with any person entitled to grant access to the material or entitled to grant entry to the premises on which the material is situated; or

     (iii) the investigation for the purposes of which the application is made may be seriously prejudiced unless a constable can secure immediate access to the material.

(4) A warrant under this paragraph shall authorise a constable to enter the premises specified in the warrant and to search the premises and any persons found there and to seize and retain any material found there or on any such person, if he has reasonable grounds for believing that it is likely to be of substantial value (whether by itself or together with other material) to the investigation for the purpose of which the warrant was issued.

(5) A warrant under this paragraph may authorise persons named in the warrant to accompany a constable who is executing it.

Explanation of seized or produced material

15. (1) A sheriff may, on an application made by a procurator fiscal, order any person specified in the order to provide an explanation of any material produced or made available to a constable under paragraph 12 above or seized in pursuance of a warrant under paragraph 14 above.

(2) A person shall not under this paragraph be required to disclose any information which he would be entitled to refuse to disclose on grounds of confidentiality in legal proceedings as being—

    (*a*) communications between a professional legal adviser and his client, or

    (*b*) communications made in connection with or in contemplation of legal proceedings and for the purposes of those proceedings,

except that a lawyer may be required to furnish the name and address of his client.

(3) A statement by a person in response to a requirement imposed by virtue of this section may only be used in evidence against him—

    (*a*) on a prosecution for an offence under section 2 of the False Oaths (Scotland) Act 1933; or

    (*b*) on a prosecution for some other offence where in giving evidence he makes a statement inconsistent with it.

(4) Sub-paragraphs (1), (2), and (5) of paragraph 13 above shall apply to orders under this paragraph as they apply to orders under paragraph 12 above.

Urgent cases

16. (1) If a police officer of at least the rank of superintendent has reasonable grounds for believing that the case is one of great emergency and that in the interests of the State immediate action is necessary, he may by a written order signed by him give to any constable the authority which may be given by a search warrant under paragraph 14 above.

(2) Where an authority is given under this paragraph particulars of the case shall be notified as soon as may be to the Secretary of State.

(3) If such a police officer as is mentioned in sub-paragraph (1) above has reasonable grounds for believing that the case is such as is there mentioned he may by a notice in writing signed by him require any person specified in the notice to provide an explanation of any materials seized in pursuance of an order under this paragraph.

(4) Any person who without reasonable excuse fails to comply with a notice under sub-paragraph (3) above is guilty of an offence and liable on summary conviction to imprisonment for a term not exceeding six months or a fine not exceeding level 5 on the standard scale or both.

(5) Sub-paragraphs (2) and (3) of paragraph 15 above shall apply to a requirement under sub-paragraph (3) above as they apply to an order under that paragraph.

Supplementary

17. (1) This Part of this Schedule is without prejudice to—

(a) any power of entry or search or any power to seize or retain property which is otherwise exercisable by a constable;

(b) any rule of law whereby—
  (i) communications between a professional legal adviser and his client, or
  (ii) communications made in connection with or in contemplation of legal proceedings and for the purposes of those proceedings,

are in legal proceedings protected from disclosure on the ground of confidentiality.

(2) For the purpose of exercising any powers conferred on him under this Part of this Schedule a constable may, if necessary, open lockfast places on premises specified in an order under paragraph 12 or 16 above or a warrant under paragraph 14 above.

(3) A search of a person under this Part of this Schedule may only be carried out by a person of the same sex.

SECURITY SERVICE ACT 1989

1 The Security Service

(1) There shall continue to be a Security Service (in this Act referred to as "the Service") under the authority of the Secretary of State.

(2) The function of the Service shall be the protection of national security and, in particular, its protection against threats from espionage, terrorism and sabotage, from the activities of agents of foreign powers and from actions intended to overthrow or undermine parliamentary democracy by political,industrial or violent means.

(3) It shall also be the function of the Service to safeguard the economic wellbeing of the United Kingdom against threats posed by the actions or intentions of persons outside the British Islands.

2 The Director-General

(1) The operations of the Service shall continue to be under the control of a Director-General appointed by the Secretary of State.

(2) The Director-General shall be responsible for the efficiency of the Service and it shall be his duty to ensure—

(*a*) that there are arrangements for securing that no information is obtained by the Service except so far as necessary for the proper discharge of its functions or disclosed by it except so far as necessary for that purpose or for the purpose of preventing or detecting serious crime; and

(*b*) that the Service does not take any action to further the interests of any political party.

(3) The arrangements mentioned in subsection (2)(*a*) above shall be such as to ensure that information in the possession of the Service is not disclosed for use in determining whether a person should be employed, or continue to be employed, by any person, or in any office or capacity, except in accordance with provisions in that behalf approved by the Secretary of State.

(4) The Director-General shall make an annual report on the work of the Service to the Prime Minister and the Secretary of State and may at any time report to either of them on any matter relating to its work.

3 Warrants

(1) No entry on or interference with property shall be unlawful if it is authorised by a warrant issued by the Secretary of State under this section.

(2) The Secretary of State may on an application made by the Service issue a warrant under this section authorising the taking of such action as is specified in the warrant in respect of any property so specified if the Secretary of State—

(*a*) thinks it necessary for the action to be taken in order to obtain information which—

    (i) is likely to be of substantial value in assisting the Service to discharge any of its functions; and

    (ii) cannot reasonably be obtained by other means; and

(*b*) is satisfied that satisfactory arrangements are in force under section 2(2)(*a*) above with respect to the disclosure of information obtained by virtue of this section and that the information obtained under the warrant will be subject to those arrangements.

(3) A warrant shall not be issued under this section except—

(*a*) under the hand of the Secretary of State; or

(*b*) in an urgent case where the Secretary of State has expressly authorised its issue and a statement of that fact is endorsed on it, under the hand of an official of his department of or above Grade 3.

(4) A warrant shall, unless renewed under subsection (5) below, cease to have effect—

(*a*) if the warrant was under the hand of the Secretary of State, at the end of the period of six months beginning with the day on which it was issued;

(*b*) in any other case, at the end of the period ending with the second working day following that day.

(5) If at any time before the day on which a warrant would cease to have effect the Secretary of State considers it necessary for the warrant to continue to have effect for the purpose for which it was issued, he may by an instrument under his hand renew it for a period of six months beginning with that day.

(6) The Secretary of State shall cancel a warrant if he is satisfied that the action authorised by it is no longer necessary.

(7) In this section "working day" means any day other than a Saturday, a Sunday, Christmas Day, Good Friday or a day which is a bank holiday under the Banking and Financial Dealings Act 1971 in any part of the United Kingdom.

4 The Security Service Commissioner

(1) The Prime Minister shall appoint as a Commissioner for the purposes of this Act a person who holds or has held high judicial office within the meaning of the Appellate Jurisdiction Act 1876.

(2) The Commissioner shall hold office in accordance with the terms of his appointment and there shall be paid to him by the Secretary of State such allowances as the Treasury may determine.

(3) In addition to his functions under the subsequent provisions of this Act the Commissioner shall keep under review the exercise by the Secretary of State of his powers under section 3 above.

(4) It shall be the duty of every member of the Service and of every official of

the department of the Secretary of State to disclose or give to the Commissioner such documents or information as he may require for the purpose of enabling him to discharge his functions.

(5) The Commissioner shall make an annual report on the discharge of his functions to the Prime Minister and may at any time report to him on any matter relating to his discharge of those functions.

(6) The Prime Minister shall lay before each House of Parliament a copy of each annual report made by the Commissioner under subsection (5) above together with a statement as to whether any matter has been excluded from that copy in pursuance of subsection (7) below.

(7) If it appears to the Prime Minister, after consultation with the Commissioner, that the publication of any matter in a report would be prejudicial to the continued discharge of the functions of the Service, the Prime Minister may exclude that matter from the copy of the report as laid before each House of Parliament.

(8) The Secretary of State may, after consultation with the Commissioner and with the approval of the Treasury as to numbers, provide the Commissioner with such staff as the Secretary of State thinks necessary for the discharge of his functions.

OFFICIAL SECRETS ACT 1989

11 Arrest, search and trial

(1) In section 24(2) of the Police and Criminal Evidence Act 1984 (*a*rrestable offences) in paragraph (b) for the words "the Official Secrets Acts 1911 and 1920" there shall be substituted the words "the Official Secrets Act 1920" and after that paragraph there shall be inserted—

> (*bb*) offences under any provision of the Official Secrets Act 1989 except section 8(1), (4) or (5);"

(2) Offences under any provision of this Act other than section 8(1), (4) or (5) and attempts to commit them shall be arrestable offences within the meaning of section 2 of the Criminal Law Act (Northern Ireland) 1967.

(3) Section 9(1) of the Official Secrets Act 1911 (search warrants) shall have effect as if references to offences under that Act included references to offences under any provision of this Act other than section 8(1), (4) or (5); and the following provisions of the Police and Criminal Evidence Act 1984, that is to say—

> (*a*) section 9(2) (which excludes items subject to legal privilege and certain other material from powers of search conferred by previous enactments); and
>
> (*b*) paragraph 3(b) of Schedule 1 (which prescribes access conditions for the special procedure laid down in that Schedule),

shall apply to section 9(1) of the said Act of 1911 as extended by this subsection as they apply to that section as originally enacted.

(4) Section 8(4) of the Official Secrets Act 1920 (exclusion of public from hearing on grounds of national safety) shall have effect as if references to offences under that Act included references to offences under any provision of this Act other than section 8(1), (4) or (5).

(5) Proceedings for an offence under this Act may be taken in any place in the United Kingdom.

DRUG TRAFFICKING OFFENCES ACT 1986

Investigations into drug trafficking

27 Order to make materials available

(1) A constable ... may, for the purpose of an investigation into drug trafficking, apply to a Circuit judge ... for an order under subsection (2) below in relation to particular material of material of a particular description.

(2) If on such an application the judge ... is satisfied that the conditions in subsection (4) below are fulfilled, he may make an order that the person who appears to him to be in possession of the material to which the application relates shall—

(*a*) produce it to a constable for him to take away, or
(*b*) give a constable access to it,

within such period as the order may specify.

This subsection is subject to section 30(11) of this Act.

(3) The period to be specified in an order under subsection (2) above shall be seven days unless it appears to the judge ... that a longer or shorter period would be appropriate in the particular circumstances of the application.

(4) The conditions referred to in subsection (2) above are—

(*a*) that there are reasonable grounds for suspecting that a specified person had carried on or has benefited from drug trafficking,
(*b*) that there are reasonable grounds for suspecting that the material to which the application relates—
  (i) is likely to be of substantial value (whether by itself or together with other material) to the investigation for the purpose of which the application is made, and
  (ii) does not consist of or include items subject to legal privilege or excluded material, and
(*c*) that there are reasonable grounds for believing that it is in the public interest, having regard—

    (i) to the benefit likely to accrue to the investigation if the material is obtained, and

    (ii) to the circumstances under which the person in possession of the material holds it,

that the material should be produced or that access to it should be given.

(5) Where the judge or, as the case may be, the sheriff makes an order under subsection (2)(*b*) above in relation to material on any premises he may, on the application of a constable ... order any person who appears to him to be entitled to grant entry to the premises to allow a constable to enter the premises to obtain access to the material.

(6) Provision may be made by Crown Court Rules ... as to—

(*a*) the discharge and variation of orders under this section, and

(*b*) proceedings relating to such orders.

(7) An order of a Circuit Judge under this section shall have effect as if it were an order of the Crown Court.

(8) Where the material to which an application under this section relates consists of information contained in a computer—

(*a*) an order under subsection (2)(*a*) above shall have effect as an order to produce the material in a form in which it can be taken away and in which it is visible and legible, and

(*b*) an order under subsection (2)(*b*) above shall have effect as an order to give access to the material in a form in which it is visible and legible.

(9) An order under subsection (2) above—

(*a*) shall not confer any right to production of, or access to, items subject to legal privilege or excluded material,

(*b*) shall have effect notwithstanding any obligation as to secrecy or other restriction upon the disclosure of information imposed by statute or otherwise, and

(*c*) may be made in relation to material in the possession of an authorised government department.

28 Authority for search

(1) A constable ... may, for the purpose of an investigation into drug trafficking, apply to a Circuit judge ... for a warrant under this section in relation to specified premises.

(2) On such application the judge ... may issue a warrant authorising a constable to enter and search the premises if he is satisfied—

(*a*) that an order made under section 27 of this Act in relation to material on the premises has not been complied with, or

(*b*) that the conditions in subsection (3) below are fulfilled, or

(*c*) that the conditions in subsection (4) below are fulfilled.

(3) The conditions referred to in subsection (2)(*b*) above are—

(*a*) that there are reasonable grounds for suspecting that a specified person has carried on or has benefited from drug trafficking, and

(*b*) that the conditions in section 27(4)(*b*) and (*c*) of this Act are fulfilled in relation to any material on the premises, and

(*c*) that it would not be appropriate to make an order under that section in relation to the material because—

   (i) it is not practicable to communicate with any person entitled to produce the material, or

   (ii) it is not practicable to communicate with any person entitled to grant access to the material or entitled to grant entry to the premises on which the material is situated, or

   (iii) the investigation for the purposes of which the application is made might be seriously prejudiced unless a constable could secure immediate access to the material.

(4) the conditions referred to in subsection (2)(*c*) above are—

(*a*) that there are reasonable grounds for suspecting that a specified person has carried on or has benefited from drug trafficking, and

(*b*) that there are reasonable grounds for suspecting that there is on the premises material relating to the specified person or to drug trafficking which is likely to be of substantial value (whether by itself or together with other material) to the investigation for the purpose of which the application is made, but that the material cannot at the time of the application be particularised, and

(*c*) that—

   (i) it is not practicable to communicate with any person entitled to grant entry to the premises, or

   (ii) entry to the premises will not be granted unless a warrant is produced, or

   (iii) the investigation for the purpose of which the application is made might be seriously prejudiced unless a constable arriving at the premises could secure immediate entry to them.

(5) Where a constable has entered premises in the execution of a warrant issued under this section, he may seize and retain any material, other than items subject to legal privilege and excluded material, which is likely to be of substantial value (whether by itself or together with other material) to the investigation for the purpose of which the warrant was issued.

29 Sections 27 and 28: supplementary provisions

(1) For the purposes of sections 21 and 22 of the Police and Criminal Evidence Act 1984 (*a*ccess to, and copying and retention of, seized material)—

(*a*) an investigation into drug trafficking shall be treated as if it were an investigation of or in connection with an offence, and

(*b*) material produced in pursuance of an order under section 27(2)(*a*) of this Act shall be treated as if it were material seized by a constable.

(2) Subject to subsection (3) below, in section 27 and 28 of this Act "items subject to legal privilege", "excluded material" and "premises" have the same meanings as in the said Act of 1984.

(3) [repealed by Criminal Justice Act 1987, s 70(2), Sch 2].

30 Disclosure of information held by government departments

(1) Subject to subsection (4) below, the High Court may on an application by the prosecutor order any material mentioned in subsection (3) below which is in the possession of an authorised government department to be produced to the court within such period as the court may specify.

(2) The power to make an order under subsection (1) above is exercisable if—

(a) the powers conferred on the court by sections (8)(1) and 9(1) of this Act are exercisable by virtue of subsection (1) of section 7 of this Act, or

(b) those powers are exercisable by virtue of subsection (2) of that section and the court has made a restraint or charging order which has not been discharged;

but where the power to make an order under subsection (1) above is exercisable by virtue only of paragraph (b) above, subsection (3) of section 7 of this Act shall apply for the purposes of this section as it applies for the purposes of sections 8 and 9 of this Act.

(3) The material referred to in subsection (1) above is any material which—

(a) has been submitted to an officer of an authorised government department by the defendant or by a person who has at any time held property which was realisable property,

(b) has been made by an officer of an authorised government department in relation to the defendant or such a person, or

(c) is correspondence which passed between an officer of an authorised government department and the defendant or such a person,

and an order under that subsection may require the production of all such material or of a particular description of such material, being material in the possession of the department concerned.

(4) An order under subsection (1) above shall not require the production of any material unless it appears to the High Court that the material is likely to contain information that would facilitate the exercise of the powers conferred on the court by sections 8 to 11 of this Act or on a receiver appointed under section 8 or 11 of this Act or in pursuance of a charging order.

(5) The court may by order authorise the disclosure to such a receiver of any material produced under subsection (1) above or any part of such material, but the court shall not make an order under this subsection unless a reasonable opportunity has been given for an officer of the department to make representation to the court.

(6) Material disclosed in pursuance of an order under subsection (5) above may, subject to any conditions contained in the order, be further disclosed for the purposes of the functions under this Act of the receiver or the Crown Court.

(7) The court may by order authorise the disclosure to a person mentioned in subsection (8) below of any material produced under subsection (1) above or any part of such material; but the court shall not make an order under this subsection unless—

(a) a reasonable opportunity has been given for an officer of the department to make representations to the court, and

(b) it appears to the court that the material is likely to be of substantial value in exercising functions relating to drug trafficking.

(8) The persons referred to in subsection (7) above are—

(a) any member of a police force,

(b) any member of the Crown Prosecution Service, and

(c) any officer within the meaning of the Customs and Excise Management Act 1979.

(9) Material disclosed in pursuance of an order under subsection (7) above may, subject to any conditions contained in the order, be further disclosed for the purposes of functions relating to drug trafficking.

(10) Material may be produced or disclosed in pursuance of this section notwithstanding any obligation as to secrecy or other restriction upon the disclosure of information imposed by statute or otherwise.

(11) An order under subsection (1) above and, in the case of material in the possession of an authorised government department, an order under section 27(2) of this Act may require any officer of the department (whether named in the order or not) who may for the time being be in possession of the material concerned to comply with it, and such an order shall be served as of the proceedings were civil proceedings against the department.

(12) The person on whom such an order is served—

(a) shall take all reasonable steps to bring it to the attention of the officer concerned, and

(b) if the order is not brought to that officer's attention within the period referred to in subsection (1) above, shall report the reasons for the failure to the court;

and it shall also be the duty of any other officer of the department in receipt of the order to take such steps as are mentioned in paragraph (a) above.

31 Offence of prejudicing investigation

(1) Where, in relation to an investigation into drug trafficking, an order under section 27 of this Act has been made or has beenapplied for and has not been refused or a warrant under section 28 of this Act has been issued, a person who,

knowing or suspecting that the investigation is taking place, makes any disclosure which is likely to prejudice the investigation is guilty of an offence.

(2) In proceedings against a person for an offence under this section, it is a defence to prove—

(a) that he did not know or suspect that the disclosure was likely to prejudice the investigation, or

(b) that he had lawful authority or reasonable excuse for making the disclosure.

(3) A person guilty of an offence under this.section shall be liable—

(a) on conviction on indictment, to imprisonment for a term not exceeding five years or to a fine or to both, and

(b) on summary conviction, to imprisonment for a term not exceeding six months or to a fine not exceeding the statutory maximum or to both.

32 Authorisation of delay in notifying arrest

(1)—(3) [amend the Police and Criminal evidence Act 1984, ss 56, 58, 65].

(4) Without prejudice to section 20(2) of the Interpretation Act 1978, the Police and Criminal Evidence Act 1984 (Application to Customs and Excise Order 1985 applies to sections 56 and 58 of the Police and Criminal Evidence Act 1984 as those sections have effect by virtue of this section.

The Criminal Justice (Confiscation) (Northern Ireland) Order 1990

Investigations into drug trafficking

Order to make material available

31 (1) A constable may, for the purpose of an investigation into drug trafficking, apply to a county court judge for an order under paragraph (2) in relation to particular material or material of a particular description.

(2) Subject to Article 34(11) if on such an application the judge is satisfied that the conditions in paragraph (4) are fulfilled, he may make an order that the person who appears to him to be in possession of the material to which the application relates shall—

(a) produce it to a constable for him to take away, or

(b) give a constable access to it,

within such period as the order may specify.

(3) The period to be specified in an order under paragraph (2) shall be 7 days

unless it appears to the judge, that a longer or shorter period would be appropriate in the particular circumstances of the application.

(4) The conditions referred to in paragraph (2) are—

(*a*) that there are reasonable grounds for suspecting that a specified person has carried on or has benefited from drug trafficking,

(*b*) that there are reasonable grounds for suspecting that the material to which the application relates—

    (i) is likely to be of substantial value (whether by itself or together with other material) to the investigation for the purpose of which the application is made, and

    (ii) does not consist of or include items subject to legal privilege or excluded material, and

(*c*) that there are reasonable grounds for believing that it is in the public interest, having regard—

    (i) to the benefit likely to accrue to the investigation if the material is obtained, and

    (ii) to the circumstances under which the person in possession of the material holds it,

that the material should be produced or that access to it should be given.

(5) Where the judge makes an order under paragraph (2)(*b*) in relation to material on any premises he may, on the application of a constable order any person who appears to him to be entitled to grant entry to the premises to allow a constable to enter the premises to obtain access to the material.

(6) Provision may be made by Crown Court Rules as to—

(*a*) the discharge and variation of orders under this Article, and

(*b*) proceedings relating to such orders.

(7) An order of a county court judge under this Article shall have effect as if it were an order of the Crown Court.

(8) Where the material to which an application under this Article relates consists of information contained in a computer—

(*a*) an order under paragraph (2)(*a*) shall have effect as an order to produce the material in a form in which it can be taken away and in which it is visible and legible, and

(*b*) an order under paragraph (2)(*b*) shall have effect as an order to give access to the material in a form in which it is visible and legible.

(9) An order under paragraph (2)—

(*a*) shall not confer any right to production of, or access to, items subject to legal privilege or excluded material,

(*b*) shall have effect notwithstanding any obligation as to secrecy or other restriction upon the disclosure of information imposed by statute or otherwise, and

(*c*) may be made in relation to material in the possessionof an authorised government department.

Appendix 6

Authority for search

32 (1) A constable may, for the purpose of an investigation into drug trafficking, apply to a county court judge for a warrant under this Article in relation to specified premises.

(2) On such application the judge may issue a warrant authorising a constable to enter and search the premises if he is satisfied—

(a) that an order made under Article 31 in relation to material on the premises has not been complied with, or

(b) that the conditions in paragraph (3) are fulfilled, or

(c) that the conditions in paragraph (4) are fulfilled.

(3) The conditions referred to in paragraph (2)(b) are—

(a) that there are reasonable grounds for suspecting that a specified person has carried on or has benefited from drug trafficking, and

(b) that the conditions in Article 31(4)(b) and (c) are fulfilled in relation to any material on the premises, and

(c) that it would not be appropriate to make an order under that Article in relation to the material because—

  (i) it is not practicable to communicate with any person entitled to produce the material, or

  (ii) it is not practicable to communicate with any person entitled to grant access to the material or entitled to grant entry to the premises on which the material is situated, or

  (iii) the investigation for the purposes of which the application is made might be seriously prejudiced unless a constable could secure immediate access to the material.

(4) The conditions referred to in paragraph (2)(c) are—

(a) that there are reasonable grounds for suspecting that a specified person has carried on or has benefited from drug trafficking, and

(b) that there are reasonable grounds for suspecting that there is on the premises material relating to the specified person or to drug trafficking which is likely to be of substantial value (whether by itself or together with other material) to the investigation for the purpose of which the application is made, but that the material cannot at the time of the application be particularised, and

(c) that—

  (i) it is not practicable to communicate with any person entitled to grant entry to the premises, or

  (ii) entry to the premises will not be granted unless a warrant is produced, or

  (iii) the investigation for the purpose of which the application is made might be seriously prejudiced unless a constable arriving at the premises could secure immediate entry to them.

(5) Where a constable has entered premises in the execution of a warrant issued under this Article, he may seize and retain any material, other than items subject to legal privilege and excluded material, which is likely to be of substantial value

(whether by itself or together with other material) to the investigation for the purpose of which the warrant was issued.

Articles 31 and 32: supplementary provisions

33 (1) For the purposes of Articles 23 and 24 of the Police and Criminal evidence (Northern Ireland) Order 1989 *(a*ccess to, and copying and retention of, seized material)—

(*a*) an investigation into drug trafficking shall be treated as if it were an investigation of or in connection with an offence, and

(*b*) material produced in pursuance of an order under Article 31(2)(*a*) shall be treated as if it were material seized by a constable.

(2) In Articles 31 and 32 "items subject to legal privilege", "excluded material" and "premises" have the same meanings as in that Order of 1989.

Disclosure of information held by government departments

34 (1) Subject to paragraph (4), the High Court may for the purpose of an investigation into drug trafficking on an application by the prosecution order any material mentioned in paragraph (3) which is in the possession of an authorised government department to be produced to the Court within such period as the Court may specify.

(2) The power to make an order under paragraph (1) is exercisable if—

(*a*) the powers conferred on the Court by Articles 13(1) and 14(1) are exercisable by virtue of paragraph (1) of Article 12, or

(*b*) those powers are exercisable by virtue of paragraph (2) of that Article and the Court has made a restraint or charging order which has not been discharged;

but where the power to make an order under paragraph (1) is exercisable by virtue only of sub-paragraph (*b*), Article 12(3) shall apply for the purposes of this Article as it applies for the purposes of Articles 13 and 14.

(3) The material referred to in paragraph (1) is any material which—

(*a*) has been submitted to an officer of an authorised government department by the defendant or by a person who has at any time held property which was realisable property,

(*b*) has been made by an officer of an authorised government department in relation to the defendant or such a person, or

(*c*) is correspondence which passed between an officer of anauthorised government department and the defendant or such a person,

and an order under that paragraph may require the production of all such material or of a particular description of such material, being material in the possession of the department concerned.

(4) An order under paragraph (1) shall not require the production of any material unless it appears to the High Court that the material is likely to contain

information that would facilitate the exercise of the powers conferred on the Court by Articles 13 to 16 or on a receiver appointed under Article 13 or 16 or in pursuance of a charging order.

(5) The High Court may by order authorise the disclosure to such a receiver of any material produced under paragraph (1) or any part of such material; but the Court shall not make an order under this paragraph unless a reasonable opportunity has been given for an officer of the department to make representations to the Court.

(6) Material disclosed in pursuance of an order under paragraph (5) may, subject to any conditions contained in the order, be further disclosed for the purposes of the functions under this Order of the receiver or the Crown Court.

(7) The High Court may by order authorise the disclosure to a person mentioned in paragraph (8) of any material produced under paragraph (1) or any part of such material; but the Court shall not make an order under this paragraph unless—

  (*a*) a reasonable opportunity has been given for an officer of the department to make representations to the Court, and
  (*b*) it appears to the court that the material is likely to be of substantial value in exercising functions relating to drug trafficking.

(8) The persons referred to in paragraph (7) are—

  (*a*) any member of the Royal Ulster Constabulary,
  (*b*) the Director of Public Prosecutions for Northern Ireland or any person acting on his behalf, and
  (*c*) any officer within the meaning of the Customs and Excise Management Act 1979.

(9) Material disclosed in pursuance of an order under paragraph (7) may, subject to any conditions contained in the order, be further disclosed for the purposes of functions relating to drug trafficking.

(10) Material may be produced or disclosed in pursuance of this Article notwithstanding any obligation as to secrecy or other restriction upon the disclosure of information imposed by statute or otherwise.

(11) An order under paragraph (1) and, in the case of material in the possession of an authorised government department, anorder under Article 21(2) may require any officer of the department (whether named in the order or not) who may for the time being be in possession of the material concerned to comply with it, and such an order shall be served as if the proceedings were civil proceedings against the department.

(12) The person on whom such an order is served—

  (*a*) shall take all reasonable steps to bring it to the attention of the officer concerned, and
  (*b*) if the order is not brought to that officer's attention within the period

referred to in paragraph (1), shall report the reasons for the failure to the High Court;

and it shall be the duty of any other officer of the department in receipt of the order to take such steps as are mentioned in sub-paragraph (*a*).

Offence of prejudicing investigation

35 (1) Where, in relation to an investigation into drug trafficking, an order under Article 31 has been made or has been applied for and has not been refused or a warrant under Article 32 has been issued, a person who, knowing or suspecting that the investigation is taking place, makes any disclosure which is likely to prejudice the investigation is guilty of an offence.

(2) In proceedings against a person for an offence under this Article, it is a defence to prove—

(*a*) that he did not know or suspect that the disclosure was likely to prejudice the investigation, or

(*b*) that he had lawful authority or reasonable excuse for making the disclosure.

(3) A person guilty of an offence under this Article shall be liable—

(*a*) on conviction on indictment, to imprisonment for a term not exceeding 5 years or to a fine or to both, and

(*b*) on summary conviction, to imprisonment for a term not exceeding 6 months or to a fine not exceeding the statutory maximum or to both.

Miscellaneous and supplemental

Disclosure of information subject to contractual restriction upon disclosure

36 Where a person discloses to a constable—

(*a*) a suspicion or belief that any property—
  (i) has been obtained as a result of or in connection with the commission of an offence to which this Order applies or, as the case may be, is used in connection with drug trafficking; or
  (ii) derives from any property so obtained or, as the case may be, from drug trafficking; or

(*b*) any matter on which such a suspicion or belief is based,

the disclosure shall not be treated as a breach of any restriction upon the disclosure of information imposed by contract.

Authorisation of delay in notifying arrest, etc., and drug trafficking offences to be serious arrestable offences

37 (1) The Police and Criminal Evidence (Northern Ireland) Order 1989 shall be amended as follows.

(2) In Article 53 (interpretation of Part VI)—

(*a*) after the definition of "appropriate consent" there shall be inserted—

"drug trafficking" and "drug trafficking offence" have the same meaning as in the Criminal Justice (Confiscation) (Northern Ireland) Order 1990"; and

(*b*) at the end of that Article there shall be inserted— "References in this Part to any person's proceeds of drug trafficking are to be construed in accordance with the Criminal Justice (Confiscation) (Northern Ireland) Order 1990".

(3) In Article 57 (right to have someone informed when arrested)—

(*a*) at the beginning of paragraph (5) there shall be inserted "Subject to paragraph (5A)"; and

(*b*) after paragraph (5) there shall be inserted—

"(5A) An officer may also authorise delay where the serious arrestable offence is an offence to which the Criminal Justice (Confiscation) (Northern Ireland) Order 1990 applies (offences in respect of which confiscation order under that Order may be made) and the officer has reasonable grounds for believing—

(*a*) in the case of an offence other than a drug trafficking offence, that the detained person has benefited from the offence and that the recovery of the value of the property obtained by that person from or in connection with the offence or of the pecuniary advantage derived by him from or in connection with it will be hindered by telling the named person of the arrest; and

(*b*) in the case of a drug trafficking offence, that the detained person has benefited from drug trafficking and that the recovery of the value of that person's proceeds of drug trafficking will be hindered by telling the named person of the arrest."

(4) In Article 59 (*a*ccess to legal advice)—

(*a*) at the beginning of paragraph (8) there shall be inserted "Subject to paragraph (8A)"; and

(*b*) after paragraph (8) there shall be inserted—
"(8A) An officer may also authorise delay where the serious arrestable offence is an offence to which the Criminal Justice (Confiscation) (Northern Ireland) Order 1990 applies (offences in respect of which confiscation order under that Order may be made) and the officer has reasonable grounds for believing—

(*a*) in the case of an offence other than a drug trafficking offence, that the detained person has benefited from the offence and that the recovery of the value of the property obtained by that person from or in connection with the offence or of the pecuniary advantage derived by him from or in connection with it will be hindered by the exercise of the right conferred by paragraph (1); and

(*b*) in the case of a drug trafficking offence, that the detained person has benefited from drug trafficking and that the recovery of the value of that person's proceeds of drug trafficking will be hindered by the exercise of the right conferred by paragraph (1)."

(5) In Article 87(2) *(a*rrestable offences that are always serious) after sub-paragraph *(a)* there shall be inserted—

"*(aa)* any of the offences mentioned in sub-paragraphs *(a)* to *(e)* of the definition of "drug trafficking offence" in Article 2(2) of the Criminal Justice (Confiscation) (Northern Ireland) Order 1990;".

CRIMINAL JUSTICE ACT 1987

PART I

FRAUD

Serious Fraud Office

1 The Serious Fraud Office

(1) A Serious Fraud Office shall be constituted for England and Wales and Northern Ireland.

(2) The Attorney General shall appoint a person to be the Director of the Serious Fraud Office (referred to in this Part of this Act as "the Director"), and he shall discharge his functions under the superintendence of the Attorney General.

(3) The Director may investigate any suspected offence which appears to him on reasonable grounds to involve serious or complex fraud.

(4) The Director may, if he thinks fit, conduct any such investigation in conjunction either with the police or with any other person who is, in the opinion of the Director, a proper person to be concerned in it.

(5) The Director may—

(*a*) institute and have the conduct of any criminal proceedings which appear to him to relate to such fraud; and
(*b*) take over the conduct of any such proceedings at any stage.

(6) The Director shall discharge such other functions in relation to fraud as may from time to time be assigned to him by the Attorney General.

(7) The Director may designate for the purposes of subsection (5) above any member of the Serious Fraud Office who is—

(*a*) a barrister in England and Wales or Northern Ireland;
(*b*) a solicitor of the Supreme Court; or
(*c*) a solicitor of the Supreme Court of Judicature of Northern Ireland.

(8) Any member so designated shall, without prejudice to any functions which may have been assigned to him in his capacity as a member of that Office, have all the powers of the Director as to the institution and conduct of proceedings but shall exercise those powers under the direction of the Director.

(9) Any member so designated who is a barrister in England and Wales or a solicitor of the Supreme Court shall have, in any court, the rights of audience enjoyed by solicitors holding practising certificates and shall have such additional rights of audience in the Crown Court in England and Wales as may be given by virtue of subsection (11) below.

(10) The reference in subsection (9) above to rights of audience enjoyed in any court by solicitors include a reference to rights enjoyed in the Crown Court by virtue of any direction given by the Lord Chancellor under section 83 of the Supreme Court Act 1981.

(11) For the purpose of giving members so designated who are barristers in England and Wales or solicitors of the Supreme Court additional rights of audience in the Crown Court in England and Wales, the Lord Chancellor may given such direction as respects such members as he could give under the said section 83.

(12) Any member so designated who is a barrister in Northern Ireland or a solicitor of the Supreme Court of Judicature of Northern Ireland shall have—

(a) in any court the rights of audience enjoyed by solicitors of the Supreme Court of Judicature of Northern Ireland and, in the Crown Court in Northern Ireland, such additional rights of audience as may be given by virtue of subsection (14) below; and

(b) in the Crown Court in Northern Ireland, the rights of audience enjoyed by barristers employed by the Director of Public Prosecutions for Northern Ireland.

(13) Subject to subsection (14) below, the reference in subsection (12)(a) above to rights of audience enjoyed by solicitors of the Supreme Court of Judicature of Northern Ireland is a reference to such rights enjoyed in the Crown Court in Northern Ireland as restricted by any direction given by the Lord Chief Justice of Northern Ireland under section 50 of the Judicature (Northern Ireland) Act 1978).

(14) For the purpose of giving any member so designated who is a barrister in Northern Ireland or a solicitor of the Supreme Court of Judicature of Northern Ireland additional rights of audience in the Crown Court in Northern Ireland, the Lord Chief Justice of Northern Ireland may direct that any direction given by him under the said section 50 shall not apply to such members.

(15) Schedule 1 to this Act shall have effect.

(16) For the purposes of this section (including that Schedule) references to the conduct of any proceedings include references to the proceedings being discontinued and to the taking of any steps (including the bringing of appeals and making of representations in respect of applications for bail) which may be taken in relation to them.

(17) In the application of this section (including that Schedule) to Northern Ireland references to the Attorney General are to be construed as references to him in his capacity as Attorney General for Northern Ireland.

2 Director's investigation powers

(1) The powers of the Director under this section shall be exercisable, but only for the purposes of an investigation under section 1 above, in any case in which it appears to him that there is good reason to do so for the purpose of investigating the affairs, or any aspect of the affairs, of any person.

(2) The Director may by notice in writing require the person whose affairs are to be investigated ("the person under investigation") or any other person whom he has reason to believe has relevant information to attend before the Director at a specified time and place and answer questions or otherwise furnish information with respect to any matter relevant to the investigation.

(3) The Director may by notice in writing require the person under investigation or any other person to produce at a specified time and place any specified documents which appear to the Director to relate to any matter relevant to the investigation or any documents of a specified class which appear to him so to relate; and—

(*a*) if any such documents are produced, the Director may—
  (i) take copies or extracts from them;
  (ii) require the person producing them to provide an explanation of any of them;
(*b*) if any such documents are not produced, the Director may require the person who was required to produce them to state, to the best of his knowledge and belief, where they are.

(4) Where, on information on oath laid by a member of the Serious Fraud Office, a justice of the peace is satisfied, in relation to any documents, that there are reasonable grounds for believing—

(*a*) that—
  (i) a person has failed to comply with an obligation under this section to produce them;
  (ii) it is not practicable to serve a notice under subsection (3) above in relation to them; or
  (iii) the service of such a notice in relation to them might seriously prejudice the investigation; and

(*b*) that they are on premises specified in the information,

he may issue such a warrant as is mentioned in subsection (5) below.

(5) The warrant referred to above is a warrant authorising any constable—

(*a*) to enter (using such force as is reasonably necessary for the purpose) and search the premises, and
(*b*) to take possession of any documents appearing to be documents of the description specified in the information or to take in relation to any documents so appearing any other steps which may appear to be necessary for preserving them and preventing interference with them.

(6) Unless it is not practicable in the circumstances, a constable executing a

warrant issued under subsection (4) above shall be accompanied by an appropriate person.

(7) In subsection (6) above "appropriate person" means—

(*a*) a member of the Serious Fraud Office; or

(*b*) some person who is not a member of that Office but whom the Director has authorised to accompany the constable.

(8) A statement by a person in response to a requirement imposed by virtue of this section may only be used in evidence against him—

(*a*) on a prosecution for an offence under subsection (14) below; or

(*b*) on a prosecution for some other offence where in giving evidence he makes a statement inconsistent with it.

(9) A person shall not under this section be required to disclose any information or produce any document which he would be entitled to refuse to disclose or produce on grounds of legal professional privilege in proceedings in the High Court, except that a lawyer may be required to furnish the name and address of his client.

(10) A person shall not under this section be required to disclose information or produce a document in respect of which he owes an obligation of confidence by virtue of carrying on any banking business unless—

(*a*) the person to whom the obligation of confidence is owed consents to the disclosure or production; or

(*b*) the Director has authorised the making of the requirement or, if it is impracticable for him to act personally, a member of the Serious Fraud Office designated by him for the purposes of this subsection has done so.

(11) Without prejudice to the power of the Director to assign functions to members of the Serious Fraud Office, the Director may authorise any competent investigator (other than a constable) who is not a member of that Office to exercise on his behalf all or any of the powers conferred by this section, but no such authority shall be granted except for the purpose of investigating the affairs, or any aspect of the affairs, of a person specified in the authority.

(12) No person shall be bound to comply with any requirement imposed by a person exercising powers by virtue of any authority granted under subsection (11) above unless he has, if required to do so, produced evidence of his authority.

(13) Any person who without reasonable excuse fails to comply with a requirement imposed on him under this section shall be guilty of an offence and liable on summary conviction to imprisonment for a term not exceeding six months or to a fine not exceeding level 5 on the standard scale or to both.

(14) A person who, in purported compliance with a requirement under this section—

(*a*) makes a statement which he knows to be false or misleading in a material particular; or

(*b*) recklessly makes a statement which is false or misleading in a material particular,

shall be guilty of an offence.

(15) A person guilty of an offence under subsection (14) above shall—

(*a*) on conviction on indictment, be liable to imprisonment for a term not exceeding two years or to a fine or to both; and

(*b*) on summary conviction, be liable to imprisonment for a term not exceeding six months or to a fine not exceeding the statutory maximum, or to both.

(16) Where any person—

(*a*) knows or suspects that an investigation by the police or the Serious Fraud Office into serious or complex fraud is being or is likely to be carried out; and

(*b*) falsifies, conceals, destroys or otherwise disposes of, or causes or permits the falsification, concealment, destruction or disposal of documents which he knows or suspects are or would be relevant to such an investigation,

he shall be guilty of an offence unless he proves that he had no intention of concealing the facts disclosed by the documents from persons carrying out such an investigation.

(17) A person guilty of an offence under subsection (16) above shall—

(*a*) on conviction on indictment, be liable to imprisonment for a term not exceeding 7 years or to a fine or to both; and

(*b*) on summary conviction, be liable to imprisonment for a term not exceeding 6 months or to a fine not exceeding the statutory maximum or to both.

(18) In this section, "documents" includes information recorded in any form and, in relation to information recorded otherwise than in legible form, references to its production include references to producing a copy of the information in legible form.

(19) In the application of this section to Scotland, the reference to a justice of the peace is to be construed as a reference to the sheriff; and in the application of this section to Northern Ireland, subsection (4) above shall have effect as if for the references to information there were substituted references to a complaint.

CRIMINAL JUSTICE (INTERNATIONAL CO-OPERATION) ACT 1990

Mutual provision of evidence

3 Overseas evidence for use in United Kingdom

(1) Where on an application made in accordance with subsection (2) below it appears to a justice of the peace or a judge or, in Scotland, to a sheriff or a judge—

(*a*) that an offence has been committed or that there are reasonable grounds for suspecting that an offence has been committed; and

(*b*) that proceedings in respect of the offence have been instituted or that the offence is being investigated,

he may issue a letter ("a letter of request") requesting assistance in obtaining outside the United Kingdom such evidence as is specified in the letter for use in the proceedings or investigation.

(2) An application under subsection (1) above may be made by a prosecuting authority or, if proceedings have been instituted, by the person charged in those proceedings.

(3) A prosecuting authority which is for the time being designated for the purposes of this section by an order made by the Secretary of State by statutory instrument may itself issue a letter of request if—

(*a*) it is satisfied as to the matters mentioned in subsection (1)(*a*) above; and

(*b*) the offence in question is being investigated or the authority has instituted proceedings in respect of it.

(4) Subject to subsection (5) below, a letter of request shall be sent to the Secretary of State for transmission either—

(*a*) to a court or tribunal specified in the letter and exercising jurisdiction in the place where the evidence is to be obtained; or

(*b*) to any authority recognised by the government of the country or territory in question as the appropriate authority for receiving requests for assistance of the kind to which this section applies.

(5) In cases of urgency a letter of request may be sent direct to such a court or tribunal as is mentioned in subsection (4)(*a*) above.

(6) In this section "evidence" includes documents and other articles.

(7) Evidence obtained by virtue of a letter of request shall not without the consent of such an authority as is mentioned in subsection (4)(*b*) above be used for any purpose other than that specified in the letter; and when any document or other article obtained pursuant to a letter of request is no longer required for that purpose (or for any other purpose for which such consent has been obtained), it shall be returned to such an authority unless that authority indicates that the document or article need not be returned.

(8) In exercising the discretion conferred by section 25 of the Criminal Justice Act 1988 (exclusion of evidence otherwise admissible) in relation to a statement contained in evidence taken pursuant to a letter of request the court shall have regard—

(*a*) to whether it was possible to challenge the statement by questioning the person who made it; and

(*b*) if proceedings have been instituted, to whether the local law allowed the parties to the proceedings to be legally represented when the evidence was being taken.

(9) In Scotland evidence obtained by virtue of a letter of request shall, without being sworn to by witnesses, be received in evidence in so far as that can be done without unfairness to either party.

(10) In the application of this section to Northern Ireland for the reference in subsection (1) to a justice of the peace there shall be substituted a reference to a resident magistrate and for the reference in subsection (8) to section 25 of the Criminal Justice Act 1988 there shall be substituted a reference to Article 5 of the Criminal Justice (Evidence, Etc.) (Northern Ireland) Order 1988.

4 United Kingdom evidence for use overseas

(1) This section has effect where the Secretary of State receives—

(*a*) from a court or tribunal exercising criminal jurisdiction in a country or territory outside the United Kingdom or a prosecuting authority in such a country or territory; or

(*b*) from any other authority in such a country or territory which appears to him to have the function of making requests of the kind to which this section applies.

a request for assistance in obtaining evidence in the United Kingdom in connection with criminal proceedings that have been instituted, or a criminal investigation that is being carried on, in that country or territory.

(2) If the Secretary of State or, if evidence is to be obtained in Scotland, the Lord Advocate is satisfied—

(*a*) that an offence under the law of the country or territory in question has been committed or that there are reasonable grounds for suspecting that such an offence has been committed; and

(*b*) that proceedings in respect of that offence have been instituted in that country or territory or that an investigation into that offence is being carried on there,

he may, if he thinks fit, by a notice in writing nominate a court in England, Wales or Northern Ireland or, as the case may be, Scotland to receive such of the evidence to which the request relates as may appear to the court to be appropriate for the purpose of giving effect to the request.

(3) Where it appears to the Secretary of State or, as the case may be, the Lord Advocate that the request relates to a fiscal offence in respect of which proceedings have not yet been instituted he shall not exercise his powers under subsection (2) above unless—

(*a*) the request is from a country or territory which is a member of the Commonwealth or is made pursuant to a treaty to which the United Kingdom is a party; or

(*b*) he is satisfied that the conduct constituting the offence would constitute an offence of the same or a similar nature if it had occurred in the United Kingdom.

(4) For the purpose of satisfying himself as to the matters mentioned in sub-section (2)(*a*) and (*b*) above the Secretary of State or, as the case may be, the Lord Advocate shall regard as conclusive a certificate issued by such authority in the country or territory in question as appears to him to be appropriate.

(5) In this section "evidence" includes documents and other articles.

(6) Schedule 1 to this Act shall have effect with respect to the proceedings before a nominated court in pursuance of a notice under subsection (2) above.

5 Transfer of United Kingdom prisoner to give evidence or assist investigation overseas

(1) The Secretary of State may, if he thinks fit, issue a warrant providing for any person ("a prisoner") serving a sentence in a prison or other institution to which the Prison Act 1952 or the Prisons (Scotland) Act 1989 applies to be transferred to a country or territory outside the United Kingdom for the purpose—

(*a*) of giving evidence in criminal proceedings there; or
(*b*) of being identified in, or otherwise by his presence assisting, such proceedings or the investigation of an offence.

(2) No warrant shall be issued under this section in respect of any prisoner unless he has consented to being transferred as mentioned in subsection (1) above and that consent may be given either—

(*a*) by the prisoner himself; or
(*b*) in circumstances in which it appears to the Secretary of State inappropriate, by reason of the prisoner's physical or mental condition or his youth, for him to act for himself, by a person appearing to the Secretary of State to be an appropriateperson to act on his behalf;

but a consent once given shall not be capable of being withdrawn after the issue of the warrant.

(3) The effect of a warrant under this section shall be to authorise—

(*a*) the taking of the prisoner to a place in the United Kingdom and his delivery at a a place of departure from the United Kingdom into the custody of a person representing the appropriate authority of the country or territory to which the prisoner is to be transferred; and
(*b*) the bringing of the prisoner back to the United Kingdom and his transfer in custody to the place where he is liable to be detained under the sentence to which he is subject.

(4) Where a warrant has been issued in respect of a prisoner under this section he shall be deemed to be in legal custody at any time when, being in the United Kingdom or on board a British ship, British aircraft or British hovercraft, he is being taken under the warrant to or from any place or being kept in custody under the warrant.

(5) A person authorised by or for the purposes of the warrant to take the

prisoner to or from any place or to keep him in custody shall have all the powers, authority, protection and privileges—

(a) of a constable in the part of the United Kingdom in which that person is for the time being; or

(b) if he is outside the United Kingdom, of a constable in the part of the United Kingdom to or from which the prisoner is to be taken under the warrant.

(6) If the prisoner escapes or is unlawfully at large, he may be arrested without warrant by a constable and taken to any place to which he may be taken under the warrant issued under this section.

(7) In subsection (4) above—

"British aircraft" means a British-controlled aircraft within the meaning of section 92 of the Civil Aviation Act 1982 (application of criminal law to aircraft) or one of Her Majesty's aircraft;

"British hovercraft" means a British-controlled hovercraft within the meaning of that section as applied in relation to hovercraft by virtue of provisions made under the Hovercraft Act 1968 or one of Her Majesty's hovercraft;

"British ship" means a British ship for the purposes of the Merchant Shipping Acts 1894 to 1988 or one of Her Majesty's ships;

and in this subsection references to Her Majesty's aircraft, hovercraft or ships are references to aircraft, hovercraft or, as the case may be, ships belonging to or exclusively employed in the service of Her Majesty in right of the Government of the United Kingdom.

(8) In subsection (6) above "constable", in relation to any part of the United Kingdom, means any person who is a constable in that or any other part of the United Kingdom or any person who,at the place in question has, under any enactment including subsection (5) above, the powers of a constable in that or any other part of the United Kingdom.

(9) This section applies to a person in custody awaiting trial or sentence and a person committed to prison for default in paying a fine as it applies to a prisoner and the reference in subsection (3)(b) above to a sentence shall be construed accordingly.

(10) In the application of this section to Northern Ireland for the reference in subsection (1) to the Prison Act 1952 there shall be substituted a reference to the Prison Act (Northern Ireland) 1953.

6 Transfer of overseas prisoner to give evidence or assist investigation in the United Kingdom

(1) This section has effect where—

(a) a witness order has been made or a witness summons or citation issued in criminal proceedings in the United Kingdom in respect of a person ("a prisoner") who is detained in custody in a country or territory outside the United Kingdom by virtue of a sentence or order of a court or tribunal exercising criminal jurisdiction in that country or territory; or

(b) it appears to the Secretary of State that it is desirable for a prisoner to be identified in, or otherwise by his presence to assist, such proceedings or the investigation in the United Kingdom of an offence.

(2) If the Secretary of State is satisfied that the appropriate authority in the country or territory where the prisoner is detained will make arrangements for him to come to the United Kingdom to give evidence pursuant to the witness order, witness summons or citation or, as the case may be, for the purpose mentioned in subsection (1)(b) above, he may issue a warrant under this section.

(3) No warrant shall be issued under this section in respect of any prisoner unless he has consented to being brought to the United Kingdom to give evidence as aforesaid or, as the case may be, for the purpose mentioned in subsection (1)(b) above but a consent once given shall not be capable of being withdrawn after the issue of the warrant.

(4) The effect of the warrant shall be to authorise—

(a) the bringing of the prisoner to the United Kingdom;
(b) the taking of the prisoner to, and his detention in custody at, such place or places in the United Kingdom as are specified in the warrant; and
(c) the returning of the prisoner to the country or territory from which he has come.

(5) Subsections (4) to (8) of section 5 above shall have effect in relation to a warrant issued under this section as they have effect in relation to a warrant issued under that section.

(6) A person shall not be subject to the Immigration Act 1971 in respect of his entry into or presence in the United Kingdom in pursuance of a warrant under this section but if the warrant ceases to have effect while he is still in the United Kingdom—

(a) he shall be treated for the purposes of that Act as if he has then illegally entered the United Kingdom; and
(b) the provisions of Schedule 2 to that Act shall have effect accordingly except that paragraph 20(1) (liability of carrier for expenses of custody etc. of illegal entrant) shall not have effect in relation to directions for his removal given by virtue of this subsection.

(7) This section applies to a person detained in custody in a country or territory outside the United Kingdom in consequence of having been transferred there—

(a) from the United Kingdom under the Repatriation of Prisoners Act 1984; or
(b) under any similar provision or arrange from any other country or territory,

as it applies to a person detained as mentioned in subsection (1) above.

Additional co-operative powers

7 Search etc for material relevant to overseas investigation

(1) Part II of the Police and Criminal Evidence Act 1984 (powers of entry, search and seizure) shall have effect as if references to serious arrestable offences in section 8 of and Schedule 1 to that Act included any conduct which is an offence under the law of a country or territory outside the United Kingdom and would constitute a serious arrestable offence if it had occurred in part of the United Kingdom.

(2) If, on an application made by a constable, a justice of the peace is satisfied—

(a) that criminal proceedings have been instituted against a person in a country or territory outside the United Kingdom or that a person has been arrested in the course of a criminal investigation carried on there;

(b) that the conduct constituting the offence which is the subject of the proceedings or investigation would constitute an arrestable offence within the meaning of the said Act of 1984 if it had occurred in any part of the United Kingdom; and

(c) that there are reasonable grounds for suspecting that there is on premises in the United Kingdom occupied or controlled by that person evidence relating to the offence other than items subject to legal privilege within the meaning of that Act,

he may issue a warrant authorising a constable to enter and search those premises and to seize any such evidence found there.

(3) The power to search conferred by subsection (2) above is only a power to search to the extent that is reasonably required for the purpose of discovering such evidence as is there mentioned.

(4) No application for a warrant or order shall be made by virtue of subsection (1) or (2) above except in pursuance of a direction given by the Secretary of State in response to a request received—

(a) from a court or tribunal exercising criminal jurisdiction in the overseas country or territory in question or a prosecuting authority in that county or territory; or

(b) from any other authority in that country or territory which appears to him to have the function of making requests for the purposes of this section;

and any evidence seized by a constable by virtue of this section shall be furnished by him to the Secretary of State for transmission to that court, tribunal or authority.

(5) If in order to comply with the request it is necessary for ant such evidence to be accompanied by any certificate, affidavit or other verifying document the constable shall also furnish for transmission such document of that nature as may be specified in the direction given by the Secretary of State.

(6) Where the evidence consists of a document the original or a copy shall be transmitted, and where it consists of any other article the article itself or a description, photograph or other representation of it shall be transmitted, as may be necessary in order to comply with the request.

(7) The Treasury may by order direct that any powers which by virtue of this section are exercisable by a constable shall also be exercisable by, or by any person acting under the direction of, an officer commissioned by the Commissioners of Customs and Excise under section 6(3) of the Customs and Excise Management Act 1979; and the Secretary of State may by order direct that any of those powers shall also be exercisable by a person of any other description specified in the order.

(8) An order under subsection (7) above shall be made by statutory instrument subject to annulment in pursuance of a resolution of either House of Parliament.

(9) In the application of this section to Northern Ireland for references to the Police and Criminal Evidence Act 1984, to Part II and section 8 of and to Schedule 1 to that Act there shall be substituted references to the Police and Criminal Evidence (Northern Ireland) Order 1989, to Part III and Article 10 of and to Schedule 1 to that Order.

20 Enforcement powers

(1) The powers conferred on an enforcement officer by Schedule 3 to this Act shall be exercisable in relation to any ship to which section 18 or 19 above applies for the purpose of detecting and the taking of appropriate action in respect of the offences mentioned in those sections.

(2) Those powers shall not be exercised outside the landward limits of the territorial sea of the United Kingdom in relation to a ship registered in a Convention state except with the authority of the Secretary of State; and he shall not give his authority unless that state has in relation to that ship—

    (a) requested the assistance of the United Kingdom for the purpose mentioned in subsection (1) above; or
    (b) authorised the United Kingdom to act for that purpose.

(3) In giving his authority pursuant to a request or authorisation from a Convention state the Secretary of State shall impose such conditions or limitations on the exercise of the powers as may be necessary to give effect to any conditions or limitations imposed by that state.

(4) The Secretary of State may, either of his own motion or in response to a request from a Convention state, authorise a Convention state to exercise, in relation to a British ship, powers corresponding to those conferred on enforcement officers by Schedule 3 to this Act but subject to such conditions or limitations, if any, as he may impose.

(5) Subsection (4) above is without prejudice to any agreement made, or

which may be made, on behalf of the United Kingdom whereby the United Kingdom undertakes not to object to the exercise by any other state in relation to a British ship of powers corresponding to those conferred by that Schedule.

(6) The powers conferred by that Schedule shall not be exercised in the territorial sea of any state other than the United Kingdom without the authority of the Secretary of State and he shall not give his authority unless that state has consented to the exercise of those powers.

23 Application of ancillary provisions of Misuse of Drugs Act 1971

(1) The Misuse of Drugs Act 1971 shall be amended as follows.

(2) In section 12(1) (prohibition direction on practitioner etc in consequence of conviction) after paragraph (*b*) there shall be inserted—

"(*c*) of an offence under section 12 or 13 of the Criminal Justice (International Co-operation) Act 1990;".

(3) In section 21 (offences by bodies corporate) after the words "an offence under this Act" there shall be inserted the words "or Part II of the Criminal Justice (International Co-operation) Act 11990".

(4) In section 23 (power to search and obtain evidence) after subsection (3) there shall be inserted—

"(3A) The powers conferred by subsection (1) above shall be exercisable also for the purposes of the execution of Part II of the Criminal Justice (International Co-operation) Act 1990 and subsection (3) above (excluding paragraph (*a*)) shall apply also to offences under section 12 or 13 of that Act, taking references in those provisions to controlled drugs as references to scheduled substances within the meaning of that Part."

SCHEDULE 3

Enforcement Powers in Respect of Ships

Preliminary

1. (1) In this Schedule "an enforcement officer" means—

(*a*) a constable;
(*b*) an officer commissioned by the Commissioners of Customs and Excise under section 6(3) of the Customs and Excise Management Act 1979; and
(*c*) any other person of a description specified in an order made for the purposes of this Schedule by the Secretary of State.

(2) The power to make an order under sub-paragraph (1)(*c*) above shall be exercisable by statutory instrument subject to annulment in pursuance of a resolution of either House of Parliament.

(3) In this Schedule "the ship" means the ship in relation to which the powers conferred by this Schedule are exercised.

Power to stop, board, divert and detain

2. (1) An enforcement officer may stop the ship, board it and, if he thinks it necessary for the exercise of his functions, require it to be taken to a port in the United Kingdom and detain it there.

(2) Where an enforcement officer is exercising his powers with the authority of the Secretary of State given under section 20(2) of this Act the officer may require the ship to be taken to a port in the Convention state in question or, if that state has so requested, in any other country or territory willing to receive it.

(3) For any of those purposes he may require the master or any member of the crew to take such action as may be necessary.

(4) If an enforcement officer detains a vessel he shall serve on the master a notice in writing stating that it is to be detained until the notice is withdrawn by the service on him of a further notice in writing signed by an enforcement officer.

Power to search and obtain information

3. (1) An enforcement officer may search the ship, anyone on it and anything on it including its cargo.

(2) An enforcement officer may require any person on the ship to give information concerning himself or anything on the ship.

(3) Without prejudice to the generality of those powers an enforcement officer may—

(a) open any containers;
(b) make tests and take samples of anything on the ship;
(c) require the production of documents, books or records relating to the ship or anything on it;
(d) make photographs or copies of anything whose production he has power to require.

Powers in respect of suspected offence

4. If an enforcement officer has reasonable grounds to suspect that an offence mentioned in section 18 or 19 of this Act has been committed on a ship to which that section applies he may—

(a) arrest without warrant anyone whom he has reasonable grounds for suspecting to be guilty of the offence; and
(b) seize and detain anything found on the ship which appears to him to be evidence of the offence.

Assistants

5. (1) An enforcement officer may take with him, to assist in exercising his powers—

(*a*) any other persons; and
(*b*) any equipment or materials.

(2) A person whom an enforcement officer takes with him to assist him may perform any of the officer's functions but only under the officer's supervision.

Use of reasonable force

6. An enforcement officer may use reasonable force, if necessary, in the performance of his functions.

Evidence of authority

7. An enforcement officer shall, if required, produce evidence of his authority.

Protection of officers

8. An enforcement officer shall not be liable in any civil or criminal proceedings for anything done in the purported performance of his functions under this Schedule if the court is satisfied that the act was done in good faith and that there were reasonable grounds for doing it.

Offences

9. (1) A person is guilty of an offence if he—

(*a*) intentionally obstructs an enforcement officer in the performance of any of his functions under this Schedule;
(*b*) fails without reasonable excuse to comply with a requirement made by an enforcement officer in the performance of those functions; or
(*c*) in purporting to give information required by an officer for the performance of those functions—
　(i) makes a statement which he knows to be false in a material particular or recklessly makes a statement which is false in a material particular; or
　(ii) intentionally fails to disclose any material particular.

(2) A person guilty of an offence under this paragraph is liable on summary conviction to a fine not exceeding level 5 on the standard scale.

BANKERS' BOOKS EVIDENCE ACT 1879

7 Court or judge may order inspection, etc

On the application of any party to a legal proceeding a court or judge may order that such party be at liberty to inspect and take copies of any entries in a banker's book for any of the purposes of such proceedings. An order under this section may be made either with or without summoning the bank or any other party, and shall be served on the bank three clear days before the same is to be obeyed, unless the court or judge otherwise directs.

INTERCEPTION OF COMMUNICATIONS ACT 1985

1 Prohibition on interception

(1) Subject to the following provisions of this section, a person who intentionally intercepts a communication in the course of its transmission by post or by means of a public telecommunication system shall be guilty of an offence and liable—

    (*a*) on summary conviction, to a fine not exceeding the statutory maximum;

    (*b*) on conviction on indictment, to imprisonment for a term not exceeding two years or to a fine or to both.

(2) A person shall not be guilty of an offence under this section if—

    (*a*) the communication is intercepted in obedience to a warrant issued by the Secretary of State under section 2 below; or

    (*b*) that person has reasonable grounds for believing that the person to whom, or the person by whom, the communication is sent has consented to the interception.

(3) A person shall not be guilty of an offence under this section if—

    (*a*) the communication is intercepted for purposes connected with the provision of postal or public telecommunication services or with the enforcement of any enactment relating to the use of those services; or

    (*b*) the communication is being transmitted by wireless telegraphy and is intercepted, with the authority of the Secretary of State, for purposes connected with the issue of licences under the Wireless Telegraphy Act 1949 or the prevention or detection of interference with wireless telegraphy.

(4) No proceedings in respect of any offence under this section shall be instituted—

    (*a*) in England and Wales, except by or with the consent of the Director of Public Prosecutions;

    (*b*) in Northern Ireland, except by or with the consent of the Director of Public Prosecutions for Northern Ireland.

2 Warrants for interception

(1) Subject to the provision of this section and section 3 below, the Secretary of State may issue a warrant requiring the person to whom it is addressed to intercept, in the course of their transmission by post or by means of a public

telecommunication system, such communications as are described in the warrant; and such a warrant may also require the person to whom it is addressed to disclose the intercepted material to such persons and in such manner as are described in the warrant.

(2) The Secretary of State shall not issue a warrant under this section unless he considers that the warrant is necessarily—

(a) in the interests of national security;

(b) for the purpose of preventing or detecting serious crime; or

(c) for the purpose of safeguarding the economic well-being of the United Kingdom.

(3) The matters to be taken into account in considering whether a warrant is necessary as mentioned in subsection (2) above shall include whether the information which it is considered necessary to acquire could reasonably be acquired by other means.

(4) A warrant shall not be considered necessary as mentioned in subsection (2)(*c*) above unless the information which it is considered necessary to acquire is information relating to the acts or intentions of persons outside the British Islands.

(5) References in the following provisions of this Act to a warrant are references to a warrant under this section.

3 Scope of warrants

(1) Subject to subsection (2) below, the interception required by a warrant shall be the interception of—

(a) such communications as are sent to or from one or more addresses specified in the warrant, being an address or addresses likely to be used for the transmission of communications to or from—
   (i) one particular person specified or described in the warrant; or
   (ii) one particular set of premises so specified or described; and

(b) such other communications (if any) as it is necessary to intercept in order to intercept communications falling within paragraph (*a*) above.

(2) Subsection (1) above shall not apply to a warrant if—

(a) the interception required by the warrant is the interception, in the course of their transmission by means of a public telecommunication system, of—
   (i) such external communications as are described in the warrant; and
   (ii) such other communications (if any) as it is necessary to intercept in order to intercept such external communications as are so described; and

(b) at the time when the warrant is issued, the Secretary of State issues a certificate certifying the descriptions of intercepted material the examination of which he considers necessary as mentioned in section 2(2) above.

(3) A certificate such as is mentioned in subsection (2) above shall not specify

an address in the British Islands for the purpose of including communications sent to or from that address in the certified material unless —

(a) the Secretary of State considers that the examination of communications sent to or from that address is necessary for the purpose of preventing or detecting acts of terrorism; and

(b) communications sent to or from that address are included in the certified material only in so far as they are sent within such a period, not exceeding three months, as is specified in the certificate.

(4) A certificate such as is mentioned in subsection (2) above shall not be issued except under the hand of the Secretary of State.

(5) References in the following provisions of this Act to a certificate are references to a certificate such as is mentioned in subsection (2) above.

4 Issue and duration of warrants

(1) A warrant shall not be issued except—

(a) under the hand of the Secretary of State; or

(b) in an urgent case where the Secretary of State has expressly authorised its issue and a statement of that fact is endorsed thereon, under the hand of an official of his department of or above the rank of Assistant Under Secretary of State.

(2) A warrant shall, unless renewed under subsection (3) below, cease to have effect at the end of the relevant period.

(3) The Secretary of State may, at any time before the end of the relevant period, renew a warrant if he considers that the warrant continues to be necessary as mentioned in section 2(2) above.

(4) If, at any time before the end of the relevant period, the Secretary of State considers that a warrant is no longer necessary as mentioned in section 2(2) above, he shall cancel the warrant.

(5) A warrant shall not be renewed except by an instrument under the hand of the Secretary of State.

(6) In this section "the relevant period"—

(a) in relation to a warrant which has not been renewed, means—
  (i) if the warrant was issued under subsection (1)(a) above, the period of two months beginning with the day on which it was issued; and
  (ii) if the warrant was issued under subsection (1)(b) above, the period ending with the second working day following that day;

(b) in relation to a warrant which was last renewed within the period mentioned in paragraph (a)(ii) above, means the period of two months beginning with the day on which is was so renewed; and

(c) in relation to a warrant which was last renewed at any other time, means—

(i) if the instrument by which it was so renewed is endorsed with a statement that the renewal is considered necessary as mentioned in section 2(2)(*a*) or (*c*) above, the period of six months beginning with the day on which it was so renewed, and

(ii) if that instrument is not so endorsed, the period of one month beginning with that day.

5 Modification of warrants etc

(1) The Secretary of State may at any time—

(*a*) modify a warrant by the insertion of any address which he considers likely to be used as mentioned in section 3(1)(*a*) above; or

(*b*) modify a certificate so as to include in the certified material any material the examination of which he considers necessary as mentioned in section 2(2) above.

(2) If at any time the Secretary of State considers that any address specified in a warrant is no longer likely to be used as mentioned in section 3(1)(*a*) above, he shall modify the warrant by the deletion of that address.

(3) If at any time the Secretary of State considers that the material certified by a certificate includes any material the examination of which is no longer necessary as mentioned in section 2(2) above, he shall modify the certificate so as to exclude that material from the certified material.

(4) A warrant or certificate shall not be modified under subsection (1) above except by an instrument under the hand of the Secretary of State or, in an urgent case—

(*a*) under the hand of a person holding office under the Crown who is expressly authorised by the warrant or certificate to modify it on the Secretary of State's behalf; or

(*b*) where the Secretary of State has expressly authorised the modification and a statement of that fact is endorsed on the instrument, under the hand of such an officer as is mentioned in section 4(1)(*b*) above.

(5) An instrument made under subsection (4)(*a*) or (*b*) above shall cease to have effect at the end of the fifth working day following the day on which it was issued.

6 Safeguards

(1) Where the Secretary of State issues a warrant he shall, unless such arrangements have already been made, make such arrangement as he considers necessary for the purpose of securing—

(*a*) that the requirements of subsections (2) and (3) below are satisfied in relation to the intercepted material; and

(*b*) where a certificate is issued in relation to the warrant, that so much of the intercepted material as is not certified is not read, looked at or listened to by any person.

(2) The requirements of this subsection are satisfied in relation to any intercepted material if each of the following, namely—

(a) the extent to which the material is disclosed;
(b) the number of persons to whom any of the material is disclosed;
(c) the extent to which the material is copied; and
(d) the number of copies made of any of the material;

is limited to the minimum that is necessary as mentioned in section 2(2) above.

(3) The requirements of this subsection are satisfied in relation to any intercepted material if each copy made of any of that material is destroyed as soon as its retention is no longer necessary as mentioned in section 2(2) above.

7 The Tribunal

(1) There shall be a tribunal (in this Act referred to as "the Tribunal") in relation to which the provisions of Schedule 1 to this Act apply.

(2) Any person who believes that communications sent to or by him have been intercepted in the course of their transmission by post or by means of a public telecommunication system may apply to the Tribunal for an investigation under this section.

(3) On such an application (other than one appearing to the Tribunal to be frivolous or vexatious), the Tribunal shall investigate—

(a) whether there is or has been a relevant warrant or a relevant certificate; and
(b) where there is or has been such a warrant or certificate, whether there has been any contravention of sections 2 to 5 above in relation to that warrant or certificate.

(4) If, on an investigation, the Tribunal, applying the principles applicable on an application for judicial review, conclude that there has been a contravention of sections 2 to 5 above in relation to a relevant warrant or a relevant certificate, they shall—

(a) give notice to the applicant stating that conclusion;
(b) make a report of their findings to the Prime Minister; and
(c) if they think fit, make an order under subsection (5) below.

(5) An order under this subsection may do one or more of the following, namely—

(a) quash the relevant warrant or the relevant certificate;
(b) direct the destruction of copies of the intercepted material or, as the case may be, so much of it as is certified by the relevant certificate;
(c) direct the Secretary of State to pay to the applicant such sum by way of compensation as may be specified in the order.

(6) A notice given or report made under subsection (4) above shall state the effect of any order under subsection (5) above made in the case in question.

(7) If, on an investigation, the Tribunal comes to any conclusion other than

that mentioned in subsection (4) above, they shall give notice to the applicant stating that there has been no contravention of sections 2 to 5 above in relation to a relevant warrant or a relevant certificate.

(8) The decisions of the Tribunal (including any decisions as to their jurisdiction) shall not be subject to appeal or liable to be questioned in any court.

(9) For the purposes of this section—

(a) a warrant is a relevant warrant in relation to an applicant if—
   (i) the applicant is specified or described in the warrant; or
   (ii) an address used for the transmission of communications to or from a set of premises in the British Islands where the applicant resides or works is so specified;
(b) a certificate is a relevant certificate in relation to an applicant if and to the extent that an address used as mentioned in paragraph (a)(ii) above is specified in the certificate for the purpose of including communications sent to or from that address in the certified material.

8 The Commissioner

(1) The Prime Minister shall appoint a person who holds or has held a high judicial office (in this section referred to as "the Commissioner") to carry out the following functions, namely—

(a) to keep under review the carrying out by the Secretary of State of the functions conferred on him by sections 2 to 5 above and the adequacy of any arrangements made for the purposes of section 6 above; and
(b) to give to the Tribunal all such assistance as the Tribunal may require for the purpose of enabling them to carry out their functions under this Act.

(2) The Commissioner shall hold office in accordance with the terms of his appointment and there shall be paid to him out of money provided by Parliament such allowances as the Treasury may determine.

(3) It shall be the duty of every person holding office under the Crown or engaged in the business of the Post Office or in the running of a public telecommunication system to disclose or give to the Commissioner such documents or information as he may require for the purpose of enabling him to carry out his functions under this section.

(4) It shall be the duty of the Tribunal to send to the Commissioner a copy of every report made by them under section 7(4) above.

(5) If at any time it appears to the Commissioner—

(a) that there has been a contravention of sections 2 to 5 above which has not been the subject of a report made by the Tribunal under section 7(4) above; or
(b) that any arrangements made for the purposes of section 6 above have proved inadequate.

he shall make a report to the Prime Minister with respect to that contravention or those arrangements.

(6) As soon as practicable after the end of each calendar year, the Commissioner shall make a report to the Prime Minister with respect to the carrying out of his functions under this section.

(7) The Prime Minister shall lay before each House of Parliament a copy of every annual report made by the Commissioner under subsection (6) above together with a statement as to whether any matter has been excluded from that copy in pursuance of subsection (8) below.

(8) If it appears to the Prime Minister, after consultation with the Commissioner, that the publication of any matter in an annual report would be prejudicial to national security, to the prevention or detection of serious crime or to the economic well-being of the United Kingdom, the Prime Minister may exclude that matter from the copy of the report as laid before each House of Parliament.

9 Exclusion of evidence

(1) In any proceedings before any court or tribunal no evidence shall be adduced and no question in cross-examination shall be asked which (in either case) tends to suggest—

- (a) that an offence under section 1 above has been or is to be committed by any of the persons mentioned in subsection (2) below; or
- (b) that a warrant has been or is to be issued to any of those persons.

(2) The persons referred to in subsection (1) above are—

- (a) any person holding office under the Crown;
- (b) the Post Office and any person engaged in the business of the Post Office; and
- (c) any public telecommunications operator and any person engaged in the running of a public telecommunication system.

(3) Subsection (1) above does not apply—

- (a) in relation to proceedings for a relevant offence or proceedings before the Tribunal; or
- (b) where the evidence is adduced or the question in cross-examination is asked for the purpose of establishing the fairness of unfairness of a dismissal on grounds of an offence under section 1 above or of conduct from which such an offence might be inferred;

and paragraph (a) of that subsection does not apply where a person has been convicted of the offence under that section.

(4) In this section "relevant offence" means—

- (a) an offence under section 1 above or under section 45 of the Telegraph Act 1863, section 20 of the Telegraph Act 1868, section 58 of the Post Office Act 1953 or section 45 of the 1984 Act;

(b) an offence under section 1 or 2 of the Official Secrets Act 1911 relating to any sketch, plan, model, article, note, document or information which tends to suggest as mentioned in subsection (1) above;

(c) perjury committed in the course of proceedings for a relevant offence;

(d) attempting or conspiring to commit, or aiding, abetting counselling or procuring the commission of, an offence falling within any of the preceding paragraphs; and

(e) contempt of court committed in the course of, or in relation to, proceedings for a relevant offence.

10 Interpretation

(1) In this Act, unless the context otherwise requires—

"the 1984 Act" means the Telecommunications Act 1984;

"address" means any postal or telecommunication address;

"copy", in relation to intercepted material, means any of the following, whether or not in documentary form—

(a) any copy, extract or summary of the material; and

(b) any record of the identities of the persons to or by whom the material was sent,

and cognate expressions shall be construed accordingly;

"external communication" means a communication sent or received outside the British Islands;

"high judicial office" has the same meaning as in the Appellate Jurisdiction Act 1876;

"intercepted material", in relation to a warrant, means the communications intercepted in obedience to that warrant;

"person" includes any organisation and any association or combination of persons;

"public telecommunications operator" and "public telecommunications system" have the same meanings as in the 1984 Act;

"public telecommunication service" means a telecommunication service provided by means of a public telecommunication system;

"statutory maximum" has the meaning given by section 74 of the Criminal Justice Act 1982;

"telecommunication service" has the same meaning as in the 1984 Act;

"the Tribunal" means the tribunal established under section 7 above;

"wireless telegraphy" has the same meaning as in the Wireless Telegraphy Act 1949;

"working day" means any day other than a Saturday, a Sunday, Christmas Day, Good Friday or a day which is a bank holiday under the Banking and Financial Dealings Act 1971 in any part of the United Kingdom.

(2) For the purposes of this Act a communication which is in the course of its transmission otherwise than by means of a public telecommunication system shall be deemed to be in the course of its transmission by means of such a system if its mode of transmission identifies it as a communication which—

(a) is to be or has been transmitted by means of such a system; and
(b) has been sent from, or its to be sent to, a country or territory outside the British Islands.

(3) For the purposes of this Act conduct which constitutes or, if it took place in the United Kingdom, would constitute one or more offences shall be regarded as serious crime if, and only if—

(a) it involves the use of violence, results in substantial financial gain or is conduct by a large number of persons in pursuit of a common purpose; or
(b) the offence or one of the offences is an offence for which a person who has attained the age of twenty-one and has no previous convictions could reasonably be expected to be sentenced to imprisonment for a term of three years or more.

11 Amendments, saving and repeal

(1) For section 45 of the 1984 Act (interception and disclosure of messages etc) there shall be substituted the section set out in Schedule 2 to this Act.

(2), (3) [amend Post Office Acts 1953, s 58; 1969, Sch 5, para 1(1)].

(4) ...

(5) Section 4 of the Official Secrets Act 1920 (power to require the production of telegrams) is hereby repealed.

12 Short title, commencement and extent

(1) This Act may be cited as the Interpretation of Communications Act 1985.

(2) This Act shall come into force on such day as the Secretary of State may by order made by statutory instrument appoint.

(3) This Act extends to Northern Ireland.

(4) Her Majesty may by Order in Council direct that any of the provisions of this Act specified in the Order shall extend to the Isle of Man or any of the

Channel Islands with such exceptions, adaptations and modifications as may be so specified.

CHILDREN ACT 1989

Removal and accommodation of children by police in cases of emergency.

46 (1) Where a constable has reasonable cause to believe that a child would otherwise be likely to suffer significant harm, he may—

(a) remove the child to suitable accommodation and keep him there; or

(b) take such steps as are reasonable to ensure that the child's removal from any hospital, or other place, in which he is then being accommodated is prevented.

(2) For the purposes of this Act, a child with respect to whom a constable has exercised his powers under this section is referred to as having been taken into police protection.

(3) As soon as is reasonably practicable after taking a child into police protection, the constable concerned shall—

(a) inform the local authority within whose area the child was found of the steps that have been, and are proposed to be, taken with respect to the child under this section and the reasons for taking them;

(b) give details to the authority within whose area the child is ordinarily resident ("the appropriate authority") of the place at which the child is being accommodated;

(c) inform the child (if he appears capable of understanding)—

(i) of the steps that have been taken with respect to him under this section and of the reasons for taking them; and

(ii) of the further steps that may be taken with respect to him under this section;

(d) take such steps as are reasonably practicable to discover the wishes and feelings of the child;

(e) secure that the case is inquired into by an officer designated for the purposes of this section by the chief officer of the police area concerned; and

(f) where the child was taken into police protection by being removed to accommodation which is not provided—

(i) by or on behalf of a local authority; or

(ii) as a refuge, in compliance with the requirements of section 51,

secure that he is moved to accommodation which is so provided.

(4) As soon as is reasonably practicable after taking a child into police protection, the constable concerned shall take such steps as are reasonably practicable to inform—

(a) the child's parents;

(b) every person who is not a parent of his but who has parental responsibility for him; and

(c) any other person with whom the child was living immediately before being taken into police protection,

of the steps that he has taken under this section with respect to the child, the reasons for taking them and the further steps that may be taken with respect to him under this section.

(5) On completing any inquiry under subsection (3)(e), the officer conducting it shall release the child from police protection unless he considers that there is still reasonable cause for believing that the child would be likely to suffer significant harm if released.

(6) No child may be kept in police protection for more than 72 hours.

(7) While a child is being kept in police protection, the designated officer may apply on behalf of the appropriate authority for an emergency protection order to be made under section 44 with respect to the child.

(8) An application may be made under subsection (7) whether or not the authority know of it or agree to its being made.

(9) While a child is being kept in police protection—

(a) neither the constable concerned nor the designated officer shall have parental responsibility for him; but

(b) the designated officer shall do what is reasonable in all the circumstances of the case for the purpose of safeguarding or promoting the child's welfare (having regard in particular to the length of the period during which the child will be so protected).

(10) Where a child has been taken into police protection, the designated officer shall allow—

(a) the child's parents;

(b) any person who is not a parent of the child but who has parental responsibility for him;

(c) any person with whom the child was living immediately before he was taken into police protection;

(d) any person in whose favour a contact order is in force with respect to the child;

(e) any person who is allowed to have contact with the child by virtue of an order under section 34; and

(f) any person acting on behalf of any of those persons,

to have such contact (if any) with the child as, in the opinion of the designated officer, is both reasonable and in the child's best interests.

(11) Where a child who has been taken into police protection is in accommodation provided by, or on behalf of, the appropriate authority, subsection (10) shall have effect as if it referred to the authority rather than to the designated officer.

MENTAL HEALTH ACT 1983

135 Warrant to search for and remove patients

(1) If it appears to a justice of the peace, on information on oath laid by an approved social worker, that there is reasonable cause to suspect that a person believed to be suffering from mental disorder—

    (a) has been, or is being, ill-treated, neglected or kept otherwise than under proper control, in any place within the jurisdiction of the justice, or

    (b) being unable to care for himself, is living alone in any such place,

the justice may issue a warrant authorising any constable ... to enter, if need be by force, any premises specified in the warrant in which that person is believed to be, and, if thought fit, to remove him to a place of safety with a view to the making of an application in respect of him under Part II of this Act, or of other arrangements for his treatment or care.

(2) If it appears to a justice of the peace, on information on oath laid by any constable or other person who is authorised by or under this Act or under section 83 of the [Mental Health (Scotland) Act 1984] to take a patient to any place, or to take into custody or retake a patient who is liable under this Act or under the said section 83 to be so taken or retaken—

    (a) that there is reasonable cause to believe that the patient is to be found on premises within the jurisdiction of the justice; and

    (b) that admission to the premises has been refused or that a refusal or such admission is apprehended,

the justice may issue a warrant authorising any constable ... to enter the premises, if need be by force, and remove the patient.

(3) A patient who is removed to a place of safety in the execution of a warrant issued under this section may be detained there for a period not exceeding 72 hours.

(4) In the execution of a warrant issued under subsection (1) above, [a constable] shall be accompanied by an approved social worker and by a registered medical practitioner, and in the execution of a warrant issued under subsection (2) above [a constable] may be accompanied—

    (a) by a registered medical practitioner;

    (b) by any person authorised by or under this Act or under section 8 of the [Mental Health (Scotland) Act 1984] to take or retake the patient.

(5) It shall not be necessary in any information or warrant under subsection (1) above to name the patient concerned.

(6) In this section "place of safety" means residential accommodation provided by a local social services authority under Part III of the National Assistance Act 1948 or under paragraph 2 of Schedule 8 to the National Health Service Act 1977, a hospital as defined by this Act, a police station, a mental nursing home or

residential home for mentally disordered persons or any other suitable place the occupier of which is willing temporarily to receive the patient.

136 Mentally disordered persons found in public places

(1) If a constable finds in a place to which the public have access a person who appears to him to be suffering from mental disorder and to be in immediate need of care or control, the constable may, if he thinks it necessary to do so in the interests of that person or for the protection of other persons, remove that person to a place of safety within the meaning of section 135 above.

(2) A person removed to a place of safety under this section may be detained there for a period not exceeding 72 hours for the purpose of enabling him to be examined by a registered medical practitioner and to be interviewed by an approved social worker and of making any necessary arrangements for his treatment or care.

Index